In Memory of

Dale Dennett

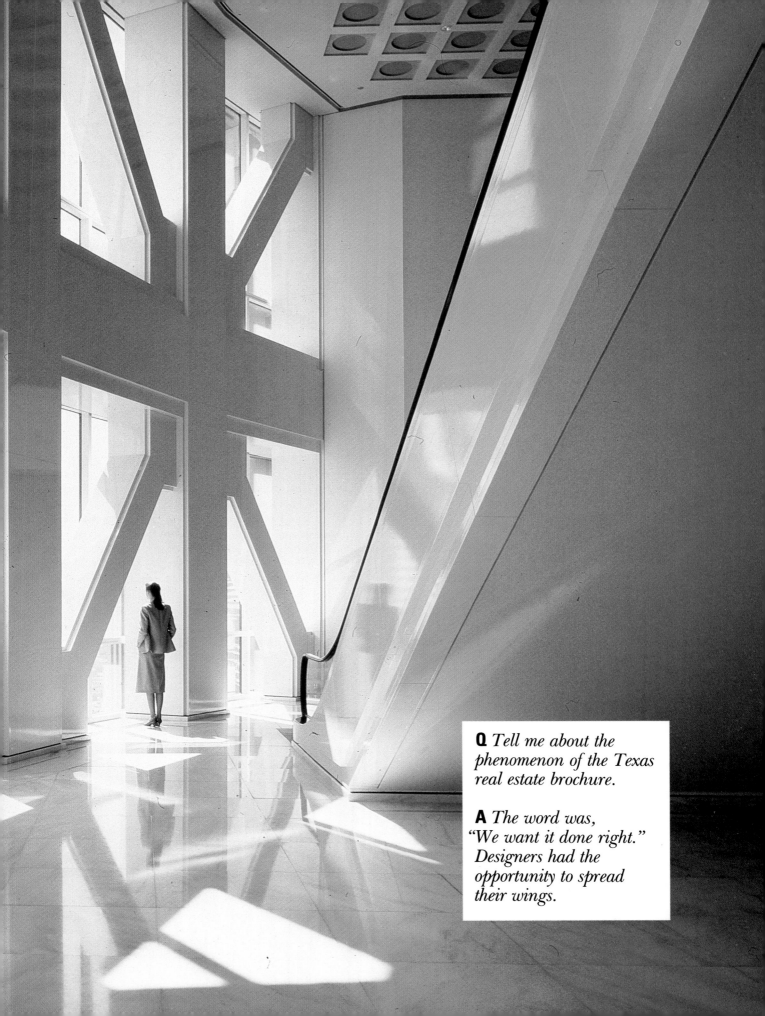

Q *Tell me about the phenomenon of the Texas real estate brochure.*

A *The word was, "We want it done right." Designers had the opportunity to spread their wings.*

can, I want to give that printer a chance at a job. So I think the old adage of doing good deeds gets its return. And it's not just doing good deeds, it's making contacts as well. I wouldn't give a designer a job simply because he or she was a friend of mine—if he or she couldn't do the job. But certainly, everyone should broaden their range of contacts.

I think it's very important that people selling design services also look outside the so-called art world. While a number of my peers are interested in art, more of my peers are involved in various civic activities—boards and organizations. To pursue this contact venue, you need to broaden your spectrum of interests. For instance, the Society for Marketing Professional Services is a group of people who are involved in marketing for the architectural, engineering, and construction industries, and that's my field. I would strongly advise designers to become active in organizations like this, because the people who buy design services are there. While it might be the CEO who sends the recommendations down to his marketing person, it's very often the marketing person, like me, who makes the decision. On a major project like the Century Corporation brochure, I made recommendations to our chairman and president. They turned to me and said, "All these people are really good. Who would you choose? Who do you prefer to work with?" So belonging to the right country club and all that is important, but belonging to the appropriate professional organization is crucial.

Given all of this, how did you meet the designer you work most closely with?

By referral! When I first joined Century three years ago, we set about to do a corporate brochure, the first of its kind in this company. I was shopping for a designer. One day I was talking to a photographer who was doing some work for us and he said, "You need to meet my friend Chris Hill; he's one of the best designers in town." And I said, "Okay, have him give me a call."

Before I met Chris, I was calling all my colleagues who do the same thing I do for other companies in town. I asked who they used and who they considered the best designers in town. Those are really two different questions because they might not have been able to afford the best ones in town. Anyway, I got a number of names. I made a list and set up a series of interviews and went from there.

How did you make your choice?

They were all excellent designers. I went with Chris because I found him to be a very easy person to work with and talk to. I found him to have a unique understanding of marketing, as opposed to just graphics.

◄**Photo for Century by Rick Gardner depicts First National Bank Plaza, a 71-story, 200,000-square-foot Houston building managed by Century's subsidiary, Property Management Systems.**

When you were undergoing your search, were designers also searching for you? Were you getting self-promotion in the mail? Were you getting phone calls?

When I joined Century, we put an announcement, a release, in the paper. I was just beseiged with calls.

But Chris could talk marketing and results and not just white space. I knew that this brochure was going to take a long time, a lot of hair pulling, and a tremendous amount of work. It was very important to me to find someone I would be comfortable with under those circumstances.

How long does it take you to make that kind of judgment about someone?

By the end of the first presentation, I know whether I'll be comfortable or not. When we were making out decision on this brochure, I narrowed it down to three firms. Two of the proposals I got were in-depth, "This is my understanding of your needs. This is how we propose to meet them." The third one was simply a quotation. There was no question that I was impressed with the two proposals that were more thorough. I felt they really analyzed my situation and my needs. They did more than put a price on the job.

Some organizations ask for proposals in order to satisfy a requirement for three bids. Everyone is giving the project a good deal of thought and racing around getting photographers, printers, and other vendors involved in pricing the project. Sometimes the client does not even call the losers to acknowledge this effort.

I read every word of the proposals that are prepared for me. To those designers who are agonizing over whether to spend a lot of time on a proposal, number one, you've got to look at the size of the job. Some jobs don't merit a mega-proposal. Sometimes a letter will do. But on the major proposals that go out—where you're talking about $100,000—designers owe it to themselves to get their thoughts clear. And the designer owes it to the client to clarify whether he or she is thinking about a $75,000 job or a $150,000 job. That's a lot of business for any designer. And that's a big chunk of a client's budget. Designers have to weigh each job and the impact it will have on their bottom line and prestige in the community.

As to how clients respond to proposals, I've been one of those who have neglected to call people. And I've regretted it. Everybody deserves to understand why they lost. I produce Century's proposals. Whether we win or lose, we always like a debriefing. It's important for our future marketing efforts and our future proposals.

To those clients out there who have gotten their three proposals, have some compassion for the people who didn't make it. But don't count on it, designers, because competition, not compassion, is the name of the game.

Century Corporation

The "Texas real estate brochure," to a certain extent, changed design in this country. All of a sudden, maybe eight years ago, books appeared that were more lavish, better photographed, and better printed than just about anything around. Can you tell me about this phenomenon?

You have to understand that this is Texas! Bigger, better, best. And the people who were in real estate then were tremendously competitive, intense entrepreneurs—Texas-style entrepreneurs. Back in the early eighties, there was a huge building boom going on, especially in Houston and Dallas. While this is not New York, Chicago, or Los Angeles, we were making big news. Whether it was skyscrapers or campus-style buildings, we did everything Texas style. And the entrepreneurial egos, at times, were so large that everything had to be perfect. Every building was "One of the Most Beautiful Buildings Ever." And the marketing books were part of the total package. There was money to be spent, and the word was "We want it done right," and that gave the designers the opportunity to spread their wings.

It's not an opportunity that comes along very often.

No. And I don't think you'll see it much anymore, even in Houston or Dallas. Construction has trickled almost to a halt in Houston, and in most Sun Belt cities there simply aren't any more buildings going up. Many of the major monuments and edifices built in the early eighties are still not 100 percent occupied. Everybody's projecting a turnaround in the market in Houston in the early nineties. But even then, I don't think we're going to see the same kind of boom times. I think we—the developers and the financial institutions—have learned a definite lesson.

What were your objectives for the Century Corporation book?

This company has a number of subsidiaries, and its story had never been pulled together before. Our objective was to be able to show the company as a total package, as a total entity. We have been in business for a long time; we have thirty major properties. Our companies provide a variety of services. Senior management uses the book in various ways. Sometimes we want to show the nationwide breadth of the company; sometimes we want to show the depth of services, sometimes the people. Whether we're dealing with financial institutions or with clients, we need to tell our story in a succinct way. This brochure accomplishes that. ∎

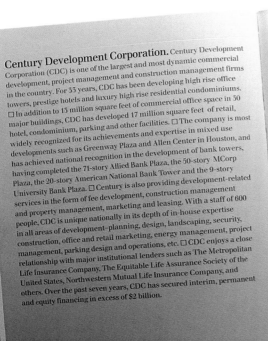

Century Development Corporation. Century Development Corporation (CDC) is one of the largest and most dynamic commercial development, project management and construction management firms in the country. For 35 years, CDC has been developing high rise office towers, prestige hotels and luxury high rise residential condominiums. □ In addition to 15 million square feet of commercial office space in 30 major buildings, CDC has developed 17 million square feet of retail, hotel, condominium, parking and other facilities. □ The company is most widely recognized for its achievements and expertise in mixed use developments such as Greenway Plaza and Allen Center in Houston, and has achieved national recognition in the development of bank towers, having completed the 71-story Allied Bank Plaza, the 50-story MCorp Plaza, the 20-story American National Bank Tower and the 9-story University Bank Plaza. □ Century is also providing development-related services in the form of fee development, construction management and property management, marketing and leasing. With a staff of 600 people, CDC is unique nationally in its depth of in-house expertise in all areas of development–planning, design, landscaping, security, construction, office and retail marketing, energy management, project management, parking design and operations, etc. □ CDC enjoys a close relationship with major institutional lenders such as The Metropolitan Life Insurance Company, The Equitable Life Assurance Society of the United States, Northwestern Mutual Life Insurance Company, and others. Over the past seven years, CDC has secured interim, permanent and equity financing in excess of $2 billion.

Four Allen Center
Houston, Texas

Chris Hacker was trained as an industrial designer at the University of Cincinnati. He was vice president of design for Dansk International Designs from 1985 through 1987, after serving as a product manager at Dansk in the late 1970s. In the interim, he was manager of design for GAF Corporation, executive design director for the Estée Lauder Company, and managed his own consulting business in product, graphic, and exhibition design. Mr. Hacker is currently vice president and director of design for Steuben Glass. Mr. Hacker's work has been published in the *ID Review*, an edition of *ID* magazine, and was shown at the Whitney Museum exhibition, "High Styles: 20th Century American Design."

Dansk International Designs is a leading importer of contemporary designs for the tabletop. The company was founded in 1953 to bring new Danish-style design to the American market. Headquartered in Mount Kisco, New York, Dansk relies on various international factories to custom-manufacture the products that are designed by the Dansk designers. The company sells products through wholesale and retail channels.

4

What Every Client Should Expect from a Designer

Carbone Smolan Associates is a New York City design firm headed by Kenneth Carbone and Leslie Smolan. The firm's broad-based clients include the Louvre in Paris, the Museum of Modern Art in New York, the Los Angeles County Museum of Art, the American Stock Exchange, and Merrill Lynch and Co. Carbone and Smolan are both graduates of the Philadelphia College of Art; Mr. Carbone began his career at Chermayeff and Geismar Associates and Ms. Smolan at Corporate Annual Reports. In 1975, Mr. Carbone joined Gottschalk + Ash International, Canada, to supervise the 1976 Montreal Olympics project. He returned to New York to establish a Gottschalk + Ash office and was soon joined by Ms. Smolan; they purchased the firm in 1980. The firm is widely known for the design of the best-selling *Day in the Life* book series. Both are active teachers and lecturers. Mr. Carbone was a treasurer of AIGA New York. Ms. Smolan is on the AIGA national board and on the advisory committee of *New York Woman* magazine.

Chris Hacker

Q *You are a designer by training, and you've been meeting with designers and choosing design firms to work for leading companies for twelve years. Do you have a special way of going about it?*

A At Steuben I'm involved in virtually all design-related activity, which means product design, graphic design, interior design, and shop detailing. I fit the scope of each project to a designer's capability. There are designers who have "overlapping" or "crossover" capabilities, beyond one field. I have tended to use those people, and try to push them in directions they haven't taken before. At Dansk, when I hired Carbone Smolan for the dinnerware project, I wanted graphic design applied to an existing product shape.

At Steuben, all our graphic design is done in-house, so I use outside designers for other, three-dimensional projects—products and architecture—which come up on a fairly infrequent basis. I tend to use people I know, either with whom I've worked with before or who have attracted my attention for one reason or another.

Do design awards ever attract your attention?

I don't select designers based on awards. But I do pay fairly close attention to the architecture and interior design magazines. I will seek people out and talk to them.

◄ "Ditto," a dinnerware pattern designed in 1987 by Carbone Smolan Associates for Dansk International Designs. Chris Hacker supplied Carbone Smolan with models of the product shape, developed by Larry Porcelli for Dansk. The assignment: to apply graphic design to product.

Carbone Smolan explored a range of possible design directions. After the initial pencil sketches were reviewed internally, two-dimensional comps were produced on foam-core board. Patterns were rendered with cut colored paper, colored pencil, and paint.

How do you feel about design professionals who hire marketing people to seek you out? People who will make cold calls?

I don't particularly care for it. I am interested in talking to principals. Let me give you a specific example. We were recently looking for an architectural firm to redesign the interior of our shop. My search essentially started where my predecessor had left off. A few years ago, he interviewed seven or eight architects; then the project was put on hold and didn't resurface until I joined the company. I started with his list and added people whose work I had seen published and had admired, or who had been recommended to me by other people. I wrote a letter to each of them, describing the scope of the project and asking them to contact me for a portfolio review.

The people who were most interesting to me were the ones who called me back directly. When a principal called, we had a conversation immediately. When I had to talk to a marketing intermediary, I couldn't seem to get the kind of information I needed to evaluate the firm. And it took longer than necessary to get to the person who could get me that information.

Many clients have said the same thing . . .

And yet every design firm in America has a marketing person.

Not quite. But it seems that when firms grow to a certain size, the principal can feel stretched to the limits.

Right, and finds it very difficult to be both the creative director and the salesperson.

And starts thinking about finding someone who can go out and sell so he or she can get back to the drawing board. From your perspective, why doesn't this always work?

Well, it's interesting. It can work, I think, for large firms who are going after large clients. And perhaps for unsophisticated clients who just need to get a job done. But a company as design-specialized as the one I work for—in fact, most of the ones I have worked for—insists on dealing with the person who's actually going to be doing the work.

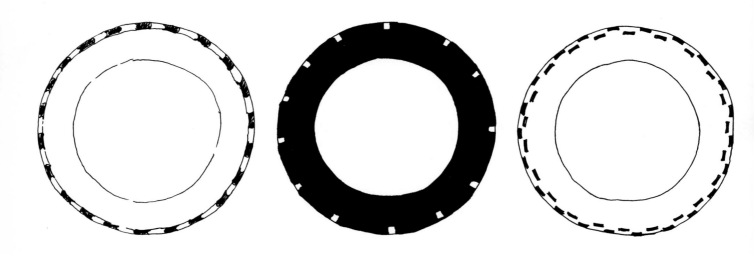

How should that relationship get started?

With an expression of interest in the project from the designer and a little conversation about just what's involved. Essentially, it's five minutes: it's here I am; we're interested; let's arrange a meeting. I am far more interested in looking at the work than in talking on the telephone.

I'm not interested in designers all talking and looking like account executives or bankers, but I'm interested in people clearly knowing what they're about. I prefer to meet with the actual project designers, who I presume will be the principals. There are marketing people in the design field whom I respect and who can communicate well, but there aren't very many of them.

There are some firm principals who have a strictly marketing function. And some firms set up this way have achieved enviable success stories. But in general, if only a marketing person showed up, would the firm be crossed off your list?

That's pretty well assured. A company like Dansk or Steuben could be such a valuable client to any firm, that I would be surprised—no, truly disappointed—if the people who were going to be doing the work didn't come. Their presence would mean that they thought enough of my project to put whatever they were doing at the office on hold. That's a little chauvinistic, but I think it's a fair view.

Are there special ways you learn of people who may have the particular capabilities you are looking for?

I'm in a network of design managers who call each other and say, "This firm or person came by and I really like their work; you might be able to use them." I do a lot of referring that way as well. If something is appealing to me and I can't use it—or even if I can use it and think someone else I know can, too—I'll pass it along. I worked for Estée Lauder for a couple of years, and I've sent a lot of people there who were more appropriate to that business than to this one. I do try to refer people judiciously so I don't burden my colleagues with interviews, but when it's appropriate, I certainly will.

Generally, what do you expect from a designer?

I want to make sure he or she will fit into our schedules and processes, which are somewhat eccentric for product design. At Steuben, instead of asking designers to develop two-dimensional presentations of new products, we develop a lot of conceptual ideas and then go directly into the factory, the blowing room, where we make prototypes. It's a very different way of working for a product designer who is used to presenting, say, five very beautiful renderings of products he might think we as a company should make. So I'm more interested in talking about the process of design rather than the end product.

Would slides be a good way to show that kind of process?

I don't want to editorialize about how work should be shown; I'm much more interested in what's *in* the presentation, and how people think and work. If they feel the best way to show that is through flat work, renderings or portfolios, great. Then, if I like their work, I immediately start talking about what we have in mind.

I think a consultant/company relationship has to be based on knowledge about what the company's about. It would be unfair to even consider involving someone who doesn't have a fair view of how things are done here. I'm very much an open book in terms of that discussion. I can remember a couple of cases where people came in and we talked about the business, what we were doing and where we were going, and they were surprised about how open I was.

When I have a specific project in mind, I narrow the field and see who I want, and then we get going immediately. And that means a discussion to get the costs in line, and an agreement about how long it's going to take and all that. I tend to say something like, "Look, I have $3,000 to spend. Can you do it?" That's because product designs have low budgets, lower than most designers expect.

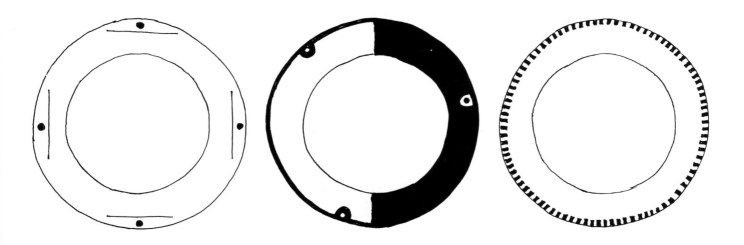

Are there occasions when you don't make up your mind right away and want to judge on the basis of a proposal?

Yes. For instance, the architecture project I mentioned earlier was exactly that case. I narrowed the field to three architects and asked each to write a proposal because I wanted to see whether, first, they understood the scope and budget of the project and, second, what kind of dollar figure each firm would come up with. I gave them each a total construction budget. I wanted to see how their fee would be structured. And how the proposal would be put together, visually. Anybody who's got the least bit of design in their blood had better pay attention to that stuff; I certainly do.

How do you define your role as director of design?

I view myself as an editor. I have an industrial design degree, and I'm perfectly capable of designing products. But I choose, for a lot of reasons, to keep out of it; the primary reason is so I can be more objective.

My career only moves in a positive direction when design work that I shepherd through the system is successful. That's one reason why I tend to hire people I've been successful with before. It minimizes the risk. Ken Carbone and his group are an interesting example of this because we've worked together on every job I've had for . . . it's probably been going on ten years. Have I made them rich? Absolutely not, but at appropriate moments I've selected them for very good projects.

If something that you did together won a design award, how would you feel about that?

Oh, it would be terrific.

Three Carbone Smolan designs were selected for further development. In addition to "Ditto," runners-up were "Rotation" and "Egypt" (far right), which were produced as plaster models on which final adjustments to form, color, and scale were made. "Ditto," which has been on the market since fall, 1988, is available at Dansk retailers and major department stores.

Here is the conflict, you say it's terrific but . . .

I don't use it to find other people to work for me. Well, it may be a bit disingenuous to say that you never select people that you see in design reviews, because anything that enhances someone's reputation is a positive thing. True, I don't go through design reviews to actually select a designer. But if over the years I've seen someone's work published, that certainly makes a cumulative impression.

And if a project I'm involved in is an award winner, I'm proud of that. Let me give you an interesting example. I brought Larry Porcelli into Dansk in 1978, when I was with the company the first time. He was incredibly durable because he consulted to Dansk for ten years, during which time nothing he did was produced. He was paid well for some of it, but some of it was on a royalty basis and he never saw a dime for it. One of those projects was the design kettle now in the Museum of Modern Art. It was originally designed in 1981, was ready to go into production, and then killed for reasons I'm still not clear on. When I rejoined the company in 1986, I found it in the closet and asked, "What is this?" and someone said, "Oh that's Larry's kettle. It was a dumb project; it was never finished." And I said, "It's the most beautiful kettle I've ever seen. Let's make it." So we did. And because it was partially tooled, we were able to get it to market a lot faster. It went on to win *Industrial Design* magazine's product of the year; it was also the Industrial Design Society of America's choice for one of their major awards. I'm very proud of that. Now I didn't have much to do with the design, but I had a lot to do with getting it made. So, yeah, I think if any project you are associated with wins an award, that's great news.

Are you also saying that for industrial or product designers who work for companies like yours, there's a certain amount of heartbreak? That they might put a lot into a design that could never see the light of day?

Industrial designers probably suffer from this more than anyone else because of the capital required to produce a product. There's a high degree of failure. Failure of a company to get a product on the market, and then failure beyond that because a company didn't market it correctly. Industrial designers are probably masochists.

And if the product is produced, it might have been changed from the original design. I've chosen to work for companies who value the output of designers. Dansk is a company, for example, whose whole premise is, "We've got these designers; we're paying a royalty; they're creating their vision; and let's try not to screw around with it too much." But even Dansk screws around. You know, they change colors, change details. Sometimes a detail will be designed that ultimately is not appropriate to the manufacturing method, and something has to be changed. But I did—and still do—try to get the designer involved in the change.

Are the companies who commission architects to design "tabletop"—dinnerware, flatware, teapots, and so forth—more in awe of someone of Richard Meier's stature? Would they tend to not change the design as much?

I've talked about this with Michael Graves, who's on Steuben's board of advisors, and he implied that he has as much trouble as every other designer in getting people to make what he wants them to make. He still has the job of convincing them that what he designed, which might have gone beyond what they originally had in mind, should not be changed. So, yes, companies tend to treat big-name architects in the same way as regular old designers. I think the trend toward using architects is an interesting one, particularly given the architects' view that they're the original artisans of the world. It all depends on the individual architect, whether it's the appropriate marriage of a design style or personality to a company, but ultimately, they don't get much respect either.

Do you think the American public is becoming more attuned to good design in everyday living?

Absolutely. We've come farther in the last ten years than ever before. There are still tremendous gaps in taste, but advances in the reality of product design are dramatic. There's a tremendous amount of good design that's being marketed by companies that weren't into good design before, like Mr. Coffee. And look at a company like IKEA. They're sort of the Swedish version of Conran's, only bigger. They have a store outside Philadelphia, a catalog warehouse operation with terrific furniture and household products, beautifully designed for the price. You can furnish a house—a first house or apartment for a young person—with great, cheap stuff.

Does this mean there will be more opportunities for industrial designers to do more and more products? And for designers from other disciplines to cross over into the field?

Oh, I think so. It's an interesting time because we've been through the phase of the great independent industrial designers of the thirties, forties, and fifties. We've been through the great corporate design office syndrome—the GMs, the JC Penneys—and now we're seeing a return to individual designers. In the next few years, there's going to be a tremendous opportunity for all kinds of designers to consult to companies who have realized that trying to operate with only a cheap internal design staff is a fantasy.

To designers who aspire to work for people like you, at companies like Dansk or Steuben, what is your advice?

Nothing can be more important than having a vision of where you want to go and the kind of work you want to do. You should only work at that level, and not settle for projects that show yourself to lesser advantage in terms of quality. ∎

Diane Cory is a teacher and facilitator. She wove together her education in journalism with her experience in public relations and in rearing four children to create innovative training and development tools that supported the Quality of Work Life process in AT&T's Atlanta Network Operations Group. Ms. Cory, who worked at AT&T from 1983 to 1988, is the author of the *AT&T Teaching Tales* (The Two Kings/The Magic Mirrors, The Dancing Stars, The Lion and the Princess, and The Harp and the Sword) and the *AT&T Teaching Verses*, which have received awards from the Dallas Society of Visual Communications, *Print* magazine and *Communication Arts* magazine (the 1988 Design Annual). Ms. Cory earned a B.A., *magna cum laude* in journalism from the University of North Texas. Currently she is working as a business consultant, trainer, and facilitator, and is finishing a new book of teaching tales.

AT&T (Network Operations Group/Atlanta, Georgia) provides global information movement and management services via telecommunications products and services to both residential and business customers in the United States and around the world.

5

Toward a New Definition of Selling

Jack Summerford is a native Texan who received his design degree from Washington University in St. Louis. After thirteen years with other design firms, including eight with Stan Richards, he founded Summerfor*design*, Inc., Dallas, which operates on a unique "one-person" basis with an expandable team of up to four designers. Jack Summerford's work has been represented in the top design shows, the Library of Congress, and *Communication Arts, Idea,* and *Print* magazines. He has served on boards of various design organizations, including the founding board of AIGA/Texas; he has spoken to design-related groups; and he has been a juror at exhibitions such as the *Communication Arts* Design Annual and AIGA Communication Graphics.

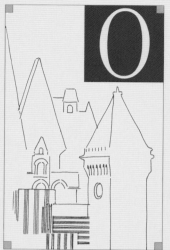

Once upon a memory, in a past that is always present,

and in a land of more than plenty, there lived twin brothers who were princes. But although they were identical physically, they were as opposite every other way as light and dark. Sun and shadow. Song and silence.

One prince thought more. One felt more. One prince related to the world through his senses. One through his intuition. One prince liked to make decisions. One liked to leave things open. One prince related outwardly. One inwardly.

As children the princes loved being reflections of each other and their opposite. Sometimes they wondered if the rest of the people who looked so different from each other were really more alike than they knew. And because the princes were children, and because they were both themselves and their opposite, they knew instinctively that the answer was both "yes" and "no."

The twins drew comfort and strength from knowing that what each was not, the other was. They passed the seemingly idle hours of childhood playing to each others'

◄ The AT&T Teaching Tales were distributed in a specially produced box. Each 12-page booklet, printed in four flat colors on textured stock, is an illustrated story by Diane Cory that uses myth and metaphor to teach corporate leadership values and skills.

The opening page of "The Two Kings/ The Magic Mirrors" begins a fairy tale about twin princes, one who "liked to make decisions," the other who "liked to leave things open." AT&T Teaching Tales are used by the Atlanta Network Operating Group to facilitate communication between union leaders and corporate managers.

Q *You have been responsible for some very unusual projects—brochures published by a corporation, but far from corporate in content and design. Can you give me a little background?*
A My career evolved from fifteen years in public relations and corporate communications into human resources training and development. My work is specifically focused around leadership—the new paradigms of leadership and management that are emerging, that are actually being called forth out of corporate America. In terms of printed materials, what I needed didn't exist, so I created the materials I wanted.

What was your inspiration?
Along the course of my growth and development I had been going through some Jungian counseling, which deals with metaphor, myth, stories, and fairy tales. The more I learned about C. G. Jung and about human psychology, the more I changed the way I communicated. It made me understand design and illustration and writing in a much more profound way. I tried to bring all that together to create the tales. I first wrote the stories as part of training and development in AT&T's Quality of Work Life process.

I developed a two-hour presentation on leadership skills that I've given over twenty times to about five thousand people—inside and outside of the business. During the presentations, I read the *AT&T Teaching Tales* out loud. I have trained other trainers and facilitators, and taught them how to use the stories in team building. When I do public speaking externally, I use the booklets as a gift to the audience.

Can you describe the value they've had for the company?
The tales give people permission to have different kinds of relationships, different from the traditional nonfunctional relationships they've had in the past. For me, they help create an environment where union leaders and managers can come together in a new way. They helped create new paradigms of what's possible, which is what stories are supposed to do.

Once you'd developed the stories, how did you go about finding the right person to create the visual format?

When I lived and worked in Dallas, I was highly involved in advertising, and I started teaching myself about design. I've always been a writer, and I wanted to know how to work best with art directors, so we could create the very best product. I had the goal of meeting all the top photographers, designers, and illustrators in Dallas.

I met Jack Summerford, and what clicked, what made the difference, was that Jack sold me on substance in addition to form. Most designers and art directors are really more flash than substance. I saw that I could have a good business relationship and human relationship with him; we were going to be able to create some really good products because I could talk to him about what I was trying to do, and it wasn't just superficial hogwash. I kept on working with him when I moved to Atlanta.

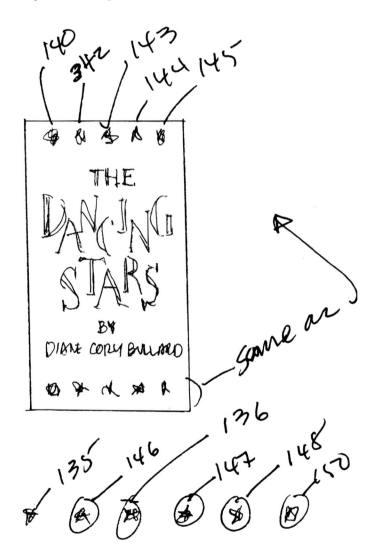

Jack Summerford, designer of the AT&T Teaching Tales, sketched each booklet's cover and opening page on tracing tissue, indicating layout and type selection to the typographer, who set all elements in position. The numbers indicate ITC Zapf Dingbats, type ornaments.

How did you initially go about your search?

I talked to a lot of people and I started going to meetings of the Dallas Society of Visual Communicators and the International Association of Business Communicators (IABC). I also went to design shows and just started asking.

Did the designers at those meetings and shows know you were a client looking for them?

No. My friends would take me around and introduce me to everybody. So I was sort of hanging out in the environment and looking at work and watching people. I also paid attention to reputations. People get reputations real fast about what they're like to deal with.

I also looked at every issue of *Communication Arts* magazine. That was part of my self-education. I would always read about designers if I liked their work. And whenever I had a project, I'd go back and scan a couple of years' worth of issues to see if I could find someone who looked like they might fit.

At first, I was interested in seeing everything and everybody. Then I reached a saturation point, when I felt like I had learned some things. I came into it very uneducated, but once I got enough exposure to designers under my belt, I became a little more discriminating. I started asking them to send me some pieces before I'd even see them. Then, I paid close attention to how they came across professionally. A lot of them were real goofy. They just had no sense of professionalism.

Have you seen things change in that regard in the last ten years?

Yes, I have. Designers present a much more professional appearance, even over the phone. And of course, a lot of designers were calling me. I also got a few rep calls. But to me, that's like a dysfunctional relationship. I don't enjoy working with reps. Their focus is on selling me something. That doesn't help me. They're not focused on meeting my needs; they're focused on meeting their own needs or meeting the needs of the person they're repping. I can sense that immediately, and then I won't deal with them. If they would just learn how to switch gears and meet my needs, then I would gladly work with them.

Anyway, I would have everybody send me their material. Even if they were goofy. If the material was good, I would give them a follow-up meeting.

What's your definition of goofy, by the way?

Someone who is not to point, not professional. They might not have the faintest idea how to approach me or what to say, or they might even act real silly. Some would be crazy creative types who don't really know how to talk. But some of them would be so polished and I'd think, "Oh, gag, this guy couldn't possibly have anything to show me." But sometimes I'd be surprised.

What was the next step?

To call them back and say, "Why don't we get together and talk?" I'd either go to their office or we'd meet somewhere for lunch. I'd spend a little time trying to get a feel for them and how they deal with their clients.

In the business I've been in, I have less time than anything. I don't need someone to tell me right off what my project is and how to do it. I need someone who understands collaborating and can interpret what it is I'm trying to communicate. And I need someone who is as balanced as he or she can be, and who understands how pressured I usually am—without letting it hurt his or her feelings. The designer has to understand the realities of my business world.

An illustration by Jack Summerford for an AT&T Teaching Verse, entitled "Black Fire," that praises "the beauty of four children/and the truth of a rock I hold/in one hand."

What was your reaction to the design shows you went to?

I really liked to see who in Dallas was winning awards. It's not that an award itself means so much to me; it's simply the exposure—I got to see the work. Awards annuals, also, are like advertising to me.

Would it be helpful to you if designers did advertise?

It would be especially helpful. It would save me a lot of time.

What about in the local papers?

Well, I need to see something better than a local paper. It just wouldn't be the same as seeing work in *Communication Arts,* in four color.

Those people who haven't yet been selected for an article in Communication Arts *can take out a color spread in a showcase book, or can create their own mailer and self-promotion. Is that of any interest to you?*

I haven't seen many promotions that tell me much. I've just seen people show off. They show off and have a great creative time with whatever they create. I don't see many who use their work for other clients to sell themselves. Instead, it's "I can be an art director, I can be real creative."

Is there something about being too creative that makes you uncomfortable?

I'm probably more creative than half the art directors, so that doesn't bother me. But I'm also extremely practical, and so I like to see that combined. I like to see creativity serving a function, instead of just for its own sake. There's a place for that, but not in what I do.

The Southwest has been getting a reputation as a very creative place, with a lot of terrific people to choose from. Do you ever see what you're looking for in several people, and then have to make a decision?

Yes, and I'll sit back and stew about my project. I'll spread the materials of all the designers out in my office and really give myself a lot of time to think it through. Then I'll trust my intuition on who would help me the most. I'll also ask for ballpark bids, based on general specifications.

When you're thinking it through, what kinds of things could get someone eliminated from the running?

First of all, I don't want to work with people who seem to be trying to impress me with a lot of status baloney. Don't try to impress me with who your other clients are, instead of how you helped them! I don't care who anyone's clients were or are; what I care about is what was done for them. Clients lists can be an indication of how good you are, but they also don't mean poop. Secondly, I find it annoying when designers boast about their offices and amenities. Thirdly, when designers try to be too nice because they really want the business. When I tell people I'm with Southwestern Bell or

AT&T, they go nuts; it runs down their legs. They have visions of projects; they go crazy. They try and talk to me about all the stuff they'd done. That really irritates me. I mean, I've been taken to more lunches and been sent more jars of jelly at Christmas, but none of that stuff plays a part in my decisions.

Once you've established a relationship with a designer like Jack, would you assume he's the one for every major new project, or would you consider other people as well?

It depends on timing and turnaround and budget. I have a good working relationship with Jack, and if it's a difficult project that I have good funding for, I'll stay with him. It's not just talent; I want to stress it's how much time and money he's been able to save me in terms of meetings and everything else.

When you began working with Jack, did you have a visual concept for the presentation of the AT&T *Teaching Tales?*

No idea. Jack came up with all of that. He presented some comps—paper stocks, colors, a basic example—and said, "This is the way I think they should look." And we had a short discussion about minor details, but basically he asked me a series of questions to find out if he was in the right direction, which, of course, he was. The design met my needs.

All designers should consider that the relationships they have with their clients can either serve the client or not. A lot of times, they only consider the design. But the business relationship is as important as the design; it's critical.

Designers should also try to act as teachers and educators. Sometimes they get too judgmental and defensive, spending their time defending a design or an illustration or a photograph. Inside corporations, people don't know much about design.

When I present things for final approval, I take the time to really explain the alternatives I looked at, and why I'm recommending a certain approach. Then, people are appreciative. I have almost always gotten approval for everything I wanted because I used the meeting as an opportunity to teach as well as to sell. ■

Diane Cory

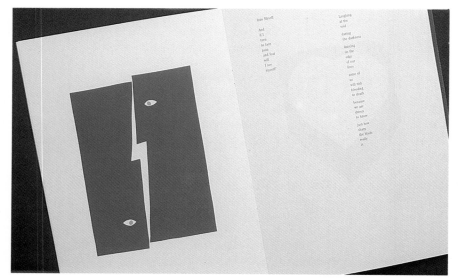

Cover and two spreads from the AT&T Teaching Verses, a 20-page book of poetry by Diane Cory. Written as a companion to the AT&T Teaching Tales, the verses are intended to reflect an "inward/outward journey ... much like the one we find in business."

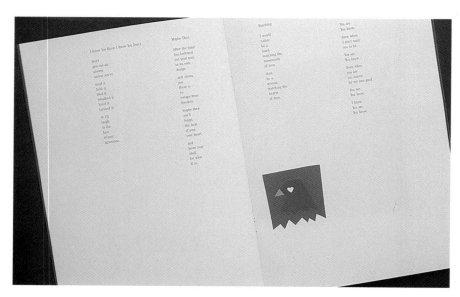

Part Two

Presentations and Proposals

Kathleen E. Zann, manager of marketing communications for James River Corporation, is responsible for advertising and promotional materials for the premium printing papers group, Southampton, Pennsylvania. She plans and develops marketing communications strategy for ten product lines and supervises the development and production of all promotional materials, including advertising and package design. Both a manager and an artist, Ms. Zann brings to her current position twelve years of experience in graphic design, advertising, and sales promotion in San Francisco and New York. She is a graduate of St. Mary's College and did postgraduate work at the Academy of Art College in San Francisco.

James River Corporation is a major integrated manufacturer of pulp, paper, coverted products, disposable food and beverage products, and coated and multilayer film products. Headquartered in Richmond, Virginia, the company has offices and manufacturing locations throughout the United States and worldwide.

6

Meetings that Set the Stage for Mutual Respect

John Waters, a native of North Carolina, received his B.F.A. from Virginia Commonwealth University and later studied at MIT, NYU, and the School of Visual Arts. He is president of Waters Design Associates, Inc., a New York firm that provides identification planning, marketing communications, environmental design, and electronically produced art. Mr. Waters is on the board of AIGA/New York and is a member of the Society of Typographic Arts (STA) and the Design Management Institute. The work of Waters Design has been represented in major exhibitions, including the Mead Annual Report Show and *Print Casebooks*. In 1985, Waters Design became the first American design firm to install a Lightspeed computer design work station, an interactive system of video input, digital image manipulation, and film recording. In addition to James River, clients of the firm include Smith Barney, Harris, Upham & Co.; Arrow Electronics; and National Distillers & Chemical Corp.

Kathleen E. Zann

Q *Paper promotion is an area where designers can stretch their creative muscles. How can they create the opportunity to meet with someone in your position?*

A I'm always impressed when someone calls and says, "I saw a particular promotion that you did, and this prompted me to call. What impressed me about this promotion was thus-and-such." This tells me that he or she looked at it, evaluated the piece, did some homework, and is prepared to talk about it. But sometimes I'll respond, "Well, I'm sorry, I don't have time to see you, but if you'll please send samples, I can take a look at them, and I promise I'll return them." Many designers refuse. Either I grant them an audience or I don't get to see their work. I find that annoying. At that point, I wonder, if the designer won't cooperate with me on the initial phone call, how are we going to work together later? Also, if someone has to be there to explain the portfolio, the work must not be able to stand on its own.

Let's say a designer does send samples, and you're impressed. What happens next?

I meet with designers all the time. I'm always looking to see if what they do might fit my needs.

To you, how can designers make that initial meeting the most productive? First of all, who should show up? Should it be one person, or would a group of two or three make a more favorable impression?

I prefer the principal of the design firm because he or she sets the flavor of the design style and the management. And I prefer to see only one person. My office is very small and very crowded. With more than one visitor, it's going to be a real zoo.

So to those designers who are planning to hire actors with three-piece suits?

Don't do it.

But wouldn't you think it strange that a principal of a firm had the time to be out seeing prospects—especially since your company is off the beaten track—rather than being back at the office managing design work? Wouldn't that make it look like he or she were not busy enough or too hungry for work?

I don't think so. My concern is to meet with the principal of the firm. What you have to do back at the office perhaps can be delegated to someone else, but I insist on meeting the principal.

And given that, what is the first thing you look for?

That you're prepared. If I were to approach a prospective client, I'd make sure I knew something about the company, to whom they market, the name of the person I'm going to see, and what he or she does. I think it's only professional. Let's say somebody comes in and says, "I really know a lot about paper; I get paper from Lindenmeyr all the time." That's great, but Lindenmeyr is a distributor and James River is a manufacturer, which

◄ **Wire-O-bound promotional piece designed by John Waters and Carol Bouyoucos of Waters Design Associates for Curtis Tuscan Antique and Curtis Tuscan Terra paper grades manufactured by the James River Corporation's premium printing papers group.**

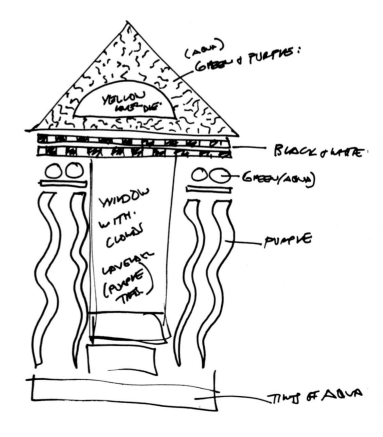

tells me you haven't done your homework. One can research a paper company by reading the annual report, talking to your local merchant, and looking at its promotions. Every mill has a sample department you can call, get swatch books, and get samples. Each of the swatch books describes a product line; look them over so you can talk intelligently when you come in. The same principles of being prepared apply when approaching any company.

What kind of a presentation do you prefer to see?

I want to see printed samples. I have no use for slides. Slides tend to hide a multitude of sins. And I also look at the print quality of the piece. Sometimes, someone will say, "I know printing inside and out," and I take a look at the piece and the binding is off; there's ghost-

ing, offsetting, and you-name-it. Or it's really a mess, dog-eared or torn. And if your presentation isn't perfect and meticulous, what is your design work going to look like? The same goes for your personal appearance. If I can't immediately take you to a board of directors meeting, I probably won't use you.

Some people might blame bad print quality on their past clients by saying, "They made me use a bad printer. I wish I could work with clients like you who use good printers."

If you have to explain a piece in your portfolio, leave it out. I suppose that sounds really tough. But if you have to say, "Well, this would have been really nice if I could have done the second tissue instead of the first tissue, and if it had been red instead of blue . . ." then you're in trouble.

In his early explorations (far left), John Waters considered texture, form, and color. His double-page-spread comps (left) demonstrated to Kathleen Zann how the designers proposed to utilize a variety of printing and binding techniques to showcase the printing characteristics of Tuscan text and cover. Comps were prepared with art generated on the Lightspeed computer design work station.

Would that demonstrate to you that the designer wasn't able to take charge and manage the project properly?

Maybe the client was a bozo. But for whatever reason, if you have to justify why a piece looks the way it does, then don't show it. What I do want to see is that every piece tells a story—what the problem was and how you solved it.

How much information do you need to know about the design firm?

I want to know the number of employees, where you're located, and the type of clients you have. You should have done some research so you're prepared to know what you want from me when you walk in, so that it's a productive meeting. I would also hope that you'll keep the meeting short, because I assume that you're as busy as I am. As I mentioned, I only want to see printed pieces. But if, for some reason, you've done a three-dimensional project or corporate identity and it won't fit in a portfolio, I would accept 4 × 5″ transparencies, nicely mounted.

Are you ever willing to come to the designer's office for the meeting?

Generally speaking, if you are selling to someone, you are the one expected to make the sales call. However, I recently visited about a dozen studios in San Francisco, and they were wildly different from each other. It gave me a perspective on each designer's environment and a sense of their aesthetics. I usually don't have the luxury of time for that, but now I have files you wouldn't believe on the designers I want to use in the future.

The pages of the Tuscan promotion show seven opaque matched ink colors, two kinds of metallic foil, and four die cuts on fourteen different stocks. The copy humorously connects the culture and arts of Tuscany with the desirable characteristics of Curtis Tuscan Antique and Terra papers.

James River Corporation

Do you think it's a good idea for the designer to use printed samples as a leave-behind at the meeting?

You can leave something behind. I have extensive files. I try to keep them current, but I can't keep everything. They may be tossed out.

So that's not the time to leave your best samples.

No, don't leave your best samples. Although, if a particular piece impressed me, I'll ask to keep it. Leave your business card. And I'd appreciate a follow-up letter; I think that's professional.

Once the initial meeting has taken place, it often takes anywhere from two to three months to two or three years to develop a client relationship. Are follow-ups, packages of new printed samples, a bonus or an annoyance to you?

I keep a mental file of not only the projects that are coming up, but the designers I would like to use. I think it's a good idea to send a new printed sample—one you're proud of—every once in while with a personal letter attached to it, so that I remember who you are and what you do. But for the most part, if your portfolio has impressed me, I'll use you anyway.

Sometimes it's difficult for people to get enough samples to send them to everyone they want to keep in contact with.

I produce very large quantities of my promotions. If we were working together and you told me at the beginning that you wanted a thousand of them, I'd be willing to negotiate with you. And I think that they would be a much better example of your capabilities than a capabilities brochure.

What do you think of an offer to take you to lunch?

Forget it. Maybe once we have a working relationship, it's nice to go to lunch, maybe have a drink, and

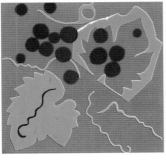

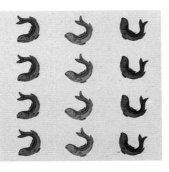

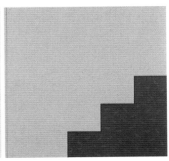

talk about the project that we're working on. But to take me to lunch to get a job . . . . it just doesn't interest me. What does interest me is learning about the advantages of using your company, and the results of your work. For example, if you redesigned a college catalog and enrollment increased 30 percent, that's worthy of mention. Then, more than a designer, you're selling yourself as a problem solver.

Can you relate this to your area, promotions produced by paper companies? Many promotional campaigns stand out in my mind as useful reference tools on a variety of subjects from fishing to the culture of Brazil. Do paper companies have an additional purpose?

It would be nice to think that we're trying to create beautiful works in print, but basically we're talking about a manufacturing operation. These are selling tools. Maybe from the designer's point of view they're more than that, but their purpose is to demonstrate performance characteristics of paper.

Do you have a list of criteria that each promotion must demonstrate?

Absolutely. We have a targeted marketing plan. Who is the end user, the specifier? In some cases, the printer will specify the sheet. In some cases it will be the designer. We've found that it might even be the corporate executive who happens to have heard, for example, the name "Curtis Flannel" and therefore has some input.

I'm very specific with designers. I'll say things such as, "This is the primary and secondary target market; these are the parameters within which you may design. Here are the features, advantages, and benefits that this piece has to demonstrate."

Do you see your role as keeping the designer on the right track?

Definitely. Here's an example: We were introducing a 100 lb. Curtis Flannel cover, and a designer wanted to double it over for the front and back covers, which would make it even heavier. I agreed that a gatefold would look beautiful. But the point of a 100 lb. cover is that it's substantial enough on its own. So I had to veto the designer's idea.

When I enumerate all the characteristics I want to get across, a designer might take off with one thing of particular interest to him or her, which might not be particularly important in the whole marketing scheme. That's why I need to see tissue sketches, so I can stop something before it gets too far along.

Are you warning designers not to take criticism too personally? It's not that this is a bad solution, just that certain objectives have to be met?

Yes, absolutely. Most designers will be disappointed when I reject a particular direction, but the real professionals realize that I don't do it arbitrarily. There are solid reasons why something won't work. I don't just say, "We have to change this." Instead, I'll say, "It would be better if we emphasized this aspect because, for these reasons, it's more important than what you've shown."

To designers who are approaching paper companies, thinking that they may get a once-in-a-lifetime opportunity to satisfy all their fantasies, then, it's not necessarily so.

It's not so. Maybe some paper companies have the kind of budgets where they can hand the designer an unlimited amount of money and say, "Do something wonderful."

Does that happen?

Honestly, I've seen some promotions that look that way. Almost without purpose. A paper promotion is not a portfolio piece for the designer! A paper company is a client like any other company.

Ego is always involved in design. But when you can separate your ego from your design—when you don't take it personally, and you realize there's a reason for making changes—then I think you become a much better designer, certainly a better businessperson.

Can computers help designers keep a project on track so that fewer changes have to be made? John Waters is recognized for being the first to install the Lightspeed system in his office. From your point of view as his client, was the system helpful?

At one point, I came into his office and saw slides showing many possible design solutions.

You just told me you hated slides!

I do hate slides when they're used to sell a designer's work, but I had already given John the project. Instead of showing me sketches, his people said, "Come on over here"; they punched some buttons, and designs came up on the monitor that previewed what they had in mind. In that respect it really helped me. And this was one of the magical projects where everything just clicked.

Do you have any rules of thumb in terms of evaluating proposed solutions?

I have found that designers are very different from each other. Some of them will take an assignment and run to such an extreme that you have to grab them by the collar and pull them back. With others, you have to keep pushing. I am finishing a project now with a design group that presented me with finished comps for eight different design directions. I sat in their office thinking, "These are beautiful, but they're just not it," and wondering how I could tell them after they put in all that time. I had to reject every single one. But each comp had something terrific about it, and if you could combine the best points of all of them, which they eventually did, it would be perfect. As it turned out, it's an outstanding promotion.

This process can be like giving birth. I later asked them, "How did you keep from strangling me?" They said that there was a mutual trust. I knew they were putting their heart into it. One of them said that I kept pushing, just kept pushing. Well, that's my responsibility as a client.

Some people might have accepted something they didn't really believe in, or started over again with another designer.

I don't think that's ethical. Recently, a designer gave me one direction. And when I said it wasn't quite right, he said, "I'm sorry. This is a solution to your problem and it works, and if you don't like it, that's it." We negotiated a percentage of his design fee, but I kept saying, "I want to work with you, let's rethink this." And he said no, he didn't have time; he had worked on it for two weeks, which he felt was sufficient. So we had to terminate the project and I had to find another designer. I was very disappointed. Once I make a commitment to work with a designer, as far as I'm concerned, we're going to work together until we solve the problem. ∎

John Waters and Carol Bouyoucos at the Lightspeed station at Waters Design Associates, New York.

Robert Moulthrop has over twenty years' experience in public relations, strategic planning, internal and external communications, and managing the process of new business proposals. Since October 1988, he has been senior marketing director for the New York office of KPMG Peat Marwick, one of the world's largest accounting, tax, and consulting firms. Previously, he was marketing director for the New York office of Deloitte Haskins & Sells, (DH&S) another Big Eight firm. He came to DH&S from Educational Testing Service in Princeton, New Jersey, where he was director of marketing and public relations. He has also served in the public relations office of the City University of New York, headquarters for the nation's largest urban college system.

Deloitte Haskins & Sells is an international firm of auditors, tax advisors, and consultants providing service to a broad range of national and multinational clients through more than a hundred offices in the United States and 450 offices worldwide. Organized as a partnership, DH&S employs more than twenty-three thousand people; there are approximately 750 partners in the United States. The New York office at One World Trade Center includes on its client list Merrill Lynch, The Equitable, and The New York Times Corporation.

7

The Written Proposal: What Matters, What Doesn't

Melanie Roher, a *cum laude* graduate of Pratt Institute, studied illustration and photography at Carnegie Mellon and Syracuse universities. She was a member of the design department staff for exhibitions and graphics at the Metropolitan Museum of Art for six years. Subsequently, she became design director of the bicentennial exhibit, "Remember the Ladies" and an art director for Mobil Corporation. Ms. Roher is currently principal of Roher Design, Inc., Ardsley, New York, which she founded in 1980. She has created interpretive graphics for clients in the United States, as well as multilingual projects in China, Japan, and Europe. She has received numerous awards for her work for museums, galleries, nonprofit institutions, corporations, and service firms such as Deloitte Haskins & Sells.

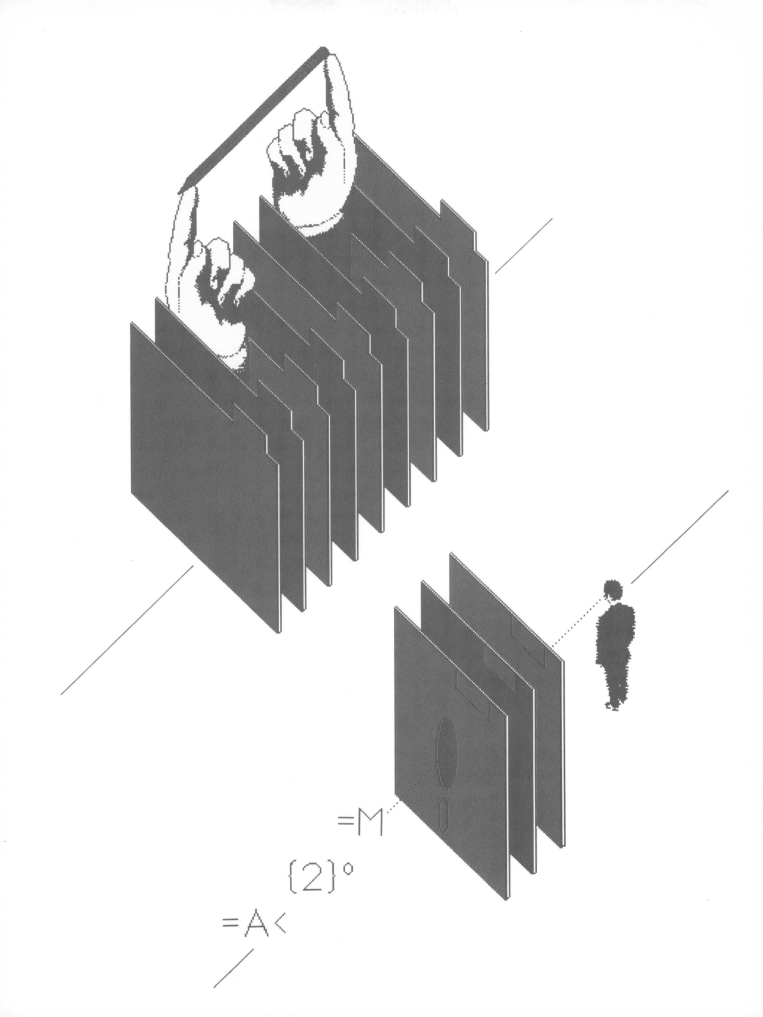

=M

{2}°

=A<

Robert Moulthrop

Q *You are a proposal maven, both as a recipient of designers' proposals for creative services and as the creator of proposals for accounting and other services offered by accounting firms. As an expert in the medium, how do you think design firm proposals should be structured?*

A I want a proposal to show me that a designer understands the project objectives; what the problem is that this particular project is going to solve. It can be structured in any way that truly accomplishes this.

To you, what is the purpose of a proposal?

To make sure there are no surprises! You may want to consider it as a kind of discussion draft. If it weren't that, it would be a contract. You must reassure me that you understand what I said in our initial meeting. You must also make sure that I am clear about the specific services you are going to provide.

The design work should, I think, be structured in phases. Once you describe what is going to be accomplished in general, outline as specifically as you can the work to be accomplished in each phase. For example: Phase I—Sketches; Phase II—Comps; Phase III—Mechanicals. You should go into some measure of detail about exactly what you propose to present to me at the completion of each phase. And finally, include an overall budget, with separate numbers for design fees and for anticipated expenses, listed by category, such as typography, illustration, and so forth. I would also like to see

some kind of transmittal document or cover letter, which needn't, depending on the size of the project, be terribly important.

Is there anything special designers should know about proposals geared to accounting or other professional service firms?

Remember that for people like me, who work at accounting firms—and since we are increasingly in need of design services, you may find yourselves working more and more for us in the future—that it's not to me alone that the proposal is addressed. It is going to be read by several other people. In my firm, that's going to be accountants. And I can't begin to tell you what they don't know about design. We need—I need—the designer's help in making sure that what is presented to them is something they not only understand, but feel comfortable with. Which means, in effect, that the way you prepare a proposal for me—or for any other service firm that is newly marketing its services—may be very different from the way you prepare a proposal for a large corporation.

Before we get into those differences, I'd like to address your comment, "You may find yourselves working for us more in the future." What kinds of projects are coming up?

Basically, we have two kinds of projects. We need designers to help us sell generic services and to help us sell specific services. Let me explain; generic services include things like an accounting firm's general capability in international tax or in telecommunications consulting. Specific services include things like providing an audit for a particular company, which we call an "engagement." The design projects that sell generic services are likely to be brochures or newsletters or an

◄**Macintosh-generated art by Mark Ulrich, commissioned by Melanie Roher to illustrate a 12-page, 1986 recruiting brochure for the New York office of Deloitte Haskins & Sells.**

Melanie Roher's first storyboard indicated photography as a key page element. The DH&S partners, however, wanted to emphasize the firm's advanced information processing capabilities and were more intrigued by Roher's concept of computer-generated illustration.

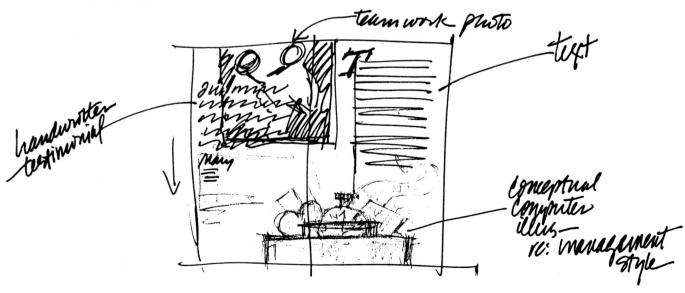

identity, for example, for our financial services area. When we are going after a specific project, designers are more likely to be called in to design a presentation format, to help design charts, or to do a lot of nitty-gritty stuff that's going to clarify our proposal to get that engagement. In that way, we'll use design to really help with our communication process, with new prospects. As far as I'm concerned, that's where the rubber hits the road. For instance, when you have a new business presentation, and it looks like hell, you give it to a designer, who looks at it and says, "Okay, we need sections and organization, and let's do this and that." He sets it up on his desktop publishing system and all of a sudden it becomes something very unique and appealing.

Are you saying that when you're competing for a significant piece of business, you will do whatever it takes to position your firm successfully against the competition, and that may include hiring designers?

Right. And it's much the same for lawyers, who need designers to help present evidence. It's a whole new ball game for professional service firms. DH&S has been in business since the late 1800s. And this type of marketing is a relatively recent development—since 1979–1980, when the American Institute of Certified Public Accountants took the wraps off the whole non-competitive thing. Some states like Texas still have rigorous noncompetitive clauses that prohibit the full range of stuff the rest of the country enjoys—everything from advertising to brochures to seminars to television commercials. One accounting company advertises on cable TV.

I've read that accounting firms have been hiring marketing people from the package goods giants.

DH&S hired a former brand manager from RJR Nabisco. The thinking was that it's possible to market services in much the same way as products. But you have to remember that accounting firms are business-to-business operations. They're not putting stuff on the shelves for consumers to buy; they are presenting professional services for other business to buy.

With that background, I'd like to return to the way you prefer design firm proposals to be prepared. Are you more interested in the content and style or the numbers? Designers often wonder whether they've invested days coming up with exacting prose to describe a project and its objectives—and whether the recipient just goes to the last page and says something like, "Ah, $29,000, here's one for $18,000," and immediately trashes theirs.

Well, make no mistake about it, it's not only accountants who care how much the fee is. Everybody is bottom-line-oriented today. Yes, of course, fee counts. But's let's assume that rather than $29,000 and $18,000, that we've got two proposals of similar quality, and one is $29,000, and the other is $27,000. Then a lot of other things are going to come into play. And writing does

count. Now, I'm not talking curlicues and style, but I want to see that you can think, that you can write English well, and that you can put a couple of sentences together to make things logical. And if you can't do that, please get someone to help you who can. It may just be writing is not your strong point, and that we're still going to get along. I happen to be very word-oriented. Don't overwrite a proposal, but do organize and structure it. And to all designers: please don't clutter up the page. I don't want a proposal that looks like an impenetrable thicket of words. What I want is something that is inviting and says what you want it to say. The proposal is a place for good design. And it's not necessarily going to be a typewritten document these days; with desktop publishing, a lot of people are doing things differently. Most important, I want a proposal that makes me glad to be involved with this particular design firm, that makes me think, "If they can do this for themselves, boy, they're really going to do great stuff for me."

So looks do count. But do you always understand the terminology and design jargon? Is terminology like "flyleaf," "gatefold," or "perfect bound" self-evident to you and your accounting partners and managers, or do designers need to explain themselves better?

Well, there is a place for jargon. That's where you can flex your muscles, where you want to say, "flyleaf" or "gatefold," so there's a sense that you are master of your mystique and know what you're talking about. But when you're proposing to non-design-oriented clients like accountants, you'll need to enclose some kind of mock-up—nothing too elaborate—so I can show the partners what they'll be getting.

You don't see that as "working on spec," considered unethical by many designers?

No. I'm just talking about giving me a visual proposal as well as a written one—especially if, say, there's a special kind of paper or a die cut involved. Remember, I'm not doing this as an exercise, to see who comes up with the best mock-up. I've basically already chosen you. Now, you must take the time to put together a little something, so I'm not left doing a tap dance with people who are wondering why it's $29,000 instead of $18,000. So that there is, indeed, some kind of justification. I think that everybody who is responsible for buying design work at accounting and law firms has the same expectation. Before the partners give the nod to go ahead, they want to know what it's going to look like; they want to know, "What am I going to be spending all this money for?" If they haven't done something just like before, it's hard for them to take the leap of faith that's required.

How should the proposal be delivered? In the mail? Or should designers air express it or send it by messenger. Does that make it look more important? Or should it be presented in person, at a meeting where there would be the opportunity to discuss it with you and the partners?

It really does depend on the deadline. I mean, if it's due today, then I don't want someone to call me at 12:00 and say, "I put it in the mail." But I don't particularly want a big production number out of the delivery of the proposal. I just want the thing there, and I want it done well, and I want it done with a minimum of fuss. And I really don't want to have a meeting until I've had the chance to go over it.

And probably after I go over it, I will call, asking, "Could you change this a bit . . . because, when I talk to the partners, this is going to raise some questions . . . so I'll need you to do thus-and-such." I want to make sure that the meeting with the partners goes smoothly. Because at my place, I have to bring you in, and you have to get tapped on the head. They have to sprinkle holy water on the project.

The process is not always as smooth as designers would hope, is it? What should come with the proposal? Is getting a contract premature at this time, or would it be helpful to explain some of the terminology and working procedures outlined in the proposal?

The contract is definitely premature and looks pushy. Obviously have it ready, but don't send it along with the proposal. I would appreciate any printed samples similar to what we've been talking about. Again, because they help me when I have to act as a translator to other people.

When and how should the proposal be followed up? Do you think designers should wait for potential clients to call back, or—after a reasonable interval—should they call you?

If you haven't heard from me by the day we agreed on, don't just sit there. By all means, pick up the phone and call to ask, "Is the project moving? What happened?" If somebody else got the project, that's life. But even if you lost out, if the process was good, your chances increase dramatically the next time up. The nod may go to you instead of someone else. It may be that a whole variety of factors led to a negative decision. But by no means should you just sit and wait for the proposal to die on the other end. Pick up the phone so that the action is complete . . . if I've been schnook enough not to call you back.

And if you do *call back?*

Be there when I call or return the call promptly, as promptly as you can. Our first conversations and meetings really are a litmus test. Everyone who has been on interviews knows that judgments are made—perhaps they shouldn't be—but judgments are made in two or three minutes. You can tell right away if it's going to work or it isn't. So, it is worth taking the time to sit down and go over everything in detail, especially if you think of it as an investment in a long-term client relationship that's going to flower. My volume is low compared to many large corporations, and my budgets are lower, too. But I'm a great believer in long-term relationships.

Do you think you're difficult to work for?

No. I like designers who beat me up. I don't respect people whose response, when I say, "Let's do it this way" is "That sounds good." That's not the point of the whole process. If I knew what I were doing, I wouldn't have to ask designers to come in and help, and be willing to pay good money for it. But when you're beating me up, I want to know why. I want to know why my idea is really not good. I want to know what your idea is going to contribute. What's really important is how much designers bring to the party—the totality of their contribution. The best projects that I've done involved designers who have really contributed a lot, I mean, a lot beyond the look of the thing and whether it's Times Roman or Garamond. And the more the designer brings to the party, the more likely it is that we're going to party again.

It's true that not only accountants care about the bottom line, but some accounting firms can typify the kind of client who is more concerned about a low price than anything else—than concept or quality. And designers are hungry for work. So they come in with a low price to get the job, hope they can do it, and get into trouble.

That means trouble for me, too.

I don't think anyone goes over budget intentionally. The clients demand the low price, they say, "We have to have it for X dollars." Then it costs more money to get it done. More for photography, for illustration, for type, and for printing.

In building long-term relationships, it's important to be realistic. If you're willing to eat your fee—if you're willing to price it at $15,000 and know it's going to cost $20,000 . . . you know you're not going to make money. You'll also have to realize that when I come back and say, "I have $15,000 for another similar project," you're going to have to say, "No, no, no, this is a $20,000 project. I ate my fee once, but I'm not doing it again."

Certain expectations have been set up.

Certain *false* expectations. Nobody is suggesting that any young designer be greedy, but I think you do have to be realistic.

Do you think it would be better to say to the client right away, or state in the proposal, "This job should be priced at $20,000, but we'll do it for you for $15,000 in order to establish our relationship on a first-time basis?"

Yes, I think that would be acceptable.

When you used the word "greedy," I was thinking that most young designers are not greedy for money. They are greedy for the opportunity to do good work. Also, in many cases, those more profitable second-time jobs rarely materialize.

The good work will happen. There are certain projects that we know are going to cost money, that we are willing to spend the money on. And if we have had a good experience with you, we will call you back. But it's a different situation if we get the bill from the printer, and it's off by a magnitude of two in terms of what we thought we heard it was going to be. When the designer says, "Oh yeah, this printer charges for 'overs,' and there was also this or that." It's just horrible when I have to confront my client inside the recruiting department or the tax partner who's going to sign the check and say, "Well, I'm sorry we're over budget, it's $5,000 more than the designer said it was going to be." As the internal marketing guy, I can do that once, maybe twice. But after that I begin to get the fish eye every time I walk in.

Let's return to your initial answer, "The purpose of a proposal is to make sure there are no surprises." We talked about terms like "flyleaf" and "gatefold." Yet other things, like "overs," can hit clients by surprise. The printer will answer, "This is industry standard." But it turns out that the client never heard of it before, because they've never done it before. Things like "sidewalk delivery" turn out to be very big issues.

And don't forget stuff like, "The photographer's fee is $1,500 a day plus expenses." Then when it's all over, we find out about the assistant, the props, the meals, the transportation, and the fifty rolls plus processing and contacts. It's a small fortune, and no one who's inexperienced at working with designers will sit still for a surprise like that.

So you're saying a proposal can't go into too much detail.
Not for me. ∎

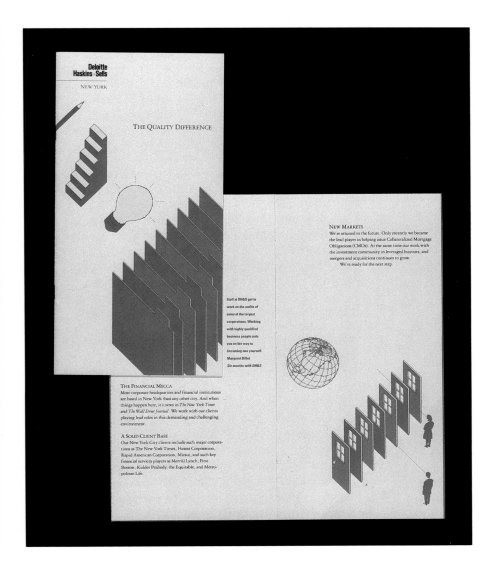

The tall, slim format was suggested by one of the DH&S partners, who wanted the brochure to stand out from the pile of recruiting literature candidates were likely to be considering.

Dr. David M. Lederman is chairman, president, and chief executive officer of ABIOMED, Inc. Dr. Lederman received a B.S. degree in engineering physics, and an M.S. and a Ph.D. in aerospace engineering, all from Cornell University. He joined the Avco Everett Research Laboratory in 1973 as principal research scientist in the medical group. In 1979, Dr. Lederman was appointed chairman of Avco's medical group, with overall technical and fiscal management responsibilities. In 1981, he formed ABIOMED, Inc. He has authored over forty scientific publications related to the cardiac assist and prosthetic valve fields and has been a principal investigator on numerous programs sponsored by the National Institutes of Health. A frequent speaker in national and international forums on advanced cardiac support and related technology, he is a member of numerous professional organizations.

ABIOMED, Inc. was founded in 1981 to develop cost-effective, innovative medical devices. Since then, the Danvers, Massachusetts, company has become a leader in the development of temporary and permanent cardiac assist systems, and is using its core technological resources to develop a range of other medical and dental products. Temporary cardiac support devices benefit patients during or after surgery, after an acute heart attack, or while waiting a donor heart for transplant; the company's BVS System 5000, in use in Europe, is undergoing clinical evaluations in the United States. ABIOMED is also developing a group of permanently implantable devices for patients with irreversible heart disease for whom donor hearts are unavailable. These devices are designed to provide a near normal quality of life. ABIOMED became a public company in 1988 with an initial public offering that raised $12 million for product development. With 1988 revenues, primarily from research and development contracts, of $4.9 million, the company employs approximately sixty-five people.

Michael Weymouth was born in Maine and studied at the New England School of Art in Boston, Massachusetts. He worked for ten years in the Boston design community prior to founding Weymouth Design in 1973. Weymouth Design produces twenty to twenty-five annual reports each year, as well as other corporate materials such as capabilities brochures and identity programs for clients including Reebok, Drexel Burnham Lambert, and the Massachusetts Industrial Finance Agency. Unlike most designers, Michael Weymouth shoots much of his own photography. His firm's design work and his photography have frequently appeared in the Mead Annual Report Show, *Print Casebooks, Communication Arts* magazine, and *PhotoGraphis*.

8

A Test for Avoiding Mediocrity

Dr. David Lederman

Q *In May 1985,* Business Week *came out with a cover story, "Small Is Beautiful: A Special Report on America's Hot Growth Companies." I wrote to the "Top 100" companies in the New York area and requested their annual reports. Upon review, I concluded that even if* Business Week *thought the financials were beautiful, the annual reports were anything but. They clearly showed that most people who make decisions about graphic communications for smaller companies manage to resist the advances of a graphic designer. In the first few years of a company, it seems that an extremely low-budget or do-it-yourself approach is considered good enough. But you've done things differently. Why?*

A Many young companies, start-ups, do not pay enough attention to the market. An annual report is a mechanism to tell the stockholders the status and prospects of their investments. But it is also a mechanism for the company to present itself to the world. If you think of yourself as being beautiful, to use *Business Week*'s word—even if it's your first year as a public company—it is important to show exactly what is beautiful about you, and it is very important to find someone who can do that well. I have been told—I don't know whether it is true—that the majority of people spend somewhere between seventeen and twenty seconds on an annual report before throwing it away, and that they only look at the chairman's letter and at the photographs—so the design becomes as important as the words.

Well, I've read it's five minutes in a couple of studies by investor relations firms.

I'm glad to hear that. I certainly spend more than five minutes on the companies I follow. Typically I ask, "Why did they decide to show that picture, that product, that person?" Or, "Why did they say this or that?" What you think of yourself, your self-image, also applies to a company. And quite frankly, I don't think that the issue of cost is the deciding element in the decision to go with a designer like Michael Weymouth. While cost consciousness and cost effectiveness are obviously concerns, when you break down the cost of making an annual report, there may be a tendency to be "penny wise and pound foolish." You may try to save on something and in the long run, it costs you more. A good annual report is always a good investment. And if a company is mature enough to realize that the marketing of the company is as important as the marketing of the products, management will pay attention to the annual report. Companies that think small are likely to stay small.

◄**Left to right: investor relations consultant Peter Feinstein, Dr. David Lederman, and designer Michael Weymouth discuss how ABIOMED's biventricular cardiac assist system, a temporary heart pump, will be pictured in ABIOMED's 1988 annual report.**

Pages from Mike Weymouth's sketchbook show how he planned to integrate product photography representing ABIOMED's major operations with illustrations and "lots of support graphs" to tell the company story. He visualized the report's binding by diagramming how several paper stocks, with printing ranging from two to six colors, would fit into a 32-page format.

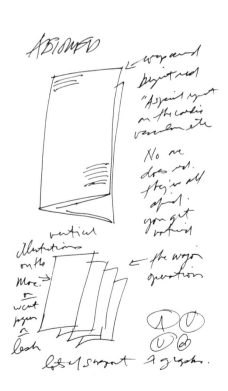

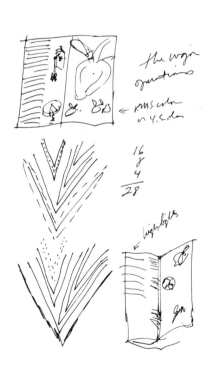

ABIOMED, Inc.

For many small, new companies, budget is the number-one consideration. If they went directly to a printer with pictures from the files and said, "Put these together with our financials, print it, and put a nice cover on it," maybe they would spend $20,000, just to use a round number. On the other hand, a graphic designer might propose, "You need original photography and a much higher level of printing quality." Perhaps the cost would then be between $75,000 and $100,000. And to the client, that would be a significant amount of money that could be spent on something else. The thinking might be, "The securities analysts and shareholders will just look at the income statement anyway, and won't care about all this stuff." Is your feeling that they do care?

Yes, but the spread you have given me could be narrower. One can get something very elegant for a lot less than $100,000. And one can go directly to printers and spend more than $20,000. Before we were a public company, we issued literature where we didn't hire a graphic designer—and it shows.

But all this is noise compared to the overall cost of going public, and the cost of maintaining a public company in terms of legal, accounting, and other related expenses. You have to put everything in the right perspective. Think of the cost of doing business as a public company, and try to assess what percentage of that should be spent on projecting your message and informing the world and your stockholders of what you have done, are doing, and are planning to do. Again, very small companies tend not to be market-driven. As they mature, companies become more market-driven, so I would think that in most cases, the successful ones will change their minds. Am I right?

Yes, but by then there might be quite a lot of bad work that will need to be undone.

Well, not for us. I am very happy we decided to go the way we did with our first report as a public company. And I have to tell you that our marketing staff is also happy because the annual report becomes more than just a financial report to the stockholders. It serves numerous functions. It also becomes a marketing instrument for our products. It is also very important for recruiting. When interviewing prospective employees, especially during the phase of building the management team, the first document candidates ask for is the annual report; sometimes they won't even schedule an interview until they've seen it. It is to their benefit to read something that presents the company fairly and accurately, and the report pays for itself in that sense.

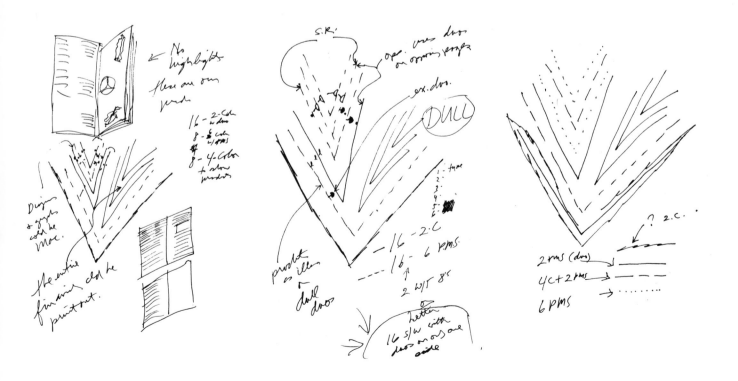

Q *Many smaller companies appear to resist the advances of a graphic designer. You've done things differently. Why?*

A *Companies that think small are likely to stay small.*

How did you meet Mike Weymouth and start to work with him; what was your interview process like? And what were your goals for the report?

Since becoming a public company, we have used an outside consulting firm, Peter Feinstein, Inc., to help us set up an investor relations program. They introduced me to four different graphic designers. Each presented to me a representative assembly of work. I was simply and overwhelmingly more impressed with Mike Weymouth's work. I have a lot of respect for good photography. Mike doesn't strike me as being the type of person who will do any annual report for any company; he apparently has to feel that there is something of real quality before he takes an assignment. There is a correspondence between the elegant kind of report he likes to do and the type of company that the report is about. It's not just a question of dollars and cents.

Our mission is to save lives, and we derive a great sense of pride from our work. Our company's success is not only measured by our ability to generate profit, but by our ability to develop medical technology that will save or improve human lives at a cost lower than comparable or existing therapies.

Mike also gets a great deal of satisfaction and pride from his work. I asked him questions, and I asked the other graphic designers that I met—I will not reveal their names of course—whether they would do certain things for me because I wanted them done a particular way. I intentionally gave them examples that, in my opinion, exhibited very poor taste. Imagine the layout or structure of a very ridiculous type of annual report. I said, "I would like something like this." They said okay; they'd do it.

Do you think that those who agreed weren't very good at what they did?

Yes. It meant to me that it wasn't important to them how the annual report was going to end up looking. If the designer doesn't have a strong feeling about his or her work, even if he or she disagrees with me, then I'm not very impressed.

You conducted something that delved much deeper than a portfolio review. You tested people to see if they were just going to be "yes people" and if your report was just going to be another job.

Correct. To me that was very important. If the others were as good as I am told—and I'm not saying that they didn't do good work—they were not consistent. They were driven by the economics of their business.

◄ **Dr. Lederman offers technical advice as Mike Weymouth photographs the biventricular assist system.**

They might also have been driven by being intimidated by past clients. The clients may have "made them do stuff" that they didn't feel was right, and they assumed that's the way these relationships had to be.

That is precisely what they said to me! When I reviewed their work, I asked them how they could do work like that, and they said that's how the client wanted it! That may be true. But if you look at Mike's work—whether you like it or not—all examples shown to me were well done and to my liking; however diverse and different, he is consistent. Working with him, he voiced strong opinions, and I learned to respect him even more.

His attitude is similar to and compatible with our corporate philosophy, our culture. I sense that Mike is a person who seeks long-term relationships. After he thought out and discussed what he recommended as the focus of our first annual report, one can sort of project what the second one should be like, and what the third one may be. I like that. I like the idea of long-term planning. For annual reports and everything else. I would be curious to know how different I am from the others you have spoken with.

Several years ago I surveyed a group of leading designers about what they found most rewarding and most problematic about client/designer relationships. And to reflect on what you're saying, most designers told me that their biggest overall business problem was that clients seemed to want mediocre solutions. "Seemed to want" is too mild a term. They described clients who demanded mediocre solutions, who were overly directive and would say, "This is the picture for the cover; this is what we want on page three." How would you address clients like that? What advice would you offer?

I consider myself to be very knowledgeable in my own field of medical device technology. I expect people whose expertise is in other areas of interest to recognize that, and acknowledge that I am better qualified to determine what is extraordinary or what is mediocre about medical device products. If you have chosen the right graphic designer, he or she should also be considered an expert. I would say that once you have chosen someone you are comfortable with, the design should be driven more by what the designer feels than by what you feel. Mike asked in the beginning, "What is it that you're trying to say? Why are you going to do this?" And then he decided how to implement that. So one must offer the direction, but once the direction is given—if you have retained the right professional—one would think that you're not doing your job if you cannot delegate the creative decisions. If you interfere and demand mediocrity, I think a smart designer would drop you and your company as a client.

Here's an example. To my thinking, photography is one of the most important elements in the report. I am personally an enthusiastic photographer; I have my own darkroom and a collection of cameras. The temptation was high to get involved and try to micro-manage. However, I pretty much left Mike alone. When the selection of photographs came up, I asked some questions, and made some recommendations. But ultimately, the choices were the shots he selected, except for one small photograph in which I suggested to Mike that something didn't look right, and I thought we should go back and reshoot. He agreed. I don't think that we disagreed about anything in the annual report; it became largely what he recommended. It was amazing. This had never happened to me before! Very seldom have I been able to interact with someone from the outside in that way, and we do interact with a lot of outside professionals that provide us with various services. There are always disagreements. Maybe it's just personality compatability or maybe that's just how a relationship should be. But I do think the decision-maker in a company must choose someone he can rely on to produce a high-quality product that represents the company well.

Sometimes a CEO delegates that to people who don't have his vision.

That's a mistake. It's shortsighted. There are certain functions that are part of a CEO's job. You used the right word, "vision," which is one of the things you want to project in an annual report. And that comes from the top. In this company, by the way, there were two people involved in the process—myself and the person with the most marketing and sales experience in the company. He is a very important member of the management team, and it is his charter and focus to sell our products. We didn't want to make a product catalog out of the annual report, but we did want to project the credibility of the company to our product customers as well as to the stockholders. ■

The 1988 ABIOMED, Inc. annual report shows investors, securities analysts, prospective employees, and customers what ABIOMED's products look like and how they work, both inside and outside the patient.

Walt Walston has been director of the Jimmy Stewart Relay Marathon, a benefit event for Saint John's Child Study Center, since 1981. Previously, he was department manager of the hospital's cardiovascular department. Formerly a medical/industrial photographer, he received his technical training in the U.S. Navy. Mr. Walston is an avid runner, running at least one marathon a year. He is very active in the running community and in road race productions. As marathon director, he annually coordinates five thousand runners, 750 volunteers, and fifty corporations that participate as sponsors and enter corporate teams.

Saint John's Hospital and Health Center is one of southern California's leading health care facilities. A 551-bed comprehensive acute-care hospital, it provides a wide variety of primary and tertiary care services including the $5 million Saint John's Cancer Center, the Heart Institute, and the Chemical Dependency Center. Approximately a thousand physicians and nearly two thousand other health care professionals are on staff. For twenty-five years, Saint John's Child Study Center has been offering comprehensive outpatient services for infants and children with emotional disturbances and developmental disabilities. Saint John's was founded in 1942 by the Sisters of Charity of Leavenworth, Kansas. The hospital is one of eight in the Sisters of Charity Health Services Corporation, the twenty-ninth largest health system in the United States.

9

Establishing the Value of *Pro Bono* Work

Morava & Oliver was founded in 1980 after Emmett Morava ended his seventeen-year association with Cross Associates, Los Angeles, where he helped guide the communications of companies such as Mattel, Fluor, and St. Regis Paper. A graduate of Pomona College and of Art Center College of Design, Mr. Morava began his career in the design department of Alcoa, Pittsburgh. His partner, Douglas Oliver, a graduate of the University of Kansas and of Art Center, came to the firm from Robert Miles Runyan and Associates, Playa del Rey. Located in Santa Monica, California, the Morava & Oliver Design Office has gained a reputation for intelligent annual reports for a range of clients in both the corporate and nonprofit sectors. Morava & Oliver have donated design services to the Jimmy Stewart Relay Marathon since 1987.

The Jimmy Stewart
Relay Marathon
with co-host Robert Wagner

The Jimmy Stewart
Relay Marathon
with co-host Robert Wagner

Walt Walston

Q *You have been responsible for communication and graphics in the nonprofit institutional world. Does that have a special meaning for designers?*

A It means that we try to get everything for free, whenever possible.

Designers are finding that there are interesting opportunities available in the nonprofit sector, say, doing recruiting or fundraising pieces for hospitals and universities. Many nonprofit institutions want—and should have—publications of a quality comparable to those of leading corporations. But there is a feeling that they want the work donated, or they're only willing to pay a fraction of the price for the same product. Designers want to do the work—see the creative potential—and yet can't run a business under those conditions. Can you address this?

If people support a particular charity or nonprofit organization—if they're an alumnus of a university or if their babies were born in our hospital—they may give us a break because they like us. Then, I think it's essential for the nonprofit organization to give back to a vendor, as much as possible, in recognition for a job well done. This can take many forms. It could be a credit on a poster, an introduction to the trustees or other alumni who may give them profitable work, and, of course, being selected for the project again the following year.

It is an honored tradition that design firms and ad agencies support charities and social causes through pro bono *work. However, as the health care industry becomes more competitive and market oriented, designers are increasingly needed for major communications projects. In those cases, do you think the design firm is entitled to normal project fees?*

◄T-shirts for the 1989 Jimmy Stewart Relay Marathon were designed *pro bono*—to benefit the Saint John's Child Study Center—by Jane Kobayshi Ritch of the Morava & Oliver Design Office.

Left to right: entry form, press kit, poster, and T-shirts for the 1988 Jimmy Stewart Relay Marathon. According to Walt Walston, projects like this give designers widespread exposure and the opportunity to make significant contacts.

Yes. When I was in the hospital's cardiovascular department, we didn't get any breaks on price at all. We were able to budget adequately for advertising and publications. We wanted to be choosy rather than in the position a lot of nonprofit organizations find themselves in—having to take whatever they can get at a discount instead of getting the best work out there.

Are you saying that you make a distinction between the special project, like the poster, that could or should be donated, and the larger project that requires specialized expertise, which you are willing to pay for?

Very much so. I'm involved with a charity now, and everything has to be donated. It's a tough job to be a fundraiser for a nonprofit organization. There are a lot of organizations out there with nonprofit status, and everybody's asking for the same dollar. Your charity has to be a good one and an authentic one, and you have to be able to give back to those people who give you discounts or donations. For instance, one local newspaper donates ad space to us. We make sure that they are first on the list to get an interview with our celebrities and to be invited to the marathon's celebrity cocktail kick-off party.

How can a charity find good designers who are willing to donate services?

I ask the business people who are affiliated with this facility. A lot of our foundation trustees work for Fortune 500 companies in the Los Angeles area. I ask them who they use, and whether they can influence that person to perhaps give us a donation. Then I may interview two or three different design companies. What really matters to me is the time line they say they can give us, how much of their staffing they'd be able to provide, and the quality of their work and their reputation. We're in a fortunate position because of the reputation of our event; we don't have to settle on just anything because it's a discount or free. If someone donates a service to us, he or she can take that project, put it in their resumé or portfolio and say, "We work for these people."

You see yourself as being able to contribute to the designer's portfolio. Is the work highly visible?

We often have national coverage. Almost everyone in the Los Angeles area—in Los Angeles, Orange, and Ventura counties—knows about the Jimmy Stewart Relay Marathon. It's held in Griffith Park, near Hollywood. We usually have about five thousand runners.

Every year, we need different graphics, a different look. The designers give us a discount or a full donation of services, and we try to make them happy enough that they might want to come back to us next year. But if the firm got stuck on last year's idea and said, "Well, we can't change it," or if they couldn't come up with a new creative idea, then I would be very quick to change firms. The only way that our event progresses every year is by becoming better, by becoming something that the participants will want to come back to over and over. It's their entry fees that support the Child Study Center.

If you felt that you needed to change designers, what would you look for?

I want to be impressed by the concept, the different idea. I've done this event for seven years, and I'm always racking my brain for a new look. If I suggested a tag line or slogan—which I would do when requesting a proposal—I would like to see how they interpreted it and if they could come up with a very creative new look that would add to what we've done in the past.

Are you referring to a comp or visualization in a proposal?

Absolutely. I'm heavily into graphics; I like to see things presented to me in a graphic sense as opposed to two or three pages of typewritten material—although I think the ability to put thoughts on paper is important, too. But perhaps even more important in selling your product is the ability to show a person what you can do graphically.

Many designers are uncomfortable with preparing visual concepts for a proposal, and consider it working on spec.

As a consumer—whether I were to pay for the work or get it donated—I would not feel comfortable with a firm that wasn't able to convey their ideas to me. I mean, I wouldn't hire a firm that said, "Oh, don't worry, we'll come up with an idea, just give us a retainer."

Let's say, for a job for which you had a budget for professional fees, you only received proposals that stated, "Phase I—Concept Development: We will present two to five concept sketches, and the fee for this work will be X." Would you accept such a proposal?

No. I would not. This may sound cold, but I think there are too many hungry people out there who would give me a concept with the proposal . . . with the hope I'd love their work and then hire them.

In addition to the hungry people, there are business owners who are engaged in current work. In order to do that concept sketch for you, they might need to allocate several days to analyzing your problem and coming up with a solution. They might feel that it wouldn't be fair, to you or to them, to show you a quick sketch if only because it wouldn't represent their best thinking.

Let me use a different analogy. Yesterday we had a long committee meeting to interview the two finalists for our public relations firm. Both public relations firms gave me proposals that contained not only background of what they had done in the past, but also what they thought they could do for us this year—new ideas, time schedules, and so forth. In other words, they had done a tremendous amount of work researching our situation. What's the difference between a public relations firm and a design company?

A design company is selling the very work—the concept sketch—that you're asking for up front. The public relations firm is explaining their plan or strategy to you, but they're not actually calling up reporters and setting up interviews or staging events. On the basis of their proposal, you will enter into a retainer agreement with one of the public relations firms to provide those services, but they haven't gotten started yet. But the design firm has completed a phase of the work. Do you think designers are unfair in making this distinction?

I'm not asking for camera-ready artwork. I'm asking them to come up with a concept, and it might just be a sketch. But if they can't grasp what I'm trying to tell them, then I wouldn't be able to use them. I'd also want to be able to call some of their previous clients. I'd ask them how easy it was to convey their thoughts to the designer: "Was the designer able to interpret your ideas, and give you what you needed?"

I understand what you're saying. It's not an ideal way to work for many designers, but it is a reality of the business world for many others. To see preliminary ideas, some clients will pay an honorarium to each of several firms. And getting references is expected.

Earlier you said you think it's essential for a nonprofit organization to give back as much as possible for a job well done. Can you elaborate?

We make sure all our sponsors and people on the board know who does our design, and that we're happy with the work. We consider Morava & Oliver a sponsor of the marathon. They're a fun, easy group to work with. Like the other sponsors, they are invited to our celebrity kick-off party where Jimmy Stewart, Robert Wagner, and a whole bunch of other celebrities are invited to meet the sponsors. The designers also get to meet representatives from our corporate sponsors such as Nike, Carnation, and AT&T. All those people are in the same room mingling and having a good time, being photographed by the media. In a couple of cases, our sponsors have utilized this event by publishing photos taken at the party in their house organs or trade magazines. So it's very advantageous for them. We want to make sure that they understand that we appreciate their donation. At the race itself, they're always given a VIP pass and parking, and invited to the VIP tent.

You're saying that perhaps charities like yours ask for a little bit more up front, but you're willing to give a lot more back. And that it would be advantageous to the designer if he or she were willing to play ball with you at the outset. Not to mention donating good work to a worthy cause, which for many people is its own reward.

Definitely. And, where appropriate, we put the designers' name on the stuff we produce. Because of the design, one of our recent posters turned out to be a very collectible item. We had kids putting them up all over southern California. So the designers had their name spread all over the place, which made the poster as great for them as it was for us. ∎

The concept sketch (left) Morava and Oliver
presented to Walt Walston gained them the
opportunity to design the promotional materials
and T-shirts (above) for the 1989 marathon.

Sharon Streger, as vice president for creative services, is responsible for creative marketing for Vestron Inc., specifically for directing the advertising, sales promotion, packaging, and broadcast/theatrical (audiovisuals) promotional materials for the video, pictures, and television divisions. Ms. Streger joined Vestron in 1982 as manager of creative services. She was promoted to creative director in 1983 and to vice president in 1984. Previously a senior copywriter for a New York-based promotion firm, Ms. Streger has been a successful freelance copywriter and creative director. She attended graduate school at New York University, and received her undergraduate degree from the State University of New York at Binghamton.

Vestron Inc., Stamford, Connecticut, is the parent company of Vestron Video, Vestron Pictures, Vestron Television, and Vestron International Group. Founded in 1981, Vestron Video rapidly became the world's largest independent home video company, with over six hundred titles, including feature films and comedy, children's, and music programs; and special programming such as National Geographic Video and the NOVA Video Library. In October 1985, Vestron Inc. became the first major home video company to go public with a successful offering of 5.4 million shares. In January 1986, Vestron Inc. launched Vestron Pictures, a theatrical film production and distribution company. Ten feature films were released in 1987, including *Dirty Dancing*, the highest-grossing independent feature film of all time, and the critically acclaimed *Anna* and *The Dead*.

10

When It Just Has to Get Done

Scott A. Mednick is president of Scott Mednick and Associates, a Los Angeles-based design and marketing firm serving clients nationwide. A graduate of the Rhode Island School of Design, Mr. Mednick's work has been exhibited worldwide, including a recent show at the Kresge Art Museum in Michigan. His design and art direction in the areas of corporate identity, poster design, collateral, and exhibitry have earned him numerous awards, including gold and silver medals from the Art Directors Club of New York. Currently president of the Art Directors Club of Los Angeles, he is a member of the architecture and design council of the Museum of Contemporary Art (MOCA) and has been selected for inclusion in *Who's Who in the West* and *Outstanding Young Men of America*.

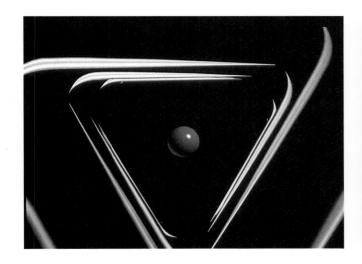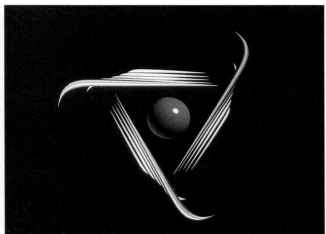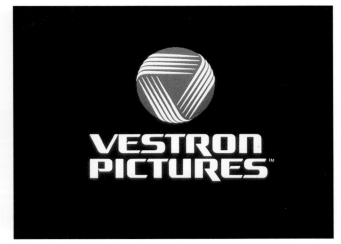

Sharon Streger

Q *When a growing, highly visible company decides to change its symbol or logo, very often there's an immediate need behind that decision. What was happening at Vestron?*

A Our situation was no exception. Vestron was a very young business, taking its first tentative steps to becoming a large-scale corporation. The original logo—two overlapping Vs with speed lines through them—had been designed by a friend of one of the first principals of the company. It had a lot of problems that I had been complaining about ever since I started working at the company. It always printed with a moiré pattern; it was so many generations removed from the original it was impossible to reproduce clearly.

One day, I was called up to the president's office, and he said, "Well, you've got your chance to do us a new logo, but we need it by day X," and it was an incredibly, incredibly tight schedule.

What was the significance of that date?

The initial public offering of our stock. We needed the logo for the tombstone ad and the prospectus. We had something like three and a half weeks to do it—design it, approve it, ink it, and finish it. So we couldn't go through some of the usual corporate identity steps. And I knew it was going to be an especially difficult

process because there were conflicting views on how to represent the company. When I started at Vestron in 1982, I was the fifteenth employee; today there are over 450 employees. Selling the core group on something that would reflect Vestron's bigger future wasn't going to be easy.

I chose Scott Mednick and Associates for many reasons. First, they had already had a relationship with the company, in many instances, performing on schedule in other time-crunch situations. The size and direction of Scott's company was also a good match for what Vestron needed. They weren't a big corporate identity firm that would insist on saying to us, "Fill out these thirty-two questionnaires and we'll come back in three months with some preliminary designs." But they also had, I felt, the background and expertise to not give us just a little boutique logo.

Did you talk to other design firms?

No, I did not. I didn't have time to look at the portfolios of people with whom I had not worked, and that would have been too risky anyway—to let people do this as a first project for me. And I didn't think that any of the other design firms that had worked on product-

◄ Animated title sequence produced by R/ Greenberg Associates gives dimension to the Vestron identity designed by Scott Mednick and Associates.

Scott Mednick originally presented fifty options for the Vestron mark to Sharon Streger; the presentation was narrowed to twenty-five, which were shown to the company's chairman and president. The second from left, top row, was the clear favorite and was developed into the final mark.

related logos for Vestron were right for this project either. My decision was based on the fact that we needed it done fast, by people we knew and who understood us; by people who had both the sense of fun that this company is all about and the sense of what makes a good corporate mark that could last us for years and years.

I didn't even have time to examine the proposal. I just asked Scott what it would take to do it, and we talked very generally. Nothing was in writing. We set up an ideal time frame, then threw it out the window, and worked with the time we had.

In terms of cost, I knew beforehand what would be too high and what would be too low. Scott did come in in the middle. He set up the initial fee in two phases, design and execution. Then we had a separate price list for the various stationery items and the corporate identity manual.

I think an identity or symbol can be the most difficult kind of project to price.

It's also a matter of editorial decisions. If we bring in a first presentation and no one likes anything, we're not in the same price ball park anymore. Feedback like, "We don't like these, do some more," leads you down all sorts of paths requiring a bigger financial commitment.

I'm glad you said that. Some clients expect designers to keep working indefinitely for the same fee . . . until they see something they like.

Many symbols introduced over the last several years have so-called speedlines; others take the form of Möbius strips; and globes and spheres are ubiquitous. The Vestron mark has all those elements, yet it is original and distinctive. It's hard to believe that it was done in just a few weeks. How did it go?

Well, Scott's first presentation gave us about fifty options—sketches—which we narrowed down to twenty-five, to show to the people who were to make the choice—Austin First, the chairman, and John Peisinger, the president.

What was their reaction?

Incredibly conflicting feedback and disagreement. The chairman felt strongly that the mark should be a "V," and should be able to be used both alone and as the beginning of the word Vestron. The president felt strongly, as I did, that the mark should *not* be a "V." My vision was that Vestron was going to become a multinational corporation, and that a "V" would be meaningless in many countries where we did business. I had the AT&T mark in my mind as a model, something with that kind of usability and vitality.

But one sticky point almost to the end was that the chairman wanted a logo that somehow made use of the mark in the wording—which might have been able to

Sharon Streger

work in the word Vestron—but then what happens when you have Vestron Television, Vestron International Group, or Vestron Benalux? Things start to get very convoluted, and very difficult in small sizes. At the time, no one really knew how big the company was going to get and how many permutations would be required.

Was the selected mark one of the twenty-five?

It grew out of one of them. We went back, did some more work, and tried to accommodate people's wishes. I spent a lot of time going up to the executive offices and arguing, coming back downstairs to work on some more refinements with Scott, and going back upstairs and arguing some more.

I think Scott fully anticipated what would take place. At the next presentation, we showed five designs. The president picked out the winner right away. He loved it, and he really got us on board for it.

How did other people in the company react?

When we introduced the mark, there was a major period of adjustment. The company was just skyrocketing. We were opening offices in every major European country and in Japan and Australia. At the time, I had wanted very much to have an internal communications program to get people comfortable with the new identity. But during that stressful growth period, we never had the time to do that. Consequently, I would see one of our feature films on the screen, for example, and the title logo would be the wrong one—the positive logo in reverse. Then I'd call our postproduction person and say, "It's used wrong," and he'd respond, "Well, I don't understand—explain it to me."

So I had to send out numerous "Get on Board" memos along with the manuals, stating how the logo's used, that it's won several design awards, and how we ought to be proud of it. Now I'm sensing that people are finally getting excited about their corporate identity and getting behind it. It's starting to happen.

And we're still working on the program. The logo was originally designed for Vestron Inc. and Vestron Video. Little did we know that a couple of weeks later we would be doing the lettering for Pictures, and a few weeks after that we would be lettering Television. We have almost a full alphabet now.

The mark's three broad strokes represent Vestron's major divisions: video, motion pictures, and television. A custom alphabet was created by Scott Mednick and Associates to accommodate division logotypes in several languages.

Vestron Inc.

Since you agreed to the price with a verbal OK, were there any conflicts about the cost of the additional design work that came up?

Unfortunately, there couldn't be—because I was a prisoner of the schedule. Sometimes that happens, you can't argue about a price because you're demanding so much overtime. The designers worked nights and weekends to get it done. What kind of price can you put on that?

How was its value perceived on Wall Street? Do you sense any difference in security analysts' perception of a company with a "modern" symbol versus a company with a homemade-type logo?

As a designer, I have to say yes. The old logo—if only because it was so poorly rendered—would have represented the company poorly. A symbol can make a psychological sell: "Management knows what they're doing; they know how to market the company and its products effectively." The chairman and president of Vestron recognized that. It's to their credit that they wanted something good in time for the initial public offering.

What was the reaction to the symbol in Hollywood and the entertainment business in general? Was it anything like, "Hey, here's a new force ready to contend with the majors?"

That reaction took a while to develop, but I think without the new logo it never would have developed; we would have always looked small and not quite having our act together. At first, there was some reaction to the similarity between our logo and New World Pictures'. Why? Because both are circular! People tend to react like that. In the entertainment business? It added a new polish to the company—particularly to the video division.

Did that new polish extend into other areas such as the type of art you commission for campaigns?

It really dressed up our sales materials. It had always looked like there was this blurry thing on our point-of-purchase material and packaging. And now there was this clean, crisp, very active, and energetic-looking mark. At the same time, we were growing at the rate that demanded better and better quality work. With *Dirty Dancing*, we released the top-grossing independent

Vestron's corporate identity manual contains reproduction art and guidelines for the use of the mark and logotypes in advertising, collateral, packaging, film, and video applications.

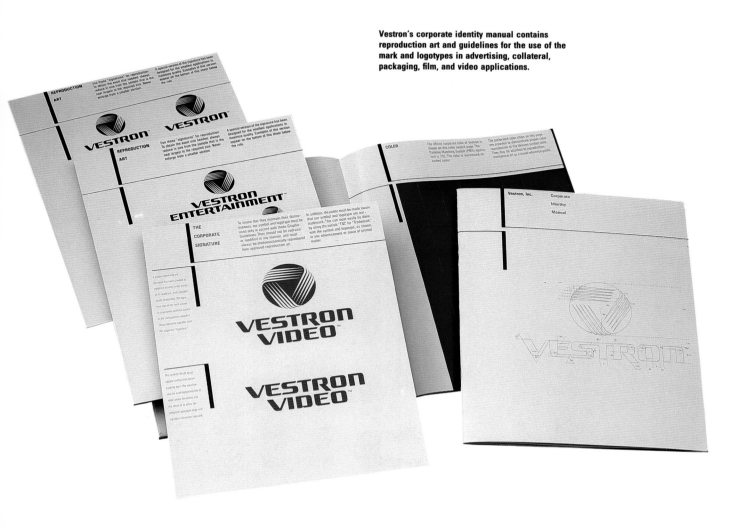

feature film of all time. We started to commission higher quality work, higher priced work. We took on the National Geographic Video line, and, of course, there was a real shine just from that name, which reflected on everything we did.

What are you involved with now?

Dozens of designers are working for us. Especially out of a small group of Los Angeles boutiques that specialize in theatrical campaigns and ancillary materials, such as ad breakdowns, brochures, trailers, and TV and radio spots. Before I had campaigns to give out, I was redoing enormous numbers of other studios' campaigns for video boxes, so I became acquainted with those design groups—primarily by word of mouth, also by doing some research. When I saw a campaign that I thought really worked or had a style I wanted to mimic,

I called up the group who did it. Finding out who-did-what was not very difficult because it's a small universe out there.

We get a lot of designers' promotional materials every week—letters, solicitations, brochures, and portfolios. I'll go through them and pass them along to my creative directors for Video and Pictures. If I get a reel, I pass it along to my creative director for AV. If we really like someone's work, we will arrange to work with them; it's as simple as that. I don't need to get bids because I've been doing this stuff so much, I know what the costs are.

Sometimes people get overwhelmed by us. Small studios will solicit us and if we like their work, we'll give them some work and some more work and some more work.

Isn't that everyone's dream?

Sure, but it can be overwhelming when you're small. I started working with Scott right after he had formed his own agency, and I began to assign enormous amounts of work to him when he was still working out of his living room.

He's not working out of his living room anymore.

I know, I know. ∎

A range of Vestron publications and promotional materials designed by Scott Mednick and Associates demonstrate the versatility of the new identity.

Part Three

Working
Relationships
that Work

John J. Dietsch joined Booz-Allen in 1981 as a director of corporate communications. Previously, he was vice president of a major international public relations firm. He holds a B.A. degree in English literature from DePauw University.

Booz-Allen & Hamilton Inc. is the world's largest international management and technology consulting firm. Founded in 1914, Booz-Allen serves corporations, financial institutions, U.S. federal agencies, and the governments of thirty-nine nations from offices in the United States, Europe, Latin America, Africa, the Middle East, and Japan. Booz-Allen's Technology Centers in Bethesda, Maryland, employ 2,500 professionals who provide systems development, acquisition, and operational support services to government and industry. The Information Technology Center focuses on information systems, telecommunications, advanced electronics technologies, and space systems. The Applied Sciences Center focuses on weapon system technology, survivability, strategic defense, avionics and aerospace systems, transportation, and environmental science.

11

Getting the Job Done Right

Shapiro Design Associates Inc. is a New York communications consulting firm that develops, writes, and produces corporate and institutional publications, including capability brochures, company magazines, annual reports, newsletters, and advertising. Ellen Shapiro, the firm's president, a *magna cum laude* graduate of UCLA's College of Fine Arts, is a member of the Communication Design faculty of Parsons School of Design. She has served as a vice president of AIGA/New York and has judged and been represented in design competitions across the United States and in Canada. Clients of Shapiro Design include nonprofit organizations as well as leading corporations such as American Express, Chemical Banking Corporation, and Schlumberger Ltd. The work for Booz-Allen on these pages was designed by Ellen Shapiro, Donald Burg, and Terri Bogaards.

The Booz·Allen Choice

For Support Staff Careers

BOOZ·ALLEN & HAMILTON

BY: CHARLES E. LUCIER

Aggressive and innovative management of mature manufacturing businesses, based on competitive leadership and differentiation, can provide attractive levels of profitability which create value for shareholders. Complacent or defensive management of mature businesses which minimizes investment and extracts cash will quickly result in a declining, unprofitable position.

The need to address fundamental problems and adopt strategies to secure a favorable competitive position is urgent. Competition in North America is intensifying: many companies are achieving dramatic improvements in their cost and quality; the most successful and desirable customers are reducing the number of their suppliers; aggressive foreign competitors are establishing U.S.-based manufacturing capacity. While the decline of the dollar continues to provide some respite for American manufacturers, companies that

A STRATEGIC DECISION TREE FOR MATURE MANUFACTURING BUSINESSES

IS THE INDUSTRY STRUCTURALLY DISADVANTAGED SO THAT NO COMPETITOR IS ABLE TO EARN ATTRACTIVE RETURNS?

YES ▶ BREAKOUT OR ASSET REDEPLOYMENT STRATEGY

NO

IS YOUR COMPANY COMPETITIVE IN COST AND QUALITY?

NO ▶ REMEDY THE COST AND QUALITY DISADVANTAGES

YES ▶ CREATE A DIFFERENTIATED STRATEGIC POSITION

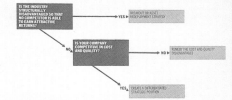

Brandan Chang "Technology Commitment"

Joyce Doria "Independence"

Walt Drozdeski "Leading Edge Projects"

Bill Shiley "Opportunities"

Don Pierce "Leadership"

Alma Wiegand "Tuition Assistance"

The Booz·Allen Choice

**For Careers in
Engineering, Science
and Technology.**

TACTICAL C³
AIRLAND,
MARITIME.

BOOZ·ALLEN & HAMILTON INC

und they need. If they're not out in the cold, if the
rpose of the project and its audience are thoroughly
derstood, they should be able to solve the problem. I
n't want to go through a lot of iterations and be pre-
nted with tons of sketches or comps. If there's enough
rbal interaction and agreement before we actually exe-
te something, there's no need for them. All I need to
e is one design concept or maybe two.

Our firm, which is in the professional and technical
rvices industry, is a partnership, privately owned
d structured much like a law firm. We have a really
nds-on entrepreneurial focus. That focus carries over
to our design philosophy. We seek—and get—original
lutions that set us apart from our competitors.

How do you achieve that?

By trying to minimize the number of decision-
akers. The managers we work with trust what my

professional basis. We don't have too many problems
with internal clients objecting to designs. Maybe we're
just lucky.

*For you, one good design concept is enough. Young
designers who are just starting out and trying to build their
practice might worry that no real client would believe they're
creative unless they bring in a presentation with at least half a
dozen different approaches; it might seem too risky to state the
problem and make one decision about the right way to go.*

I find overkill a waste of time. I like to work with a
small number of designers. They know me and I know
them; they understand our firm pretty well; they know
the kind of look we want and they give it to us. Also, I
try to minimize my actual involvement in the design
process. Once I tell the designer what the project is all
about and they fully know the requirements, I leave the
creative work to them. I don't see myself as a micro-
manager.

distinctive color palette and selection of
efaces unifies publications produced for Booz-
en by Shapiro Design Associates. Projects
clude recruiting brochures, a scientific journal,
d "Viewpoints," a monograph series.

Booz-Allen & Hamilton Inc.

One strength Booz-Allen sells is the ability to analyze a problem and say, "This is the way it ought to be solved." Since your firm is used to thinking that way, it clarifies your approach to design.

We're results-oriented. I want a solution. I think the designers we work with understand that and like working that way.

There are many cases in which exploring alternative solutions is useful—and necessary—for both the client and the designer. Do you see the need for that?

I think the best way to answer that is to look at a recent project, a marketing piece that presented the environmental services our firm offers, which are quite extensive. We had never done a piece for this particular group, but had determined that the project would be ambitious in scope. We didn't know how far our ambition was taking us, and we really had to find a budget. So the designers came back with three different covers, which, in retrospect, was unusual for us. I evaluated them and was attracted to the one that proved to be the

Ellen Shapiro developed three alternative covers (left) for a 1987 brochure on Booz-Allen's environmental consulting capabilities. Although John Dietsch agreed that the layers of the earth's environment made the most powerful statement, he vetoed the shots of space and the ocean floor. He also requested that the smokestacks be changed to recovery drums, which depict a solution to the problem.

most elegant and the most ambitious. I kept another in reserve, in case the budget didn't support the first choice. When the designer came down to meet with me and my client, I said, "Look, I think this one is the way to go; I think you do, too, so now go in and sell it to these people." And the designer did.

Are you also saying that creative disagreements will be minimized if the designer is capable of selling the concept?

That's their job, and they know their business much better than I. It's much more credible when a designer can do that, whereas, if you rely on an intermediary, even someone like the communications director within the client's organization, it doesn't work as well.

Disagreements arise when a designer doesn't really understand the kind of work we need. We deal with complex technical material that primarily relates to the defense and aerospace industries. A lot of designers have difficulty adapting to the technical nature of the projects and may come up with something inappropriate or too soft for our market. In most cases, it's a matter of getting them to understand the requirements of the project itself, and its audience. I try to instruct and educate designers to be able to translate the information, the copy, into the kind of look we need.

Let's say you think the look is right; the problem has been solved, but the designer isn't satisfied yet. He or she wants to refine it or add detailing you don't think is necessary. When designers talk about creative disagreements, that's pretty typical.

I agree. But if they can convince me that what they want makes sense, I usually go along.

A 1988–89 series of ads designed by Terri Bogaards of Shapiro Design describe Booz-Allen's consulting engineering work in space exploration, defense, computer technology, the environment, and several other areas.

As an example, a designer may recommend a photographer, but the client might respond that photographer B, who charges a lot less, is good enough. The designer disagrees and believes that the effectiveness of the book is based on the quality of the photography, and doesn't want to sacrifice it. It comes down to: "Whose project is it, anyway?"

When it's an issue like the choice of photographer, my tendency is to defer to the designer—unless I have personal knowledge of the expertise of photographer B, which is probably unlikely.

But I will say that designers can get too carried away with design for design's sake rather than really understanding the importance of making an effective piece for your business. There are cases where things are done more elaborately than are necessarily appropriate. Sometimes designers are onto something in terms of a particular effect. From our standpoint, that can be kind of hard to take. Everyone has to understand that the piece is a combination of content and presentation, and that they have to work together. Sometimes it's not easy.

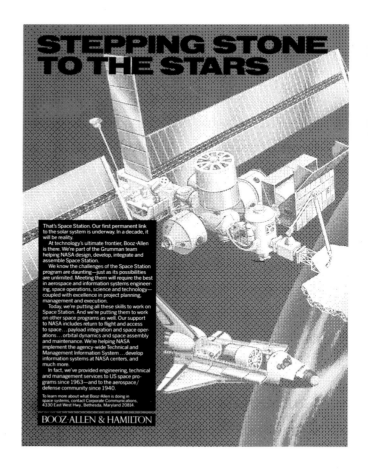

What could cause you to lose confidence in a design firm?

Booz-Allen has the philosophy that whatever it takes, we can get it done, despite deadline pressures or whatever. I expect the designers and other creative people I work with to accept that and to produce, not to become exasperated by it. I see the designers I work with as essentially part of my team, helping me achieve my goals and carry out my purpose. They have to think of themselves as part of the team and function that way and not as some bizarre creative resource that we pull in. They need to be aware of overall team goals, beyond a specific job, as well as the project nuances. I would tend to lose confidence if surprises happened or if the routine was basically undisciplined.

We spoke before about situations in which the designer isn't satisfied with something the client's basically happy with. But it's even trickier when the designer thinks the problem's solved and the client does not. The client wants it done over.

Sure, that's happened. But a client always has control over what's going to happen. If something is missed in translation and the client wants to change it, it's the client's problem. If I've screwed up, I've got to pay to get it fixed. If you screw up, it's on you.

One design group I know learned a lot about that from a massive "screw-up" on a project that had been laid out with the approval of the communications director. When the president of the organization looked at it, he wanted certain sections emphasized. He apparently was very presidential in his demeanor, and they weren't going to argue with him. They worked over the weekend and came up with a solution that gave him what he wanted. It required adding several pages to the book. But nobody wrote a memo dealing with how much those pages would cost in design time, mechanicals, and printing. After the client got the bill, the design group lost the account . . . and the communications director lost her job. The designer told me that, in retrospect, the work should have been held up until the president had a chance to evaluate the options. Perhaps those changes wouldn't have been so essential once the cost was known.

That designer is correct. I tell my internal clients what the budget is going to be and get that squared away up front. I'm careful to tell people over and over again that the meter keeps running. That's essential.

You say a client always has control over what's going to happen. But not all clients feel that way. Sometimes they sense that projects are going out of control. What advice would you give them?

As I said earlier, good projects start with good communication. Make sure the designer has the best possible understanding of the project's requirements—up front. On complex projects, it's also important to stay in constant touch with the designer. On occasion, it seems like the designer and I have talked endlessly before anything's committed on paper. So, getting things nailed down from the get-go is the best way to avoid disaster down the road.

Let's return to something you said earlier, about the highly specialized nature of your work. How can other clients in your position help designers understand complex technological material?

It's not easy. The technologies themselves are complex, the issues associated with them are complex, and the terminology used to describe them is specialized. To come up with an optimal solution, a designer needs to grasp all three things.

For example, we are involved with something called Neural Technology, which is both a computer and software technology as well as a program language; I would say that virtually no designer would know anything about it. In order to produce a capabilities brochure, we would have to teach them what it is and what it's used for, as well as what we're trying to say and whom we're trying to reach, before they could come up with any sort of effective design. Clients in my position must take the time to do that.

Information technologies are abstract, basically electrons moving around. They appear on screens and go through wires, but are hard to grasp in a tangible way, which is particularly challenging for a designer.

Might that lead to an abstract piece of artwork as a solution?

That's right. As long as it's an acceptable symbol to someone who *is* familiar with it. Our client or prospect, usually someone with extensive technical knowledge, would have to see an evident relationship, even if he or she knew nothing about art.

I have been talking with several clients about far-out, leading edge design that "pushes the edge of the envelope." Given the subject matter, can you foresee a place for that in your work?

Pushing the envelope doesn't necessarily mean something overdesigned or outlandish. It can be something very, very simple. Just take a look at some of the ads we've done. ∎

Sandra J. Ruch, a leader in the area of corporate support of the arts, began her career as chief curator of the American Craft Museum. She then owned an art gallery and served as visual arts director of crafts for the National Endowment for the Arts. Subsequently, she became a senior vice president at Ruder, Finn & Rotman Fine Arts, where she produced visual and performing arts projects for such corporations as Philip Morris, ITT, Bristol Myers, Bulova, and Mobil. For eleven years, Ms. Ruch was responsible for all of Mobil's cultural programs, including the "Masterpiece Theatre" and "Mystery" television series, and Mobil-sponsored museum exhibitions. Ms. Ruch is presently vice president of public relations event marketing for The House of Seagram, where she is responsible for consumer and trade marketing, public relations, and special events.

Mobil Corporation, a $54.9 billion public company headquartered in New York City and operating worldwide, is in the integrated petroleum, chemicals, mining and minerals, and real estate businesses. Mobil characterizes its petroleum businesses as "upstream" (exploration and producing) and "downstream" (refining and marketing). In addition, it operates Mobil Chemical Company. Mobil is in the forefront of corporate advocacy, communicating with opinion leaders and the public through advertisements on the op-ed pages of major newspapers. In addition to the sponsorship of many cultural and community programs, Mobil has sponsored "Masterpiece Theatre" on public television for eighteen seasons. The series has won twenty-two Emmys.

12

Why It's Smart to Be Demanding

Ivan Chermayeff, a designer, painter, and illustrator, was born in London, studied at Harvard and the Institute of Design in Chicago, and graduated with a B.F.A. from Yale University School of Art. A past president of the AIGA, he serves on many boards of directors, including the International Design Conference in Aspen. He founded Chermayeff and Geismar Associates in 1960 with Thomas Geismar; Stephen Geissbuhler and John Grady are now partners. The firm has a staff of thirty designers and architects and is active in corporate identification, exhibitions, and graphics for architecture. Mr. Chermayeff was named to the New York Art Directors Club Hall of Fame in 1982; in 1979, he received the AIGA Gold Medal (with Tom Geismar). The firm has developed trademarks and identity programs for over 150 clients, including Mobil, Xerox, Chase Manhattan Bank, the Museum of Modern Art, NBC, and PBS.

WAR AND PEACE

A dramatization of the Tolstoy novel presented on PBS-TV

Beginning November 20 Made possible by matching grants from

National Endowment for the Humanities & Mobil Oil Corporation

CRIME AND PUNISHMENT

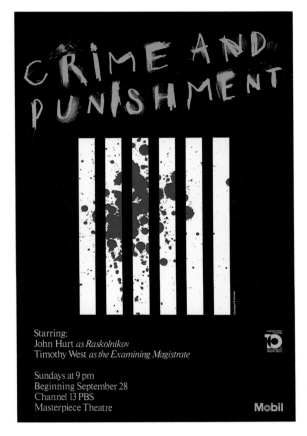

Starring:
John Hurt *as Raskolnikov*
Timothy West *as the Examining Magistrate*

Sundays at 9 pm
Beginning September 28
Channel 13 PBS
Masterpiece Theatre

Mobil

Mobil Showcase presents

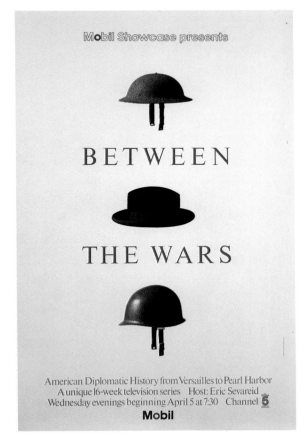

BETWEEN

THE WARS

American Diplomatic History from Versailles to Pearl Harbor
A unique 16-week television series   Host: Eric Sevareid
Wednesday evenings beginning April 5 at 7:30   Channel 5

Mobil

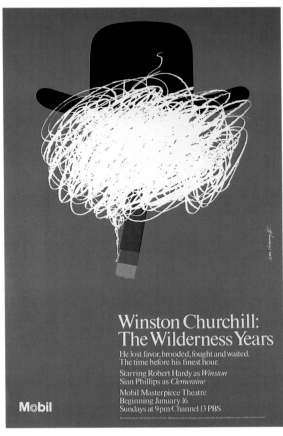

Winston Churchill: The Wilderness Years

He lost favor, brooded, fought and waited.
The time before his finest hour.

Starring Robert Hardy as *Winston*
Sian Phillips as *Clementine*

Mobil Masterpiece Theatre
Beginning January 16
Sundays at 9 pm Channel 13 PBS

Mobil

Sandra J. Ruch

Q *On a poster for a television show, one graphic image has to entice millions of people. When you were at Mobil, how many design ideas did you want to see? Was one good enough?*
A It depended on the artist. I have worked with designers who never gave me more than one design. There were others who always came in with two or three ideas, fairly well-executed, almost to completion.

When a person's style melded with what the show was all about, it worked. I have had some run-ins with some well-known names, who will remain nameless. And there have been times when it took us almost four or five months before we came up with the image. I'm talking about four or five months of working it over and over to the point where, in one case, the designer farmed it out to an illustrator, because we just weren't hitting on the feeling of the show. But in the end, the design—and the "Masterpiece Theatre" series—were very successful.

Do you just know when something's right? What's your secret?

I don't have any rules. And because I go after a certain approach, it doesn't mean the artist is treated like a vendor. I am not a designer; I am not an illustrator. But I do have a strong gut feeling that a show should be represented by such-and-such a kind of image or illustration; that it should have this or that mood. I verbalize what I feel before the designer starts working. There is no secret. For instance, for each "Masterpiece Theatre" show, the designers are given a series of cassettes to take home, or if they don't have a VCR, they can watch them in Mobil's video room; the entire series, sometimes thirteen hours. Then he or she is given a series of color transparencies or black-and-white stills, and it is discussed.

There were times when the designer returned with a concept, and I said, "It's absolutely perfect; I won't change a thing. It goes beyond my expectations." Then there were times when it was off the mark and we had to start again. And sometimes my boss, who had strong opinions also, was not satisfied.

Even war, crime, and family feuds take on an extraordinary charm at the hand of Ivan Chermayeff, who has designed and illustrated over one hundred posters for Mobil's "Masterpiece Theatre" television series.

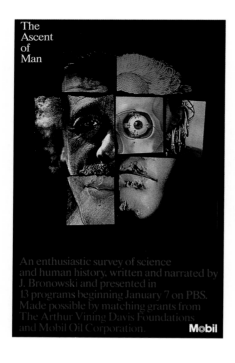

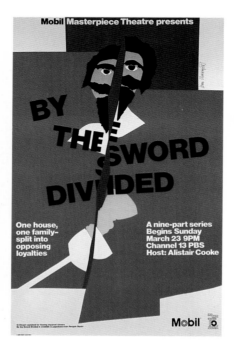

Sometimes, designers didn't share my point of view. And I would say, most of the time when that happened, the designers did win. I was very fortunate to have been able to use a lot of excellent outside talent, because, I think, it maintained a freshness that we wouldn't have had if we had our own designers doing the same work over and over again.

When there are creative disagreements with a designer, what do you think is the best way to handle them?

Directly. I think I'm very blunt and can say, "This doesn't work." But I've never had to fire anybody. At Mobil, I frequently had disagreements with designers, mostly over the fact that my copy was constantly cut by them—and my copy was short. Vert short. If you look at the one-liners on "Masterpiece Theatre," they are usually six to ten words long. I felt that I had something to sell in terms of a story idea that had to go beyond the visuals. For instance, I wanted Alistair Cooke's name in my poster, and not down on the right-hand corner, tiny. Also, we fought constantly about the size of the logo with certain people. And we lost constantly. Most of the time, I thought "Mobil" was too small. You may disagree with me, but it's really smaller than what I wanted. But all those things worked out. I don't think I have a bad reputation. I have a difficult reputation, demanding.

Don't you think it's your right to be demanding?

Yes. There's nothing wrong with that. All people earn a certain description or profile of themselves. Being demanding is what people respond to—if your demands are reasonable and can be met, and your expectations are realistic. I'm demanding of myself. And I'm demanding of the people that work with me and for me. And I think it works.

Did you treat long-established stars like Ivan Chermayeff any differently from someone who was newer to the profession?

I had to. Ivan is such a part of Mobil. He knows so many things that I didn't have to explain much to him.

And he didn't need to be sent back to the drawing board?

That's not true at all! He went back to the drawing board on occasions when he couldn't come up with something that we all felt equally was what we wanted. I remember Ivan going back many times, and Seymour Chwast going back many times on "Nicholas Nickleby." There's nothing wrong with that.

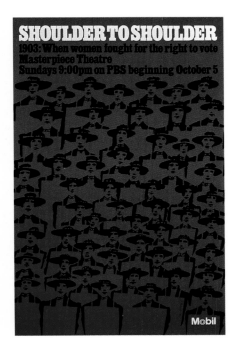

These superstars don't have a problem with that?

Well, they may have. But they still did it. Most of them felt that what they brought in was perfect. But that didn't mean that something couldn't be worked out if it wasn't exactly what we needed to communicate.

Some of the illustrators who have worked for "Masterpiece Theatre" also have reputations as difficult personalities. Do you continue to work with someone who is difficult if you get what you want, ultimately, out of it?

Sure. Absolutely. I had about ten new television programs a year, most of which went to people I already used—because I liked what they did for me.

You've emphasized that when you have a concept in mind for a particular project, you go after the person who can do it. Have you ever been pleasantly surprised when someone came back with another idea, a different concept?

Yes. Sometimes it comes out completely different than what I thought of, and it's better. I like that. I'm always open to that. Ivan does that. He has very strong ideas and a visual sense of how something should be translated. His ideas are often different from mine, and he often takes them further. It goes both ways.

Is there a relationship between quality art and a successful show? Can you relate the overall sophistication of what you were doing to the intellect of the PBS audience?

There's no question about it. Think of the nature of the subject matter; if you're doing Cheerios, it's different from doing *War and Peace* by Tolstoy. Your market is different. The content of "Masterpiece Theatre" is on a level that makes it relatively easy to do imaginative things.

Have you discovered and launched any new talents?

Yes. Norm Walker was one person we used a lot for "Mystery." We also gave Edward Gorey a chance that no one else did. When we started the "Mystery" series, we commissioned him to do the opening graphics and animate them, which he was dying to do his whole life.

A pencil drawing by Ivan Chermayeff for "The Last Place on Earth," a 1986 "Masterpiece Theatre" series, was rejected by Sandra Ruch in favor of the selected concept (far right).

He had always wanted to do a full-length feature animated film, which at some point Mobil may do with him.

How friendly can designers and illustrators get with you? People have said over the years, "Well, it's your connections. That's how you get clients." There is some disagreement among clients about this.

I think I'm particularly antisocial in that way. I don't invite lunches or dinners or drinks. And I do resent printers who try to wine and dine me. I must have broken fifty lunch dates with printers. Because in the final analysis, just show me your work. If you're good, you're good. I cannot stand having lunch and talking to people with whom I have nothing to discuss other than the project, which I would rather talk about over my desk.

I like people to come to my office. At Mobil, my office and the halls were filled with all our work over the last twenty-five years. There was no better way for me to show you Mobil's image, graphically, than to walk you around the halls and show you 250 examples of poster design for Mobil's television series. Not everybody has seen everything. And sometimes I would say, "I like the

look of this, and this is what I want to capture again."

But socializing? I've never given anyone a job because I socialized with them. Sometimes, I've met designers in a social context, and they've introduced me to someone else. But that has never caused me to work with someone.

Is there a point at which you'll visit the designer's office?

Sure. Sometimes I'm curious to see what it's like. But it's not necessary. I don't care what their space is, as long as they deliver. And I also don't care how they dress. You're not going to meet Mobil's chairman because he trusts the communications managers to understand about design. In fact, one well-known illustrator dresses so much like a vagrant that the security guards stop him every time he comes in. But this didn't bother me at all.

What's the key that that keeps you coming back for more?

The whole experience. The projects I had—and now have—are fun. They're the cream of the crop. If someone can come in and engage my imagination, I look forward to that. The best people are pleasant to work with. They're open. They're strong in their own opinions and in what they want to do. And they deliver. It is an enjoyable experience for both of us. ∎

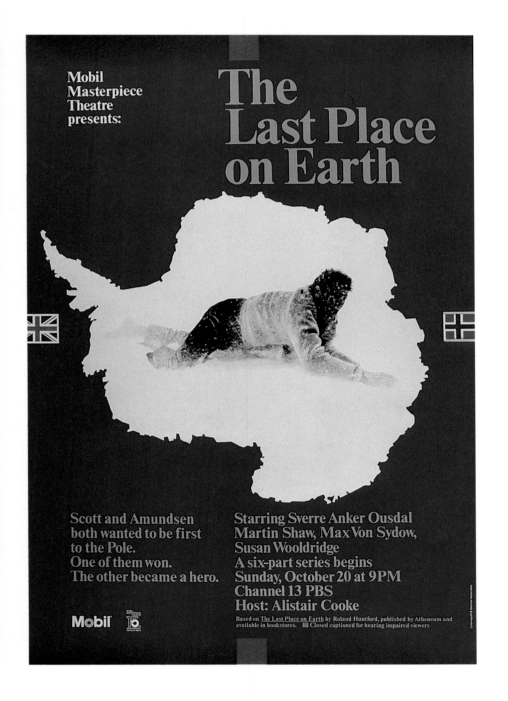

John Schwartz and Bill Schwartz have been in the restaurant business since 1970, when Bill Schwartz decided that the office park development company he worked for might have an easier time attracting tenants if it had a restaurant. So Bill opened The Butcher, a steakhouse in Benaroya Business Park in Bellevue, Washington. His brother, John, joined him, beginning his food-service education in the kitchen. The Butcher was an instant success with the business-lunch clientele, and today it alone is responsible for over $1.4 million in annual sales. John and Bill Schwartz, natives of Washington state, are both active in professional and charitable organizations. They attribute the success of their company to a personal philosophy: "Do everything possible to take care of your customer and everything else will fall into place."

Schwartz Brothers Restaurants has expanded from the original Butcher to twenty restaurants and has become a $30+ million-in-sales company. One of their newest and most ambitious restaurants, Chandler's Crabhouse and Fresh Fish Market, opened in March 1988 and features "the freshest live Dungeness crab, oysters, clams, mussels, and lobster in town," available on the menu and for retail sale. Other restaurants in the group, which spans Washington, Oregon, and California, include The Sandwich Shop and Pie Place, casual cafeterias in shopping malls; Henry's Off Broadway, specializing in Northeast regional cuisine; Daniel's Broiler; Benjamin's open kitchen restaurants; Benji's Fish and Chips, with a tugboat-shaped fish bar, and Benji's Deli Express. In July 1988, the Schwartz Brothers opened their latest restaurant, Cucina! Cucina! Italian Cafe, featuring wood-fired ovens from Italy.

13

The Ingredients of a Successful Collaboration

Tim Girvin, principal of Tim Girvin Design, Inc., Seattle, built his office on a reputation for unique and elegant typographical design, calligraphy, and illustration. Creative director for the graphic design aspects of Chandler's Crabhouse and other Schwartz Brothers restaurants, Tim Girvin supervises a staff of seventeen. Trained initially as a marine biologist, Girvin, a graduate of Evergreen State College in Washington, founded his firm in 1977. He has traveled extensively in the United States, Great Britain, Europe, and the Soviet Union as a student, guest speaker, and design competition judge. The firm's diverse client list includes Bloomingdales, CBS Entertainment, Disney Studios, Revlon, and United Airlines.

John and Bill Schwartz

Q *Today, opening a new restaurant seems almost like making a film, with a theme, a star (the chef), a cast (the waiters and maitre d'), a set, lighting, and music. You've been in business since 1970 and have seen many changes in the industry. When did you first think about hiring a graphic designer?*

A In the mid-seventies we got a bit more sophisticated. Before that we just dealt with an advertising person. Now, all our restaurants have different concepts. They range from a tugboat-shaped fish-and-chips stand to one of Seattle's most elegant fine dining establishments. Chandler's Crabhouse and Fresh Fish Market has a spectacular Seattle waterfront setting and a nineteen-thirties kind of style.

At what point does a graphic designer become involved in a new restaurant concept?

Ideally, at the very beginning. The first thing we have to do is establish a logo. Because each of our restaurants is unique, the logo must be unique. The sign that goes on the restaurant is the first and most important application of that logo. Then, the logo is used throughout the restaurant in various customer supplies—menus, napkins, matchbooks, coasters—and in interior signage. We attract attention with billboards and print advertising, which are produced by an advertising agency, but with the look set up by the designer.

Are you working with the architect and interior designer at the same time the initial look and graphics are established?

Actually, the architect is on board first. He more or less controls the project; the interior designer is one of the principals in the architectural firm we work with. We think of the graphic designer as part of the team. But we want him to have input beyond the scope of the logo and the way it's used. We want all our team members involved in the total concept.

When the graphic designer gets involved is the color scheme and architectural style already established?

Yes.

Are there ever disagreements between the architects and the graphic designers?

We encourage disagreements. We encourage communication, input from all parties. If the architect doesn't like the work of the graphic designer, we will listen. But if we think the designer's ideas are correct, we're going to make that clear to the architect. We make the decisions.

When we establish a working relationship with designers, it's very important that they learn our company culture and visit all our restaurants to get a feel for our style and how we like to operate. Then, as we're discussing a new assignment like Chandler's Crabhouse, we will review the floor plans and the menu ideas. We give designers a clear idea of what we want the restaurant to be like. Then, we leave it to the designers. For this type of project, we want to see eight to ten logo ideas. It

◄ **Tim Girvin's distinctive hand lettering enlivens Crab Bar and Fresh Fish Market chalkboards at Chandler's Crabhouse.**

100

would be absolutely unacceptable if someone came in and announced, "Here it is; here's your logo." We need to see options, but they don't necessarily have to be eight to ten completely different solutions. A few variations enable us to say, "Yeah, we like this one," or "Maybe you need to go back and refine these two." Sometimes if we like several designs, we might ask the designer to take a particular aspect from one and combine it with another.

Have you ever worked with designers who insisted, "This design can't be changed like that?"

No.

I'm not talking about prima donnas, but many designers will stand behind the integrity of a particular solution.

Of course, we like to get somebody's opinion. But with Tim Girvin, we have no problem. In the case of our company logo, as well as the one for Chandler's, he liked a different one from the one we ended up with. He had his reasons, and we wanted to hear them. But in the final analysis, he went along with us. That's the kind of give-and-take we like.

It doesn't sound like you would accept an idea you weren't quite sure of if the designer was convinced it was great and would work for you. You know what you want.

Well, except that we really do rely on a designer's professional expertise. And again, in the case of Chan-

dler's, we were looking to recreate a style, an East Coast twenties or thirties sort of look. Now, we don't know about typefaces and so forth, so we left it up to the designer to come up with something that reflected that era.

What is the time frame for a typical project? Let's say from the time you're starting to evaluate the logo designs until the restaurant opens its doors?

Six months. And a lot has to be done: the sign, all the customer supplies, and the preopening advertising. It requires coordination and service. Our deadlines are tight. We need to deal with people who are available on short notice. Many elements have to come together to open a restaurant. Design is just one of them, but designers must be team members and be willing to work evenings and weekends to meet the deadlines, so the whole project comes together on time. In fact, Girvin's firm helped get the architect and interior designer to meet their deadlines.

Do you insist on working only with principals?

Working with employees is just fine as long as we know the principal cares and is involved from the beginning. There is an advantage to not dealing only with the principal, which is that a staff designer may be able to devote more time to the project. A principal might have several things going, business problems or whatever, and we want someone who's available whenever we need to be in contact.

To enhance the Schwartz Brothers' concept, Tim Girvin chose American wood typefaces of the 1930s. Although Girvin favored a version with many crabs in motion, the Schwartz Brothers preferred the crab as a central symbol.

On your projects, do you typically agree to a flat fee with the design firm?

We want the fees to be broken down by each piece, so that we know the logo is X amount, the menu is Y amount, and so forth.

Is overtime expected to be included in the fee?

Yes. The designer knows the schedule and has to provide the design for the fee, even if there is a lot of overtime. If we start with an itemized budget, we know our options. There are always changes. Let's say we originally commissioned designs for three menus: a lunch menu, a regular menu, and a bar menu. Then we'll decide we want a deck menu. On the other hand, there might be some things we ultimately choose not to do; we might cut back on the interior signage.

How do you like to be informed of the billing changes that result from those changes?

Right away. And we want the whole story. The best way is by a phone call, or in person if there's a meeting scheduled. There should be a follow-up letter.

For items that are specified by the designer—whether printed menus or manufactured signs—do you prefer them to be billed directly by the vendors or can they be listed on the designer's invoices as out-of-pocket expenses? And how do you feel about agency commissions and markups?

No markups. We simply want to agree on a fee. Whether it's the designer, architect, or advertising agency, we want to pay for their services and be billed directly by the suppliers.

Six months of work are in place and the restaurant opens its doors. Let's look at three aspects: the food, the service, and the design. In terms of pleasing customers, how do you rank them?

Obviously all three are important. But design—and advertising—is what initially gets people into a restaurant. We use radio and outdoor advertising to let people know a restaurant is going to open. We believe there's kind of a pent-up curiosity: People have driven by; they've heard about it; they've seen the sign, the advertising, and all of it connotes a certain image in their minds. We want them to think, "This looks really great, here's a new restaurant I've just got to try." In the early stages, most work-of-mouth referrals are from people who say things like, "You've got to check out this neat restaurant, and don't miss the murals." People aren't quite as picky about the food and service in the first month or so.

In the long run, though, what keeps people coming back month after month, year in and year out, is good food and good service. There is sort of a role reversal with the design.

The selected logotype. Girvin subtly modified the type forms and "distressed" the surface. The diamond-shaped crab insignia was developed for use as a separate design element.

Schwartz Brothers Restaurants

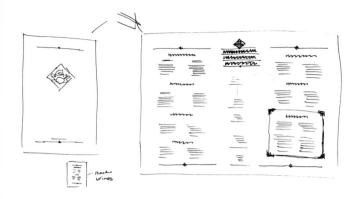

Sketches for menus and wine list (above) by Laurie Vette of Tim Girvin Design show the crab insignia as a cover design.

A custom alphabet, also styled after a 1930s typeface, was created for the restaurant's exterior marquee. The letters were hand-drawn and silkscreened on individual plastic rectangles so the message could change on a daily basis.

Do you remember the great old Horn & Hardart campaign, "You Can't Eat Atmosphere?"

Today it's got to be the atmosphere. At the outset, the food and the service simply aren't known. If a restaurant happens to be on the water like Chandler's, that's great. People in our area want to be on the water, in a terrific location. But that does lose importance after a while.

When you can gauge the public's reaction, do you make changes in the restaurant?

There are always changes. The more traditional the restaurant, the more it stays the same. But in our restaurants, we're always changing the decor a little bit, the menus, the lighting. When we find out what needs to be improved, we improve it.

In the Seattle area, when a waiter asks, "Is everything okay?" people tend to answer, "Yes, everything's okay," even if it isn't. Not like in New York. Here, typically, people just don't come back to the restaurant; you don't hear about it. That's why we encourage our customers and employees to tell us when things are wrong. We want to know; we want to turn a negative into a positive. If we've screwed up, tell us, and we'll do what we can. Customers comment about the design, the logo, even the name. We listen.

AABCDEFGHIJKL
MNOPQRSTUVW
XYZ&.,.:;-´`!?/$¢
1234567890

Q *Do you remember the great old Horn & Hardart campaign, "You can't eat atmosphere"?*

A *Today it has to be the atmosphere. At the outset, the food and service simply aren't known.*

Martin E. Zimmerman, president, chairman, and chief executive officer of The LINC Group, has been a leader in the leasing industry for almost twenty years. Before founding the LINC Group in 1975, he established Telco Marketing Services, Inc., an organization that helped pioneer the hospital equipment leasing field. Mr. Zimmerman earned a B.S. degree in electrical engineering from the Massachusetts Institute of Technology, and an M.B.A. in finance from Columbia Graduate School of Business, where he was elected a Kennecott Copper fellow and a McKinsey scholar. He is a trustee of Business Volunteers for the Arts, and a member of the dean's advisory council and trustee of the alumni association of the Columbia Graduate School of Business. He has been responsible for completing more than $500 million in lease and other debt financing.

The LINC Group, Inc. is an independent financial services organization, providing equipment leasing, investment banking, property financing, consulting, equipment remarketing, and associated capabilities to the health care and communications industries. Headquartered in Chicago, with offices in other major U.S. cities, The LINC Group has six operating units: LINC Financial Services, Inc., LINC Capital Corporation, LINC Management Services, LINC Equipment Services, LINC Capital Management, and LINC Scientific Imaging.

14

The Goal Is Innovation, Not Imitation

Rick Valicenti is principal of Thirst, the Chicago design firm he founded in 1980. Valicenti, a graduate of Bowling Green University, received his M.F.A. in design and photography from the University of Iowa. In 1988, he won nine awards from STA-100, a new record. He is a member of the 27 Chicago Designers. Mr. Valicenti worked on these projects in conjunction with Todd Lief, a Chicago communications consultant and writer who specializes in the creative process in organizations. Mr. Lief, the cofounder and leader of the "Mindsprouts" creativity training seminars, is involved in marketing strategy, communications planning, and conceptual packaging.

EQUIPMENT LEASING

CAPITAL FINANCING

LEASE INVESTMENT BANKING

Q *What were your key objectives for your company's printed communications?*

A I wanted to influence people's thinking about us. Our printed communications are a means for closing a sale at the second level after we've been recommended at the first level. It's common in selling to hospitals, for example, that you sell to the person you're initially in touch with, usually a technical or a financial officer. Then he goes to a committee and makes a recommendation—maybe of two alternatives—and the committee or the administrator who is his superior will make a decision. You can't get at that second level directly. You have to get at it through advertising or printed materials.

Are you competing against big-name investment banks?

We're competing against big-name commercial banks, big-name leasing companies, and in some cases, big-name investment banks. We call our business "lease investment banking" because it's more than leasing. But it's not typically long-term financing; it's typically medium term. We're a smaller company competing with large institutional-type players. We have to be able to explain why it is an advantage for an institutional user to work with someone other than an institutional supplier.

Institutional suppliers, and by that I assume you mean banks, often request a design approach they think will appeal to their clients—a low-key, restrained look. Some people like to use the term "plain vanilla."

That's changing to some extent, but it's still largely true. In many companies, there tends to be a kind of committee approach to design. Our approach is more forward-thinking, more on the leading edge. We sell the firm with this concept: We're more specialized, we've got all the experience, but we're not as large; along with our smaller size comes flexibility and responsiveness and more attention by senior people. The whole idea is to have a serious appearance that suggests a serious and responsible approach to solving problems, but one that is more creative.

◄ **Rick Valicenti created a series of highly original illustrations for the LINC Group's 1987 corporate capabilities brochure, "Money with Spirit." The illustrations were also used as covers for the individual operating company pieces.**

You have been successful in achieving that. How much direction did you give your design group?

Quite a bit. First of all, we voiced our philosophy. That took a series of meetings. We have content objectives that we need to accomplish with a given piece of collateral or advertising. A certain type of content or editorial approach suggests a certain type of design approach. But we don't want to be totally pinstriped, so I'll give the designer flexibility in terms of the imagery. The whole idea is to create a feeling of success and sophistication. We want to be known as a creative-type financing source, where people can get new concepts for existing problems. There are lots of problems out there, but there are not too many fresh ideas on how to solve them. We're the guys people come to for the tough ones. With that reputation, I hope we'll be called on for the easier ones, too. So the idea is to get on everybody's bid list and have a shot at getting new business, not simply by virtue of a low price but by virtue of more value-added.

You are the chairman of the company. I am impressed that you deal directly with designers.

I don't like to work through someone else. I want the designer to be there, and he appreciates it because he's got a chance to defend himself. I might comment on what I think is wrong or right. Then he'll say, "Here's what I've been trying to do," or "Here's why I did it." And sometimes I'll step back. I don't dictate to designers—ever—particularly if a designer feels strongly about something. By the same token, most designers are sensible enough to know that their client has a sense of what he wants to communicate; that he wants something fresh, attractive, and interesting; and that he wants to avoid the dull, repetitious stuff that both bores him and, ultimately, bores the reader.

Do you ever criticize a particular detail, such as "Why do we need this little red line right here?"

If I think something's extraneous, sometimes I'll ask why it's used, and sometimes I'll get an answer. I usually don't fight that kind of thing. I do pay a lot of attention to things like legibility of subheads—the layout from the point of view of the reading public. Sometimes a designer will devise a layout that is simply hard to read, or will use reverse type, or type that's not bold enough. For example, in our brochure, one of the major problems is that the lead-off heads have been screened back too far. Small matter, but it's something that impacts legibility. Now, when we reprint, we're not going to change much, but we'll make those heads darker. Ordi-

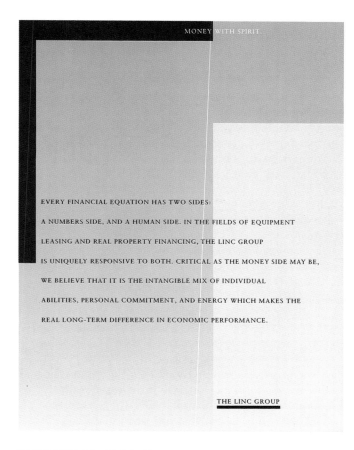

MONEY WITH SPIRIT.

EVERY FINANCIAL EQUATION HAS TWO SIDES:
A NUMBERS SIDE, AND A HUMAN SIDE. IN THE FIELDS OF EQUIPMENT
LEASING AND REAL PROPERTY FINANCING, THE LINC GROUP
IS UNIQUELY RESPONSIVE TO BOTH. CRITICAL AS THE MONEY SIDE MAY BE,
WE BELIEVE THAT IT IS THE INTANGIBLE MIX OF INDIVIDUAL
ABILITIES, PERSONAL COMMITMENT, AND ENERGY WHICH MAKES THE
REAL LONG-TERM DIFFERENCE IN ECONOMIC PERFORMANCE.

THE LINC GROUP

REAL PROPERTY FINANCING

INVESTMENT BANKING SERVICES

SPECIALTY LEVERAGED LEASING

narily, though, I wouldn't say anything about little red lines. I want the designer to feel that it's his design, and that it hasn't been all gouged up by the client. So I refrain from commenting on design issues that don't directly pertain to the communication of the copy.

What was the industry response to the brochures?

Quite positive, on the whole. Actually, our own people found them a little sophisticated at first, but they've gotten used to them. Have they changed the way our clients think about us? There's no doubt in my mind. They've been very, very important to us. Our ads have, too, and they reflect the sophistication of the brochures.

Do you view your brochures as an investment? Very often, to accomplish something this ambitious, designers have to do a huge selling job on the client, who might not be able to project the benefit of printing techniques like matte and gloss varnish to his business. Did you have to be sold?

Well, I certainly looked at the pros and cons of those decisions. Ultimately we look at something major like this brochure series as having at least a two-year life. We're dealing in an area where the difference of $5,000 or $10,000 can be made up for by just one sale. So if I can see something that might get me a sale over the course of one year or two years, it's much easier to justify. For example, I know that varnish, which is a significant extra cost, protects the piece and prevents fingerprinting. Since we hope each brochure will be seen and handled by several people, this is an important consideration.

Can you relate specific things like additional ink colors to making a sale? Or do you feel, instead, that high quality in general makes a subliminal sell to a prospective customer?

Both. We want to make sure that our stuff looks as good as that of any bank or investment bank. I mean, you decide how you want to spend your money! A six- or seven-color job was appropriate in this case because it was an omnibus corporate brochure. We made it go further by using the imagery in the individual operating company pieces. So we spent a lot of money on the images, but this cost was amortized over many different pieces. And sometimes we do produce one- or two-color pieces. And then it's especially important that the design is striking and enhances the message.

Both the cover of the LINC Group brochure (above) and the illustration representing LINC Capital Corporation (below) demonstrate an approach that positions LINC as a creative financing source.

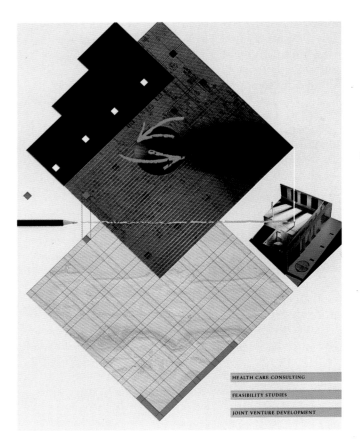

HEALTH CARE CONSULTING

FEASIBILITY STUDIES

JOINT VENTURE DEVELOPMENT

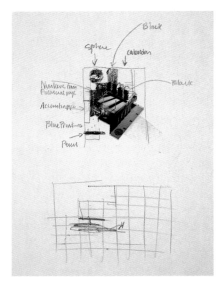

Marty Zimmerman, Rick Valicenti, and Todd Lief discussed the tools of the trade and the symbols that would best express each brochure's content; that would make the intangible tangible. Working from meeting notes, Valicenti developed each collage by cutting photographs out of "scrap," in this case (above) for the LINC Management Services illustration.

If other clients wanted to educate themselves about using the available marketing tools and talent to impact their businesses in a positive way, how would you suggest they go about it?

I think you learn a lot by interviewing the smartest, most successful practitioners around. I got my first designer by calling a housewares specialty retailer in Chicago, Crate & Barrel, that had—and still has—wonderful design. I knew Gordon Siegal a little bit, and I asked, "Gordon, who do you use for design? Who's terrific?" And he said, "Here's the guy." That's how I got started, and from there it was just constant interviewing, constant talking to people, and constant looking. Making sure that I kept up with some of the good stuff that's being done.

You ended up being in the forefront of it.

If you get lucky, you're able to do that.

I don't think you got lucky. You had a plan, and you followed it.

I'd like to discuss another issue, which is the line between industry expertise and real or perceived conflict of interest. First, industry expertise. Would it matter to you if your designer had never done a brochure for a company in the leasing business?

It wouldn't matter a bit. In fact, I'd rather they had never done one. What concerns me is whether the designer had worked for companies that wanted to achieve the kinds of objectives we want to achieve. I'm concerned that the designer know the kind of look I identify with as an emerging growth-type company, trying to be leading edge in a conservative market. Being able to reflect that image is more important than knowing anything about the technical side of my business.

One designer I know recently submitted a proposal to one of the major airlines for a series of international tour brochures. Apparently, the airline was impressed with the presentation, but because the firm's portfolio didn't include another travel brochure exactly like what they were looking for, they chose another designer. What would you say to a client like that?

I would tell a client like that that you are setting yourself up to get a repetition of what somebody else— your competitor—has already used! The advantage of using someone who has done effective communication in a similar opportunity or problem area, for another industry, is that you can translate someone else's success into something fresh and new to your industry.

That is a perfect answer. But if the designer had said that, the client might not have believed it.

That's what separates really successful businessmen who don't make many mistakes from guys who do. Let me explain. The way of avoiding mistakes is to take a proven concept and use it in another industry. To

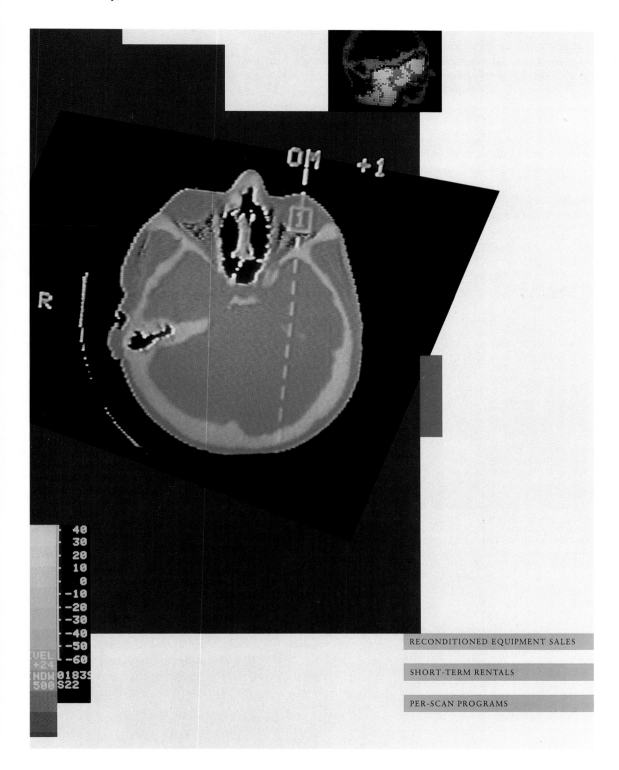

RECONDITIONED EQUIPMENT SALES

SHORT-TERM RENTALS

PER-SCAN PROGRAMS

come up with a concept that's never been used anywhere is risky, because you don't know whether it will work at all. But it's a lot less risky, for example, to introduce McDonald's in Uruguay when you know it has worked in Brazil and all over the United States. Do you follow?

Yes.

That's what we do to minimize risks. It's not always possible, but I've borrowed lots of ideas from computer leasing and from investment banking. I try to bring them into the context of health care finance and our other activities. Our corporate structure reflects the structure of one of the most successful computer manu-

LOW LEASE RATES?

NOBODY DOES IT SMARTER.

LINC IS A UNIQUE COMBINATION OF FINANCIAL SERVICES FOR THE HEALTH CARE INDUSTRY, A THINK TANK WITH POWERFUL RESOURCES OF EXPERIENCE, CAPITAL AND CREATIVITY.

WE KNOW THE BUSINESS SIDE, THE FINANCING SIDE, THE TAX CONSEQUENCES. WE STRIVE FOR AN OPTIMAL BALANCE OF LOW COST INSTITUTIONAL DEBT, POOLED EQUITY FUNDS, AND ACTIVE REMARKETING CAPABILITIES, WHICH MEANS LOWER EQUIPMENT LEASE RATES, HIGHER REVENUES, LESS RISK. TO FIND OUT MORE, SIMPLY CALL OR WRITE.

LINC FINANCIAL SERVICES, INC.

303 East Wacker Drive Chicago, Illinois 60601 (312) 467-5100. Or toll-free 1-800-233-LINC Other companies in the LINC Group include LINC Management Services, Inc., LINC Equipment Services, Inc., LINC Capital Corporation, LINC Capital Management, Inc.

facturers, a very successful emerging growth company. Why? Because I've seen it work, and I'm close enough to what that company's done to know that it's a sensible corporate structure for us, even though I also know that there's no other corporate leasing company in the country that uses it. To me, it's been proven. I'm just applying it to a different industry.

When a prospective client says, "You've never done one for someone exactly like us before," I bet a lot of designers wish they could make an argument as articulate as yours. Is there any suggestion you could make to a designer in that situation?

If a person knows they might not be able to respond persuasively, the easiest thing to do is to refer to an expert.

Here are three ideas: One way—and this is not the solution for everyone—is to work with a marketing or communications consultant. Our consultant, Todd Lief, who works as the interface between us and our designer, was formerly a principal at a couple of major Chicago boutique agencies. Designers are constantly faced with marketing issues that are difficult for them to respond to, and they just don't have the credibility of people like Todd, with a full-scale marketing background. So it's very helpful for a designer to have someone like that on board. Then the designer can say, "Look, it's worked here, and our marketing expert recommends it for your situation. Why don't you discuss it with him?"

The second thing the designer could do is tell the client directly that it's very effective to apply something that's been used in another industry. In reality the problem's the same, but it will give the client something fresh and not a rehash of what his competition has done. The last thing we want is something another leasing company has done!

A third way to sell a concept is to ask the client in your initial conversation, "What company in another industry would you model yourself on?" It may be that someone would model his company on Federal Express. Then when you come back, you can make that comparison and say, "Federal Express has used this technique and this kind of a look to distinguish themselves, and we're suggesting that you use something a little bit like that, but updated." Comparative selling can work very well. It depends on the person you're trying to sell.

You suggest working with a marketing person. Many clients I've spoken to are opposed to the kind of marketing person who sells design services. But you are talking about a different role: Someone who is perceived as working on behalf of the client rather than selling for the designer.

Yes, exactly. The marketing person we work with is an independent professional. He's on our team, so to speak, as well as on the designer's team. Together, they provide many of the services of an agency. From Rick Valicenti's standpoint, I think, Todd not only writes the copy, he helps to translate our objectives and sharpen the focus of the materials. Rick doesn't waste time going down creative blind alleys; the work is on target.

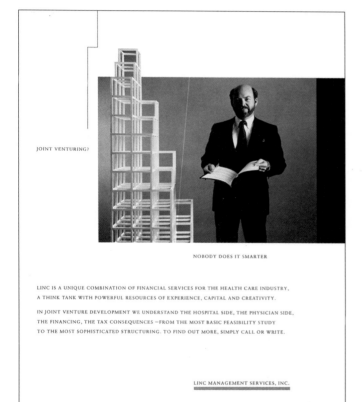

JOINT VENTURING?

NOBODY DOES IT SMARTER

LINC IS A UNIQUE COMBINATION OF FINANCIAL SERVICES FOR THE HEALTH CARE INDUSTRY, A THINK TANK WITH POWERFUL RESOURCES OF EXPERIENCE, CAPITAL AND CREATIVITY.

IN JOINT VENTURE DEVELOPMENT WE UNDERSTAND THE HOSPITAL SIDE, THE PHYSICIAN SIDE, THE FINANCING, THE TAX CONSEQUENCES –FROM THE MOST BASIC FEASIBILITY STUDY TO THE MOST SOPHISTICATED STRUCTURING. TO FIND OUT MORE, SIMPLY CALL OR WRITE.

LINC MANAGEMENT SERVICES, INC.

303 East Wacker Drive, Chicago, Illinois 60601 Toll-free phone 1-800-223-5462 (LINC) also Albuquerque, Nashville, Los Angeles Other companies in THE LINC GROUP include LINC Financial Services, Inc., LINC Equipment Services, Inc., LINC Capital Corporation, LINC Capital Management, Inc.

The forward-thinking approach of LINC's brochures extends to its black-and-white print advertising campaign, also produced by Valicenti, in which a few well placed design elements suggest LINC's sophisticated positioning in the financial services industry.

How to market services is always a dilemma for the really good independent designer. An agency has its own people to market its services—the account managers, the senior guys, whatever, and design is provided within the context of the overall solution. But I think a more interesting issue is how an independent designer markets his services, and does he use a marketing person? It can work if the marketing person is not just a salesperson, but an adviser to the client.

Let's talk a bit about the flip side of "You've never done it before," and that's, "You've done too much of it." Many clients, I think, especially in the service and financial sectors, are worried about conflict of interest. The same designer who didn't have specific tour brochure experience went to see a large accounting firm. His firm had done several projects for Big Eight firms, and the reaction to the presentation was, "You work for other accounting firms. We can't possibly use you; the partners would never go for that because of conflict of interest." He couldn't win! Here's what is seen as a potential problem by the client: "You talk to our competitors. You're going to let our secrets out."

It's a problem shared by agencies, a complicated issue. I don't really have an answer for that, because it's all in the individual's mind. Why do certain clients resign if the agency gets another client in the same industry?

How would you feel if your designer/consultant team also worked for one of your competitors?

I probably wouldn't want it if it were the same direct market, with the same customers, with the same kind of product. If it were a different product, or a different market, I wouldn't have a problem.

My thought would be that a designer, having worked closely with several competing firms, could see their differences clearly and would be better positioned to give them different looks, different approaches. Does the concept of industry expertise have any value for you?

Yes, except I use a designer, frankly, for ideas as well as for visuals. And I want to make sure that other people don't have access to those ideas. In terms of a product design or a stationery design, it really wouldn't be a problem. But I use a designer for considerably more, such as coming up with thoughts and observations as well as reflections on marketing communications. I don't want to get thoughts that are reflective of what someone else is doing. There's no easy answer. If my designer were heavily involved with a direct competitor, would I use him? No. If he did an occasional piece of work for a company in the same general industry, I'd have no problem. ■

Douglas P. Whaley is graphics coordinator for the San Diego Natural History Museum. He has worked as a production artist, graphic designer, and an art director. With a background in computer graphics and experience in interior design and video production, he joined the museum in 1987 to assist in its efforts to "turn a formerly musty museum into a dynamic center of interest." He is currently creating and heading up an in-house graphics department and developing a new graphic identity and image for the institution.

San Diego Natural History Museum, located in Balboa Park, was founded in 1874. The second-oldest scientific institution in the western United States, it features the plants, animals, and geology of southern California and parts of Arizona and Mexico. The museum is divided into three areas: research, education, and exhibits. The research staff collects specimens and studies biological problems, often of direct importance to local residents. The education department produces classes, lectures, seminars, nature walks, and tours, and maintains a loan library of over 1,200 mounted specimens available to artists, teachers, and museum members. The exhibits department is involved in the renovation of the museum's 25,000 square feet of temporary and permanent exhibit space. The museum is currently embarking upon a $12 million expansion project and is planning to transform its environment into an interactive experience for visitors.

15

When an "Outside" Designer Joins an In-House Team

Gerry Bustamante founded StudioBustamante, San Diego, on a simple philosophy—stay small, remain involved in every phase of each project, and adhere to uncompromising standards of quality. Since 1985, StudioBustamante has designed and illustrated printed pieces, clothing, three-dimensional inflatables, and exterior signage for local, regional, and national accounts. A graduate of San Diego State University's graphic communications department, Mr. Bustamante has received awards of excellence on both the national and local levels. His work is included in the permanent collection of the Library of Congress.

Douglas P. Whaley

Q *You are a designer, and you are also a client who hires outside designers. When you choose designers to work with you, do you look for people who are experienced in projects for museums?*

A Not necessarily. It is helpful, though, if a designer is able to demonstrate experience in areas such as interior design, architecture, signage, and/or theatrical set design. A knowledge of how things are constructed can be extremely valuable. When I review portfolios—usually with our exhibit designer, Mark Donnelly—we look for work that demonstrates the ability to expand a graphics program over a range of applications. We look for visual excitement that would appeal to a wide group of people. There is quite a range of interests, ages, and education levels that makes up our visitors. A person's ability to work with color and to incorporate color into a three-dimensional environment is also important; so is the ability to organize and simplify information and ideas that are easily understandable. A knowledge of typography is essential. Unless it's a temporary exhibit, we try to stay away from trendy looks. We need something that won't go out of style. We also look at portfolio samples that have been sold in retail environment: T-shirts, posters, postcards. We are not only designing an exhibit, we are marketing products around it. So it's really important to find somebody who's versatile.

As I understand it, many museum exhibition staffs number thirty or more people, including exhibit and graphic designers like yourself, production artists, scriptwriters, coordinators, technicians, and so forth. When you hire an outside graphic or exhibition designer, what is that person's relationship to your staff?

◀ "Dinosaurs!" banner by Gerry Bustamante welcomes summer, 1988, visitors to the San Diego Natural History Museum.

The "Dinosaurs!" logo was designed by Bustamante to work in color and in black and white, to appeal to adults as well as to kids, to fit a variety of shapes and formats, and to harmonize with both the exterior of the museum building and with the design of the exhibition itself. Client/art director Doug Whaley scanned Bustamante's original drawing into his computer to produce black-and-white repro art (near right) for use on press releases and print ads.

They are definitely part of our team. Only the largest museums have internal design staffs adequate for most projects. The majority of museums are like ours and have a real need for continuing outside help. We invite portfolios, and see everybody who calls. But I know that many other museums are not as hospitable. They just don't have the time or the staff.

How do you present the assignment to the designer? How does the work flow go?

At our museum, the department heads get together to brainstorm ideas for possible exhibitions. After the content has been established, a committee will be formed ranging from four to fifteen people. It will be made up of someone from the exhibit design staff, someone from our education department, a scientific curator, and the public programs director who oversees the project and reports to the museum director. Additional committee members might include the museum director, our fundraising person, the public relations specialist, the copywriter, the gift shop manager, and sometimes someone from the construction staff who will build the exhibit. An outside designer will usually get involved after the preliminary floor plan has been approved.

Do all these people give input and direction to the designer? And do they all evaluate the designer's presentation—each from his or her own perspective?

Yes. Both.

I'm going into this much detail because I read in a recent book that there are over 5,000 museums in the United States that attract 500 million people a year, which is six times as many people as attend professional ball games. It's becoming a huge market, and you say you're looking for talent. Do designers know that?

We don't get as many designers coming in here to show their work as we'd like. Part of the problem might be that most museums in the United States are non-profit organizations. They don't have a lot of money to spend. When we hired Gerry Bustamante for the "Dinosaurs!" exhibition, we hoped his work for us would not only attract visitors, but other designers of his caliber as well.

You are describing two potential problems for designers: One, you might not have much money, and, two, a big crowd might be involved in approving the design.

True, these can be problems. But even though the budget might not be as large as we'd like, these projects can be really interesting and fun for the designer, and create a lot of exposure. As far as approvals go, many people do have input, but the exhibits department is ultimately in charge of the look of the show. If there is ever a dispute, the museum director is the ultimate decision-maker.

Tell me about the "Dinosaurs!" exhibition.

First of all, this year's show is geared toward children and includes many interactive, hands-on activities. There's a giant sandbox where kids can dig for dinosaur bones. We have a huge trackway of dinosaur footprints where they can run around and compare their foot size to dinosaur feet. We have a video theater that features an award-winning Claymation® video. Our Dinostore is a gift shop that exclusively sells dinosaur items. The education department has been featuring all kinds of events and classes, from weekend films to something called "Build-a-Beast," where kids search for scattered dinosaur bones and assemble them into a giant stegosaurus. The greatest things are the lifelike and fully animated dinosaurs. They range from about one-third to two-thirds actual size; the tallest, tyrannosaurus rex, being about thirteen feet tall. They move, they roar, and they breathe. Kids love them, even though a few do get scared. Adults seem to enjoy watching the kids as much as watching the exhibit. This is our third dinosaur exhibit, and we were worried that people would be dinosaured-out. But we're back by popular demand. We've designed each year's exhibit differently. Even if people come back twice, each time would be a totally different experience.

What were the specific responsibilities of the graphic designer?

When we started to work with Gerry, it was already established that we would divide the exhibit into seven specific, color-coded areas. We wanted our exterior signage to utilize those seven colors and harmonize with the exterior color of the building. We were looking for a fresh, versatile look that would appeal to kids as well as to adults. The logo image had to work in both color and black and white. Since we hang banners in front of the museum to attract attention, the image had to fit a long, vertical format. But it had to work in several other formats, such as on square buttons and on horizontal postcards; we had to be able to change around the proportions. Other applications included black-and-white

print ads, press releases, promotional posters, and graphics within the exhibit area. We were looking for colors that were summery, emblematic, and contemporary. That was one of the reasons Gerry was chosen—because of his look. I had seen his work before in awards shows.

Which shows do you follow?

His work was in the last two shows for the communicating arts group here in San Diego. I had admired it, and chose him because he was an up-and-coming local artist with experience designing promotional products for large public events. He demonstrated a good color

The museum's "Dinostore," a gift shop adjacent to the exhibition, sells dinosaur-related items and contributes additional revenue to the museum. The interior signage by Doug Whaley and Mark Donnelly incorporates the typography Bustamante established for the exhibition graphics.

sense and a very graphic illustration style. We needed something that was quick and easy to reproduce. We had a low budget and a short time frame, and had to build the entire exhibit and fabricate all the signage in-house.

In general, our museum is trying to get away from the traditional, stuffy approach used by other natural history museums. You know, wildlife paintings. We're trying to develop a new image. Plus, we're competing for dollars with the San Diego Zoo, which is right next door, and with Sea World, Wild Animal Park, and other nearby tourist attractions. So there's a real need to stand out in any way we can.

Has this competition caused museums everywhere to be more aggressive?

Yes. They have to. It's necessary for them to survive. People seem to think our museum is supported by city taxes. In reality, the amount of money we get from the city is very minimal. We're just like any other business. If we don't meet our operating expenses, we'll cease to exist. One of the ways to generate additional revenue is to sell items in the gift store, something new to this museum. The T-shirts are one example. I believed in them so strongly that I financed them myself. The museum had spent its entire budget on the show and didn't have the money to invest in dinosaur T-shirts. So I took $1,500 of my own money and created camera-ready artwork. I drove a hundred miles to a shirt wholesaler up in Los Angeles, bought shirts, found a silkscreener, paid his expenses, and went ahead and produced a seven-color shirt on my own. It's a big seller.

Not many people would put their own cash and their own time on the line like that.

I felt strongly enough about the appeal of Gerry's work that I didn't think there was anything to lose. As a designer, you have to have an appreciation for other artists, a respect for them. Gerry gave us a favor; he charged us a rate lower than his normal fee. I appreciated his attitude of wanting to help us out in any way he could. We usually don't have large budgets, so when the budgets are low, I try to find other ways to reward designers, such as design freedom and royalties. ∎

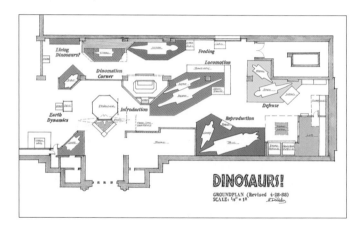

When the museum staff began working with Gerry Bustamante, it was already established that the exhibition would be divided into seven color-coded areas (above). Bustamante applied the seven colors to a range of exhibition graphics, including the platforms on which the dinosaur models were mounted.

Doug Whaley financed seven-color "Dinosaurs!" T-shirts himself in order to promote the museum and the work of Gerry Bustamante, who receives a royalty for each shirt sold.

Christian Plasman is president of Hickory Business Furniture (HBF). He came to the company from Herman Miller, Inc. in 1983. Born in Grand Rapids, Michigan, Mr. Plasman received his B.A. from Hope College. In 1988, he successfully completed the executive program at the Darden School of Business at the University of Virginia.

Hickory Business Furniture is a Hickory, North Carolina, company that manufactures and markets inventive, high-qualify furniture for the contract market. Founded in 1980 as a division of the Lane Company, HBF won immediate acclaim for its innovative product lines and woodcrafter-quality workmanship. Its offerings draw freely upon styles of the past such as Arts and Crafts, Regency, Chippendale, and the classic school chair. HBF updates these styles in luxurious woods for today's environment. Designers who have done prize-winning work for HBF include Massimo and Lella Vignelli, Orlando Diaz-Azcuy, Wayne Braun, and Michael Vanderbyl. HBF's Chicago showroom, which opened in 1983, has won awards from the American Society of Interior Designers and *Interior Design* magazine; a New York showroom in the International Design Center, New York (IDCNY) opened in 1986. In 1986, the Lane Company was purchased by Interco, Inc. HBF employs over two hundred people.

16

How One Designer's Diverse Talents Helped Build a Company

Michael Vanderbyl received a B.F.A. in graphic design from the California College of Arts and Crafts in 1968. Today he is dean of its School of Design. His company, San Francisco-based Vanderbyl Design, founded in 1973, is internationally known for graphics, packaging, signage, interiors, showrooms, furniture, textiles, and fashion apparel. The firm's clients also include Esprit, Bernhardt Furniture Company, Simpson Paper, and the San Francisco Museum of Modern Art. Mr. Vanderbyl is a frequent guest speaker at conferences and design organizations, and has been a visiting instructor at colleges and universities. He has served on the national board of the AIGA. Work by Vanderbyl Design has been included in every major design competition in the United States and Europe and is in the permanent collections of the Cooper Hewitt Museum and the Library of Congress.

Christian Plasman

Q *Would it be fair to characterize Hickory Business Furniture as a relatively new company that has been successful in marketing antique reproductions as well as new furniture designs? And that your success has been largely achieved through the efforts of one designer?*

A We started the company by calling HBF "The New Tradition." New Tradition meant that we didn't necessarily make copies of eighteenth-century-style furniture, but rather took elements from pieces with a historical perspective and reinterpreted them to achieve what was necessary in today's market. Michael Vanderbyl has been instrumental in the formation of the image of this company—in promotion, advertising, showrooms, and now on to the furniture itself. There is a design consistency through the entire company, and Vanderbyl Design plays an important role in this process.

Michael Vanderbyl told me that he feels he holds "the destiny of your company in his hands." He did not seem to be bragging, just stating a fact. How did the relationship get started?

A previous general manager of this organization was familiar with Michael's work for Modern Mode. We approached Michael six years ago—two months after I joined the company—with some pretty crummy black-and-white catalog sheets and said, "We'd like to do a poster." We were planning to announce our new representatives in Texas; the idea was to stage a promotional event for HBF in the Texas market. Michael came back to us and said, "I also have an idea for how you should show your product." He laid it out, and it all made immediate sense. It was a consistent presentation of HBF, way beyond posters, from our brochures to the binders that hold the brochures, to the showrooms; a presentation that encompassed everything we do.

◄ HBF's showroom in Chicago's Merchandise Mart, designed by Michael Vanderbyl, displays furniture along grand colonnades.

The poster that launched a company (and a worldwide graphic design trend). This 1983 poster, Michael Vanderbyl's first project for HBF, introduced HBF to the Dallas market. A series of stylistically similar posters followed.

Hickory Business Furniture

You are describing a situation in which a designer's unsolicited concept was accepted and ultimately contributed a great deal to your company's success. Many designers are afraid to go out on a limb like that. They're worried that their time and effort won't be appreciated, and that—if they've virtually already given their work away—the client will not want to pay for it. Yet it's important for designers to be able to present original concepts.

I agree. A lot of companies have not allowed that to happen. For it to take place, you've got to allow the designer the opportunity and the flexibility to become involved with an organization on more than a single project. And you've got to be able to move from project to project and make sure there is a consistency between all of them. Your image becomes much more solid when you can establish a long-term relationship with a designer who does more than a one-time job for you.

Let's say, though, the designer comes back with a prototype of something that you don't want to do, that you don't think is quite right for you. Do you think the designer should be paid for the time and materials that went into doing that work?

Only if we gave the designer the project. We hire people to do the things we feel need to be done, not necessarily the things that they need to do for us. It has to be agreed upon ahead of time.

Perhaps I misunderstood, but I thought the original presentation was Michael's initiative.

And we bought it.

Are you saying that if it was something that you did not want to go ahead with, you would not have bought it?

That's right. It was his investment in establishing a relationship.

A silhouette of North Carolina–born President Andrew Jackson, "Old Hickory," was Vanderbyl's concept for the company symbol.

Could that investment happen at various times along the line?

Certainly. It does all the time. We often work from thumbnail sketches to keep somebody from going to a great deal of expense before we know whether we're going to go forward with something.

The February 1987 issue of Interiors *magazine describes Michael Vanderbyl as "probably the most celebrated multidisciplined designer in the United States," and goes on to say that "clients nationwide are drawn by a special California attitude toward design marketing and business." Do you think there's any validity to the idea of a California attitude?*

I don't think people look at HBF and say, "That's California design." I think people look at HBF and say, "That's design that works." Certainly the designs that have been done for HBF are recognized far beyond the borders of the United States as good design. But I won't disagree with people who recognize that there's a tremendous amount of design talent in California right now.

Can you tell me about your first showroom at IDCNY? How did the concept of the striped tubes come about?

Elements of columns have been with HBF since the beginning of the company. Prior to the opening of IDCNY, we used columns very effectively in the Chicago showrooms. And the first poster Michael did for us was an illustration of a Corinthian column with splashes of color. The idea of using the black-and-white striped columns in New York made a lot of sense. First of all, from an economic standpoint, you could move them. They weren't anchored to the floor. Yet they divided the space beautifully and provided an opportunity to do some things that didn't take a lot of renovation when we were through. All we had to do was pick them up and take them out, and we had a totally clean space again. Second, they were easy for us to do. We bought them in white, painted them here, shipped them up to New York, and put them in place. Third, they were extremely striking. It was our first showroom in New York; we felt it was very, very important to make as striking a presentation as we could for the Designer's Saturday opening.

HBF's looseleaf brochures for individual product lines are produced by Vanderbyl Design. All the brochures can be assembled into a binder, which comprises the company's catalog.

Hickory Business Furniture

Can you describe the overall effect you were trying to achieve?

To intrigue people; to bring them in. The outside of our New York space is entirely opaque. It's black marble, decorated only with a gold-leaf HBF monogram and the profile of Andrew Jackson, "Old Hickory." So it's sort of like being outside of Tiffany's. We didn't want a glass storefront, where people could take a look inside, and then just walk by. You really have to come inside to see what it's all about. And it's worked very, very well.

Michael told me that he had never designed a showroom like yours before. Some clients think it's necessary to see something very close to what they want in a designer's portfolio in order to trust that designer's capability. I'd like to hear your thoughts on that.

You can never understand the total benefit of a design until you're standing in it. You can look at things for other clients, at models and renderings, but you will never experience its full impact until it's done. I think you just have to trust your designer. As long as you have expressed yourself well to someone who's worked on a number of consistent projects across a number of different fronts, I think it will be what you want it to be.

What about clients who have one designer for their employee publications, another for their shareholder communications, and a different agency for their sales promotion and advertising? The interior design would most likely be handled by yet another firm. Do you see a need for, or a trend toward, multidisciplinary capabilities?

Personally, I think that it would be very inefficient for a company to hire one designer for one project and another designer for the next project; one designer to do the interiors, and another for the annual report. It seems to me there could be a built-in inconsistency because there might be an immediate competition among the designers.

A company's first obligation is to its customer. The idea is to sell the product, and everything else should fall in line with that. If you're putting your best foot forward with your customer, why wouldn't you want to do that with your plant employees and everybody else? I mean, it should be consistent. To me, it all can come from the same person.

The Orlando Diaz-Azcuy furniture collection was unveiled in October 1985 at a spectacular New York event. When the Orlando textiles were launched the next year, the company continued the "unveiling" or "unwrapping" theme.

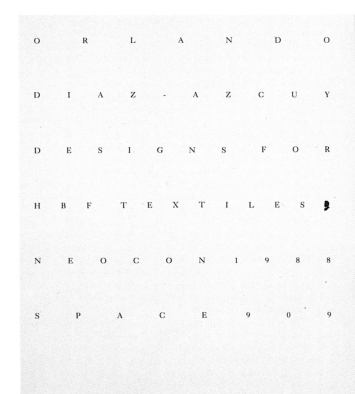

ORLANDO

DIAZ-AZCUY

DESIGNS FOR

HBF TEXTILES

NEOCON 1988

SPACE 909

Q *What do you think of companies that use different designers for different projects?*

A *A company's first obligation must be to its customers. To sell a product, everything should be consistent.*

Christian Plasman

For you, that person is not local. Obviously that has not been a handicap.

It may be an advantage because that person, not located in Hickory, North Carolina, certainly views the world from a different perspective. I enjoy the possibility of having that perspective come into consideration, as opposed to someone from a town of twenty-five thousand trying to make an interpretation as to what the rest of the world would like to see. Secondly, given the way we communicate in the electronic age, it's not much of a problem. Fax and air express have dramatically changed the way people do business today.

Do you consider Bernhardt, another of Michael's clients, your competitor? As I understand it, Bernhardt is also located in Hickory, North Carolina, and manufactures similar furniture for the contract market. Clients have strong, but conflicting, opinions about whether their designer should be working for their direct competitors.

No, I don't consider Bernhardt my competitor. But even if I did, I would trust a good designer's ability to see the distinctions between us and be able to communicate them. There is value to in-depth knowledge of an industry and its market.

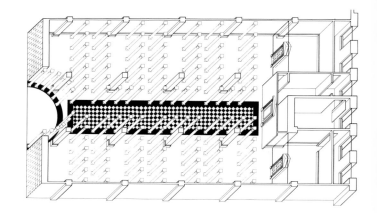

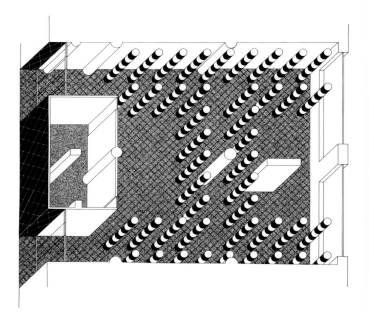

◄ HBF's showroom at IDCNY, Long Island City, New York, which opened in 1986, displays "Athenee" and "Miami" chairs from the Orlando Diaz-Azcuy Collection against dramatic black-and-white tubes specified by Michael Vanderbyl.

Isometric plans for HBF's Chicago showroom (top) and for HBF's IDCNY showroom (center).

The opaque facade of HBF's IDCNY showroom (right) is designed to intrigue people. According to Christian Plasman, it has been extremely effective. At the entrance stands a Cambridge Series chair designed by Michael Vanderbyl.

130

Hickory Business Furniture

What inspired you to ask Michael to design furniture?

I guess as much as anything, it is the fact that Michael always has ideas. He said, "Instead of this, why didn't they do that?"

Do you mean that when he looked at the furniture that was going in the catalog, he wasn't completely pleased with what he saw?

It was always constructive criticism, and most of his suggestions were minor. I think Michael finally got to the point where he said, "You know, if I had done it, I would have done it this way." And finally we said, "You know, Michael, why don't you do it?" And he has, and has done quite well. So it was a natural outflowing of his creative talent. There are a lot of people in the world who have that capability. I don't think that if you're a good designer it means you're just a good graphic designer or just a good interior designer. In fact, the majority of the furniture we've introduced over the last five years has not been done by product designers or industrial designers. Almost exclusively, it was done by interior designers or interior architects or, in the case of

Michael, a graphic designer. We find that most of these people, whether they've aspired to it or not, have been multidisciplined; they specify furniture for various spaces, and have a number of different ideas as to what, physically, furniture should look like. So it all flows together very nicely.

The article in Interiors *concludes, "For HBF, a modernist colonial look was developed using black and white. The technique worked. Following the launch of the Orlando Diaz-Azcuy furniture collection, sales increased by 200 percent."*

That's right. Every year we continue to grow. We are now five-fold bigger than we were then. And graphics has been one of the keys to that. From that standpoint, it all fits together. Our growth would not have happened if we had only come to the market with some very good furniture designs. Our growth occurred because we had some very good furniture designs that we presented very well to the specifying public. ∎

Michael Vanderbyl's Colonnade Series conference and occasional tables were introduced in June 1985 with this print ad. The line has enjoyed excellent sales.

Patrice I. Boyer has been a professional communicator for almost fifteen years. Before becoming director of marketing and communications for the world's largest YMCA, she served as an account executive at Daniel J. Edelman and Burson-Marsteller, both international public relations agencies. She also developed college textbooks for Little, Brown and Company, and edited *Yankee Oilman*, a trade journal for the heating industry. Ms. Boyer holds a B.A. in English from the University of Pennsylvania and an M.A. in English from the University of Manchester, England.

The YMCA of Metropolitan Chicago is a private, non-profit social service organization providing child care, community development, family activities, health enhancement, and leadership development programs to half a million people. Its mission is to aid in the development of Christian values and to support the physical, mental, and spiritual well-being of individuals and families in order to improve their quality of life. In 1988, it celebrated its 130th year in Chicago.

17

The Advantages of a Long-Term Alliance

Pat and Greg Samata, a husband-and-wife team, are partners in Samata Associates, Dundee, Illinois. Graduates in design communications from the Chicago Academy of Art, the Samatas formed their firm in 1974. They create award-winning corporate trademarks, identity programs, financial publications, and exhibit and packaging design. A. Gregory Samata is on the board of directors of the Society of Typographics Arts (STA), and the AIGA, and is a member of the 27 Chicago Designers. Patricia G. Samata is also active in many professional organizations, including Women in Design. The work of the Samatas has been recognized in many major design publications and competitions.

Patrice I. Boyer

Q *Can you tell me what first got the Chicago Y interested in design?*

A We needed to make an impact with our primary audiences in Chicago: the civic community, the corporate community, and of course, the general population. It was a transitional period, we had a new president, and wanted to create a whole new look to stress quality, professionalism, and forward movement. We have a volunteer board of managers, and one of the board members recommended Pat and Greg Samata because they had done some work for his company, Illinois Bell. The Samatas were hired. Then I was hired. So we were all new, including the president. It was a new beginning.

What is special, unique about the Chicago Y?

We're a leader with a prominent position in the international and national YMCA movement. For example, we have developed guidelines and working models for community development, and not all Ys are strong in this area. We're very large, and we use the Y as a leadership force within the community, as a model for smaller organizations. Together with them, we form neighborhood coalitions to solve local issues. One of our Ys, for instance, is part of a coalition of many agencies in an extremely low-income neighborhood. It works with hospital, churches, and other groups to create programs for the residents, who would not be served as well by independent agencies.

When I say very large, if you count everything we do—every camp, every outreach center, every social service agency Y, and every full facility swimming pool and gym Y—it adds up to forty Ys in the Chicago metropolitan area.

Did you need to change people's perceptions about what a Y is?

To answer, let me describe a few of the programs we are working on. We're testing a model program we've developed for youth fitness. When I was a kid in school, we had President Kennedy's physical fitness programs, which are now defunct. So we've created a program called Healthy Heroes, which should be running within the year. Another program is called Youth And Government. It draws students from each of the city's seventy high schools and matches them with an adult counterpart in city government. The students go through months of after-school education in the workings of government, including holding their own elections. On the last day, they take over the city council chambers, and Chicago's mayor and other elected officials meet with the kids. This took quite a bit of work within the local political structure to organize. In addition, our president is involved in partnerships with Ys around the world to exchange resources and expertise. We have set up a fund for the Ys in Africa, which supports local initiatives in areas such as agriculture and job training.

You used the words "leadership force." One might say that your annual reports are a leadership force in design—in typography, color, and imagery. Was there a conscious decision on the part of the Y to achieve this?

We always strive for leadership; that's a main goal of ours.

◄ **"Core Program" posters donated by Pat and Greg Samata hang in every Chicago YMCA.**

The first report the Samatas did for the Y in 1983, a 36-page book, marked the organization's 125th anniversary, highlighted ten special programs, and called for rebuilding the inner city Ys. Photography: Robert Tolchin.

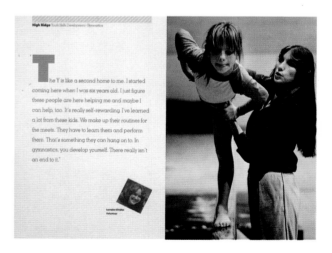

Take a typical spread—there's a photograph of a boy with a basketball silhouetted against a huge lavender-pink letter "M" bleeding of the page. The boy is acutely foreshortened, the type is at an angle, and there are tiny pink initial caps. There are six or seven things right here that a client might have problems with, they might say, "We can't do that; people wouldn't react well. It makes this kid look all out of proportion." What makes your organization willing to say, "Hey, this looks terrific; this is exciting," and not knock it down?

I think the secret of our success is the strength of our relationship with the Samatas. I'm the primary liaison with them. We completely trust their judgment, and we have very few levels of approval here. We're extremely busy in other areas, and we don't have time to sit around and pick apart design. It's my philosophy that you let the experts do what they're good at. They make me look good, and I make the organization look good.

What would you say to clients around the country to whom designers show a comp, and the clients start taking it apart and saying, "We've got to be more conservative; I'm afraid to show this to my boss; the trustees aren't going to understand it"?

The first thing I would say is that the job of communications belongs in the communications department. I believe that a certain strength of direction and opinion should reside with my counterparts at other companies and agencies. I'm not afraid to present things. Secondly—I've learned this not only at the Y but at my previous positions—in any business you've got to rely on people to help you do your job. In some cases, you pay those people; you call them suppliers and they call you clients. But once you find people who are trustworthy, they will deliver what you need. If you have good chemistry with them, and they have the skills and taste and whatever else you're looking for, stay with them. You can build a growing, rewarding relationship. I support the Samatas within my own organization, not

that I have to overcome anybody's resistance to them because everybody here just loves their work . . . even though they can certainly make more money working for other clients. One point I want to make is we don't pay them the full price of what these books cost to produce. We can't.

Can we talk about the budget in context of the format? It's ranged from a six-panel folder to a thirty-six-page perfect-bound book. Did those decisions derive from budget constraints, or were they editorial decisions based on the amount of information you had to present?

It was both budget and editorial. The first year, when we were new to each other, we did the perfect-bound book, and we did pay what I imagine was the full freight of the job. It was a lot of money for us, but we felt that it was well spent because we had a major change to announce, and we had to reestablish the Y as a vital organization worth contributing to. We wanted to make a substantial and highly visible impact on the corporate community. The second year we spent a bit less, but it was still a considerable sum. The third year, we saw that our image was beginning to take root in the community and in the Chicago centers of industry, business, and politics. So we felt we could go with something a bit more modest but still with good design and solid concept. This was the book that announced our strategic plan, so it was more of a thoughtful working document, and we wanted to present it in a simpler, more pared-down way.

That was the year that your photography also changed from a journalistic style to shots that were clearly set up.

The 1983 report was all candid. The photographer just took what was happening in front of him.

The 1984 report noted a financial turnaround and focused on youth programs. Photography: Tim Bieber; illustration: Tony Reinwald.

The second year, 1984, was the overhead shots, or in the case of the pool, under water. The idea was to have sort of an overview of things—to tie in the leadership theme—showing a whole scene from a fairly distant vantage point. Those photographs were not exactly candid because the photographer was up on a ladder, but they still showed the action taking place.

And then in 1985, we went to studio shots and portraits to try to portray the goals of our strategic plan. There were, I believe, nine goals, and we just didn't have the room and the money to show nine different things, so we had people who represented one area holding pictures of people representing another goal. For instance, there's a photograph of a senior woman holding a day care picture. We hoped to convey both programs and the age spectrum in an economical way.

In 1986, it was still lifes of the whistle, the marshmallow on a stick, and so forth. It looks like it was a lower budget solution, and a very appealing one.

That was definitely low-budget. We had so much success with the other books and with the new image that we decided to pare down even more. It's funny to put it this way, but there was a confidence that led to that decision; there was a confidence that we didn't need to do major pieces every year. In fact, by the time we got to the fold-out, we were firmly rooted in our belief that the whole identity was working, and we could get away with a piece that was less expensive and elaborate. We did that one for probably a third or a fourth of what the first one cost, so we're talking about a big price difference.

Then, in passing conversation, the Samatas mentioned that they wanted to continue doing the more substantial pieces, which gave them a bit more opportu-

nity for their own design expression. In order to do this, they agreed to make up the cost difference.

Can you share your perspective on how designers can work successfully for nonprofit organizations?

I've worked both for nonprofits and the corporate sector, and I don't think there is any real difference—other than designers are more turned on by what the Y does than they would be if we sold computers or airplane engines. We provide them with an opportunity to

Photo by Mark Joseph from the 1987 report depicts one of the 14- to 18-year-olds who join in sports and recreational activities at the thirty-four Ys and six camps operated by the YMCA of Metropolitan Chicago.

In 1985, the Samatas worked with the Y on a smaller book that set out new program goals. Photography: Jean Moss and Robert B. Tolchin.

design pieces of a different type. It's more people-focused, our products are programs and services for people. The content gives them greater creative leeway. I think—and they'll have to back this up—that they're willing to exchange the lower fees for the goodwill of helping an organization they believe in, and also for the creative freedom of taking photographs of little girls holding paper dolls. That stuff is more fun for them.

Also, we don't hack their designs to pieces. I don't think they'd be working with us if they brought in a design and we said, "Let's change this, we don't like these colors, and let's do without these photos." I mean, that would be the end.

Or, "Here are the photos in our files. Please design something with them." There are institutions that want both: donated or partially donated work and total control of the design.

The philosophy I have—and I'm really surprised more people don't have it—is that we all do what we're good at. I'm good at writing. I'm good at coordinating for the overall production. I'm not good at designing or picking photographs. I write my copy according to the designers' specs. For instance, if they're doing illustrated initial caps and want to use a kid's athletic sock, the quote has to start with an *L* because it's a sock shape. So

A six-panel foldout for 1986 (below) celebrated the Y's third year with a balanced budget. Even in this modest format, credit is given to: the designers, Pat and Greg Samata; the writer, Patrice Boyer; the photographers, Dennis Dooley and Jean Moss; and the printer, Great Northern Design.

In 1987, the Samatas created a daring photographic layout (bottom) that introduced the Y's six Core Programs and became the foundation of the poster series.

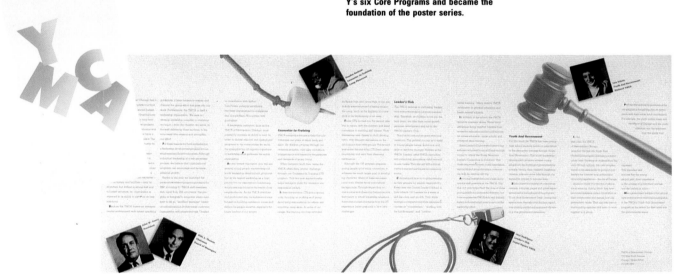

I start my sentence with an *L.* We're very much a team, and the ultimate piece we create is the goal. No one is in charge. I don't feel that because I'm the client, I'm the big boss.

You commented that after the Samatas did the fold-out, they let it be known that it was more interesting for them to work on a bigger book. The next year, 1987, there was indeed a bigger book. Was that decision made to meet the Y's need or because you wanted to give them the project they suggested?

The way they proposed it, it was a way of donating services. It wasn't, "We'd rather do bigger books." It was, "We'd be willing to supplement whatever your budget is to do a more substantive piece." They have always been supporters of the Y, either in the donation of money or in the donation of services. So they basically said, "We really like the piece we did last year, but we don't at all mind supplementing your budget with an in-kind contribution."

How is the contribution recognized?

They are recognized as corporate partner of the Y. This year they also offered, both as a contribution and to have some fun, to do a series of posters completely free of charge—the photography, the paper, the printing, everything. I said, "That's wonderful; let me see what guidelines I can give you." At that time, we were creating what we call our Core program. A volunteer committee looked at our hundreds of program offerings to group them into a handful of categories that would be more easily identifiable by the public. Coinciding with the offer of the poster series, we came up with the six

Core programs: Family Life, Child Care, and so forth. So I said, "Why don't we use the programs as the theme of the posters?" It was also annual report time, so the projects evolved jointly. The posters are now hanging in every Chicago Y.

They've also done model T-shirts and sweatshirts, which have not been produced, primarily for financial reasons. But we are intending to continue the identity in other ways.

And I should tell you that every year I go to a national conference for YMCA marketing and public relations professionals from around the country. As the years go by, more and more people I don't know come up to me when they find out I'm the Chicago person. They just fall all over me and say things like, "We love your stuff. You can't believe how much you've helped me convince my boss and board of directors that we need to pay attention to what we're doing in graphics."

That must make you feel great.

It does. People in Ys across the country know of the work we do here, and value it because it helps them. I get many requests for copies of the annual report. I also take the reports to the corporations we work with. Right now, we're doing a major promotion with Sears, McDonald's, Marriott, and a number of other large companies. The way that I introduce them to the Y is by showing them our publications. The corporate people ask me, "Who did these? These are wonderful." So referrals are happening, even informally, in this way.

To me, all of this is about the most basic and simple thing: very talented people doing great work with a good organization that's smart enough to let them do what they do best. We benefit from that. What I can't understand is why that's news. My relationship with designers is that they come as problem-solvers. They are more than people who figure out how wide the margins should be. I use them as expert consultants in the highest sense. ■

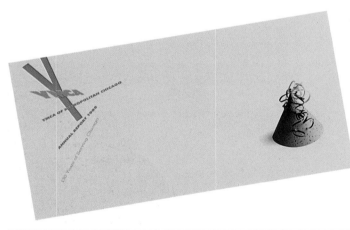

The 1988 report playfully celebrates the institution's 130th birthday. Photography: Mark Joseph.

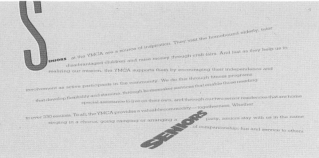

Part Four

Results Rewards and the Future

David Bither has been vice president–international of Elektra Entertainment, part of Warner Communications' recorded music group, since 1987. Previously, he was director of corporate communications for Warner; his responsibilities included production of the corporation's annual reports from 1984 to 1986. Prior to that, he was director of corporate relations at the Brooklyn Academy of Music, producing a variety of fund-raising and audience development materials as well as annual reports. Mr. Bither earned a B.S. in journalism from the University of Illinois and an M.A. in arts administration from the University of Wisconsin. In his present position, Mr. Bither is responsible for the international marketing of such artists as Anita Baker, Tracy Chapman, 10,000 Maniacs, and the Kronos Quartet for Elektra/Asylum/Nonesuch Records.

Warner Communications Inc. (WCI), one of the world's leading communications and entertainment corporations, celebrated its twenty-sixth year as a public company in 1988. In 1962, revenues were $17 million; in 1988, they totalled approximately $4 billion. WCI's Filmed Entertainment division includes Warner Bros., Warner Bros. Television, and Warner Home Video; the Recorded Music Group includes Warner Bros., Atlantic, and Elektra/Asylum/Nonesuch Records, and Warner/Chappell Music; Cable and Broadcasting is led by Warner Cable Communications. WCI also owns Warner Books, *Mad* magazine, and DC comics. The corporation, based in New York, has operations worldwide. In March 1989, Warner Communications announced that it would merge with Time Inc. to form the largest media and entertainment company in the world, Time Warner.

18

Why Take the Risk on Leading-Edge, Experimental Work?

Pentagram is an international partnership, providing services in identity, information, packaging, and product and environmental design. Thirteen partners and over a hundred staff operate from offices in New York, San Francisco, and London. Each partner has individual areas of expertise, giving the company a broad base for design activities. Pentagram opened its New York office in 1978; currently it has four design partners and a staff of twenty-five serving clients including Drexel Burnham Lambert, Knoll, The '21' Club, and Chase Manhattan Bank. Peter Harrison is the partner in charge of the Warner Communications annual reports. London-born Mr. Harrison specializes in combining graphics with three-dimensional design. Senior designers on the reports shown here were Susan Hochbaum and Harold Burch.

David Bither

Q *You have produced annual reports that can only be called radical and experimental within a traditional corporate annual report context. Not many chairmen of the boards of Fortune 100 companies allow their portraits to be decorated with collagelike elements. Tell me about Warner's philosophy.*

A Warner Communications is mostly about two things: quality and creativity. During the years I was involved with and ultimately responsible for the annual reports, the company was at first riding at the highest peak of a roller coaster; we were enormously profitable, and the annual reports didn't even have a budget that I knew of. It was just, "Let's do the best possible thing we can." And we spent an enormous amount of money doing just that. These were the big books of the late seventies and early eighties. Then, Warner's Atari company went down the other side of the roller coaster, and we lost a great deal of money. The annual report budget was cut by about 75 percent . . . even though we were producing the same number of books. So we went from trying to be creative on a big budget to trying to be creative on a restricted budget.

◄A collage by California artist John Van Hammersveld commissioned by Pentagram for the cover of the 1987 Warner Communications annual report.

Steven J. Ross, WCI's chairman and chief executive officer, as he was pictured on the "letter to shareholders" pages in his company's 1984, 1985, and 1987 reports.

How did that downswing affect design decisions?

In 1984, after Warners lost all that money, we tried to emphasize that the bedrock of the company was the creative people we worked with: the musicians, the film stars, the directors, and the writers. We did a very sober book with black-and-white photography by Neal Slavin. It was of high quality, but there was a certain message we were trying to convey—that this was a stable company that, despite serious losses, was not going to fold up and blow away.

Then Warners sold off Atari and made a strong comeback; we were liberated by the idea that we could think of the future again. So the 1985 book expressed our desire to be as creative as possible after a year of really strong earnings and said to our shareholders, "Look, this is what we're all about. We take risks."

My thinking at the time was: We can make an optimistic and dramatic statement without spending the kind of money we used to, if we spend it wisely and make the kind of book that graphically presents the story of this company, which is about pushing forward in terms of filmmaking and music and the arts in general—the popular arts at least. If anybody could take those chances, we could. And I thought we had the responsibility to. The book reflects my own taste to some degree. Which is almost too simple an answer. But I wanted an annual report that didn't look like anyone else's annual report had ever looked before. I wanted to push the medium farther than it had ever been pushed.

You have to remember, though, that we are not talking about radical innovation here. The design was unusual for a corporate annual report, but I don't want to give you the impression that we invented something that the world had never seen before. The illustrators, Su Huntley and Donna Muir, were at that time quite well known in the European design world. It was more a question of context.

Within the corporate structure, did you have to do anything extraordinary to get people to accept the idea of pushing the medium?

One thing that made it easy, ironically, was that during the period of losses, Warner's corporate staff was streamlined dramatically. Before that, six to eight people were responsible for putting the report together, and fifteen different people had to pass judgment on it. In 1985, it was essentially me working with the designers at Pentagram, Peter Harrison and Susan Hochbaum, and then presenting the results to our chairman, Steve Ross. There was very little bureaucracy. It was a matter of Ross saying, "Yes, you can do it. You've done these annuals before, and you've done them well and I trust you." I reported directly to one other executive, Geoff Holmes, who also basically said, "You make your own decisions, and I'll say 'yes' or 'no.'" But he didn't interfere at all. He was very supportive and let me "have my own head." It boils down to one word—freedom. And, of course, there was the critical trust between my office and Pentagram in terms of the work that they'd done for us in the past.

What was the initial internal reaction to the book?

The first three phone calls I got when it came off the presses were from executives within the company who said, "How could you have possibly done this? This is the most outrageous thing I've ever seen."

Did that worry you?

The end of the story is that a few weeks later, when we started to get a lot of favorable reaction and even press about this book, the same guys were carrying it around to meetings, asking people, "Have you seen our annual report? Isn't this the most incredible thing you've ever seen?"

Did those guys need favorable press reaction to be comfortable with the 1986 book?

By then, we had definitely broken down the walls internally about what you could do with an annual report. And I think everybody had sort of redefined, in their own heads, the kind of image that we wanted to present about ourselves as a company. I would say 1986 was, frankly, not as much fun as 1985 because we had already taken the risks and had succeeded. We had won quite a few awards and all that. Even though we were even more optimistic about Warner's future prospects, it was sort of like, "What do we do for an encore?" And I think the book reflects that a little bit. It was kind of a holding action. After the 1985 book, I told everyone that we should all move on to something else. And after 1986, I did.

But in 1986, didn't you start a few trends, too? Vellum pages with photograms?

We were hard on ourselves because there had been that exhilarating feeling the year before. But we did take some steps that moved in another direction; we were still trying to create imagery that had not been seen in an annual report before; we were still trying to look aggressive. That was—and continues to be—the posture of the company. There had been some occasional use of photograms in the past, but we decided to devote the whole book to them. One of the ways that we had streamlined the books in terms of cost was to use one consistent image—instead of commissioning all kinds of photography, writing special essays, and creating additional elements.

Let's talk about the 1987 report. It makes a statement about tape; this company's put together with masking tape.

(Laughs.) We tried not to let that be the suggestion. Or that the company is nearly exploding off of the page into chaos.

It also makes me think of clients who ask designers to use existing photography from the files. That's not such a horrible prospect if a designer can find a new way to treat the images.

No, it's not. We did it because we returned to the stand-alone essay section, a twenty-five year history of the company. We wanted to give a sense of what Warner's had been, what it had become. Interestingly, things the company had done back in the sixties were being revived in new configurations—albums were becoming cassettes or compact disks; Otis Redding CDs rereleased

The 1984 annual report portrayed stars of film, music, and publishing under contract to WCI. "A very sober book," according to David Bither, "that showed a stable company that was not going to blow away." Photography: Neal Slavin.

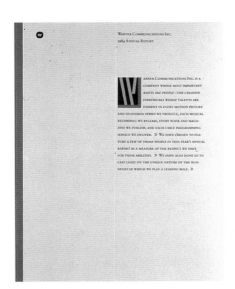

in 1987 had been recorded in 1966 when the company that had become WCI was only five years old. This sort of continuity or lifeline ran through the company history. You can't go back and take photographs of 1966; you've got to use existing imagery. But how could we update that imagery and keep it in the new tradition of what we had done in the last couple of years? The answer was to treat the photographs in an unusual way.

There are a lot of people's favorite pictures in here, icons.

Yes, and some that had become clichés; you've seen them so many times. But we made them new by giving them a new context, splattering paint on them and taping them to the wall. And that was the implicit message: You can reinvent icons by giving them a new context.

Did anyone complain that this book is hard to read?

I did. One of the sections I wrote is almost unreadable, and I think in retrospect that is a failure of the special section. It is tilting toward being pure image as opposed to telling a story in text and in pictures.

Is it reasonable to think that other designers working with other companies—other kinds of companies—might be able to achieve equally startling and successful results?

I have to think that it is. Pentagram is a very good design company; the fact that we have worked together for ten years tells you what we think of them. But there are other very good design companies in the world. Certainly, my ambition was to try to push this as far off the

edge as possible, but there are probably other clients who have similar points of view.

How about a nonentertainment company for whom a designer is dying to tear paper and splash paint, or to create a totally new kind of imagery? And the client looks at the comps and says, "You've got to be kidding." Or how about a company for whom this kind of solution is totally inappropriate; the designer is just doing it to imitate Warners? What would you say in those situations?

First, to the client I would say, never underestimate your audience. People tend to do that on all fronts, not just in making annual reports but in creating products, in running companies. One of the fears that we had when we started on that 1985 book was that our shareholders were going to be offended. In fact, by and large, we didn't hear anything from them. And those people we did hear from were very positive; they thought it was fresh and unusual. We took something that had become pretty stale in some people's minds and gave it a whole new image. Ours jumped off the pile of reports that sat on an analyst's or an investor's desk. So give your readership or your clients or your shareholders or your public, the benefit of the doubt. They have minds of their own, and you don't have to play it so safe.

To the designer: You, too, can't be afraid to present your strengths as they are. Assuming they are *your* strengths and you are not imitating. As soon as you start tailoring your proposal, your ideas, to fit—I have also found this in the music business and it seems to be a consistent pattern—as soon as you start thinking about what your audience wants to see or hear, you start compromising. I would rather risk losing the job. I know it's real easy for me to say this because I don't have my own design firm with overhead to meet, and I don't need to get an annual report job to establish my firm. But, any-

In 1985, Steven Ross's letter praised "tremendous efforts and a remarkable financial recovery." Following David Bither's direction to "push the medium farther than it had ever been pushed," Pentagram commissioned English artists Su Huntley and Donna Muir to produce a series of mixed-media illustrations.

way, don't be afraid to take the risk. You've got to present yourself in a way that's true to your ideals. These books were about ideals, not about making compromises. About 80 percent of the time, you'll run into serious problems and will get compromised. But I think at least 20 percent of the world is willing to take chances. I would encourage designers to keep open, keep trying.

Another message, to both clients and designers, is not to take all of this so seriously. These things can be fun, and that's part of what we were trying to do.

What would you think about a designer coming in with two comps, a daring one and a safer one?

I would think he or she was quite prepared to accept the safer one.

Is that negative or positive?

It's negative. I think any client, any good client—is certainly willing to work through give-and-take. There was a lot of give-and-take on all these books. If you try to guess what they're not going to like, then you're going to begin by compromising before you even get started. ■

"1986," says Bither, "was a holding action." The book (above) featured color and black-and-white photograms by Scott Morgan.

Pentagram turned on all its creative juices for 1987 (below) and combined the printed word with collages by John Van Hammersveld in a 16-page 25th-anniversary special section.

The Rev. George H. Martin, formerly pastor of St. Luke's Episcopal Church in Minneapolis, started a new congregation in the suburb of Eagan in 1986. Rev. Martin is a graduate of Hobart College and Bexley Hall Seminary, and has done graduate work at the University of Nebraska and at Virginia Theological Seminary, where he is a consultant to the national Episcopal Church in the area of communications and new church development. As executive director of the Episcopal Ad Project, he has given presentations on religious advertising throughout the country.

The Episcopal Ad Project is an independent, nonprofit ministry that in 1979 began to offer print advertising for other churches to use. The initial market for the ads focused on Episcopal churches, and interest from many other churches led the project to release its ads for use in all denominations. No national church body is responsible for the Ad Project; the executive director of the project reports to an independent board of directors. The Ad Project also produces posters, Christmas cards, and calendars. Lay people and clergy have been involved in suggesting many of the ideas, which have evolved into award-winning ads and posters.

19

Great Work: to Influence People or to Win Awards?

Fallon McElligott is a Minneapolis advertising agency founded in 1981 by account manager Pat Fallon, copywriter Tom McElligott, and art director Nancy Rice. Now part of the Ogilvy Group, the agency quickly gained a reputation as a daring and imaginative shop. Not long after it opened, *Advertising Age* magazine named it "Agency of the Year," and it has garnered numerous awards and national accounts including the Federal Express Corporation, Timex Group Ltd., and Porsche U.S.A. The ads on these pages were originally designed by Nancy Rice, now of Rice and Rice, Minneapolis, and by Dean Hanson.

Every Sunday, millions of Americans confuse greener lawns with greener pastures.

This Sunday, come join the Episcopal Church in the love, fellowship and worship of Jesus Christ. You may be surprised to find the grass is actually greener on our side of the fence.

The Episcopal Church

Will you come back to church if we promise not to throw the book at you?

In the Episcopal church we believe in a loving and forgiving God. Come and join us this Sunday when we open up the Good Book in worship.

The Episcopal Church

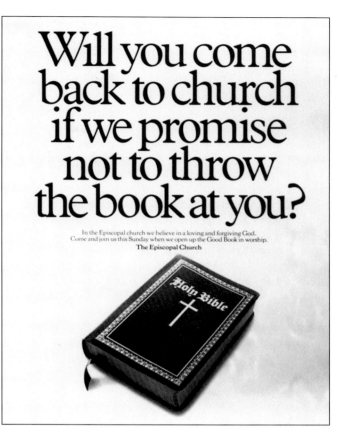

2000 years later, Christianity's biggest competition is still the Lions.

Before you sit down for an afternoon with the Lions, Bears, Dolphins, Rams, Cowboys or Vikings, come spend an hour with some very nice Christians in the love, worship and fellowship of Jesus Christ.

The Episcopal Church

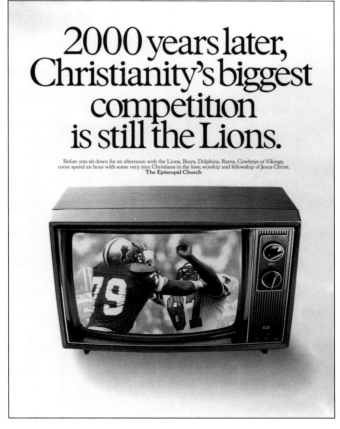

In a religion that was born in a barn, an open door goes without saying.

The Episcopal Church invites you to join us this Sunday in the worship and fellowship of Jesus Christ. The door is always open.

The Episcopal Church

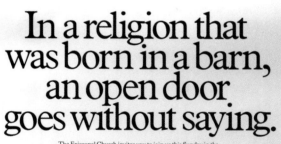

The Rev. George H. Martin

Q *What inspired you to first think about advertising?*
A I wanted to reach the unchurched people in the immediate neighborhood of the church I served. The original purpose of the campaign was to change people's Sunday morning habits. We had a community newspaper, and I figured some good advertising might set us apart and bring badly needed attention to our church.

Here's one ad that shows Moses and the Ten Commandments. The headline reads, "For fast, fast, fast relief, take two tablets." Some people would say you are selling religion like Alka-Seltzer. Do you think that's a necessity in a culture brought up on TV commercials?

When I read the prophets, the sermons of Paul, and the parables of Jesus, what I find is language that was contemporary at the time. I don't think we're doing anything new under the sun. I mean, you don't have to use religious language to communicate about God. You use ordinary language and ordinary examples. Jeremiah once took a pot and smashed it and said, "This is going to happen to us if we don't change our ways." That's great advertising.

Did any clergy of any other churches or people in your congregation object to the ads?

There are always people who look at things from a myopic point of view. They're too concerned with appearances. For me, if we disturb some of the purist types within the institution, it's almost like a litmus test that says we must be doing something right. Getting people upset is not our primary mission, but I've learned not to be disturbed by it.

When you began your relationship with Fallon McElligott, who approached whom?

I went to Tom McElligott, we had lunch together, and I presented the case, as it were. At the time, my urban congregation wasn't in a terrible section of town, but it certainly wasn't in a growing area. We needed to attract new people. I presented an advertising problem, and he was intrigued by the idea. Our first ads were done on the side.

◄ The first ads produced by Fallon McElligott for the Episcopal Ad Campaign have achieved remarkable success in getting people who had "left the fold" to change their Sunday morning habits and come back to church.

On the side of what?

On the side of his regular work. At the time, he was employed at Bozell and Jacobs. He and Pat Fallon had a side business called "Lunchtime Limited" or something like that. They had a few clients they took on the side, and we became one of them. An initial set of six ads was developed, and we've kept within that same basic format. There has been evolution and change and, I think, greater sophistication throughout the history of the project.

When you saw the presentation of those first six ads, what was your initial reaction?

I really enjoyed them because they had a sense of humor and a fresh, snappy quality. They addressed the key issue we identified, which was how to get people who are not in the habit of going to church to at least give it a try. As time went by, we also confronted some of the more troubling aspects of our secular culture and its values. We also turned our attention to certain people within the religious world who were giving religion a bad name.

Have you ever rejected any headlines or artwork as too far out?

Yes. There was one that showed a picture of the devil. It was an attempt to say something about free speech, which wasn't an issue we needed to deal with at the time. Another one had a picture of Jim Jones back in the days when we were questioning cults, and I remember the headline saying something like, "Before you accept Christ into your life, make sure it's really Christ." It was just too blatant.

Can you usually tell what's right or not from a gut reaction?

Yes. Here's an example, we had a monumental struggle with the agency folks over an ad headlined, "Where Women Stand in the Episcopal Church." It took them two years to understand what I was saying; why we needed an ad that addressed the fact that women participate fully in the ministry and life of our church. In many churches, especially the Roman Catholic, women are excluded. We needed to make our position clear and positive to people with feminist concerns.

The struggle with the agency was over the visual. They wanted a pulpit and I wanted an altar, and we went 'round and 'round. They kept saying, "It's got to be a pulpit." I kept saying, "You don't know who we are if you say that." I wouldn't give on it, and we finally shot it as an altar. It was an award-winning ad that has really worked well. They were real stubborn, but I wouldn't go along with them because we're not a pulpit-centered church; we're a sacramental church.

Can you explain the distinction?

In a pulpit-centered church, which tends to be true of many Protestant churches, the most important thing that happens is the sermon. In our church, the most important thing that happens is the Eucharist, or the communion. In the Catholic tradition (whether Episcopal or Roman), you have to be an ordained priest to celebrate.

Did you want to show a woman offering a wafer or wine at the altar?

The neat thing about that ad, and what makes it work so well, is it doesn't show anybody. It just shows an altar—a very clearly identifiable Christian altar. In the parlance of the trade, it's a "quick read."

You say it was an award-winning ad. I'm going to read you a quote from a recent New York Times *article headlined, "Ad Agencies' Obsession with Winning Awards":*

"Many executives also detect a frenzied effort among agencies, particularly new ones, to do work strictly for its award potential. The strategy, they say, was perfected by Fallon McElligott in Minneapolis. . . .

"Part of Fallon's strategy, executives of other agencies said, was to seek out small clients and pro bono accounts (among them a Minneapolis barber shop and, more recently, the Episcopal Church) for which the agency could do highly creative, even daring, work without risking the client's rejection. The strategy paid off in a spate of Gold Pencils at the One Show. It also helped the agency win Advertising Age's *agency-of-the-year award in 1983."*

For fast, fast, fast relief take two tablets.

In the Episcopal Church, we believe that some of the oldest ideas are still the best.
Like the regular worship of God. Come join us as we celebrate this Sunday.
The Episcopal Church

"You can use contemporary language to communicate about God," says The Rev. Martin.

There are a lot of questions that come to mind. First of all, I want to address the phrase, "highly creative and daring work without risk of the client's rejection." The assumption is because they did the work for free, you had to accept it. Were you in that position?

No. It's true that Fallon and McElligott don't want to work through layers of committees. They want to know who has the responsibility for approval, and if it involves a huge process that takes months and various meetings, they avoid that client. In terms of our relationship, I'm the only one who says "yea" or "nay" to things. But I do, occasionally, reject things.

According to that article, there is the feeling in some agency circles that the work they did for you was used to attract national accounts—that you were used, so to speak.

We have one of the most distinctive campaigns in the history of advertising! I like Fallon McElligott's commitment to awards. That's how we know that they think, "We're not just in it for the bucks; we're in it for our quality." There's a freedom, too, for the people who work on our campaign. They can get real tired of writing copy for cereal. An account like this comes along, and it turns on their creative juices. And it has not all been easy. Once you move beyond creating ads to doing a successful campaign, there has to be a momentum to keep it going. We struggle to keep freshness in it because the history of advertising is the history of campaigns losing their edge.

Then you don't see awards as creative people patting each other on the back? To you they really are a mark of excellence, acknowledged excellence.

Absolutely. What's interesting is that when Fallon McElligott goes to pitch a client like *The Wall Street Journal* or Armour Foods, they take our religious stuff along. You might think they would say, "We better not show that God work."

Here's another quote from the Times *article, "Awards create imitation." They show a couple of award-winning campaigns and how they were knocked off by other agencies, other products. Did other churches or nonprofit organizations copy your advertising concept?*

Not directly. There are a few other examples of sparkling religious advertising. But that's it, a very few.

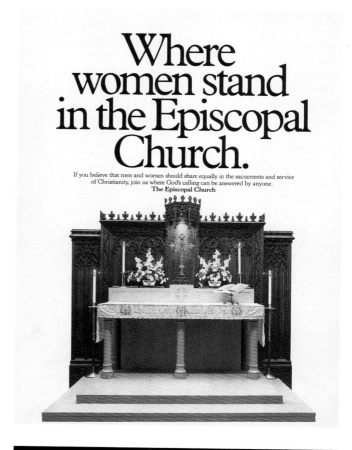

I'm surprised that we have had the field to ourselves for so long. But we have a willingness to express a sense of humor. Some people say, "You shouldn't laugh at religion." There's a risk factor that we assume most institutions are not willing to take on, which is why so much advertising with institutional connections is bland and boring and dull.

Did you meet your initial objectives?

The ultimate tragedy is that we have these wonderful materials, and yet, in terms of individual churches, there still is the issue of how do we begin to make use of them?

Do you mean that they can't afford the ad space?

Yes. We're dealing with small organizations, individual churches, that for the most part have limited discretionary budgets. It's too bad because my experience is that when we do run an ad, the results are astounding. When our diocese could pay for it, we had the ads blown up into billboards at our local airport. I have seen the arresting quality of this work. It literally stops people in their tracks in the middle of a busy airport. Their heads jerk back and they say, "What did I see?" And they stop and they read it.

It says in your brochure that the Episcopal Ad Project was founded in 1979 at St. Luke's Episcopal Church. There's kind of a success story there, too.

We started by running the ads in a community newspaper. Then, we saw the average age of the congregation gradually drop lower and lower; the hair in the congregation turned from gray to varying colors as they exist in God's world. We saw the Sunday school grow.

"Where women stand in the Episcopal Church" (above left) came about after a lengthy dispute over the visual between the client and the agency.

One of several posters (left) displayed in airports and other public places that "literally stop people in their tracks."

People would say, "I never heard of the Episcopal Church before, but I came to check this church out because I wanted to see if you really matched up with what the ads were saying." Or, "I'd been away from church; I didn't think that anything could get me started again, but gee those ads were good."

Was your thinking that if the ads spoke the twentieth-century American vernacular, people would sense that the priest would, too? That the church would, too? And that the people who would be attracted might not necessarily be Episcopalians to start with?

Exactly. They were all kinds of Christians who had "left the fold," so to speak. We do have some people who are still part of the old, stuffy Episcopal Church, and they'd like to keep it that way.

So it wasn't just that you ran some ads. You made some fundamental changes in the church.

That's true across the board. The Episcopal Church has been changing. It isn't just the church of the establishment anymore.

The irony of this is that we have no control over accuracy. The Episcopal Ad Project distributes these ads, and we have no way of saying, "You can only use these ads if the reality of your particular church matches what the ads say." But I think there tends to be a fair correspondence between a church that has vision enough to use our ads and what goes on inside. I know that there are some real medieval places, but they're probably not going to use our material.

Let's say you were addressing people with administrative responsibilities for other churches or service organizations that weren't attracting enough people. What advice would you give about advertising and promotion?

I'd say, you've got to be willing to be provocative and approach things with a sense of humor, or you're not going to get people to pay attention. We really err when we take ourselves so doggone seriously all the time. But the willingness to provoke and to ask the tough questions has got to be there. And you always have to keep up the struggle to keep the campaign fresh. ∎

Rick Berg has spent over fifteen years marketing a wide variety of consumer packaged goods, as both a client-side marketer and an advertising executive. He has held key marketing positions with Van de Kamp's Frozen Foods, TreeSweet Products, and Halley's Fine Foods. As a vice president at BBDO Los Angeles, he worked on Sizzler Restaurants, Hughes Supermarkets, Bumble Bee Seafoods, Gillette's Oral-B Laboratories, and numerous new products. He recognizes that not all marketers can win the "share battle" by outspending their competitors. Rather, he believes in identifying and personifying what makes each product special.

TreeSweet Products Company has marketed a variety of frozen and ready-to-drink juices for over fifty years. TreeSweet orange juice, grapefruit juice, and juice blends are sold across the United States. These products include frozen concentrate, ready-to-drink bottled and canned juices, and refrigerated cartons; most are available in supermarkets and through food-service operators. In 1985, the Santa Ana, California, company was taken private by a Houston-based investment group.

20

Can Design Excellence Pay Off at the Checkout Line?

Primo Angeli, a student of Buckminster Fuller, received a B.F.A. and an M.S. in communication from the University of Southern Illinois. He moved to San Francisco in 1959 and established Primo Angeli, Inc. in 1967. In providing corporate identity, packaging, and environmental design to an international clientele, Mr. Angeli has received more than four hundred awards, including gold and silver medals from the Art Directors Club of New York, and awards of excellence from the Package Design Council and the San Francisco Society of Communicating Arts. A number of Angeli designs are in permanent collections worldwide. Mr. Angeli's client list includes General Mills, Carnation, Shasta Beverages, and Christian Brothers Winery, as well as leading corporations, financial institutions, airlines, hotels, and retailers. A creative director, poster designer, and fine artist, Mr. Angeli is the author of *Twelve Stories*.

Q *Strolling down a typical supermarket aisle, one would think that bad design is what attracts consumers. TreeSweet is one company that saw things differently. Why was that?*
A In the orange juice business, there was a big gap between the slick and commercial look of Citrus Hill and Minute Maid, and Tropicana's less serious—almost kid-ified—package. We wanted to fill that gap.

Wasn't the old TreeSweet pretty corny, too, with little smiling oranges?

Without a doubt. That package was definitely stuck in the fifties. And we had a shelf staple juice product in a blue-and-green modified version that I thought was even worse. By some quirk of fate, it won a packaging award years earlier, and the former president of the company kind of latched on to it as a reason for not having to spend money on another redesign. His real mission was to keep the company alive so it could be sold off. When the company was finally sold, we wanted to make a statement about new leadership and being more market-oriented and progressive, so the opportunity for redesign surfaced in a serious way.

The packages that are selected for design annuals are often for specialty gourmet foods and other products that seem to be targeted to an upscale, sophisticated buyer. But when it comes to mass-market items there are very few packages that designers would consider well designed. Is there a feeling that the American public, the average supermarket shopper, is not attracted to good design?

One of the concerns is what kind of pricing statement your package makes. The boutiquey designs, the specialty products, have a lot of personality but also promise high price. For the average grocery product, price sensitivity is an issue. When you're playing in nationally branded product categories, generally, all brands are the same price, so one of the things you don't want a package to say is, "This product is going to cost more."

So even if it happened to cost less to design or produce a particular package, if somehow it made the product itself look more expensive, a manufacturer wouldn't go that route?

They would certainly be sensitive to that. There's a lot of testing that can be done to figure that out. I worked on a bottled salad dressing priced comparatively with Kraft and Wishbone, but it had an image of costing five to ten cents more. It didn't. And we didn't have a great package design. It was just that the image seemed to project that it came from a dressing specialist, not from a national conglomerate. So people figured that it had to cost more because it was probably made in smaller batches and so forth. That's how these things get strung together in the consumer's mind.

Then why wouldn't the consumer—looking at TreeSweet, which is beautifully designed with elegant hand lettering, handsome colors, and illustration—why wouldn't the consumer think, "This is more expensive juice"? Or is juice different somehow?

Frozen orange juice is very much a commodity category. Over 55 percent of the frozen orange juice sold in this country is private label store brands. This reflects a widespread perception of parity: "So why not buy the

◄ **Logo for TreeSweet is hand-lettered by Ray Honda of Primo Angeli, Inc.**

Primo Angeli (left) evaluates TreeSweet's existing packaging with Mike Dinuzzo and Michael Prone of Primo Angeli, Inc.

At a client meeting, John Crane, Michael Prone, and Doug Haddenberg review preliminary design concepts.

least expensive?" The same attitude exists among branded users. The TreeSweet design was a solid attempt to break that perception of parity.

Orange juice concentrate is traded on the commodity and futures markets. Does it all come out of the same vat, so to speak?

You could say that. The same sources sell products to most of the different manufacturers.

People swear they can taste the difference. Even though it is a parity product, did you want TreeSweet to project a more upscale image?

Upscale? No. Unique, maybe better? Yes. We wanted to provide an image that said we were the "vintage juice brand," the brand that had been around a long time. The name itself has a lot of good qualities, but it hadn't been heavily advertised for many years. The emphasis on trying to create a richer image was to make it distinctive versus the competition. By going back to this vintage juice brand, it called up some of the history and "good old feelings" of adults remembering when they were kids.

And by "vintage," were you referring to graphics reminiscent of old produce crate labels?

Yes. And the hope was that you would get some of those good attitudes, like fresh-squeezed, farm-fresh, just-picked, and all that, coming through with a warmer execution. And because the other guys weren't doing that, there was a readily apparent gap; anyone who could bring a little humanity and nostalgia into the game would look distinctive in the competitive setting. Primo Angeli is excellent at this, at helping brand personality stand out from the field by appealing to our emotions.

The result is packaging that makes you say to yourself, "That's a product for me."

Primo's promotional material states that TreeSweet presented his firm with four objectives for the project: 1. Develop a high-quality, fresh-looking brand identity; 2. Create strong shelf impact; 3. Reflect the company's fifty-two-year-old established authority in the juice market; 4. Differentiate flavors in the line.

Right. If you look at the old package versus the new, you'll see that we also gave him carte blanche. For example, we told him, "As far as we're concerned, on the frozen products, you can change the color of the lids; you can color code the pull string. Do anything to make us an alternative in this category. If we can look special and still have comparable pricing, we should get more than our fair share of sales."

How long has the new packaging been in the market?
About three years.
How would you categorize consumer acceptance?
I'd say it was terrific.
Was it launched with an advertising campaign?
The package served as a focal point in print and outdoor advertising and as a rallying point for motivating employees, sales brokers, and the trade. Because there was new ownership, there was a chance to rekindle an awful lot of enthusiasm for the products, for the company, and for the new management.

Magic marker comps of the selected design direction are scanned into the computer for further refinement.

Several logo variations are inked and hand-colored by Mark Jones.

Q *Did you want
TreeSweet to project a
more upscale image?*

A *We wanted to
create a richer image
that made the temptation
to buy a real solid
temptation.*

TreeSweet's press release reads: "On January 1, 1985, a search was launched for a firm to create a new visual identity for the fifty-two-year-old citrus juice company. After extensive interviews and many elaborate presentations, the design firm of Primo Angeli Inc. was chosen." Can you tell me how you conducted the interviews and evaluated the presentations?

(Laughs.) Well, my recollection is—unless somebody else was running around on the side looking at a bunch of firms—that three firms were considered. One was the incumbent. One happened to be a Los Angeles design firm that two other guys in the marketing group had worked with before. And the other was Primo. The new management people met with each of those groups, and Primo came out on top. So in terms of how extensive and scientific the process was . . . in reality, it was short, it was sweet, it was easy, and it worked.

What were you looking for in the presentations?

The most important thing, I think, is that a designer project the ability to understand the culture of the company, and demonstrates an understanding of the marketing conditions that the package has to survive in. We need to be able to see that a designer can grasp our objectives as quickly as possible. Not all packaging assignments are the kind of open door we gave Primo. Many, well you know what they are: "Give me a little twist to make this more modern, but I need the equity of this package to keep working, so I don't want to give anything up."

There's an old axiom in the marketing community: "Just because you change a package doesn't mean you're going to sell one more box." The people who cite that refer to some of the oldest brands in the country that have had few or very minor packaging changes over the years. People will even cite Proctor & Gamble items as examples of bad packaging that achieved number-one status in their categories. So it's kind of like, "How important is package design, really?" I don't think anybody knows. It varies from product to product. What I try to get out of packaging designers and their marketing people is whether they're in touch with what's going on in the consumer's mind. I want to find out if their perceptions of my company's image can be translated into the consumer's language, and how they foresee going about it.

Are you interested in seeing examples of "befores" and "afters"?

Yes. And it helps to take people through your thought processes, too. A designer friend of mine worked on a very unique product that offered a lot of opportunity to explain that it was new to its category. It needed to be clearly shown that this was different from a regular frozen dinner. But the package turned out like any Stouffer or Banquet or Le Menu kind of product, and, I thought, it really misled the consumer. It wasn't until about a year later, when my friend asked me to help pull together his own new business presentation that I got to see the other concepts that he had put on the table in front of the client. There were some outstanding things, but the client was not that creative, and all the good work wound up in somebody's back room.

◄ "What happens when you see it on the shelf is the real test of good packaging," says Rick Berg.

The finished, ready-to-drink product line.

My friend wanted to know if he should show the things that were rejected. I told him, "Definitely. They show me exactly what was going on in your mind at the time. And even though I don't like the end product, you've got great work here that shouldn't be kept under wraps."

Several clients have said that they only want to see real, printed samples. But you're saying that there's nothing wrong with showing slides of rejects if they demonstrate how you think, not necessarily what a client bought.

There's nothing wrong with it. It's also an opportunity to add a little show business, too.

You said, "Primo came out on top." What were the key strengths of his presentation?

First of all, he didn't make the initial presentation. It was made by his sales rep, who happened to have been in Los Angeles.

But it showed that Primo has a really terrific instinct for getting inside people's lives. In the advertising world, we believe that good advertising has to touch your life in order to register and work. In other words, even the most carefully crafted ad, with all the right reasons why a product is good for you, won't sell until you touch somebody's life. But if a designer can really make the message relevant, and bring to life the emotional aspects of what's in it for the user, you probably will make a sale.

Primo has the ability to make products look like you would want to own them. And he does it repeatedly. He can produce complex richness in such a personable way that there's a real solid temptation to buy a product.

If management thought a package really did the job, would you do a focus group; in effect subjecting the package to a group of "typical consumers?"

I wouldn't. Focus groups aren't a perfect research solution. At best, they're a disaster check for radical departures. Big companies might want to test the daylights out of packaging, but I think they're only looking for the negative aspects. They don't want to make a mistake, but they're clearly not going to hit a home run, either. In focus groups, when ten or twelve people are set up as a group of critics, they turn into sheep real easily. And when we ask them to say what they think about a certain product, they know they're there in the role of expert, and they start looking for things that are wrong. They become the designers and tell you how they would do it if it were their package. Unless the focus group picks a clear-cut winner or loser, what you get is some pretty convoluted and nebulous feedback.

So would your advice be, "Know what you're doing and then trust your instincts?"

Usually. But, I think, the real test of good packaging is what happens when you see it on the shelf. Designers are paid to produce things that are aesthetically pleasing and communicate some key brand facts. The acid test is to put the package in the section where it has to operate. We create an artificial section in the office and stock the shelves. You can see right away if a package grabs your attention and easily communicates what is important. If it does, you may have that home run. ■

"Lite" shelf staple juice drinks, refrigerated juice drinks, and frozen concentrates.

According to Rick Berg, "By carefully combining traditional nostalgia with contemporary graphics, Primo Angeli, Inc., brought strong shelf impact and taste appeal into the competitive setting."

Murray Pearlstein is president of Louis, Boston. Mr. Pearlstein attended Middlebury College and received his B.A. from Harvard. He has worked in the family business since 1960 and became president in 1972.

Louis, Boston. is a retailer of fine men's and women's clothing and accessories. Its three stores are located in Back Bay and Chestnut Hill, Boston, and Fifty-seventh Street, New York City. The New York store opened in August 1988. Louis was founded in 1924 by Sol and Nathan Pearlstein, Murray Pearlstein's father and uncle. The company, which remains privately held, was named after his grandfather. With 170 employees, Louis is currently expanding into its newest location, the former Museum of Natural History in Boston. A totally vertical organization, Louis buys its own wools, silks, and cottons from mills worldwide, and has suits, jackets, trousers, overcoats, shirts, and neckwear tailored to specification. Louis also sells sportswear, knitwear, leather, and accessories by several internationally respected artisans and designers.

21

Fashioning an Image for Long-Term Performance

Tyler Smith is an art director and graphic designer who lives and works in Providence, Rhode Island. He has won numerous national and international awards, including a gold and silver medal from the New York Art Directors Club. Feature articles on his work have appeared in *Communication Arts*, *Art Direction*, *Photo/Design*, and *Print* magazines. He has lectured at the Smithsonian Institution and has judged design and photography shows across the United States. Several of his posters are represented in the permanent collection of the Cooper-Hewitt Museum, New York. In 1984, he designed the "Health Research" postage stamp for the U.S. Postal Service and was also named Rhode Island School of Design's Alumnus of the Year. In addition to Louis, Boston., Mr. Smith's clients include E F Hutton, Estée Lauder, Southwick Clothing, Ann Taylor, Evan-Picone, and Reebok.

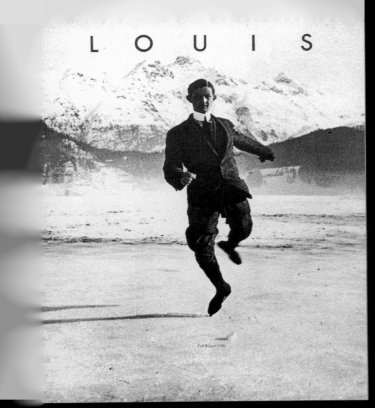

LOUIS

Fall Winter 1986

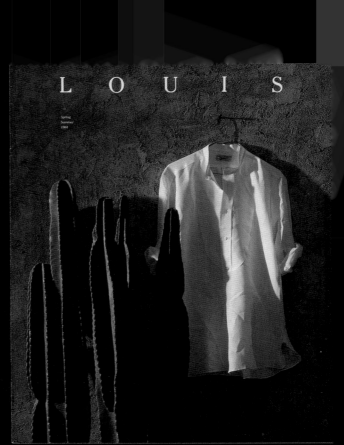

LOUIS

Spring
Summer
1984

LOUIS

LOUIS

Fall Winter 1987

Murray Pearlstein

Each of the Louis brochures reflect a certain attitude toward quality and taste. Spring/Summer 1985 takes the reader through a wordless tale of the friendship of a particular *menage à trois*. Photography: Clint Clemens.

How high-society people played at St. Moritz was the theme for Fall/Winter 1986. Photography: John Goodman; copy: Craig Walker.

Fall/Winter 1987 offered a glimpse of the style of the people of the Langhe region of the Italian Piedmont. Photography: Aldo Fallai; copy: Lee North.

◄ Five of the ten brochures Tyler Smith has designed and art directed to educate Louis, Boston.'s customers about "a more European way of dressing."

Louis, Boston.

Q *I've heard that your customers will fly to Boston just to buy clothes at your store.*
A Some of them do. But others may be visiting Boston for other reasons. Some of them may make a stopover here between the West Coast and Europe. Some of them are driving up to Vermont. Many New Yorkers like to come up to Boston for the weekend. But all of them are loyal and will visit the store. It is part of their itinerary. The kind of clothing we have makes it worth a trip from almost anywhere.

That's why we advertise in national magazines. We've been able to achieve this kind of loyalty largely through our advertising. Or I should say, through our media, because it includes a special kind of direct mail brochure.

We don't publish catalogs. We never mention price. And our advertising never begs people to come in the store, to buy anything. We take a much softer, more low-key approach. Instead, our advertising presents what we have to offer, which is a level of taste, a style, a mood, a European approach to clothing.

We comb Europe for all the most unusual, striking things; the special things our customers will respond to. We don't sell big name designers—the Calvin Kleins, the Ralph Laurens. As much as I admire their talents, they are mostly merchandising organizations now, and people can get the clothing in many other places.

Our customers, both men and women, want a much more European way of dressing, of choosing clothes. We help them. That's where our people come in. They are the second thing that makes a visit to our store worth a trip to Boston. They are knowledgeable. Many of them have been with us for years. They know our customers' wardrobes and what pieces might be missing or what additions might be most appreciated. Unlike some retailers, we don't change our styles drastically from season to season. You can build your wardrobe here.

As I understand it, you are the president of a fifty-year-old family-owned business.

Closer to sixty. My father started the company. We are opening our first store in New York right now. After sixty years. There are businesses that expanded much too quickly, opened forty stores, and went bankrupt. We have a different way of doing things.

Which reminds me of something other entrepreneurs, heads of private companies, have stated: that you can make much more effective business decisions when you stay family-owned.

I agree. We don't have to make decisions based on what we think other people will say, or how we think they might react. We are not hired hands of large corporations, where managers have to worry about jobs that depend on next quarter's bottom line. Our jobs depend on how we perform over the long run. And sometimes what's good over the long run can be very negative over the immediate short term. I often talk with people in corporations who are frustrated because they can't follow their instincts, their taste. We couldn't work that way. When you have to report to stockholders, to committees, your decision-making can't be subjective. It has to be objective. That can lead to mediocrity.

Sometimes we look at ads from other retailers and see too many pictures, too much copy, credit card logos, store hours. That is not the way you sell to our market.

When you look at our ads, you see an image. You are not asked to buy anything. Admittedly, we are not dealing with a huge segment of the population. Our customers are an elite group—wealthy, mobile. I'm not saying we are snobs. I would like everyone to come into our stores. But this is the way we have positioned our business.

The success of your business to design seems to relate to two kinds of design: the design of the clothing and the design of the ads and the collateral.

We want the ads to capture the clothing. I believe in beautiful photography, but I don't want the photographer's style to obscure the detailing, the lines of the clothing. In so many ads today, there's a mood, there's action—but you can't see the clothes. I want people to be able to visualize the cuts, the fabrics, the textures. We never airbrush, take wrinkles out of suits or anything like that. The essence of our ads is restraint, taste, and creativity.

Tyler Smith has had a lot to do with this. Although we know pretty much what we want, the tone and the look, he has educated us over the years. It has been a ten-year relationship. And it has given us something we had never been able to achieve with an ad agency. We worked with several of them. As soon as an agency got too large, or was acquired, forget it. We were lost in the shuffle. And we were never comfortable with a system in which we couldn't deal directly with the creative people, the art director and the copywriter. Account executives try hard and mean well, but that's not who we want to work with. We were with one or two larger agencies, but they were always changing people on us—a new art director, a new copywriter. There was no continuity. And sometimes those people were not on the right track at all; they seemed to be following their own agenda, not ours. We ended up educating them. They were supposed to be there to serve me. It wasted a lot of time.

How did you meet Tyler and begin to work with him?

One of my employees was talking to a group of market research people and happened to mention that we were not happy with our agency. They said, "We know a great free-lance art director, Tyler Smith. Why don't you give him a call?" I did.

Did it matter to you whether he had done similar work for other clothing stores or apparel companies?

I didn't look at his work.

You hired a designer, sight unseen?

I talked to him on the phone. I liked what he said. He said all the right things. That's what I mean about decision-making. We have a personal kind of relationship by now. I think we understand each other very well. He is not a full-service agency; he hires free-lance copywriters, but I have no problem with that. He is unconventional. So am I.

For example, we have an unconventional approach to advertising. Although sometimes we have to, we prefer not to advertise in fashion magazines or other publications that run a lot of clothing advertising. We advertise in *Vanity Fair*, *Esquire*, and *The New York Times Magazine*. We also advertise in *Gourmet*. That strategy has worked very well for us. Sometimes too well.

One of our ads in *Gourmet* showed an Italian silk dress. The dress sold for $700, and we had seventy of them to sell. We got a thousand phone calls and letters from people who wanted that dress. It sold out instantly. The rest of the people were furious. They accused us of false advertising and everything else under the sun.

Why would you choose to run a full-page ad in a national magazine if the profit from the sales could barely cover the cost of the ad?

We want the ad to intrigue people, to bring them into the store, not to sell that dress. Louis is not in the mail-order business. What if we had bought a thousand dresses and only seventy people wanted them? Or what if no one wanted one?

You are describing the use of advertising and design to achieve a long-range goal, not an immediate return.

Correct. To continue to build our image and long-term customer relationships.

Right now, we are beginning to advertise the new store we will be opening in two weeks in New York, which will be on Fifty-seventh Street and Lexington Avenue. It will have a kind of thirties or forties look and ambiance. We used several pages in our fall brochure to show architecture; the art deco architecture of the building and of nearby buildings on Fifty-seventh Street. There is a mood, a time, and a place. In all our design and advertising, restraint is the byword. We will never do anything aggressive.

Can you relate how the elements of graphic design—paper, type, color, image—can create the right mood for you?

That's Tyler's area. I leave it to him. He's done a wonderful job. You should see our new magazine. It is elegant. .

The March 1987 issue of *Gourmet* carried a Louis, Boston. ad for a 1930s style silk dress by Luciano Barbera. The ad drew hundreds of requests. In September 1988, Louis achieved similar results with a *New York Times Magazine* ad (right) for a Scottish wool sweater and a challis skirt by Mariano Rubinacci.

Louis, Boston.

(Three Weeks Later)

I visited your new store on Fifty-seventh Street; I'm intrigued by your ad campaign, especially "The Eastern Shuttle Will Never Forgive Me" ad. How is it all working out?

We've had an amazingly good reception in New York so far. Retail business is generally soft now, but we're way ahead of expectations. The advertising is provocative; it makes people think. It doesn't sell anything specific, just the idea of visiting Louis. There's no clothing shown, no discounted prices, no hoopla, no special promotion like "If you come in the first five days, we'll give you a free whatever." It's just an interesting and low-key way of introducing a new organization to the people of New York. And I think the right kind of people were attracted, because those I've seen come in seem to be very quality-oriented, and not the type of people who are looking for a deal.

Do you think the traffic on the shuttle flights to Boston has slowed down?

There may be fewer stops in Boston because a lot of our customers were New Yorkers. But I don't think the New York store is going to change the habits of customers from other parts of the country, who've formed attachments to certain salespeople. And the merchandise selection in our store in Boston is still better and deeper. The New York store may change the habits of New Yorkers, though.

I don't think you will see too many companies that advertise the way we do. We're not a big company, and we went in *The New York Times Magazine* with double-page spreads twice in the same month. I think it's quite a ballsy approach. To blow that kind of space on one message, to me, is a very important statement. Yet it was very, very beautifully executed. Especially the typeface Tyler used—that typeface had a certain tone to it, which reflects the quality of our products. There are a lot of subliminals in the way these ads look. They seem to say "visit us." I want the consumer to be curious enough to come to us and find out what's inside the store. It's working. Again, it's an approach that's tied into the long-term health of our company.

You have referred to your brochure a "magazine." Does that relate to your concept of introducing clothing over a series of seasons; you can present it in magazinelike editorial layouts.

The magazine is as much a teaching tool as anything else. For example, we were probably the first major store to carry pleated trousers to the exclusion of plain trousers. And I'm going back twelve, fourteen years. Some of our customers thought we were crazy when we started this trend. But I see the most conservative stores doing it now.

Right now, the very short skirt has certain messages we don't particularly feel comfortable with. We're showing long, soft skirts. We just got in an unbelievable skirt that wraps and puffs and goes in four hundred directions. It looks fabulous when you put it on. You should come in and take a look. ∎

The theme of the Fall/Winter 1988 edition of the Louis magazine (top) is "A Tale of Two Cities." Heralding the opening of Louis' New York store, it chronicled the legend of Babe Ruth: "From a Boston Red Sox hero to the greatest New York Yankee of them all." "Babe Ruth's New York," reads the copy, "embodied much of what we value most." The "Dear Lily" ad in *The New York Times Magazine* (left) and the "Eastern Shuttle" ad in *The New York Times* drew the type of quality-oriented customer Louis seeks.

Edwin Simon is president of the Pelican Group, Inc., a New York City public relations and corporate communications consulting firm he founded in 1986. Previously, he was vice president and senior communications officer of Sikorsky Aircraft, where he was responsible for public and media relations, advertising, marketing support, and employee communications. Prior to joining Sikorsky, he was with its parent company, United Technologies, where in addition to his advertising and investor relations responsibilities, he administered corporate arts and cultural programs in the United States and Europe. Mr. Simon has also been director of corporate communications at Avon Products, manager of corporate public relations at Bristol-Myers, and a vice president of Ruder & Finn, the public relations agency. He has been responsible for the writing, design supervision, and production of over twenty corporate annual reports.

United Technologies designs and manufactures high technology products and systems, and provides related services to customers around the world. Headquartered in Hartford, Connecticut, the corporation employs 190,000 people, operates three hundred plants, and maintains sales and service offices in fifty-seven countries. Sales in 1988 were over $18 billion. United Technologies' products include Pratt & Whitney aircraft engines, Carrier air-conditioning systems, Otis elevators, Sikorsky helicopters, and Hamilton Standard aerospace systems. The company's Sikorsky Aircraft division, with sales of $1.5 billion and fourteen thousand employees, is the world's leading designer and manufacturer of helicopters. A pioneer in vertical flight technology, Sikorsky's military models are flown by all branches of the U.S. military, and by thirty-five other nations.

22

How Smart Companies Judge Whether a Project Is Really Effective

Arnold Saks studied design at Syracuse University and did graduate work at the Yale University School of Art. His office, Arnold Saks Associates, has been a major graphic design resource for over twenty years. Its clients include many of the best known industrial service companies in the world, such as Alcoa, Avon, Burlington Industries, General Foods, Monsanto, RCA, and Seagram. The firm's work covers a broad range of graphics: annual reports, trademarks, recruiting and capabilities brochures. Mr. Saks is listed in *Who's Who in America* and is a member of Alliance Graphique Internationale and the Century Association. His firm's work has received hundreds of design awards and has been published extensively throughout the world.

Edwin Simon

Q *Some people have said that the role of a designer is to make the client into a hero within his or her company. Within the context of a typical large corporation, is that a correct assumption?* **A** In a word, yes. I'm living, breathing evidence of that, because I've been fortunate in dealing with a lot of very good graphic designers who've done a lot of good work for me.

The hard reality is that within most large corporations, the chairman, the president, and other people in senior management are seldom aware of who's actually doing the designing. The aura of the good work that's produced tends to surround the person within the company who seems to be responsible for it. And that's either the corporate communications director or the public relations director, depending on the structure of the company. So the good work tends to be part of one's implied portfolio. If you've been able to collaborate successfully with designers, it enhances your whole professional life and career.

I'm certainly indebted to the designers who've made me look good, and I've returned the favor by being loyal to them.

This is a process that is essential for anybody in the design business to accept wholeheartedly. Now don't think to yourself; "My work will become part of my client's 'implied portfolio' and the chief executive won't even know I did it." Forget it. It's not important. As long as you've done a great piece, you'll probably get another assignment. And that's all you really need to know. Besides, most chief executives know painfully little about design, and you shouldn't value their opinion too much anyhow. What's important is that you have a good client as your contact within the company. It is that person's opinion you should be most concerned with, because that's the person with whom you have fought the battle, and who will give you the next assignment.

◄A photograph by Eric Meola for "Experience the S-76," a 36-page, oversized, six-color brochure designed in 1983 by Arnold Saks for United Technologies' Sikorsky Aircraft division.

168

United Technologies

You've been in situations where you were able to spend top dollar for photography and printing. Can a successful product be achieved without those budgets?

Absolutely. Excellence is not necessarily a function of budget. It's a function of attitude. When budgets are low, that's the perfect time to propose something a little bit different. And I think it's *always* important for designers to look for the opportunity to suggest an approach that goes beyond the usual.

Is this a realistic attitude today? Many designers and photographers are saying, "With all the mergers, acquisitions, and divestitures, every company just wants to cut back and do things as cheaply as possible."

The thinking is very different today. There's no question.

Would you say that it's wise for companies—even when they're cutting back in certain areas—to still make a significant commitment to quality corporate communications? Take IBM as an example, which suggests that although economic trends peak and valley, consistency in image pays off over the long term.

You and I, from our vantage points, can say yes. And certainly I would say "yes" with a great deal of conviction. But the fact is, the environment has changed in a fundamental way. In most cases, management has changed and the CEOs are a different breed; they're more the "bean counter" types, much less amenable to a plea from their communications director for $200,000 for a brochure. There are companies around that are still willing to come up with budgets for first-class design and first-class photography, first-class writing, printing, and so forth—but there are fewer of them.

I'd like to return to the question, "Can a successful product be achieved without those budgets?" You used the number, $200,000. But let's just say a company could only budget a quarter to half that amount for a capabilities or product brochure. Do you think a superb piece could still be produced?

Yes. And risk-taking now comes into the picture more often, simply because if you don't have a huge budget, you don't have the luxury of applying as much money to each facet of the process. You have to leverage, and leverage can come from creativity on the part of the designer.

Ultimate achievement in helicopter design—sleek styling, engineering excellence and advanced technology in total harmony.

No matter what the budget, can what was thought to be a successful end product be considered by management to be not-so-successful once the designer's final bill arrives . . . if the bottom line is bigger than the number on the proposal?

It really depends on the company. I think smaller companies still tend to be more budget-conscious than larger ones. My personal attitude toward budget has always been this: If you produce a winner, people aren't going to care if you're a little over budget. And if you produce a loser, the fact that you came in on or under budget is not going to help a bad situation. I mean, you've got graphic evidence, thousands of printed copies that just ain't so hot. But if you produce a magnificent piece and the budget exceeds whatever, most people won't care. In my experience, anyhow, they have not cared. They've been so delighted with the result that the fact that it was $10, $15, or $20,000 over was not a big deal.

You're stating one advantage of working for certain large and powerful corporations! By what standards does such a company judge a piece to be "magnificent"?

There are several criteria. One would obviously be that the piece meets both the design objectives and the business objectives that were set out in the beginning. You'd like it, ideally, to come in on or under budget.

And you want it to please management. I touched on that before and it's tricky. Because, again, management is not involved in the process; they don't know why you made the decisions you made; and they may have formed a conception of it that may no longer be in concert with reality. The project could have evolved over time to be very different from what was expected. But if you've been consistent to the original objectives, and it *looks* magnificent, that shouldn't be too much of a problem.

And being responsible for that kind of product could, indeed, make you into a hero?

A client's job is to produce—or produce through quality people—quality work, so there is certainly going to be some reflective glory in it. That's not what we're really after, though we certainly take it when it comes along. By the same token, it works the other way around just as easily. If, for example, the particular project that we've worked on is not a success, the design firm will go on to other clients. In terms of the client, it can be a more lasting problem. And a more difficult one to overcome.

"You're appealing as much to ego as you are to the practical nature of the purchase," says Ed Simon.

*E*xtending busy days into elegant nights with luxury and convenience. The priceless comfort of complete mobility.

Have you heard of people who have lost their jobs or suffered in their careers because designers or agencies didn't come through for them?

No. That's not to say it hasn't happened. But it's more likely to happen on the advertising side because the stakes are so much higher than the corporate communications or the graphics side.

Tell me about the Sikorsky brochure. How did the designer's proposal to do something a little bit different come about?

We started by looking at the market and determining that corporate aircraft were usually sold in a technical way, pilots selling to pilots. We reasoned that with a helicopter—certainly a premiere corporate helicopter—you're appealing as much to ego as you are to the practical nature of the purchase in terms of fuel economy, range, quiet, and other technical considerations. Taking that theory as a point of departure, we realized that we had to market it like a luxury car or yacht. We had to position it in such a way that a layman—the target being chief executives and very, very wealthy self-made people—could look at the brochure and project themselves right into that helicopter. Could look at it and say, "This is up to my standards. I want to see myself in this aircraft." At the same time, we clearly delineated the technical aspects—that it's safe; that it has the most advanced electronics and dual engines and is operated by two pilots; and that it has all the things that are reassuring from the standpoint of safety and operational quality. We began to create an image that said, "This is the very best; this is, in effect, the Rolls Royce of helicopters."

Did you develop this approach before you met with the designer?

Yes. We used feedback from the field, from the salespeople, many of whom were pursuing entrepreneurial types and oilmen and bankers and landowners in Texas. The sales force told us they needed a prestige piece that would appeal to that kind of person. It was very much an ego sale.

Then we all sat down with Arnold Saks and said, "Okay, let's talk about how we can execute this." He came up with a concept we liked very much, which included picking a photographer with an advertising and graphic sense who would depict the helicopter in a way that would go beyond simply allowing the viewer to lovingly admire the helicopter's lines.

At the time, how much did the helicopter cost?

That's a useful statistic because it tends to get people to take notice. You're talking major purchase, about $4 million.

And your budget for the brochure was approximately?

About $200,000.

So it's miniscule compared to one sale.

Oh, absolutely.

Designers sometimes have a problem that perhaps advertising agencies with research departments don't, which is knowing what percentage of a client's overall marketing budget for a product or service should be spent on a sales brochure. Is there a rule of thumb, such as, "When you're planning to sell or make X, then you have to spend Y?"

That's very hard to do, because on a relative basis, the cost of a brochure does tend to be miniscule. It is more customary to come up with measures for advertising. I don't think there's a benchmark. You have to intuitively look at your product and say, "Okay, what is required?" and then budget what's called for in terms of executing it, for example, extraordinary photography.

In this case you chose Eric Meola.

Right. Eric has excellent credentials. He is known for his graphic and powerful advertising images. He approached the assignment not just saying, "I'm going to photograph some nice-looking helicopters," but he was really sensitive to the total environment in which the helicopters should be pictured. He also had the right feel for the elegance and leadership that are the basic themes of the brochure.

You used the word "credentials" when you described Eric, and I think that's something that's been key to Arnold Saks's success, also. Hand-in-hand with a particular quality level comes a certain corporate comfort level. But how can new people break in?

It's very difficult. It takes courage. It takes persistence on the designer's part, and it takes courage on the part of their counterpart within the company, usually the corporate communications director. Friends of mine who are good designers have asked me, "I know you're working with designer X, but why can't we get that work?" And I'll respond very simply, "Because you don't have the kind of name that would provide the right comfort level, the feeling that the company is using someone appropriate to its size and importance." Admittedly, it is not easy for a designer to make that kind of name for him or herself; there's no simple solution. The most likely way to begin is to leave the big fish alone and go after some of the smaller fish in terms of smaller projects. A designer should try to develop a track record with a client, and reach the point where there's a trust and a sense of his or her capabilities. Then it's easier to build up to the big projects.

Edwin Simon

How do you feel about design awards?

Design awards mean nothing to me. I may be insulting a lot of people, but I look at design societies as mutual support associations. They tend to be very political; you have people who seem to take the attitude, "It's my turn this year, your turn next year."

And there's another problem. I don't believe that what is regarded as excellence is always excellence in terms of solving the client's problem. There is a very, very sharp difference, which you have to be alert to. A designer can do something that he or she will think is wonderful, and it can be a total bomb from the client's point of view. For a lot of reasons. It may just be overdesigned. It may not meet the expectations of the chairman of the board or of senior managers who are not close to the process, people who don't know why all the decisions were made that lead to the final product.

For example, I went to the Mead Annual Report Show this year and was very disappointed because I thought the books that I saw there were entirely too tricky, too clever, too gimmicky, and too subtle. I only saw two or three pieces that, from my experience, would have successfully solved the client's problem. Now I understand why designers liked those pieces and why they won awards. But remember that that can be very, very different from successfully serving the client. That's why I really never have paid much attention to awards. I trust my judgment enough to evaluate the work of the people who are coming to see me, and to decide accordingly.

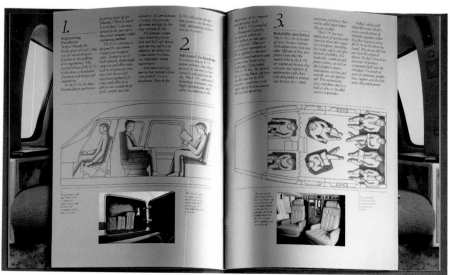

Eric Meola, known for his color-saturated advertising images, traveled to Arizona, California, Connecticut, Nevada, New York, Oklahoma, Texas, and England on this assignment.

The brochure's 8-page, short-cut center section presents—in illustration and photography—the helicopter's amenities, such as cabin size, baggage compartment, warranty, and training.

But can't design awards be cited as credentials to the CEOs and other decision-makers who need the reassurance you've been talking about?

No. They don't know what the standards are for these awards, and aren't going to take the time to find out. They're simply not interested. I really believe it's irrelevant in large corporations, where people are much more interested in knowing the names of clients for whom the designer has worked for in similar, related businesses. That's meaningful.

You have been saying that awards aren't important, performance is. I'd like to hear your thoughts on the phrase, "Good design is good business." In your experience, how has design effected the overall success and performance of companies like United Technologies?

From my own experience, good design and careful attention to how a corporation presents itself to all its key audiences is definitely good business. Thomas Watson of IBM was right. In the midseventies, few people had heard of, much less knew anything about, United Technologies. Then, the chairman, Harry Gray, decided to use corporate advertising and other graphic media, such as arts sponsorships, to build awareness of the company and to convey an image of quality and imagination. It worked.

For example, the communications department created a series of full-page ads that featured all-type statements on subjects of human—not business—concern. They ran in *The Wall Street Journal* once a month for six years and generated hundreds of thousands of requests for reprints. Some, like the "Let's Get Rid of the Girl" ad, became famous—because we had the guts to argue that women should be referred to respectfully.

The company also initiated the classic, now much imitated, ad campaign with spectacular Jay Maisel photos that abstractly illustrated the application of various United Technologies products. The ads appeared in *The New Yorker* and in the Sunday *New York Times Magazine*, environments where corporate advertising isn't usually found. Yet those magazines are read by business and government leaders; the audiences we wanted to reach most. They gave United Technologies excellent exposure.

As long as there are case histories like those of United Technologies, IBM, Mobil, and a host of other companies that have successfully and imaginatively employed good design, I am optimistic about the future of the design and communications business.

And what about smaller companies like those you're serving now at the Pelican Group?

The values that have worked for larger companies will work for the smaller ones as well. Their budgets may not be as big, and their needs are more limited, but I'm convinced that there's a growing number of emerging companies that either know instinctively or can be taught the value of good design as a competitive tool in the marketplace. A good example is Steven Jobs of Apple Computer fame, who hired Paul Rand to do the logo for his new company, Next. In my view, these companies, as much as the larger, more established corporations, represent the future potential of design. ■

The ultimate test of the S-76 comes in the sky. Only an actual flight can adequately demonstrate for you how unique this aircraft is. Because we know that it will exceed your expectations, we invite you to experience that uniqueness yourself. You will recognize that the S-76 has achieved the ultimate in responding to business air transport's need for a fast, convenient, comfortable aircraft for short- and middle-distance flights.

Consider, then, what satisfying returns this investment might provide for you.

Index

Acknowledgments

My sincerest thanks to everyone who helped make this book possible; to all the clients and designers who contributed so much of their time, energy, and distinguished work; and to:

Mary Suffudy, Sue Heinemann, and Andrew Hoffer, of Watson-Guptill, for their continual encouragement and superb editing.

My colleagues of AIGA/NY, Willi Kunz, for his astute leadership of the Design Management Seminars; and Michael Beirut, Dean Morris, Christy Trotter, Jan Uretsky, and Roger Whitehouse, for reviewing the manuscript and offering excellent suggestions.

My colleagues at Shapiro Design Associates, Terri Bogaards and Sara Holbrook, for their invaluable design assistance; and Shari Sperling for her tireless word processing.

And, with special admiration, to Primo Angeli, for his stunning jacket design; and Tony DiSpigna, for hand lettering it so exquisitely.

Photography and Illustration Credits

Preface
P. 7-Reprinted by permission of Harper & Row Publishers, from Management: Tasks, Responsibilities, Practices, © Peter Drucker, 1973.

Chapter 1
P. 10-Richard Frank; p. 15-illustrations by Jim Silks and Randall Lieu; p. 17-all Calculator Chronicle exhibition photography by Neuhart Donges Neuhart.

Chapter 2
P. 18-Paul Warchol; p. 26 (top left) Ullstein Bilderdienst and Hans-Peter Siffert, (top center) Christian Coigny; p. 27 (top right) Tom Vack and Corrine Pfister.

Chapter 3
P. 28-Kay Marvins; p. 29-Jim Simms; pp. 32-33 and 35-Rick Gardner; p. 35-still life by Gary Faye.

Chapter 4
P. 36-Frank Petronio; p. 37-Irv Blitz.

Chapter 5
P. 42-Marilyn Futterman; pp. 43-48-illustrations by Jack Summerford; p. 43-still life by John Katz; p. 48-still life by Gary McCoy.

Chapter 6
Pp. 51 and 53-Richard Fried; p. 57-Todd Weinstein.

Chapter 7
P. 58-Ellen Shapiro; pp. 59 and 63-illustrations by Mark Ullrich.

Chapter 8
Pp. 64-71-all photography by Michael Weymouth.

Chapter 9
Pp. 73-77-all photography by Elyn Marton.

Chapter 11
P. 86-Bob Randolph; pp. 87-89-still lives by Peggy Barnett; p. 87-portraits by Steve Kahn; p. 88 (left) all photographs © The Image Bank (top to bottom); NASA, David W. Hamilton, Alex Stewart, Kaz Mori, Gary Cralle, Fernando Bueno, Burton McNeely (center); illustration by David Suter (right); NASA; p. 89 all photographs except recovery drums © The Image Bank (top to bottom) Pete Turner, Eric Meola, Kaz Mori, Fernando Bueno; p. 90-courtesy of NASA.

Chapter 13
P. 98-Louis Bencze; pp. 99, 104-105, 107-Robert Pisano.

Chapter 14
P. 108-François Robert; pp. 109-113-collages using stock photography and illustration by Rick Valicenti of THIRST; pp. 114-115-portraits by François Robert.

Chapter 15
P. 116-Jim Coit; pp. 117 and 120-Carina Shoening; pp. 119 and 121-Jim Coit.

Chapter 16
P. 122-Setzer Studios; p. 123-Sadin Photogroup; p. 126-still life by Roger Lee; p. 127-wrapped chair by Stone & Steccati; pp. 128-129-Sharon Risedorph; p. 130 (bottom) Sharon Risedorph; p. 131-Stone & Steccati.

Chapter 17
P. 132-Warren Browne; p. 133-Mark Joseph; p. 134-Robert Tolchin; p. 135-Tony Reinwald; p. 136 (bottom left) Jean Moss and Robert Tolchin, (center) Mark Joseph; p. 137 (top) Dennis Dooley and Jean Moss, (bottom) Mark Joseph; p. 138-Mark Joseph.

Chapter 18
P. 140-George Bennett; p. 141-collage by John Van Hammersveld; p. 142-portraits by (top) Neal Slavin, (middle) Neal Slavin, hand-colored by Huntley/Muir, (bottom) Scott Morgan, illustrated by John Van Hammersveld; p. 143-Neal Slavin; p. 144-illustrations by Huntley/Muir; p. 145 (top) Scott Morgan, (bottom) collages by John Van Hammersveld.

Chapter 19
P. 146-Tim Peterson; p. 147-photography for "Greener Pastures," "Throw the Book," and "Christianity's Biggest Competition" by Rick Dublin; "Where Women Stand" by Tom Bach, Marvy Photography.

Chapter 20
P. 152-Wiener; pp. 153-159-Ming Louie.

Chapter 21
P. 160-John Goodman; p. 161 (clockwise from top right) Myron, illustration by Ken Maryanski, Clint Clemens (2); p. 162 (top to bottom) Clint Clemens, John Goodman, Aldo Fallai, illustration by Fritz Dumville; p. 164-"Gourmet" cover by Christopher Barry, fashion photographs by Myron; p. 165 (clockwise from top left) Babe Ruth courtesy Baseball Hall of Fame, illustration by Anthony Russo, photographs by John Goodman.

Chapter 22
Pp. 167-173-all photography by Eric Meola; still lives of S-76 brochure by Peggy Barnett.

This book was designed by Ellen Shapiro; graphic production by Ellen Greene; typeset in ITC New Baskerville and Univers 67.

Magic Toyshop

For Eliza
Special thanks to Val Wilding

First published in 2012
by Faber and Faber Ltd
Bloomsbury House
74–77 Great Russell Street
London WC1B 3DA

Printed and bound by CPI Group (UK) Ltd, Croydon, CR0 4YY

Series created by Working Partners Limited, London W6 0QT

A CIP record for this book
is available from the British Library

978–0–571–25984–7

FSC
www.fsc.org
MIX
Paper from
responsible sources
FSC® C101712

2 4 6 8 10 9 7 5 3 1

Magic Toyshop

The Rabbit Rescue

By Jessie Little

Illustrated by Penny Dann

ff

faber and faber

WHO LIVES IN SUMMERTOWN?
MEET THE HOOZLES!

This is
Willow and Toby

Here are Freddie
and Wobbly

Auntie Suzy
owns the toyshop!

The Hoozle Council – Grouchy, Wizard and Lovely

Smooches the
rabbit is new!

Nasty Croc is the
only mean Hoozle

'Tidy-up time!' said Willow. She loved it when the Best Toy Shop in the World closed its doors, and she and Auntie Suzy made everything perfect, ready for the next day.

Willow sat her blue Hoozle bear, Toby, on the shop counter and

found her brother, Freddie, a picture
book to read. Then she sorted a
basket of glove puppets and tidied
the doll's house display. Toby stayed
still and silent, as he always did
when other people were around.

Freddie picked up Wobbly, his lion
Hoozle, and asked if he could take
the book to his bedroom.

'Of course,' said Auntie Suzy. 'I'll
come, too. It's time I put the kettle
on. Willow, turn the shop door sign
to "Closed", would you?' She and
Freddie went upstairs.

Willow shut the front of the dolls'
house and picked Toby up. But
before she could reach the shop
door, it was thrown wide open.

A tall woman walked in. She had
long, glossy, conker-coloured hair
with a glittering diamond slide at

the back, and following her was
a girl of about Willow's age. They
were both beautifully dressed in
white and carried matching pink
handbags, sewn with silver sequins.
The girl's bag had something pink
and fluffy poking out through the
top.

Willow felt Toby wriggle with
excitement. 'The girl's got a Hoozle
in her bag!' he whispered.

Willow still got a special thrill
when her Hoozle spoke to her. Just
a few weeks before, she'd discovered

the Hoozle secret – they could move
and talk. Willow wondered if the
girl knew that all Hoozles were just
as alive as she was.

Auntie Suzy
poked her head
into the shop and
when she saw the
glamorous woman
she rushed over
and flung her arms
round her. 'Ellie!'
she cried. 'I haven't seen you
for ages.'

Willow whispered to Toby, 'Let's go and find out who her Hoozle is.' She went up to the girl, who was looking at a basket of cute furry animals as if they were the dullest thing she'd seen all day and said, 'Hi, I'm Willow.'

'Oh, hello,' said the girl. 'My name's Clementine.' She smoothed the skirt of her spotless white dress. 'You can call me Clemmie.'

Willow pointed to the handbag. 'Who's your Hoozle?'

Clemmie opened the bag wide

and Willow looked inside. The white
bunny-rabbit Hoozle had soft, pale
pink ears, dark gold eyelashes and
wore a pink collar, studded with
glittering glass jewels of all different
colours. 'This,' said Clemmie, 'is
Smooches.'

'Hi Smooches,' said Willow,
stroking the soft velvety coat. 'She's
beautiful, Clemmie.' She held Toby
out. 'This is my Hoozle.'

'He's nice,' said Clemmie, but
Willow didn't think she was all that
interested. She didn't even ask his
name.

Willow held out Toby's paw. 'Shake hands with Smooches, Toby,' she said.

Clemmie quickly pulled her bunny rabbit back. 'No, don't,' she said. 'Your Hoozle looks grubby. He might dirty Smooches's lovely clean fur.'

Willow couldn't believe anyone could say that about Toby. He wasn't grubby! He just looked as if he was loved a lot, which was true. She gave him an extra-loving cuddle.

Auntie Suzy put an arm round Willow's shoulders. 'Ellie,' she said, 'this is my niece, Willow, and I'm very lucky, because she and her brother, Freddie, are staying with me while their parents are working abroad.' She turned to Willow. 'Ellie and I were at school together,' she said. 'She's a famous actor now.'

Willow looked at Ellie a little more carefully. 'Are you a film star?'

'Watch!' Ellie swept up her
hair, then laughed loudly.

Willow gasped. 'You were
the beautiful witch in *Magic Millie*,
weren't you? I love that film.'

Ellie nodded and smiled. 'I'm
taking a break from movies so
Clemmie and I can spend a few
months at our beach house in
Summertown. I hope you two will
be friends.'

Auntie Suzy invited Ellie upstairs

for a cup of tea and off they went, still talking.

'Come and see where the Hoozles are made,' Willow said to Clemmie. 'Auntie Suzy's planning to start a new one after tea.'

She showed Clemmie the shiny pink sewing machine and the red Hoozle workbag, full of colourful fabrics, threads and buttons. 'Every Hoozle in the world is made by Auntie Suzy,' she said proudly, and pointed to three Hoozles sitting on a shelf right above the counter.

'They're known as the Hoozle
Council, and one of them is the first
ever Hoozle. I'll show you.'

She carefully lifted down a grey-
and-white owl Hoozle. He had a
kindly expression. 'This is Wizard,
and he belongs to Auntie Suzy.'

'He's quite nice, I suppose,'
Clemmie said. 'And the penguin's
rather sweet.'

'That's Grouchy,' said Willow.
'And this is Lovely.' She lifted down
a pink pony Hoozle with a silky
purple mane and eyelashes as long

as Smooches's. 'She's my mum's.'

Clemmie laughed. 'That pony's not half as lovely as my Smooches.'

Willow was stunned. Clemmie certainly wasn't nice to other Hoozles. How must poor Lovely feel after hearing that?

As Clemmie wandered round the shop, examining the toys, Willow made sure the Hoozle Council were safely back on their shelf and mouthed, 'Sorry.' Then she whispered in Toby's ear. 'One thing's for sure, Clemmie

doesn't have any idea that Hoozles are alive, or she wouldn't be mean about them.' Willow couldn't understand anyone not adoring Hoozles. They were all so friendly and loving — well, all except a certain orange crocodile Hoozle, called Croc.

Toby pressed her hand. 'Only special people know the Hoozle secret — like you.'

Willow dropped a kiss on his nose and went to talk to Clemmie. But what was that? Something moved behind a display of robot dinosaurs. Yes! There it was again! A flash of orange.

Oh no! She knew exactly who it was. 'Toby,' Willow whispered, 'it's Croc! What's that naughty Hoozle doing in the shop?'

'Something bad, of course,' Toby replied in his growly whisper. 'Let's chase him away.'

'No!' said Willow. 'We mustn't! Not in front of Clemmie!'

'If we don't,' growled Toby, 'one thing's certain. There'll be trouble.'

Chapter Two

Willow had to stop Croc causing
trouble. But she also had to make
sure Clemmie didn't see. 'We have
to keep her on the other side of the
shop,' she whispered to Toby. 'You
know Croc. If he sees Smooches,
he'll try to steal her pocket heart.'

Toby looked very serious and put
his paw over his own pocket heart.
All Hoozles were given a special
object by their owners, which was
a symbol of the love they had for

each other. A Hoozle without a pocket heart was a sad and sorry Hoozle.

'Willow, don't let Clemmie put her bag down,' Toby growled softly. 'If she does, Croc will be in there faster than a sneeze.'

'OK.' Willow raised her voice. 'Clemmie,' she said, 'why don't you have a look at the dolls' house, over by the counter? You can open it up if you like. It's got such cute things in it.'

'All right,' said Clemmie. 'I like

dolls' houses. Come on, then.'

Willow thought quickly. 'Um, I – um, I'm going to dust the stegosaurus,' she said. 'Won't be a moment! Oh, don't put your lovely bag on the floor. It hasn't been swept yet.'

She knew that would make Clemmie hold on to her handbag. She turned towards the place where she'd last seen Croc.

'Hey!' said Clemmie. 'There's a cat in here. Have you got a ginger cat?'

Willow knew exactly what Clemmie had seen. It must have been Croc. 'I expect it's just wandered in,' she said. 'You know what cats are like. They love playing with soft toys.'

Clemmie stroked Smooches's ears. 'I think you should get rid of it,' she said. 'I don't want bits of ginger fur getting into Smooches's lovely white coat.' She wandered away to look in the hobbies section.

Willow searched around.
Suddenly Croc's orange head
popped up from behind a train set.
He grinned at her and disappeared
again.

She sat Toby on the counter
where he'd be safe from Croc,
then looked for something to keep

Clemmie
busy
while she
hunted for
the naughty
Hoozle.

She went to the crafts section.

'We've got some sample felt tips,' Willow said. 'Big, fat ones, and there's every colour you could think of. Anyone's allowed to colour one of the pictures in this tray.'

'Ooh, can I?' Clemmie asked. 'Mum says I'm very artistic.'

As Willow reached up for the pot of pens, she heard a faint scurrying sound and spun round. Crash! The pot tipped over and all the pens bounced from shelf to shelf, on to the floor. All except one.

'Oh, look what you've done!'
cried Clemmie.

Willow stared in horror at a long
jagged line of bright yellow felt
tip all down the side of Clemmie's
white dress. 'I'm sorry!' she
said. 'Let me see if I
can get it off.'

Clemmie was
furious. 'Don't
you dare
touch it! I'm
going to find
my mother.'

She dumped her handbag on the chair by the counter, propped Smooches up inside it, and held the skirt of her dress out with both hands. 'It's ruined,' she cried, and stormed upstairs.

'Wow!' said Toby, from the counter. 'She's scary when she's cross.'

'It's Willow's fault for making her cross,' said a small, but firm, voice.

'Smooches!' said Willow. She knelt down to speak to the bunny Hoozle. 'I'm sorry, but it was an accident.'

Toby jumped down on to the chair and said, 'It really was, Smooches.'

The bunny Hoozle ignored him. 'What sort of a place is this, anyway?' she said. 'An unswept floor? Pens flying all over the place? An uninvited cat?'

That reminded Willow that Croc was still loose in the shop. While she searched the shelves, Toby tried to explain to Smooches about the naughty crocodile. All the time, Willow could hear the bunny grumbling.

'Look at those Hoozles up there
on that shelf getting dusty. Why
do their owners leave them there?
Don't they care about them? You –
Toby – help me out of this handbag.
Ooof! That's better.'

Willow smiled to herself.
Smooches sounded
a little bit like
Clemmie.

What
was that?
She saw a
streak of

orange race across the floor towards the counter. 'Toby!' she cried. 'Look out!'

Before she could reach the Hoozles, Croc leapt on to the chair. He turned to laugh at Willow, then snatched a sparkling pink glass bead from Smooches's pocket and jumped down.

'Her pocket heart,' cried Willow. 'Come back here, Croc!'

But the bad Hoozle ran behind the counter, through the store room, and out into the alley behind the shops.

Smooches twitched her nose. 'What a ruffian! How dare he touch me?'

Willow stroked her. 'Oh, Smooches,' she said gently. 'I'm so sorry.' She tried to explain that Croc didn't want other Hoozles to be happy, and that's why he stole their pocket hearts, but the bunny wasn't listening.

Instead, Smooches turned on Toby. 'It's your fault,' she said. 'You should have stopped him. You go and fetch my pocket heart back at once.'

'I'm sorry, Smooches,' spluttered Toby, 'but it's not my fault. He's so quick! Willow and I will do our best to find him, really we will.'

'Oh, you're far too slow,' said Smooches. 'You should have

grabbed him straight away.
Excuse me!' she added, pushing
past Toby.

Willow guessed what she was
going to do. 'Stop!' she cried, but
Smooches leapt down from the
chair and ran
to the back
door.

'If you won't
go after him,'
she said, 'then I
will!'

Willow ran

out into the alley. 'Smooches, come back!'

Oh, no, she thought. What's Clemmie going to say?

Chapter Three

Willow scooped Toby up and rushed
after Croc and Smooches. She had
to bring back the bunny-rabbit
Hoozle – and her pocket heart –
before Clemmie realised they were
gone. She'd never be able to explain
this away. And suppose Croc hid

the pink glass bead where no one could find it! Willow imagined poor Smooches without her pocket heart – she could hardly bear the thought.

As she turned out of the alley on to the seafront, she spotted the two Hoozles. Croc had stopped to tease Smooches by waving the pink glass bead. 'I'm going to put your pocket heart where no one will ever be able to get it,' he taunted. 'At the top of the tallest tree in Summertown!' And he was off again.

Willow called and called for

Smooches to stop, but the little
white bunny rabbit just kept going

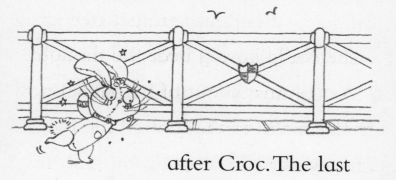

after Croc. The last
Willow saw was a flash of
her tail as she disappeared round
the corner by the library.

'We'll have to find
them, Toby,' said
Willow. 'I just hope
Clemmie doesn't go

down into the shop
before we get back.'

'Where's the tallest tree in Summertown?' Toby asked.

'It must be in the park,' Willow decided. 'Let's go!'

As she ran along, Toby said, 'It's strange, Willow. When Freddie's Hoozle, Wobbly, lost his pocket heart —'

'When Croc stole it, you mean,' panted Willow.

'Yes, well, Wobbly was sad and weak

and cold until he got
it back. But Smooches
is as lively as ever.'

Willow could see the
park gates now. 'Maybe the
pocket heart Clemmie gave
Smooches isn't right for her,' she
said. 'Perhaps there's something
wrong with it, and that's why
she was mean to the other
Hoozles.' They turned into the
park. 'Look!' Willow cried
in dismay.

Croc was already

halfway up a big old chestnut tree – the tallest tree in Summertown. And Smooches was climbing up after him. As Willow and Toby drew near, they could hear her shouting up at Croc.

'She does go on, doesn't she?' Willow murmured.

'You horrid crocodile,' Smooches was yelling. 'I can't believe you've made me come after you. Just look at the state of my fur!'

Croc laughed. 'You didn't have to follow me.' He jumped on to a

higher branch,
but wobbled
and nearly
toppled off.

Willow caught her breath.
Bad as he was, she didn't want him
to be hurt.

Croc steadied himself. His face
turned angry.

Willow had seen that look before.
It meant Croc was feeling especially
mean and spiteful.

'I'm doing it for your own good,
bunny rabbit,' he said. 'That Clemmie

girl will soon get tired
of you when some
flashy new toy comes along.'
Smooches kept on climbing
as Croc taunted her.
'Clemmie only likes new,
clean things. She hates
grubby things!'

Smooches paused in
her climb.

'She's gone quiet,' said
Toby.

'I think what Croc said
has upset her,' said Willow.

'Oh, I must help her.' She looked around. If only there was a ladder, or something she could stand on so she could reach the first branch. Smooches and Croc's little paws could grip the ridges and bumps and knobbly bits on the tree trunk, but she'd never be able to get a handhold at all.

Smooches struggled onwards, yelling as she climbed higher and higher, and getting angrier and angrier with Croc.

Croc was almost at the top of

the tree. He laughed. 'Why don't you stop all that shouting and save your energy for the long climb down? You're just making yourself dirty. Look at the state of your paws.'

Smooches lifted a paw to look and

lost her grip. She cried out as she slithered back a little way.

Willow's heart leapt. 'We have to do something!'

Willow struggled to climb up to the lowest branch of the chestnut tree, but it was impossible. She couldn't get a grip on the trunk. 'I just can't do it,' she said miserably, sinking to the ground. 'I've never been good at climbing trees.'

Toby climbed on to her shoulder and touched her face with his soft paw. 'I'll help Smooches,' he said. 'Lift me as high as you can, and I'll jump up on to that branch.'

Willow hugged him. 'I know you can do it,' she said as she lifted him up. He sprang into the air and landed neatly on the first branch.

Willow was relieved and proud

at the same time. You're such a
brave little bear, she thought as she
watched him climb steadily up the
trunk, pulling himself from branch
to branch, never looking down.
When he reached Smooches, she
gave a little cheer to herself.

'I'll help you go the rest of the
way,' she heard Toby say.

Willow watched the two Hoozles
working together, climbing higher
and higher, helping each other
over difficult branches. All the time,
she could hear Croc taunting and

teasing them.

'Needed a
friend to help
you, did you,
Smoochy-
woochy? Watch
you don't fall.
I shouldn't look
down, if I were
you.'

But Smooches
did look down.
Willow saw the
little white figure

wobble and heard her frightened squeal. She gasped. Smooches was falling! But she needn't have worried. Brave Toby caught hold of the bunny and helped her to wedge herself safely where a branch joined the trunk.

Smooches closed her eyes. 'I don't think I want to go any higher,' she said. Her voice trembled.

'Willow,' Toby called. 'I'm leaving Smooches here, and I'm going on up alone. I'll get her pocket heart.'

'Please be careful, Toby,' Willow cried. She watched him climb, ever higher.

Just as Toby reached the branch below Croc, a prickly chestnut pod hit him on the nose, 'Ow! You stop that, Croc!'

More chestnut pods rained down on him, but Toby kept going.

'See, Croc?' shouted Willow, dodging falling chestnuts. 'You can't stop my Hoozle.'

The same thought must have occurred to Croc, because he began

to edge along the branch, away
from Toby, saying, 'Get back!'

'Give me that pocket heart!' Toby
demanded, crawling on his tummy
along the branch.

'No!' snapped Croc. 'It's none of
your business.'

'If any Hoozle needs help, it's my

business,' said Toby, standing up.
He took three quick steps, reached
for Croc and grabbed him. They
struggled for a moment.

Willow could hardly bear to look
and, when Toby lost his footing and
slipped, she cried out. 'Be careful!'

But the valiant little bear regained
his balance and reached for Croc
again. 'Give me that pocket heart,
Croc. You can't escape.'

Croc realised he was trapped.
'Back off!' he shouted, his tail
lashing from side to side. 'Or else.'

Willow gasped. High above her, Croc was holding out the pink glass pocket heart.

'Back off!' he said again. 'Or do you want me to let it go?'

'Please don't drop it!' cried Willow. She stood beneath him, her hands ready to try to catch the glass bead, and never took her eyes off him.

Croc jumped down to the branch below and looked back up at Toby. 'You stay in the tree if you want to,' he said. 'I'm off, and you won't catch up with me this time.'

The orange
crocodile dropped
from one branch
to another. Willow
held her breath. Be
careful, Croc, she
thought. Hold it
tightly.

Toby's voice was
strong and growly
as he shouted
down, 'He's too
fast. I can't keep

up with him, Willow. Don't let him escape.'

'I won't,' she promised. 'He's not getting out of this tree with Smooches's pocket heart.'

'That's what you think,' Croc sneered. He held out the glass bead once more. 'Move away from the tree — or I throw it!'

Chapter Five

Willow did what Croc wanted
and moved slowly backwards. But
only because she'd seen what was
happening above him. Smooches
still sat where Toby had left her,
with her paws over her eyes, but the
daring bear was creeping down the

tree, closer and closer to the orange crocodile.

'Croc,' she called, hoping to stop him looking up. 'Um, mind you don't slip.'

He ignored her, and Willow tried desperately to think of something else to say. She bent down and picked up an odd-shaped stone. 'Look, Croc,' she cried. 'This looks rather like a

crocodile's tail, don't you think?'

He paused. 'No,' he said. 'It looks like a bear's nose.' He peered upwards through the leaves. 'Speaking of bears, where's that —'

'Croc!' Willow said hurriedly, hoping he hadn't spotted Toby. 'You look stuck. Are you stuck?'

'No!'

Over Croc's shoulder, Willow saw Toby drop down and reach towards the glass bead. He was almost there . . . almost . . . and then he stepped on a dry twig.

CRACK!

The twig snapped.

Croc spun round and saw Toby. Willow gasped in horror as the crocodile reached up, grabbed Toby's paw, and pulled him off balance. She gave a little scream as he tumbled down, down through the branches and then – PLOP! –

safe into her outstretched arms.

'Oh, Toby!' said Willow in a shaky
voice.

Croc mimicked her. 'Oh darling
Toby! Well, nah nah na-na nah!'
And with that, he threw the pocket
heart away from the tree as hard as
he could.

Willow rushed to catch it, but
she couldn't get there fast enough.
The glass bead hit the ground and
shattered.

From high in the tree there was a
squeal of despair.

Willow looked up. 'Oh, Smooches, I'm sorry! I tried!'

Croc laughed, then hurtled down the tree and away across the grass. His gleeful giggles faded as he disappeared through the park gate.

Smooches was still high in the tree, sobbing. 'Clemmie won't love me any more now I haven't got my pocket heart. Oh, what's going to happen to me?'

Willow and Toby did their best to comfort her, but she was too upset.

'It's safe to come down now,
Smooches darling,' said Willow
gently. 'Croc's gone.'

But Smooches refused to move.
'I've got no one to love me, so I'm

staying in this tree
for ever and ever,' she
wailed.

'Uh oh,' Toby said to
Willow. 'Now what are
we going to do?'

'We've got to
persuade her to come
down, somehow.'

Willow thought for
a moment and decided
there was only one thing
to do. Get Clemmie. She
told Smooches she'd be

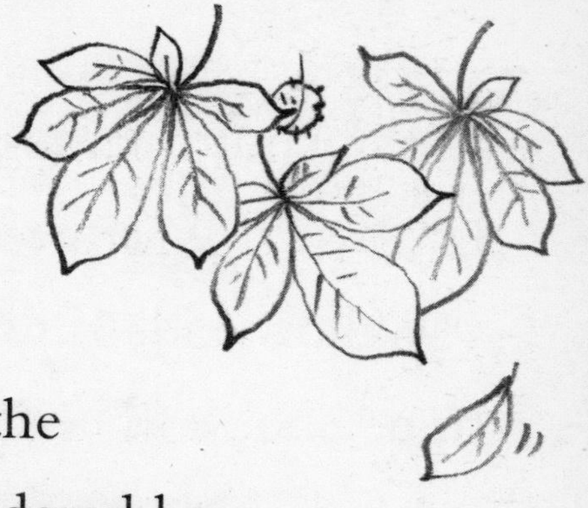

back soon, and
then she and
Toby raced to
the toy shop. All the
way, Willow wondered how
on earth she was going to explain
why Smooches was stuck up a tree
without her pocket heart.

Clemmie was flouncing down the
stairs when they arrived. There was
a damp patch on her dress. 'We've
managed to get the mark out,' she
said. 'You'll be glad to know those
pens have washable ink.' She went

to the chair and picked up her handbag. 'Where's Smooches?'

Willow took a deep breath and said, 'She's not here.'

Clemmie's eyes narrowed. 'What have you done with my Hoozle?'

Willow still didn't know how to explain. 'I'm really sorry, but she's stuck up a tree in the park,' she began.

'Oh no!' said Clemmie. 'It was that ginger cat, wasn't it? It stole my Smooches!'

Willow expected Clemmie to burst into tears and start yelling, but she didn't. Instead she clasped her hands together and said, 'Oh, why did I leave her down here where anything could happen to her?' She turned to Willow. 'You must take me to Smooches at once. Come on.'

And without waiting for a reply, she hurried out of the door. Willow went after her, and they ran together to the park.

As they drew near to the chestnut tree, Clemmie cried out when she

saw the bunny rabbit so high up.
'Poor Smooches!' she cried. 'It's all
my fault.'

Willow knew that wasn't true.
'It's not your fault,' she began, but
Clemmie interrupted.

'I won't leave Smooches up there a moment longer,' Clemmie declared. 'I should never have left her alone with a stray cat, just because my dress was dirty. Dresses aren't important.' She looked Willow up and down. 'I'm taller than you. If you give me a boost I could reach that branch.'

And with that, she kicked off her pink strappy sandals and said, 'I'm going up.'

Chapter Six

Willow watched in amazement as
Clemmie hauled herself on to the
first branch.

Clemmie muttered and grumbled
as she made her way up the tree.
Twigs hooked themselves into her
hair and at one point, Willow heard

a ripping
sound. Oh no!
she thought.
Clemmie's
beautiful
white dress.
'Poor
Smooches
must be really
scared,' Toby
growled.
Willow
hugged him,
knowing he

would be anxious until Smooches and Clemmie were safely down. 'She'll be fine, you'll see,' she said.

At last, she saw Clemmie reach out for her Hoozle and lean against the trunk.

'I've got her!' she shouted.

'Well done, Clemmie,' Willow called back.

'I'm tying her to my belt. Here I come!'

Toby gripped Willow's thumb until Clemmie reached the bottom-most branch and dropped down beside them.

'That was amazing,' said Willow. 'You're a brilliant climber.'

Clemmie didn't reply. She whisked bits of leaf off Smooches and gave the bunny Hoozle a most enormous hug. 'I'm so happy to have you back, darling Smooches,' she whispered.

As Clemmie brushed herself down, Willow saw that the expensive white dress had a long tear in it. She held her breath, waiting for the explosion.

But Clemmie didn't explode.
She shrugged and said, 'It doesn't
matter. It's worth it, just to have
my Smooches back. Willow,' she
continued, 'I'm really glad you
spotted the cat stealing my Hoozle.
I'm sorry I got so mad about the

marker pen on my dress.'

And to Willow and Toby's surprise, Clemmie put her arms round them both and gave them a hug, too.

On their way back to the Best Toy Shop in the World, Clemmie invited Willow to come over to her house next day. 'My mum has loads of costumes from her movies, and she lets me dress up in them. You can too. If you want,' she added shyly.

Willow grinned. 'That would be

fantastic!' Then she remembered something. 'Clemmie, I'm really sorry, but Smooches's pocket heart is gone.'

'I don't care,' said Clemmie. 'Those sort of beads went out of fashion ages ago. I'll find something else.'

Suddenly, Willow realised why Smooches wasn't affected when her pocket heart was stolen. The glass bead wasn't special to Clemmie. 'A Hoozle's pocket heart should really

mean something,' she said. 'It should be very important to you both.'

Clemmie frowned. 'That's true. But what could it be?'

Toby's blue paw patted Willow's hand. She looked at him in surprise. He never normally moved when someone else was around. It must be important. She dropped back a little and lifted him to her ear.

'There's a chestnut pod caught in Clemmie's hair,' he whispered in his soft, growly voice.

Willow grinned at him, and

reached up to untangle the chestnut pod. She broke it open and showed Clemmie the glossy brown chestnut inside. 'It's from the tree you climbed to save Smooches, and it's exactly the same colour as your hair!'

They smiled at each other, then Clemmie said, 'Willow, don't you think this would be the perfect pocket heart? It would always remind me of when Smooches was taken away from me and of how happy I was to get her back.'

Willow thought that was perfect, and so did Toby, judging by the cheeky wink he gave her as Clemmie slipped the chestnut into Smooches's pocket. At that very moment, Willow thought she glimpsed a flickering golden glow around them both. She moved away and whispered to Toby, 'Croc was trying to break them apart, but he's made the Hoozle bond even stronger than before.'

Clemmie hugged Smooches to her, linked arms with Willow, and they skipped off back to the toy shop.

Willow held the back door open for them, and noticed Smooches mouth a silent,

'Thank you!' to Toby.

Clemmie wasn't bad at all. In fact,

Willow was beginning to like her. It looked as if it would be fun having a new friend in Summertown!

Magic Toyshop

Get ready for even more

Magic Toyshop adventures!

DIMITRI D. LAZO

*Japanese Culture
and Behavior*

Japanese Culture and Behavior
SELECTED READINGS

EDITED BY
TAKIE SUGIYAMA LEBRA
AND
WILLIAM P. LEBRA

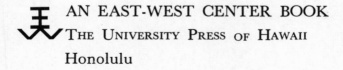 AN EAST-WEST CENTER BOOK
THE UNIVERSITY PRESS OF HAWAII
Honolulu

Contents

Introduction

Many books have been written on Japanese culture and have contributed to an understanding of the subject. In the course of teaching, however, we came to realize that there is not a single book that satisfies all necessary conditions for an adequate reader. Those available seemed lacking in comprehensiveness, coherence, parsimony, or cross-cultural objectivity. Such deficiencies are particularly striking in the area of behavior, where the dynamism of Japanese culture should be fully shown.

This reader is an outgrowth of several years of our perusal of publications on Japan, discussion and argument as to their relative value, and our personal observation of Japanese behavior. The articles selected are intended to fit together so that Japanese culture as manifested in behavior will emerge as a system in our readers' minds. Special attention in selection was given to surmounting the aforementioned deficiencies. We particularly sought to include a greater number of Japanese authors who might add balance to a limited Western perspective.

Our emphasis upon systematic coherence should not be misconstrued as acceptance of existing stereotypes of Japanese often held by Westerners—especially stereotypes that are static and simplistic. We want to stress the complexity, variety, conflict, and dynamism inherent in Japanese culture, and we believe that herein lies the intellectual challenge, for us at least, in studying this culture instead of a simpler one.

This volume consists of four parts. Part I provides an initial orientation to the subject from the point of view of generalized beliefs and values. Pelzel describes the cosmological and ethical beliefs that he has inferred from the Japanese myths of antiquity, which, he claims, have not disappeared in the contemporary scene. Mythological symbolism is extrapolated into a general ethos of Japanese culture in a remarkable contrast to Chinese culture. Ishida characterizes Japanese emotions by comparing them with Western counterparts, labeling the latter "a culture of love and hate." Although the comparative references are thus different, we note an intriguing convergence between the two papers, one by an American, the other by a Japanese. They both stress Japanese indifference to or repulsion from dogmatic assertions and unequivocal extremism, whether the matter in question is cognitive, moral, or affective.

While Pelzel and Ishida rely primarily upon literature as well as on their personal impressions and intuitions, Caudill and Scarr systematically follow methodological precision and empirical fidelity in arriving at conclusions on Japanese values. Applying the theory of value orientations originally developed by Kluckhohn and Strodtbeck, this study presents a profile of the Japanese based upon rank-ordered preference distributions in "relational," "time," and "man-nature" dimensions. The results are far from simple and stereotypic. Lebra explores moral values with a focus on faith in compensative justice, that is, the expectation of, or commitment to, the fair distribution of rewards for moral actions. A sentence-completion test is used as the instrument. Both the paper by Caudill and Scarr and the paper by Lebra consider intergenerational differences with an aim of suggesting the direction of culture change. The results do not substantially confirm many of the conventional speculations on the generation gaps that are often alleged to be unique to today's Japan and otherwise unheard-of throughout its history. While Lebra characterizes the Japanese sense of justice as anchored primarily in the expectation of social sanction, DeVos captures Japanese morality from the standpoint of internalized sanction, namely, guilt, which, however, is not bound or generated by an abstract moral standard or superego. DeVos' conceptualization of the Japanese sense of guilt, on the one hand, thus exposes the ethnocentrism of Western scholars revealed in their definitions of guilt, and on the other, offers a needed antidote to Benedict's "shame culture" label for the Japanese.

Although each author approaches Japanese culture and behavior in his or her own way, Part I should convey the overall impression that the Japanese are human-centered and relativistic. It is the editors' belief that human-centricity boils down to socio-centricity and that socio-centricity is the very explanation for relativism. Part II, therefore, is intended to set forth a cultural elaboration of patterns of social interaction and communication. This part should be regarded as a more specific extension of Part I.

Doi's article on *amae* elucidates the Japanese attitude toward dependency and captures its subtleties in a way that only a "native" psychiatrist can, with his complete familiarity with the language. Closely related to *amae* dependency is Nakane's depiction of Japanese behavior in terms of group cohesion, which she compares with the more individualistic quality of Hindu behavior. Nakane finds the same family-like interaction pattern replicated by every kind of group, traditional and modern, domestic and industrial. This somewhat overgeneralized picture, perhaps admitted as such by the author herself, may well be compared with the above-mentioned paper by Caudill and Scarr, particularly with regard to the "relational" area involving preference among "lineal," "collateral," and "individualistic" orientations. The following article by Brown renders support for Nakane's viewpoint by setting forth a number of essential attributes of Japanese management that together forge an enterprise into a unified "community." The basic frame of reference for the next two papers by Lebra and Befu is the norm of reciprocal exchange and obligation widely shared and deeply internalized by the Japanese. Lebra focuses on the concept of *on*, which constrains Japanese behavior in two opposite ways—in favor of asymmetric social relationship and of symmetric give-and-take. Befu sheds light upon the more overt convention of gift-giving, which lends insight into Japanese social structure.

Given the normative patterns of interaction and communication as described in Part II, there must be a set of culturally shared ways of internalizing them. Part III thus views the individual longitudinally, with an emphasis on socialization and developmental change.

The article by Caudill and Weinstein suggests that a cultural difference between American and Japanese behavior emerges as early as the third month of life, a result of a culturally biased pattern of interaction between mother and infant. Caudill and Plath report their study of sleeping arrangements, pointing out the preference for co-sleeping among the Japanese, and draw inferences as to the relationship between this and other aspects of life. Ikeda's study illuminates the cultural indispensability of birth-order hierarchy as a mechanism of socialization, where twins pose a uniquely disturbing problem. A syndrome associated with a critical stage of life, graduation, is analyzed by Kasahara with reference to undergraduate students who procrastinate graduating. Rohlen presents a modern Japanese version of initiation rites given for new employees of a company, which are intended to achieve a radical transfer of dependency and solidarity from the family to the company. From the way it is conducted, the orientation program appears more like brainwashing than socialization in its ordinary sense. Partially overlapping with this article, and integrating all the above articles on socialization, is Kiefer's analysis of interrelationship among the three socialization agencies the individual passes through—the family, school, and bureaucracy—intercepted by "examination hell," the latter regarded as crisis rites.

The first three parts all refer to dominant, normative orientations that are shared expectations among the Japanese. Nonetheless, it goes without saying that not all Japanese follow, nor does any individual always follow, normative models. Moreover, normative models themselves undergo change over time, which is likely to disrupt commitment to the old norms. Some instances of deviancy may be attributable solely to idiosyncracies of the individual. What concerns us, however, is the kind of deviancy that can be viewed as a product of stress and conflict, either embedded in the dominant, normative part of culture or resulting from its change. Part IV attempts to delineate cultural stress, deviant or extreme responses to that stress, and mechanisms for correcting deviancy or transforming undesirable behavior patterns, whether deviant or not.

Kato presents an epidemiological analysis of suicide that may be considered a useful map for locating what strata of the population, particularly by age and sex, have been under severe stress. This article also suggests a direction of social and cultural change over recent years as reflected in the changing patterns of suicide. Juvenile delinquency and criminal behavior are discussed by Iwai with reference to underworld groups organized on a ritual kinship basis— a notable example of deviancy that expresses a cultural ideal in an extreme form. In contrast to such social deviancy are pathological forms of deviancy. Kasahara analyzes neurotic patients suffering from the "fear of eye-to-eye confrontation," which seems to be extreme response to the culturally demanded social sensitivity, especially shame sensitivity, in interaction situations. The following two articles discuss psychotherapeutic methods that we consider significant not because they are used by many therapists but because they bring into relief some of the dominant values that were characterized in Parts I through III. Miura and Usa give a concise summary of Morita therapy, a psychotherapy credited as a unique contribution of Japan to this field. As analyzed by Murase, Naikan therapy, also a Japanese invention, suggests the mobilizability of guilt for therapy or rehabilitation of Japanese patients and deviants. The last two papers are concerned with the most recent worldwide social issue, campus unrest, as it has emerged on the Japanese scene. Owada, Gleason, and Avery introduce a dramatic aspect of the most radical student movements involving a total reversal of authority and the forcible brainwashing of professors. Complementary to this is Doi's article, which singles out a psychological mechanism that he believes students strategically manipulated toward their triumph over helpless professors. The whole argument is ultimately related to *amae*, the concept described in another paper in this volume by the same author.

These papers by no means exhaust all that should be included in a book on Japanese culture and behavior, and we regret that there are many other articles which were reluctantly excluded because of space limitations. But we hope that this volume will help students toward a better understanding of Japanese culture and behavior.

TAKIE SUGIYAMA LEBRA
WILLIAM P. LEBRA
HONOLULU, 1972

PART I
Values and Beliefs

Human Nature in the Japanese Myths

JOHN C. PELZEL

What follows is an attempt to describe one traditional Japanese literary view of human nature, that pictured in the myth portions of the *Kojiki* and *Nihongi*. Though the quality seen in man is the main interest here, it has seemed desirable to describe also the myths' view of his context—the nature of the world and of mankind's role in it.

These sources constitute only one of the models that the basic literary tradition made available to later generations of Japanese. Buddhist and lay Chinese conceptions were in time absorbed, and in recent centuries ideas from the West, and we must assume that throughout history the native talent reworked the body of perceptions it had before it in varying ways. Nevertheless, the myths are the earliest repositories of this tradition, and in spite of many additions to Japanese eschatological literature and numerous fluctuations of fashion, the myths have not been rewritten, nor have they ceased to be well known and viewed with at least some measure of respect by even moderately well-educated Japanese. They are thus the most persistent, and at least one of the basic, sources of native literary views on these matters.

The behavioral relevance of such a model is an interesting problem. One may wish to argue that a society's basic literature offers cognitive limits and patterns according to which the native mind tends to build up its understanding of the world and of man. As values, the views of prestigious literature may be accepted by native individuals as proper judgments and can even affect the choices through which, in part, they form their own personalities.

From *Personality in Japanese History,* A.M. Craig and D.H. Shively, eds. (Berkeley: University of California Press, 1970); reprinted by permission of The Regents of the University of California.

Nevertheless, and critical as the question of behavioral relevance undoubtedly is in many contexts, it is beyond the scope of the present paper, which will confine itself to the attempt to discern the mythic model itself.

What the *Kojiki* and the *Nihongi* have to say about the cosmos and man was not set out in any self-conscious or reasoned statement. These books are art forms, a mixture of narrative legend and poetry. But in this they are characteristic of the main form of the Japanese literary tradition, which in this respect contrasts so sharply with the Chinese corpus as to merit a reminder.

The bulk of the respected literature of China has been a formal ethics, identified with individual professional philosophers, and a history deliberately written to illustrate the conclusions of the philosophers. Chinese literature is thus rational and intellectualized, as well as didactic. Its thrust, moreover, is such as to counsel agnosticism about the nature of the cosmos, earthly pragmatism about the role of man therein, and disinterest in most aspects of human nature except the moral. Japanese literature, by way of contrast, has from its beginnings in the myths taken forms—such as poetry, fiction, and the drama—which are best suited to an approach by intuition and imagination rather than reason. This literature has been much given, moreover, to questioning and picturing the place of individual men in a cosmos that includes, but that goes far beyond, earthly society. Certainly, then, what the Chinese and the Japanese sources have to say about man differ not alone in the traits of personality they discern or emphasize, but even more basically in the approach to the human condition that they illustrate. Chinese literature had faith in conscious moral will and exhorted man to be what he should be in one overwhelmingly important segment of life. Japanese literature instead had faith in intuition and described men in terms of the whole existence they were seen to lead.

The context and the events of life are thus basic to the interpretation of the Japanese myths, and their narrative accordingly deserves to be recapitulated here. In details, the stories of the two books under consideration vary slightly, but both were well known and had roughly equal prestige.[1] The retelling that follows attempts to combine important elements from both tales, noting the textual divergence only when this seems to have a particular significance.

The myths fall into several cycles, most centering on certain major figures and events and roughly sequent to one another in terms of myth chronology. We may broadly divide this chronology into three myth eras, namely, Before the Creation of the Earth, the Creation of the Earth, and the Ordering of the Earth.

THE ERA BEFORE THE CREATION OF THE EARTH

This first segment of the myths is extremely brief and, in contrast with what follows, aesthetically unrewarding. The story starts with heaven already in existence,[2] though we are told virtually nothing about it until the third and final era, and with the earth still a formless thing, floating about below heaven "medusalike," "like drifting oil." The first precursor of creation was the growth of a "thing like a reed shoot," which in its turn gave rise to three or four (varying with the source) deities described as "single," that is, each existing alone, at a different time, without discernible relation to the others, and, it may be added, without our learning anything about them other than their names.[3] These were followed by four or five generations, each of which comprised a pair of gods, one male and one female, described as "brother and sister." The last such pair, Izanagi (the brother) and Izanami, were the creator gods par excellence.

THE CREATION OF THE EARTH

With this segment, the story comes to life. The creator siblings stood on the "floating bridge of heaven," stirred the formlessness below with the "heavenly jewel spear," and watched the brine dripping from its point curdle into an island, Onogoro. Descending to it, they erected there the "pillar of the center of the land" and proceeded to the work of creation.

In part, they created as their exuviae, articles of their clothing, and so forth turned into progeny. But in part they created through normal mammalian sexual reproduction, which is given by far the greater attention in this cycle. As it turns out, they must discover or invent sexual reproduction, and they perform a ritual to accompany it, a marriage rite, as well.

Izanagi, as though casting about for a method of creation, asked his sister how her body was formed. She replied that in one place it was "not complete." Noting that his own body at one point had "something left over," he then proposed, "How would it be if we were to fill in the place on your body that is not complete with the spot on mine where something is left over, and so give birth to the land?" She replied simply, "That would be good."

Izanagi likewise devised a ritual, which consisted in their circumambulating the pillar of the center of the land from opposite directions, he from the left and she from the right; on meeting on the other side, they would "perform the acts of the honeymoon chamber."[4] On the first attempt, however, the sister exclaimed first, on the far side of the pillar, "What a fine, lovely youth!"—a forwardness which her brother considered a breach of the proper male-female relationship. He therefore had them perform the circumambulation again and exclaim on one another's loveliness in the proper sequence. As a result of the breach of etiquette that had occurred, however, one of their children was born deformed.[5]

By sexual reproduction and something approaching parthenogenesis, therefore, the siblings created a large number of deities, many identifiable with the seas, islands, rivers, mountains, and vegetation of Japan and others (for example, the Sun Goddess) deities who came later to occupy key positions in heaven or in the process by which the created earth was put into order.

Only the *Kojiki* and certain variants cited by the compilers of the *Nihongi*, but not the text of the *Nihongi* itself, tell a version of the common Old World tale of Orpheus and Eurydice in Hades. According to the Japanese version, Izanami was badly burned by the birth of the Fire God and died, going to the "world of darkness." Mourning for her and wishing to persuade her to come back and continue the unfinished work of creation, Izanagi followed her, but when he met her he violated her order not to look at her and saw her in the corruption of her body. Frightened, he fled toward the upper world while she, in shame, sent avenging deities after him. He was able to trick them, however, and in the end took leave of his sister-wife at the Even Pass of Hades in enmity, she threatening to strangle earthly people, and he boasting that he could easily replace such losses, building "1,500 parturition huts a day." Back on earth, according to the *Kojiki*, he then saw other deities created from his exuviae, and according to both books he retired to a life of perpetual quiet on the islands of Japan.

THE ORDERING OF THE EARTH

Much the longest and most circumstantial, this segment of the myths consists of several cycles depicting the events whereby the created earth was ordered into the particular life forms we know. Not only is it richer in detail than what goes before, there also is repeated variation between the two main texts, and numerous variants are cited by the compilers of the *Nihongi*.

The story begins with a cycle depicting the relations in heaven between the Sun Goddess, now ruling there on the authority of her parent(s), and her younger brother Susanoo (the meaning of whose name we do not know). Susanoo had from birth been a selfish, cruel, and unruly god, whose very presence "withered mountains and dried up rivers and seas" and encouraged the "sound of bad deities to be like flies in the fifth moon." His parent(s) therefore had ordered him to proceed to the nether world (or the sea) to be its ruler where he could not harm the things of earth, but instead, at the start of this cycle, he had risen up to heaven.

His rising made so fierce a commotion it alerted and alarmed his sister, who wondered if he came "with good intentions" or to rob her of her kingdom. Fearing the latter, she dressed and armed herself like a man, gave a battle cry, and went to question him on the "redness of his heart," i.e., his sincerity. He protested his innocence, saying he had only wished to bid his sister good-bye before leaving to take up his own realm far away. To test the purity of his intentions, however, brother and sister engaged in an ordeal which amounted to a symbolic act of incest. She chewed up his sword and spat out its pieces as children, while he did likewise with the jewels of her regalia. They then exchanged children, those treated as hers and as inheritors of her authority and ancestors of the imperial family being the sons her brother spat out from her regalia.

The result of the ordeal was accepted as vindication of his intentions, and he remained a visitor in heaven. However, he continued to perform acts which were aggressive and destructive— breaking down the dikes around his sister's rice fields, letting a piebald colt loose in her fields at harvest time, defecating on the floor of her palace, and so forth. The Sun Goddess did not protest these acts, however, in each case finding an excuse for them that was acceptable to her. For example, she decided that in tearing down the dikes among her fields he had been moved by a helpful intent, impractical as it was in actuality, merely to increase the area that could be planted to rice, and she imagined that what looked like excrement on her floor was really nothing but vomit that he had brought up during an otherwise forgivable bout of drunkenness.

Eventually, however, Susanoo broke a hole in her roof while she was weaving, and threw in the corpse of a piebald colt flayed backwards. She (or her maids) was so startled that she jumped up and wounded herself (or themselves) on the shuttle. Indignant at this personal outrage and harm, she withdrew into a cave, locked the door, and so reduced heaven to darkness. Thereupon, the *Kojiki* adds, the "voices of the myriad [evil?] deities were like the flies in the fifth moon as they swarmed, and myriad portents of woe all arose."

The heavenly deities met together in a riverbed and consulted on how to end this intolerable situation. They collected a number of objects and performed various rituals, but they also did things to pique the Sun Goddess's curiosity and vanity. Having birds fill the air with song, they also had a goddess perform a noisy dance so lewd ("pulling out the nipples of her breasts and pushing down her skirt-string to her private parts") that they all laughed. Hearing the sounds of apparent revelry outside and wondering how the deities could make merry with herself absent and the world dark, the Sun Goddess stuck her head out to see what was happening. A mirror was immediately pushed up in front of her face, and she was told that it was a "deity more illustrious than" herself. Quite upset, she came out farther until she could be grasped and was implored by the deities not to deprive them of herself again. The heavenly deities then took upon themselves the judgment of Susanoo. Fining him for the pollution he had caused, they banished him from heaven, in effect voting for the continued rule of the Sun Goddess.

In the next cycle, Susanoo descended to earth, at a spot known historically as Izumo, and after saving the daughter of a pair of "earthly deities" from a monstrous dragon, produced from her a progeny that was to rule earth for a period, the principal descendant being the so-called Master of the Land. Susanoo himself then proceeded to the nether world he had for so long avoided.

At this point, the sources vary considerably. It is clear from all that the earth was still untamed. As one variant says, "This central land of reed-plains had always been waste and wild. The very rocks, trees, and herbs were all given to violence." The text of the *Nihongi* notes that "earth had numerous deities which buzzed like flies. There were also trees and herbs, all of which could speak." This subcelestial world had to be "constructed . . . for the sake of the visible race of man as well as for beasts . . . in order to do away with the calamities [that occur to] birds, beasts, and creeping things," and all texts make it clear that the progeny of the Sun Goddess, who were eventually to rule Japan, did not want to take on so noisome a place until it had been made habitable.

However, the *Kojiki* and several of the variants cited by the compilers of the *Nihongi* have most of this taming task performed by the Master of the Land, earth-born scion of Susanoo, before the Sun Goddess's emissaries descended, and tell a number of tales in which he exerted his humanizing influence on earth. The *Nihongi* itself, in contrast, gives very little space to Susanoo's progeny and has the humanizing work performed by ministers of the Sun Goddess and the heavenly deities, thus implying the dereliction of Susanoo's line. It is in this that the text of the *Nihongi* perhaps most clearly edits the record in a way ennobling to the imperial family, which claimed descent from the Sun Goddess. The tales told of the Master of the Land by the *Kojiki* and the variants add much that is of cultural interest, however, and because they also were available to all readers of the myths they will be recapitulated here.

In one, the Master of the Land is pictured as at first the despised servant of his eighty lusty, aggressive, and selfish brothers, relegated by them to carrying their baggage while they go in pursuit of a desirable female. On the way, they met a hare which had lost its fur. The elder brothers, as a cruel joke, told it to bathe in sea water, but when it did and the water dried, its skin cracked and put it in great pain. The Master of the Land, feeling pity for it, told it to roll in pollen, which formed a soothing cloak, and the hare in gratitude promised him the hand of the princess. Angered because she therefore accepted him rather than themselves, the eighty brothers twice killed the Master of the Land, once by striking him with a searing hot stone and once by catching him in the fork of a split tree, but each time his own mother brought him back to life.

Going to the nether world, the Master of the Land married his half-sister, the daughter of his father, Susanoo. His cruel parent then submitted him to several tortures. Once confined in a pit of snakes and once in a house filled with centipedes and wasps, the son was in each case saved by a scarf, given him in secret by his wife, which served to ward off these loathsome creatures. Again, Susanoo shot an arrow into the moor and sent the Master of the Land to fetch it, but then set fire to the moor grass to kill him. The Master of the Land again was saved, this time by a mouse that showed him a hole in which to hide while the fire passed overhead and then showed him the location of the arrow, which he therefore was able to return to his father as ordered. In the end, Susanoo fell asleep while the Master of the Land was performing the filial task of picking lice out of his hair, which the son therefore tied to the rafters and, stealing his father's sword, bow and arrows, and lute, fled with his own wife. Starting up, Susanoo was delayed long enough by his hair's entanglement that the refugees were able to get past the Even Pass of Hades. Thereupon Susanoo, giving the accolade to success, called to the Master of the Land that he must become the ruler of the earth and put his eighty unruly elder brothers to death, which he did.

The *Kojiki* continues its special attention to the progeny of Susanoo, competitors-to-be of the imperial line, by picturing a series of love affairs the Master of the Land had with several women on earth after he had returned to it in the company of his wife. He took up again with the princess he had earlier won from his eighty elder brothers. Again, telling of his courtship of another girl, the myth is able to paint the type of scene that was to be popular in Heian literature at least three centuries later. The Master of the Land is shown standing all night outside her bedroom, rattling her locked door and imploring her to let him in, while she replies that she is "like a drooping plant, my heart . . . a bird on a sandbank," and that she will not let him in until the next night, when she promises that his "arms white as rope of paper-mulberry bark shall softly pat [my] breast soft as the melting snow."

Predictably, the wife of the Master of the Land became jealous and must have threatened to leave him, for he sang that if she indeed left, her "weeping shall. . . . rise as the mist of the morning shower." She, trying then to appeal to his sympathy, offered him a drink and sang "[Thou], being a man, probably hast on the various island headlands that thou seest, and on every beach, . . . a wife like the young herbs. But as for me, alas! being a woman, I have no man except thee. . . ." In spite of this appeal, the *Kojiki* ends this cycle of amorous tales by listing the numerous progeny the Master of the Land subsequently had with still other girls.

The same sources that tell the story of Susanoo's progeny on earth, moreover, ascribe to the Master of the Land a series of the humanizing tasks. It is said that "for the sake of the visible race of man as well as for beasts, [he and his helper] determined the method of healing diseases," and also that they, "in order to do away with the calamities of birds, beasts, and creeping things, established means for their prevention and control." Again, it is noted that whereas formerly "the very rocks, trees, and herbs were all given to violence," the Master of the Land has "now reduced them to submission, and there is none that is not compliant.... It is I, and I alone, who now govern this land."

In any event, there begins here the cycle of tales according to which, with only slight variations, all sources agree that in spite of the Master of the Land's ministrations the earth was still not a suitable place, and tell of the steps by which the Sun Goddess's descendants take over its control. Japan "is still painfully uproarious," "violent and savage earthly deities are numerous," and rocks and vegetation still have the power of speech. In sum, "that country... is a tumbledown land, hideous to look on," and the Sun Goddess's progeny refuse to descend to it as they are ordered until things have been put right there.

In consequence, when the Sun Goddess decided that the son her brother spat out from her regalia (or, in other versions, when another god decided that her grandson through that son) shall rule the earth, a congress of heavenly deities has first to be convened to decide which of the gods should be sent to make the land fit for the divine children. The emissaries so dispatched, it turned out, were not faithful, but instead curried favor with the ruling Master of the Land, settled down with earthly goddesses, and did not even report back to heaven. Ultimately, however, a pair of emissaries was found who asked the Master of the Land to stand down in favor of the heavenly line. Consulting his own son, the incumbent ruler decided not to resist the intercession and "became concealed" forever in the shrine of Izumo, still one of the principal spots of state Shinto worship. In all versions, Ninigi no mikoto, grandson of the Sun Goddess, is the first of the heavenly line to descend and rule the earth, after the emissaries who received the submission of the Master of the Land pacified it and made it a fit place to live.

Among the heavenly grandchild's first acts on earth was his mating with a beautiful girl. The *Kojiki* and some variants also say that he refused to mate as well with this girl's ugly elder sister, and that because of this act of uncharity the emperors of Japan were doomed to be mortal. In all versions, Ninigi no mikoto made his wife pregnant in only one night and therefore expressed doubts that he could possibly be the father. Piqued, and submitting herself to an ordeal to prove his paternity, she set fire to her parturition hut and the children born therein were unharmed. At his death, the heavenly grandchild was the first of the long line of early emperors who were buried in the great *kurgans*, many of which are still known in western and central Japan.

In a final cycle, the two sons born to Ninigi no mikoto proved to have gifts for fishing and the sea, and hunting and the land. They decided to exchange tools and occupations for awhile, but soon became bored and the fisherman elder brother asked for his hooks back. The clumsy younger brother, however, had lost them, and though he made offers of restitution nothing would satisfy the overbearing elder brother except the return of the very hooks lost. The younger brother was in despair, but eventually made his way to the palace of the Sea God, at the bottom of the sea. Marrying the Sea God's daughter and recovering the lost hooks, he returned to land with his wife and a jewel that gave him control of the tide, which he used to make his elder brother liege to him. One of the sons (or, according to a variant, one of the grandsons) of the younger brother and the daughter of the Sea God came to be known as Jimmu Tennō, taken by traditional Japanese historiography to have been the founder of the imperial Japanese family.

At this point, what the Japanese considered to be the mythic portion of the tales ends. Though much of what follows in the *Kojiki* and *Nihongi* still smacks more of legend than of history, it is perhaps permissible to abandon the story here and turn to the attempt to analyze the myths.

COSMOLOGY

On the whole, the cosmos pictured by the myth-makers is the earth the Japanese knew, and only the earth they knew. The features of the realm called "the land" are of course those of the Japanese islands, often given the place names they still had in historical times, and only one or two remarks indicate even an awareness of other regions of the globe, including those parts of the nearby continent known to Japanese long before the dates at which the present texts of the *Kojiki* and *Nihongi* were compiled.

The homogeneity and familiarity of the mythic cosmos go far beyond this, however. Realms other than earth are indeed pictured—heaven, nether world(s), and a land beneath the sea—but only in the tale describing Izanami's dark and physiologically corrupted hades is any of these shown as at all different from man's own world. Certainly the High Plain of Heaven is nothing but the mold from which the earth was cast—a land of familiar vegetation, rivers, and mountains; of villagers subsisting by irrigated rice agriculture and making their clothing in weaving halls; of government by a ruler who is little more than the executive of consensuses reached in town meetings; of a religion of familiar ritual and pollution taboos; and of gods who feel the same joys and pains, and exhibit the same aptitudes, as individual men on earth do.

If the forms of the cosmos are thus almost everywhere the same, so too are the processes at work in it, those that men find in their own experiences to be natural. Most features of the environment, and most gods, are born by normal mammalian reproduction, discovered as even human children left to themselves can discover it. Most behavior conforms either to cultural conventions quite like those of men or to individual motivations understandable to the human reader.

There are some events that do not have this familiarity—the aboriginal generation of something "like a reed shoot," the creation of certain beings by parthenogenesis, the resurrection of the Master of the Land, the "concealment" of some deities, the primeval mobility of plants and rocks, whatever force it may be that renders ordeals effective, and so forth. Yet many of these instances need not be considered unnatural. If immortality is natural for gods, then so is their "concealment," which it is clear is only the process by which they change from one form of life to another. Izanami's is the only such case in which the alter life included physical change, but she continued to be active, even though in hades. In other examples, because the deity in question reappears later leading a normal life in heaven or the nether world, one must conclude that "concealment" amounted to no more than a physical transportation from one to another location. In still other instances, the "hidden" god in fact remains alive in this world, as the Master of the Land continues to farm his rice fields and to live with a retinue in his palace-shrine. He has merely, as the result of a spirit change, quite literally "hidden himself" from the eyes of others and taken on a role that no longer obtrudes itself on them. In the same vein, there is no suggestion, in the telling of the ordeal of Susanoo, that its efficacy needs to be guarded by supernatural, rather than human, means. It can be considered to be a form of the promise, a transaction between men, accepted or rejected in terms of the probity, the will, and the faith in one another of its human participants.

Other exceptions, unfamiliar to human experience as they may be, are presented as being irrelevant to men. The noisiness and aggression of plants and rocks was the state of affairs of antiquity, but had been corrected by the time the heavenly deities and their descendants came to occupy earth. Clearly also, the myth-makers treat the distinction between mammalian birth and parthenogenesis as immaterial. Even though the myths seem to have been compiled in part as a political apologia for the temporal supremacy of the imperial family, the two sources differ without comment on the form of birth, and the source of authority, of even the Sun Goddess. One has her created parthenogenetically and sent to rule heaven by her father alone; the other makes her the result of the mating of the creator siblings, and her rule take its legitimacy from the order of both these primal gods.

The earthly condition as men know it is thus presented by the myths as all but universal and, in any event, the only context men need seriously consider. Moreover, once the heavenly dynasty has taken possession of the world, there is little evidence that other regions of the cosmos can any longer even have much effect on men's realm. In the past, it is true, the gods came from heaven, and all Japanese are their genealogical descendants. The main political emphasis of the myths was to establish the biological tie between the ruler of heaven and the rulers of earth, but the descent of noble Japanese families from other deities was also, within that context, accepted. By the beginning of recorded history, at the latest, very large segments—if indeed not all—of the Japanese people may well have been considered genealogically related to the gods, presumably through some form of adoption to the aristocratic lines if not biologically.[6] Nevertheless, the myths tend to assure us that these physical links now have been broken, and give no evidence that the two realms are any longer in a position to affect each other very substantially.

Similarly, the main impression a reader receives of the nether world(s) is that it is significant only for those beings who must be excluded from the normal community—whether because of the kind of polluting physical accident that maimed Izanami, or for the qualities of personality that made Susanoo a source of constant trouble for those around him. There is here no suggestion that normal gods or men need expect this exile. Moreover, though hades can to a certain extent affect this world—as is clear from Izanami's threat to destroy earth's inhabitants—its impact also can be nullified from earth, for Izanagi maintains that he can easily repair her ravages. All things considered, the nether world(s) is merely a distant island, much like the major islands on which men and the gods live, where those who are beyond the social pale can live out their lives without harming their fellows.

In sum, the Japanese myths show few of the workings of a "metaphysical" imagination, and give a resounding priority and value to things of this world. Except for a very few, and surely Sinified, exegeses, there is no suggestion of impersonal or unearthly processes, such as the Yin-Yang, karma, or even the absolute law of God, which have made much in the continental Asian cosmologies an engine amoral to and/or beyond the understanding of man.

Similarly, there is no hint that such cosmic forces as do exist can overpower life as man proposes to live it. The gods do not have arbitrary powers; an earth-nurturing Izanagi can counteract an earth-threatening Izanami, and the heavenly deities were able to take control of earth only with the agreement of its previous masters. Even the imagery of the myths shows us little to fear or to marvel at. The only monsters appear in Izanami's hades—but not in that of Susanoo—and in the form of the eight-headed eight-tailed dragon, a brief nightmare, easily destroyed. The godly captiousness of so humanistic a mythology as that of Greece—Zeus of the thunderbolt or Hera of the jealous eye—have no counterparts in the Japanese stories, where gods and events pursue a gentle and sociable, an almost homely, course. Only the Sun Goddess's younger brother acts arbitrarily, and he is banished for behavior that conforms more to that of the American Peck's Bad Boy than to that of a devil.

The moral of the myths thus seems to be that life for men can be expected to follow courses that are almost wholly intelligible and actionable in earthly and human terms. More, one can expect them to run along a fairly even way, in sight of neither the abyss of frustration nor the mountain of miracle. One need not fear terror or hope for ecstasy of any ultimate proportions.

THE HUMAN WORLD

It is tempting to say that the myths thus show the world to be "good," and indeed in one very important sense they do. Nevertheless, it is a kind of "good" for which the English adjective is not an apt translation.

Except for those who are physically maimed, there is no different world with which to contrast our own. For the generality of men and gods, even the "nonworld" of death is not clearly pictured, individuals either disappearing from the narrative without explanation, being exiled to other worlds much like ours, or "concealing" themselves in a new form of our life. We may wish to assume that the strict pollution taboos we know surrounded death in early Japan led the myth-makers to avoid mention of any different kind of life after death; their silence then would not indicate that they also refused to admit of mortality. Certainly much later Japanese literature seems bemused by a fear of death. Yet such an interpretation is also arbitrary, and it seems as economical to conclude that the myth-makers quite simply denied death as a final or different state, that they saw life, essentially as we know it on earth, universal in time as it is in space. The preoccupation of later Japanese literature with the waste of death can be seen as a natural reaction of a people with the myth-fed faith in the hopefulness and permanency of life, who subsequently have had to take cognizance of the imported South Asian heresy—that life is pain and its end to be sought.

If there are no states other than those of our world and our life, we must conclude that at this point in Japanese history the idea of fundamental value alternatives—of "good" and "evil" as an elemental dualism—did not exist. On this basis, it is meaningless to characterize the mythic view of the things of our experience as merely "good." Far more basically, they "are," and are compatible with one another.

So existential a view does not, of course, preclude evaluation. The myths do judge a great many things positively or negatively and together with the verbal judgment justify appropriately cathectic behavior—avoidance or expiation of the ritually unclean, joyous mating with the beautiful girl, and so forth. There is no sense, however, of that massive concentration of "evil" at one point and time, and of "good" at another, which is so characteristic of Chinese thought and of the theory of the dynastic cycle on the continent. Instead, what is evaluated in the myths are particular states, individual events, and beings, which one runs into only at random. We shall do well, therefore, to interpret things so evaluated simply as items in the "is-ness" of life which are appreciably above or below the mean and average, rather than as things foreign to life. Even the "evil" Izanami and Susanoo are merely banished to realms where they can live out more fully the particular characteristics that make them "evil" for most men. "Evil" thus is not destroyed. Indeed, to the extent that we are correct in our general understanding of this philosophy, the denial or destruction of evil, its removal from the cosmos of what "is," would be inconceivable. One can think only to isolate its harmful effects from the rest of life.

It is congruent with this kind of evaluation, clewed as it is only to the standards of life, that the judgments of particular things handed down in the myths recognize no priority among all the possible types of "good" and "bad." Rather than subordinating other cathexes to a metaphysical, or a moral, or any other single kind of good, the texts name what is valued in each case differently, isolating verbally now one, now another, kind of standard. Sometimes they call it by the catchall, as well as moral, terms "good" and "evil," but as often they call it "lucky" or "unlucky," "bright" or "dark," "clean" or "dirty," "beautiful" or "ugly," "good-hearted" or "evilhearted," and so forth. It seems most useful to interpret such terminology as the expression of a catholic and on the whole unbiased appreciation of the many kinds of value a thing can have to the lives of men, and thus basically to an appreciation of things in terms of their facilitation or inhibition of human life.

It is not strange to find in this world, where life is the only criterion of value, that the state of being is equivalent to the possession of spirit, that impersonal or will-less forces do not exist. Gods and men of course are spirit, but one of the most nearly central, and unique, elements of the myth story records that at an early date plants and what we call "inorganic" matter also had identical attributes of life and spirit. For many plants and features of the topography we are given the genealogy, facts of birth, and names that personify them. For all, we are assured that they once possessed the powers of speech, movement, and violence.

Their use of these attributes was as troublesome to life for men as was Susanoo's behavior. The heroes of the Japanese myths therefore remedied this defect. Like many another cultural charter, therefore, the myths of Japan also celebrated the heroes of the significant process by which an aboriginal earth was made fit for men, and in the celebration validated a line of rulers and a system of rule.

Yet how enormously different are the Japanese and, for example, the Chinese myths in this regard! In the Chinese myths, physical nature is pictured as only a passive entity. It is troublesome for man because he still, at that early date, lacked the cultural artifacts to exploit its inertness for his own benefit. The continental heroes were therefore inventors of artifacts and custom—of ditches to drain the swamps, of plows to tear the grass-matted soil, of techniques for growing grain. The Chinese view thus assumed an absolute gulf of nature between man and even beasts, let alone the "lower" orders of life. Man adores man, and only man.

In the Japanese myths, in contrast, human culture much as it persisted well down into historical times is taken as already given, its origins of no interest, its celebration of no utility. The natural world has life and will that are all but identical with those of man, save that like Susanoo they often use these to antisocial ends. The task of the culture heroes was to make nature civil, removing from it the troublesome qualities of speech, mobility, and violence.

We must note that there is no suggestion that in doing so the heroes reduced physical nature to a lifeless and spiritless state, or made it into an order unworthy of man's attention. The myths are filled with an appreciation of the flora and topographic features of the islands of Japan, and the message of the hero tale is that this world is a harmonious union of the life of man with the life of nature. One sees here, in other words, the first literary expression of that acute and comradely sensitivity to physical nature that has been a hallmark of the customs of Japanese life down to our own day. One feels that as early as the time at which the myths were told, the Japanese genius already had avoided Rilke's "mistake of drawing too sharp distinctions."[7] This view persists, so that it is not strange for even a contemporary Japanese novelist to say of his heroine, "Looking around her garden, a little gone to seed [after a week's absence], . . . she felt that each of its plants and trees, each in its own language, was speaking to her."[8]

HUMAN NATURE

There is as yet, in the myths, as little evidence of what Gilbert Murray called a "failure of nerve" about man's capacity to achieve a satisfactory fate in this world as there was among the early Greeks. Nor need there be. The universe conforms to worldly and human experience and provides no more justification to the fatalist than it does to the Pollyanna. Events oscillate fairly evenly about a mean that for man as a whole is life-sustaining, and thus encourage neither pessimism nor optimism. In time, Buddhist and continental imports, with their visions of other worlds and idealized goals, would prepare the soil for those clichés about the "transiency" of life, "regret" for the unrequited, and *akirame* ("giving up") the unattainable that were to be so characteristic of later Japanese literature. But one senses that in the mythic view it is the fate of mankind to succeed, with reasonable effort, in grappling with the very material problems of daily life, as indeed it is his unconsciously accepted goal.

Individual fates do differ, some men attaining more, others fewer, of those earthly experiences and attributes that are "good" or "bad" because they are above or below the mean. There is as yet, however, no hint of Buddhist or Chinese explanations of these differences in terms of karma or "hidden good and evil." There is no picture of differences in individual fate so thoroughgoing as to impress one with the contrast between misery and blessedness.

We thus sense no ontological gulfs dividing men or gods into fundamentally different types. This is, of course, congruent with the myth's view of the descent of all men from the gods. The most basic element of man's nature is his spirit—that bit of the godhead dwelling in each Japanese, derived from one primal common source, and thus in the most basic sense alike in all men. The myth-makers even extend their universalism in a way that is cross-cultural-ly quite rare, for to them mankind shares his descent from the gods, and his nature as spirit, with all other things of this world. The way was thus open not only for that sense of kinship with nature which has continued to characterize the Japanese, but also for such modifications of imported concepts as the doctrine which allowed Buddhahood even to what continentals considered "lower" orders.[9]

It is also true that later, as Japanese came to have contact with other peoples, for whom a kindred descent from the gods could not be claimed, they were forced into that pervasive ethnocentrism so characteristic of many isolated tribal peoples—an ethnocentrism that cannot accord even human status to others. In somewhat the same vein, the emphasis in the myths on man's nature as spirit would lead Japanese thinkers, from Shōtoku Taishi to men of our own day, into almost compulsive attempts to try to define what it is that best describes the "Japanese spirit." It even seems possible to argue that the stress on success in attaining worldly "goods" inevitably validated that hierarchialism which has been so charac-teristic of Japanese social relations; he who succeeds knows no reason for tempering his satisfaction or for querying its rightness, just as he who falls behind finds no legitimation for his resentment. The man who succeeds is patently, and in a most pervasive sense, "better" than the failure.

The assumptions of the myths about man's fate and nature thus would conduce to particularisms that other peoples and times would find corrosive or petty. But the compilers of the myths wrote as if they were unaware of these possibilities, and we as well must admit the real universalisms at home here.

It is against this background of a common nature and fate for all created things that the myths were able effectively to concentrate their attention on individuality. Each actor has particular charac-teristics—of beauty or strength, of skill, of sociability, and so forth. We remember clearly the sympathy of the Master of the Land for the naked hare and his elder brothers' cruel prankishness, the quickness of hand of the god who seized the Sun Goddess from her cave, the hunter and fisher sons of Ninigi no mikoto, the womanly pique of the Sun Goddess when she imagined that her neighbors could enjoy themselves even in her absence, Susanoo's irascibility. These texts do not, it is true, draw so full and unique a picture of each character as the best modern fiction does. But the Sun Goddess and her brother come close enough, and as Kroeber has pointed out, the later literature of Japan approached that of the West more closely than most in this respect.[10] The actors in the myths are pictured much as we think of the members of our own family or closest friends—alike, but in ways so fundamental as seldom to arouse awareness, all our interest being concentrated on the quite individual quirks by which each person is stereotyped for identification by his intimates.

It was above all the emotions of the actors that excited the interest of the myth-makers, and it thus seems possible to say that at the individual level human nature was defined heavily in emotional terms. The principal emotions portrayed, moreover, fall into two opposing sets—love for the other person and love for oneself. Susanoo concentrates into his character most of the extreme examples of the latter, but love for others is described repeatedly, for numerous actors, and in a variety of forms. One can only conclude that in the mythic view love for others is the more common quality of mankind, as it is unhesitatingly, with no apparent *arrière-pensées* at all, judged "good."

A quite uncomplex sexual love reappears again and again, and in terms that forced the Victorian sensibilities of Chamberlain to render whole passages of the *Kojiki* into Latin. These are all cases, be it noted, of physical attraction at first sight, with immediate pleasurable copulation as their straightforward aim. To generalize the myth phraseology, when a boy and girl meet and are pleased with each other, almost his first remark is the simple "Let's go to bed. How about it?" and very few refusals are recorded.

In this picture of sexual love, mutuality is obviously the standard. There is no suggestion of brutal initiatives, of sadism or rape, of neurosis, and if a person refuses it is simply because he finds the other unattractive. The myths even make it clear that it is improper to deny a person who proposes love his or her pleasure merely because the attraction is not reciprocated, for the emperors of Japan are not immortal, it is said, because the Sun Goddess's grandson would not sleep with one goddess whom he found ugly. The aim of love is not merely to gain pleasure but, as important, to give it.

At no point do the myths picture sexual love as in conflict with social "goods," or as conditioned by the requirements of society. Kinsmen are not shown as having anything to do with one another's marriages, let alone love affairs, and there is no suggestion that the community need judge sexual relations. This emphasis on the absolute goodness and individual autonomy in judgment of the bond of pleasurable love is carried even to the point of an uncritical portrayal of what we, and at least historical generations of Japanese, were to consider brother-sister incest. The creator deities are of course full brother and sister. Though the relationship between the Sun Goddess and her brother may be considered to have been masked by the only symbolic form of their incest, the Master of the Land married his half-sister without attracting the myth-makers' condemnation. As late as the reign of the Emperor Ingyō, what the traditional Japanese view treats as history records the union of Crown Prince Karu with his full sister, and though they are punished by the exile of one (or both) of them, their relationship is described with some sympathy as a case of a true love.[11]

It seems quite clear that this presentation of sexual love as something that does, and should, well naturally and undenied from the hearts of two people has remained the basic norm of the Japanese people to our time. In Heian literature, upper-class manners are shown as more complex, and in the upper class of the Tokugawa some currency was given to the imported Chinese convention that sexual love is legitimate only when harnessed, through the arranged marriage, to the machine of family politics. But by and large, the view of the myths that sexual love is an unconditional good, subject only to the mutual wills of those who share it, has continued to exert a strong appeal in the literature and the daily customs of the Japanese. *Yobai*, the visit of a youth to his girl's bedroom, is first acted out by the Master of the Land, and the curiously aroused mutuality (if not the constraint) of the modern geisha and her customer would not seem out of place if described in the myths. Even where the family-haunted conventions of China at last reduced the Japanese spirit, the values first celebrated in the myths have tempered them, for in Japan the principals play a far larger role in the marriage arrangement, just as their wishes help account for the great prevalence even into modern times of the *naien* or common-law marriage.

Sexual love, however, is only one of a variety of gentle loves that characterize the relation of men or gods in the story. In a real sense, one can argue that it is love between individuals that begets all communal and societal morality. The Master of the Land, it will be recalled, helped the hare; he likewise determined the methods of healing diseases "for the sake of the visible race of man as well as for beasts." The bond between parents and children is never pictured as other than one of love, and the unilateral social obligation of filial piety that was so obtrusive in Chinese thought about this key bond never put down deep roots in Japan. Above all, the mechanism through which harmony is achieved and maintained within the social community can only be described as the working out of a steady mutuality among not merely the rights but, more important, the sensibilities of its members.

No doubt the formal social institutions of the village of the gods—the town meeting with its decisions reached by consensus, the obvious limitation on the ability of the Sun Goddess to make important decisions arbitrarily—were such as externally to constrain the individual to cooperation with his fellows, without any necessary commitment of his will to this end. No doubt also the form of the myths, as a creation of art rather than of reason, inhibited their statement of social duty in terms of abstract moral principles, and the absence of such statements is not evidence that these principles were not also operative. Nevertheless, even in later ages Japanese were not attracted to the Chinese habit of trying to produce moral behavior through conscious obedience to abstract principles. Moreover, in *giri*—a duty to a specific person —and in the compulsions ascribed to *ninjō*, as in the legal importance given confession, the Japanese have shown an interest in morality as a matter of the emotional commitment of the individual to others. It seems not inappropriate, therefore, to interpret the myths in the same terms, as a portrayal of morality achieved, or denied, in the personal relations of individuals.

Where behavior takes the form shown by Susanoo it is "evil." He makes loud noises that frighten others and acts impulsively, without the warning that would at least save their being startled. He tricks people, promising to be considerate but breaking his word, perhaps with intent to do so from the outset. He does not shrink from inflicting physical harm on others or from harming them through their possessions. Yet there is no suggestion that his behavior results form either long plotting or a perverted pleasure in harm for its own sake, as there is little evidence that he aims through his actions to gain any special material rights for himself. In other words, he is either a complete egoist or an emotional cripple. Needing only to express himself, he makes the freedom to do so his goal, so that in the end he admires his son for having exploited the same freedom to thwart him. He cannot, or will not, empathize with the pain his actions bring to others. He shows no capacity whatsoever to give, or to receive, consideration.

The quality of the Sun Goddess is not morally upright in any self-conscious sense. Rather, she shows understanding of how to mold herself with the people around her in a harmony that still does not deny the individuality of each. It seems no accident that she is typically termed "bright," a sign perhaps more of her humane than her astral attributes. She does not obtrude herself markedly on the lives of others, on the whole seeming to live and let live. When she acts as heaven's chatelaine, she asks more than she orders the behavior of others, letting hereslf be guided in major things by the consensus of the gods and gaining her ends by persuasion. She overlooks or forgives small errors and accepts their consequences, willing to give her brother and her recreant messengers to earth every benefit of the doubt. Yet she is not cowardly, and when she suspects her brother of evil she is willing to fight if need be. Nor does she lose the sense of the inner borders of her own individuality, for when her brother has clearly violated her trust she withdraws from society, sick at a world in which she can no longer maintain a minimal dignity. She is lured out of this withdrawal only by the firm evidence that her fellow gods are lonely without her, and are willing to act to change that world back to the one of reciprocal emotional trust that alone she can abide.

It thus does not seem amiss to say that morality lies in the total sympathy of one person for another, in the desire to give, not humanitarian "rights," but human fulfillment, even as he receives the same common and essential gift. In a real sense, morality derives from the forms of love.

Against this background, we should perhaps restate the myth's evaluation even of sexual love. It is not merely that they show no sense of "wrongness" attaching to this act and thus reduce it to the level of the behavior of the human animal. Instead, wherever man and woman want one another it is a "good" to take and give this pleasure, and perhaps even the most nearly idealistic of all rapports. One needs some such interpretation to explain the enduring romanticism of the Japanese literary treatment of this relation.

The emphasis given here to morality as emotional rapport between individuals comports poorly with the frequent contemporary view that Japan's is a "shame culture." If such a culture is one in which improper behavior is frequently prevented or punished by the negative reactions of other persons, the description of Japan in these terms is apt. As every Japanese child soon learns, if he errs in propriety or fails in an effort, he will be "laughed at," and ridicule, however gently applied by Western or Chinese standards, is unbearable. Likewise, if he sins deeply or repeatedly against others, he will be "abandoned," emotional as well as material support being withdrawn from him.

Nevertheless, it is nonsense to squeeze one's description of morality down to only negative sanctions against improper behavior. It is surely as much the habit of modern Japanese as it was that of their ancestors as portrayed in the myths to engage for the most part in proper acts, impelled thereto by positive sanctions—again, in the myths, to gain and earn consideration for themselves as sentient beings, as well as to give that consideration, and not merely by the fear of losing it.

The myths make it seem as clearly partial to claim that the main sanctions, whether negative or positive, are those imposed by other persons. Susanoo is not judged in terms of whether he did objective good or evil, and not even according to the opinion of the other gods on his actions. He was judged, rather, according to his own intentions—his will or "heart"—to do good or evil to others. The point of his ordeal is that it seemed to confirm his profession that his heart was "clean," and his sister was willing for a long time thereafter to forbear from judging what was in fact his disruptive behavior. She overlooked the harm he caused the fields as due to his ignorance of the field economy. She assumed that he was drunk when he vomited behind her chair; the seat of the moral will lies in that part of the mind that is given a vacation in drunkenness, and even today Japanese law and custom consider it not only forgivable but "good" that an individual give himself this holiday occasionally.

Susanoo ultimately was judged "evil" only when the Sun Goddess and her neighbors came to understand that he either wanted to visit evil upon them or was incapable in his own heart of distinguishing good from evil, crimes so polluting that he must pay an expiatory fine and be banished. The basic sanction to morality is thus the individual's own conscience, his compassion that not only, as Mencius put it, "cannot bear to see the sufferings of others," but wishes them joy.

Much of this view of the matter is still built deeply into the Japanese legal system. Its emphasis is not on whether an objective crime has or has not been committed, and not on restoring equity or punishing the offender, but on gaining from him that self-realization and repentence that is the true meaning of the confession so sought at every legal level.[12] The myths seem already to have contributed to this system the view that social evil is the failure, as good is the common success, of the individual will to be compassionate with others.

NOTES

1. One man, Ō no Yasumaro, was the key amanuensis for both books, which were completed in A.D. 712 (the *Kojiki*) and in 720 (the *Nihongi*). Neither book is represented as other than a compilation from then-extant sources, not now identifiable but apparently consisting primarily of the archives of various noble families (including the imperial family) and oral traditions and documents, many of the latter having themselves been written down from oral tradition. Both compilations were made at imperial order, at a time when the throne was coming into a position to assert the cultural supremacy of the centralized state over the feudalism or tribalism of the noble families and at a time when Chinese influence over the lives and thought of the upper class was rapidly increasing.

   The *Kojiki* is said to be the transcript of a record dictated to Yasumaro by one Hieda no Are, a person famous for the ability to memorize, though twenty-five years after he (or she) had been set to the task of committing at least some part of the extant sources to memory. The *Nihongi* is represented as having been compiled entirely from then-existent documents by Yasumaro and Prince Toneri. The forms of the books we have are consistent with the origins imputed to them. The *Kojiki* is a smoothly flowing narrative in colloquial Japanese though transliterated by Chinese characters used phonetically), whereas the *Nihongi* is written in the Chinese language itself, which was used then for all official documents, and includes quotations as well as numerous variants from the differing sources said to have been used.

   The question has been raised of whether the *Kojiki* we have is not a much later forgery. In evidence against this view, the book shows very few of those Chinese influences which were at the time of its reputed compilation only becoming known in Japan, but which were soon to become an inseparable part of the intellectual furniture of later generations of Japanese. Moreover, the *Kojiki* also is said to preserve many archaic Japanese linguistic usages which were not known to later generations. Thus, most authorities believe the *Kojiki* to be what it pretends to be. Probably equally authentic, the *Nihongi*, however, contains many more usages and ideas derived from the continent, and thus represents a further stage of that cultural fusion which was becoming fashionable during the generation and a half that the compilers say separated the original of these texts.

   The English translations used and quoted here are, for the *Kojiki*, Basil Hall Chamberlains' "Kojiki, Records of Ancient Matters,"

Transactions of the Asiatic Society of Japan, supplement to vol. 10 (1882), and for the *Nihongi,* W. G. Aston's *Nihongi, Chronicles of Japan from the Earliest Times to* A.D. *697,* supplement to *Transactions and Proceedings of the Japan Society* (London, 1896). The Japanese text of the *Kojiki* used is that of Kurano Kenji, ed., *Kojiki taisei,* vol. 6: *Hombun-hen* (Tokyo, 1957).

2. The *Nihongi* states baldly that heaven emerged before earth as a "united body" out of an original chaos, "like an egg which was of obscurely defined limits and contained germs," but all commentators consider this a Sinified exegesis.

3. The *Kojiki* lists three "single gods" in existence in heaven prior to the appearance of the reed shoot, but none is given any prominence.

4. The text of the *Kojiki* is slightly less euphemistic than that of the *Nihongi.* The term here translated *"acts* of the honeymoon chamber" is glossed by Kurano, p. 53, as having meant "to exchange glances and consummate a marriage."

5. The *Kojiki* and a variant cited in the *Nihongi,* but not the text of the *Nihongi* itself, state that Izanagi and Izanami were commanded to their task of creating the earth by the "heavenly deities" and took counsel with them to discover, through their divination, the breach that had produced the deformed child. I have omitted these evidences of a complete and guiding heaven, however, for it is not shown as deeply involved in the creation of earth.

6. At least this is one interpretation that can be made of the evidence on the family system of the day. See Ariga Kizaemon, "Nihon kodai kazoku," in Tanabe Juri, ed., *Shakaigaku taikei,* vol. 1: *Kazoku* (Tokyo, 1948), pp. 103–150.

7. Ranier Maria Rilke, *Duino Elegies,* tr. and ed., J. B. Leishman and Stephen Spender (New York, 1939), "First Elegy," line 81.

8. Osaragi Jirō, *Munakata kyōdai* (Tokyo, 1952), pp. 184–185.

9. See Nakamura Hajime, *Ways of Thinking of Eastern Peoples* (Honolulu, 1964), chap. 34, especially pp. 356–360.

10. A. L. Kroeber, "The Novel in Asia and Europe," *University of California Publications in Semitic Philology,* 11: (1951) 233–241.

11. Aston, *Nihongi,* pp. 323–325.

12. Arthur von Mehren, ed., *Law in Japan* (Cambridge, Mass., 1963), pp. 426–427.

A Culture of Love and Hate

EIICHIRŌ ISHIDA

One autumn after the war, I stopped my car in a small village near the Alps in southern Germany and dropped in at the cemetery behind the church. I had no particular aim in view, but soon I found myself drifting irresistibly among the graves, absorbed in reading the words of affection chiselled on each stone.

Dear wife, dear Ilse whom I can never forget,
rest in peace!

The grief common to all human beings who have lost what is dearest to them on earth strikes at the wayfarer's heart with a particular poignancy; the wild flowers offered up to the lately deceased are also affecting. Before I knew it, my own eyes were moist with tears.

But my memory also goes back to my life in Germany and Austria just before the war:

Juden sind verboten!
Nur Arier!

"Jews forbidden, Aryans only." The theaters, cinemas, restaurants, cafes, park benches, plastered with the lurid posters. The merciless seizure of property, the arrests and the detentions. I saw a man dragged about the town by the Nazi S.A. with a large placard about his neck saying, "I bought at a Jew's shop." He had gone shopping at a store with a poster proclaiming "Jüdisches Geschäft." Even at that time, things had already gone too far for me to understand, let alone sympathize. What, then, of the appalling massacre of six million people which was revealed to the world after the war, and fresh aspects of which are still being exposed today, at

Reprinted from *Japan Quarterly* 8 (1961): 394–402.

the Eichmann trial? It is intolerably depressing to think that the same people who carved such poignant words of affection on those gravestones also perpetrated—or at least permitted—the massacre.

Do all human beings, then, have the possibility of these two extremes? One suspects that they do. Miss Inukai Michiko, who was present during part of the Eichmann trial, tells the following story:

"An American woman reporter sitting next to me prodded my elbow just as the trial was about to begin. 'Oh, he's only an ordinary man!' she said. Her face betrayed a certain disappointment."

"Things would be much simpler," Miss Inukai adds, "if he were a devil.... That is the terrifying thing; that he is, indeed, no devil, but an ordinary man. It is because he is the kind of ordinary man you might see anywhere that Eichmann is far more devilish than any devil."

The Japanese army itself committed atrocities "far more devilish than any devil" on the Chinese mainland and in the Philippines. The same factor that, under a particular set of conditions, can make the "ordinary man" commit unparalleled cruelty—the ordinary man who, leading the humdrum life of the ordinary citizen, would probably be an ideal husband and father—undoubtedly lurks within all human beings. Among members of the Nazi S.S. that I have met personally there were those whose character and abilities would have given them an honorable place among the elite of whatever society they found themselves in.

Yet despite this, many Japanese, when they see horrifying scenes of mass slaughter in films of the last war, feel with a shudder "a Japanese could never do such things." I do not believe one can dismiss this as merely Japanese hypocrisy or complacency. It is connected rather, I suspect, with a feeling many Japanese have about the particular quality of European reactions—with the opinion, often expressed privately, that Westerners are egotistic and unrelenting. If I may quote from an essay I wrote recently for a newspaper:

> The European is far more conscious of the distinction between friend and foe than the Japanese. This is true not only of everyday life. Religious and political conflict and struggles, for instance—as during the Reformation and the age of the Nazis—have time and again driven men into a world of terrible hatred. The Japanese are by contrast far more willing to compromise. The reverse side of the willingness to compromise, however, is half-heartedness. For example, love as portrayed in Western literature is deep, intense, and full-blooded in a way that leaves far behind the gentle pathos of its Japanese counterpart; it has its roots in the very nature of Western civili-

zation, with its thoroughgoing loves and hates. My memories of life in Europe are an odd compound of inexhaustible goodwill and kindness on the one hand and an implacable severity in human relationships on the other. To study this question further one would have, I suspect, to go back to the very bedrock and mainsprings of the cultures of East and West.

I hope sometime to tackle this vast theme in a scholarly fashion, from the viewpoint of the cultural anthropologist or the cultural historian. So far, however, I am not qualified to do so. All I can attempt here is to outline the ideas that have long been germinating in my mind as hints or as possible pointers to a working hypothesis for the academic solution of the question, and to invite the criticisms of those who have themselves been brought up inside Western civilization. I would point out here that I have striven to keep what I write, whether dealing with Western or Japanese civilization, free from all personal, emotional, value judgments.

About the same time that I published the piece from which I quote above, the critic Takeyama Michio wrote something relevant to the question in "The City of the Barbed Wire," an article in the July, 1961, issue of the periodical *Bungei Shunjū* recording his impressions of Berlin today.

"Europe is part of Christendom, yet no trace of the Sermon on the Mount is to be found in these parts. The history of Europe affords few examples of forgiveness towards the enemy. Nor were the mighty humble before men. . . . The Christian peoples have persisted in blatant preying on the weak. In what sense, and to what extent, one wonders, are the people of Europe Christians?"

I have myself remarked before on the lack of tolerance to be found in practice in the history of Christianity, supposedly the religion of love, and of Christian civilization. This lack of tolerance, however, is not peculiar to Christianity. Hebraism, from which it sprang, as well as Islam—which draws on the springs of Hebraism and Christianity and worships a supreme god of the same generic type—both have elements in common with it; and despite the merciless struggle between the rival creeds, the characteristics with which each has stamped its own civilization all bear a family likeness.

God, teaches Christianity, is love. Yet in actual history the Christian God in whose name the witch hunts, the Inquisition, and the suppression of the Copernican theory took place was the same jealous God that sent thunder and hail to destroy the unbeliever and the heretic. During the conquest of the New World, Cortes converted the Aztec king Cuauhtemoc to Catholicism by force, and Pizarro did the same to Atahuallpa, emperor of the Incas—then both the converts were put to death. One cannot read any history of the Crusades or of the Orders of Knighthood without noticing the resemblances to the expeditions of Mahomet, made with sword and the Koran in his hand, to protect the cause of Allah against the infidel. Such things are far from the doctrine of, at least, the New Testament—from the spirit of Christ who said, "Love thine enemy."

Perhaps, then, one should seek the source of the fierce intolerance and implacable hatred of the foe that pervades European history not so much in Christianity as in some broader and deeper cultural stratum that created the whole spiritual framework of which Christianity is but one section—a cultural stratum which, one suspects, formed the nature of Christianity and its civilization with a force far mightier and more overwhelming than that of any reforms of a single prophet of Nazareth.

To turn back to the case of the Germans, one at once comes up against the Germanism which the Nazis extolled as the peculiar tradition of the German people prior to Christianity. Woden (Odin), the god of the storm who occupied chief place in the pantheon of the Germanic tribes at the time of Tacitus, together with Thor, the god of thunder, and Tyr, whom the Romans identified with Mars, were all gods of war. The very name Woden, the principal god who led the phantom *wütendes Heer* of dead warriors as they thundered through the stormy night skies, derives from a word signifying "rage" or "frenzy" and corresponding to the modern German word *wüten*. Nor is this quality confined to myths and legends and heroic epics: the strains of battle and victory, defeat and revenge echo throughout the whole history of the formation of the Germanic peoples. In time, the Christian cross—like the Nazi swastika later—was to become the symbol that spurred on the knights of the Middle Ages into the Holy Wars.

The tough, untamed quality of the ancient Germans is still today—as is their language—deeply rooted in the psychologies of the peoples of Western civilization. Even in England, one form of punishment until the comparatively recent past consisted of tying the criminal between two horses which then tore him apart, while as late as the reign of Elizabeth I it is said that a crowd castrated a man in the streets of London. Even the thoroughgoing way in which the British, till the beginning of this century, repressed any resistance from the peoples of the colonies of the British Empire betrays, one suspects, something of the same quality.

However, the Germanic peoples and their culture do not, any more than Christianity, supply the sole mainstream of modern Western civilization. The civilization of Greece, as it was transmitted through the legacies of the Roman Empire, forms one of the bases of Western culture alongside Hebraism. One cannot, in particular, understand modern thought and the modern outlook since the Renaissance without tracing its genealogy back to classical Greek civilization, a civilization which saw a unique flowering on the bed of the ancient civilization that stretched from the Orient to the Mediterranean.

One thing that can be said for certain, though, is that Greeks and Romans alike belonged in their language to the same Indo-European family as the Germans, the "barbarian tribes of the North," and that originally they spread across the southwestern portion of the Eurasian continent from a common source. There is no space here to discuss the academic question of where precisely this source lay, but the Indo-European peoples who in the first half of the second millenium before Christ began a mass move with their horses and chariots into Mesopotamia to the south, Iran and India to the east, and the Mediterranean and Danube areas to the west show marked common features in the breeds of horses, the form of their chariots and their gods of the chariot; and their culture exhibits many of the military qualities—the mobility and the organizing power—to be seen in the warlike nomadic peoples of historical times.

Now if one considers the derivation of our modern cultures very roughly in terms of spheres or strata of culture, the basic culture of the Indo-European peoples who have created modern European civilization cannot be called agrarian in the sense in which the word applies to the peoples of the Japanese archipelago or of Southeastern Asia. Their living habits put them closer to the nomadic peoples of Inner Asia than to the rice-cultivating peoples of the damp, rainy regions. They slaughtered large numbers of domestic animals, tanned their hides, spun their fur, made dairy products of every kind and even blood sausages, and cut and ate their meat with knives and forks, while their dress was derived from the horseman's trousers and narrow-sleeved jacket. Moreover, the Semitic peoples who gave birth to Judaism, Christianity, and Islam were still more dependent on animal breeding than the Indo-Europeans.

If one looks at ethnic culture in this way, as a number of layers piled on each other in chronological sequence, then Hebraism and the cultures of the Indo-Europeans, including the Greeks, Romans, and Germanic peoples, will be seen to have a common underlying basic stratum. I do not, of course, believe that the breeding of animals originally grew up on the grasslands in the interior of the Eurasian continent independently of and parallel with the agricultural culture of the southern fringes of the continent. The nomadic peoples and their characteristic culture as they appear in history were not born, I believe, until later than the agrarian culture of the Orient. Even so, it is undeniable, even assuming that the discovery of animal raising was made in sedentary agricultural settlements, that once the nomadic people who relied on large flocks of animals for the greater part of their livelihood began to range over the boundless plains in search of grass and water, a cultural sphere was formed that was essentially different from that of the older agricultural society.

Nor were the differences confined to those, such as food, clothing and housing, which were dictated by differing environments and subsistences. The preeminence of the male in social and economic life led to a strong patriarchal authority, and the nomadic peoples, in contrast to the farming peoples who looked to the earth as the mother of generation and fertility, came to look on the heavens that reigned above their heads as in themselves constituting the supreme male god. Where the view of the world held by the farming peoples was non-rational or supra-rational, that of the nomadic peoples tended towards a coherent, monotheistic belief in a clear-cut providence ordering the whole world. The stubborn religious fight put up by the Jewish prophets who insisted that there was no god but Jehovah and ordered the destruction of the idols of Astarte, Baaloth, and other Mother Goddesses was surely a challenge aimed by the monotheists at polytheistic heresies.

The belief in a single providential Heaven of this kind can hardly have been unconnected with what they saw about them in their daily lives, as they wandered without let across the vast plains through the dry, clear air, constant witness to the orderly revolution of the crystalline arc of heaven. And I suspect that these cultural characteristics, which were common—so far as one can judge from historical sources—to all the nomadic peoples of the Eurasian continent, have given Western culture its present nature, even after a historical process which entailed multiple fission into Hebraism, Hellenism, Germanism, and the like.

This cultural-historical interpretation of Western civilization is reinforced still further by comparison with other, different cultural spheres. At a discussion on how the civilizations of Europe and Africa could understand each other, held at the Round-Table Conference on Civilization in Rome in February, 1960, the poet Leopold Sedar Senghor, later President of the Republic of Senegal, pointed up vividly the differences between the culture of the white man and the black man in terms of their different attitudes to the world and things. In Europe, he said, men were creatures of will, fighters, birds of prey, and as such they distinguished clearly between things. Black people, however, lived in a primitive night, dark as their skins. Black people did not *see* others, they felt them, for in the night all elements are alive.

This contrast with the civilization of Europe, made by a member of a culture born out of the dense depths of the vegetation of Negro Africa, awakes a considerable sympathetic response in us Japanese, who carry on an agrarian culture in common with Southeast Asia. The volume of the *Nihon Shoki* (*The Chronicles of Japan*) dealing with the Age of Gods says that, before the descent of the August Grandson Ninigi-no-Mikoto, the "Middle Land Where Reeds Grow Luxuriantly"—i.e., the Japanese archipelago—was filled with "numerous deities which shone with a lustre like that of fireflies, and evil deities which buzzed like flies. There were also trees and herbs all of which could speak."[1]

This land of animistic *kami*, in which men and Nature were indistinguishable, is a far cry from that other realm where the bright light of day illumines so clearly the distinction between the self and others; it is a perfect specimen of a "night where all elements are alive."

The Buddhist culture from the continent which was to be superimposed on this cultural foundation was in itself the product of distinctly non-Aryan sources. In his *Travel Diary of a Philosopher* (1919), Count H. Keyserling declares that the phenomenology of Buddhism, which stresses the never-ending cycle of change to which all things are subject, could only have been understood against a background such as that of India, with its terrifyingly swift, never-ceasing proliferation of vegetable life. Buddhism, he says, is the gospel of the tropics, the doctrine of vegetable growth. Such cultural traditions, one feels sure, still live on in the feelings and actions of the Japanese today.

Here we must turn again to the love of compromise and the pliability—in a different light, the lack of consistency—of the Japanese which I referred to at the outset, and compare it with the tenacity and intolerance of the European. My knowledge of European society is, of course, imperfect, but it is safe to assert that there, even among close friends, likes and dislikes, "yes" and "no," are expressed with great clarity; one may hunt dictionaries of European languages in vain for the equivalent of, say, *haragei* ("belly-play"). As a result of this Western way of doing things, the other man may sometimes be temporarily put out—yet the question is thereby got over with, leaving no particular aftermath.

A Japanese, however, even when he means "no," will sometimes equivocate because the other's expression, he fancies, seems to require it. And that strange phenomenon, the "Japanese smile," though it may smooth over the surface at the time, is often the prelude to an unpleasant, ambiguous kind of relationship. Even where, for a European, soundly berating someone in a loud voice would be an end to the matter, for the Japanese it can often be the beginning of a new question. To the former, the way the Japanese feels is incomprehensible; to the latter, Europeans do not show enough respect for others' feelings in their speech.

Whatever happens in theory, one wonders how far ideas such as "hate the crime but not the man" or "virtue and vice go hand in hand" play any part in actual society and politics in Europe. On this score, at any rate, Japanese society is astonishingly lenient. For instance, even though a man may have committed many times what amounts to fraud—a crime, according to accepted social ideas—yet if he has virtues and abilities in other spheres he may yet be esteemed socially as a leader in the political, financial, or even sometimes the academic world. A man fired for embezzling public funds may very shortly be taken on by the organization next door. I do not know to what extent similar phenomena occur in Occidental society, but the fate of individual leaders at times of serious political conflict—for example, in the totalitarian states— suggests that society as a whole is less easygoing, more rigorous and demanding.

Where the question of war crimes is concerned, for instance, the Germans' feelings are far less pliable than those of the Japanese. No sooner had the war ended than the Japanese could switch quite effortlessly from talk of "American and British devils" to talk of "repentance of the whole nation." The atrocities the Japanese committed on the neighboring continent, too, were quite forgotten in ten years or so. The occasional dragging to light of such matters in books or magazines is frowned on as somehow being an unnecessary reopening of one's fellows' wounds.

In Germany, however, the courthouse where the Nürnberg trials were held was defaced with constantly recurring swastikas. On the other hand, only recently—a full fifteen years after the war—some 200,000 feet of film about the Nazis have been collected in West Germany with the aim of compiling a new documentary tracing the history of Germany's own crimes. Again, on May 11, the West German television station broadcast an hour-long film, entitled "Trial of the Executioner," on the life of Eichmann. "All these things," the announcer pointed out repeatedly as scene of horror succeeded scene of horror, "were done in the name of the German people."

The swastikas and the self-accusation—these two contrasting phenomena reveal very clearly the nature of Western civilization: the proud stubbornness, and the insistence on pursuing every question through to its logical conclusion. The two things almost certainly spring from the same cultural roots.

There have been quite a few well-known writers in modern Japan, Tanizaki Junichirō and Nagai Kafū among them, who fell under the spell of European civilization in their youth, only to return to things Japanese in the latter half of their lives. They respect and envy Western culture for its indomitable will to live and its fierce affirmation of human existence, yet in the end the pace proves too much for them, or they react against the unrelentingness, the excessive emphases of Western culture, and come to seek spiritual relief in an "Oriental" tranquillity. In the European's frantic pursuit of life, on the other hand, one senses an almost terrifying thoroughness.

A man in whose life I feel a strong interest, and who seems to me to stand for the typical European, is Heinrich Schliemann, the first to excavate Troy and Mycenae. Born the son of a poor pastor in a small village in northern Germany, he was excited as a child by the legends of knights, giants, and ghosts that clung to the old tombs in the village and the ruins of its medieval castle, and he conceived an extraordinary fascination for the unknown and the mysterious. Hearing the Homeric tales of the Trojan wars from his father, he decided at the age of eight that the mighty walls of Troy must still survive somewhere, and resolved that he would one day discover them for himself. Through a life full of difficulties in which he worked as shop assistant, steward on a ship, and messenger for a trading company among other things, he continued his studies in the hope of realizing his childhood dream. Finally, after building up a fortune as a merchant, he was at last able, in his late forties, to take spade in hand and set about making his life's dream come true.

The account of his thwarted love for the girl Minna—described quite briefly in the first chapter of his autobiography—strikes the reader with a purity of heart and a nobility that the *hakanai koi* ("fleeting love") of the Japanese language cannot express. The warm sympathy that germinated between the two as children led to a vow, made with a childish simplicity, to love and be faithful to each other forever; thereafter, the hope that Minna would accompany him in his excavations of Troy was a constant spur to his enthusiasm. When, after many years of separation, he achieved economic independence and proposed to Minna, he learned that she had married another man only a few days previously. In Schliemann's plain, unadorned account of this episode, commonplace in itself, I seem to sense something fundamental to the nature of all Europeans. In the fact that it was this same German people that produced Hitler and Eichmann I found the first incentive to write this article.

I am well aware that the above brief notes may be criticized as betraying a one-sided view. I have merely compared the culture of the West with that of the Japanese and deliberately avoided such words as "Oriental culture," since this involves too many different streams. I have not mentioned how a long history of conflict and struggle within a comparatively limited area distinguishes the civilization of Europe from that of America and has helped give it its characteristically uncompromising quality. Nor must it be forgotten that what I have lumped together as "Western civilization" itself includes strong currents of pre-Indo-European cultures from the Orient and the Mediterranean. I have not touched on the differences among individuals common to both East and West, and I foreswore from the outset any attempt to discuss the "human nature" common to all mankind in any part of the world. It goes without saying, moreover, that national character, patterns of culture, and the like are not eternally fixed and immutable. Even so, even after all these points have been taken into consideration, it seems to me, at least, that the individual characteristics of the cultures of both Europe and Japan harbor certain basic elements that will not easily prove susceptible to change.

NOTE

1. Aston's translation.

Japanese Value Orientations and Culture Change

WILLIAM CAUDILL

HARRY A. SCARR

This article presents an analysis of Japanese value orientations based on data gathered in 1955 through use of a theory and a method coming from the work of Florence Kluckhohn. It is appropriate that our analysis of the Japanese data follows the recent publication (Kluckhohn and Strodtbeck 1961) of a thorough discussion of her research.

The motivation for our investigation was threefold. First, information was desired about Japanese value orientations in order to help provide cultural perspective on the symptoms of psychiatric patients and types of treatment in Japan (see Caudill 1959, 1961). Second, we wished to obtain data which would give some indications of the directions of change taking place in Japanese value orientations. Third, we hoped to build on the work of Kluckhohn by attempting to make a further contribution to the theoretical understanding and measurement of variations in value orientations. We were especially sensitized to the question of systematic variation because, although such variation exists at any point in a culture's history, the question becomes a crucial one during periods of apparent culture change as in Japan today.

JAPANESE BACKGROUND

In the ten years since Japan regained full sovereignty in 1952, the country has been subject to many political and social upheavals, and this period was preceded by the American Occupation, which was a massive effort to bring about cultural change. Although the

Reprinted from *Ethnology* 1 (1962):53–91.

changes under the Occupation were essentially imposed from the outside, they were not dissimilar in their thoroughness to the re-alignment of the structure of Japanese society which took place in the late nineteenth century under the Meiji Reformation, ending 250 years of comparative cultural stability during the Tokugawa period. Yet the Tokugawa period began early in the seventeenth century only after the strenuous efforts, in succession, of Oda No-bunaga, Toyotomi Hideyoshi, and Tokugawa Ieyasu to unify the country. Looking back at these transition periods of rapid cultural realignment, one can say, "Yes, things changed at that point under Hideyoshi, Ieyasu, Meiji, MacArthur, and are even changing in the present as a result of the struggles between the Socialists and the Liberal Democrats." But, one wonders, what in such realignments is truly new, and what is essentially the repetition of old ways of behaving in different forms?

Western writers on Japan have often been accused of over-emphasizing "traditional" aspects of Japanese culture, and of not attending to the great changes that were taking place. Benedict (1946), in particular, has been criticized for placing too much emphasis on the hierarchical structuring of interpersonal relations, the importance of obligations over human feelings, and the role of the family over that of the individual. Reischauer (1957), however, stresses many of the same things as does Benedict, and, indeed, so do quite a few Japanese writers, e.g., Kawashima (1948) and Takagi (1957).

After World War II there was a widespread popular reaction in Japan against "traditional" values and what was called "feudalis-tic" behavior, and a rather loudly voiced enthusiasm for "hu-manism" and "democracy." Writers often expressed the belief that the old values were outmoded, and, although the determined pleas-ure-seeking of a not inconsiderable proportion of the population was viewed with some alarm, it was felt that the country was at least moving toward individualism and democracy (see Kato 1959; Stoetzel 1955).

In more recent years, there have been a number of attempts to describe the blending or clashing of "traditional" and "modern" values and behavior patterns in postwar Japan. Dore (1958, 1959) has written excellent accounts for both urban and rural life. Matsu-moto (1960) has made a careful analysis of public opinion polls, which is especially relevant as background for this article, as is also the discussion by Pelzel and Kluckhohn (1957) of changing Japa-nese values. Although the general picture is still unclear, there does seem to be agreement that Japan is not moving evenly in all spheres of behavior toward individualism, but rather has retained a strong emphasis on the importance of the group, even though this may be expressed today in humanistic and socialistic terms instead of in terms of filial obligation and loyalty to one's superiors.

This article takes a position similar to that in other recent studies, but we feel that a certain lack of clarity evident in the literature may, in part, be a result of the duality inherent in the contrast between "traditional" and "modern" values and in the assumption that such values are necessarily blending or clashing. It seems to us that a theory of variations in value orientations may help to bring greater clarity to the problem of culture change by avoiding the trap of either-or propositions while still allowing for systematic and empirical treatment of data.

THEORY OF VALUE ORIENTATIONS

Kluckhohn develops the idea that *ordered variation* in value orientations is a key factor in the understanding of any culture. She defines value orientations as follows: "Value orientations are complex but definitely patterned (rank-ordered) principles, resulting from the transactional interplay of three analytically distinguishable elements of the evaluative process—the cognitive, the affective, and the directive elements—which give order and direction to the ever-flowing stream of human acts and thoughts as these relate to the solution of 'common human problems' " (Kluckhohn and Strodtbeck 1961: 4).

Three major assumptions underline Kluckhohn's classification of value orientations. The first is that there is a limited number of common human problems for which all people at all times must find solutions. The second is that there is a limited range of variability in the solutions to problems. The third assumption is that all variations of recurring solutions are, with varying degrees of emphasis, present in all societies at all times. There will be, therefore, in every society not only a dominant value orientation for each of the common human problems, but also one or more variant value orientations for each problem. Moreover, the theory emphasizes that variant value orientations are not only permitted, but are required in any society for its successful functioning. It is the dynamics of the relation between dominant and variant value orientations that provides, for us, the flexibility and special usefulness of this theory.

Kluckhohn, to date, has defined five common human problems for which people in any society must find solutions. These five problems concern the nature of man himself, his relation to nature and supernature, his place in the flow of time, the modality of human activity, and the relationship man has to his fellow human beings. The names given to the areas of value orientation relating to each of these problems are *human nature, man-nature, time, activity,* and *relational* (see Kluckhohn and Strodtbeck 1961: 10–20, 340–344).

In the schedule devised to gather data on value orientations in five cultures in the Southwestern United States, Kluckhohn and her co-workers tested for four of the five areas of orientation, omitting items on *human nature*. Because the original schedule was adapted for use in Japan, we shall not refer again to the area of human nature. Also, although Kluckhohn's theory postulates a three-position ranking of solutions in each area of value orientation, the original schedule provided for only a two-position ranking on the items in the *activity* area. The items in the *activity* area were included in the Japanese schedule but will not be analyzed here. Our analysis will concentrate upon the three value-orientation areas —*relational, time,* and *man-nature*—for which data are available on a three-position ranking.

For handling the Japanese data, we arranged the main theoretical concepts and terms in an order appropriate for our procedures, and hereinafter we shall use these concepts and terms as they are defined in the following paragraphs. Our definitions are essentially the same as those of Kluckhohn and Strodtbeck (1961), but we have, in several respects, attempted to build on the types of analyses presented by them, particularly in our elaboration of the concept of *distance* between value orientations and the implications of this for cultural change.

We define a *value-orientation area* as coinciding with one of Kluckhohn's five common human problems. Specifically, we shall deal with the *relational* area, the *time* area, and the *man-nature* area, which we shall abbreviate, respectively, as R, T, and MN (see Table 1).

In each area, Kluckhohn postulates that there are three solutions to the common human problem being considered, and that, although all solutions are always present, the order in which they are emphasized may vary from one society to another, from one social class to another, from one generation to another, and so on. We shall designate each of the three solutions to a common human problem as a *position* in a value-orientation area.

The three positions in the *relational* value-orientation area are Lineal, Collateral, and Individualistic, abbreviated, respectively, as L, C, and I. Lineal relations are those that stress the descent from parent to child. Authority passes, for example, from the father to the eldest son in a tight hierarchical arrangement. In behavior spheres other than family life, Lineal relations emphasize superior and subordinate positions in the exercise of authority. The familial basis for Collateral relations is found in the ties among siblings. In the exercise of power and the making of decisions, Collaterality is exhibited in a preference for general group discussion until consensus is reached. Individualism is rooted in the uniqueness (whether physical, psychological, or cultural) which each person has when compared with another. Practically speaking, an emphasis on Individualism means that each person essentially makes his own decisions and acts on these in a manner relatively independent of other persons.

The three positions in the *time* value-orientation area are Past, Present, and Future, abbreviated, respectively, as Pa, Pr, and Fu. These terms scarcely need elaboration. Kluckhohn illustrates the ordering of these positions by noting that Spanish Americans emphasize the Present, Chinese (in earlier historical periods) emphasized the Past, and Americans emphasize the Future.

The three positions in the *man-nature* value orientation area are Subjugation-to-Nature, Harmony-with-Nature, and Mastery-over-Nature, abbreviated, respectively, as S, W, and O. The Subjugation-to-Nature position involves a feeling of fatalism; there is little man can do about such problems as fire, storm, and illness except to accept them as inevitable. In the Harmony-with-Nature position there is no real separation between man and nature, and a sense of completeness and well-being derives from their unity. In the Mastery-over-Nature position, natural forces of all kinds are to be overcome; rivers are to be spanned; illness is to be controlled; and life is to be lengthened.

Kluckhohn's definition of value orientations, cited earlier, begins with the key statement: "Value orientations are complex but definitely patterned (rank-ordered) principles...." Following this, we define a *value orientation* as a ranking of the positions in a value-orientation area; for example, $I > C > L$ is one of the possible value orientations in the *relational* area. The symbol $>$ indicates that one position is ranked higher than another, thus expressing an order of preference. We shall speak of *first-rank*, *second-rank*, and *third-rank* positions in a value orientation.

In our analysis we shall consider only value orientations which are complete rankings and shall not be concerned with rankings involving ties in positions (called incomplete rankings on Tables 4–13). In the administration of the schedule, the respondent was instructed that he might include ties in his numerical preference ranking of the three alternative solutions given for the life situation represented in each item. Empirically, however, tied rankings were infrequent in the responses from our sample (see Tables 4–13), and also in the data presented by Kluckhohn and Strodtbeck (1961: 416–437). Tied rankings pose interesting theoretical questions, but we shall not consider these in this article.

Six complete rankings are possible for the three positons in the *relational, time,* and *man-nature* value-orientation areas. Thus, using our definition of a value orientation as a ranking of positions in a value-orientation area, the six *value orientations* in each of the three areas in our analysis can be listed as follows:

Relational	Time	Man—nature
I>C>L	Fu>Pr>Pa	O>W>S
I>L>C	Fu>Pa>Pr	O>S>W
L>I>C	Pa>Fu>Pr	S>O>W
L>C>I	Pa>Pr>Fu	S>W>O
C>L>I	Pr>Pa>Fu	W>S>O
C>I>L	Pr>Fu>Pa	W>O>S

The respondents in the sample did not, of course, indicate their value-orientation preferences in this way. There was no identification of items in the schedule by value-orientation area, and no identification of positions was given. Each *item* merely presented a hypothetical life situation followed by three alternative solutions which the respondent was asked to rank numerically (including the opportunity for ties) in order of preference. In coding the items for analysis, this numerical ranking was translated into a ranking of value-orientation positions, thus yielding the respondent's value orientation for that item. The *schedule* consisted simply of a series of items; its construction is discussed in full by Kluckhohn and Strodtbeck (1961: 77–104).

We come now to our final conceptual tool for dealing with variations in value orientations. In addition to speaking of the six value orientations from a single item as different (the one from the other), we are also going to speak about the *distance* between them. By distance between two value orientations we mean *the smallest number of adjacent position rank reversals required to turn one into the other.*

To illustrate the concept of distance we may refer to Figure 1, which presents the percentage distribution of value orientations in our total sample of 619 respondents on Item R2, Help in Case of Misfortune (see Table 1 and the English text of this item cited below). We shall discuss the logical properties of Figure 1 before turning to the empirical results.

Figure 1: Item R2: Help in Case of Misfortune

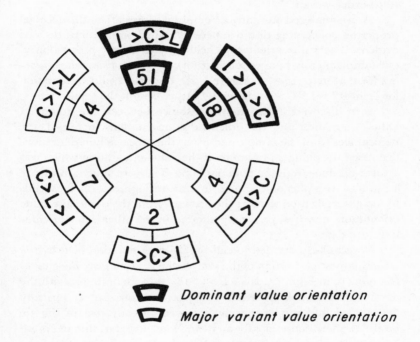

▱ *Dominant value orientation*
▱ *Major variant value orientation*

What is the distance between I > C > L and L > I > C? Starting with I > C > L, we reverse the ranks of C and L, thus obtaining the orientation I > L > C (which in Figure 1 lies between I > C > L and L > I > C); then, working with I > L > C, we reverse the ranks of I and L, thus obtaining the orientation L > I > C. Since two reversals were required in this process, we say that I > C > L and L > I > C are a *two-distance* apart. Note that I > C > L and I > L > C are a *one-distance* apart, as also are I > L > C and L > I > C. This concept of distance applies to all possible pairs of orientations in Figure 1 and makes statements such as the following meaningful: "C > L > I is further from I > C > L than I > L > C is from I > C > L"; or, "L >

C > I is further from I > C > L than is any other value orientation."

As a convention, we call orientations which are a one-distance from the orientation under consideration *first-order variants;* those which are at a two-distance we call *second-order variants;* and that orientation which is at a three-distance, the farthest possible, we call the *third-order variant.* Thus, from the point of view of I > C > L in Figure 1, C > I > L and I > L > C are first order variants: C > L > I and L > I > C are second-order variants; and L > C > I is the third-order variant.

As we analyzed our data, an empirical correlate to these logical properties concerning distance between value orientations became evident. The value orientation held by the largest proportion of our sample on any item we decided to call the *dominant value orientation* for that item (thus, in Figure 1, the dominant value orientation for Item R2 is I > C > L, chosen by 51 per cent of the total sample). We then discovered that, as the distance between the dominant value orientation and the other value orientations increased, the percentages from the sample endorsing the other value orientations decreased, reaching a minimum at the value orientation which was a three-distance from the dominant one. The percentages in Figure 1 illustrate this phenomenon, as do those in Figures 2–4. This leads to the generalization that, as the distance from the dominant value orientation increases, percentages found in the other value orientations decrease.

We similarly decided to call the value orientation held by the second largest proportion of the sample the *major variant value orientation* (which, in Figure 1, is I > L > C). By these definitions, both the dominant and major variant value orientations are empirically determined and might conceivably occur as any two of the six possible value orientations for an item. Note, however, that in Figure 1 the major variant value orientation, I > L > C, is also one of the two logically deduced first-order variants, I > L > C and C > I > L, of the dominant value orientation, I > C > L. This follows necessarily if our generalization concerning the relation of distance and percentage distribution is true. Figures 2–4 reveal that, for all eighteen items analyzed, the major variant value orientation coincides, in fact, with one of the logically deduced first-order variants of the dominant value orientation.

THE INSTRUMENT AND THE SAMPLE

The instrument we used was a schedule devised by Kluckhohn and her co-workers (see Kluckhohn and Strodtbeck 1961: 77–120).

The final version of Kluckhohn's schedule consisted of twenty-two items, while the Japanese schedule had twenty-three items, retain-

Table 1. Items from the Japanese Language Form of the Value-Orientation Schedule Used for Analysis in this Article

Item Series Number (this number is the same as that used in Kluckhohn and Strodtbeck, 1961 [hereafter K&S], p. 140)	Place of Item in the Sequence of Administration in the Japanese Form of the Schedule	Short Title
Relational items:		
R1	2	Bridge Building (adapted from K&S, p.80, Well Arrangements item)
*R2	7	Help in Case of Misfortune
*R3	8	Family Work Relations
*R4	10	Choice of Delegate
*R5	13	Wage Work
R6	21	Personal Property Inheritance (adapted from K&S, p. 88, Livestock Inheritance item)
R7	22	Land Inheritance
Time items:		
T1	3	Child Training
*T2	5	Expectations about Change
*T3	12	Philosophy of Life
*T4	15	Ceremonial Innovation
T5	23	Water Arrangements (adapted from K&S, pp. 89–90, Water Allocation item)
†T6	9	New Factory
Man-Nature items:		
MNI	4	Crop Damage (adapted from K&S, pp. 81–82, Livestock Dying item)
MN2	6	Facing Conditions
*MN3	11	Use of Fields
MN4	14	Belief in Control
*MN5	18	Length of life

*In the text, these nine items are given more intensive analysis than the others.

†This item was not used by Kluckhohn in the final form of her schedule, but it was used in the Japanese form of the schedule.

ing an additional item in the *time* area from an earlier version of the Kluckhohn schedule. The twenty-three items in the Japanese schedule were divided among the value-orientation areas as follows: seven *relational* items, six *time* items, five *man-nature* items, and five *activity* items. For the reasons noted above we have dropped the five *activity* items.

The eighteen items analyzed here are listed in Table 1. The content of several of the items was slightly altered from that in the Kluckhohn schedule, but such alteration was minimal and consisted, for example, of substituting the problem of bridge building for that of well arrangements, since bridge building was a more realistic situation in Japan. In the sequence of administration, items from the various value-orientation areas were distributed throughout the sequence, and within items in a particular area the three value-orientation positions represented by the three solutions for a life situation were systematically rotated.

The Japanese schedule contained a face sheet for the collection of background characteristics of the respondent, instructions for the ranking of the alternative solutions (including the allowance for ties), and a set of boxes for each item in which the respondent placed his numerical rankings. Space limitations make it impossible to give the full English text of the eighteen items from the Japanese schedule which are analyzed here. (It is available from the authors upon request.) The following English text for three items, one in each of the value-orientation areas, will, however, give a feeling for the content of the schedule. The pre-defined value-orientation positions and the item series numbers are enclosed in brackets to indicate that they did not appear on the form of the schedule given to the respondent. The number to the right of the title indicates the place of the item in the sequence of administration:

[R2] *Help in Case of Misfortune* 7

A man had a crop failure, or, let us say, had lost most of his cattle. He and his family had to have help from someone if they were going to get through the winter. There are different ways of getting help, as in the following.

[Coll] Would it be best if he depended on his brothers and sisters or other relatives all to help him out as much as each one could?

[Ind] Would it be best for him to try to raise the money on his own, without depending upon anybody?

[Lin] Would it be best for him to go to a boss or to his head house (*honke*), and ask for help until things got better?

[T6] *New Factory* 9

People in a community heard that there might be a new factory built very close to where they lived. When the people talked about this they said different things.

[Pres] Some people say they never know about these things. It may turn out to be a good thing or it may not. They want to wait and see how it works out.

[Fut] Some people are all for the factory and do all they can themselves to get it brought in. They feel that new things like this are always good and will bring improvements to the whole region.

[Past] Some people do not want to have the factory moved into the area. They say that it will change things and people too much. They don't want to upset the old ways.

[MN2] *Facing Conditions* 6

There are three different ways of thinking how God (or Buddha) is related to man and to nature. The word nature means the weather and all other natural conditions which influence the harvest. Here are three possible ways of thinking about this.

[With] God and people work together all the time, and all the conditions which make the crops and animals good or bad depend upon whether people do the proper things to keep themselves in harmony with their God and with the forces of nature.

[Over] God does not directly use his power to affect the growth of crops or animals. It is up to the people themselves to figure out the ways conditions change and to try hard to find the ways of controlling them.

[Subj] Just how God will use his power over all the conditions which affect the growth of crops and animals cannot be known by man. It is useless for people to think they can change conditions. The best way is to take conditions as they come and do as well as one can.

During the fall of 1954, the Kluckhohn schedule was translated into Japanese, using as a model the Japanese translation which had been made by Mrs. Kimiko Hara under the direction of Professor Seiichi Izumi of the University of Tokyo. The schedule was then given to a Japanese scholar who had had nothing to do with the translation, and he translated the Japanese schedule back into English. The results of this check were encouraging since the translation from Japanese was almost the same, considered word for word, as the original English version (on this problem see Kluckhohn 1960).

The procedure followed in administering the schedule was to use senior high schools (contacts were made originally through the Ministry of Education) and to obtain material from twelfth grade students (who, on the average, were eighteen years of age) by group administration in the classroom. After the students had completed their schedules, fresh schedules were distributed, and the students were asked to have their parents fill these out and return them to the school within a week. We specifically asked the girls to have their mothers fill out the schedules, and asked the boys to have their fathers do so. We requested the students not to prompt their parents in this task. There are several reasons for believing that the students complied with this request: first, and most cogently, the most significant differences we obtained were between generations (see Tables 5–23 below); second, scholarly research has considerable prestige in Japan, and there was no indication that the students and parents did not perform their tasks seriously.

During the spring of 1955, a pilot study was carried out with 464 respondents, who were fairly equally distributed by residence in a rural village, a medium-sized city, and a ward area of Tokyo. Through an error in administration, only first choices to the alternative solutions on the items were obtained in the pilot study. This error was corrected in a second study, carried out in the fall of 1955, in which the sample was drawn from three similar, but entirely separate, communities. In this study, utilizing 619 respondents, a ranking of the three positions was obtained for all items. When comparisons were made between the first choices of respondents, the two samples replicated almost exactly. We shall consider here only the results from the second study. The respondents in this study are classified by sex, generation, and place of residence in Table 2.

The first of the three communities selected for study was Ome, a small city (population 55,218 in 1955) located about 25 miles northwest of Tokyo. Here we chose a senior high school drawing its student body largely from farming families residing in nearby villages (79 per cent of the fathers of students in the Ome sample were farmers). The second selection was Chiba (population 198, 116 in 1955), the capital of Chiba Prefecture, located about 20 miles southeast of Tokyo. In the senior high school we chose in Chiba, the students came from economically better-than-average families, but there were no students from well-to-do families. In Tokyo (population in all *ku*, or wards, 6,969,104 in 1955) we chose two senior high schools located in different, but economically broadly similar, areas. The sample of boys and their fathers was obtained in Fukugawa, a downtown (*shitamachi*) working-class area (see Dore 1958). The sample of girls and their mothers was obtained in

Table 2. Distribution of Total Sample of 619 Respondents According to Sex, Generation, and Place of Residence*

	Ome (rural area)		Chiba (city)		Tokyo (metropolis)		Total Three Communities
	Males	Females	Males	Females	Males	Females	
Old	24	38	42	62†	56	55	277
Young†	25	44	58	61	85	69	342
Total	49	82	100	123	141	124	619

*These numerical values are the sub-sample sizes for all percentage distribution tables in which this breakdown of respondents occurs.

†A young respondent is a boy or girl who completed the schedule in his school classroom. An old respondent is a man or woman who completed a schedule brought home to him by a young respondent. Old respondents are almost always (241 out of 277 cases) mothers of young girls or fathers of young boys, in accordance with instructions given to the young respondents.

†There are more old than young respondents among Chiba females, since some of the schedules obtained from young respondents were not usable.

a white collar and working-class part of Shinjuku, a large ward area with an economically highly variegated population.

All of the younger generation in our sample were students in the last year of senior high school; in the older generation, the parents of the students, the average educational level in each of the communities was between eight and nine years of education completed. In regard to religion, which is normally considered more a family than an individual matter in Japan (see Dore 1958; Matsumoto 1960), most respondents gave "none" as their own religion, and overwhelmingly listed "Buddhist" as the family religion. Occupations, pertinent of course only to the older generation, were classified into two types, traditional and modern (see Rosovsky and Ohkawa 1961). Traditional occupations are those which were important in pre-industrial Japan as well as today, e.g., farmers, craftsmen, and small shopkeepers. Modern occupations are those associated with increased industrialization and formal education or technical training, e.g., white collar workers, machine operators in factories, and professionals such as engineers, doctors, and lawyers. The three communities revealed interesting differences in the proportions of traditional and modern occupations. In Ome the major concentration was in traditional occupations (92 per cent of the fathers of sons were farmers). In Tokyo there was an approximately even split between traditional and modern occupations (49 per cent of the fathers of sons were small shopkeepers). In Chiba, only about one-third of the older respondents (32 per cent of the fathers of sons) were in traditional occupations, the remainder (68 per cent, of the fathers of sons) being engaged in modern occupations mostly as white collar or skilled factory workers.

One further characteristic of our sample, length of residence in the community, is especially important in the case of Ome. Among our respondents from both Chiba and Tokyo, the modal length of time which families had lived in the area was six to ten years. In contrast, families from the rural area surrounding Ome city had lived there much longer; among the fathers of sons the modal length of residence was 41 years or more and among the mothers of daughters it was 21 to 25 years. The greater residential stability of males reflects both a family farming system and a marriage pattern in which the wife comes to live in the home of her husband's family. In comparisons of value orientations by place of residence, therefore, we shall think of Ome as more representative of a folk way of life, of Chiba and Tokyo as more representative of an urban way of life.

Prior to the collection of any of the data, the senior author in consultation with his Japanese assistants made predictions for each item on the schedule in terms of the expected dominant value orientation for the total sample. Of the eighteen items analyzed in this article, predictions involving ties in positions were made for six items, and completely ranked predictions were made for twelve items. Table 3 presents the results of the use of two criteria in checking the accuracy of the twelve completely ranked predictions.

The first criterion simply states that if the predicted value orientation is an important one among Japanese, then it should be over-chosen a statistically significant number of times in the total sample. As shown in Table 3, three of the items fail to satisfy this criterion, while nine of them meet it.

The second criterion, though more stringent theoretically, is difficult to deal with in a formal statistical fashion. This criterion requires that if the predictions are true, then no predicted dominant orientation should be other than the empirical dominant orientation or one of its first-order variants. In Table 3, all predicted dominant orientations satisfy this criterion; five are the same as the empirical dominant value orientation, and seven are one of its first order variants (see Figures 2–4 below).

The results presented in Table 3 are encouraging. First, it seems that two of the value-orientation areas are dealt with success-

Table 3. Predicted Dominant Value Orientations and Their
Occurrence in Responses from the Total Sample on Twelve
Items in the Japanese Schedule

Item Number	Predicted Dominant Value Orientations	Did the predicted dominant value orientation occur as a statistically significant proportion of responses from the total sample?*	Did the predicted Dominant Value orientation occur as the empirical dominant value orientation or as one of its first-order variants in responses from the total sample?†
R1	I>L>C	No	Yes
R3	C>I>L	Yes	Yes
R4	I>C>L	Yes	Yes
R5	I>C>L	Yes	Yes
R6	C>I>L	Yes	Yes
T3	Pr>Fu>Pa	Yes	Yes
T4	Pr>Pa>Fu	No	Yes
T5	Fu>Pr>Pa	Yes	Yes
T6	Pr>Fu>Pa	No	Yes
MN1	O>S>W	Yes	Yes
MN3	O>W>S	Yes	Yes
MN4	O>W>S	Yes	Yes

*Assuming that 1/6 of the responses should be the predicted dominant orientation on the basis of chance alone (since there are six ways to rank three positions, completely), a "yes" in this column means that significantly more than 1/6 of the respondents (at the .05 level or better) chose the predicted dominant orientation.

†Defining the value orientation receiving the largest percentage of responses as dominant, and the two orientations adjacent to it on either side as its first-order variants, a "yes" in this column means that the predicted dominant orientation in fact turned out to be one of these three value orientations. With six possible orientations per item, hitting on any one of three pre-defined orientations should occur about 1/2 the time (in the most null case) by chance. Hitting on 12 items out of 12 is a significant result, statistically, by any standard technique, such as the sign test, which might be applied.

fully: the *man-nature* and the *relational*. The accuracy of predictions within each of these areas suggests that our initial grasp of Japanese value orientations was fairly sound. In the *man-nature* area the predictions for each of the three items turned out to be the empirical dominant value orientation. In the *relational* area, the predictions could have been better had not the strength of the Lineal and Collateral positions been underestimated for Items R3, R4, and R5, and overestimated for Items R1 and R6. To see this clearly the reader should examine the percentage distributions for the *relational* items in Table 4. The least success was obtained with predictions in the *time* area. Even in this area, however, the predictions were satisfactory on the basis of the second, and more theoretical, criterion. It is interesting in this connection that Kluckhohn has expressed the opinion that the items designed to test in the *time* orientation area were the least successful in the schedule (Kluckhohn and Strodtbeck 1961: 91).

GENERAL RESULTS

The consensus among respondents is statistically significant for each of the eighteen items (see Table 4). The unevenness of the distribution of responses over the six value orientations from each item, with a sample as large as ours, almost guaranteed such significance. Though this formal characteristic of the overall patterning is an important aspect of our data, we are even more concerned with the generalization discussed earlier under the concept of distance, according to which, in a single item, as the distance between the dominant value orientation and the other value orientations increases, the proportion of the sample endorsing the other value orientations decreases.

The distributions in Table 4 are presented in Figures 2–4 in a form which emphasizes our generalization concerning percentage distribution and distance from the dominant orientation. The generalization holds for Items R1, R2, R4, R5, and R7 from the *relational* area, Items T1, T3, T4, and T5 from the *time* area, and Items MN1, MN2, and MN3 from the *man-nature* area. Of the items departing from the generalization, only Item MN4 involves drastically "misplaced" percentages. Item T2 would not be expected necessarily to behave regularly over the total sample, for it was administered in a different form to the two generations—one version for young respondents and another for old. The "out of line" percentages in Items R3, R6, T6, and MN5 are slight enough to suggest that some minor extraneous characteristic may have caused the deviation. We will now discuss the patterning in each of the value-orientation areas.

The Relational Value-Orientation Area.

Among the seven items in this area, only one—Item R3, Family Work Relations—had the value orientation $C > L > I$ as dominant (49 per cent of the respondents chose it). The major variant value orientation was $C > I > L$, chosen by 23 per cent of the respondents.

Table 4. Percentage Distribution of Value Orientations in Total Sample of 619 Respondents on Eighteen Items in the Schedule

Relational

Item	I>C>L	I>L>C	L>I>C	L>C>I	C>L>I	C>I>L	Incomplete Rankings**	Total Percent*	Significance Level†
R1	[40]‡	15	2	2	4	(33)	3	99	.001
R2	[51]	(18)	4	2	7	14	4	100	.001
R3	11	3	2	9	[49]	(23)	3	100	.001
R4	(25)	12	7	9	16	[27]	4	100	.001
R5	(21)	2	0	1	5	[64]	5	98	.001
R6	[45]	12	5	7	4	(22)	4	99	.001
R7	[32]	13	9	7	10	(24)	4	99	.001

Time

Item	Fu>Pr>Pa	Pr>Fu>Pa	Fu>Pa>Pr	Pa>Fu>Pr	Pr>Pa>Fu	Pa>Pr>Fu	Incomplete Rankings	Total Percent*	Significance Level†
T1	(23)	2	0	2	7	[62]	4	100	.001
T2	(24)	[35]	6	7	8	12	7	99	.001
T3	(21)	3	1	1	8	[62]	4	100	.001
T4	(28)	3	0	4	16	[41]	6	98	.001
T5	[45]	(38)	2	0	1	6	6	98	.001
T6	[65]	8	1	3	2	(13)	6	98	.001

Man-Nature

Item	O>W>S	O>S>W	S>O>W	S>W>O	W>S>O	W>O>S	Incomplete Rankings	Total Percent*	Significance Level†
MN1	(27)	[50]	11	4	0	3	4	99	.001
MN2	(26)	[31]	16	8	5	6	7	99	.001
MN3	[54]	10	3	3	4	(23)	2	99	.001
MN4	[35]	8	4	9	12	(27)	4	99	.001
MN5	[56]	14	5	3	2	(15)	4	99	.001

*By rounding error, total per cent often does not equal 100. †Significance of distribution for each item is based on Kendall's Coefficient of Concordance (W). ‡Dominant value orientation for each item is enclosed in brackets, [ ]; major variant value orientation is enclosed in parentheses, ( ). **Incomplete rankings are responses involving tied ranks (e.g., I>C>L, or Fu>Pr=Pa, or O=S=W).

Thus, 72 per cent of the respondents held a value orientation with Collaterality in a first-rank position—an emphasis which is in line with previous literature on Japanese family life. The unpopularity of orientations with first-rank Lineality in this item suggests a commitment to corporate family effectiveness, rather than to intra-family lineal authority, though this may not have been true in the past. Present Japanese wages and salaries are seldom sufficient to permit an individual to live "by himself." They reflect an under-lying premise that the individual is part of a corporate family unit to which all members who are able contribute financially. Factors such as this may account for the reaction against the tyranny of Lineality in the recent past, and for wishful fantasies of an Indi-vidualistic nature in the present, but they certainly demonstrate the reality of the pressures toward Collaterality today.

Given the intermeshing of the economy of the family with that

Figure 2: Percentage Distribution of Value Orientations for Total Sample of 619 Respondents on *Relational* Items

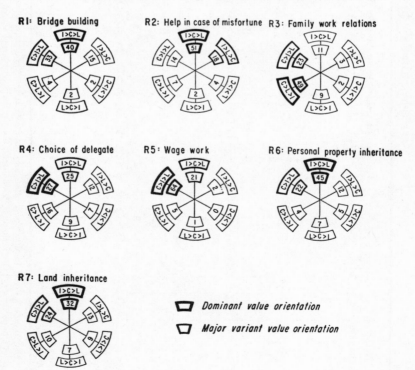

RI: Bridge building   **R2:** Help in case of misfortune   **R3:** Family work relations

R4: Choice of delegate   **R5:** Wage work   **R6:** Personal property inheritance

R7: Land inheritance

Dominant value orientation

Major variant value orientation

of the business world, together with the extent of personal involvement of the employer in the lives of his employees in Japan (Abegglen 1958), it is not surprising that orientations appropriate to family relations are also seen as appropriate to the occupational world. Item R5, Wage Work, dealing specifically with employer-employee relations, has the dominant value orientation C>I>L, chosen by 64 per cent of respondents. The major variant value orientation, I>C>L (chosen by 21 per cent of respondents), points to the commitment of a sizable part of the population to a more contractual, Individualistic view of employer-employee relations. The rejection of first-rank Lineality orientations (chosen by less than 2 per cent of the respondents) is an expression of the postwar Japanese reaction against traditional pseudo-familial work relations, often characterized by the epithet "feudalistic." Though spoken of derisively today, these relations nevertheless continue, in various forms, to be of importance in getting and keeping a job. This may help to account for the bitter smile which often accompanies

Figure 3: Percentage Distribution of Value Orientations
for Total Sample of 619 Respondents on *Time* Items

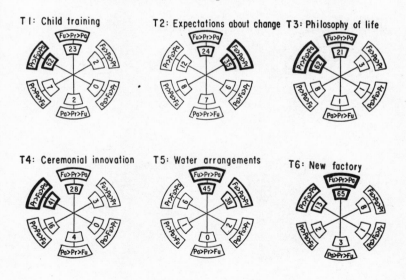

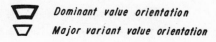

Dominant value orientation
Major variant value orientation

verbal reference to them (see Ishino 1953; Dore 1958; Matsumoto 1960).

Four of the remaining five items in the *relational* area have I > C > L as the dominant value orientation. Two of these, R1 and R2, are concerned with rural activities—Bridge Building and Help in Case of Misfortune. The other two, R6 and R7, deal with inheritance practices—Personal Property Inheritance and Land Inheritance. The first-rank Individualistic responses to Items R1, R2, and R7 suggest that the land reform movement, revivified and accelerated under the Occupation, facilitated the holding of an Individualistic position in at least two respects: first by helping to free the farmer from his dependency as a tenant upon the landlord (thus de-emphasizing Lineality), and, second, by providing him with a buttress against some of the group pressures involved in village life (thus to a degree de-emphasizing both Lineality and Collaterality). Dore (1959: 343–350), however, in discussing the persistence of group ties in village life, makes a point which suggests caution in

Figure 4: Percentage Distribution of Value Orientations for Total Sample of 619 Respondents on *Man-Nature* Items

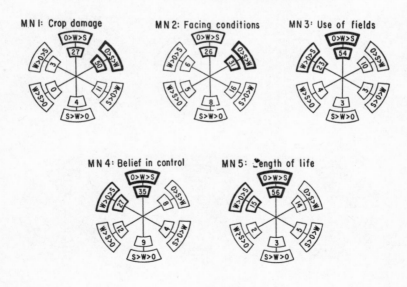

Dominant value orientation
Major variant value orientation

accepting rural Individualism at face value. Village members, he finds, frequently act in a "collateral" manner in order to reach a decision to be "individualistic," especially while participating in "democratic" community meetings.

In the case of Item R6, Personal Property Inheritance, the legal reform initiated during the Occupation, which changed the system of inheritance from one based on primogeniture to one based on a principle of more equitable distribution among the surviving heirs (see Ministry of Justice 1954), may have played a role in accounting for the dominance of the value orientation I > C > L.

In the *relational* area, only on Item R4, Choice of Delegate, did we observe two value orientations in approximately equal competition for dominance, with I > C > L chosen by 25 per cent of the respondents and C > I > L by 27 per cent. This item is directly relevant to the problem of evaluating the decision-making process in Japan discussed by Dore (1959) and referred to above. The conflict between value orientations in the decision-making process occurs not only at the village level but throughout the political sphere in postwar Japan. It is well illustrated by the bitterness with which Socialist party representatives in the National Diet complained, in the spring of 1960, about the "tyranny of the majority" under the Kishi government at the time of the renewal of the security treaty with the United States. This phrase was the euphemism used by the Socialists to express their dislike of a procedure where a decision had not been reached in a Collateral manner prior to being formally endorsed by vote in the National Diet.

More generally, the responses to Item R4, Choice of Delegate, might be considered to summarize value orientations in the *relational* area. Two competing kinds of orientations—those with first-rank Collaterality and those with first-rank Individualism—are, in their interplay, providing the context in which the relations of man to fellow man are being acted out in contemporary Japanese society.

The Time Value-Orientation Area

Two items in the *time* area—T5, Water Arrangements, and T6, New Factory—yielded the dominant value orientation Fu > Pr > Pa. Responses to both items indicate a forward-looking, innovative set toward technological matters. On T5, for instance, a total of 83 per cent of respondents endorse the two orientations with a first-rank Future position. A similar emphasis is found on T6, where 65 per cent of the sample endorses the orientation Fu > Pr > Pa.

In contrast, the dominant orientation for Items T1, T3, and T4 is a first-rank Present orientation: Pr > Fu > Pa. The major variant orientation on these latter three items is, however, Fu > Pr > Pa, which, as noted, is the dominant orientation on T5 and T6. The content of Items T1, T3, and T4 (Child Training, Philosophy of Life, and Ceremonial Innovation) deals with the more emotional, philosophical, and ceremonial aspects of everyday life. With this shift in content, the dominant first-rank Future position in technological matters changes to a dominant first-rank Present position. The expression of this preference in social activities today has its analogue in earlier times. An emphasis on the small pleasures of life, whether these be minor triumphs in social interaction or momentary physical indulgences, has been a continuous theme among the Japanese from Tokugawa times to the present.

Item T2, Expectations about Change, will be discussed more fully in the section dealing with behavior sphere variation since, as mentioned, it was administered in a different form to the two generations. It is of interest here mainly because it reflects the same first-rank Future position as do the technological items. Value orientations in the *time* area may be summarized in terms of two emphases. First, value orientations having a first-rank Future position are pervasive in technological matters and also have considerable potency in social activities. Second, a first-rank Present orientation, Pr > Fu > Pa, is dominant in the social sphere but has little representation in the responses to items concerned with technology.

The Man-Nature Value-Orientation Area

Three value orientations dominate the responses to all five items in the *man-nature* area. Perhaps the most traditional of these three orientations, W > O > S, is the major variant value orientation for Items MN3, MN4, and MN5. The most popular orientation, however, is O > W > S, which is the dominant value orientation for these same three items and is also the major variant value orientation for Items MN1 and MN2. The third orientation, O > S > W, is the dominant orientation for Items MN1 and MN2.

The dominance of the Mastery-over-Nature position in the more workaday aspects of Japanese life is apparent from the content of Items MN1, MN3, and MN5, which concern, respectively, Crop Damage, Use of Fields, and Length of Life. Item MN4, Belief in Control, the most abstractly phrased item in the *man-nature* area, reveals a heavier emphasis upon the Harmony-with-Nature position than do any of the remaining items. The anomalous item in this area is MN2, Facing Conditions, which, though abstractly phrased, shows no great emphasis upon the Harmony-with-Nature position. The strong emphasis on the Mastery-over-Nature position, with a weak but discernible emphasis on the Harmony-with-Nature position, sums up our analysis of the *man-nature* area in the Japan of today.

PATTERNING OF VALUE ORIENTATIONS IN FOUR BEHAVIOR SPHERES

Kluckhohn and Strodtbeck (1961: 24–32) suggest three classes of determinants which exercise a major influence in accounting for variations in value orientations: culture, social structure, and behavior sphere. In their book, the focus was on differences between cultures in accounting for differences in value orientations. Our Japanese material represents the description of a sample from a single culture comparable to those obtained by Kluckhohn and Strodtbeck from each of their groups. The size of our sample permits us to investigate some aspects of the other two classes of determinants—social structure and behavior sphere—in a systematic fashion. Kluckhohn assigns the term *behavior sphere* to those broad categories of activities (economic-technological, religious, recreational, and so forth) which are essential to the functioning of any society. The theory of behavior sphere differentiation has not, as yet, been worked out fully, and we shall use the term in its common-sense meaning.

We began by choosing nine items from the schedule which, from their content, fell most clearly into the four behavior spheres of *family life* (Items R3 and T2), *political life* (Item R4), *occupational life* (Items R2, R5, and MN3), and *religious life* (Items T3, T4, and MN5). Because the schedule was not designed with behavior sphere variation in mind, the items are not distributed evenly over the spheres, either by value-orientation area or by number of items. Thus, while we can say something about all four spheres, it will be with varying degrees of thoroughness. Our second operation was to break down the total sample according to three social structural characteristics: *generation, sex,* and *place of residence.* This breakdown has been presented in Table 2 in conjunction with the description of the sample.

We shall now examine differential preferences for value orientations in the several behavior spheres according to generation, sex, and place of residence. Our method is to hold two of these variables constant while discussing effects of the third. Thus, when discussing generational differences, we make six old-young comparisons, using the following groups: Ome males, Ome females, Chiba males, Chiba females, Tokyo males, and Tokyo females. Similarly, when testing for sex differences, we made six male-female comparisons, using the following groups: Ome old, Ome young, Chiba old, Chiba young, Tokyo old, and Tokyo young. Finally, when making comparisons by place of residence, we work with four groups: old males, old females, young males, and young females.

Using this method for testing for the effects of any one of our three variables, our statistic will be the number of times the proportion of respondents in one group in a comparison is greater than the proportion of respondents in the other group. For example, we can say that the old are more likely than the young to hold the orientation $L > C > I$ on Item R3 (see Table 5), since in all of the six possible controlled comparisons between old and young for this orientation, the proportion of old endorsing $L > C > I$ is greater than the proportion of young endorsing it.

We shall introduce the items in each behavior sphere by asking and answering the question, Do the value orientations found to be the dominant and major variant orientations for the total sample (see Table 4) remain the dominant and major variant orientations for the twelve sub-samples created by all combinations of our three social structural variables? (See Table 5.) Primarily, however, in this section, we wish to consider all six possible value orientations on each item. Our choice in the preceding paragraph of the example of the orientation $L > C > I$ on Item R3 was deliberate, precisely because this orientation is held by only 9 per cent of the total sample. We shall thus be concerned with the systematic differences that appear on any orientation in terms of our three variables.

Family Life

On Item R3, Family Work Relations, the orientation $C > L > I$, which is the dominant orientation for the total sample, remains the dominant orientation for all twelve of the sub-samples (Table 5). The major variant orientation, $C > I > L$, maintained its major variant status for ten of the twelve sub-samples. On our second items in the sphere of Family Life, Item T2, Expectations about Change, the dominant orientation, $Fu > Pa > Pr$, remains dominant in eleven of the twelve sub-samples (Table 6), while the major variant orientation, $Fu > Pr > Pa$, persists as the major variant in nine of the twelve sub-samples.

Table 5. Percentage Distribution of Value Orientations on *Relational* Item 3, Family Work Relations, for Total Sample of 619 Respondents, Controlling for Generation, Place of Residence, and Sex*

Ranking of Value-Orientation Positions	Old						Young						Total Sample	
	Ome (rural area)		Chiba (city)		Tokyo (metropolis)		Ome (rural area)		Chiba (city)		Tokyo (metropolis)			Number of Respondents
	M	F	M	F	M	F	M	F	M	F	M	F	Percent	
I>C>L	17	(24)	(24)	11	14	13	4	0	9	5	12	6	11	68
I>L>C	0	5	2	3	9	5	0	2	0	0	5	0	3	18
L>I>C	0	3	0	0	2	5	4	5	0	0	0	3	2	10
L>C>I	13	16	14	11	9	(18)	8	14	0	8	4	3	9	55
C>L>I	[46]	[37]	[40]	[58]	[43]	[33]	[48]	[48]	[62]	[49]	[55]	[59]	[49]	307
C>I>L	(21)	11	17	(14)	(21)	(18)	(36)	(32)	(29)	(34)	(19)	(25)	(23)	141
Incomplete Rankings	4	5	2	2	2	7	0	0	0	3	6	4	3	20
Total Percent	101	101	99	99	100	99	100	101	100	99	101	100	100	—
Number of Respondents	24	38	42	62	56	55	25	44	58	61	85	69	—	619

*Dominant value orientations are indicated by brackets, [ ], and major variant value orientations are indicated by parentheses, ( ), in the body of Tables 5–13.

The effects of generaiton made the most difference in the patterning of preferences on the value orientations from the two items, R3 and T2. A greater preference among the old for the orientations I > C > L, I > L > C, L > C > I, and Fu > Pr > Pa, contrasts with a greater preference among the young for the orientations C > I > L, C > L > I, Pa > Pr > Fu, Pa > Fu > Pr, and Pr > Pa > Fu.

The nature of these systematic differences between the generations is striking. One has heard a good deal, since the end of World War II, about a movement toward Individualism among the younger generation in Japan. This "revolt" against the older generation, as it is often called, has not materialized in our data on family life, although in political life such a movement does seem to be occurring (see below). Rather, the emphasis among the young which differentiates them from their elders in the sphere of family life takes the form of a greater preference for first-rank Collateral orientations. Indeed, it is among the old that a preference for Individualism in family life occurs, as well as the more expected emphasis on the "traditional" value orientation L > C > I.

A commitment by the young to the present and the past, to a greater extent than is true for the old, is reflected in the relative preferences for the orientations Pa > Pr > Fu, Pa > Fu > Pr, and Pr > Pa > Fu, all of which are more heavily endorsed by the young (Table 6). The older group, by contrast, systematically has a greater proclivity for the orientation Fu > Pr > Pa. Though these contrasts may reflect differences in the phraseology of this item as it was administered to the young and the old, the nature of the emphasis placed upon the orientations by these two generations here is so similar to that in other behavior spheres, e.g., religious life, that we have reasonable confidence in its reality. In general, a greater emphasis upon first-rank Present orientations (Pr > Pa > Fu on Item T2) is a characteristic of Japanese youth today (see Schorer 1956; Matsumoto 1960) which our data support.

The only discernible effects of sex and place of residence on Items R3 and T2 were these: males seemed to prefer the I > C > L orientation more than females, and residents of Ome expressed a greater disposition for the Pr > Pa > Fu orientation than did residents of Chiba or Tokyo.

In the family life behavior sphere, in fine, only generational differences, among the three variables with which we are dealing, exert a marked effect upon the patterning of value orientations.

Table 6. Percentage Distribution of Value Orientations on *Time* Item 2, Expectations About Change, for Total Sample of 619 Respondents, Controlling for Generation, Place of Residence, and Sex

Ranking of Value-Orientation Positions	Old						Young						Total Sample	
	Ome (rural area)		Chiba (city)		Tokyo (metropolis)		Ome (rural area)		Chiba (city)		Tokyo (metropolis)		Percent	Number of Respondents
	M	F	M	F	M	F	M	F	M	F	M	F		
Fu>Pr>Pa	(29)	[45]	[36]	(37)	(29)	(25)	(32)	14	(19)	15	(13)	(16)	(24)	148
Fu>Pa>Pr	[50]	(29)	[36]	[40]	[38]	[40]	[40]	[25]	[33]	[39]	[35]	[30]	[35]	220
Pa>Fu>Pr	0	3	0	0	4	0	0	14	15	10	5	13	6	37
Pa>Pr>Fu	4	3	0	2	2	0	0	16	7	(16)	8	(16)	7	43
Pr>Pa>Fu	8	5	7	3	4	4	20	(18)	10	5	12	12	8	53
Pr>Fu>Pa	8	11	5	16	13	16	8	11	15	10	11	10	12	72
Incomplete Rankings	0	5	17	3	13	15	0	2	0	5	17	3	7	46
Total Percent	99	101	101	100	103	100	100	100	99	100	101	100	99	—
Number of Respondents	24	38	42	62	56	55	25	44	58	61	85	69	—	619

Table 7. Percentage Distribution of Value Orientations on *Relational* Item 4, Choice of Delegate, for Total Sample of 619 Respondents, Controlling for Generation, Place of Residence, and Sex

Ranking of Value-Orientation Positions	Old						Young						Total Sample	
	Ome (rural area)		Chiba (city)		Tokyo (metropolis)		Ome (rural area)		Chiba (city)		Tokyo (metropolis)		Percent	Number of Respondents
	M	F	M	F	M	F	M	F	M	F	M	F		
I>C>L	13	(21)	21	[26]	(20)	15	[28]	[39]	[36]	[38]	[28]	(17)	(25)	159
I>L>C	8	16	10	14	5	18	4	11	10	11	13	14	12	74
L>I>C	8	5	7	5	14	7	16	0	9	2	6	6	7	41
L>C>I	17	16	10	18	9	18	4	2	0	5	5	7	9	54
C>L>I	(25)	11	[24]	11	18	[20]	[28]	9	15	18	15	13	16	101
C>I>L	[29]	[26]	[24]	[26]	[30]	[20]	20	(36)	(28)	(26)	(26)	[32]	[27]	168
Incomplete Rankings	0	5	5	0	4	2	0	2	2	0	7	10	4	22
Total Percent	100	100	101	100	100	100	100	99	100	100	100	99	100	—
Number of Respondents	24	38	42	62	56	55	25	44	58	61	85	69	—	619

Youth presses for an emphasis on Collaterality and the Present; age for Individualism and the Future.

Political Life

As can be seen in Table 7 for Item R4, Choice of Delegate, the dominant orientation C > I > L for the total sample remains dominant for the six older and one of the younger sub-samples. The major variant I > C > L for the total sample becomes the dominant orientation for five of the six younger sub-samples and one of the older sub-samples (because of ties the number of older sub-samples does not add to six).

As the effects of generation were so obviously potent on Item R4, dealing with political life, our interest centers on the two orientations just referred to, C > I > L and I > C > L, chosen respectively by 27 and 25 per cent of the respondents. We took note of this item earlier as the only one on which we observed two orientations in competition for dominance, and we now learn that this competition is largely between generations, with the old preferring a first-rank Collateral position and the young a first-rank Individualistic position. Such a one-distance shift seems in line logically with "normal" value-orientation change, but considerable dissension between the generations may accompany it.

In the Japanese political world of today, this dissension between the generations may be expressed in terms of two rather contradictory ideological grounds: first, Collaterality may be thought of as more "traditional" and Individualism as more "modern"; second, Collaterality may be thought of as more "socialistic" (or, in the versions of some scholars in Japan, as more "humanistic") and Individualism as more "democratic." On the first ground, the old would plump for Collaterality and the young for Individualism; on the second ground, the old would favor Individualism and the young Collaterality. Such a confusion seems to be evident on the contemporary scene, and it often appears to be resolved in particular cases on the basis of expediency; in some situations the old adopt Collaterality, while in others they chose Individualism, and vice versa for the young.

In general, however, we find the old preferring the orientation C > I > L, while the young prefer I > C > L. Among the other orientations on Item R4, generational differences appear in the greater relative preference of the old over the young for the orientations L > C > I and C > L > I.

A sex difference involving a conflict similar to that between generations also appears in the sphere of political life. Males prefer the orientation L > I > C more often than do females, while the converse is true for I > L > C. This may reflect the postwar struggle between males and females over the rights of women in the political sphere, in which males tend to take a more "conservative" position (L > I > C) and women a more "radical" one (I > L > C).

These two differences, the one generational and the other sexual, were the only systematic effects which our variables had upon the patterning of value orientations in the behavior sphere of political life.

Occupational Life

The dominant value orientation on Item R2, Help in Case of Misfortune, is I > C > L, and it remains dominant over all twelve of the sub-samples. The major variant orientation I > L > C remains the same for the six older and one of the younger sub-samples, while in four other younger groups C > I > L becomes the major variant. On Item R5, Wage Work, the dominant orientation C > I > L remains dominant for eleven of the twelve sub-samples, and the major variant I > C > L persists for ten of the twelve sub-samples. Finally, for Item MN3, Use of Fields, the dominant pattern O > W > S is also dominant for eleven of the twelve sub-samples, and the major variant W > O > S remains the same for eight of the twelve sub-samples.

The three orientations I > L > C, I > C > L, and C > I > L are the most interesting in the configuration of responses to Item R2, dealing with rural occupational matters, and Item R5, dealing with urban occupational concerns. Both old and young groups have I > C > L as their dominant orientation on Item R2, with the major variant among the old being I > L > C, while among the young it is C > I > L. With the shift to an urban situation (in Item R5), both old and young groups have C > I > L as dominant and I > C > L as the major variant. Thus, as one goes from rural to urban matters, a shift toward first-rank Collaterality, led by the young, takes place at an accelerating rate from I > L > C through I > C > L to C > I > L.

The effects of generation upon relational orientations in the occupational world support the hypothesis of a movement toward Collaterality led by the young. The old prefer I > L > C on both

Table 8. Percentage Distribution of Value Orientations on *Relational* Item 2, Help in Case of Misfortune, for Total Sample of 619 Respondents, Controlling for Generation, Place of Residence, and Sex

Ranking of Value-Orientation Positions	Old						Young						Total Sample	
	Ome (rural area)		Chiba (city)		Tokyo (metropolis)		Ome (rural area)		Chiba (city)		Tokyo (metropolis)		Percent	Number of Respondents
	M	F	M	F	M	F	M	F	M	F	M	F		
I>C>L	[58]	[37]	[69]	[52]	[47]	[36]	[56]	[27]	[58]	[71]	[52]	[52]	[51]	318
I>L>C	(25)	(29)	(17)	(35)	(25)	(35)	8	11	5	10	6	(14)	(18)	110
L>I>C	4	5	2	3	5	5	8	7	2	2	1	4	4	23
L>C>I	0	3	0	2	4	5	0	7	0	2	2	3	2	14
C>L>I	4	13	2	3	2	7	8	(25)	9	2	8	3	7	42
C>I>L	4	8	7	5	13	5	(20)	20	(24)	(16)	(20)	(14)	14	85
Incomplete Rankings	4	5	2	0	5	5	0	2	2	0	11	9	4	27
Total Percent	99	100	99	100	101	98	100	99	100	101	100	99	100	—
Number of Respondents	24	38	42	62	56	55	25	44	58	61	85	69	—	619

Table 9. Percentage Distribution of Value Orientations on *Relational* Item 5, Wage Work, for Total Sample of 619 Respondents, Controlling for Generation, Place of Residence, and Sex

Ranking of Value-Orientation Positions	Old						Young						Total Sample	
	Ome (rural area)		Chiba (city)		Tokyo (metropolis)		Ome (rural area)		Chiba (city)		Tokyo (metropolis)		Percent	Number of Respondents
	M	F	M	F	M	F	M	F	M	F	M	F		
I>C>L	(41)	(13)	(36)	(21)	[47]	(25)	(32)	5	(19)	(11)	(14)	(13)	(21)	132
I>L>C	0	8	5	2	5	5	0	0	0	0	1	0	2	13
L>I>C	0	0	2	0	0	2	0	0	0	0	0	0	0	2
L>C>I	0	3	2	0	2	4	0	0	0	0	1	3	1	8
C>L>I	4	3	2	11	4	9	0	(7)	2	7	0	6	5	29
C>I>L	[50]	[60]	[48]	[66]	[43]	[49]	[68]	[86]	[77]	[82]	[68]	[70]	[64]	403
Incomplete Rankings	4	13	5	0	0	5	0	2	2	0	15	9	5	32
Total Percent	99	100	100	100	101	99	100	100	100	100	99	101	98	—
Number of Respondents	24	38	42	62	56	55	25	44	58	61	85	69	—	619

Table 10. Percentage Distribution of Value Orientations on *Man-Nature* Item 3, Use of Fields, for Total Sample of 619 Respondents, Controlling for Generation, Place of Residence, and Sex

Ranking of Value-Orientation Positions	Old Ome (rural area) M	Old Ome (rural area) F	Old Chiba (city) M	Old Chiba (city) F	Old Tokyo (metropolis) M	Old Tokyo (metropolis) F	Young Ome (rural area) M	Young Ome (rural area) F	Young Chiba (city) M	Young Chiba (city) F	Young Tokyo (metropolis) M	Young Tokyo (metropolis) F	Total Sample Percent	Total Sample Number of Respondents
O>W>S	[50]	[45]	[79]	[69]	[54]	[47]	[44]	[32]	[57]	[52]	[65]	[44]	[54]	336
O>S>W	13	16	5	8	13	5	12	18	10	10	7	7	10	64
S>O>W	0	13	2	0	2	4	0	5	0	2	1	0	3	16
S>W>O	0	5	5	5	2	5	8	2	3	2	0	4	3	18
W>S>O	8	8	5	0	5	2	8	7	2	3	2	7	4	26
W>O>S	(29)	(8)	(2)	(18)	(23)	(35)	(28)	(36)	(28)	(30)	(15)	(36)	(23)	144
Incomplete Rankings	0	5	2	0	2	2	0	0	0	2	9	1	2	15
Total Percent	100	100	100	100	101	100	100	100	100	101	99	99	99	—
Number of Respondents	24	38	42	62	56	55	25	44	58	61	85	69	—	619

Items R2 and R5 more than do the young, while the opposite effect occurs with respect to C > I > L on these items. In addition, the old prefer the I > C > L orientation more than do the young on Item R5. Thus we encounter again the difference centering about first-rank Collaterality versus first-rank Individualism which divides old and young in family life as well as here in the occupational world. The only remaining generational effects find the old, on Item MN3, more disposed toward S > W > O and O > W > S than the young, who prefer the orientation O > S > W.

The most interesting sex differences show females, on Item R2 which has the more rural content, preferring L > C > I and I > L > C; these orientations are also supported by the old on this item. In Item R5 with a more urban content, however, the allegiance of females shifts to C > I > L and C > L > I, and females find strong support here in the greater relative preference given C > I > L by the young. This reflects, probably, the reality of the situation for females relative to males in these two different occupational domains; they are still bound to the older generation in rural concerns, but are struggling, together with the young, in an urban setting to bring about change in ways of earning a living. In Item MN3, a female emphasis upon W > O > S, versus a male emphasis on O > W > S, is the final systematic effect of sex as a determinant in occupational life.

The effects of place of residence occur primarily in the *man-nature* area in a way which makes sense in the occupational sphere. The systematic variation on Item MN3, Use of Fields, occurs in two orientations, O > W > S and O > S > W, which have in common the Mastery-over-Nature position as a first-rank position. Ome residents prefer O > S > W to a greater extent than do the residents of Chiba or Tokyo, while the reverse is true for O > W > S. Since the content of this item is directly pertinent to rural life, it is interesting that the actual rural people, residents of Ome, see themselves more Subjugated-to-Nature than do urban dwellers (that is, as between the two orientations residents of Ome prefer the one which has Subjugated-to-Nature ranked higher). The urban dwellers take a more benign, perhaps even classical Japanese, position toward nature and see themselves more in harmony whit it (because, one might surmise, their livelihoods are less dependent on its whims).

Religious Life

The data from the three items in the sphere of religious life are presented in Tables 11–13. Both the dominant orientation Pr > Fu > Pa and the major variant orientation Fu > Pr > Pa, for Item T3, Philosophy of Life, remain dominant and variant respectively for all twelve sub-samples. On Item T4, Ceremonial Innovation, the dominant orientation Pr > Fu > Pa remains dominant for nine of the twelve sub-samples, while the major variant orientation Fu > Pr > Pa persists for seven of the twelve sub-samples. Finally, for Item MN5, Length of Life, the dominant orientation O > W > S remains dominant for all twelve sub-samples, and the major variant orientation W > O > S is also the major variant for eight of the twelve sub-samples.

Differences by generation occur on Items T3 and T4 in the *time* area, while differences by sex are more pronounced on Item MN5 in the *man-nature* area. The young endorse the orientation Pr > Fu > Pa more than do the old on both Items T3 and T4, while the reverse is true for Pr > Pa > Fu on Item T3, and Fu > Pr > Pa on Item T4. This emphasizes again the general preference for first-rank Present orientations by the young, and for first-rank Future orientations by the old.

On Item MN5, the greater relative preference of the old for O > S > W, and of the young for W > O > S, reflects the content of this item, which is concerned with lengthening life via scientific means; the Mastery-over-Nature position most strongly affirms this possibility. The responses may thus indicate a lesser concern of the young about the problem of death. Despite the high suicide rates found among both old and young in Japan (Okazaki 1958), our data point to a less resigned attitude about death, at least among the old, than these rates might lead one to suspect. The minor trends just mentioned, however, occur in the context of a rather overwhelming preference for first-rank Mastery-over-Nature orientations among both generations.

Females seem to prefer value orientations emphasizing a Subjugated-to-Nature position more than do males in the sphere of religious life. This is seen most clearly in the two orientations, O > S > W and O > W > S, where the orientation with a second-rank Subjugation-to-Nature position is preferred by females more than males, while the reverse is true for the orientation with a second-rank Harmony-with-Nature position. There were no systematic effects according to place of residence.

CULTURE CHANGE AND VALUE ORIENTATIONS

We turn now to a more detailed consideration of questions of

Table 11. Percentage Distribution of Value Orientations on *Time* Item 3, Philosophy of Life, for Total Sample of 619 Respondents, Controlling for Generation, Place of Residence, and Sex

Ranking of Value-Orientation Positions	Old						Young						Total Sample	
	Ome (rural area)		Chiba (city)		Tokyo (metropolis)		Ome (rural area)		Chiba (city)		Tokyo (metropolis)		Percent	Number of Respondents
	M	F	M	F	M	F	M	F	M	F	M	F		
Fu>Pr>Pa	(25)	(26)	(21)	(23)	(25)	(20)	(12)	(9)	(29)	(23)	(21)	(19)	(21)	133
Fu>Pa>Pr	8	11	5	2	0	5	4	2	0	2	0	4	3	18
Pa>Fu>Pr	0	0	0	0	0	4	4	0	0	0	0	1	1	4
Pa>Pr>Fu	0	3	0	2	0	2	0	0	0	0	0	1	1	4
Pr>Pa>Fu	21	3	10	10	11	16	12	0	5	3	11	1	8	49
Pr>Fu>Pa	[46]	[55]	[62]	[64]	[63]	[49]	[68]	[89]	[64]	[72]	[58]	[61]	[62]	388
Incomplete Rankings	0	3	2	0	2	4	0	0	2	0	11	12	4	23
Total Percent	100	101	100	101	101	100	100	100	100	100	101	99	100	—
Number of Respondents	24	38	42	62	56	55	25	44	58	61	85	69	—	619

Table 12. Percentage Distributions of Value Orientations on *Time* Item 4, Ceremonial Innovation, for Total Sample of 619 Respondents, Controlling for Generation, Place of Residence, and Sex

Ranking of Value-Orientation Positions	Old						Young						Total Sample	
	Ome (rural area)		Chiba (city)		Tokyo (metropolis)		Ome (rural area)		Chiba (city)		Tokyo (metropolis)			Number of Respondents
	M	F	M	F	M	F	M	F	M	F	M	F	Percent	
Fu>Pr>Pa	[46]	[37]	[36]	[40]	(27)	(29)	[40]	14	(17)	(36)	17	(22)	(28)	173
Fu>Pa>Pr	4	3	5	2	4	9	0	2	5	2	1	4	3	21
Pa>Fu>Pr	0	0	0	0	2	2	0	0	0	0	0	0	0	2
Pa>Pr>Fu	4	3	0	6	5	7	16	0	5	3	4	4	4	28
Pr>Pa>Fu	13	18	7	18	20	13	8	(18)	(17)	10	(18)	(22)	16	98
Pr>Fu>Pa	(33)	[37]	[48]	(34)	[36]	[35]	(36)	[64]	[52]	[44]	[45]	[33]	[41]	257
Incomplete Rankings	0	3	5	0	7	5	0	2	3	5	17	14	6	40
Total Percent	100	101	101	100	101	100	100	100	99	100	102	99	98	—
Number of Respondents	24	38	42	62	56	55	25	44	58	61	85	69	—	619

Table 13. Percentage Distribution of Value Orientations on *Man-Nature* Item 5, Length of Life, for Total Sample of 619 Respondents, Controlling for Generation, Place of Residence, and Sex

Ranking of Value-Orientation Positions	Old Ome (rural area) M	Old Ome (rural area) F	Old Chiba (city) M	Old Chiba (city) F	Old Tokyo (metropolis) M	Old Tokyo (metropolis) F	Young Ome (rural area) M	Young Ome (rural area) F	Young Chiba (city) M	Young Chiba (city) F	Young Tokyo (metropolis) M	Young Tokyo (metropolis) F	Total Sample Percent	Total Sample Number of Respondents
O>W>S	[79]	[42]	[64]	[56]	[72]	[40]	[68]	[36]	[58]	[64]	[64]	[48]	[56]	352
O>S>W	8	(24)	(14)	16	(16)	(20)	8	(20)	12	7	8	(17)	14	88
S>O>W	0	16	2	6	2	5	4	9	3	5	4	9	5	34
S>W>O	0	3	0	3	0	5	0	5	5	2	4	1	3	16
W>S>O	0	5	5	0	0	5	0	2	0	2	0	4	2	12
W>O>S	(13)	11	12	(18)	7	(20)	(20)	(20)	(14)	(21)	(12)	14	(15)	93
Incomplete Rankings	0	0	2	0	4	4	0	7	7	0	9	6	4	24
Total Percent	100	101	99	99	101	99	100	99	99	101	101	99	99	—
Number of Respondents	24	38	42	62	56	55	25	44	58	61	85	69	—	619

culture change, using the same items as in the preceding section on behavior spheres and omitting Item T2, the one administered in a different form to the two generations. Throughout our discussion so far we have referred to questions of culture change indirectly, particularly when speaking about differences between generations. If we assume that, within the structure of the family, most parents wish to instill in their children values similar to their own, then some summary expression of the success of parents in this task is one indicator of the persistence (and, obversely, of the change) of values over time in a society.

Our sample was collected with this idea in mind. Among the 619 respondents are 253 identifiable parent-child pairs. A father and his son constitute 109 of these pairs, and a mother and her daughter the remaining 144. Our criterion of the success of the parent in instilling his values in his child is the *distance* between the value orientations of the parent and the child (see the previous discussion of Figure 1). Parent-child pairs which are a zero-distance apart represent the greatest success by the parent in transmitting his values to his child. Such success decreases progressively as parent-child pairs are a one-distance, a two-distance, and a three-distance apart. The distance between the members of a parent-child pair is taken as a measure of the amount of *change* which has occurred from the orientation of the parent to that of the child. The extent to which Japanese parents have been successful in transmitting their value orientations to their children is expressed in Table 14.

On the whole, Japanese parents have been highly successful in transmitting their value orientations to their children. Considering only the most extreme definition of success—a zero-distance change for an item—the average proportion of parent-child pairs achieving this degree of success on any one item is 42 per cent, or two and one-half times the average chance expectancy (16 per cent). If we liberalize our criterion of success to include pairs at a one-distance in addition to those at a zero-distance, the average rate of success becomes 81 per cent, as compared with the average chance expectancy of 50 per cent. Before the construction of Table 14, moreover, we ascertained that there are no differences in these respects between father-son and mother-daughter pairs.

A second question concerning shifting value orientations between the generations is, In what areas have parents had the least success in holding their children to their value orientations? Table

Table 14. Percentage Distribution of All Identifiable
Parent-Child Pairs from the Total Sample According to
the Distance Between the Value Orientations of Parent and
Child on Selected Items from the Schedule

Item Number	Distance between Parent and Child (distance increases from 0 to 3)				Total Per cent	Number of Parent-Child Pairs
	0	1	2	3		
R2	36	40	18	6	100	236
R3	42	33	19	5	99	236
R4	23	42	26	9	100	238
R5	53	39	8	0	100	227
T3	51	39	9	1	100	237
T4	35	45	17	3	100	224
MN3	43	36	15	6	100	243
MN4	51	35	9	5	100	233
Average Per cent of Pairs at Each Distance	42	39	15	4		

15 rearranges some of the data from Table 14 in a manner designed
to provide an answer to this question.

The items in Table 15 are arranged in order of decreasing percentage of very distant parent-child pairs on an item. We define
a *very distant pair* as one with a two-distance or a three-distance between the orientations of parent and child. Thus, under the assump-

Table 15. Items Arranged According to Decreasing
Percentage of Very Distant* Parent-Child Pairs

Item Number	Per cent Very Distant Pairs
R4	35
R2	24
R3	24
MN3	21
T4	20
MN5	14
T3	10
R5	8

*Percentage of very distant parent-child pairs is defined simply as the percentage
of parent-child pairs a distance of 2 or 3 apart, according to our value-orientation distance concept.

tion that distance equals change, the items range from those in which there has been a great deal of change in orientations between parents and children to those in which there has been very little. With the data in this form, we can test in an exploratory way several hypotheses about possible correlates of this ordering in the attempt to discover where parents have had the least success in value transmission.

We first grouped the eight items in Table 15 according to value-orientation areas, and ascertained that the mean rates of change for items in the *relational, man-nature,* and *time* areas are, respectively, 23, 18, and 15 per cent. Second, we grouped the same items according to behavior sphere, and found the mean rates of change for items in the *political* (R4), *familial* (R3), *occupational* (R2, R5, MN3), and *religious* (T3, T4, MN5) spheres to be, respectively, 35, 24, 18, and 15 per cent. Tentatively, the behavior spheres, more than the areas, seem to separate the items according to the rates at which orientations are changing from parents to children, but many more items in all areas as well as spheres would be needed before definitive conclusions could be reached.

The nature of the variance of children from their parents in the several behavior spheres will now receive attention. Almost all differences noted in the preceding section turn out to be, in fact, movements away from parental orientations. By controlling for family membership, however, we begin to discern the actual process of movement—first in terms of its sheer extent, as was done in our discussion of Tables 14 and 15, and second in terms of its content and direction, as we now undertake through a consideration of Tables 16–23. Our estimate of the expected distribution of orientations held by the children on an item is simply the actual distribution held by their parents on that item. Several other models for computing the expected distribution for children were tried and discarded because they yielded no more information about the nature of change than does the model we are using.

What is the nature of change in the behavior sphere of political life? As can be seen in Table 16, on Item R4, Choice of Delegate, the two orientations with a first-rank Individualism, considered together, gained the most in the movement from parent to child. The orientation $I > C > L$ increased among the children relative to its frequency among their parents to become the dominant orientation for the children. The orientation $I > L > C$ maintained its standing. Among the remaining four orientations, increase or decrease in relative frequency from parents to children depended upon whether

Table 16. Frequency Distribution of Value Orientations Among Children Controlling for Value Orientations Among Parents over 238 Parent-Child Pairs on *Relational* Item 4, Choice of Delegate

Value Orientations of Parents	Value Orientations of Children						Distribution of Parents
	I>C>L	I>L>C	L>I>C	L>C>I	C>L>I	C>I>L	
I>C>L	[19]*	9		2	6	14	50
I>L>C	14	[4]	1	1	1	7	28
L>I>C	5	2	[5]		3	6	21
L>C>I	6	2	3	[2]	9	15	37
C>L>I	12	5	2	2	[8]	11	40
C>I>L	24	5	2	3	12	[16]	62
Distribution of Children	80	27	13	10	39	69	238 Total†

*The frequency of identical child-parent value orientations is indicated by a set of brackets, [ ], for each value orientation in Tables 16–23.
†Totals for number of children, number of parents, and number of pairs are identical, of course, within each table, for Tables 16–23.

Table 17. Frequency Distribution of Value Orientations Among Children Controlling for Value Orientations Among Parents over 236 Parent-Child Pairs on *Relational* Item 3, Family Work Relations

Value Orientations of Parents	Value Orientations of Children						Distribution of Parents
	I>C>L	I>L>C	L>I>C	L>C>I	C>L>I	C>I>L	
I>C>L	[7]			2	18	12	39
I>L>C	2	[]			8	3	13
L>I>C			[2]	1	2		5
L>C>I		2		[3]	19	9	33
C>L>I	7	1	1	5	[69]	22	105
C>I>L			1	4	18	[18]	41
Distribution of Children	16	3	4	15	134	64	236 Total

Table 18. Frequency Distribution of Value Orientations Among Children Controlling for Value Orientations Among Parents over 236 Parent-Child Pairs on *Relational* Item 2, Help in Case of Misfortune

Value Orientations of Parents	Value Orientations of Children						Distribution of Parents
	I>C>L	I>L>C	L>I>C	L>C>I	C>L>I	C>I>L	
I>C>L	[70]	8	5	3	7	25	118
I>L>C	40	[10]	2		6	13	71
L>I>C	5	1	[1]	1	3	1	12
L>C>I	3		1	[]	1	1	6
C>L>I	7			1	[1]	3	12
C>I>L	9	2			2	[4]	17
Distribution of Children	134	21	9	5	20	47	236 Total

Table 19. Frequency Distribution of Value Orientations Among Children Controlling for Value Orientations Among Parents over 227 Parent-Child Pairs on *Relational* Item 5, Wage Work

Value Orientations of Parents	Value Orientations of Children						Distribution of Parents
	I>C>L	I>L>C	L>I>C	L>C>I	C>L>I	C>I>L	
I>C>L	[12]	1			3	50	66
I>L>C		[]				9	9
L>I>C	1		[]			1	2
L>C>I				[]	1	3	4
C>L>I	1				[3]	12	17
C>I>L	19			1	4	[105]	129
Distribution of Children	33	0	0	2	11	180	227 Total

Table 20. Frequency Distribution of Value Orientations Among Children Controlling for Value Orientations Among Parents over 243 Parent-Child Pairs on *Man-Nature* Item 3, Use of Fields

Value Orientations of Parents	Value Orientations of Children						Distribution of Parents
	O>W>S	O>S>W	S>O>W	S>W>O	W>S>O	W>O>S	
O>W>S	[79]	15	1	1	7	39	142
O>S>W	9	[7]				6	22
S>O>W	4		[ ]			5	9
S>W>O	3	1		[1]	1	4	10
W>S>O	5	2			[1]	3	11
W>O>S	19	7	4	2	1	[16]	49
Distribution of Children	119	32	5	4	10	73	243 Total

Table 21. Frequency Distribution of Value Orientations Among Children Controlling for Value Orientations Among Parents over 237 Parent-Child Pairs on *Time* Item 3, Philosophy of Life

Value Orientations of Parents	Value Orientations of Children						Distribution of Parents
	Fu>Pr>Pa	Fu>Pa>Pr	Pa>Fu>Pr	Pa>Pr>Fu	Pr>Pa>Fu	Pr>Fu>Pa	
Fu>Pr>Pa	[16]				2	39	57
Fu>Pa>Pr		[1]				10	11
Pa>Fu>Pr	1		[ ]			1	2
Pa>Pr>Fu				[ ]		2	2
Pr>Pa>Fu	4	1			[2]	18	25
Pr>Fu>Pa	29	1	1	1	7	[101]	140
Distribution of Children	50	3	1	1	11	171	237 Total

Table 22. Frequency Distribution of Value Orientations Among Children Controlling for Value Orientations Among Parents over 224 Parent-Child Pairs on *Time* Item 4, Ceremonial Innovation

Value Orientations of Parents	Value Orientations of Children						Distribution of Parents
	Fu>Pr>Pa	Fu>Pa>Pr	Pa>Fu>Pr	Pa>Pr>Fu	Pr>Pa>Fu	Pr>Fu>Pa	
Fu>Pr>Pa	[30]			2	13	38	84
Fu>Pa>Pr	4	[ ]		1	1	4	10
Pa>Fu>Pr			[ ]				0
Pa>Pr>Fu	1			[1]	2	7	11
Pr>Pa>Fu	7	3		2	[4]	20	36
Pr>Fu>Pa	17			6	16	[44]	83
Distribution of Children	59	4	0	12	36	113	224 Total

Table 23. Frequency Distribution of Value Orientations Among Children Controlling for Value Orientations Among Parents over 223 Parent-Child Pairs on *Man-Nature* Item 5, Length of Life

Value Orientations of Parents	Value Orientations of Children						Distribution of Parents
	O>W>S	O>S>W	S>O>W	S>W>O	W>S>O	W>O>S	
O>W>S	[94]	14	2	3	2	22	137
O>S>W	18	[11]	3		1	7	40
S>O>W	2	1	[4]	1		2	10
S>W>O	3			[ ]		1	4
W>S>O	4		1	1	[ ]	1	7
W>O>S	20	2	2	1	1	[9]	35
Distribution of Children	141	28	12	6	4	42	233 Total

Individualism was in a second-rank or third-rank position. Thus, between the two orientations $L>I>C$ and $L>C>I$, which decreased their frequency from parents to children, $L>I>C$ decreased less than did $L>C>I$. And between the two orientations $C>I>L$ and $C>L>I$, the orientation $C>I>L$ gained more. We have already discussed the possible causes of this increasing emphasis upon Individualism in the sphere of political life among the young.

In the behavior sphere of family life, represented by Item R3, Family Work Relations, in Table 17, a substantial gain occurs in Collaterality in the movement from parents to children. That is, both $C>L>I$ and $C>I>L$ increase in the children's responses. Among the four orientations, $C>L>I$, $C>I>L$, $I>L>C$, and $I>C>L$, the Lineal position also plays an important secondary role. In both pairs of orientations having the same first-rank position— $C>L>I$, $C>I>L$, and $I>L>C$, $I>C>L$—the orientation with a second-rank Lineality in each pair gains more or loses less than does the orientation with a third-rank Lineality.

With reference to this secondary emphasis on Lineality among the children in the sphere of family life, it must be remembered that orientations with first-rank Lineality lost consistently in the movement from parents to children, while orientations with first-rank Collaterality gained consistently. What we are saying, to phrase it in more metaphorical terms, is that the children rejected Lineality when it was presented to them in a blatant form and chose Collaterality instead, but in so doing a certain covert fondness for Lineal value orientations rode along with the dominant Collaterality. Thus, the younger generation in Japan, so often vociferous in its rejection of "traditional" values, may not be so "modern" as it would like to appear, at least in the sphere of family life.

Occupational life is represented here in Tables 18–20 by Items R2, R5, and MN3, which are, respectively, Help in Case of Misfortune, Wage Work, and Use of Fields. As can be seen in Table 18, there is a consistent gain in Collaterality among the children on Item R2, and both first-rank Collateral orientations increase their representation. A secondary trend occurs in the other four orientations when they are compared in terms of pairs of orientations having the same first-rank position. Between $I>C>L$ and $I>L>C$, the orientation $I>C>L$ gains, while the orientation $I>L>C$ loses considerably; and between $L>C>I$ and $L>I>C$, the orientation $L>C>I$ loses less than the orientation $L>I>C$. In other words, in both pairs of orientations, that with a second-rank Collaterality gains more or loses less than that with a third-rank Collaterality.

In general, however, on Item R2, the orientation I > C > L, with a first-rank Individualistic position, remains dominant for both parents and children.

As revealed by Item R5, Wage Work, in Table 19, both parents and children strongly endorse Collaterality, in the orientation C > I > L, with the children laying the heavier emphasis upon it. It is interesting that, although the total distributions of responses over the orientations look very different on Items R2 (in Table 18) and R5 (in Table 19), the same movement toward a greater emphasis on Collaterality for the children can be discerned on both items.

On Item MN3, Use of Fields, in Table 20, the most noticeable shift between parents and children is the increase in concentration among the children on the first-rank Harmony-with-Nature orientation, W > O > S, mainly at the expense of the first-rank Mastery-over-Nature orientation, O > W > S. The latter remains, however, the dominant orientation in both generations.

In the behavior sphere of religious life, in Tables 21 and 22, the children move away from first-rank Future orientations and toward the first-rank Present orientation Pr > Fu > Pa, on both Item T3, Philosophy of Life, and Item T4, Ceremonial Innovation. Although on Item MN5, Length of Life, as presented in Table 23, there are some slight shifts in frequency from parents to children on several of the orientations, the distributions of the two generations are very similar.

Three facts about culture change in Japan can be stated as a result of the foregoing analysis. First, in terms of sheer amount, children have moved away from the value orientations of their parents relatively little. Second, this little movement is distributed unequally over the four behavior spheres; most of it occurs in political life, moderate amounts in family and occupational life, and only a slight amount in religious life. Third, by controlling for parental value orientation, we have been able to show how the generational differences which were found in the preceding section were the consequence of shifting value orientations as parents, with a greater or lesser degree of success, attempted to fulfill their roles as transmitters of culture.

CONCLUSION

In this article we have presented data on Japanese value orientations from a sample of 619 respondents. Both the schedule and the theory used originated in the work reported by Kluckhohn and Strodtbeck (1961). This theory enabled us to analyze some of the subtleties in Japanese values described by earlier writers, but for which they had neither the theoretical ideas to consider variation systematically nor the instrument with which to measure it. Without such a theory and instrument we could not have discerned some of the most interesting contrasts that appeared.

We wish to make one final comment concerning our concept of distance in relation to culture change. In the world of today one society often exerts a considerable influence upon another, and it would be useful to be able to predict the degree of success in such influence. So far as value orientations enter into such predictions, our analysis would indicate that it is not only a similarity or difference in first-rank positions that is involved but that second-rank and third-rank positions should also be taken into consideration.

For example, Americans (as exemplified by the Texans in Kluckhohn and Strodtbeck 1961: 258) seem to prefer the orientation $I > C > L$ on both Items R3 and R5, which deal with Family Work Relations and Wage Work and fall, respectively, into the behavior spheres of family and occupational life. On the other hand, Japanese (as exemplified by our sample) seem to prefer the orientation $C > L > I$ on Item R3, Family Work Relations, and the orientation $C > I > L$ on Item R5, Wage Work. The first-rank positions on both of these items are Individualism for Americans and Collaterality for Japanese. Yet we would predict that Americans and Japanese would have more trouble eventually getting together on Item R3, Family Work Relations, than on Item R5, Wage Work. The reason for this is that, in terms of our concept of distance, the American orientation of $I > C > L$ on Item R3 is a two-distance apart from the Japanese orientation of $C > L > I$, whereas the American orientation of $I > C > L$ on Item R5 is only a one-distance apart from the Japanese orientation of $C > I > L$. If the two behavior spheres are indeed represented by these items, it should be easier for Americans and Japanese to get together on occupational matters than for them to do so on family life.

Finally, when one reads analyses of culture change, it often sounds as if the change came from "out of nowhere" into prominence in a society, whether from internal or external influences. Given an array of value orientations and a reasonable estimate of the proportion of people who hold to them, it is possible to see empirically that there is always some segment of the population that is congenial to the adoption of almost any change. Such a segment does not necessarily have to subscribe to the dominant or major variant value orientations of the society in order to make itself felt.

We must forego a discussion of the complex problem concerning the place of minor segments of a population in the social and power structure of a society. What we do want to emphasize is that it does not make sense to consider value orientations, especially with regard to questions of change, in terms of "either-or" propositions. It is not, for Japan, merely a question of whether Collaterality or Individualism is the preferred value, but it is rather a question of the relative ranking of these positions in an array of value orientations, as these have been defined in this article.

BIBLIOGRAPHY

Abegglen, J. C. 1958. The Japanese Factory. Glencoe.

Benedict, R. 1946. The Chrysanthemum and the Sword. Boston.

Caudill, W. 1959. Observations on the Cultural Context of Japanese Psychiatry. Culture and Mental Health, ed. M. K. Opler, pp. 213–242. New York.

———— 1961. Around the Clock Patient Care in Japanese Psychiatric Hospitals. American Sociological Review 26: 204–214.

Dore, R. P. 1958. City Life in Japan. London.

———— 1959. Land Reform in Japan. London.

Ishino, I. 1953. The Oyabun-kobun: A Japanese Ritual Kinship Institution. American Anthropologist 55: 695–707.

Kato, H., ed. 1959. Japanese Popular Culture. Tokyo.

Kawashima, T. 1948. Nippon shakai no kazokuteki kōsei (The Familial Structure of Japanese Society). Tokyo.

Kluckhohn, F. R. 1960. A Method for Eliciting Value Orientations, Anthropological Linguistics 2: 1–23.

Kluckhohn, F. R., and F. L. Strodtbeck. 1961. Variations in Value Orientations. Evanston.

Matsumoto, Y. S. 1960. Contemporary Japan: The Individual and the Group. Transactions of the American Philosophical Society 50: Pt. 1. Philadelphia.

Ministry of Justice. 1954. The Civil Code of Japan (as of 1954). EHS Law Bulletin Series 2: No. 2100. Tokyo.

Okazaki, A. 1958. Jisatsu no kuni (Land of Suicide). Tokyo.

Pelzel, J., and F. Kluckhohn. 1957. A Theory of Variation in Values Applied to Aspects of Japanese Social Structure. Bulletin of the Research Institute of Comparative Education and Culture, Kyushu University, English Edition 1: 62–76.

Reischauer, E. O. 1957. The United States and Japan. Rev. ed. Cambridge.

Rosovsky, H., and K. Ohkawa. 1961. The Indigenous Components in the Modern Japanese Economy. Economic Development and Cultural Change 9: 476–501.

Schorer, M. 1956. Japan's Delinquents: Children of the Sun and Moon. Reporter, October 18, pp. 35–38.

Stoetzel, J. 1955. Without the Chrysanthemum and the Sword. New York.

Takagi, M. 1957. Nihonjin no seikatsu shinri (The Psychology of Japanese Life). Osaka.

Intergenerational Continuity and Discontinuity in Moral Values among Japanese

TAKIE SUGIYAMA LEBRA

Hypothetical Statement

This paper attempts to fathom the depth of the generation gap in contemporary Japan, with a special focus on moral values. The two generations selected for comparison are removed from each other by the Second World War and are labeled "prewar generation" and "postwar generation." The prewar generation refers to those "adults" who had completed basic education prior to 1945, and the postwar generation includes those "youth" who were born after 1945.

There are good reasons to believe that there exists a gap in moral orientation between the prewar and postwar generations thus defined. Three factors are considered here as possible explanations for the assumed generation gap.

In the first place, the termination of the war in Japan's defeat inaugurated a systematically planned, authoritatively enforced change in the moral system. The traditional values rooted in feudal Japan, reinforced after the Meiji Restoration (though not consistently) and carried to perverse extremes under Shōwa militarism, were abruptly replaced by a new set of moral ideals that were derived from Western culture as it was visibly represented and imposed by the Occupation Forces. This change amounted to a total reversal of the old system in many respects. The traditional emphasis upon group solidarity was replaced by the sacredness of individuality; discipline, endurance, and conformity were sup-

To appear in *Youth, Socialization, and Mental Health,* W. P. Lebra, ed. (Honolulu: The University Press of Hawaii) forthcoming.

planted by freedom, spontaneity, and variety; the taboo of hierarchy and rank distinction was lifted by equalitarian ideology involving demotion of the emperor to human status; the deeply inculcated sense of debt and obligation to others had to give way to the claimed autonomy of self armed with basic human rights; the wartime faith in the omnipotence of the Japanese spirit was downgraded as stupidity, while faith in science and rationality came into ascendency; veneration for tradition, ancestors, and elders lost ideological ground, and youth was upgraded by virtue of its innovative potential. In schools the moral education curriculum called *shūshin* ("self-discipline") was abolished and replaced by "social study"; sexual equality and intimacy were encouraged not only through the introduction of coeducation but also by compulsory seating arrangements; teachers converted themselves from official representatives of the government to unionized "proud laborers," with varying degrees of class-consciousness. The supreme expression of these new values is the new constitution, which declares not only the people's sovereignty but also Japan's commitment to peace. The old value system was denounced as feudalistic, authoritarian, and oppressive, while the new system was hailed as modern, liberal, and democratic.

How deeply the new moral ideals have taken root in Japanese culture and personality is not easy to determine. Some Japanese intellectuals who are personally committed to a progressive ideology claim that the larger part of the Japanese population has accepted and even internalized the new moral values. They do acknowledge the existence of *gyakkōsu* ("backward course") and *fukko-chō* ("revivalistic tendency") in today's Japan, as evidenced, for example, by the great demand for reprints of prewar school textbooks in bookstores. This reactionary trend, in their view, however, is not a sign of cultural resistance to change but rather a product of a deliberate policy designed by men of power, especially by the conservative government, to re-create a docile people. Another view is that postwar Japan has lacked moral instructors both at home and at school because the sudden value change deprived parents and teachers of the authority necessary for the moral education of children. Parents, lacking confidence, only spoiled their children, while teachers avoided the touchy issue of moral education and preferred to devote their efforts to preparing students for entrance examinations. Postwar socialization, in this view, is characterized by a lack of discipline, which dismays both progressive and conservative adults, although the former group attributes it to the inefficacy of postwar democratic education and the latter, conversely, to the very success thereof. Campus radicalism today, characterized by violence and anarchism, is often ascribed to this lack of discipline among students.

The problem of determining the effectiveness of the new, democratic values is made more complex when the second possible source of a generation gap is taken into consideration. This second factor lies in the worldwide techno-environmental change involving all industrial and postindustrial societies. Unlike the first factor, where the change in moral values was designed and enforced, the moral change brought about by industrialization is an unplanned by-product. What impact this change has had upon youth and on youth-adult relations has been of popular as well as professional concern. The widely shared argument is that techno-environmental change at the present rate and in the present form only results in moral deterioration and alienation among youth. The alienated youth may choose different means of expressing themselves: violence-oriented protest movements, hallucinatory trips, dropping out of school, delinquency, rock music, joining hippie communes, and "occult" (Greeley, 1970) behavior. Nonetheless, these are all accentuated expressions of intergenerational discontinuity and "counterculture" (Denisoff et al., 1970) indicative of youth's readiness for "a kind of soc'al bulldozing" (Mead, 1970:85) of the social order and values inherited from the parental generation.

Even though the alleged connection between techno-environmental change and youth's alienation may be taken for granted as nothing more than platitudinous, the reasoning behind this connection is far from simple and consistent, especially insofar as postindustrial societies are concerned.

Youth's alienation in contemporary U.S. or other high-energy societies is attributed by many authors (Mays, 1961; Keniston, 1965, 1967; Flacks, 1967; Murphy, 1971) to the unprecedented affluence, security, freedom, and leisure that have been conferred by technological advancement. Murphy, for instance, offers a persuasive argument, drawing upon Maslow's theory of the hierarchy of needs and self-actualization, that the satiation of lower-level needs—simply put, too much comfort—made the youth of the 1960s more aware of their higher-level needs such as belongingness and thus drove them toward protest movements. On the other hand, some observers (Meyerson, 1966; Eisner, 1969) stress the contemporary youth being worse-off than ever, more constrained by the authoritarian, elitist, conformist, or other pressures from the adult world. Probably closer to the truth is that most adult observers of campus unrest are not quire sure which position to take, and therefore tend to be ambivalent as to whether the Establishment should concede to the demands of young dissenters or take a firm stand against them (Margaret Mead, 1970, may be an exception with her prophetic conviction that the roles of teacher and pupil are to be reversed between old and young in the "prefigurative" age). Even a sophisticated observer like Lipset (1970) seems to vacillate between the two opposite positions, leaving his readers perplexed as to what he recommends as a solution to campus unrest.

Such contradiction or confusion is understandable in view of the complexity of the phenomenon we are facing. It is neither exclusively satiation nor deprivation that underlies alienation and intergenerational conflict. It is rather the structural dilemma in which the very same thing that benefits today's youth to an unprecedented degree and thus makes them a privileged class distinct from their parents also frustrates them to an extent unknown to their predecessors. The same social structure that needs highly trained young personnel and thus can gratify the aspirations of the competent young puts pressures upon the coming generation for increasingly higher-level performance, upgrades the standard of success, intensifies competition, and escalates the strain for underachievers. The prolonged universal school education, afforded only by affluent societies, is a blessing in giving opportunities to motivated individuals and in rectifying inequalities among families. Yet, it is undoubtedly an anathema when seen as responsible for "irrelevance" of the existing educational system and for keeping youth socially useless (Special Committee on Campus Tensions, 1970). Furthermore, the same development-committed society that cherishes the independence and innovative spirit of young individuals, and thus tends to be permissive toward them, also reduces them to a humiliating status, totally dependent upon adults, for an increasingly longer period, particularly upon the conservative sectors of adult society, namely, family and school embedded in a residential community (Parsons, 1965). The parental aspiration for the child reflects the structural dilemma of a mobility-oriented society: the parent expects the child to surpass him and yet to remain under parental control. Such a dual expectation puts the child in a double bind: "If youth succeeds, it emasculates the parent. As a result, youth cannot feel successful—partly out of guilt, and partly because he cannot be sure if it was he or his parent who wanted him to succeed" (Bettelheim, 1965:85). Lastly, we must face the classical problem of anomie in the Durkheiman sense, as it is interlocked with widened freedom of choice. The likely response to this situation by youth would be "a duality of orientation" as manifested in their peer-group behavior, namely, "compulsive independence" and "compulsive conformity" (Parsons, 1965:130–31).

The structural dilemma discussed above reminds us of what might be regarded as a psycho-social parallel with the current issue of industrial pollution. Alienation among youth as well as intergenerational conflict may thus be regarded as psycho-social pollutions that await adequate disposal.

Japan is among those countries that are confronted with this dilemma of industrialization, especially in the area of information technology and mass media. Economic growth and a labor shortage through the 1960s have allowed the average Japanese to enjoy unheard-of affluence, security, and leisure. Moral apathy among the young, linked with this techno-environmental change, is further aggravated by the fierce examination system for college entrance, which compels the whole school education to be geared for the maximal production of successful candidates. Tashiro (1970), for instance, noted the motivational impoverishment of today's high school students in anything other than "passing the entrance examination."

The third and final source of a generation gap transcends historical time and place. It relates to human maturation or the human life cycle. Intergenerational value differences could be attributed to a difference in the stage of life. One generation is simply more mature, more experienced, less egocentric, more realistic than the other. If there are generational conflicts, they may arise from the conflicting emotions peculiar to the transitional stage called adolescence. Conflicting emotions, aside from the Oedipal-rebellion hypothesis, which has been largely discredited (Special Committee on Campus Tension, 1970), may include mastery vs. dependency, frivolity vs. seriousness, loyalty vs. rebellion, or as Erikson (1965) puts it, "fidelity" vs. "diversity."

One might also look at this critical phase of life in the light of a social system rather than an intrapersonal system. Eisenstadt (1965:32) characterizes youth as "role moratorium," and Bettelheim (1965) sees the generation conflict as struggle over succession—the older generation resisting "moving over" and the younger anxious to take over the headship of a social unit.

If maturation or life stage is considered the predominant variable, we might well accept demographic explanations for the counterculture among American youth of the 1960s (as a result of the 1940s "baby boom") (Drucker, 1971) and for significant roles played by youth in social movements and innovations in history (Watanuki, 1966; Moller, 1968). Nor would it be unreasonable to find historical parallels in the current youth movements, or to see cultural persistence, as Seidensticker (1970) did, in "pulverizers" (destroyers of everything in existence) among Japanese students. One might also well agree with Feuer that there is nothing surprising in the postgraduation conversion of the former Zengakuren leaders, who championed "filiarchy" against the gerontocracy of Japan, to core employees of the Establishment. The reason for such an abrupt transformation is obvious: "political action founded on obscure emotions of generational rebellion tends to terminate with the end of that generational phase" (Feuer, 1969:214).

It is more likely, however, that the universal problem of life stage and generational turnover is closely linked with the second factor mentioned above, namely, techno-environmental change. I am tempted to agree with Bettelheim when be contends that the generational succession struggle has become more severe with technological development, which eliminates the natural condition for smooth takeover.

I am in no position, however, to say with confidence how all three factors—Japan's postwar democratization, worldwide techno-environmental change, and the universal problem of life cycle—influence one another; whether they reinforce one another to widen a generation gap, or whether one counteracts another to stabilize or narrow the gap. I do suggest a threefold hypothesis, derived from the above considerations, regarding the manifestations of a gap in moral orientation presumably lying between prewar- and postwar-generation Japanese. First, the postwar generation is more apathetic or skeptical toward moral order in general; second, it is more resistant to a culturally inherited moral order; third, once morally committed, the postwar generation is more compulsive, fastidious, and short-circuited, whereas the prewar generation tends to be more compromising or "realistic."

The following presentation of empirical data will delineate where one generation diverges from the other, and where the two converge, along this hypothesis. Explanations for such divergences and convergences will be derived, I hope, from one of the above three factors or from interaction among them.

SAMPLE AND METHOD

The sample was drawn from residents of a provincial city with a population of around 60,000, around 120 kilometers southwest of Tokyo. Known as a resort, the city consists of an urban center primarily oriented toward tourism—mainly commerce, hotel business and entertainment—and a rural periphery dominated by farming and fishing industries. The city does not rank high in degree of urbanization, but compared with what it was two decades ago, it has become urbanized at a striking pace, acquiring overdeveloped motorization and so-called urban sprawl, which astonishes the residents themselves.

A sample of the prewar generation was taken from members of the city's women's association, whose cooperation was secured with the aid of the city government. Since there was no men's association equivalent to the women's, the members' husbands were also included in the sample, although only one person, wife or husband, represented each household. For the postwar sample, I obtained the cooperation of the senior-year students of the city's secondary high school. While this sample is uniform in age, the prewar sample varies widely, with a minimal age of 40.

These representatives of the two generations were given a sentence-completion test that I designed to elicit responses relevant to morality.[1] Twenty-nine sentence fragments were presented, to be incorporated into complete sentences. The youth sample was administered the test in their classrooms by teachers, while the adult respondents received the test sheets through district leaders of the association and returned them by mail. The voluntary nature of the latter test situation, compared with the classroom situation, was reflected in the low response rate (117 out of 300). For the same reason, however, the adults' responses turned out to be more complete than those of the youth. The research was conducted in the summer of 1970.

Table 1 shows the distribution of the two samples, A (adults) and Y (youth), by age and sex. Although sex does not concern us, our tabulation will differentiate it because the two samples are not well balanced in the distribution of this variable. Despite the wide age variation of the adult sample, we shall deal with adult respondents as if they all belonged to a single generation.

Space permits us to refer to no more than eight sentences of the test. Since each sentence consists of two parts, S (stimulus part) and R (response part), let the eight sentences be identified as S1, S2,... S8, and R1, R2,... R8. S's selected are as follows, as translated

Table 1. Number of Adult (A) and Youth (Y)
Respondents, Distributed by Age and Sex

	A				Y		
Age	Male	Female	Both	Age	Male	Female	Both
40–49	21	27	48	17–18	49	49	98
50–59	13	27	40				
60–69	7	4	11				
70–79	0	1	1				
Total(%)	41(41)	59(59)	100*(100)	Total(%)	49(50)	49(50)	98(100)

*Out of the 117 returned responses, 17 were eliminated either because of incomplete information (e.g., sex, age) or because the respondents turned out not to belong to the prewar generation as defined in this paper.

from Japanese[2] (labels are given in parentheses):

S1. If you persevere through all the hardships that you encounter....(Perseverance)

S2. Perhaps because I experienced suffering when I was young....(Suffering)

S3. If you are kind to others....(Kindness)

S4. If you carry out obligations of filial piety....(Filial Piety)

S5. That we can live as happily as we do....(Happy Life)

S6. Because I once received *on*[3] from that person....(*On*)

S7. In order to build an ideal home life....(Ideal Home)

S8. In order to be respected by others....(Respect)

As might be noted, these vary in the degree of closure, both logical and cultural. Logically, S's 1, 2, 3, 4 and 6 are more closed or structured than the others in that they impose more constraint upon the structure of the R's; culturally, S6 may be said to be most closed in the sense that it is loaded with the traditional values of Japanese culture and is part of the cultural idiom, although some other S's, too, are more or less culturally charged. Closure in S's will be reflected in limited variation in R's.

The responses were coded in accord with categories designed for the purpose of this research and analyzed on the basis of percentage distributions, as will be shown below. The results of a Chi-square test for between-sample differences by generation as well as for within-group differences by sex will be given only insofar as the data are amenable to such a test and where statistical confirmation is specially called for.[4]

ANALYSIS

Moral commitment depends upon faith in the efficacy of a

moral order, and the latter, in turn, is based upon fair distribution of rewards and punishments in accord with moral and immoral actions. Moral frustration, and hence moral apathy, results from the perceived randomness of distribution of rewards, material and nonmaterial, or more so, from a perceived inverse correlation between moral action and reward. The following analysis concentrates on this single dimension of moral order, namely, the fair distribution of rewards and punishment, or what might be called "compensative justice."

Compensative justice, as accepted or rejected by our subjects, will be elucidated from a number of angles.

Compensation for Energy-investment

Perseverance. First, we shall analyze expected compensation for perseverance as a form of morally charged energy-expenditure. In Japanese culture, perseverance, *gaman*, is considered one of the major moral ingredients of a rewarding outcome. Responses to S1 ("If you persevere through all the hardships that you encounter") indicate that an overwhelming number of respondents (96.9 percent of 99 adults; 93.6 percent of 94 youth) affirmed or expected positive compensation for perseverance, with the youth only slightly less positive than the adults. Six percent of youth and 2 percent of adults denied or questioned a positive outcome. Examples of those responses are, "That does not necessarily bring about a good thing"; "You will be a fool." It further turns out that if there is any generational divergence, it is only within the male sample, with almost no difference between female adults and female youth. Whether this is a consistent characteristic or not is an important question to keep in mind as we go along. Regardless, however, there is little intergenerational difference in connecting perseverance with a reward.

When the analysis goes further into specific forms of compensation, we come upon a wider discrepancy between generations (see Table 2). What is meant by each category of R1 may be understood from the examples quoted.

First, the "relaxation" outcome (category 1) is mentioned more frequently by adults, which implies that adults are more confident, from their retrospective view of life, of relaxation following the tensions of perseverance. Second, "functional utility" (2) and "achievement" (4) are reversed in frequency between the two groups: youth stress achievement more than adults, while adults see more functional utility in perseverance. Both are goal-oriented, but youth are oriented toward the end result and adults, particularly

Table 2: Consummative Forms of Compensation for Perseverance

S1: If you persevere through all the hardships that you encounter ...

RI	Male		Female		Total	
	A	Y	A	Y	A	Y
1. Relaxation or gratification "You will have an easy life" "Happiness will follow" "There will be pleasure"	23.1	14.3	25.0	21.7	24.2	18.2
2. Functional utility "You will develop self-confidence" "It will be useful for your self-improvement" "It will be beneficial for your adulthood"	20.5	7.1	3.6	2.2	10.5	4.5
3. Desensitization to pain "You will come to feel nothing" "Once passed, it will be come a pleasant memory" "The habit will become part of your personality"	10.3	16.7	8.9	6.5	9.5	11.4
4. Achievement "You can achieve anything" "You can certainly succeed"	5.1	14.3	8.9	13.0	7.4	13.6
5. Metaphorical outcome "Some day it will blossom" "It will bear fruit" "The fruit will be sweet"	5.1	2.4	7.1	4.3	6.3	3.4
6. Social result "You will receive cooperation" "You will be recognized" "Every problem will be solved harmoniously"	5.1	0.0	1.8	2.2	3.2	1.1
7. Other specific outcome	0.0	0.0	1.8	0.0	1.1	0.0
8. Unspecific outcome "Something good will come" "You will be rewarded" "The result will be good" "There will be a good time" "There is something you can gain"	30.8	45.2	42.9	50.0	37.9	47.7
Total (N)	39	42	56	46	95	88

NOTE: Figures in this and all following tables indicate percentages, except for the N's in the "Total" row.

male adults, toward the means. Here is a sign of more short-circuited orientation among youth. Third, although both groups show a high frequency of "unspecific outcome" (8), the youth group is higher. These three points of difference may derive primarily from the life-cycle factor. Categories 5 and 6 carry culturally loaded responses

preferred by more adults. Adults seem to have the culturally inherited taste for allegorical description of human affairs in terms of
natural phenomena (5), such as the growth of a plant; one may
further argue that the sense of moral order for the adult group is
embedded in the sense of natural order. "Social result" (6) is
noteworthy in that 5 percent of male adults but no male youth
responded with such social sensitivity. On the other hand, male
youth ranks highest in "desensitization to pain" (3). In this category
too, difference by sex is as noticeable: males seem more prone to
desensitization than females.

The Chi-square test cannot be used for Table 2, since some
categories contain frequencies lower than required.

Suffering. Let us examine responses to S2 ("Perhaps because
I experienced suffering when I was young"). While perseverance
is an active aspect of energy-expenditure, suffering, *kurō*, is more
passive. Unlike S1, which involves future-oriented expectations, S2
elicits retrospective consequences of past experience. Suffering as
such is not a moral act, to be sure, but it has culturally profound
moral implications in its connection with "moral masochism"
(DeVos, 1960) and its capacity for instilling guilt in its observers.
As anticipated, youth showed definitely more resistance to the idea
of suffering as either moral or a profitable investment than to perseverance. The generational gap in this respect is wide enought to
be statistically significant (p < .01): adult responses indicate
75.9 percent associate suffering with a beneficial outcome, and
9.6 percent with an injurious result, whereas the two figures for the
youth group are 58.1 percent and 29.1 percent, respectively. The
higher rejection by youth of suffering, compared with perseverance,
may be because suffering, as stated in S2, was taken by youth as
symbolic of parental righteousness, a familiar complaint that
generates both antagonism and guilt in them. As for the sex variable,
here again we find a wider generational gap in the male sample than
in the female sample.

Further details of S2 are shown in Table 3.

Note first, category 1, where many youth relate suffering to
physiological deterioration, totally devoid of moral significance.
Conversely, more adults refer to economic or occupational success
and gratification, as shown in category 2. Categories 3, 5, and 6
were given subcategories to show the variety within each category,
without affecting the Chi-square test. While there is no generational
difference in category 3 as a whole, where both groups are of
highest frequency, it turns out that youth are more markedly oriented toward 3b, a maturation outcome, compared with adults, than

Table 3: Compensation for Suffering

S2: Perhaps because I experienced suffering when I was young ...

R2	Male		Female		Total	
	A	Y	A	Y	A	Y
1. Natural, physiological outcome "I am gray-haired" "My body aches"	5.4	27.9	6.0	15.9	5.7	21.8
2. Economic, occupational outcome "I can now live an easy life" "I have become president of a big company"	10.8	2.3	16.0	6.8	13.8	4.6
3. Personal gratification	32.4	27.9	44.0	45.5	39.1	36.8
(3a) Relaxation "I am happy now"	(10.8)	(7.0)	(22.0)	(4.5)	(17.2)	(5.7)
(3b) Maturation "I have come to understand what life is" "I have developed good judgment in appraising people"	(18.9)	(20.9)	(20.0)	(31.8)	(19.5)	(26.4)
(3c) Social gratification "People trust me" "I am old and happy, being well taken care of by my children"	(2.7)	(0.0)	(2.0)	(9.1)	(2.3)	(4.6)
4. Desensitization to suffering "Suffering no longer affects me" "I don't feel suffering as suffering"	10.8	16.3	10.0	13.6	10.3	14.9
5. Concern for others' suffering	21.6	16.3	18.0	6.8	19.5	11.5
(5a) Sensitization to others' suffering "I cannot help offering help when someone is in trouble" "I do not want my children to suffer"	(13.5)	(7.0)	(16.0)	(4.5)	(14.9)	(5.7)
(5b) Concern for fair share of suffering "I find today's children spoiled" "I am strict with children"	(8.1)	(9.3)	(2.0)	(2.3)	(4.6)	(5.7)
6. Other	18.9	9.3	6.0	11.4	11.5	10.3
(6a) Negative psychological outcome "My mind is warped" "I cannot trust people"	(8.1)	(7.0)	(4.0)	(6.8)	(5.7)	(6.9)
(6b) Other "I want to retire early" "I did not suffer"	(10.8)	(2.3)	(2.0)	(4.5)	(5.7)	(3.4)
Total (N)	37	43	50	44	87	87

Intergenerational difference: $X^2 = 14.92$ (p $<$ .02)

Within-group sex differences: Adult $X^2 = 5.83$ (p $<$ .50) $\Big\}$ DF = 5
Youth $X^2 = 6.09$ (p $<$ .30)

toward 3a, relaxation. This difference, incidentally, appears more noticeable between female youth and female adults, unlike most categories, where the male sample exhibits a greater generational gap. There is frequency reversal between generations in categories 4 and 5. Here again youth, especially male youth, are oriented toward desensitization. Most interesting is category 5, where one's own suffering is related to others' suffering. We note two kinds of such orientation: one is compassion for others' suffering as a result of one's own experience (5a), and the other is concern for what might be labeled "distributive justice," which stipulates an equal share of suffering (5b). It will be further noted that the generational difference in 5 stems from 5a only. Adults are more susceptible or capable of empathy, whereas youth are as resentful as adults, if not more so, of today's youth who do not share suffering equally with yesterday's generation. The latter point implies that compensative justice for youth is more egalitarian-biased, although compensation and equality are logically distinct.[5] The generational difference in categories 4 and 5a is remarkable in that suffering leads to desensitization for one generation and to sensitization for the other.

The difference between A and Y covering the six categories (disregarding subcategories) turns out to be significant ($p < .02$), with no significant difference within each group by sex.

Compensation for Social Investment

Both perseverance and suffering are nonsocial in that they refer to no person other than the acting Ego. How would our subjects react to social action involving Alter? This question is particularly relevant in view of the traditional preoccupation of Japanese culture with gratifying social interaction (for this reason I have described Japanese culture as "sociocultic"—Lebra, 1971). Furthermore, social stimuli should be expected to elicit more complex and more variable responses than nonsocial stimuli, simply because action here is not unilateral but doubly contingent on Ego's and Alter's expectations.

Kindness. S3 (Kindness) was intended to elicit responses to this traditionally stressed social contribution to generalized "others," *hito.* Although the majority of both A and Y responded to "If you are kind to others" by expecting a desirable consequence, adults turned out to have significantly higher expectations. Table 4 shows this difference and more details.

In response to S3 ("If you are kind to others"), two kinds of positive consequences of kindness are distinguished. Categories 1,2,

Table 4: Compensation for Kindness
S3: If you are kind to others...

R3	Male		Female		Total	
	A	Y	A	Y	A	Y
1. Reciprocal return of kindness "You will be treated kindly by others"	7.5	11.1	8.5	13.0	8.1	12.1
2. Reciprocal return in other forms "You will be helped when in trouble" "You will be rewarded" "You will be thanked"	30.0	35.6	30.5	28.3	30.3	31.9
3. Circulatory return "It will turn around and around and eventually come back to you"	12.5	0.0	8.5	0.0	10.1	0.0
4. Autistic satisfaction "You will feel better" "Your feelings will be enriched"	35.0	28.9	33.9	39.1	34.3	34.1
5. Societal gratification "The world will be at peace" "Society will become easier to live in"	7.5	2.2	11.9	4.3	10.1	3.3
6. Negative result "You will only lose" "It will be returned with viciousness" "You should not expect to be reciprocated"	0.0	20.0	1.7	10.9	1.0	15.4
7. Other	7.5	2.2	5.1	4.3	6.1	3.3
Total (N)	40	45	59	46	99	91

Intergenerational difference: $X^2 = 26.38$ (p $<$ .001) DF $= 6$
Within-group sex differences: Adult $X^2 = 1.78$ (p $<$ .95) DF $= 6$
Youth $X^2 = 3.00$ (p $<$ .70) DF $= 5$

and 3 refer to compensative justice in the narrower sense of the word, i.e., payoff being assured for the kind actor, whereas categories 4 and 5 do not involve such payoff directly for the actor. As far as compensative return is concerned, category 1 shows more youth referring to "homeomorphic reciprocity" (Gouldner, 1960) in the sense of "kindness for kindness." On the other hand, some adults but no youth conceived compensation in terms of circulatory return, and more adults than youth referred, as in category 5, to the extension of benefit to the whole society or world. These differences suggest that adults are more confident of the existence of a moral order that transcends the simple dyadic bond. One respondent mentioned the Buddhist idea of causal chain, presumably as the regulator of circulation of goods.

Table 5: Compensation for Filial Piety
S4: If you carry out obligations of filial piety . . .

R4	Male		Female		Total	
	A	Y	A	Y	A	Y
1. Autistic satisfaction "You will not regret" "You will feel at peace"	27.0	17.1	21.1	38.9	23.4	27.3
2. Gratifying result from child "You, too, will be the receiver of filial piety" "Your child will emulate you"	32.4	0.0	45.6	2.8	40.4	1.3
3. Parental satisfaction "Your parents will be pleased"	5.4	22.0	1.8	30.6	3.2	26.0
4. Other gratification	8.1	39.0	14.0	11.1	11.7	26.0
(4a) Gratifying result from parents "You will receive more allowance"	(0.0)	(4.9)	(0.0)	(2.8)	(0.0)	(3.6)
(4b) Social approval "Neighbors will praise you"	(5.4)	(14.6)	(1.8)	(2.8)	(3.2)	(9.1)
(4c) Societal gratification "Through family harmony, human relations will carry on smoothly and everyone will be happy"	(0.0)	(4.9)	(8.8)	(0.0)	(5.3)	(2.6)
(4d) Gratification of both Ego and others "Both parents and yourself feel good"	(2.7)	(14.6)	(3.5)	(5.6)	(3.2)	(10.4)
5. Naturalness of filial piety "It will be only natural"	13.5	7.3	8.8	11.1	10.6	9.1
6. Other	13.5	14.6	8.8	5.6	10.6	10.4
(6a) Negative result or appraisal "Nothing will come out" "Can you go to heaven?"	(0.0)	(7.3)	(1.8)	(2.8)	(1.1)	(5.2)
(6b) Other "It would be a good thing" "It will be my way of repaying for their having brought me up"	(13.5)	(7.3)	(7.0)	(2.8)	(9.6)	(5.2)
Total (N)	37	41	57	36	94	77

Intergenerational difference: $X^2 = 49.86$ (p $<$ .02) ⎫
Within-group sex differences: Adult $X^2 = 3.87$ (p $<$ .70) ⎬ DF = 5
Youth $X^2 = 12.61$ (p $<$ .05) ⎭

The higher frequency of youth in category 6 appears self-evident except that this category includes not only the negative consequences of kindness but also disapproval of expectation of reward; this relates to a sense of morality different from compensative justice. Furthermore, that youth and adults are equally high in the frequency of "autistic satisfaction" seems to suggest either the cultural persistence of the belief that social dedication assures mental well-being or the particular attraction for youth of what might be called "moral autism," which derives gratification from Ego's own action, independently of Alter's reaction. These points are raised here as a warning that there are kinds of justice or order other than compensative, which will be touched upon again.

The between-group difference in Table 4 proves to be highly significant (p < .001).

Filial Piety. We shall turn to another form of social investment, filial piety. We find to our surprise that both generations responded to S4 ("If you carry out obligations of filial piety") overwhelmingly with a positive appraisal of this traditional virtue. Even negative responses took such mild forms as, "Your life will become rigidly stereotyped"; "It will be worthless, since eternal happiness is not thereby guaranteed for your parents." How can we explain this difference between R3 (Kindness) and R4 (Filial piety)?

My interpretation is that filial piety involves specific, tangible Alters, namely parents, toward whom not only adults but also youth can orient themselves, whereas response to kindness is oriented toward *hito*, others, who may be too abstract or intangible. (The youth in prewar Japan, having learned moral virtues ideationally through *shūshin*, might have bridged the gap between personal experiences and the intangible, yet unexperienced world.) Furthermore, given physical and emotional intimacy between parent and child, filial piety may be regarded more as a natural feeling than as an obligatory norm. This interpretation is grounded on such responses as, "You will feel good"; "The parents will be happy"; "That is only natural." Another possibility is that urbanization and the breakdown of the local Gemeinschaft have been accompanied by consolidation of nuclear family ties, as reflected in the Japanized half-English phrase widely used, *mai-hōmu-shugi* ("my-home-ism").

A closer examination, however, reveals intergenerational differences clearly present in those responses that associate filial piety with positive compensation, as shown in Table 5.

What stands out in this table is that the parental generation sees the investment in filial piety paid off in the same filial piety or through their children's emulation of parental behavior, as in category 2 whereas very few youth think of filial piety in that light. The latter most frequently see in filial piety autistic satisfaction (1), satisfaction of parents as receivers of filial piety (3), and other gratification (4), especially social approval (4b) and gratification of both filial Ego and parental or other Alters (4b).

The homeomorphic payoff (filial piety for filial piety) that seems to be a major orientation among adults is not based on the rule of reciprocity. What is invested in one's parents is returned from one's child, which involves a lineal triad rather than a reciprocal dyad. The generations under study diverged in their perception of the lineal succession of debtor- and creditor-status as the basis for compensative justice. Youth tend to think of filial piety more in dyadic terms (except in the case of "social approval," where the source of gratification lies outside the parent-child dyad) but without expecting reciprocal payoff. It remains to be seen whether this difference implies value change presently taking place throughout the society and therefore means a real generation gap or only reflects different stages in the life cycle. Youth do assume for themselves the role of the child in filial-piety responses, while adults take the parental role as the receiver of filial piety. Although Table 5 yields a statistically significant difference ($p < .001$) between A and Y, this by no means reflects a value conflict but rather value complementarity between the two generations.

Social Indebtedness

Compensative justice for social investment can be effective only where the social investee or debtor is aware of his obligation of repayment. Indeed, Japanese culture is known for its emphasis upon sensitization to one's debt in terms of *on* (a fusion of bestowed benefit and incurred debt), which compels its receiver to be aware of his debtor's status. The compelling sense of generalized *on* has been in fact a stronghold for maintaining morality among the Japanese (for a psychosocial analysis of *on*, see my other chapter in this volume). This section analyzes the debtor's point of view as the complement of previous sections, where compensative justice was looked upon from the investor's point of view.

Acknowledgement of Indebtedness. For the sense of debt to be operative as a morally binding force, one must have an internalized proclivity for crediting whatever one enjoys to others, rather than to oneself, regardless of whether or not a particular creditor-bene-factor can actually be identified. S5 ("That we can live as happily as we do") was intended to elicit the sense of debt deep-seated at such a latent level. Table 6 shows, first, that both groups share an equal intensity of national identification and attribute their happiness to one or another special quality or performance of

Table 6: Social Indebtedness for a Happy Life
S5: That we can live as happily as we do . . .

R5	Male		Female		Total	
	A	Y	A	Y	A	Y
1. Japanese, nation "Is because Japan has become a great country"	28.2	31.7	20.7	15.2	23.7	24.3
2. The deceased	15.4	2.4	27.6	0.0	22.7	1.4
(2a) Ancestors "Is thanks to the heritage from our ancestors"	(12.8)	(2.4)	(20.7)	(0.0)	(17.5)	(1.4)
(2b) Forerunners and other deceased "Is thanks to those who fought for the country and were killed"	(2.6)	(0.0)	(6.9)	(0.0)	(5.2)	(0.0)
3. Parents "Is thanks to our parents"	7.7	24.4	1.7	39.4	4.1	31.1
4. Other people "Is because of sacrifices made by so many people" "Is thanks to you, everyone"	17.9	7.3	13.8	9.1	15.5	8.1
5. Creditors not mentioned "Is a product of industriousness" "The country has its center, the family has its center"	23.1	29.3	31.0	30.3	27.8	29.7
6. Other "We should think about whom we owe this" "Is not because of Prime Minister Sato"	7.7	4.9	5.2	6.1	6.2	5.4
Total (N)	39	41	58	33	97	74

Intergenerational difference: $X^2 = 35.47$ (p < .001)
Within-group sex differences: Adult $X^2 = 5.13$ (p < .50) } DF = 5
Youth $X^2 = 4.31$ (p < .70)

Japanese as a people or a country (category 1). "We" in S5 was evidently identified as "we Japanese." We cannot delve into nationalism in this paper, but let it be noted that some responses to other S's also revealed a sense of national solidarity still thriving across the generations. In category 1 the debtor and the creditor are mutually identified so that the sense of indebtedness merges with the feeling that one "deserves" the life being enjoyed.

Intergenerational difference stands out in categories 2 and 3, where frequencies are so distinctly reversed. Adults find themselves indebted to those who have passed away, especially to (2a) ancestors, whereas almost no youth are ancestrally oriented but rather feel indebted to parents. (Intergenerational divergence here is more distinct in the female than in the male sample.) This is, as in R4 (Filial piety), no real gap but a beautiful example of an intergenerational shift in role identification along lineality. The two generations are alike in that they both feel benefited from the generosity of the preceding generation. This interpretation may have to be qualified, however, in that the sense of indebtedness on the part of youth may be confined to parents only and may not be capable of extending itself, when the time comes, to the endless bloodline, either toward ancestors or future descendants, as prewar Japanese were accustomed to. At any rate, the latent indebtedness to parents spontaneously expressed by youth is a confirmation of what we observed in regard to filial piety. Besides the reasons speculated there for the lack of alienation from parents, we may well contend that this is a result of the inevitable sense of economic dependency on adults, particularly within the nuclear family, since youth today are totally out of circulation in the labor market because of their prolonged school education.

If the lineal extensibility of indebtedness on the part of youth is doubtful, horizontal extensibility beyond the nuclear family is certainly limited, as shown in category 4. More adults than youth refer to horizontal indebtedness to "other people." This also underscores the skepticism expressed by youth toward kindness, as we saw in R3, invested in generalized "others."

Prewar students would have referred to teachers side-by-side with parents as major benefactors. The sense of debt concentrated in parents may be understood as another sign of the atomization of the unit of solidarity down to "my home."

Debtor's Disposition. Once a debt is incurred and acknowledged, the debtor's behavior is expected to be affected thereby and generally to conform to the rule of reciprocity. In S6 ("Because I received *on* from that person"), I wanted to know whether and how the subjects would express the sense of indebtedness to an explicitly mentioned benefactor who is clearly other than Ego's parents. The result is shown in Table 7.

The large portion of both A and Y responded to the *on* debt with the intent of repayment, as shown in categories 1 and 2. That intent, however, was expressed more frequently by adults in voluntaristic (2) rather than obligatory (1) terms, granted that both groups rank highest in "willingness to repay." This difference takes a more striking form of contrast in categories 3 and 4, where

Table 7: Attitude toward *On* Benefactor

S6: Because I once received on from that person...

R6	Male		Female		Total	
	A	Y	A	Y	A	Y
1. Obligation to repay "I must repay him some time"	15.0	22.9	7.0	15.2	10.3	19.1
2. Willingness to repay "I want to help him" "I will do my best to return the *on*"	57.5	37.5	59.6	52.2	58.8	44.7
3. Inhibition, constraint "I must be patient with him" "I cannot talk back to him"	5.0	25.0	3.5	21.7	4.1	23.4
4. Acknowledgment, unforgetfulness "I must not forget that under any circumstances" "I am grateful"	17.5	4.2	21.1	4.3	19.6	4.3
5. Other	5.0	10.4	8.8	6.5	7.2	8.5
(5a) Ego's achievement "I want to succeed so that he will be pleased with me"	(0.0)	(2.1)	(1.8)	(0.0)	(1.0)	(1.1)
(5b) Obligation denied, disapproved "I don't feel any need to repay" "To think that way is too restrictive"	(0.0)	(2.1)	(1.8)	(6.5)	(1.0)	(4.3)
(5c) Other "We are good friends"	(5.0)	(6.3)	(5.3)	(0.0)	(5.2)	(3.1)
Total (N)	40	48	57	46	97	94

Intergenerational difference: $X^2 = 26.83$ (p $<$ .001)

Within-group sex differences: Adult $X^2 = 2.21$ (p $<$ .70) }DF = 4

Youth $X^2 = 2.39$ (p $<$ .70)

adults express acknowledgment and gratitude, while youth incline toward inhibition and circumspection. This seems to be a remarkable summation of the *on* complex involving a wide range of feelings from positive to negative. The compulsion for repayment of *on*, I think, derives from two sources: gratitude and burdensomeness; compelled by gratitude, one wishes spontaneously to repay, while, pressed under the burden, one wishes to repay as soon as possible in order to get rid of the load. Youth seem to regard *on* as a burden that constrains freedom of action, requires circumspection, and thus can arouse hostility toward the benefactor; adults give more morally and spontaneously inclined responses in the form of gratitude.

Youth may acknowledge their debt spontaneously, as in R5, but at the same time may be easily sensitized to the negative, constraining aspect of *on* once a specific person is identified as their benefactor, as in R6. I am not certain whether this is an indication of alienation on the part of contemporary youth from the *on*-based norms of traditional culture, or whether this type of split in reaction to *on* is typical of youth-adult differences in general. The likelihood of alienation from *on* as such seems quite low, however, in view of the negligible number of negative responses (5b), even among youth.

The statistical test of Table 7 shows a significantly wide generation gap ($p < .001$).

Investor's Resources and Motives

Given compensative justice as an effectively operating part of the moral order, the remaining question is whether one is willing to invest at all, and if so, what resources are available to the investing actor.

Investment for Home Life. S7 ("In order to build an ideal home

Table 8: Resources for Investment in Home Life
S7: In order to build an ideal home life...

	Male		Female		Total	
R7	A	Y	A	Y	A	Y
1. Energy expenditure "I will work hard" "I make every effort"	14.6	42.2	22.0	23.9	19.0	33.0
2. Moral resolution "I shall live faithfully" "Self-discipline is necessary"	43.9	13.3	27.1	15.2	34.0	14.3
3. Rationality, planning, ability "First plan, and then act"	4.9	8.9	1.7	6.5	3.0	7.7
4. Cooperation, communication "Let us better understand each other" "All family members must cooperate"	29.3	28.9	44.1	47.8	38.0	38.5
5. Other (including external conditions such as "Money is necessary")	7.3	6.7	5.1	6.5	6.0	6.6
Total (N)	41	45	59	46	100	91

Intergenerational difference: $X^2 = 13.18$ ($p < .02$)
Within-group sex differences: Adult $X^2 = 5.11$ ($p < .30$) } DF = 4
                                          Youth $X^2 = 4.66$ ($p < .50$)

life") was intended to elicit the subjects' willingness and resources for investing in a personal home life. All respondents, with a negligible few exceptions, either expressed willingness for or implied acceptance of such an investment by indicating necessary efforts or external conditions. Let us look at what kinds of resources were identified, particularly those resources internal to the actor.

Table 8 reveals that youth, particularly male youth, have more faith in physical energy to be expended (category 1), whereas adults, male adults especially, incline toward moral resources (2). It appears as if the two generations are capitalizing, this way, upon their respective points of strength. Category 3, "rationality," is represented more among youth, but we are unable to generalize, because of the negligible frequency, that this reflects the importance of rationality in postwar education. Category 4 refers predominantly to cooperation within the family and is overrepresented by the female respondents across the generations.

Table 9: Moral Legitimacy of Respect-invoking Action
S8: In order to be respected by others . . .

R8	Male		Female		Total	
	A	Y	A	Y	A	Y
1. Approval or association with desirable action "You must polish yourself" "You should respect others first"	76.9	56.8	85.5	70.7	81.9	63.5
2. Negative response	23.1	43.2	14.5	29.3	18.1	36.5
(2a) Disapproval or association undesirable action "It would be repulsive to do something (in order to . . .)" "Pretend to be better than what you really are" "You overstretch yourself and end up being unfaithful to yourself"	(12.8)	(25.0)	(7.3)	(17.1)	(9.6)	(21.2)
(2b) Indifference "I don't make special effort (in order to...)" "I am not aware (of doing things in order to...)"	(5.1)	(18.2)	(7.3)	(9.8)	(6.4)	(14.1)
(2c) Other	(5.1)	(0.0)	(0.0)	(2.4)	(2.1)	(1.2)
Total (N)	39	44	55	41	94	85

Intergenerational difference: $X^2 = 7.69$ (p < .01)
Within-group sex differences: Adult $X^2 = 1.12$ (p < .30) } DF = 1
Youth $X^2 = 1.77$ (p < .20)

The generational differences in Table 8 seem to stem from different resources unique to the different qualities of respondents, such as the physical prowess of male youth, the moral discipline of adults, and the socioemotional sensitivity of the female sex. By and large, we are impressed by the lack of a generation gap; both generations are clearly positive toward the notion of building an ideal home life.

Investment for Gaining Respect. When we come to S8 ("In order to be respected by others"), a totally different picture emerges. Here we find a strong refusal by youth to go along with the given stimulus. While 81.9 percent of adults show a willingness to invest in or approve of respect-invoking action, only 63.5 percent of youth are so inclined (see Table 9). Conversely, disapproval of or indifference to such action is expressed much more strongly by youth, particularly by male youth. Quite symbolically, one youth respondent pointed to the "impurity" and another to the "hypocrisy" of such purposeful action. Respect should come only as a result of action, they seem to be protesting, not be intended as its goal. Here the legitimacy of social investment as such was brought into question, and accusation was made of the investor's immoral motive.

This takes us back to what we noted before regarding R3 (Kindness): negative responses to kindness more frequently observed among the youth sample fall in two categories—denial of payoff and disapproval of expectation of reward. The former rejects the idea of compensative justice from an egoistic point of view as illustrated by, "You will only lose (if you are kind to others)." The latter case, on the other hand, as exemplified by, "You should not expect to be reciprocated," rejects compensative justice from a selfless, disinterested point of view. It seems that doing something good in anticipation of a reward repels the moral fastidiousness, or "fidelity," of youth. If the egoistic rejection of compensative justice is a sign of either postwar socialization or demoralization, refusal to anticipate a reward suggests a strong moral commitment suggestive of altruism.

How can we reconcile altruistic fidelity with egoistic resistance to moral control, both present more frequently in the youth sample? We realize that the apparent discrepancy between these two orientations is not any more than what they share in common. Both altruism and egoism in their extremes claim the actor's autonomy of "social" feedback, social contingency, or considerations of social equilibrium. Social insensitivity in this sense seems to account for the discrepancy between adults and youth, as observed in R2 (Suffering), in the frequency of empathy for others' suffering as a product of one's own suffering. Indeed, the negative responses we are discussing here appeared more often in reaction to those S's that have social references, be they social investment, such as "kindness" (S3), or social motive, such as gaining "respect" (S8). Similarly, ambivalence toward the benefactor as expressed in R6 (*On*) suggests youth's resistance to social expectations.

This does not deny that a conflict between egoism and altruism can exist where moral strain overlaps with natural inclination. Perhaps it is this mechanism that was working when youth gave such positive responses, almost totally free of skepticism or cynicism, to S's referring to the family, noted in R4 (Filial piety) and R7 (Ideal home life). This means that what we said about the social insensitivity of youth applies only to remote, impersonal relationships, not to intimate, personal interactions. The latter are typically found within the nuclear family and probably in a small-scale peer group as well.

Conclusion

The foregoing analysis has focused on compensative justice as it is regarded by an actor who expects compensation for his social investment, who is indebted to others, or who might invest for a particular purpose. Our findings have not led to a clear-cut continuity or discontinuity between two generations under study. Keeping this uncertainty in mind, we may still draw some tentative generalizations.

First, our data suggest that the difference between youth and adults lies not so much in the former's alienation from moral values in general as in their resistance to the traditional morality of Japan. The traditional morality, as I see it, has been regulated primarily by the "social radar" built in each actor. The higher social insensitivity found among youth tends to express itself in two seemingly contrasting directions: egoistic indulgence and compulsive denial of self-interest. Such unilateral extremism of youth contrasts with the social relativism binding adults' orientations. It may be that social morality as conceived here is more vulnerable than other types of morality to the simultaneous influence of the three factors presented in the introduction—postwar resocialization, industrialization, and life cycle.

Second, in spite of the attenuation of the socially controlled moral system, youth do not diverge from adults in attachment to family ties even when they are responding to such a traditional stimulus as filial piety. Alienation from social morality as pointed out above, therefore, applies only to social units larger than or outside the nuclear family. Positive identification with the nuclear family may be a sign of, among many others, the prolonged and exclusive dependency of today's youth on their parents, as well as of the atomization of solidarity units into the smallest, most intimate interaction unit. Interpreted this way, consolidation of the nuclear family is seen not as a contradiction to, but rather as causally interlocked with, the impairment of "social radar."

Third, what generation gap appeared was found to exist more between male adults and male youth than between female counterparts, especially when the gap implied a real discontinuity or even conflict. This leads to two hypotheses: generation conflict is derived, as Bettelheim claims, mainly from the succession syndrome affecting the male holder of an authority position and his male successor such as father and son, only; as far as Japanese culture is concerned, its traditional values have been identified with or insisted upon more strongly by men than by women.

Lastly, despite the above findings, our overall impression is that the two generations do not diverge as widely as anticipated. They share, we found, the same moral orientation, judging from the responses of the majority. Divergences showed up in minority responses: we saw frequency reversal only in those categories of second, third, or lower frequency, not of the highest. We might conclude that the two generations are continuous in dominant patterns and discontinuous in more extreme orientations. This statement does not contradict the prevailing keen sense of a generation gap, because it is extreme patterns that draw observers' attention and because only difference, not sameness, conveys messages. Moreover, what appeared to be a gap often turned out to be a complementary difference attributable to different life stages.

It is possible that intergenerational continuity in dominant patterns, as hypothesized here, reflects the bias of our data. Methodologically, it may be argued that projective tests like sentence-completion tests tend to reveal the most conservative aspect of behavior. If so, it only confirms the unique merit of a projective test. More serious would be the bias of our sample. It may be that the subjects selected here do not represent the Japanese population in terms of the degree of urbanization. This possibility will be either accepted or rejected when a more urban sample is collected in my next project, which is under way on a cross-cultural scale.

ACKNOWLEDGMENTS

I wish to acknowledge support by the National Institute of Mental Health (Grant # MH09243) that made this research possible. Thanks are also due the Social Science Research Institute, University of Hawaii, for providing assistance in writing this paper.

NOTES

1. I have benefited from a methodological review of the SCT given by Goldberg (1965).
2. The problem of translation alone would require detailed discussion, but suffice it to point out the following: S5 might well be translated, "We can live as happily as we do because." However, such reasoning is only implied and thus can be ignored in the Japanese original. "You" in S's 1, 3, and 4, used as a generic person, has no equivalent in Japanese. "That person" in S6 was used instead of "him" or "her" because the Japanese word does not distinguish sex.
3. This word will be clarified in the text when we deal with social debt.
4. I wish to acknowledge the statistical advice rendered by my colleague, Michael Agar, although responsibility for the interpretation of the data is entirely mine.
5. Gouldner's (1960) confusion in his theory of reciprocity derives, I believe, from his failure to distinguish these.

REFERENCES

Bernard, J. 1961. Teenage culture: an overview. Annals of the American Academy of Political and Social Sciences 338:1–12.
Bettelheim, B. 1965. The problem of generations. *In* The challenge of youth. Erik H. Erikson, ed. Garden City, New York, Doubleday.
Brown, W. N. 1968. Alienated youth. Mental Hygiene 52:330–36.
Denisoff, R.S., and M.H. Levine. 1970. Generations and counter-culture: a study in the ideology of music. Youth and Society 2:33–58.
DeVos, G. 1960. The relation of guilt toward parents to achievement and arranged marriage among the Japanese. Psychiatry 23:287–301.
Drucker, P.F. 1971. The surprising seventies. Harper's, July 1971.
Eisenstadt, S.N. 1965. Archetypal patterns of youth. *In* The challenge of youth. Erik H. Erickson, ed. Garden City, New York, Doubleday.
Eisner, V. 1969. Alienation of youth. The Journal of School Health 39:81–90.
Erikson, E.H. 1965. Youth: fidelity and diversity. *In* The challenge of youth. E.H. Erikson, ed. Garden City, New York, Doubleday.
Feuer, L.S. 1969. The conflict of generations. New York, Basic Books.
Flacks, R. 1967. The liberated generation: an exploration of the roots of student protest. Journal of Social Issues 23, 3:52–75.
Glazer, N. 1970. The six roots of campus trouble. Harvard Bulletin, September 21, 1970:23–30.
Goldberg, P.A. 1965. A review of sentence completion methods in personality assessment. *In* Handbook of projective techniques. B.I. Murstein, ed. New York, Basic Books.
Gouldner, A.W. 1960. The norm of reciprocity: a preliminary statement. American Sociological Review 25:161–78.
Greeley, A.M. 1970. Implications for the sociology of religion of occult behavior in the youth culture. Youth and Society 2:131–40.
Keniston, K. 1965. The uncommitted: alienated youth in American society. New York, Harcourt, Brace and World.

————. 1967. The sources of student dissent. Journal of Social Issues 23:108–37.

Lebra, T.S. 1971. The social mechanism of guilt and shame. Anthropological Quarterly 44:241–55.

Lifton, R.J. 1962. Youth and history: individual change in postwar Japan. Daedalus 91:172–97.

Lipset, S.M. 1970. American student activism in comparative perspective. American Psychologist 25:675–93.

Matza, D. 1961. Subterranean traditions of youth. Annals of the American Academy of Political and Social Sciences 338:102–18.

Mays, J.B. 1961. Teenage culture in contemporary Britain and Europe. Annals of the American Academy of Political and Social Science 338:22–32.

Mead, M. 1970. Culture and commitment, a study of the generation gap. New York, Natural History Press.

Meyerson, M. 1966. The ethos of the American college students: beyond the protests. Daedalus 95:713–39.

Moller, H. 1968. Youth as a force in the modern world. Comparative Studies in Society and History 10:237–60.

Murphy, H.B.M. 1971. Mass youth protest movements in Asia and the West: their common characteristics and psychiatric significance. Presented at the Conference on Culture and Mental Health in Asia and the Pacific. Social Science Research Institute and East-West Center, Honolulu, Hawaii, March 15–19, 1971.

Oppenheimer, M. 1968. The student movement as a response to alienation. Journal of Human Relations 16:1–16.

Parsons, T. 1965. Youth in the context of American society. *In* The challenge of youth. E.H. Erikson, ed. Garden City, New York, Doubleday.

Riesman, D. 1958. Leisure and work in postindustrial society. *In* Abundance for what. D. Riesman, ed. Garden City, New York, Doubleday (1965).

Seidensticker, E. 1970. The pulverizers. Encounter 34(6):81–87.

Special Committee on Campus Tensions. 1970. Campus tensions: analysis and recommendations. American Psychologist 25:694–725.

Tashiro, S. 1970. Kokosei (Secondary high school students). Tokyo, Iwanami. [In Japanese.]

Watanuki, T. 1966. On generation. Sociologia Internationalis 4:197–203.

World Assembly of Youth. 1967. Youth and urbanization in Asia. Based on the WAY Asian Regional Seminar, Singapore, April 16–30, 1967.

The Relation of Guilt toward Parents to Achievement and Arranged Marriage among the Japanese

GEORGE DEVOS

This paper, based on research materials gathered in Japan, suggests certain interpretations concerning the structuring of guilt in Japanese society.[1] Especially pertinent are Thematic Apperception Test (TAT) materials in which the subjects invent stories about a series of ambiguous pictures, which were taken from Niiike, an agricultural village of central Honshu. It is possible to obtain from the stories involving themes of achievement and marriage relationships indirect verification of hypotheses concerning the nature of inter-

From *Psychiatry* 23 (1960):287–301. Copyright 1960 by The William Alanson White Psychiatric Foundation, Inc. Reprinted by special permission of the Foundation.

The author is indebted to Hiroshi Wagatsuma for his able assistance and collaboration in the analysis and interpretation of basic materials. The materials on which the following interpretations are based were obtained by the author as a member of a large interdisciplinary project in cooperation with the Human Relations Interdisciplinary Research Group of Nagoya under the direction of Dr. Tsuneo Muramatsu, Professor of Psychiatry, Nagoya National University. This research, which is continuing in Japan under Professor Muramatsu's direction, was sponsored in part by the Center for Japanese Studies of the University of Michigan, the Foundation Fund for Research in Psychiatry, and the Rockefeller Foundation. The author, who takes full responsibility for the views expressed in the present paper, based on material from a single village, participated in the Human Relations Interdisciplinary Research Group as a Fulbright research scholar in Japan from September, 1953, to July, 1955. Subsequent research on these psychological materials in the United States was assisted in various stages by a faculty research grant from the University of Michigan, the Behavioral Science Division of the Ford Foundation, and the National Institute of Mental Health. The Human Relations group hopes to be able to make more definitive statements than those of the present paper upon completion of its analysis of comparable primary material taken from three villages and two cities.

nalization of the Japanese social sanctions that have been influenced by the traditional neo-Confucian ethics sustained by the dominant samurai class in the past.

A central problem to be considered is whether the Japanese emphasis on achievement drive and on properly arranged marriage may possibly have its motivational source in the inculcation of shame or guilt in childhood. It is my contention that this emphasis is not to be understood solely as a derivative of what is termed a "shame" orientation, but rather as stemming from a deep undercurrent of guilt developed in the basic interpersonal relationships with the mother within the Japanese family.

The characteristic beliefs, values, and obligatory practices that provide emotional security and are usually associated in the West with religious systems and other generalized ideologies—and only indirectly related to family life[2]—are related much more directly to the family system of the tradition-oriented Japanese. The structuring of guilt in the Japanese is hidden from Western observation, since there is a lack of empathic understanding of what it means to be part of such a family system. Western observers tend to look for guilt, as it is symbolically expressed, in reference to a possible transgression of limits imposed by a generalized ideology or religious system circumscribing sexual and aggressive impulses. There is little sensitivity to the possibility that guilt is related to a failure to meet expectations in a moral system built around family duties and obligations.

Piers and Singer, in distinguishing between shame and guilt cultures,[3] emphasize that guilt inhibits and condemns transgression, whereas shame demands achievement of a positive goal. This contrast is related to Freud's two earlier distinctions in the functioning of the conscience. He used *shame* to delineate a reaction to the ego ideal involving a goal of positive achievement; on the other hand, he related *guilt* to superego formation and not to ego ideal. A great deal of Japanese cultural material, when appraised with these motivational distinctions in mind, would at first glance seem to indicate that Japanese society is an excellent example of a society well over on the shame side of the continuum.

Historically, as a result of several hundred years of tightly knit feudal organization, the Japanese have been pictured as having developed extreme susceptibility to group pressures toward conformity. This strong group conformity, in turn, is often viewed as being associated with a lack of personal qualities that would foster individualistic endeavor.[4] In spite of, or according to some observers because of, these conformity patterns, which are found imbedded in governmental organization as well as in personal habits, the Japanese—alone among all the Asian peoples coming in contact with Western civilization in the nineteenth century—were quickly able to translate an essentially feudal social structure into a modern industrial society and to achieve eminence as a world power in fewer than fifty years. This remarkable achievement can be viewed as a group manifestation of what is presumed to be a striving and achievement drive on the individual level.

Achievement drive in Americans has been discussed by Riesman,[5] among others, as shifting in recent years from Puritan, inner-directed motivation to other-directed concern with conformity and outer-group situations. Perceived in this framework, the Japanese traditionally have had an other-directed culture. Sensitivity to "face" and attention to protocol suggest that the susceptibility to social pressure, traced psychoanalytically, may possibly derive from underlying infantile fears of abandonment. Personality patterns integrated around such motivation, if culturally prevalent, could possibly lead to a society dominated by a fear of failure and a need for recognition and success.

Intimately related to a shift from Puritan patterns in America were certain changes in the patterns of child-rearing. Similarly, it has been observed in Japan that prevailing child-rearing practices emphasize social evaluation as a sanction, rather than stressing more internalized, self-contained ethical codes instilled and enforced early by parental punishment. In spite of some earlier contentions to the contrary based on a few retrospective interviews,[6] the child-rearing patterns most evident in Japan, in deed, if not in word, manifest early permissiveness in regard to weaning and bowel training and a relative lack of physical punishment.[7] There is, moreover, considerable emphasis on ridicule and lack of acceptance of imperfect or slipshold performance in any regard. There is most probably a strong relationship between early permissiveness and susceptibility to external social sanctions. In line with the distinctions made between shame and guilt, the Japanese could easily be classified as shame oriented, and their concern over success and failure could be explicable in these terms. Somehow this formula, however, does not hold up well when reapplied to an understanding of individual Japanese, either in Japan or in the United States.[8] Emphasis on shame sanctions in a society does not preclude severe guilt. While strong feelings of anxiety related to conformity are very much in evidence, both in traditional as well as present-day

Japanese society, severe guilt becomes more apparent when the underlying motivation contributing to manifest behavior is more intensively analyzed. Shame is a more conscious phenomenon among the Japanese, hence more readily perceived as influencing behavior. But guilt in many instances seems to be a stronger basic determinant.

Although the ego ideal is involved in Japanese strivings toward success, day-by-day hard work and purposeful activities leading to long-range goals are directly related to guilt feelings toward parents. Transgression in the form of "laziness" or other nonproductive behavior is felt to "injure" the parents, and thus leads to feelings of guilt. There are psychological analogs between this Japanese sense of responsibility to parents for social conformity and achievement, and the traditional association sometimes found in the Protestant West between work activity and a personal relationship with a deity.[9]

Any attempt to answer questions concerning guilt in the Japanese raises many theoretical problems concerning the nature of internalization processes involved in human motivation. It is beyond the scope of this paper to discuss theoretically the complex interrelationships between feelings of shame and guilt in personality development. But the author believes that some anthropological writings, oversimplifying psychoanalytic theory, have placed too great an emphasis on a direct one-to-one relationship between observable child-rearing disciplines culturally prevalent and resultant inner psychological states. These inner states are a function not only of observable disciplinary behavior but also of more subtle, less reportable, atmospheric conditions in the home, as well as of other factors as yet only surmised.

Moreover, in accordance with psychoanalytic theory concerning the mechanisms of internalizing parental identification in resolving the Oedipal developmental stage, one would presume on an a priori basis that internalized guilt tends to occur almost universally, although its form and emphasis might differ considerably from one society to another. This paper, while guided by theory, is based primarily on empirical evidence and a posteriori reasoning in attempting to point out a specifically Japanese pattern of guilt. Developmental vicissitudes involved in the resolution of Oedipal relationships are not considered. Concisely stated, the position taken in this paper is as follows:

Guilt in many of the Japanese is not only operative in respect to what are termed superego functions, but is also concerned with what has been internalized by the individual as an ego ideal. Generally speaking, the processes involved in resolving early identifications as well as assuming later adult social roles are never possible without some internalized guilt. The more difficult it is for a child to live up to the behavior ideally expected of him, the more likely he is to develop ambivalence toward the source of the ideal. This ideal need not directly emphasize prohibited behavior, as is the case when punishment is the mode of training.

When shame and guilt have undergone a process of internalization in a person during the course of his development, both become operative regardless of the relative absence of either external threats of punishment or overt concern with the opinions of others concerning his behavior. Behavior is automatically self-evaluated without the presence of others. A simple dichotomy relating internalized shame only to ego ideal and internalized guilt to an automatically operative superego is one to be seriously questioned.

Whereas the formation of an internalized ego ideal in its earlier form is more or less related to the social expectations and values of parents, the motivations which move a developing young adult toward a realization of these expectations can involve considerable guilt. Japanese perceptions of social expectations concerning achievement behavior and marriage choice, as shown in the experimental materials described in this paper, give ample evidence of the presence of guilt; shame as a motive is much less in evidence.

Nullification of parental expectations is one way to "hurt" a parent. As defined in this paper, guilt in the Japanese is essentially related either to an impulse to hurt, which may be implied in a contemplated act, or to the realization of having injured a love object toward whom one feels some degree of unconscious hostility.

Guilt feelings related to various internalization processes differ, varying with what is prohibited or expected; nevertheless, some disavowal of an unconscious impulse to hurt seems to be generic to guilt. In some instances there is also emphasis on a fear of retribution stemming from this desire to injure. Such seems to be the case in many of the Japanese. If a parent has instilled in a child an understanding of his capacity to hurt by failing to carry out an obligation expected of him as a member of a family, any such failure can make him feel extremely guilty.

In the following materials taken from the rural hamlet of Niiike,[10] an attempt will be made to demonstrate how guilt is often related to possible rebellion against parental expectations. Two possible ways for the male to rebel are: (1) Dissipating one's energies in some sort of profligate behavior rather than working hard, or neglecting the diligence and hard work necessary for obtaining some achievement goal. (2) Rejecting arranged marriage by losing oneself in a marriage of passion, a so-called "love marriage."

In women, guilt seems related to becoming selfish or unsubmissive in the pursuit of duties involved in their adult role possibilities as wife and mother. This could mean, as in the case of men, refusal to accept the parents' marriage arrangement, or, after marriage, failure to devote oneself with wholehearted intensity, without reservation, to the husband and his purposes and to the rearing of the children. Failure to show a completely masochistic, self-sacrificing devotion to her new family is a negative reflection on the woman's parents. Deficiencies in her children or even in her husband are sometimes perceived as her fault, and she must intrapunitively rectify her own failings if such behavior occurs. TAT stories taken from the Niiike sample bring out in both direct and indirect fashion evidence to support these contentions.

THE RELATION OF GUILT TO ACHIEVEMENT

The Japanese mother has perfected the technique of inducing guilt in her children by quiet suffering. A type of American mother often encountered in clinical practice repeatedly tells her children how she suffers from their bad behavior but in her own behavior reveals her selfish motives; in contrast, the Japanese mother does not to the same extent verbalize her suffering for her children but lives it out before their eyes. She takes on the burden of responsibility for her children's behavior—and her husband's—and will often manifest self-reproach if they conduct themselves badly. Such an example cannot fail to impress. The child becomes aware that his mother's self-sacrifice demands some recompense. The system of *On* obligation felt toward the parents, aptly described by Ruth Benedict,[11] receives a strong affective push from the Japanese mother's devotion to her children's successful social development, which includes the standards of success set for the community. As discussed in a previous paper,[12] the educational and occupational achievements of Japanese-Americans also show this pattern, modified in accordance with American influences.

The negative side of accomplishment is the hurt inflicted on the parent if the child fails or if he becomes self-willed in marriage or loses himself in indulgence. Profligacy and neglect of a vocational role in Japan—and often in the West as well—is an attack on the parents, frequently unconsciously structured.

The recurrence of certain themes in the TAT data, such as the occurrence of parental death as a result of disobedience, suggests the prevalence of expiation as a motive for achievement.[13] Themes of illness and death seem to be used not only to show the degree of parental, especially maternal, self-sacrifice, but also seem to be used as self-punishment in stories of strivings toward an ideal or goal with a single-minded devotion so strong that its effects may bring about the ruin of one's health.

These attitudes toward occupational striving can also be seen in the numerous examples in recent Japanese history of men's self-sacrifice for national causes. The sometimes inexplicable—to Western eyes at least—logic of the self-immolation practised in wartime by the Japanese soldier can better be explained when seen as an act of sacrifice not resulting only from pressures of group morale and propaganda stressing the honor of such a death. The emotions that make such behavior seem logical are first experienced when the child observes the mother's attitude toward her own body as she often exhausts it in the service of the family.

To begin the examination of TAT data, the relation of guilt to parental suffering is apparent in certain TAT stories in which the death of the parent follows the bad conduct of a child, and the two events seem to bear an implicit relationship, as expressed in the following summaries (*W* indicates a woman, *M* a man):[14]

> *W, age 16, Card J13:* A mother is sick; her son steals because of poverty; mother dies.
>
> *M, age 41, Card J6GF:* A daughter marries for love against father's will; she takes care of her father, but father dies.
>
> *W, age 22, Card J6GF:* A daughter marries against her father's opposition, but her husband dies and she becomes unhappy.
>
> *M, age 23, Card J18:* A mother strangles to death the woman who tempted her innocent son; the mother becomes insane and dies. The son begs forgiveness.

In such stories one may assume that a respondent first puts into words an unconscious wish of some kind but then punishes himself by bringing the death of a beloved person quickly into the scene.

One could also interpret such behavior in terms of cultural traditions. Punishing or retaliating against someone by killing or injuring oneself has often actually been done in Japan in both political and social arenas. Such self-injury or death became an accepted pattern of behavior under the rigid feudal regime, where open protest was an impossibility for the suppressed and ruled. Numerous works on Japanese history contain accounts of the severe limitations on socially acceptable behavior and spontaneous self-expression.

Understanding the "emotional logic" of this behavior, however, requires psychological explanations as well as such valid sociological explanations. This "moral masochistic" tendency, to use Freud's terminology, is inculcated through the attitudes of parents, especially of the mother. Suffering whatever the child does, being hurt constantly, subtly assuming an attitude of "look what you have done to me," the Japanese mother often gains by such devices a strong control over her child, and by increasing overt suffering, can punish him for lack of obedience or seriousness of purpose. Three of the above stories suggest that a mother or father is "punishing" a child by dying. Parents' dying is not only the punishment of a child, but also more often is the final control over that child, breaking his resistance to obeying the parental plans.

This use of death as a final admonishment lends credence to a story concerning the Japanese Manchurian forces at the close of World War II. The young officers in Manchuria had determined to fight on indefinitely, even though the home islands had surrendered. A staff general was sent by plane as an envoy of the Emperor to order the troops to surrender. He could get nowhere with the officers, who were determined to fight on. He returned to his plane, which took off and circled the field, sending a radio message that this was the final directive to surrender. The plane then suddenly dived straight for the landing field, crashing and killing all on board. The troops then promptly surrendered.

It is not unknown for a mother to threaten her own death as a means of admonishing a child. In a therapy case with a delinquent boy,[15] the mother had threatened her son, with very serious intent, telling him that he must stop his stealing or she would take him with her to the ocean and commit double suicide. The mother reasoned that she was responsible and that such a suicide would pay for her failure as a mother, as well as relieve the world of a potentially worthless citizen. The threat worked. For the man, this kind of threat of possible suffering becomes related to the necessity to work hard in the adult occupational role; for the woman, it becomes related to working hard at being a submissive and enduring wife.

In other of the TAT stories the death of a parent is followed by reform, hard work, and success. Examples of these stories are:

> *W, age 16, Card J7M:* A son, scolded by his father, walks out; the father dies; son works hard and becomes successful.

> *M, age 39, Card J5:* A mother worries about her delinquent son, becomes sick and dies; the son reforms himself and becomes successful.

> *M, age 54, Card J13:* A mother dies; the son changes his attitude and works hard.

> *W, age 17, Card J7M:* A father dies; son walks out as his mother repeatedly tells him to be like the father; when he meets her again, she dies; he becomes hard-working.

> *W, age 38, Card J9:* Elder brother is going to Tokyo, leaving his sick mother; his sister is opposed to his idea; his mother dies; he will become successful.

> *M, age 15, Card J6M:* A son becomes more thoughtful of his mother after his father's death; he will be successful.

Emphasis on hard work and success after the death of parents clearly suggests some expiatory meaning related to the "moral masochistic" attitude of the mother in raising her child. The mother's moral responsibility is also suggested by other stories, such as a mother being scolded by a father when the child does something wrong, or a mother—not the father—being hurt when the child does not behave well. The feeling experienced by the child when he realizes, consciously or unconsciously, that he has hurt his mother is guilt—because guilt is generated when one hurts the object of one's love. The natural ambivalence arising from living under close parental control supplies sufficient unconscious intent to hurt to make the guilt mechanism operative.

The expiatory emphasis on hard work and achievement is also evident as a sequel in TAT stories directly expressing hurt of one's mother or father:

> *M, age 17, Card J11:* A child dropped his father's precious vase. The father gets angry and scolds the mother for her having allowed the child to hold it. The child will become a fine man.

> *M, age 53, Card J18:* A child quarreled outside; his mother is sorry that his father is dead. The child makes a great effort and gets good school records.

> *M, age 24, Card J11:* A mother is worrying about her child who has gone out to play baseball and has not yet come back. When he comes home he overhears his mother complaining about his playing baseball all the time without doing his schoolwork. He then makes up his mind not to play baseball any more and to concentrate on his studies.

Although the realization of having hurt one's parents by bad conduct is not stated in the following story, it is another example of the use of working or studying hard—obviously as the means to achievement—to expiate possible guilt:

> *W, age 17, Card J3F:* A girl worries about the loss of her virginity, consults with someone and feels at ease. She studies hard in the future.

In the same context, if one fails to achieve, he has no way to atone. He is lost. The only thing left is to hurt himself, to extinguish himself—the one whose existence has been hurting his parents and who now can do nothing for them. Suicide as an answer is shown in the following stories:

> *M, age 57, Card 3BM* [original Murray card]: A girl fails in examination, kills herself.
>
> *W, age 32, Card J3F:* Cannot write a research paper; commits suicide.

On the level of cultural conditioning, the traditional teaching of *On* obligations enhances the feeling of guilt in the child, who is repeatedly taught by parents, teachers, books, and so forth, that his parents have experienced hardship and trouble and have made many sacrifices in order to bring him up. For example, financial strain and, significantly, ill health because of overwork may haunt the parents because of this child. Of course the child did not ask for all this sacrifice, nor does he consciously feel that he has intentionally hurt the parents, but there seems no way out; all this suffering takes place somewhere beyond his control, and he cannot avoid the burden it imposes. Certainly the child cannot say to himself, "I did not ask my parents to get hurt. Hurt or not, that is not my business," because he knows his parents love him and are also the objects of his love. What can be done about it then? The only way open to the child is to attain the goal of highest value, which is required of him; by working hard, being virtuous, becoming successful, attaining a good reputation and the praise of society, he brings honor to himself, to his parents, and to his *Ie* (household lineage), of which he and his parents are, after all, parts. If he becomes virtuous in this way, the parents can also receive credit. Self-satisfaction and praise from society go to them for having fulfilled their duty to *Ie* and society by raising their children well. The pattern repeats itself; he sacrifices himself masochistically for his own children, and on.

My assumption is, therefore, that among many Japanese

people such a feeling of guilt very often underlies the strong achievement drive and aspiration toward success. If this hypothesis is accepted, then it can easily be understood that the death of a parent—that is, the culmination of the parent's being hurt following some bad conduct of a child—evokes in the child a feeling of guilt which is strong enough to bring him back from delinquent behavior and to drive him toward hard work and success. This is what is happening in the TAT stories of parental death and the child's reform.

GUILT IN JAPANESE MARRIAGE RELATIONSHIPS

The feeling of *On* obligations generated in the family situation during childhood is also found to be a central focus in Japanese arranged marriages. This feeling of obligation is very pronounced in women. In a sense, a woman expresses her need for accomplishment and achievement by aiming toward the fulfillment of her roles as wife and mother within the new family she enters in marriage. The man does not face giving up his family ties in the same way. Interview data suggest that for a Japanese woman, failure to be a dutiful bride reflects on her parents' upbringing of her, and therefore any discord with her new family, even with an unreasonable mother-in-law, injures the reputation of her parents.

Marriages which go counter to family considerations and are based on individual passion or love are particularly prone to disrupt the family structure; they are likely to be of rebellious origin, and any subsequent stresses of adjustment to partner and respective families tend to remind the participants of the rebellious tone of the marriage and, therefore, to elicit guilt feelings.

The TAT stories give evidence of guilt in regard to both types of "unacceptable" marriage behavior—they show the wife's readiness for self-blame in marriage difficulties with her husband, and they express self-blame or blame of others, on the part of both men and women, for engaging in possible love marriages.

The Wife's Self-Blame in Difficulties with Her Husband

Of the stories involving discord between a man and his wife, several indicate a woman's feeling herself to be wrong in a situation which in America would be interpreted as resulting from the poor behavior of the husband. There are no cases of the reverse attitude —of a man's being blamed in an even slightly equivocal situation.

Four of five such stories are given by women. The man's story involves a need for reform by both partners, who are united in a love marriage and therefore apparently conform to the guilt pattern of such marriages, which I shall discuss shortly. In summary, the four women's stories are:

> *W, age 26, Card J3F:* A wife quarreled with her husband when he returned from drinking. She leaves her house to cry, feels guilty for the quarrel.

> *W, age 54, Card J4:* A husband and wife quarrel because the former criticized her cooking. The wife apologizes to him.

> *W, age 37, Card J4:* A husband and wife quarrel, and after it the wife apologizes to her angry husband.

> *W, age 22, Card J5:* A husband comes home very late at night; the wife thinks it is for lack of her affection and tries hard; he finally reforms.

Such attitudes also seem to be reflected in other test data, such as the "Problem Situations" material[16] collected in Niiike village. It is especially interesting to note that a husband's profligacy can be attributed by women to the wife's failure. It seems that the husband's willfulness—as is also true of a male child—is in some instances accepted as natural; somehow it is not his business to control himself if he feels annoyed with his wife. The wife nonetheless has to take responsibility for her husband's conduct. In one therapy case of a psychotic reaction in a young wife,[17] the mother-in-law blamed the bride directly for her husband's extramarital activities, stating, "If you were a good and satisfying wife, he would have no need to go elsewhere."

In connection with this point it may be worth mentioning that on the deepest level probably many Japanese wives do not "give" themselves completely to their husbands because the marriage has been forced on them as an arrangement between the parents in each family. Wives often may not be able to adjust their innermost feelings in the marital relationship so as to be able to love their husbands genuinely. They may sense their own emotional resistance and believe that it is an evil willfulness that keeps them from complete devotion as dictated by ethical ideals of womanhood. Sensing in the deepest level of their minds their lack of real affection, they become very sensitive to even the slightest indication of unfaithful behavior by the husbands They feel that the men are reacting to the wives' own secret unfaithfulness in withholding. They cannot, therefore, blame their husbands but throw the blame back upon themselves. They may become very anxious or quickly reflect upon and attempt to remedy their own inadequacies—as when their husbands happen to be late in getting home. Another hypothetical interpretation is that, lacking freedom of expression of their own impulses, Japanese women overidentify with male misbehavior; hence, they assume guilt as if the misbehavior were their own.

This propensity for self-blame in women is not necessarily limited to the wife's role. In the following story a younger sister somehow feels to blame when an older brother misbehaves.

W, age 17, Card J9: An elder brother did something wrong and is examined by the policeman; he will be taken to the police station, but will return home and reform. The younger sister also thinks that she was wrong herself.

One might say, in generalization, that the ethical ideal of self-sacrifice and devotion to the family line—be it to father or elder brother before marriage, or to husband and children after marriage—carries with it internalized propensities to take blame upon oneself and to express a moral sensitivity in these family relationships which no religious or other cultural sanctions compel the men to share.

Love Marriages and Other Heterosexual Relationships

Of the Niiike village TAT stories involving marriage circumstances,[13.] 13 directly mention an arranged marriage and 24 mention a love marriage. While 9 of the 13 arranged marriage stories show no tension or conflict between the people involved, only 2 of the 24 stories mentioning love marriage are tension-free. The rest all contain tension of some kind between parents and child or between the marriage partners. In other words, many of the men and women in Niiike who bring up the subject of love marriage still cannot see it as a positive accomplishment but, rather, see it as a source of disruption. As mentioned, love marriage carried out in open rebellion against the parents is punished in certain stories by the death of a beloved person.

M, age 41, Card J6F: They are father and his daughter. The mother has died. The daughter is sitting on a chair in her room. The father is looking in, and she is turning around to face him. He is very thoughtful of his daughter, and as she is just about of age [for marriage], he wants to suggest that she marry a certain man he selected. But she has a lover and does not want to marry the man her father suggests. The father is trying to read her face, though he does know about the existence of the lover. He brought up the subject a few times before, but the daughter showed no interest in it. Today also—a smile is absent in her face. The father talks about the subject again, but he fails to persuade her. So finally he gives in and agrees with her marrying her lover. Being grateful to the father for the consent, the daughter acts very kindly to him after her marriage. The husband and the wife get along very affectionately also. But her father dies suddenly of apoplexy. The father was not her real father. He did not have children, so he adopted her, and accepted her husband as his son-in-law. But he died. He died just at the time when a baby was born to the couple.

W, age 22, Card J6: The parents of this girl were brought up in families strongly marked with feudal atmosphere—the kind of family scarcely found in the present time. So they are very feudal and strict. The daughter cannot stand her parents. She had to meet her lover in secret. She was seeing her lover today as usual, without her parents knowing it. But by accident her father came to find it out. She was caught by her father on the spot. When she returned home her father rebuked her severely for it. But she could not give up her lover. In spite of her parents' strong objection, she married him. [*Examiner:* Future?] The couple wanted to establish a happy home when they married. But probably she will lose her husband. He will die—and she will have a miserable life.

There are a number of stories about unhappy events in the lives of a couple married for love. Many of these are found in response to Card 13 of the TAT, which shows a supine woman, breasts exposed, lying on a bed. A man in the foreground is facing away from the woman with one arm thrown over his eyes. A low table with a lamp is also in the room. Since responses to this card bring out in clear focus some basic differences between guilt over sexuality in Americans and in the Japanese, it will be well to consider them in some detail. Card J13 in the Japanese series is a modification of the original Murray TAT Card 13, with furniture and facial features altered.

Comparing Japanese and American responses to Card 13, it is obvious that while Americans rarely express remorse in connection with a marriage, the Japanese of Niiike express remorse in a heterosexual situation *only* in the context of marriage. In Americans, Card 13 is apt to evoke stories of guilt related to intercourse between partners not married to each other, with the figure of the woman sometimes identified as a prostitute, or sometimes as a young girl. When the figures are identified by Americans as married, the themes are usually around the subject of illness. In contrast, in the sample of 42 stories given in response to this card in Niiike village, not one story depicts a theme of guilt over sexuality between unmarried partners. Remorse is depicted only when it is related to regret for having entered into a love marriage.

Most of the Japanese stories given about this card fall into one of three categories: sex and/or violence (10 stories); marital discord (10 stories); and sickness or death (20 stories). Some striking differences in themes are related to the age and sex of the subjects.

Card 13: Sex and/or violence.—Six stories involve themes of extramarital sexual liaison. In three, the woman is killed by the man. Five of the six stories are given by men, who were with one exception under 35 years of age, and one is given by a woman under 25. The young woman's story depicts a man killing a woman because she was too jealous of him. One young man sees a man killing an entertainer who rejects him. Another sees a man killing a woman who was pursuing him "too actively." Another young man gives the theme of a student and a prostitute. In this story the man is disturbed by the prostitute's nakedness, not by his feelings of guilt over his activity.

The man over 35 sees the picture as depicting disillusion in a man who unexpectedly calls on a woman with whom he is in love, only to find her asleep in a "vulgar" fashion. As is true in the stories of other men over 35, which pertain to marital discord, the man is highly censorious of the woman's position on the bed. The Japanese woman is traditionally supposed to be proper in posture even when asleep. To assume a relaxed appearance reflects a wanton or sluttish nature.

Japanese men are apt to split their relationships with women into two groups: those with the wife and those with entertainers. Other evidence, not discussed here, supports the conclusion that for many men genuine affection is directed only toward maternal figures. Conversely, little deep affection seems freely available toward women perceived in a sexual role. Moreover, the Japanese male must defend himself against any passivity in his sexual relationship, lest he fall into a dependent relationship and become tied. By maintaining a rude aloofness and by asserting male prerogatives, he contains himself from involvement.

Men can resort to a violent defense if threatened too severely. Younger women especially tend to see men as potentially violent. Three women under 35 see a man as killing a woman, in two cases his wife. In addition to the jealousy mentioned before, the motives are the wife's complaint about low salary (a man must be seen as particularly sensitive about his economic prowess if such a complaint results in murder), and regret for entering a love marriage. The latter story, which follows, is particularly pertinent to understanding how guilt is related not to sexuality per se but to becoming "involved."

W, age 22: He got married for love with a woman in spite of opposition by his parents. While they were first married they lived
happily. But recently he reflects on his marriage and the manner in
which he pushed his way through his parents' opposition—and the
present wife—he wishes his present wife would not exist—he attempts
to push away the feeling of blame within his breast. One night on the
way home he buys some insect poison and gives it to his wife to drink
and she dies. What he has done weighs on his mind. He gives himself
up to the police. He trustfully tells his story to them. He reflects on
how wicked he has been in the past. He completes his prison term and
faces the future with serious intent.

This story indirectly brings out a feeling of guilt for attempting
to carry out a love marriage. Since such a marriage is psychologically forbidden fruit, the tasting of it brings upon the transgressor
punishment, much like what happens for sexual transgressions out
of wedlock in the fantasies of some more puritanical Westerners.

Card 13: Marital discord.—The nature of the stories concerning
marital discord is unique to the Japanese. Seven of the 21 Niiike
men giving stories about Card 13 mention marital discord. Five of
these men and all three women giving such stories are between 35
and 50 years of age. The men tend to see the marriage as ending
badly, whereas the women are more optimistic about seeing the
discord resolved. Both sexes usually place the blame for the discord
on the women.

As in one of the stories mentioned previously, the men take a cue
for their stories from the position of the woman in the bed. Rather
than seeing the woman as ill, as do many of the women responding
to this card, the men use the woman's posture as a basis for criticiz-
ing her. One of the chief complaints found in these stories is that
such a woman obviously does not take "proper care" of her man.
The following stories bring out the nature of some of the feelings
leading to the castigation of the wife for "looseness" and lack of
wifely concern for her husband. The man, too, is castigated in some
of the stories, but not with the strength of feeling that is turned toward the woman.

M, age 39: This is also very difficult for me. What shall I say—I
can't tell my impressions—what shall I say—it seems to me that they
do not lead a happy life. The man often comes back home late at
night, I suppose. But his wife does not wait for her husband. She has
decided to act of her own accord, I suppose—he is back home late
again, and his wife is already asleep. He thinks that it might be well
to speak to her. I suppose there is always a gloomy feeling in this
family. Well, if they lead a peaceful life, such a scene as this would
never occur. It is customary that a wife takes care of her husband as

she should when he comes home—and afterward she goes to bed. But, judging from this picture, I suppose this wife wouldn't care a bit about her husband. Such a family as this will be ruined, I think. They should change their attitude toward each other and should make happy home. [*Examiner:* What about the future?] They will be divorced. It will be their end. [*Examiner:* Do you have anything to add?] Well, I expect a woman to be as a woman should be. A man also should think more of his family.

M, age 41: This is also—this man is a drunkard, and his wife also a sluttish woman. And the man was drunk, and when he came back his wife was already asleep—and, well—finally, they will be ruined. They have no child. They will become separated from each other. This wife will become something like *nakai* or a procuress. The husband will be held in prison—and the husband will kill himself on the railroad tracks. And—the wife will work as a *nakai*, and after contracting an infectious disease will die. An infectious disease which attacks her is dysentery. They worked together in a company and were married for love. That is their past. [*Examiner:* What does it mean that they will be ruined?] He became desperate. He became separated from his wife, so that he became desperate. If a man committed a bad thing, nobody cares for him. He could not hope for any help, so that he killed himself.

M, age 35: Well, this man and woman married for love. The woman was a café waitress and married the man for love. But they have not lived happily, so the man repents the marriage very much. Well, this man used to be a very good man, but he was seduced by the waitress and lost his self-control, and at last he had a sexual relationship with her. Afterwards, he becomes afraid that he has to think over their marriage. If their married life has any future at all, I hope they will maintain some better stability. But if this woman doesn't want to do so, he needs to think over their marriage, I suppose.

The latter story especially brings out strong feelings of guilt related to an attempt to carry out a love marriage. The story directly depicts the guilt as being related to losing self-control and becoming involved with an unsuitable woman, not with the sexual activity per se.

Implied, too, is the criticism that any woman who would make a love marriage is not really capable of being a very worthy wife. Therefore, in addition to depicting guilt for going counter to the parents in a love marriage, Card 13 indicates the potential avenue for projecting guilt on to the woman who is active enough to enter a love marriage. Such a woman's conduct obviously does not include the proper submissiveness to parental wishes and attention to the needs of her spouse.

This castigation of the woman is therefore directly related to an expectation that the wife, rather than being a sexual object, should be a figure fulfilling dependency needs. The man sees his wife in a maternal role and is probably quick to complain if his wife renders him less care and attention than were rendered him by his mother. Since the wife-mother image tends to be fused in men, there is little concept of companionship per se, or sharing of experience on a mutual basis. Also, the wife's acting too free sexually excites aspects of sexuality toward the mother that were repressed in childhood. The wife-mother image cannot be conceived of in gross sexual terms. It is speculated by some that the mistress is a necessity to some men, because their sexual potency toward their wives is muted by the fused wife-mother image. Certain free sexual attitudes on the part of the wife would tend to change the mother image of her to a prostitute image and cause castigation of her as morally bad.

One may say that this fusion of images has a great deal to do with the conflict often arising between the young bride and her mother-in-law. The mother-in-law's jealousy is partially due to her fear of being directly replaced in her son's affection by the bride, since they are essentially geared to similar roles rather than forming different types of object relationship with the man. The wife becomes more intimate with the husband after she becomes a mother, and essentially treats him as the favorite child.

These sorts of attitudes were present in Hirano's case, mentioned previously, wherein a woman's psychotic episode was precipitated by her mother-in-law's attacks, including the interpretation that the dalliance of her son with other women was further proof of the wife's incompetence. It was interesting to note that during the wife's stay in the hospital the husband was able to express considerable feeling of concern for her. There was no doubt that he loved her. In effect, however, this feeling was more for her as a maternal surrogate than as a sexual partner. His mother knew she had more to fear from the wife in this respect than from liaisons with other women, with whom the husband never became too involved. He, on the other hand, had no manifest guilt for his sexual activities—in effect, they were approved of by his mother in her battle with the wife.

Card 13: Sickness or death of wife or mother.—In six instances (five women, three of them teen-agers), Card 13 is interpreted as a mother-son situation with the mother either sick or dead. The son is pictured specifically as working hard or studying; in one story the son steals because they are so poor. The younger girls especially seem to need to defend themselves from the sexual implications of the card by inventing a completely desexualized relationship. Unable to make the card into a marital situation, much less a more directly sexual one, some fall back on the favored theme of a sick mother and a distraught, but diligent, son. Emphasis on studying hard suggests the defensive use of work and study to shut out intrapersonal problems. Diligent work to care for the mother is again unconsciously used to avoid any feelings related to possible guilt. The way out is the one most easily suggested by the culture. Seeing Card 13 as a mother-son situation is rare in American records, even in aberrant cases.

Seeing Card 13 as illness or death of a wife is the most characteristic response of women; fourteen women, most of them over 35 years of age, gave such stories. Six men, including four of the five in the sample over 50, selected this theme. The middle-aged women were strongly involved in their stories about the death of a wife. Such stories were the longest of any given to the card. In sharp contrast to the derogatory stories directed toward the women by the men, the women use respectful concepts, such as *Otoko-naki* ("manly tears"), in referring to the men. On certain occasions it is expected that "manly tears" are shed. Although a man is usually expected not to cry freely when sober, the death of a wife is an occasion on which he is expected to cry. Much emphasis is placed on the imagined love felt toward the wife by a husband, on his loneliness, and on his feeling of loss because of the absence of wifely care. Concern with potential loneliness and possible loss of such care is certainly reflected in the fact that the older men in most instances select similar themes. The women in all but one case see the wife as dead or dying; the man is frequently seen as remarrying. Conversely, the men are more optimistic about recovery of a wife from illness and more pessimistic about remarriage if she does not recover.

One woman constructs a story of the noble self-sacrifice of a sick wife who commits suicide so as not to be a burden to her husband. This type of story, which recalls many sentimental novels written in Japan, is considered very moving by the Japanese, since it is supposed to reflect the degree of devotion of a wife for her husband and his goals and purposes. Tears are brought to the eyes of the older members of a *Kabuki* audience when such a story unfolds. To the Westerner, the stories seem to be excessively masochistic and overdrawn. The Japanese ethical ideal of the self-sacrificing role of woman is here emphatically displayed.

The foregoing materials from a farming village, which other

evidence suggests is deeply imbued with traditional attitudes, are consistent with the interpretation that the potentiality for strong guilt feelings is prevalent in the Japanese. Such feelings become evident when there is failure in the performance of expected role behavior. Guilt, as such, is not as directly related in the Japanese to sexual expression as it is in the persons growing up within cultures influenced by Christian attitudes toward sexuality. As first pointed out by Benedict,[19] there is little pronounced guilt or otherwise negatively toned attitude directed toward physical expression of sexuality per se. Rather, there is concern with the possible loss of control suffered by becoming involved in a love relationship that interferes with the prescribed life goals of the individual.

From a sociological standpoint, Japanese culture can be considered as manifesting a particularistic or situational ethic as opposed to the more universalistic ethic built around moral absolutes found in Western Christian thought.[20] This evaluation can be well documented but does not mean that the Japanese evidence a relative absence of guilt in relation to moral transgressions. Whereas the applicability of the more universalistic Western ethic in many aspects may tend to transcend the family, the Japanese traditional ethic is actually an expression of rules of conduct for members of a family, and filial piety has in itself certain moral absolutes that are not competely situationally determined, even though they tend to be conceptualized in particularistic terms. This difference between family-oriented morality and a more universalistic moral system is, nevertheless, a source of difficulty in thinking about guilt in the Japanese.

Another reason for the failure to perceive guilt in the Japanese stems from the West's customary relation of guilt to sexuality. Missionaries in particular, in assessing the Japanese from the standpoint of Protestant moral standards, were often quoted as perplexed not only by what they considered a lack of moral feeling in regard to nonfamilial relationship but also—and this was even worse in their eyes—by a seeming absence of any strong sense of "sin" in their sexual relationships. It seems evident that the underlying emotional content of certain aspects of Christianity, in so far as it is based on specific types of repression and displacement of sexual and aggressive impulses, has never appealed to the Japanese in spite of their intellectual regard for the ethics of Christianity. Modern educated Japanese often recognize Christianity as advocating an advanced ethical system more in concert with modern universalized democratic ideas of man's brotherhood. As such Christianity is favored by them over their more hierarchically oriented, traditional system with its rigidly defined, particularistic emphasis on prescribed social roles. To the educated Japanese, however, the concept of sin is of little interest in their attitudes toward Christianity. The lack of interest in sin is most probably related to the absence of childhood disciplines that would make the concept important to them.

Traditional Western disciplinary methods, guided by concern with the inherent evil in man, have been based on the idea that the child must be trained as early as possible to conquer evil tendencies within himself. Later, he learns to resist outside pressures and maintain himself as an individual subject to his own conscience and to the universalist laws of God. The traditional Western Protestant is more accustomed in certain circumstances to repress inappropriate feelings. "Right" thoughts are valued highly, and one generally tries to repress unworthy motives toward one's fellow men. Justice must be impartial, and one must not be swayed by the feelings of the moment or be too flexible in regard to equity.

In Japanese Buddhist thought one finds a dual concept of man as good and evil, but in Shinto thought, and in Japanese thinking about children generally,[21] the more prevailing notion is that man's impulses are innately good. The purpose of child training is merely the channeling of these impulses into appropriate role behavior.

The definitions of proper role behavior become increasingly exacting as the child grows and comes into increasing contact with others as a representative of his family. As such, he learns more and more to be diplomatic and to contain and suppress impulses and feelings that would be disruptive in social relations and put him at a disadvantage. He is not bringing a system of moral absolutes into his relations with others any more than the usual diplomat does in skillfully negotiating for the advantage of his country. The Japanese learns to be sensitive to "face" and protocol and to be equally sensitive to the feelings of others. He learns to keep his personal feelings to himself as a family representative. It would be just as fallacious to assume, therefore, that the Japanese is without much sense of guilt as it would be in the case of the private life of a career diplomat.

The fact that so much of conscious life is concerned with a system of social sanctions helps to disguise the underlying guilt system operative in the Japanese. This system, which severely represses unconscionable attitudes toward the parents and superiors, is well disguised not only from the Western observer but also from the Japanese themselves. The Westerner, under the tutelage of

Christianity, has learned to "universalize" his aggressive and other impulses and to feel guilt in regard to them in more general terms. The modern Japanese is moving toward such an attitude but is affected by the traditional moral structure based on the family system, or if expanded, on the nation conceived of in familial terms.

Lastly, some difficulty in perceiving Japanese guilt theoretically, if not clinically, is due to the fact that psychoanalysis—the psychological system most often consulted for help in understanding the mechanisms involved in guilt—tends to be strongly influenced by Western ethical values. Psychoanalytic writers, in describing psychosexual development, tend to emphasize the superego on the one hand and concepts of personal individuation and autonomy on the other. A major goal of maturation is freedom in the ego from irrational social controls as well as excessive internalized superego demands. In understanding the Japanese, this emphasis is somewhat out of focus. Maturational ideals valued by the traditional Japanese society put far more emphasis on concepts of "belonging" and adult role identity.

In studying the Japanese, it is helpful, therefore, to try to understand the nature of internalization of an ego ideal defined in terms of social role behavior. Concern with social role has in the past been more congenial to the sociologist or sociologically oriented anthropologist,[22] who in examining human behavior is less specifically concerned with individuation and more concerned with the patterning of behavior within a network of social relations.

However, the sociological approach in itself is not sufficient to help understand the presence or absence of a strong achievement motive in the Japanese. It is necessary to use a psychoanalytic framework to examine the psychological processes whereby social roles are internalized and influence the formation of an internalized ego ideal. The ideas of Erikson,[23] in his exploration of the role of "self-identity" in the latter stages of the psychosexual maturation process, form a bridge between the psychoanalytic systems of thought and the sociological analyses which cogently describe the place of role as a vital determining factor of social behavior. The avenue of approach taken by Erikson is a very promising one in understanding the Japanese social tradition and its effect on individual development.

NOTES

1. This paper will not discuss subcultural variations. Niiike village is representative of a farming community that has well internalized the traditional, dominant values held by the samurai during the Tokugawa period (about 1600–1868). Other local rural traditions emphasize other values. For example, material from a fishing community wherein the status position of women is higher than in the farming community considered shows far different results in the projective tests. Women are perceived in TAT stories as more assertive, even aggressive, toward their husbands. Guilt is not expressed in stories of self-sacrificing mothers. Love marriages are accepted and not seen in the context of remorse, and so on. A comparison of the attitudes of the farming village with those of the fishing village is presented in detail in the following article: George De Vos and Hiroshi Wagatsuma, "Variations in Traditional Value Attitudes Related Toward Status and Role Behavior of Women in Two Japanese Villages," submitted for publication, *Amer. Anthropologist*.

2. Abram Kardiner, *The Individual and His Society;* New York, Columbia Univ. Press, 1939; pp. 89–91.

3. Gerhart Piers and Milton B. Singer, *Shame and Guilt;* Springfield, Ill., Charles C. Thomas, 1953. See also Thomas M. French, "Guilt, Shame, and Other Reactive Motives," an unpublished paper.

4. See, for example, Lafcadio Hearn's statement that Japanese authoritarianism is that of "the many over the one—not the one over the many." *Japan. An Attempt at Interpretation;* New York, Macmillan, 1905; pp. 435ff.

5. David Riesman, *The Lonely Crowd;* New Haven, Yale Univ. Press, 1950.

6. For example, Geoffrey Gorer, "Themes in Japanese Culture," *Transact. N.Y. Acad. Sciences* (1943) 2:106–124.

7. See, for example, the empirical reports by Betty B. Lanham, "Aspects of Child Care in Japan: Preliminary Report," pp. 565–583; and Edward and Margaret Norbeck, "Child Training in a Japanese Fishing Community," pp. 651–673; in *Personal Character and Cultural Milieu*, edited by Douglas G. Haring; Syracuse, Syracuse Univ. Press, 1956. A forthcoming publication by Edward Norbeck and George De Vos, "Culture and Personality: The Japanese," will present a more comprehensive bibliography, including the works of native Japanese, on child-rearing practices in various areas in Japan.

8. The five clinical studies of Japanese-Americans in *Clinical Studies in Culture Conflict* (edited by Georgene Seward; New York, Ronald Press, 1958) consistently give evidence of depressive reactions and an inability to express hostile or resentful feelings toward the parents. Feelings of guilt are strongly related to an inability to express aggression outwardly, leading to intrapunitive reactions. Feelings of worthlessness also result from the repression of aggressive feelings. The Nisei woman described by Norman L. Farberow and Edward S. Schneidman in Ch. 15 (pp. 335ff.) demonstrates the transference to the American cultural situation of certain basic intrapunitive attitudes common in Japan related to woman's ideal role behavior. The Kibei case described by Marvin K. Opler in Ch. 13 (pp. 297ff.) well demonstrates a young man's perception of the manifest "suffering" of Japanese women. The case described by Charlotte G. Babcock and William M. Caudill in Ch. 17 (pp. 409ff.) as well as other unpublished psychoanalytic material of Babcock's, amply demonstrates the presence of deep underlying guilt toward parents. Such guilt is still operative in Nisei in influencing occupational selection

and marriage choice. Seward, in a general summary of the Japanese cases (p. 449), carefully points out the pervasive depression found as a cohesive theme in each of the cases. She avoids conceptualizing the problems in terms of guilt, perhaps out of deference to the stereotype that Japanese feel "ashamed" rather than "guilty." She states, "Running through all five Japanese-American cases is a pervasive depression, in three reaching the point of suicidal threat or actual attempt." Yet she ends with the statement, "Looking back over the cases of Japanese origin, we may note a certain cohesiveness binding them together. Distance from parent figures is conspicuous in all as well as inability openly to express resentment against them. In line with the externalization of authority and the shame-avoidance demands of Japanese tradition, hostility is consistently turned in on the self in the *face-saving devices* of depression and somatic illness." (Italics mine.)

9. Robert Bellah, in *Tokugawa Religion* (Glencoe, Ill., The Free Press, 1957), perceives, and illustrates in detail, a definite relationship between prevalent pre-Meiji Tokugawa period ethical ideals and the rapid industrialization of Japan that occurred subsequent to the restoration of the Emperor. A cogent application of a sociological approach similar to that of Max Weber allows him to point out the obvious parallels in Tokugawa Japan to the precapitalist ethical orientation of Protestant Europe.

10. See the comprehensive, five-year study of this village by means of various social science disciplines by members of the Center for Japanese Studies of the University of Michigan. Richard K. Beardsley, Robert Ward, John Hall, *Village Japan;* Chicago, Univ. of Chicago Press, 1959.

11. Ruth Benedict, *The Chrysanthemum and the Sword;* Boston, Houghton Mifflin, 1946.

12. William Caudill and George De Vos, "Achievement, Culture, and Personality. The Case of the Japanese Americans," *Amer. Anthropologist* (1958) 58:1102–1126.

13. Hiroshi Wagatsuma, *Japanese Values of Achievement—The Study of Japanese Immigrants and Inhabitants of Three Japanese Villages by Means of T.A.T.;* unpublished M.A. thesis. Dept. of Far Eastern Studies, University of Michigan, 1957.

14. The TAT cards used in the Japanese research were in most instances modifications of the Murray cards, with changed features, clothing, and background to conform to Japanese experience. The situations in the original Murray set were maintained. New cards were added to the modified set to elicit reactions to peculiarly Japanese situations as well. The numbers given for the stories used illustratively in this paper refer to modified cards resembling the Murray set with the exception of J9 and J11, which represent original Japanese family scenes.

15. Reported in unpublished material of a Japanese psychiatrist, Taeko Sumi.

16. This test included items specifically eliciting a response to a hypothetical disharmony between wife and mother-in-law. In such cases the results indicate that the wife often sees herself as to blame for failing in her duty as a wife. She "should" conduct herself so as to be above reproach.

17. Described by the Japanese psychiatrist Kei Hirano.

18. A total of 80 persons gave 807 stories: 33 persons gave one or more stories involving marriage circumstances.

19. See footnote 11.

20. See Talcott Parsons, *The Social System;* Glencoe, Ill., The Free Press,

1951; p. 175, for a description of the particularistic achievement pattern. This category suits traditional Japanese culture very well.

21. It is significant that the Japanese usually use Shinto ceremonials in regard to marriage and fertility, and to celebrate various periods in childhood, whereas Buddhist ceremonials are used mainly in paying respect to the parents—that is, in funerals and in memorial services at specified times after death. It must be noted that the material in this paper does not include any reference to fear of punishment in an afterlife; although present in traditional Buddhism in the past, such feelings are not much in evidence in modern Japan. Relatively few modern Japanese believe in or are concerned with life beyond death. (See George De Vos and A. Wagatsuma, "Psycho-cultural Significance of Concern over Death and Illness Among Rural Japanese," *Internat. J. Social Psychiatry* (1959) 5:6–19; especially pp. 13*ff.*) It is my contention that fear of punishment either by the parents, society, or God is not truly internalized guilt. Insofar as the punishment is perceived as external in source, the feeling is often fear or anxiety, as distinct from guilt.

22. This approach is also evident in the theorist in religion. Also, the recent interest in existentialist psychiatry is one attempt to bring in relevant concepts of "belonging" to the study of the human experience.

23. Erik H. Erikson, "The Problem of Ego Identity," *J. Amer. Psychoanal. Assn.* (1956) 4:56–121.

PART II
Patterns of Interaction

Amae: A Key Concept for Understanding Japanese Personality Structure

L. TAKEO DOI

I am particularly interested in the problem of personality and culture in modern Japan for two reasons. First, even though I was born and raised in Japan and had my basic medical training there, I have had further training in psychiatry and psychoanalysis in the United States, thus exposing myself for some time to a different culture from that of Japan. Second, I have had many opportunities of treating both Japanese and non-Japanese (mostly American) patients with psychotherapy. These experiences have led me to inquire into differences between Japanese and non-Japanese patients and also into the question of what is basic in Japanese character structure. In this paper I shall describe what I have found to be most characteristic in Japanese patients and then discuss its meaning in the context of Japanese culture.

The essence of what I am going to talk about is contained in one common Japanese word, *amae*. Let me therefore, first of all, explain the meaning of this word. *Amae* is the noun form of *amaeru*, an intransitive verb that means "to depend and presume upon another's benevolence" (Doi, 1956). This word has the same root as *amai*, an adjective that means "sweet." Thus *amaeru* has a distinct feeling of sweetness and is generally used to describe a child's attitude or behavior toward his parents, particularly his mother. But it can also be used to describe the relationship between two adults, such as the relationship between a husband and a wife or a master and a subordinate. I believe that there is no single word in English equivalent to *amaeru*, though this does not mean that the psychology

Reprinted from *Japanese Culture: Its Development and Characteristics*, R.J. Smith and R.K. Beardsley, eds. (Chicago: Aldine Publishing, 1962) Copyright © 1962 by Wenner-Gren Foundation for Anthropological Research, Inc.

of *amae* is totally alien to the people of English-speaking countries. I shall come back to this problem after describing some of the clinical material through which I came to recognize the importance of what this word *amae* signifies.

It was in my attempt to understand what goes on between the therapist and patient that I first came across the all-powerful drive of the patient's *amae*. There is a diagnostic term in Japanese psychiatry, *shinkeishitsu*, which includes neurasthenia, anxiety neurosis, and obsessive neurosis. Morita, who first used *shinkeishitsu* as a diagnostic term, thought that these three types of neuroses had a basic symptom in common, *toraware*, which means "to be bound or caught," as by some intense preoccupation. He considered *toraware* to be closely related to hypochondriacal fear and thought that this fear sets in motion a reciprocal intensification of attention and sensation. In psychoanalytic work with neurotic patients of the *shinkeishitsu* type, I have also found *toraware* to be a basic symptom, but I have evolved a different formulation of its significance (see Doi, 1958). I have observed that during the course of psychotherapy the patient's *toraware* can easily turn into hypersensitivity in his relationship with the therapist. This hypersensitivity is best described by the Japanese word *kodawari*. *Kodawari* is the noun form of *kodawaru*, an intransitive verb meaning "to be sensitive to minor things," "to be inwardly disturbed over one's personal relationships." In the state of *kodawari* one feels that he is not accepted by others, which suggests that *kodawari* results from the unsatisfied desire to *amaeru*. Thus, *toraware* can be traced back through *kodawari* to *amae*. In my observations, the patient's *toraware* usually receded when he became aware of his *amae* toward the therapist, which he had been warding off consciously and unconsciously up to then.

At first I felt that if the patient became fully aware of his *amae*, he would thereupon be able to get rid of his neurosis. But I was wrong in this assumption and came to observe another set of clinical phenomena following the patient's recognition of his *amae* (see Doi, 1960). Many patients confessed that they were then awakened to the fact that they had not "possessed their self," had not previously appreciated the importance of their existence, and had been really nothing apart from their all-important desire to *amaeru*. I took this as a step toward the emergence of a new consciousness of self, inasmuch as the patient could then at least realize his previous state of "no self."

There is another observation that I should like to mention here. It is about the nature of guilt feelings of Japanese patients (see Doi, 1961). The word *sumanai* is generally used to express guilt feelings, and this word is the negative form of *sumu*, which means "to end." *Sumanai* literally means that one has not done as he was supposed to do, thereby causing the other person trouble or harm. Thus, it expresses more a sense of unfulfilled obligation than a confession of guilt, though it is generally taken as an indication that one feels guilty. When neurotic patients say *sumanai*, I have observed that there lies, behind their use of the word, much hidden aggression engendered by frustration of their wish to *amaeru*. So it seems that in saying *sumanai* they are in fact expressing their hidden concern lest they fall from the grace of *amae* because of their aggression. I think that this analysis of *sumanai* would also apply in essence to the use of this word by the ordinary Japanese in everyday life, but in the case of the neurotic patient *sumanai* is said with greater ambivalence. In other words, more than showing his feeling of being obligated, he tends to create a sense of obligation in the person to whom he makes his apology, thus "forcing" that person eventually to cater to his wish.

I have explained three clinical observations, all of which point to the importance of *amae* as a basic desire. As I said before, the state of *amae* originally refers to what a small child feels toward his mother. It is therefore not surprising that the desire to *amaeru* still influences one's adult years and that it becomes manifest in the therapeutic situation. Here we have a perfect example of transference in the psychoanalytic sense. But then is it not strange that *amaeru* is a unique Japanese word? Indeed, the Japanese find it hard to believe that there is no word for *amaeru* in European languages; a colleague once told me that he could not believe that the equivalent for such a seemingly universal phenomenon as *amae* did not exist in English or German, since, as he put it, "Even puppies do it, you know." Let me therefore illustrate the "Japaneseness" of the concept of *amaeru* by one striking incident. The mother of a Eurasian patient, a British woman who had been a long-term resident of Japan, was discussing her daughter with me. She spoke to me in English, but she suddenly switched to Japanese, in order to tell me that her daughter did not *amaeru* much as a child. I asked her why she had suddenly switched to Japanese. She replied, after a pause, that there was no way to say *amaeru* in English.

I have mentioned two Japanese words that are closely related to the psychology of *amae*: *kodawaru*, which means "to be inwardly disturbed over one's personal relationships," and *sumanai*, which means "to feel guilty or obligated." Now I should like to mention a few more words that are also related to the psychology of *amae*. First, *amai*, which originally means "sweet," can be used figuratively to describe a person who is overly soft and benevolent toward others or, conversely, one who always expects to *amaeru* in his relationships with others. Second, *amanzuru*, which is derived from *amaeru*, describes the state of mind in which one acquiesces to whatever circumstances one happens to be in. Third, *tori-iru*, which means "to take in," describes the behavior of a person who skillfully maneuvers another into permitting him to *amaeru*. Fourth, *suneru* describes the behavior of a child or an adult who pouts and sulks because he feels he is not allowed to *amaeru* as much as he wants to, thus harboring in himself mental pain of a masochistic nature. Fifth, *higamu* describes the behavior of a child or an adult who feels himself unfairly treated compared to others who are more favored, often suggesting the presence of a paranoid feeling. Sixth, *tereru* describes the behavior of a child or an adult who is ashamed of showing his intimate wish to *amaeru*. Seventh, *hinekureru* describes the behavior of a child or an adult who takes devious ways in his efforts to deny the wish to *amaeru*.

One could readily say that the behaviors or emotions described by all these Japanese words are not unknown to Westerners and that they appear quite frequently in the therapeutic situation with Western patients. But there remains the question I raised before: Why is there no word in English or in other European languages that is equivalent to *amaeru*, the most central element in all these emotions? To this, one might answer that the absence of a word like *amaeru* is no inconvenience, since it can easily be represented by a combination of words such as the "wish to be loved" or "dependency needs." That may be so, but does not this linguistic difference point to something deeper? Perhaps it reflects a basic psychological difference between Japan and the Western World. Before discussing this problem further, however, I would like to mention a theory of Michael Balint, a British psychoanalyst, which has much bearing on what I am talking about now.

In his psychoanalytic practice Balint observed that "in the final phase of the treatment patients begin to give expression to long-forgotten, infantile, instinctual wishes, and to demand their gratification from their environment" (Balint, 1952a). He called this infantile desire "passive object love," since its primal aim is to be loved; he also called it "primary love," since it is the foundation upon which later forms of love are built. I imagine that he must have wondered why such an important desire is not represented by one common word, for he points out the fact that "all European languages are so poor that they cannot distinguish between the two kinds of object-love, active and passive" (Balint, 1952b).

By now it must be clear that the "primary love" or "passive object-love" described by Balint is none other than the desire to *amaeru*. But then we have to draw the curious conclusion that the emotion of primary love is readily accessible to Japanese patients by way of the word *amaeru*, while to Western patients, according to Balint, it can become accessible only after a painstaking analysis. In my observations I have also noticed that the recognition of *amae* by Japanese patients does not signify the final phase of treatment, as it did in Balint's patients. I think that we have to try to solve this apparent contradiction very carefully, because therein lies, in my opinion, an important key to understanding the psychological differences between Japan and Western countries.

The reasoning behind Balint's observation that primary love appears in its pure form only in the final phase of treatment is as follows: The primary love of an infant is bound to be frustrated, leading to the formation of narcissism; as though he said to himself, "If the world does not love me enough, I have to love and gratify myself." Since such narcissism is part of the earliest and most primitive layer of the mind, it can be modified only in the last stage of treatment, at which time the long-repressed urge to be loved can re-emerge in its pure state. Then what shall we say about the Japanese, to whom this primary desire to be loved is always accessible? Does it mean that the Japanese have less narcissism? I think not. Rather I would say that the Japanese somehow continue to cherish the wish to be loved even after the formation of narcissism. It is as though the Japanese did not want to see the reality of their basic frustration. In other words, the Japanese, as does everybody else, do experience frustration of their primary love, as is well attested to by the existence of the rich vocabulary we have already encountered relating to the frustration of *amae*. But it seems that the Japanese never give up their basic desire to *amaeru*, thus mitigating the extent of violent emotions caused by its frustration.

In this connection I want to mention an interesting feature of the word *amaeru*. We do not say that an infant does *amaeru* until he is about one year old, thereby indicating that he is then conscious of his wish to *amaeru*, which in turn suggests the presence of a budding realization that his wish cannot always be gratified. Thus, from its inception, the wish to *amaeru* is accompanied by a secret fear that it may be frustrated.

If what I have been saying is true, then it must indicate that there is a social sanction in Japanese society for expressing the wish to *amaeru*. And it must be this social sanction that has encouraged in the Japanese language the development of the large vocabulary relating to *amaeru*. In other words, in Japanese society parental dependency is fostered, and this behavior pattern is even institutionalized into its social structure, whereas perhaps the opposite tendency prevails in Western societies. This seems to be confirmed by recent anthropological studies of Japanese society, notably that of Ruth Benedict, who said: "The arc of life in Japan is plotted in opposite fashion to that in the United States. It is a great U-curve with maximum freedom and indulgence allowed to babies and to the old. Restrictions are slowly increased after babyhood till having one's own way reaches a low just before and after marriage" (Benedict, 1961). It is true that the restrictions Benedict spoke of do exist for adults in Japanese society, but it should be understood that these restrictions are never meant to be drastic so far as the basic desire to *amaeru* is concerned. Rather, these restrictions are but channels through which that desire is to be duly gratified. That is why we can speak of parental dependency as being institutionalized in Japanese society. For instance, in marriage a husband does *amaeru* toward his wife, and vice versa. It is strongly present in all formal relationships, including those between teacher and student and between doctor and patient. Thus William Caudill (1961), in his observations on Japanese psychiatric hospitals, spoke of the mutual dependency he encountered in all relationships.

In this connection I cannot resist mentioning an episode that happened when I gave a talk on some characteristic Japanese words to a professional group in the United States. *Amaeru* was one of those words. After my talk, one distinguished scholar asked me whether or not the feeling of *amaeru* is something like what Catholics feel toward their Holy Mother. Apparently he could not recognize the existence of such a feeling in the ordinary mother-child relationship. And if his response is representative of Americans, it would mean that in American society the feeling of *amaeru* can be indulged in perhaps only in the religious life, but here also very sparingly.

I would now like to mention a study by a Japanese scholar, Hajime Nakamura, professor of Indian philosophy at the University of Tokyo and an authority on comparative philosophy. In his major work, *Ways of Thinking of Eastern Peoples* (1960), he presents a penetrating analysis of thought patterns of Indians, Chinese, Japanese, and Tibetans on the basis of linguistic studies and observations on variations in Buddhist doctrine and practice in these four countries. What he says about the Japanese pattern of thought is parallel to what I have been saying here, though he reaches his conclusions from an entirely different source. He says that the Japanese way of thinking is greatly influenced by an emphasis on immediate personal relations and also that the Japanese have always been eager to adopt foreign cultural influences, but always within the framework of this emphasis on personal relations. To state this in psychoanalytic terms: the Japanese are always prepared to identify themselves with, or introject, an outside force, to the exclusion of other ways of coping with it. This character trait of the Japanese was touched upon by Benedict, too, when she said that "the Japanese have an ethic of alternatives" and "Japan's motivations are situational," referring particularly to the sudden complete turnabout of Japan following the defeat of the last war.

This leads, however, to the very interesting and important question of whether or not Japanese character structure has changed at all since the war. I think that Benedict was quite right in assuming that Japan as a whole willingly submitted to unconditional surrender because it was the Emperor's order, that Japan wanted only to please the Emperor, even in her defeat. But it cannot be denied that things have been changing since then. For instance, the Emperor had to declare that he no longer wished to be considered sacred. Also the Japanese have been disillusioned to find that the paramount virtue of *chū*, that is, loyalty to the emperor, was taken advantage of by the ultranationalists, who completely failed them. With the decline of *chū* there was also a decline of *kō*, that is, of filial piety. In other words, the tradition of repaying one's *on*, that is, one's spiritual debts to an emperor and to one's parents, was greatly undermined. Thus there developed the moral chaos of present-day Japan.

I think, however, that the nature of this chaos has a distinctly Japanese character and can best be understood by taking into account the psychology of *amae*. It seems that heretofore the stress upon the duty of repaying one's *on* to the emperor and to one's parents served the purpose of regulating the all too powerful desire of *amae*. Since the Japanese were deprived of this regulating force after the war, it was inevitable that their desire to *amaeru* was let loose, with its narcissistic element becoming more manifest. That perhaps explains why we now find in Japan so many examples of lack of social restraint. I wonder whether this recent tendency has also helped to increase the number of neurotics. I think it has, though we have no reliable statistics to confirm it. But I am quite certain that an analysis of the psychology of *amae* such as I am attempting here would not have been possible in prewar days, because *amae* was concealed behind the duty of repaying one's *on*. It certainly was not visible to the outside observer, even to one as acute as Ruth Benedict. I would like to give you one clinical example to illustrate this point.

One of my recent patients, who was a student of law, revealed to me one day his secret thoughts, saying, "I wish I had some person who would take the responsibility of assisting me." The remarkable thing about this confession was that the Japanese word that he used for "assist" was a special legal term *hohitsu*, which was formerly used only for the act of assisting the emperor with his task of governing the nation. In saying this, as the patient himself explained, he wanted, like the emperor, to appear to be responsible for his acts but to depend completely on his assistant, who would really carry the burden. He said this, not jokingly but, rather, with complete seriousness. It is obvious that this confession revealed his secret desire to *amaeru*, about which he spoke more clearly on another occasion. But what I would like to point out here is that in prewar days the patient could hardly have made such a confession, using a special term reserved only for the emperor. Of course, this is a special case, and the fact that the patient was a law student accounted for his use of such a technical term. Yet I think that this case illustrates the point that I want to make, that is, the more emphasis placed upon repaying one's *on*, the less clearly seen is one's desire to *amaeru*.

In this connection, let me say a few words about the nature of so-called emperor worship, which served as the Japanese state religion in prewar days. It is true that the emperor was held sacred, but the element of taboo was greater than that of divinity. It is really tempting to apply what Freud said about taboo to the Japanese emperor worship. As a matter of act, he did mention the Japanese emperor in his book on *Totem and Taboo,* but not from the viewpoint of what is being discussed here. I will not go into this subject any further now, except to add one more comment concerning the effect of elimination of the emperor taboo and its related system, apart from the already discussed release of the desire to *amaeru.* Some Japanese critics voiced the opinion that the tight thought control deriving from the emperor and the family system in prewar days stifled development of healthy selfhood, that one could assert himself in those days only by way of *suneru* and *higamu,* which are interestingly enough the very same Japanese words that I have described before as indicating frustration of *amae* (Maruyama, 1960; Isono, 1960). I agree that this opinion is generally true, but I do not believe that elimination of the emperor and family system alone can lead to development of healthy selfhood or personality. This is shown by many patients, who confess that they are awakened to the fact that they have "not had self" apart from the all powerful desire to *amaeru*. Then what or who can help them to obtain their "self"? This touches upon a very important problem of identity, which I will not attempt to discuss in detail. I can say only that the Japanese as a whole are still searching for something, something with which they can safely identify themselves, so that they can become whole, independent beings.

In closing I should like to make two additional remarks. First, it may seem that I am possibly idealizing the West in a way, since I have looked at the problem of personality and culture in modern Japan from the Western point of view. I do not deny that I have. In fact I could not help doing so, because Japanese culture did not produce any yardstick to judge itself critically. I really think that it is a fine thing for the West to have developed such a yardstick for critical analysis. And it seems inevitable that it involves a kind of idealization when the non-Westerners attempt to apply such a yardstick to themselves. I know, however, that in the psychoanalytic circles of Western countries, idealization has a special meaning and is not something commendable. So they would certainly not call their use of the analytical method idealization. But I wonder whether they are entirely right in assuming that their use of the analytical method stands on its own without involving any idealization on their part.

Second, though I have stated that there is no exact equivalent to the word *amaeru* in all European languages, I do not say that *amaeru* is unique to the Japanese language. I have some information that the language of Korea and that of Ainu have a word of the same meaning. There seems to be some question about whether or not the Chinese language has such a word. I am now most curious to know whether or not the Polynesian languages have a similar word. I have a feeling that they may have. If they do, how would their psychology compare with that of the Japanese? It is my earnest hope that these questions will be answered by anthropological and psychological studies in the not-too-distant future.

BIBLIOGRAPHY

BALINT, MICHAEL

1952a "The Final Goal of Psychoanalytic Treatment." In *Primary Love and Psychoanalytic Technique*. London: Hogarth Press.

1952b "Critical Notes on the Theory of the Pregenital Organizations of the Libido." In *Primary Love and Psychoanalytic Technique*. London: Hogarth Press.

BENEDICT, RUTH

1961 *The Chrysanthemum and the Sword*. Boston, Houghton Mifflin Co.

CAUDILL, WILLIAM

1961 "Around the Clock Patient Care in Japanese Psychiatric Hospitals: The Role of the *tsukisoi*," *Amer. Soc. Rev.*, 26:204–14.

DOI, L. TAKEO

1956 "Japanese Language as an Expression of Japanese Psychology," *Western Speech*, 20:90–96.

1958 "Shinkeishitsu no seishinbyori" ("Psychopathology of *shinkeishitsu*"), *Psychiatria et Neurologia Japonica*, 60:733–44.

1960 "Jibun to amae no seishinbyori" ("Psychopathology of *jibun* and *amae*"), *Psychiatria et Neurologia Japonica*, 61: 149–62.

1961 "Sumanai to Ikenai ('*Sumanai* and *Ikenai*')—Some Thoughts on Super-Ego," *Jap. J. Psychoanal.*, 8:4–7.

ISONO, FUJIKO

1960 "Ie to Jigaishiki" ("Family and Self-consciousness"). In *Kindai Nippon Shisōshi Kōza* ("History of Thought in Modern Japan"), Vol. 6. Tokyo: Chikuma Shobo.

MARUYAMA, MASAO

1960 *Chūsei to Hangyaku* ("Loyalty and Rebellion"). In *Kindai Nippon Shisōshi Kōza* ("History of Thought in Modern Japan"), Vol. 6. Tokyo: Chikuma Shobo.

NAKAMURA, HAJIME

1960 *Ways of Thinking of Eastern peoples*. Japanese National Commission for UNESCO (comp.). Tokyo: Japanese Government Printing Bureau.

Criteria of Group Formation

CHIE NAKANE

1 ATTRIBUTE AND FRAME

The analysis uses two basic contrasting criteria or concepts, namely *attribute* and *frame*, which are newly formulated by myself, assuming them to be most effective in the analysis of Japanese society in comparison with other societies. These two terms, with the manner in which the distinction is employed, might lead the reader to that of the customary European thought, but they are used in a quite different way, and the resemblance is merely superficial.

According to my view, groups may be identified by applying the two criteria: one is based on the individual's common *attribute*, the other on situational position in a given *frame*. I use *frame* as a technical term with a particular significance, as opposed to the criterion of *attribute*, which, again, is used specifically and in a broader sense than it normally carries. *Frame* may be a locality, an institution, or a particular relationship which binds a set of individuals into one group; in all cases it indicates a criterion which sets a boundary and gives a common basis to a set of individuals who are located or involved in it. In fact, my term *frame* is the English translation of the Japanese *ba*, the concept from which I originally evolved my theory, but for which it is hard to find the exact English counterpart. *Ba* means 'location', but the normal usage of the term connotes a special base on which something is placed according to a given purpose. The term *ba* is also used in physics for 'field' in English.

Let me indicate how these two technical terms can be applied to various actual contexts. 'Attribute' may mean, for instance, being a member of a definite descent group or caste. In contrast, being a member of X village expresses the commonality of 'frame.'

Reprinted from *Japanese Society*, C. Nakane (Berkeley: University of California Press, 1970). Copyright by George Weidenfeld & Nicholson, Ltd.

Attribute may be acquired not only by birth but by achievement. Frame is more circumstantial. These criteria serve to identify the individuals in a certain group, which can then in its turn be classified within the whole society, even though the group may or may not have a particular function of its own as a collective body. Classifications such as landlord and tenant are based on attribute, while such a unit as a landlord and his tenants is a group formed by situational position. Taking industry as an example, 'lathe operator' or 'executive' refers to attribute, but 'the members of Y Company' refers to frame. In the same way, 'professor', 'office clerk' and 'student' are attributes, whereas 'men of Z University' is a frame.

In any society, individuals are gathered into social groups or social strata on the bases of attributes and frame. There may be some cases where the two factors coincide in the formation of a group, but usually they overlap each other, with individuals belonging to different groups at the same time. The primary concern in this discussion is the relative degree of function of each criterion. There are some cases where either the attribute or the frame factor functions alone, and some where the two are mutually competitive. The way in which the factors are commonly weighted bears a close reciprocal relationship to the values which develop in the social consciousness of the people in the society. For example, the group consciousness of the Japanese depends considerably on this immediate social context, frame, whereas in India it lies in attribute (most symbolically expressed in caste, which is fundamentally a social group based on the ideology of occupation and kinship). On this point, perhaps, the societies of Japan and India show the sharpest contrast, as will be discussed later in greater detail.

The ready tendency of the Japanese to stress situational position in a particular frame, rather than universal attribute, can be seen in the following example: when a Japanese 'faces the outside' (confronts another person) and affixes some position to himself socially, he is inclined to give precedence to institution over kind of occupation. Rather than saying, 'I am a type-setter' or 'I am a filing clerk', he is likely to say, 'I am from B Publishing Group' or 'I belong to S Company'. Much depends on context, of course, but where a choice exists, he will use this latter form. (I will discuss later the more significant implications for Japanese social life indicated by this preference.) The listener would rather hear first about the connection with B Publishing Group or S Company;

that he is a journalist or printer, engineer or office worker is of secondary importance. When a man says he is from X Television one may imagine him to be a producer or cameraman, though he may in fact be a chauffeur. (The universal business suit makes it hard to judge by appearances.) In group identification, a frame such as a 'company' or 'association' is of primary importance; the attribute of the individual is a secondary matter. The same tendency is to be found among intellectuals; among university graduates, what matters most, and functions the strongest socially, is not whether a man holds or does not hold a Ph.D. but, rather, from which university he graduated. Thus, the criterion by which Japanese classify individuals socially tends to be that of particular institution rather than of universal attribute. Such group consciousness and orientation fosters the strength of an institution, and the institutional unit (such as school or company) is in fact the basis of Japanese social organization.

The manner in which this group consciousness works is also revealed in the way the Japanese uses the expression *uchi* (my house) to mean the place of work, organization, office or school to which he belongs; and *otaku* (your house) to mean a second person's place of work and so on. The term *kaisha* symbolizes the expression of group consciousness. *Kaisha* does not mean that individuals are bound by contractual relationships into a corporate enterprise while still thinking of themselves as separate entities; rather, *kaisha* is 'my' or 'our' company, the community to which one belongs primarily, and which is all-important in one's life. Thus, in most cases the company provides the whole social existence of a person and has authority over all aspects of his life; he is deeply emotionally involved in the association.[1] That Company A belongs not to its shareholders but rather belongs to 'us', is the sort of reasoning involved here, which is carried to such a point that even the modern legal arrangement must compromise in face of this strong native orientation. I would not wish to deny that in other societies an employee may have a kind of emotional attachment to the company or his employer; what distinguishes this relation in Japan is the exceedingly high degree of this emotional involvement. It is openly and frequently expressed in speech and behaviour in public as well as in private, and such expressions always receive social and moral appreciation and approbation.

The essence of this firmly rooted, latent group consciousness in Japanese society is expressed in the traditional and ubiquitous concept of *ie*, the household, a concept which penetrates every nook and cranny of Japanese society. The Japanese usage *uchi no* referring to one's work place indeed derives from the basic concept of *ie*. The term *ie* also has implications beyond those to be found in the English words 'household' or 'family'.

The concept of *ie*, in the guise of the term 'family system', has been the subject of lengthy dispute and discussion by Japanese legal scholars and sociologists. The general consensus is that, as a consequence of modernization, particularly because of the new postwar civil code, the *ie* institution is dying. In this ideological approach the *ie* is regarded as being linked particularly with feudal moral precepts; its use as a fundamental unit of social structure has not been fully explored.

In my view, the most basic element of the *ie* institution is not that form whereby the eldest son and his wife live together with the old parents, nor an authority structure in which the household head holds the power, and so on. Rather, the *ie* is a corporate residential group and, in the case of agriculture or other similar enterprises, *ie* is a managing body. The *ie* comprises household members (in most cases the family members of the household head, but others in addition to family members may be included), who thus make up the units of a distinguishable social group. In other words, the *ie* is a social group constructed on the basis of an established frame of residence and often of management organization. What is important here is that the human relationships within this household group are thought of as more important than all other human relationships. Thus the wife and daughter-in-law who have come from outside have incomparably greater importance than one's own sisters and daughters, who have married and gone into other households. A brother, when he has built a separate house, is thought of as belonging to another unit or household; on the other hand, the son-in-law, who was once a complete outsider, takes the position of a household member and becomes more important than the brother living in another household. This is remarkably different from societies such as that of India, where the weighty factor of sibling relationship (a relationship based on commonality of attribute, that of being born of the same parents) continues paramount until death, regardless of residential circumstances; theoretically, the stronger the factor of sibling relationship, the weaker the social independence of a household (as a residence unit). (It goes without saying, of course, that customs such as the adopted son-in-law system prevalent in Japan are nonexistent in Hindu society. The same is true of Europe.) These facts support the theory that group-forming criteria based on functioning by attribute oppose group-forming criteria based on functioning by frame.

Naturally, the function of forming groups on the basis of the element of the frame, as demonstrated in the formation of the household, involves the possibility of including members with a differing attribute, and at the same time expelling a member who has the same attribute. This is a regular occurrence, particularly among traditional agricultural and merchant households. Not only may outsiders with not the remotest kinship tie be invited to be heirs and successors, but servants and clerks are usually incorporated as members of the household and treated as family members by the head of the household. This inclusion must be accepted without reservation to ensure that when a clerk is married to the daughter of the household and becomes an adopted son-in-law, the household succession will continue without disruption.

Such a principle contributes to the weakening of kinship ties. Kinship, the core of which lies in the sibling relation, is a criterion based on attribute. Japan gives less weight to kinship than do other societies, even England and America; in fact, the function of kinship is comparatively weak outside the household. The saying "the sibling is the beginning of the stranger" accurately reflects Japanese ideas on kinship. A married sibling who lives in another household is considered a kind of outsider. Towards such kin, duties and obligations are limited to the level of the seasonal exchange of greetings and presents, attendance at wedding and funeral ceremonies, and the minimum help in case of accident or poverty. There are often instances where siblings differ widely in social and economic status; the elder brother may be the mayor, while his younger brother is a postman in the same city; or a brother might be a lawyer or businessman, while his widowed sister works as a domestic servant in another household. The wealthy brother normally does not help the poor brother or sister who has set up a separate household, as long as the latter can somehow support his or her existence; by the same token, the latter will not dare to ask for help until the last grain of rice is gone. Society takes this for granted, for it gives prime importance to the individual household rather than to the kin group as a whole.

This is indeed radically different from the attitudes to kin found in India and other Southeast Asian countries, where individual wealth tends to be distributed among relatives; there, the kin group as a whole takes precedence over the individual household, and nepotism plays an important role. I have been surprised to discover that even in England and America brothers and sisters meet much more frequently than is required by Japanese standards, and that there exists such a high degree of attachment to kinfolk. Christmas is one of the great occasions when these kinfolk gather together; New Year's Day is Japan's equivalent to the Western Christmas, everyone busy with preparations for visits from subordinate staff, and then, in turn, calling on superiors. There is little time and scope to spare for collateral kin—married brothers, sisters, cousins, uncles and aunts, and so on—though parents and grandparents will certainly be visited if they do not live in the same house. Even in rural areas, people say, 'One's neighbour is of more importance than one's relatives' or 'You can carry on your life without cousins, but not without your neighbours'.

The kinship which is normally regarded as the primary and basic human attachment seems to be compensated in Japan by a personalized relation to a corporate group based on work, in which the major aspects of social and economic life are involved. Here again we meet the vitally important unit in Japanese society of the corporate group based on frame. In my view, this is the basic principle on which Japanese society is built.

To sum up, the principles of Japanese social group structure can be seen clearly portrayed in the household structure. The concept of this traditional household institution, *ie*, still persists in the various group indentities which are termed *uchi*, a colloquial form of *ie*. These facts demonstrate that the formation of social groups on the basis of fixed frames remains characteristic of Japanese social structure.

Among groups larger than the household, there is that described by the medieval concept *ichizoku rōtō* (one family group and its retainers). The idea of group structure as revealed in this expression is an excellent example of the frame-based social group. This is indeed the concept of one household, in which family members and retainers are not separated but form an integrated corporate group. There are often marriage ties between the two sides of this corporate group, and all lines of distinction between them become blurred. The relationship is the same as that between family members and clerks or servants in a household. This is a theoretical antithesis to a group formed exclusively on lineage or kin.

The equivalent in modern society of *ie* and *ichizoku rōtō* is a group such as 'One Railway Family' (*kokutetsu ikka*), which signifies the Japanese National Railways. A union, incorporating both workers and management, calls this 'management-labour harmony.' Though it is often said that the traditional family (*ie*) institution has disappeared, the concept of the *ie* still persists in modern contexts. A company is conceived as an *ie*, all its employees qualifying as members of the household, with the employer at its head. Again, this 'family' envelops the employee's personal family; it 'engages' him 'totally' (*marugakae* in Japanese). The employer readily takes responsibility for his employee's family, for which, in turn, the primary concern is the company, rather than relatives who reside elsewhere. (The features relating the company with its employees' families will be discussed later.) In this modern context, the employee's family, which normally comprises the employee himself, his wife and children, is a unit which can no longer be conceived as an *ie*, but simply a family. The unit is comparable to the family of a servant or clerk who worked in the master's *ie*, the managing body of the pre-modern enterprise. The role of the *ie* institution as the distinguished unit in society in premodern times is now played by the company. This social group consciousness symbolized in the concept of the *ie*, of being one unit within a frame, has been achievable at any time, has been promoted by slogans and justified in the traditional morality.

This analysis calls for a reconsideration of the stereotyped view that modernization or urbanization weakens kinship ties and creates a new type of social organization on entirely different bases. Certainly industrialization produces a new type of organization, the formal structure of which may be closely akin to that found in modern western societies. However, this does not necessarily accord with changes in the informal structure, in which, as in the case of Japan, the traditional structure persists in large measure. This demonstrates that the basic social structure continues in spite of great changes in social organization.[2]

2 EMOTIONAL PARTICIPATION AND ONE-TO-ONE RELATIONSHIPS

It is clear from the previous section that social groups constructed with particular reference to situation, i.e. frame, include members with differing attributes. A group formed on the basis of commonality of attribute can possess a strong sense of exclusiveness, based on this homogeneity, even without recourse to any form of law. Naturally, the relative strength of this factor depends on a variety of conditional circumstances, but in the fundamentals of group formation this homogeneity among group members stands largely by its own strength, and conditions are secondary. When a group develops on the situational basis of frame, the primary form is a simple herd, which in itself does not possess internal positive elements which can constitute a social group. Constituent elements of the group in terms of their attributes may be heterogenous but may not be complementary. (The discussion here does not link to Durkheimian theory as such; the distinction is between societies where people stick together because they are similar and those where they stick togther because they are complementary.) For example, a group of houses built in the same area may form a village simply by virtue of physical demarcation from other houses. But in order to create a functional corporate group, there is need of an internal organization which will link these independent households. In such a situation some sort of law must be evolved to guide group coherence.

In addition to the initial requirement of a strong, enduring frame, there is need to strengthen the frame even further and to make the group element tougher. Theoretically, this can be done in two ways. One is to influence the members within the frame in such a way that they have a feeling of 'one-ness'; the second method is to create an internal organization which will tie the individuals in the group to each other and then to strengthen this organization. In practice, both these modes occur together, are bound together, and progress together. They become, in fact, one common rule of action, but for the sake of convenience I shall discuss them separately. In this section I discuss the feeling of unity.

People with different attributes can be led to feel that they are members of the same group, and that this feeling is justified, by stressing the group consciousness of 'us' against 'them', i.e. the external, and by fostering a feeling of rivalry against other similar groups. In this way there develops internally the sentimental tie of 'members of the same troop'.

Since disparity of attribute is a rational thing, an emotional approach is used to overcome it. This emotional approach is facilitated by continual human contact of the kind that can often intrude on those human relations which belong to the completely private and personal sphere. Consequently, the power and influence of the group not only affects and enters into the individual's actions; it alters even his ideas and ways of thinking. Individual autonomy is minimized. When this happens, the point where group or public life ends and where private life begins no longer can be distinguished. There are those who perceive this as a danger, an encroachment on their dignity as individuals; on the other hand, others feel safer in total-group consciousness. There seems little doubt that the latter group is in the majority. Their sphere of living is usually concentrated solely within the village community or the place of work. The Japanese regularly talk about their homes and love affairs with co-workers; marriage within the village community or place of work is prevalent; the family frequently participates in company pleasure trips. The provision of company housing, a regular practice among Japan's leading enterprises, is a good case in point. Such company houses are usually concentrated in a single area and form a distinct entity within, say a suburb of a large city. In such circumstances employees' wives come into close contact with and are well informed about their husbands' activities. Thus, even in terms of physical arrangements, a company with its employees and their families forms a distinct social group. In an extreme case, a company may have a common grave for its employees, similar to the household grave. With group-consciousness so highly developed, there is almost no social life outside the particular group on which an individual's major economic life depends. The individual's every problem must be solved within this frame. Thus, group participation is simple and unitary. It follows then that each group or institution develops a high degree of independence and closeness, with its own internal law which is totally binding on members.

The archetype of this kind of group is the Japanese 'household' (*ie*) as we have described it in the previous section. In Japan, for example, the mother-in-law and daughter-in-law problem is preferably solved inside the household, and the luckless bride has to struggle through in isolation, without help from her own family, relatives, or neighbours. By comparison, in agricultural villages in India, not only can the bride make long visits to her parental home but her brother may frequently visit her and help out in various ways. Mother-in-law and daughter-in-law quarrels are conducted in raised voices that can be heard all over the neighbourhood, and when such shouting is heard, all the women (of the same caste) in the neighbourhood come over to help out. The mutual assistance among the wives who come from other villages is a quite enviable factor completely unimaginable among Japanese women. Here again the function of the social factor of attribute (wife) is demonstrated; it supersedes the function of the frame of the household. In Japan, by contrast, 'the parents step in when their children quarrel' and, as I shall explain in detail later, the structure is the complete opposite to that in India.

Moral ideas such as 'the husband leads and the wife obeys' or 'man and wife are one flesh' embody the Japanese emphasis on integration. Among Indians, however, I have often observed husband and wife expressing quite contradictory opinions without the slightest hesitation. This is indeed rare in front of others in Japan. The traditional authority of the Japanese household head, once regarded as the prime characteristic of the family system, extended over the conduct, ideas, and ways of thought of the household's members, and on this score the household head could be said to wield a far greater power than his Indian counterpart. In Indian family life there are all kinds of rules that apply in accordance with the status of the individual family member; the wife, for instance, must not speak directly to her husband's elder brothers, father, etc. These rules all relate to individual behaviour, but in the sphere of ideas and ways of thought the freedom and strong individuality permitted even among members of the same family is surprising to a Japanese. The rules, moreover, do not differ from household to household but are common to the whole community, especially among the members of the same caste community. In other words, the rules are of universal character, rather than being situational or particular to each household, as is the case in Japan.[3] Compared with traditional Japanese family life, the extent to which members of an Indian household are bound by the individual household's traditional practices is very small.

An Indian who had been studying in Japan for many years once compared Japanese and Indian practice in the following terms:

> Why does a Japanese have to consult his companions over even the most trivial matter? The Japanese always call a conference about the slightest thing, and hold frequent meetings, though these are mostly informal, to decide everything. In India, we have definite rules as family members (and this is also true of other social groups), so that when one wants to do something one knows whether it is all right by instantaneous reflection on those rules—it is not necessary to consult with the head or with other members of the family. Outside these rules, you are largely free to act as an individual; whatever you do, you have only to ask whether or not it will run counter to the rules.

As this clearly shows, in India 'rules' are regarded as a definite but abstract social form, not as a concrete and individualized form particular to each family/social group, as is the case in Japan. The individuality of the Indian family unit is not strong, nor is there group participation by family members of the order of the emotional participation in the Japanese household; nor is the family as a living unit (or as a group holding communal property) a closed society, as in the case of the Japanese household. Again, in contrast to Japanese practice, the individual in India is strongly tied to the social network outside his household.

In contrast to the Japanese system, the Indian system allows freedom in respect of ideas and ways of thought as opposed to conduct. I believe for this reason, even though there are economic and ethical restrictions on the modernization of society, the Indian does not see his traditional family system as an enemy of progress to such a degree as the Japanese does. This view may contradict that conventionally held by many people on Indian family. It is important to note that the comparison here is made between Japanese and Hindu systems focused on actual interpersonal relationships within the family or household, rather than between Western and Indian family patterns in a general outlook. I do not intend here to present the structure and workings of actual personal relations in Japanese and Hindu families in detail, but the following point would be some help to indicate my point. In the ideal traditional household in Japan, for example, opinions of the members of the household should always be held unanimously regardless of the issue, and this normally meant that all members accepted the opinion of the household head, without even discussing the issue. An expression of a contradictory opinion to that of the head was considered a sign of misbehaviour, disturbing the harmony of the group order. Contrasted to such a unilateral process of decision-making in the Japanese household, the Indian counterpart allows much room for discussion between its members; they, whether sons, wife, or even daughters, are able to express their views much more freely, and they in fact can enjoy a discussion, although the final decision may be taken by the head. Hindu family structure is similar hierarchically to the Japanese family, but the individual's rights are well preserved in it. In the Japanese system all members of the household are in one group under the head, with no specific rights according to the status of individuals within the family. The Japanese family system differs from that of the Chinese system, where family ethics are always based on relationships between particular individuals such as father and son, brothers and sisters, parent and child, husband and wife, while in Japan they are always based on the collective group, i.e., members of a household, not on the relationships between individuals.

The Japanese system naturally produces much more frustration in the members of lower status in the hierarchy and allows the head to abuse the group or an individual member. In Japan, especially immediately after the Second World War, the idea has gained ground that the family system (*ie*) was an evil, feudalistic growth obstructing modernization, and on this premise one could point out the evil uses to which the unlimited infiltration of the household head's authority were put. It should be noticed here, however, that although the power of each individual household head is often regarded as exclusively his own, in fact it is the social group, the 'household', which has the ultimate integrating power, a power which restricts each member's behaviour and thought, including that of the household head himself.

Another group characteristic portrayed in the Japanese household can be seen when a business enterprise is viewed as a social group. In this instance a closed social group has been organized on the basis of the 'life-time employment system' and the work made central to the employees' lives. The new employee is in just about the same position, and is in fact received by the company in much the same spirit, as if he were a newly born family member, a newly adopted son-in-law, or a bride come into the husband's household. A number of well-known features peculiar to the Japanese employment system illustrate this characteristic, for example, company housing, hospital benefits, family-recreation groups for employees, monetary gifts from the company on the occasion of marriage, birth, or death, and even advice from the company's consultant on family planning. What's interesting here is that this tendency is very obvious, even in the most forward-looking, large enterprises or in supposedly modern, advanced management. The concept is even more evident in Japan's basic payment system, used by every industrial enterprise and government organization, in which the family allowance is the essential element. This is also echoed in the principle of the seniority payment system.

The relationship between employer and employee is not to be explained in contractual terms. The attitude of the employer is expressed by the spirit of the common saying, 'the enterprise is the people'. This affirms the belief that employer and employee are bound as one by fate in conditions which produce a tie between man and man often as firm and close as that between husband and wife. Such a relationship is manifestly not a purely contractual one between employer and employee; the employee is already a member of his own family, and all members of his family are naturally included in the larger company 'family'. Employers do not employ only a man's labour itself but really employ the total man, as is shown in the expression *marugakae* ('completely enveloped'). This trend can be traced consistently in Japanese management from the Meiji period to the present.

The life-time employment system, characterized by the integral and lasting commitment between employee and employer, contrasts sharply with the high mobility of the worker in the United States. It has been suggested that this system develops from Japan's economic situation and is closely related to the surplus of labour. However, as J. C. Abegglen has suggested in his penetrating analysis (*The Japanese Factory*, 1958, Chapter 2), the immobility of Japanese labour is not merely an economic problem. That it is also closely related to the nature of Japanese social structure will become evident from my discussion. In fact, Japanese labour relations, in terms of surplus and shortage of labour, have least affected the life-time employment system. In fact, these contradictory situations have together contributed to the development of the system.

It might be appropriate at this point to give a brief description of the history of the development of the life-time employment system in Japan. In the early days of Japan's industrialization, there was a fairly high rate of movement of factory workers from company to company, just as some specific type of workmen or artisans of pre-industrial urban Japan had moved freely from job to job. Such mobility in some workers in pre-industrial and early industrial Japan seems to be attributed to the following reasons: a specific type of an occupation, the members of which consisted of a rather small percentage of the total working population and the demand for them was considerably high; these workers were located in a situation outside well-established institutionalized systems. The mobility of factory workers caused uncertainty and inconvenience to employers in their efforts to retain a constant labour force. To counteract this fluidity, management policy gradually moved in the direction of keeping workers in the company for their entire working lives, rather than towards developing a system based on contractual arrangements. By the beginning of this century, larger enterprises were already starting to develop management policies based on this principle; they took the form of various welfare benefits, company houses at nominal rent, commissary purchasing facilities, and the like. This trend became particularly marked after the First World War, when the shortage of labour was acute.

It was also at the end of the First World War that there came into practice among large companies the regular employment system by which a company takes on, each spring, a considerable number of boys who have just left school. This development arose from the demand for company-trained personnel adapted to the mechanized production systems that followed the introduction of new types of machinery from Germany and the United States. Boys fresh from school were the best potential labour force for mechanized industry because they were more easily moulded to suit a company's requirements. They were trained by the company not only technically but also morally. In Japan it has always been believed that individual moral and mental attitudes have an important bearing on productive power. Loyalty towards the company has been highly regarded. A man may be an excellent technician, but if his way of thought and his moral attitudes do not accord with the company's ideal, the company does not hesitate to dismiss him. Men who move in from another company at a comparatively advanced stage in their working life tend to be considered difficult to mould or suspect in their loyalties. Ease of training, then, was the major reason why recruitment of workers was directed more and more towards boys fresh from school. (There is an excellent statement of conditions in Abegglen, *The Japanese Factory,* Chapter 1.)

Recruitment methods thus paved the way for the development of the life-employment system. An additional device was evolved to hold workers to a company, for example, the seniority payment system based on duration of service, age, and educational qualifications, with the added lure of a handsome payment on retirement. The principle behind this seniority system had the advantage of being closely akin to the traditional pattern of commercial and agricultural management in pre-industrial Japan. In these old-style enterprises, operational size had been relatively small—one household or a group of affiliated households centred on one particular household, the head of which acted as employer while his family members and affiliated members or servants acted as permanent employees. Thus, the pattern of employment in modern industrial enterprise has close structural and ideological links with traditional household management.

The shift towards life-employment was assisted in the second and third decades of this century by developments in the bureaucratic structure of business enterprises; a proliferation of sections was accompanied by finer gradings in official rank. During these twenty years there appeared uniforms for workers, badges (lapel buttons) worn as company insignia, and stripes on the uniform cap to indicate section and rank. Workers thus came under a more rigid institutional hierarchy, but they were also given greater incentives by the expectation of climbing the delicately subdivided ladder or rank.

During the war, this system was strengthened further by the adoption of a military pattern. Labour immobility was reinforced by government policy, which cut short the trend to increased mobility that had been the result of the acute shortage of labour. The prohibition on movement of labour between factories was bolstered by the moral argument that it was through concentrated service to his own factory that a worker could best serve the nation. The factory was to be considered as a household or family, in which the employer would and should care for both the material and mental life of his worker and the latter's family. According to the 'Draft of Labour Regulations' (Munitions Public Welfare Ministry publication, February 1945):

> The factory, by its production, becomes the arena for putting into practice the true aims of Imperial labour. The people who preserve these aims become the unifiers of labour. Superior and inferior should help each other, those who are of the same rank should co-operate and with a fellowship as of one family, we shall combine labour and management.

Thus, the factory's household-like function came about, in part, at the behest of state authority. In this context, a moral and patriotic attitude was regarded as more important than technical proficiency. Against shortages in the commodity market, the factory undertook to supply rice, vegetables, clothing, lodging accommodation, medical care, etc.

Familialism, welfare services, and extra payments supplied by the company were thus fully developed under the peculiar circumstances of war, and they have been retained as the institutional pattern in the post-war years. It is also to be noted that the process was further encouraged by post-war union activity. Unions mushroomed after the war, when 48,000 unions enrolled 9,000,000 members. These unions were formed primarily within a single company and encompassed members of different types of occupation and qualification, both staff and line workers. It is said that, in some aspects, a union is like the wartime Industrial Patriotism Club (*Sangyō-hōkoku-kai*), lacking only the company president. Thus it can serve as part of the basis of familialism. The establishment of welfare facilities, company housing schemes, recreation centers at seaside or hill resorts, etc., are all items demanded by the unions along with wage increases. Above all, the single most important union success was the gaining of the right of appeal against summary dismissal or lay-off. In the period immediately after the war, dismissal meant starvation; this, together with the swiftly increasing power of the union movement, accounts for the unions' success in acquiring this tremendous privilege. Thus, life employment, a policy initiated by management, has reached its perfected form through the effect of post-war unionism. Again, to combat the shortage of younger workers and highly trained engineers which is felt so acutely today, management policy is moving further towards attempts at retaining labour by the offer of more beneficial provisions.

As it has shown in the course of its development, life-time employment has advantages for both employer and employee. For the employer it serves to retain the services of skilled workers against times of labour shortage. For the employee it gives security against surplus labour conditions; whatever the market circumstances, there is little likelihood of the employee finding better employment if he once leaves his job. This system has, in fact, been encouraged by contradictory situations—shortage and surplus of labour. Here is demonstrated a radical divergence between Japan and America in management employment policy; a Japanese employer buys future potential labour and an American employer buys labour immediately required. According to the Japanese reasoning, any deficiencies in the current labour force will be compensated by the development of maximum power in the labour force of the future; the employer buys his labour material and shapes it until it best fits his production need. In America, management buys ready-made labour.

Familialism, another offspring of the operational mechanism of modern industrial enterprise, is the twin to life employment. Attention was drawn above to the concept of the 'One Railway Family', which was advocated as early as 1909 by the then President of the National Railways, Gotō Shimpei. The concept was strengthened during the war years, and it has appeared in such favourite slogans of post-war management as 'the spirit of love for the company' and 'the new familialism'. According to so-called modern and advanced management theory, a genuinely inspired 'spirit of love for the company' is not merely advocated but is indeed an atmosphere resulting from management policy, so that 'whether the feeling of love for the company thrives or not is the barometer of the abilities and talents of management staff'. Even in the coining of expressions which may seem antithetical—'we must love our company' and 'the spirit of love for the company is silly'—the underlying motivation remains the securing of the employee's total emotional participation.

In summary, the characteristics of Japanese enterprise as a social group are, first, that the group is itself family-like and, second, that it pervades even the private lives of its employees, for each family joins extensively in the enterprise. These characteristics have been cautiously encouraged by managers and administrators consistently from the Meiji period. And the truth is that this encouragement has always succeeded and reaped rewards.

A cohesive sense of group unity, as demonstrated in the operational mechanism of household and enterprise, is essential as the foundation of the individual's total emotional participation in the group; it helps to build a closed world and results in strong group independence or isolation. This inevitably breeds household customs and company traditions. These in turn are emphasized in mottoes which bolster the sense of unity and group solidarity, and strengthen the group even more. At the same time, the independence of the group and the stability of the frame, both cultivated by this sense of unity, create a gulf between the group and others with similar attributes but outside the frame; meanwhile, the distance between people with differing attributes within the frame is narrowed, and the functioning of any group formed on the base of similar attributes is paralysed. Employees in an enterprise must remain in the group, whether they like it or not. Not only do they not want to change to another company; even if they desire a change, they lack the means to accomplish it. Because there is no tie between workers of the same kind, as in a 'horizontal' craft union, they get neither information nor assistance from their counterparts. (This situation is identical with that of the Japanese married-in bride as described above.) Thus, in this type of social organization, as society grows more stable, the consciousness of similar qualities becomes weaker and, conversely, the consciousness of the difference between 'our people' and 'outsiders' is sharpened.

The consciousness of 'them' and 'us' is strengthened and aggravated to the point that extreme contrasts in human relations can develop in the same society, and anyone outside 'our' people ceases to be considered human. Ridiculous situations occur, such

as that of the man who will shove a stranger out of the way to take
an empty seat, but will then, no matter how tired he is, give up the
seat to someone he knows, particularly if that someone is a superior
in his company.

An extreme example of this attitude in group behaviour is the
Japanese people's amazing coldness (which is not a matter just of
indifference, but rather of active hostility), the contempt and
neglect they will show for the people of an outlying island or for
those living in the 'special' *buraku* (formerly a segregated social
group, now legally equal but still discriminated against). Here the
complete estrangement of people outside 'our' world is institutionalized. In India there is a lower-class group known as 'untouch-
ables', but although at first glance the Indian attitude towards a
different caste appears to resemble Japanese behaviour, it is not
really so. The Indian does not have the sharp distinction of 'them'
and 'us' between two different groups. Among the various Indian
groups, A, B, C, etc., one man happens to belong to A, while
another is of B; A, B, C, and so forth together form one society.
His group A constitutes part of the whole, while, to the Japanese,
'our' is opposed to the whole world. The Indian's attitude towards
people of other groups stems from indifference rather than hostility.

These characteristics of group formation reveal that Japanese
group affiliations and human relations are exclusively one-to-one;
a single loyalty stands uppermost and firm. There are many cases
of membership of more than one group, of course, but in these cases
there is always one group that is clearly preferred while the others
are considered secondary. By contrast, the Chinese, for example,
find it impossible to decide which group is the most important of
several. So long as the groups differ in nature, the Chinese see no
contradiction and think it perfectly natural to belong to several
groups at once. But a Japanese would say of such a case, 'That man
is sticking his nose into something else', and this saying carries with
it moral censure. The fact that Japanese pride themselves on this
viewpoint and call it fastidiousness is once again very Japanese.
The saying 'No man can serve two masters' is wholeheartedly sub-
scribed to by the Japanese. In body-and-soul emotional participation there is no room for serving two masters. Thus, an individual
or a group has always one single distinctive relation to the other.
This kind of ideal is also manifested in the relationship between the
master and his disciple, including the teacher and student today.
For a Japanese scholar, what he calls his teacher (master) is always
one particular senior scholar, and he is recognized as belonging

linearly to that scholar. For him to approach another scholar in competition with his teacher is felt as a betrayal of his teacher and is particularly unbearable for his teacher. In contrast, for the Chinese it is the traditional norm to have several teachers in one's life, and one can learn freely from all of them in spite of the fact that they are in competition.

Thus, in Japanese society not only is the individual's group affiliation one-to-one but, in addition, the ties binding individuals together are also one-to-one. This characteristic single bond in social relationships is basic to the ideals of the various groups within the whole society.

NOTES

1. I find it difficult to choose an English equivalent for *kaisha*; though "company" or "enterprise" correspond etymologically, they do not have the social implications that the word *kaisha* has for a Japanese.
2. I think that, in this analysis, it is effective and convenient to employ the differentiated concepts *social structure* and *social organization,* as proposed by Raymond Firth ('Social Organization and Social Change,' *Journal of the Royal Anthropological Institute,* vol. 84, pp. 1–20, 1954; the same paper appears as Chapter III of *Essays on Social Organization and Values,* 1964).
3. Certainly there exists what may be called a standard norm or commonality which is shared by Japanese households as a whole (or, more precisely, by a local community or different strata), but within this context each individual household normally has its own ways to regulate the behaviour and speech of individual members.

Japanese Management:
The Cultural Background

WILLIAM BROWN

Since the end of the Pacific War the "modernization" of Japanese ways of life has emerged as a national goal. One expression of this ideal can be found in the efforts to rationalize the management practices of large and small businesses. During recent months, under the stimulation of the "technical revolution" taking place in production methods and the increasing integration of Japan into the international economy, the problem of rationalization has become a major concern of both government and industry. Journalists have been particularly vigorous in their castigation of the "feudalistic" and "premodern" characteristics of personnel administration. Works like "familism" and "paternalism" have become epithets stigmatizing those elements in Japanese human relations sanctioned by traditional management practices. It is widely assumed that these traditional patterns of work-relationships constitute an intolerable obstacle to the rationalization of the economy and a serious impediment to economic growth.

In reaction to this attitude, some students of the situation have taken a more "realistic" approach and advocated a compromise between the ideal of rationalization and the more intractable elements of Japanese society rooted in a long tradition.

In this paper I would like to present an aspect of the situation from a position somewhere between these two points of view. I do not wish to deny that there are some features of present management practices which indeed present obstacles to the goals of economic growth and international competition which Japan has necessarily set herself. Nor on the other hand do I reject the view that some features cannot be changed but must be accepted and put up with. I rather prefer to center my attention on those elements

Reprinted from *Monumenta Nipponica* 21 (1966): 47–60.

of Japanese social relations which actually have proved quite "rational" in the past and promise to do so in the future.

In the course of consideration I will take up those features of Japanese managerial practices which have been most severely criticised and I will investigate the two systems alleged as their causes, the promotion system and the lifetime employment system. Then I shall present some features which seem to have been overlooked in the criticism of Japanese management. The paper concludes with a sketch of what I believe to be important cultural and ethical roots of the Japanese approach to work.

LENGTH OF SERVICE

Foreign students of Japanese management have frequently observed that the age of executives in Japanese companies appears much higher than that of, say, executives in American companies. Few men ever become executives before the age of fifty. In a survey of 235 companies in 1958 it was found that the average age of 3,277 executives was 57.2 years old. A little more than 10% were below the age of fifty, while about one-third were above the age of sixty.[1] It was also found that the ages differ quite clearly according to the rank held.

It appears that the ages of those occupying these positions vary little from company to company. In other words, promotions take place at regular intervals, the basic qualification for promotion being the length of time spent in the service of the company. Seniority is also the basic unit for determining wages. Thus a man on the day he enters a company can predict with fair accuracy his wage and position in that company at any given year in the future.

This so-called "escalator system" of promotion has for some time been under attack by those who urge a more rationalistic promotion system. The proponents of change, by now far in the majority, argue that the efficient operation of a company depends to a large extent on the discovery, reward, and promotion of ability to get work done. Since 1958 many attempts have been made to change this system by introducing various methods of job-evaluation and skill-evaluation. These attempts have met with many obstacles. In a survey published in 1963 it was found that 87% of the 484 companies surveyed were still employing the length-of-service and age standard; 20% of the companies interviewed were employing a job-rank system, while 65% were trying an ability-rating system.[2] Nevertheless, the companies using combinations of these systems paid 68% of the total salaries for length-of-service considerations and only 21% for job-ability.[3] Even where the job-skill system is employed, there is no clear distinction in evaluation between skill and length-of-service,[4] and in the job-evaluation system 29% of the companies have deliberately included length-of-service considerations in their evaluation categories.[5]

It seems clear that so far attempts to modify the length-of-service system, accepted by both employers and employees, have met with only modest success. Indeed there seems to be a kind of moral pressure upon employers to see that men who entered the company together are advanced to positions of equal importance more or less at the same time.[6] Nevertheless, it must be admitted that there are other minor factors which establish slight but decisive differences in rank and prospects of further advancement among members of a group which entered the company together.[7]

LIFE EMPLOYMENT

Lifetime commitment of the employee to his company is a phenomenon nearly universal (92%), and the larger the company the more firmly is it entrenched.[8] Only about one-quarter of the companies questioned in 1963 were inclined to do much about it.[9] Opinion as to whether this system was likely to change very easily was evenly divided.[10] Those who believed that the life-employment system was likely to change expected that it would give way under modernization of management practices or the attempts to cope with the technical revolution. Most of the companies which took, shall we say, a more pessimistic view felt that the "familistic mentality" of the Japanese, upon which this system is thought to be based, is not likely to change.[11] The *defects* of this system were considered to be the inability to lay off superannuated or unnecessary labor, the "preservation of the length-of-service system," the fostering and spread of that prudential attitude which prompts workers to seek their own security first and the tendency toward indifferentism. But this system is believed to have its good points too: more than half the companies questioned (53%) thought that the life-employment system produces a sense of security among the employees. Nearly as many companies (47%) said that the system provides a "basis for nourishing the spirit of a cooperative body (*kyōdōtai teki seishin*) in the enterprise."[12]

This lack of mobility in the work force is strikingly reflected in the top levels of management. It is quite rare for the board of directors to contain many directors who entered as directors from another company. According to a survey of 159 companies made in

1956 by Ono Toyoaki, only 6.5% of the executives came from out-side the company.[13] Another survey of 235 companies made in 1958 by the Dōyūkai found that of 2,428 executives, 324 (11.8%) were from other companies.[14] Sometimes an executive of a bank or high-ranking government official who has been looking after the interests of a company may be invited to join that company on the executive level (*yokosuberiyaku*). Professor Noda Kazuo estimates that as many as 10% of Japanese executives in industrial enterprises get their jobs in this way.[15] In another survey by the Dōyūkai, only 5.7% of the companies reported that they had representatives of major stockholders on their board, and even fewer (2.3%) reported representatives from their financial agencies.[16]

The life-employment system and the seniority system are intimately related and appear to be two expressions of the typical social structure of a Japanese company. We will examine the nature of this social structure in more detail later, but here I would like to call attention to the closely knit relations among employers and employees. Such close relations would naturally be expected where the members of an organization realize that they will be together for the rest of their working lives. They also expect that promotions, instead of separating them, will keep them close together. The re-lation with superiors is also usually quite close. The superiors in a company feel obliged to call their subjects together frequently for an informal talk and they make it a point to be present at company outings and other forms of recreation.[17]

Authority and Responsibility

Foreign observers are invariably amazed at the lack of a clear definition of authority and responsibility, not only for the various sections of a company but also for the members of middle and top management.

Many of the usual means for marking out areas of authority are slow to catch on. The organization chart is by no means univer-sal. According to the 1960 Dōyūkai survey, 26.2% of the companies questioned did not have one. Small companies would conceivably have less use for an organization chart than large ones, but even among the biggest companies (capital of over 20 billion yen), 12.2% had none.[18] The existence of a set of rules delineating an official's authority is far less common. In the same survey, 66.3% of the companies replied that they had no such rules for the chief of the general affairs division (*sōmu buchō*) or for the chief of the accounting division (*keiri buchō*).[19] In a survey made by the Japan Productivity

Center in 1959, 36 out of 54 companies replied that they had no stipulations for areas of authority connected with various jobs.[20]

Not only is there a lack of clarity in areas of authority. Frequently the nature of the job itself is not clear. We saw above that Japanese companies have not been very successful in introducing job-rank and job-qualification systems. Even of the companies actually using some form of job-rank system, only 48.5% make the job analysis necessary for this system.[21] The list of difficulties these companies encountered in introducing the job-rank system is enlightening: "the difficulty in standardizing job content," "lack of agreement on the social evaluation of equal work," "individual differences in workers' efficiency," "lack of job-consciousness among employees."[22] This last item is not without significance. It has been noted more than once that when a Japanese is asked what his job is, instead of saying what he does, he is likely to reply that he is a member of such and such a company.[23]

So far we have considered the theoretical disadvantages of the length-of-service system, the life-employment system, and the lack of clear areas of responsibility and authority. Now let us consider those factors which tend to offset these disadvantages.

TALENT

The usual objections to the systems described above are that they tend to impede the discovery and development of talent and that the incompetent are allowed to reach positions of high authority. In reality, however, the incompetent rarely reach such important positions and the larger enterprises are assured of a generous supply of really able persons.

The supply of talent (*nōryoku*), as we might surmise, is taken care of by a careful selection of candidates in the beginning. Large firms usually call upon a certain few famous and highly rated universities to present candidates for the company entrance exam.[24] These candidates first must present a record of their experience, their academic record, information about their family, and the names of those whom they know in the company who are willing to sponsor them. Then they are informed whether they may be admitted to the exam. Perhaps one-tenth of these may pass the exam and thus be admitted to the firm for life.[25]

But the selection by the company is only the final stage in a long process. In reality, the educational system, and with it the greater part of the population, is mobilized toward the one purpose of providing industry and government with the cream of Japanese talent. Few other nations in the world can show a comparable example of such perfect rationalization. A separate study of the history and social psychology of the Japanese notion of "success" (*risshin shusse*) would be required to explain the intensity of the competition for these routes to the company entrance examinations.[26] The way lies through a rigorous series of elimination contests in the form of entrance examinations into the best high schools, the best middle schools, the best grammar schools, and even the best kindergartens.[27]

A priori then we can expect that Japan's business elite should be an elite in the true sense of the word. Recent research has provided a posteriori proof of this fact. Although 7% of the population between the ages of 50 to 69 obtained higher education, 71% of the industrial elite had the equivalent of a college education or above. We realize what a high percentage this is if we compare this figure with two other countries of high industrial and educational levels. According to M. Newcomer, as of 1950, 62% of the American business elite had obtained a college education or above, while in England, according to G.H. Copeman, only 36% of the business elite had an equivalent education. Mannari and Abegglen estimate that within another generation the figure will reach 100%.[28]

The fact that more than seventy percent of the Japanese business elite have had a college education tells only half the story of just how select this elite is. It was mentioned above that large companies ask only certain universities to present candidates for their entrance exams. These are the institutions which have a long tradition, superior educational facilities, and by far the best students. There are today more than 250 colleges and universities (compared with 45 before World War II), but less than a dozen of these have supplied Japanese industry with more than two-thirds of its executives.[29]

Seen in this light, the traditional Japanese promotion system is not the enemy to talent that it is alleged to be. The initial recruitment of extremely capable and industrious young men every year solves the problem at the outset. Given the general range of human intelligence, it might be safely presumed that the variation of ability in this group is not great enough to warrant the employment of a promotion system based mainly on this one discriminatory factor. After all, the white collar employee in Japan gained his job in competition with literally millions of other Japanese. Presupposing, then, that the company is staffed by a group of highly intelligent young men, it would appear more reasonable to promote them according to the *experience* which they have been intelligently accumulating.

RETIREMENT

Let us now turn our attention to another factor operating in the selection of talented managers. This is the mandatory retirement age system (*teinen seido*). In spite of the seniority system, obviously not everyone is made a president nor even a director. Most employees are retired first at the age of fifty-five.[30] Only those who have attained the title of director by the age of fifty can feel assured that they will be allowed to stay on after the mandatory retirement age, and even then it is not certain. The decisive factor in a man's career is whether he can reach the position of division head in the home office; accordingly, more care is exercised in choosing men for this post than for others.[31]

DECISION-MAKING

Even granting, then, that the length-of-service system and life-employment systems are not such obstacles to the promotion of talent as is often supposed, there remains another and more serious objection to the organization of the Japanese company. This is, as noted above, the lack of clarity in defining authority, responsibility, and the rarity of delegation of authority.

The evidence seems to indicate that the real authority of a company rests in the hands of a few, for example, the Regular Affairs Committee (*jōmukai*), or more frequently only one, the president or board chairman.[32] The decisions are made by these few and this authority is rarely if ever delegated to subordinates on the division and section level.[33]

A closer examination of the way this planning and decision process is actually carried out will show us many things about the locus, function, and conception of authority in Japan. If we take up one of the papers (*ringisho*) that are constantly crossing an executive's desk we find that it has received fourteen, sixteen, or more seal impressions. These seals are a record of the journey of this paper from section to section, division to division, from subordinate to officials to the president. This circulation of papers is the life of the decision-making process in the Japanese company. What are the characteristics of this system? Professor Noda describes them for us:

1. *The drafting of a plan by middle management.* Certainly when the

initiator is below the middle management level, and even when the initiator is a member of the highest managerial level, the drafting of the plan is always carried out in the name of an organizational unit of middle management (the section, for example) or its administrator.

2. *A careful horizontal consideration.* Before the *ringisho* is submitted to higher officials, it is sent around to related organizational units of the same rank, where it is confirmed, perhaps after additions or corrections. Sometimes, before the plan is drawn up in a formal *ringisho* the related organizational units of the same rank are called together for previous discussion.

3. *A careful vertical consideration.* The submitted *ringisho* does not receive the independent authorization of a particular individual; it receives the authorization of several people in succession along the order of occupational rank.

4. *The formality of affixing the seal.* Regarding the above-mentioned confirmation or authorization, since it is carried out by the affixing of the responsible person's seal, it is feared that the confirmation or approval of the contents of a *ringisho* may fall into a mere formalism.

5. *The lack of clarity in authority and responsibility.* The nature of the act of confirmation or approval is very vague in its relation to the enactment and effects of the items in the *ringisho*. In other words, this is a skillful device for obscuring both the locus of authority for carrying out the plan and the locus of responsibility for its effects.[34]

Almost every company has some form of this system. About 94% of the two hundred companies surveyed in 1961 were employing this system, and of these only 19% were thinking of doing away with it.[35] To abolish the system, or even to make changes in it, usually requires major changes in other organs of management in the company. This is an indication of how deeply interlaced this system is in the network of the company.[36] Although few firms think they can get along without it, almost all are trying to perfect this system, either by clarifying what matters are to be treated in this way, or by simplifying the routes of the *ringisho*.[37] In an attempt to focus responsibility for the origins of plans, 52% of the firms have rules determining who is authorized to draw up a *ringisho*.[38]

Theoretically, if a matter to be decided is within the competence of a subordinate, there should be no need to resort to the *ringi* system. Nevertheless, in those companies which have rules defining this authority (65%), in nearly half the cases a *ringisho* is sent around anyway, sometimes as a mere notification, but more usually in order to get the superior's approval.[39]

It is widely assumed that authority is concentrated in the person of the president. This phenomenon is probably explained by the fact that the final approval of proposals is given by the president. Professor Noda, however, makes the rather unexpected assertion that the Japanese company is in effect managed by subordinates. In fact, he goes so far as to claim that, because of the *ringi* system, "Japanese management is middle management":

> The essence of the *ringi* system lies in the fact that the middle management level conceives, plans, and can actually carry out almost all of the affairs which pertain to administration. It certainly appears that, insofar as approval of superiors is required, authority is formally located on the upper level. Supposing, however, that the superior merely goes through the formality of placing his stamp upon the *ringisho*, which has been submitted to him after obtaining the confirmation of each organizational unit concerned, it can be said that, in effect, authority *has been delegated to the middle-management level*.[40]

Noda goes on to develop this opinion convincingly, but his whole thesis rests on the supposition that the superior gives his approval automatically and as a mere formality. This is an assumption that should definitely be proved. Why must we suppose that the superiors do not take their job as seriously as their subordinates? (It would be interesting to know how frequently plans are turned down by superiors.)

I feel that Professor Yoshino Yotarō of Stanford University comes closer to the actual state of affairs:

> *Ringi* management is said to be a centralization of authority and so it is—formally; but in actual fact one has the strong impression that it neither centralizes authority nor decentralizes it, but rather disperses it throughout the enterprise.[41]

The difficulty in grasping the locus of authority really comes from attempting to discover what corresponds to the Western concept of authority in a non-Western social organization. The *ringi* system shows the course of the decision-making process, but does not establish it. Ideas and plans are worked up, developed, and polished in informal discussions among men who have been working in close association for years. The *ringi* system appears essentially to be a means of knitting together as many people as possible into the vital activity of the company. All are given an opportunity to make their contribution and most do so. The *ringisho*, with all its seals affixed, is the concrete manifestation of a unity of wills, a unanimous consent. The same phenomenon can be observed in committee meetings. More often than not they are an organ for the explicitation and "celebration" of a unanimous consent previously existing in a general and implicit state. The real decision-making process is frequently carried on in an area subliminal to the formal apparatus of organizations and is catalyzed by the harmonious spirit of what is known as the *kyōdōtai*.

THE ENTERPRISE AS KYŌDŌTAI

In the preceding description of Japanese management processes I have confined the discussion to the "phenomenology" of the situation, without entering into the cultural causes. In the following pages I would like to present in outline an area of the cultural background of Japanese management which I think merits further study.

If we suppose the fundamental economic unit of contemporary Japan to be the large company, it might be instructive to compare it with the fundamental economic unit of pre-Meiji Japan, the village *kyōdōtai*.[42]

The theme of mountains and water is perhaps the most frequent and beloved in Japanese art and literature from ancient times. The Japanese terrain has until recent times defined not only their aesthetic life but their economic life as well. The agrarian culture of Japan began with the Yayoi period and the introduction of wet-rice culture. As is well known, the cultivation of rice requires a constant and abundant supply of water, which in Japan could only be insured by an elaborate system of irrigation. Since the numerous canals, dams, etc., which make up this system could not be built nor maintained by individuals, cooperative forms of labor were needed. The mountains surrounding the village supplied building materials, fuel, and fertilizer, but careful cooperation was required for the development and conservation of these resources. The village, through the cooperation of its members, was economically independent from other villages, just as it was physically separated from them by geographical conditions.

The ecology of Japan, then, indicates how the social and cultural patterns developed in dependence upon mountains and water. Old village records vividly illustrate the social and legal life of the village centered around these geographical features.[43] Watsuji Tetsurō, in his famous work on the history of ethical thought in Japan, argues convincingly that the basic Japanese ethical attitudes had already been established in the primitive village *kyōdōtai* life and that all the other social institutions which grew up throughout the nation's long history were characterized by these same ethical patterns.[44]

Professor Kamishima Jirō has made a very interesting study of the relationship between the social and psychological structure of the village and its influence on urban life in Japan. Let us consider his concepts of "primary village" and "secondary village" in reference to the problem we are now examining, the cultural roots of the modern large enterprise in Japan.

The Primary Village (*dai ichi mura*)

The sociocultural principles of the way of life in the village of the Tokugawa period are enumerated by Kamishima:

1. "Mental Autarky": The economic independence of the outside and the internal interdependence produced a social, cultural, and psychological self-sufficiency, a group solidarity, and group consciousness. All the necessities of life could be supplied by the group. In short, economic autarky produced mental autarky.
2. Shintoism (not the state-sponsored religion, but that of the common people): The Shintoism of village life was focused on the *matsuri* or festival. The many annual festivals played an important part in village life. Their function was to supply the emotional unification necessary for smooth functioning of the *kyōdōtai*.
3. "Gerontology": In a self-sufficient and unchanging society, wisdom is equated with memory and experience. These qualities naturally grow with age. Thus older people are truly wiser and are the natural leaders. Such a situation is supported by the youth: all they need do is obey and wait to take their position of leadership when the time comes.
4. Familism: The extended family unified by the authority of the family head was the social unit of the village. Members were not necessarily blood relations.
5. Feudalism: Families, being the basic social element of the village, were obliged to participate as units in the preparations and celebrations of the main village activity, the festival. Roles were assigned to each family, and it was by this that family status was determined. An individual's worth was determined by the standing of the family to which he belonged, and the family's standing was determined by the

extent of its *participation* in the festival. With the decline of the family system, personal status came also to be more closely identified with age, since age was the only immutable criterion for quality.

The Secondary Village (*dai ni mura*)

The rapid development of bureaucracy and industry consequent upon the Meiji Restoration demanded a swift mobilization of manpower. This was supplied by the rural areas (villages). No social organization can function without generally recognized and accepted social patterns of behavior. There was no time to form new ones; the required social patterns were supplied by the villages.[45] The former villagers instinctively adapted the only patterns they knew to the situation in which they found themselves.[46]

The enterprise as secondary village. Let us now apply the sociocultural principles described above to the modern Japanese company viewed in the light of a "secondary village."[47]

1. "Mental Autarky": The departmentalization and lack of communication between divisions in a firm can be partially explained by this notion.[48] The emotional bonds which exist in a typical Japanese company may have strong social and psychological roots in the parent social unit, the village.

2. Shintoism: Shintoism as an explicit religious belief and practice is no longer very vital in upper classes. Although there are no more religious festivals to lubricate the friction points and strengthen the emotional ties necessary for the smooth operation of the company *kyōdōtai*, the function of the festival is fulfilled by company outings, sports events, and afterwork gatherings with office companions.

3. "Gerontology": The principle of seniority was established early in Japanese bureaucracy and has not been questioned until recently. Now the need for innovative talent and ability to appraise risk, not usually associated with older people, begin to threaten the length-of-service system. As was pointed out above, however, experience is still perhaps the most valuable discriminatory factor and is justly rewarded by promotions.

4. and 5. Familism and Feudalism: In the village a person's character or worth was determined by the status of the family to which he belonged. But under the impact of social changes just previous to and after the Meiji Restoration the large family system declined. In the large cities the small

nuclear family was relatively insignificant as a social unit. It could no longer provide identity and status. Its place has been taken by the government ministries and later by the large private enterprises. So it is that a man's worth, his character, or his status is determined by the extent of his firm's participation in the economic life of the nation. More than perhaps salary, position, or any other single factor, the standing (size) of the firm indicates personal success (*shusse*).

In brief, gerontology may be viewed in principle as the cultural origin of the length-of-service system. The close cooperative or *kyōdōtai* spirit may be explained in terms of mental autarky as the traditional approach to a work situation. Life employment may reflect mental autarky, familism, and feudalism.

Kyōdōtai Ethics

The cultural sources of life employment and also the peculiar concepts of the superior-subordinate relationship, of authority and responsibility, may ultimately be found in typical Japanese ethical attitudes. Robert Bellah, in his book *Tokugawa Religion* attempts to find in Japanese ethico-religious attitudes at least a partial explanation of the country's economic development in recent times. Presupposed is an animistic or pantheistic approach to nature. The basic religious drive is to union with this nature thus achieving union with the Absolute. The Japanese tends to regard the society of which he is a member as the expression for him of Nature. From this society or group he receives benefits, all that he has and values. He feels obliged to express his gratitude to this group by dedicating himself to its advancement. In this way, by complete self-forgetfulness, he manages to achieve a kind of mystical union with his group (Nature, the Absolute).[49]

Watsuji, in his intriguing analysis of early Japanese myths, considers the leader of the group as a kind of mediator, one representing the Absolute to the group and the group to the Absolute.[50]

Bellah and Watsuji show how the group-oriented ethics of Japan have a long history and go very deep. This ethic may ultimately explain the particularism of Japanese economic life as well as its dynamism, but as yet the surface of this aspect of Japanese culture has hardly been scratched.

CONCLUSION

It is precisely the group-orientation of the members, the cohesion, and the insistence on harmonious personal relations which,

I submit, are the strength of Japanese organizations and the source of their efficiency. Such a type of organization gives an individual's particular talents and abilities a wide range of play. Furthermore, one man's deficiencies are obscured because they are made up for by his companion's strong points. Finally, a sense of satisfaction is achieved through the awareness of a real contribution to and participation in the vital activity of the company.

In spite of the strong attraction exerted by imported management theories, the Japanese, persuaded perhaps by their own common sense rooted in a long tradition, have resisted the urge to parcel out a firm's myriad operations in neat little bundles of authority and responsibility. The Japanese approach to the work situation dictated by modern industry seems to me much more realistic than the habit of mind which insists on designating one individual as the responsible scapegoat for a plethora of details which he could not conceivably have contributed. In effect, responsibility is automatically distributed in proportion to the demands of the task, in degrees impossible to isolate and measure. According to foreign notions of work allotment, men are pegs which must be fitted into preexisting holes. Once a man's area of responsibility has been marked out it becomes his territory. As a result, any attempt by a fellow worker to make up for his inevitable shortcomings or oversights is tantamount to an invasion. Only recently have foreign efficiency experts come to realize how much heat is generated by these friction points. The Japanese work force, on the other hand, might be compared to a jigsaw puzzle. Compared with the polished pegs, the individuals seem very irregular, "irrational." But the pieces themselves, through their intimate knowledge of one another's peculiar shape and coloring, fit together neatly and a clear picture emerges. To the Westerner, the lack of work rules, job analysis, lack of definition of responsibility, etc., are evidence of the Oriental's lack of a sense of individualism. The Japanese approach to the work situation is not only an illustration of a certain degree of individualism but a means of preserving it and developing it. The executives of companies are instinctively aware of this native trait. On paper all authority appears to be in their hands, but as the operation of the *ringi* system shows, the trust and approbation of the subordinates' collective good sense and initiative is the most accurate delegation of authority possible.

Recently some voices have been raised in opposition to what has been called an infatuation with theories of management rationalization developed in the West. Professor Tsuchiya Takao is particularly

vigorous in his attack upon this form of "worship of the West."[51]
One cannot help feeling that there is indeed among some Japanese
students of management a certain implicit trust in formulas which
have proved successful in the West and a deep distrust of Japanese
"feudal" traditions. It cannot be denied that in Japan there is a
strong tendency to consider the science of management as another
form of technology which can be imported just as it is. It is also
possible to discern in this attitude what Professor Maruyama
Masao has called "faith in theory," the tendency to hypostatize
theories and to trust in the complete effectiveness of the perfect
system. In the political sphere "faith in theory" appears in the
emphasis on "structural reforms."[52] In the economic sphere we
may see the same phenomenon in the emphasis on the rationalization of management as an ultimate goal.

On the other hand we can also perceive in some quarters a
hidebound traditionalism, an insistence on the traditional way of
doing things because it is traditional. This type of thinking is based
on a misunderstanding of what tradition is.

> Real traditions are not principles from which one can draw con-
> clusions as to one's lines of conduct in new circumstances. They are
> ways of existence incorporated into a temperament, which deter-
> mines a way of reacting more than they dictate a solution. A true
> tradition is constitutive, not constituted.[53]

The real test for the rationality of a system is not to be found in
any one theory or any set of historical facts. It can be found only by
considering results and comparing them with the goal to be achieved
The process of rationalization is nothing other than adapting means
to ends. A productive system is to be judged by its efficiency, not in
terms of some abstract formula.[54] If a formula is after all required,
it must be worked out by the Japanese themselves through their
own experience of their encounter with the demands of reality. The
questions they need ask themselves are simple: "What are we really
trying to do, and are we really doing it?" Only in this way will this
great nation, which has learned much from Western experience,
contribute the richness of its own experience to the West. Meanwhile, Western observers would do well to take a harder look at the
Japanese way of doing things in terms of results, remembering a
saying dear to the pragmatic Anglo-Saxon heart: "There is more
than one way to skin a cat."

NOTES

1. Cf. Keizai Dōyūkai 1958 Survey Report, "Wagakuni daikigyō ni okeru top management no kōzō" (The Structure and Function of Top Management of Large Enterprises in Japan), reproduced in Noda Kazuo, *Nihon no jūyaku* (Big Business Executives in Japan), Diamond Press, Tokyo, 1960, pp. 317, 320–21. The Committee for Economic Development (Keizai dōyūkai) has just finished a five-year survey on management practices in Japan. Most of the figures in this paper are taken from reports on this survey.

2. Keizai Dōyūkai Survey, "Wagakuni kigyō ni okeru keiei ishi kettei no jittai (IV): rōdō shijō no henka to kigyō katsudō" (Management Decision Process in Japan (IV): Changes in the Labor Market and Enterprise Behavior), Tokyo Center for Economic Research, Tokyo, 1963, p. 88. Hereafter referred to as *Dōyūkai* IV.

3. *Ibid.*, p. 89.

4. *Ibid.*, p. 230.

5. *Ibid.*, pp. 92, 231.

6. Cf. Ono Toyoaki, "Nōryoku-shugi jidai no ningen kanri" (The Management of People in the Age of Talentism) *Bessatsu chūō kōron: keiei mondai*, Spring, 1964, pp. 34–35. Also Ishikawa Hiroyoshi and Ujigawa Makoto, *Nihon no white collar* (Japan's White Collar), Japan Productivity Center, Tokyo, 1961, pp. 90–92.

7. Kamata Isao, "Chūkan sarariman no shōshin to shōkyū" (Advancement and Pay Raises of the Middle Level Salaryman), *Bessatsu chūō kōron: keiei mondai*, Spring, 1964, pp. 74–85.

8. *Dōyūkai* IV, p. 22.

9. *Ibid.*, p. 29.

10. *Ibid.*, p. 31.

11. *Ibid.*, p. 23.

12. *Ibid.*, p. 25.

13. *Ibid.*

14. *Ibid.*, pp. 170–174.

15. *Ibid.*, pp. 170–174.

16. "Wagakuni kigyō ni okeru keiei ishi kettei no jittai" (The Actual Condition of Management Decision Processes in Japanese Enterprises), Keizai dōyūkai, Tokyo, 1960, pp. 26–28. Hereafter referred to as *Dōyūkai* I.

17. *Dōyūkai* IV, pp. 233–235.

18. *Dōyūkai* I, p. 42.

19. *Ibid.*

20. Cited in Noda, *Jūyaku*, p. 372.

21. *Dōyūkai* IV, pp. 91, 230.

22. *Ibid.*, pp. 92, 231.

23. Ōno Tsutomu, *Bijinesu man* (Business Man), San'ichi shobō, Tokyo, 1964, p. 42.

24. Cf. Noda, *Jūyaku*, pp. 160–165.

25. Personality, ideology, health, and academic achievements are listed among the most highly desirable qualities. Cf. *Dōyūkai* IV, p. 42.

26. For an interesting study of *risshin shusse* cf. Kamishima Jirō, *Kindai Nihon no seishin kōzō* (The Spiritual Structure of Modern Japan), Iwanami shoten, Tokyo, 1961, pp. 269–290.

27. This phenomenon, popularly known as *shiken jigoku* ("examination hell"), is described by Ezra F. Vogel, *Japan's New Middle Class*, University of California Press, Berkeley, 1963, pp. 40–67.

28. H. Mannari and J. Abegglen, "Nihon no sangyō shidōsha to kakureki" (The Educational Background of Japan's Industrial Leaders), *Bessatsu chūō kōron: keiei mondai,* Winter, 1963, pp. 190–197.

29. In 1959 the Japan Productivity Center in a survey of 900 executives found that of these, 32% were graduates of Tokyo University, 10% from Hitotsubashi University, 8% from Kyoto University, and 7% and 4% from the private universities, Keiō and Waseda, respectively. Survey reproduced in Noda, *Jūyaku,* pp. 345–381.

30. An idea of how low the Japanese retirement age is can be gained by comparing it with that of other countries: France, 60; England, 65; America, 65; West Germany, 65; Switzerland, 65; Norway, 70; Canada, 70. Cf. Ishikawa and Ujigawa, *White Collar,* p. 185.

31. *Dōyūkai,* IV. pp. 67, 224–226.

32. The board of Directors, the organ established by law for the direction of Japanese companies, has, for various reasons, during the past several years become more or less a mere formality, its function being taken over by regular affairs committees. Cf. *Top management no soshiki to kinō: wagakuni kigyō ni okeru keiei ishi no jittai,* II, *Keizai dōyūkai,* Tokyo, 1961, pp. 18–26, 73–77. Hereafter *Dōyūkai* II. Cf. also Sakaguchi Akira, *Keieisha* (Managers), Kawade shobō shinsha, Tokyo, 1964, pp. 79–82.

33. Cf. *Dōyūkai* I, pp. 18–24.

34. Noda, *Jūyaku,* pp. 115–117. (All translations are the author's unless otherwise stated.)

35. *Dōyūkai* II, pp. 50, 57. Even by 1964, of 397 companies again questioned about this system 92% said they employed the system and 5% said they did not. *Wagakuni kigyō ni okeru keiei ishi kettei no jittai* (v): *keiei rinen to kigyō katsudō* (The Actual Condition of Management Decision Processes in Japanese Enterprises: Management Ideology and Enterprise Behavior), Tokyo Center for Economic Research, Tokyo, 1964, pp. 116–117. Hereafter referred to as *Dōyūkai* v.

36. *Dōyūkai* II, p. 52.

37. *Ibid.,* pp. 56–57.

38. Usually the division head or section chief, *ibid.,* p. 53.

39. *Ibid.,* p. 55.

40. Noda, *Jūyaku,* p. 117. Emphasis added.

41. "Soto kara mita Nihonteki keiei" (Japanese-style Management as Seen from Outside), *Bessatsu Chūō Kōron: keiei mondai,* Summer, 1964, p. 98.

42. This term is more easily described than translated. It refers primarily to cooperative and mutual-assistance organizations, and is frequently translated simply, "community."

43. Cf. Matsuyoshi Sadao, *Mura no kiroku* (Village Records), Iwanami shoten, 1961.

44. *Nihon rinri shisōshi* (The History of Japanese Ethical Thought), *Watsuji Tetsurō senshū* (Collected Works of Watsuji Tetsurō), Iwanami shoten, Tokyo, 1962, XII, XIII.

45. It must be admitted that the extent to which peasants from the village were a constituent part of the new bureaucratic system is disputed. Former samurai and merchants were probably *leaders* in the development of these institutions, but the question is whether they also were responsible for the social patterns which appeared in these institutions.

46. Kamishima Jirō, *Kindai Nihon,* pp. 22–164.

47. One must be careful to avoid the idea that a "modernized" or "rationalized" system is one which is free from the taint of rural sociocultural patterns. The continued popularity in America of the famous "Turner

Thesis" is an indication that most Americans are proud of the role the rural past has played in their country's modernization.

48. On the "vertical organization" of Japanese firms, cf. Ono Toyoaki, "Nōryoku-shugi," pp. 103–112.

49. Robert Bellah, *Tokugawa Religion: The Values of Pre-Industrial Japan,* The Free Press, Glencoe, 1957.

50. Watsuji Tetsurō, *Nihon rinri,* xii, 55–95.

51. Tsuchiya Takao, *Nihon keiei rinenshi* (The History of Japanese Management Ideology), Nihon keizai shimbun, Tokyo, 1964, pp. 3–95.

52. Maruyama Masao, *Nihon no shisō* (Japanese Thought), Iwanami shoten, Tokyo, 1961.

53. Yves Montcheuil, *For Men of Action,* Geoffrey Chapman, London, 1957, p. 152.

54. It is not impossible that many of the real difficulties which harass Japanese management flow from an imperfect understanding of the built-in goals of industry as such. It must be remembered that technology and industry have grown up in a culture in which, due to philosophical and theological traditions, man is considered to be distinct from the natural world precisely because he is a creator and manager of it.

Reciprocity and the Asymmetric Principle: An Analytical Reappraisal of the Japanese Concept of On^1

TAKIE SUGIYAMA LEBRA

I. GENERAL IMPLICATIONS OF RECIPROCITY

Reciprocity as a useful frame of reference for understanding or explaining social phenomena has been well demonstrated in anthropology and sociology. There seems to be general agreement as to the basic characteristic of reciprocity, namely, the symmetric relationship of partners involved. The symmetric relationship can be summarized by the following interrelated aspects of social action between two individuals, A and B: (1) Bilateral contingency (A acts in a certain way provided B is to respond in an expected way, or A's favor for B creates B's obligation to repay, and vice versa); (2) interdependence of partners for mutual benefit (A gives something away to B because B has something else which A needs, and vice versa); (3) equality of exchanged values (What A gives is equivalent to what he receives). These symmetric aspects of reciprocity were emphasized by Malinowski (1959), for instance, when he characterized reciprocity in terms of "sociological dualism," economic give-and-take, and mutual legal obligations of repayment. The point (3) above in particular with reference to fair (non-exploitative) distribution of rights and duties was insisted upon by Gouldner (1960) in his distinction of "reciprocity" from the Parsonian notion of "complementarity."

What makes reciprocity powerful as a conceptual tool and also difficult to deal with seems, however, to derive from the dynamic interlocking between the symmetric strain of reciprocity and the asymmetric, generalized aspect involved in actual social trans-

Reprinted from *Psychologia* 12 (1969): 129–38.

actions. In our definition, the asymmetric relationship in its pure form involves: (1) unilateral commitment or obligation (A's devotion, compliance, or generosity toward B in disregard of B's past or future action); (2) one-way dependence for benefit (A is dependent upon what B can do for him, but not vice versa); (3) inequality of exchanged values (What A gives is more than what he receives). Needless to say, both symmetry and asymmetry are difficult to conceive except in relative terms.

The occurrence of asymmetric transaction may be accounted for by various factors. It may be due to motivational inclinations such as desire for display and publicity (Malinowski, op. cit.); to an internalized moral or religious creed governing the actor more or less independently of his partner—the essential point in Parsons' action theory (1937); and/or to the hierarchical social relationships which precludes the equality of bargaining power at the outset of interaction. In addition to these, symmetrical reciprocity may be made difficult to maintain by the fact that social debt and credit are not always quantitatively ascertainable. Indeed, some writers (Herskovits, 1952; Lévi-Strauss, 1957; Polyani cited in Bohannan, 1966: 231–232) stressed the non-economic, diffuse aspect of objects exchanged in reciprocity such as prestige, honor, or emotion, and distinguished reciprocity from market exchange. Firth (1967a; a personal comment, 1969) reminds us of the social, symbolic, or metaphorical values involved in reciprocal exchange, pointing out the importance of a non-material, indirect, covert, or long-range form as well as a material, direct, overt, or short-range form of reciprocity. Given such subtlety and incalculability of exchanged values, one may be tempted to discard the idea of symmetry as the necessary criterion of reciprocity. For Sahlins (1965) symmetry represents only one type of reciprocity, when he proposes the whole "spectrum" of reciprocities ranging from the generalized, through the balanced, to the negative reciprocity according to "kinship distance."

Thus, the dynamic interchange between symmetric and a-symmetric tendencies may be said to be inherent in reciprocity. The compulsion to maintain or restore the balance between give and take may generate as well as counteract strain toward asymmetry. A detailed analysis (Blau, 1964) was given of the process by which initial symmetry inevitably gives way to the unilateral obligation of compliance, the process of power generation out of reciprocity. Conversely, anthropological literature (Malinowski,

1959; Firth, 1956 and 1967; Mauss, 1967) abounds with evidence indicating that what appears as the operation of a unilateral, asymmetric principle is in fact governed by the rule of symmetric reciprocity.

It is proposed here that each culture provides mechanisms which keep within a limit the tension generated in the mutual constraint between symmetry and asymmetry. It is further argued that if symmetric reciprocity represents the primary value of a culture, the existence of asymmetric relations must be justified or tolerated within a framework consistent with the symmetric norm. Likewise, if asymmetry is the most pronounced sector of a cultural system, there must be some less explicit norms allowing for symmetric orientations which do not directly contradict with the asymmetric value pattern. The following is an attempt to apply the concept of reciprocity to the Japanese idea of *on* and to search for the culturally imbedded mechanisms whereby symmetric and asymmetric tendencies constrain each other without creating excessive tension. Such mechanisms may be identified as compensatory (Gouldner, 1959 and 1960), error-correcting, warning devices, or merely as historically accumulated consequences from the bipolar tendencies simultaneously at work.

II. *On* AS AN ASYMMETRIC NORM

The concept of *on*, which has played an essential role in Japanese culture, has become widely known through Benedict's work (1946). The term, as far as its contemporary usage is concerned, refers at once to a favor granted by A to B and to a resultant debt B owes to A. An *on* must be accepted with gratitude since it is an evidence of the giver's benevolence or generosity, at the same time it must be carried as a burden because the *on*, once granted, makes the receiver a debtor and compels him to repay.

The *on* can thus be defined in the language of reciprocity such as debt and repayment, and, indeed, some writers stressed the symmetric, mutual aspect of *on*-reciprocity. Sakurai (1961: 96–137) characterized *on* as a contractual relationship between a master and his subordinate bound by the double contingency of expectations: the master bestows an *on* provided the subordinate performs loyal service, whereas the subordinate fulfills the obligation of loyalty on the condition that the master rewards him with an *on*. In stressing the active participation of both parties in their mutual obligation, he criticized Benedict for correlating *hō-on* (repaying an *on*) with *ju-on* (receiving an *on*), and replaced the latter with *shi-on* (bestowing an *on*). Basically agreeing with this argument, Kawashima (1957: 88–125) distinguished *on*-reciprocity as a feudal-istic norm from piety as a patriarchical norm. The former is charac-terized by an obligation of loyalty contingent upon the *on* bestowed, while the latter represents the non-contingent, unilateral obligation of obedience.

Nonetheless, reciprocity involved in *on*, as far as it is symbolized in the most explicit part of culture, is strikingly asymmetric. One might say that the *on*-norm as a part of the dominant cultural style is characteristically unilateral. Although *on*-granting action must precede the reciprocal obligation of repayment, *on* as a Japanese cultural idiom refers disproportionately more to the debtor's obligation than to the creditor's benevolence. While *on*-granting is a matter of choice, *on*-repayment is obligatory, as far as the "official" definition goes. It is asymmetric in that the *on* is considered limitless and unpayable and that the receiver feels urged to return at least "one-ten-thousandth" of the received sum through total, sometimes life-long, devotion to the donor. Bellah (1957: 73) paid special attention to this relentless demand of *on* which puts one in the status of a permanent debtor, and equated it to the idea of original sin with all its dynamic potentialities.

The unilateral, asymmetric obligation imposed by *on* has been culturally stabilized and reinforced by systematic indoctrination of indebtedness and gratitude, which the individual was hardly free to accept or refuse: he is reminded of the fathomless *on* he owes to his parents, ancestors, country, and countless fellow human beings, alive and deceased, known and unknown to him, for his life, and for what he is today. The Buddhist idea of *shujō no on* (the *on* one owes to all living beings) only highlights the unilaterality of *on*-obligation (Sato, 1959). Bellah was right, therefore, in delineating the religious implications of *on*. More importantly, the asymmetric norm of *on* has been socially determined by the cultural emphasis upon status hierarchy. Ordinarily an *on* is granted by a superior-status holder and the burden of repayment falls on the inferior person's shoulders; hence, the *on* reinforces the inferior's loyalty and obedience to the superior. The hierarchical relationship underlying the *on* is reminiscent of the historically specific meaning of *on*, that is, the territorial grant or stipend bestowed by the feudal lord upon his vassal. In modern Japan every Japanese was supposed to owe the heaviest *on* to the emperor as the sovereign. This does not, however, preclude the possibility that *on*-reciprocity takes place between equals. In this case, status hierarchy is generated after an *on* is granted rather than the other way around as is a more common case.[2] The point is that *on*-reciprocity is inseparably entangled with status difference and status orientation in general, whether status hierarchy precedes or is preceded by *on*-granting.

Given such an asymmetric ethic of *on* permeating Japanese culture,[3] it is easy to understand why the highly conventionalized daily speech of Japanese is rich in expressing the feelings of a permanent debtor toward omnipresent creditors. Particularly to be noted is how often the Japanese express their humility and embarrassment, how they acknowledge their being helpless or a nuisance thrust upon others, indebted and unable to repay fully, and how they solicit forgiveness. It is another characteristic of the Japanese to present themselves as bound by obligations and duties rather than as motivated by rights and choice. Kawashima (1967), a specialist in the sociology of law, observed that in their orientation toward law the Japanese are obligation-centered (*gimu-chūshin*), lacking a sense of their rights.

III. Balancing Mechanisms

If the asymmetric principle of *on* points up a dominant, "official" pattern of Japanese culture, there must be some mechanisms, I have argued, however implicit or subtle they may be, which enable the rule of symmetric reciprocity to operate against this dominant strain without open clash. It is paradoxical that, despite the unilateral obligation of *on* stressed, the *on* ethic with its reciprocal language such as "returning the *on*," describing seemingly voluntary action, tends to perpetuate preoccupation with fair payoff.[4] The following are considered as balancing mechanisms.

(1) Triadic reciprocity. Since the asymmetric norm fixes A and B as a debtor and a creditor on a long-range basis, A may feel unable to correct his debtor's status vis-à-vis B, however he tries to repay, even when he feels his debt overpaid. A thus tends to seek compensation from a third person, C, who may or may not relate to B in reciprocal obligations. What is overpaid by A to B is demanded back from C. It is true that the same logic of triadic reciprocity can be used, as is often done, to underscore the debtor's unlimited obligation as well: when the *on* which A received from B is such that he decides it to be unpayable within his lifetime, A lets C, his successor or substitute, take over the unfulfilled obligation on his behalf, or "exchange shoulders" (*kata gawari*); similarly, if A's *on* (debt) to B cannot be repaid within the benefactor's lifetime, A extends his obligation to B's successor or substitute. The main

point in the present discussion is that a culturally endorsed logic of reciprocity transference allows strain toward symmetric payoff to creep into the dominant asymmetric obligation norms.

Such compensative transference of reciprocal partners may take many forms, but two seem more prevalent. One is transference through generational succession: what is overpaid by A to B in the ascending generation, e.g. A's parent, is demanded back from C in the descending generation, A's child. At a certain stage of life cycle the individual turns from a debtor into a creditor by shifting his reciprocal partner and thus without violating the asymmetric norm. In this light we can understand both the well-contented old person as the receiver of gratitude and esteem, and the retaliatory mother-in-law who finds compensation in punishing the daughter-in-law. As long as the rule of such rotation is generally followed and remains stable, one's acceptance of a debtor's status will eventually meet with payoff.

The other form of transference occurs across a hierarchical order of status holders in various institutions such as occupational, governmental, military bureaucracies. A's unilateral obligation toward a superior B is compensated for by his demand for unilateral compliance by an inferior C. If A holds the lowest status, compensation may be sought in his authoritative position within his household. This is what Masao Maruyama called *yokuatsu no ijō*, the transference of repression, in his characterization of Japanese political behavior (1956: Vol. 1, 21). Triadic reciprocity across a status hierarchy entails the natural concomitant that humility is only one side of social orientation, and the other side reveals self-inflation (Iga, 1966); one and the same person may act out humility and assert dominance depending upon whether he is facing upward or downward. Structurally, repression transference corresponds with the typically feudalistic system where the lord-vassal relationship is replicated at every level in every area of society.

(2) Avoidance of reciprocal involvement. The culturally built-in proclivity toward generalization of indebtedness is checked and balanced off by the warnings against such involvement. The Japanese are, as far as the vocabulary of their popular culture is concerned, almost cynical in articulating the undesirability of the *on*-receiver's status, equating the gained *on* to the sold freedom, taking pride in being unbound by any *on*, and resenting the unsolicited *on*-donor who signals that he has granted an *on* which is to be remembered. *Arigata meiwaku*, a thanked-for nuisance, refers to an unwelcome favor, and *enryo*, the virtue of reserve and modesty,

can mean the polite, culturally sanctioned refusal of an offer. The *on*, once granted, they are warned, must be returned as soon as possible before it grows into an unmanageable burden.

The negative side of *on* was closely followed by Benedict with reference to one category of obligation, *giri*, differentiated from another, *gimu*. Both *gimu* and *giri*, according to Benedict, refer to obligation to return an *on* in that *on*-receiving implies either *gimu* or *giri*. *Gimu* corresponds with a limitless *on* and *giri* with a limited, payable *on*. This distinction between *gimu* and *giri* as well as their alleged equivalence to *on* were severely criticized even by those reviewers who praised Benedict's work on the whole (Ariga, 1949; Kawashima, 1959; Beardsley, 1951; Sakurai, 1961: 129–137). It is apparent that Benedict erred in her effort to clarify these culture-loaded terms for her own purposes at the expense of their "emic" definition. Her *gimu-giri* distinction does indicate, however, that she rightly took note of the bipolar strains of the *on*-ethic— asymmetric and symmetric. She thus saw in the concept of *giri* a warning against *on* involvement which tends to generate asymmetric obligations. *Gimu* and *giri*, thus understood, can be viewed as mutually balancing, one neutralizing or controlling the other within a dynamic whole (for the culture-loaded meaning of *giri*, see Kawashima, 1951).

The warning against *on*-reciprocity results in encouraging avoidance not only of accepting but of granting an *on* to the extent that unsolicited generosity is likely to be resented or suspected to contain an ulterior motive. The value system of Japanese culture thus includes an idealization of social withdrawal under the assumption that loneliness or being an uninvolved stranger is a necessary condition for freedom and autonomy. Here the strain to neutralize asymmetric obligation may take such a negative form of disengagement as social retirement and anchoritism. This seems significant particularly in view of the fact that the dominant value held by the Japanese lays a distinct emphasis upon togetherness and solidarity.

(3) Manipulation of dependency-dependability expectation. As we characterized asymmetric reciprocity in terms of one-way dependency, the *on*-relationship tolerates or even presupposes one party's total dependence upon the other. The benefactor will see to it that his favor is accepted, or else he suffers a loss of face. Dependency, therefore, which generates receptivity to an *on* is a status-appropriate expectation of a potential *on*-receiver. It was a psychiatric insight that found a relationship between *on* and depend-

ency, especially a particular Japanese type of dependency called *amaeru*, which means "to depend and presume upon another's benevolence" (Doi, 1962). According to Doi, the indoctrination of one's duty to repay his *on*, particularly the *on* to the emperor and to one's parents, functioned in pre-war Japan to regulate the otherwise all powerful desire of *amae* (the noun form of *amaeru*), keeping the latter concealed. He attributed the post-war social disorder to *amae* now being let loose from *on*-obligation. My argument is not so much for the regulative function of the *on* against dependency as for dependency being simply inherent in the *on* norm. I am contending that the *on* ethic feeds or encourages, rather than reduces, dependence. To *amaeru* is a structurally imposed norm, not just a wish, violation of which is punished (Iga, 1966).

Correspondingly, no less expected than dependency on the part of the *on*-receiver is dependability on the part of the potential benefactor. If to have one's offer of a favor refused means a loss of face, the inability to gratify a request made by a humble solicitor brings as much disgrace. The dependability of the person solicited is displayed in proportion to the frank admittance by the solicitor of his need for dependency as well as to the distance he is willing to descend from his original status to accept the inferior status of a beggar, so to speak. Thus, an *on*-giver would say, "I cannot say no when someone bows so low asking for help as you do" (*Sonna ni atama o sagete tanomareruto iya towa ienai*). It looks as if the expressed solicitousness were a social price which, when paid by a debtor, could neutralize the creditor-debtor relationship. The same social price, if paid in advance, could even promote the beggar to the creditor's status and obligate the potential benefactor to gratify the former's wish. It is not only that demonstration of dependability is normatively required but that to be depended upon is also emotionally desirable. Thus, the reciprocal of *amaeru* is *amayakasu*, to gratify someone's desire to *amaeru* an ego.[5] Ogino (1968) sees not so much unilateral dependency in *amae* as mutual bargaining between the person who *amaeru* and the person who *amayakasu*.[6]

Given such cultural expectation, it is possible for an inferior person as a potential or actual *on*-receiver to manipulate the expected dependability of a superior in such a way as to secure payoff for his unilateral obligation. If the above-discussed point (2) refers to a negative method of avoidance, manipulation of the dependency-dependability expectation means positively taking advantage of dispositions revolving around the asymmetric principle.

(4) Glorification of mother, the selfless benefactor. The cultur-

al stress on filial piety, which is often symbolized by an *on*-governed son working to the point of exhaustion in support of a sick or drunken father, finds its counterpart in an equally extolled unilateral benevolence which seeks no repayment. The latter is embodied in the figure of the self-sacrificing, long-suffering mother. The Japanese mother's "masochistic" role has been singled out as providing singular insight to Japanese culture (De Vos, 1960). The mother with her self-blame for others' faults, it was noted, subtly induces profound guilt in the child, and that guilt provides an impetus for achievement in later life and prepares readiness for arranged marriage. The Japanese way of conceiving death and illness was also viewed in light of the mother's "moral masochism."

The mother eventually receives payoff through either vicarious gratification from her son's success or direct satisfaction from his guilt-driven filial piety. What is significant in the present context, however, is not the mother's actual payoff, but the cultural idealization of the mother as all-giving and without any expectation of reward. Mother is an inexhaustible source of *on* and yet demands no repayment. Glorification of this selfless benefactor may be considered as a subtle, yet effective way of controlling the more common-type benefactor who demands gratitude and repayment from the beneficiary. Furthermore, the fact that the mother is conceived not merely as sacrificing but as of the inferior sex in the male-dominant society helps dissociate *on*-bestowal from superiority in status.

(5) Reversal of hierarchical pressure. It was stated that *on*-reciprocity is conditioned by the hierarchical structure of interpersonal relationships. There are ways of neutralizing or even reversing hierarchical pressure, however, and here I suggest two alternatives. One may be conceptualized as bipolarization of formal status and activities incumbent upon the status including power manipulation. In Japan there has been a tendency for the formal status holder to be segregated from the scene of activities associated with that status; status in name thus has tended to exist in parallel with status in operation. The dual political system of the Shogunate and the Imperial Court was a distinct example at the highest level. Similar duality tends to be replicated at lower levels as well. A person, on assuming a formal status, becomes sanctified beyond the mundane tasks called for by the status, and this is the more so the higher the status. Furthermore, dependency, the cultural norm described above, is not expected of one's inferior alone but of one's

superior as well, though in a somewhat different sense. The higher the status, the more dependent is the person expected to be on his attendants for personal services. Doi (1966) describes one of his patients who wanted to be assisted by someone assuming the responsibility of *hohitsu*. *Hohitsu* is a legal term specially used for the role of assisting the emperor with his government. The patient saw, in Doi's interpretation, "the absolute gratification of dependency wishes" in the emperor's status. Such association of high status with sanctity and dependency may place an inferior in a position of control over a superior and enable his taking over the power vested in the superior's status, without violating the asymmetric norm of *on*.

The other mechanism for reversing hierarchical pressure may be termed the long-range social investment in anticipated benevolence. By showing persistent and unequivocal dedication and loyalty to a superior over and beyond an expected degree, an inferior can gradually build up a public expectation that an *on* is eventually to be granted. The anticipated *on* may never be promised explicitly, yet it comes to reduce the number of alternatives the superior can take for future action. The latter will finally find himself caught up by social pressure to grant the anticipated *on*, thus overruling the voluntary principle of benevolence. The implicit fact that loyalty is a long-range social investment becomes revealed when the superior fails to meet the invested expectation and provokes the investor's revolt. As the scope of loyalty is unlimited, so is the scope of the anticipated *on* to be granted. Hence, the possibility of reversing the flow of hierarchical influence.[7]

Reversal of hierarchical pressure as described here seems to provide a basis for what is commonly understood as *gekokujō* ("control of the superior by the inferior") and for what was labelled as *tōsakuteki-demokurashii* ("topsy-turvey democracy") (Masao Maruyama, 1956: Vol. 1, 108), where the formal authority is oversensitive to the voice of the anonymous mass. In the context of the present paper this is meaningful as a check against the *on*-bound system of obligations and privileges which would only reinforce the institutional hierarchy.

(6) Segregation of the *on*-loaded from the *on*-free social areas. While the burden of *on*, by virtue of its diffuse nature, tends to permeate every area of social interaction, occasional relief is offered by the segregation of two areas, *on*-bound and *on*-free. Segregation typically takes the form of one role expectation prevailing in the serious work-place clearly separated from the scene of frivolous play govern-

ed by quite another role expectation. A university student bound by an *on* to a professor on campus or an employee obligated to his boss in the office is temporarily freed from the burden and can speak on fictively "equal" terms with the benefactor at an annual gathering held at a restaurant, for example.

In a scene of pure play, etiquette-free behavior is endorsed and spontaneous speech is encouraged often with the help of alcoholic drinks. Indeed it is on such occasions that latent resentment and dissatisfaction felt by the obligation-loaded inferior against the superior may be brought to the surface. Wherever such dissatisfaction is collectively shared, this gives an opportunity to attain popularity and leadership by speaking up to the superior in behalf of the discontented group. Needless to say, such "ungrateful" action is permissible only on the condition that the rule of segregation is understood by both parties. (*Sake no ue no kenka*, argument triggered by drink, must be forgotten when one is back to sobriety.) It might be added that the person who does not understand this rule but brings the norm of work into the play scene is frowned upon or made fun of as inordinately *kyūkutsu* ("rigid") or *hanashi no wakaranu* ("unable to understand the way things are").

IV. Conclusion

I have suggested six mechanisms to be operating in counteraction to the asymmetric bias of *on*. These are far from exhaustive, nor do I claim that my attempt is any more than a step toward construction of testable hypotheses as to the operation of *on* in Japanese society. Enough has been shown, I do hope, however, that one must be on guard against a simplistic interpretation of the concept of *on* entirely based upon the "official" articulation of it. I intended to conceptualize *on* as a part of a complex, dynamic cultural system. As Firth (1967a) warns us, what appears to be a rigid obligatory norm (e.g., the obligation to repay an *on*) is likely to allow an area of choice and uncertainty; conversely, what seems a voluntary action (*on*-granting) may in fact be fulfillment of an obligation under heavy social pressures. This implies that the *on*-norm not only constrains but also can expedite the actor's pursuit of interest; thus, the norm can be both restrictive and instrumental.

It must be asked how the two tendencies—the symmetric strain to be effected through the above mechanisms and the asymmetric strain of *on* as an official doctrine—interact with each other within a total system of reciprocity. To answer this question at a tangible level is beyond the scope of this paper, and I can only suggest a general theoretical proposition in cybernetic terms. System stability is maintained insofar as the two tendencies fluctuate only within a limited range. When one increases beyond the limit, it will be over-reacted against by the other in such a way that the former in turn must increase even more to counteract the overreaction. If the asymmetric norm of *on* is imposed with excessive rigidity, the balancing mechanisms will be overactivated to the extent that invocation of the even more rigid virtue of unilateral obligation may be necessitated in order to put down the threat of disorder. This is the beginning of a vicious circle or what is called "positive feedback" operating toward system degeneration (Magoroh Maruyama, 1963). If the social system is to be maintained in spite of such breakdown of negative feedback, the dilemma may affect the personality system of the individual.

Post-war Japan has witnessed the asymmetric principle of *on* under severe attack as feudalistic and undemocratic. Moral education in schools has stressed that every human being is born with basic rights instead of obligations and debts. The result seems, along with the attenuation of the sense of generalized obligation, to involve breakdown of some of the balancing mechanisms as well. This is understandable since these mechanisms are subsystems functioning within the asymmetric system. The heaviest impact seems felt upon the mechanism of triadic reciprocity, particularly the payoff expected from the descending generation. Compensation based on the intergenerational rotation of debts and credits is no longer insured, given the unbridgeable generation gap and the general trend to discredit the aged as obsolescent and to find asset in youth. An increasing number of members of the older generation seem to be getting trapped in a position of continued sacrifice, instead of getting repaid by the younger generation, after having carried out their portion of obligation to their (the older generation's) parents.

Nonetheless, it would be far from the truth to say that the norm of *on* has completely broken down. What contemporary Japanese are experiencing is uncertainty, confusion, and disagreement, rather than the denial, as to the concept of *on*. This seems reflected in a recently conducted study of Japanese national character including attitudes toward *on* and *giri* (Tōkei Sūri Kenkyū-jo, 1961).[8] In regard to the sense of *on*-obligation, it was found that there was a gap between what the respondent would choose in a given conflict situation and what he thinks would be others' evaluation of his choice, and a gap between his preference and what he would recommend to others. The popular version of the above study (Hayashi et al., 1965: 86), which generally reflects the repondents' conscious denigration of pre-war values, indicates that the social bondage created by *on*-obligation is stronger than kinship ties.[9] Another study on the Japanese consciousness of *on* (Yoshida et al., 1966) demonstrated that the concept of *on* was differentially conceptualized depending upon the social roles under consideration. *On* was associated, for instance, with true love with reference to parent-child relationship; with tradition and custom for the relationship between the main house and the branch house; with a contractual obligation for the employer-employee relationship. The authors concluded that the sense of *on* based on external, economic, political pressures is declining while a positive re-evaluation is underway of the *on* derived from inner, emotional attachment or rational reasoning.

Whatever predictions may be made regarding the future status of *on*, the complexity of the problem should be kept in mind, and I hope this paper will be taken as a reminder of such complexity.

NOTES

1. I wish to express my gratitude to Professor and Mrs. Raymond Firth for their enlightening criticism on an earlier draft of this paper. At their suggestion some basic modifications have been made, although this by no means denies that responsibility for any errors and inadequacy found in this paper rests entirely upon me. Support in preparing this paper was provided by NIMH Grant Number MH-09243 which is gratefully acknowledged.

2. In this respect, I do not agree with Sakurai, who rules out the relationship between equals from the concept of *on;* he contends that an *on* is given always by a superior to an inferior and thus constitutes a samurai ethic which stresses the hierarchical order. This is another point where he disagrees with Benedict who does not make ac lear distinction between *on* and *giri* (obligation to repay an *on*) in terms of the presence and absence of status difference. According to Sakurai, *giri* refers to obligatory relationship between equals, obtaining among the *chōnin* (the commoner class of townsmen occupationally identified as traders and artisans). Thus, *giri* is contrasted as a *chōnin* ethic to *on* as a samurai ethic (Sakurai, op. cit.). I am arguing that, given the hierarchical structure as a cultural model for establishing an *on*-relationship, the model can be invoked, by doing a favor, to create a hierarchical relationship out of equals.

3. The degree of permeation may be appraised from the method of therapy called *naikan* ("looking within"), which was originally used for rehabilitation of prison inmates. In this method, according to a research report (Kitsuse, 1962), the inmate's sense of obligation to return his unlimited *on* to his parents, teachers, employers, and others is systematically mobilized and reinforced. Now the *naikan* method is said to be used

not only for psychotherapy in general but for moral education in some rural schools.

4. While Americans would rather conceal or obscure their intention of repaying a social debt as bad taste even when they are in fact repaying, the Japanese tend to let the payee know of such an intention of *okaeshi* (return).

5. Mr. Kazuo Yamamoto of the National Institute of Mental Health in Japan reminded me of the importance of *amayakasu* as the complement to *amaeru*.

6. Such bargaining would be impossible unless *amaeru* and *amayakasu* had commodity values, unless they were not only desirable but their supply were limited. As a matter of fact the Japanese are not always willing to *amaeru* or *amayakasu* but are selective in terms of choice of alters and situations. This means that dependency needs, though overwhelming sometimes, are not completely devoid of ambivalence. Ambivalence can be partly accounted for by the second balancing mechanism, avoidance of reciprocal involvement. It is also likely that dependency needs are repressed by preoccupation with face and dignity. To *amaeru* may involve too much sacrifice of dignity for the solicitor to endure.

7. It would be interesting to see how such readiness for long-range commitment to the future relates to the past-bound fatalism and resignation as noticeable in Japanese behavior. Both attitudes seem to stem from the awareness of the irreversible sequence of events over time; what makes one resigned to what has happened in the past may be also responsible for the belief that how one starts determines every future event and that the future therefore must be well planned and invested at the earliest possible date.

8. The Institute of Statistical Mathematics produced *Nipponjin no kokuminsei* (A Study of Japanese National Character). With regard to *on* and *giri*, the respondent was presented with conflict situations demanding choice between repayment of an *on* (e.g., recommending the son of a benefactor for employment) and demonstration of honesty (refusing to recommend him because he is not fitted for the job). (Tōkei Sūri Kenkyū-jo Kokuminsei Chōsa Iinkai 1961: 222–233, 423–427, 454, 488–489.)

9. The subjects were asked to assume themselves to be the president of a company which has given an examination for new employment. The president is free to choose between two candidates: the candidate who ranks highest in the examination and the candidate who is second highest but the president's relative. Seventy-five percent of the respondents chose the first candidate, and only 19 percent favored the relative. In response to the next question, which replaced the relative by a child of the president's *onjin* (benefactor), the proportion changes to 48 percent (in favor of the highest candidate) vs. 44 percent.

REFERENCES

Ariga, Kizaemon. 1949. "Nippon shakai kōzō ni okeru kaisō-sei no mondai" (Benedict's conception of hierarchy in Japanese social structure). *Minzoku-gaku Kenkyū*, 14, 4, 13–22.

Beardsley, R.K. 1951. "The household in the status system of Japanese villages." Center for Japanese Studies, *Occasional Papers*, 1, 62–73. University of Michigan, Ann Arbor.

Bellah, R.N. 1957. *Tokugawa Religion*. Glencoe, Ill.: The Free Press.

Benedict, Ruth. 1946. *The Chrysanthemum and the Sword: Patterns of Japanese Culture*. Boston: Houghton Mifflin.

Blau, P.M. 1964. *Exchange and Power in Social Life.* New York: Wiley.

Bohannan, P. 1966. *Social Anthropology.* New York: Holt, Rinehart and Winston.

De Vos, G. 1960. "The relation of guilt toward parents to achievement and arranged marriage among the Japanese." *Psychiatry,* 23, 298–301.

Doi, L. Takeo. 1962. " 'Amae': A key concept for understanding Japanese personality structure," in R.J. Smith and R.K. Beardsley, eds., *Japanese Culture: Its Development and Characteristics.* Chicago: Aldine, 132–139.

———. 1966. "Giri-ninjō: An interpretation." *Psychologia,* 9, 7–11.

Firth, R. 1956. *Elements of Social Organization.* London: Watts. 2nd Edition.

———. 1964. *Essays on Social Organization and Values.* London School of Economics Monographs on Social Anthropology No. 28. University of London, The Athlone Press.

———. 1967. *Tikopia Ritual and Belief.* Boston: Beacon Press.

———. 1967a. "Themes in economic anthropology: A general comment," in R. Firth, ed., *Themes in Economic Anthropology.* London: Tavistock. 1–28.

Gouldner, A.W. 1959. "Reciprocity and autonomy in functional theory," in L. Gross, ed., *Symposium on Sociological Theory.* Evanston: Row Peterson. 241–270.

———. 1960. "The norm of reciprocity: A preliminary statement." *American Sociological Review,* 25, 161–178.

Hayashi, Chikio, S. Nishihara and T. Suzuki. 1965. *Zusetsu nipponjin no kokuminsei* (Japanese national character with illustrations). Tokyo: Shiseido.

Herskovits, M.J. 1952. *Economic Anthropology: A Study in Comparative Economics.* New York: Alfred A. Knopf.

Iga, Mamoru. 1966. "Relation of suicide attempt and social structure in Kamakura." *International Journal of Social Psychiatry,* 12, 221–232.

Kawashima, Takeyoshi. 1949. "Hyōka to hihan" (Evaluation and criticism). *Minzoku-gaku Kenkyū,* 14, 4, 1–8.

———. 1951. "Giri." *Shisō,* September, 759–766.

———. 1957. *Ideorogii toshite no kazoku-seido* (The institutional system of family as an ideology). Tokyo: Iwanami.

———. 1967. *Nipponjin no hō-ishiki* (The Japanese consciousness of law). Tokyo: Iwanami.

Kitsuse, J.I. 1962. "A method of reform in Japanese prison," *Orient-West,* 7, No. 11, 17–22.

Lévi-Strauss, C. 1957. "The principle of reciprocity," in L.A. Coser and B. Rosenberg, eds., *Sociological Theory.* New York: MacMillan. 74–84.

Malinowski, B. 1959. *Crime and Custom in Savage Society.* Paterson, N.J.: Littlefield.

Maruyama, Magoroh. 1963. "The second cybernetics: deviation-amplifying mutual causal processes." *American Scientist,* 51, 164–179.

Maruyama, Masao. 1956–57. *Gendai seiji no shisō to kōdō* (Ideology and action in contemporary politics). Tokyo: Miraisha. 2 vols.

Mauss, M. 1967. *The Gift: Forms and Functions of Exchange in Archaic Societies.* New York: Norton.

Nakane, Chie. 1967. *Tate shakai no ningen kankei* (Human relations in a vertical society). Tokyo: Kodansha.

Ogino, Kōichi. 1968. "Amae riron (Doi) o megutte" (On Doi's amae theory). *Seishin Bunseki Kenkyū,* XIV, No. 3, 5–9.

Parsons, T. 1937. *The Structure of Social Action.* New York: McGraw-Hill.

Sahlins, M.D. 1965. "On the sociology of primitive exchange," in M. Banton, ed., *The Relevance of Models for Social Anthropology.* New York: Praeger. 139–236.

Sakurai, Shotaro. 1961. *On to giri* (*on* and *giri*). Tokyo: Asahisha.

Sato, Koji. 1959. "The concept of 'on' in Ruth Benedict and D.T. Suzuki." *Psychologia,* 2, 243–245.

Tōkei Sūri Kenkyū-jo Kokuminsei Chōsa Iinkai (Research Committee of Japanese

National Character, The Institute of Statistical Mathematics). 1961. *Nipponjin no kokuminsei* (A study of Japanese national character). Tokyo: Shiseido.

Yoshida, Masaaki, Kazuko Fujii, and Junko Kurita. 1966. "Nipponjin no onishiki no kōzō" (Structure of a moral concept *on* in the Japanese mind). *Shinri-gaku kenkyū*, 37, 74–85; 195–203.

Gift-Giving in a Modernizing Japan

HARUMI BEFU

INTRODUCTION

The prevalence of gift-giving in Japan is well known. Even the casual visitor sojourning in Japan for a few weeks will find himself presented with a gift from his Japanese friends or business associates. The full-page ads of midyear-gift (*chūgen*) sales by major department stores, the rows of gift shops in any resort town, the displays of gift-wrapped presents in stores at railroad stations, these are among the innumerable indications of the extent to which the Japanese are involved in gift exchange. Although no one knows for sure how much the Japanese spend on gifts every year, since no adequate statistics are available, the figure is undoubtedly high.[1]

Indeed, gift-giving is a minor institution in Japan, with complex rules defining who should give to whom, on what occasions he should give, what sort of gift is appropriate on a given occasion, and how the gifts should be presented. To take an example, a properly wrapped gift for a happy occasion should bear an intricately folded decoration known as *noshi* (nowadays, however, it is enough to have its picture printed on the wrapping); but a gift on an inauspicious occasion would not have the decoration on the wrapping. This practice goes back to the days when *noshi* was a strip of abalone, which, when attached to a gift, indicated that the occasion did not call for abstention from meat owing to death or other misfortune in the family. It is for this reason that a dried fishtail or fin is used in some rural areas as a substitute. For the same reason, a gift of fish does not require a *noshi*, since the nature of the gift itself indicates that abstention is not necessary and that the occasion is a felicitous

Reprinted from *Monumenta Nipponica* 23 (1968): 445–456.

one.[2] Most Japanese, particularly young urbanites, are no longer aware of this origin of *noshi*, which indicates the extent to which gift-giving customs have changed. In this paper I wish to explore the origin of gift-giving in Japan and consider recent changes in it. I hope that this little exercise will help clarify the process and the present status of Japan's modernization.

METHODOLOGICAL REMARKS

Reconstructing the past is not easy—even for a culture like Japan's which has a long written history—when the task is to outline the origin and development of a commonplace custom like gift-giving, which few literati and historians have thought worthy of documentation or study. Rather than to the historians and historical documents, then, we must turn to the folklorists and folk customs. As in so many instances, it has been the Yanagita school of folklore study that has contributed most in unraveling the past of the custom of gift-giving. To accomplish this, Yanagita and his students have had to analyze varied but similar and related gift-giving practices in many different regions of rural Japan, often in isolated communities and on offshore islands, to compare these variant practices, to dip into the etymologies of terms related to gifts and gift-giving, and to juxtapose past customs remembered by oldtimers with present practices.

One major methodological problem that confronts us in using folklorists' data and interpretations concerns the temporal referent and sequence, a blind spot in folklore study which the anthropologist Eiichirō Ishida has noted in his sympathetic assessment of Yanagita's scholarly contributions.[3] Folklorists, working almost exclusively with oral tradition and unrecorded folk practices, have generally been reluctant to specify the definite point in time for any event. They discuss events of the past in terms simply of the "past," without indicating the absolute time referent. Consequently, it is extremely difficult to work out a sequence of stages or of events leading up to the present.

What follows is a composite picture of how in general gift-giving practices have originated and developed in Japan over an undefined period of time, based in good part on the findings of folklorists and also on a comparison of rural and urban practices. Urban data were mostly obtained through the writer's own investigation.[4]

THE SUPERNATURAL PAST

The custom of offering foods to gods and other supernatural beings—still a common practice in Japan—may seem unrelated to our concern, but in fact is an appropriate starting point.[5] Examples are numberless. In many households today, rice is offered to family ancestors at the household altar every morning. Village Shinto shrines and roadside *jizō* shrines are offered glutinous rice cake and óther foods from time to time. The New Year is the time to offer rice cake to the New Year's god. And so on. Folklorists have shown that such food offerings are historically related to *naorai*, the custom according to which gods and mortals shared foods together[6] *Naorai* is now commonly understood to refer to the feast held after a religious ritual proper, but this is evidently a later modification. In the original form of *naorai*, offerings to gods were gifts to gods, and these gifts were returned by gods as their gifts for mortals to share with them, so that the mortals might partake of the divine power of the gods to whom gifts were originally offered.[7] The symbolic significance of communal eating has been well argued by DeVos in his recent study of outcasteism.[8] He argues that the abhorrence of commensalism with members of an outcaste group is an essential psychodynamic ingredient of outcasteism. For us, this abhorrence is simply the other side of the "deeply social act [of eating together] symbolizing a form of communion, whether it exists as part of a ritual or as part of the daily habits of life."[9]

The ritual importance of sake is also apparent, as the practice of offering it to gods is still very much alive. Originally, the sake was first offered to gods, and then shared by mortals in *naorai*.[10] This custom is still alive in Shirakawa, Gifu Prefecture, where once a year *doburoku* (a type of raw sake) is prepared in a large tub, offered to the tutelary god of the village, and consumed communally by all villagers and also by visitors who wish to receive supernatural power from the local god.

The pervasive custom in Japan of giving the first crop of the field to neighbors and relatives is also derived from the past practice of offering the first fruits to gods, and thereafter sharing them among the community.[11] The word *otoshidama*, which nowadays refers to the New Year's present to children (usually money), also originally denoted offerings to the god of the New Year, which were later eaten by men as the god's gift.[12]

It is because communion with supernatural beings was achieved primarily through commensality that offerings to gods were, and still are, largely foodstuff, and also that even now food is considered the traditional type of gift in Japan and that in fact it is the most popular type of gift.[13]

In the past, commensality was not only a device for transferring supernatural power to man, but also a means by which members of the community could partake in one another's power and be brought into a mystical union. After all, the gulf between mortals and gods was not felt to be great; what gods were capable of, men were capable of, too, to a lesser extent. Otherwise, how could men hold communion with gods in *naorai*? Indeed, because of the belief that men are simply less powerful gods, but still susceptible to magical contagion through commensality, it happened that when *naorai* came to be separated in time and place from the ritual proper, the feasting retained its supernatural efficacy. The belief in magical contagion accounts for the banquet held for a person of an unlucky or "calamitous" year (*yakudoshi*), in which the combined power of all the guests was believed to dispel the danger of misfortune.[14] In addition to the magical function, such communal feasting of course served to reinforce the social solidarity of the group.[15]

If magical power could be shared by mortals through a communal meal, as Yanagita has argued, it could also be shared by the giving and the receiving of a gift of food. For example, folk medicine practiced in many rural areas of Japan until recent years prescribes that a person suffering from an eye disease should go to houses in the neighborhood and beg for food.[16] By consuming food from families in which no one was suffering from the disease, one could absorb magical power from these families to help cure the disease. In fact, giving a food gift to a sick person—something frowned upon in the U.S. for medical reasons—was generally thought to be a way of giving the power of health inherent in the giver, so that the sick might recover from illness through the power of the healthy. Another custom related to gift-giving to a sick person is also based on the magical power of a food gift. Ordinarily, when a gift is given in Japan, the receiver returns a token gift, such as a box of matches or a bundle of paper, at the time the gift is made.[17] When the gift is to a sick person, however, the custom is not observed owing to the belief that such a return gift has the power of making the healthy person sick. The same belief in ritual pollution through commensality with a ritually impure person explains the customs of avoiding gifts from a person of an unlucky or calamitous year.[18] The customs of giving food gifts to a newborn baby and of having a seven-year-old child solicit food from seven neighbors, which have been seen in many rural areas of Japan until recently, are also believed to be means of building up strength by "borrowing" power from others.[19]

The folklorists' work on the supernatural origin of gift-giving has tended to give the impression that the origin of gift-giving in Japan was entirely magical and religious. To claim that gift-giving in Japan used to be entirely supernatural in its significance is to claim an unproven and probably false proposition. We have discussed the supernatural aspects of some gift-giving customs only because most of us know Japanese gift-giving in its secular forms. It is important to note that in rural Japan these gift-giving practices, whether supernatural or secular, were, and still are, imbedded in the traditional social structure, in which we find the household as a basic social unit, the values of *giri* and *on*, and the principle of social reciprocity. Let us examine the ways in which gift-giving is related to these elements of the traditional Japanese social organization. (I do not suggest that this social framework operates only in rural Japan. It is very much alive in urban Japan, too; but there one finds new social elements manifested in gift-giving practices, as we shall see later.)

The importance of the household as a basic social institution in Japan has been reiterated by generations of anthropologists, both Japanese and Western, and scarcely needs emphasis here. Suffice it to add that even when a gift is seemingly intended for one individual—e.g., a sick member of a household—and is sent from a certain individual—e.g., the sick person's uncle—the gift is still regarded as a gift from the uncle's household as a corporate unit to the sick person's household as another unit. Magically, as we saw above, such a gift may be intended for a given individual; but in terms of the working of the society, it is a gift to a group, of which the individual is merely a member. The significance of this fact will be seen when we consider how the principle of reciprocity operates.

In rural Japan, probably the most important motivating force behind gift-giving is the concept of *giri*. *Giri* is a moral imperative to perform one's duties toward other members of one's group. Gift-giving falls squarely in the sphere of *giri*; one is morally obligated to give a gift when custom demands it. *Giri* is bound up with the institution of gift-giving in another way, namely, reciprocation. To the extent that one man's relation to another in Japanese rural society is defined in reciprocal terms, in which the give-and-take of social relations should be fairly rigidly balanced, the concept of *giri* evokes in the tradition-minded rural Japanese the obligation to reciprocate. Since gift-giving is an act of *giri*, and since *giri* requires reciprocation, a gift naturally calls for a return gift. The moral obligation to give, to receive, and to return gifts is as much a part of traditional Japan as it is of the archaic societies with which Marcel Mauss concerned himself in his famous essay on the gift.[21]

So important is the concept of *giri* in gift-giving that many rural Japanese interpret *giri* to mean strict observance of the etiquette of gift-giving.[22] Dore's account of Shitayamachō in Tokyo shows how important the concept is in the operation of gift exchange even in cities.[23]

We have seen that the institution of gift-giving requires that giving be balanced by returning. The operation of this principle of reciprocity in its most elementary form is readily seen in the customary donation of "incense money" (*kōden*) at funerals. The family of the deceased keeps a careful record of each donation, and when death occurs in a family which has given incense money, an identical amount of money is returned.[24] Similarly, when the roof of a farmhouse is to be rethatched, neighbors and relatives donate labor and materials, such as bundles of grass and rope. When the time to rethatch the house of one of the helpers comes around, exactly the same amount of labor and material is returned.

Reciprocation, however, need not be in kind. A gift may be given for a favor done, or vice versa. When the relationship between households is a vertical, hierarchical one, this type of "heterogeneous" exchange is likely to take place. A man brings gifts to his *oyakata* in the New Year, or to his landlord at *o-bon* in thanks for the *on*—the past favor granted and assistance received. Or again, a recovered patient may bring a gift—in proportion to the seriousness of his illness—to this doctor to thank him for the medical attention given. On such a gift-giving occasion, the social superior does not reciprocate with a gift of the same type or value. For the gift is already a return for the past favor, and to return in kind and in value would reduce the status of the superior to that of the giver.

In short, in rural Japan, whether and how well a person observes the rules and etiquette governing the who, the what, the when, and the how of gift-giving are important ways of judging his social character. One who observes them meticulously is a responsible, trustworthy individual; he is *giri-gatai*. If, on the other hand, a person sent a gift disproportionately cheaper than the social equation of gift-giving calls for, people would gossip about the cheapness not only of the gift but also of the giver's character.

Modern Changes and Innovations

In modern urban Japan, the religious origin and significance of gift-giving discussed above has been forgotten by most people. By contrast, the social context in which gift-giving is practiced in rural areas is still of critical importance for the city dwellers. They are quite conscious of the concept of the household as a unit in gift-giving, and the continuation of their household-based customary gift exchange is very much motivated by the concept of *giri*.

This is not to say that city people uniformly approve of the traditional etiquette of gift-giving. The more educated urbanites feel very much constrained by the social obligation of *giri*, which they contemptuously label "feudalistic." It is because *giri*-based gift-giving is looked on as a nuisance and with disfavor that the Japanese often scarcely consider the appropriateness of the content of a gift. Instead, gift-giving is treated as an empty formality. One simply buys a piece of merchandise of proper monetary value. Or, as it so often happens in returning from an extended trip, one simply buys so many dozens of the same kind of gift to be distributed among those to whom one by *giri* owes a gift, irrespective of the individual tastes of the receivers. It is in this context that we can understand the practice of *taraimawashi*, in which a gift that a person receives, for which he (and anyone else, for that matter) would have no conceivable use, is simply passed on to another to meet the obligation of giving and returning. One reason why *giri*-based behavior, including gift-giving, persists in cities, in spite of the negative attitudes toward it, is that such behavior is social insurance, as Dore puts it.[25] In case of an emergency, a person just might have to depend on neighbors and friends. If he had been recalcitrant and ignored *giri*-based etiquette, he might not be able to expect a helping hand at critical moments.

The strain of tradition thus presses heavily upon urbanites. And city life, which does not depend very much any more on the kind of solidarity maintained by the traditional human relations and values of rural society, has to some extent permitted the discontinuation of the gift-giving that symbolized such solidarity. For example, in rural areas, at *o-bon* a social inferior traditionally makes a gift to his superior, such as a branch family to its main family or tenants to the landlord. In cities, the counterpart would be for employees to present gifts to their superior at work. While this custom does prevail widely, there are also a large number of city people who no longer practice it. In some business firms it has become an established practice not to give gifts to superiors at *o-bon;* in others certain superiors have explicitly prohibited the practice.

City dwellers, however, have not merely let old customs fall into disuse. They have added new practices or at least elaborated on existing customs and made them popular. One such practice is gift-giving between individuals *qua* individuals, without encumbering their households. This is not likely to occur in one's neighborhood, between relatives, etc., where households are already the interacting units. It is more likely to occur at work or at school, where individuals have opportunities to interact as individuals. School friends and work mates give gifts on birthdays, at weddings, and on other occasions. In marked contrast to the traditional type of gift-giving, in which social obligation (*giri*) is the prime mover of gifts, the motivating force in individual-to-individual gift-giving tends to be one's personal affection for the receiver. It is *ninjō,* if you like, rather than *giri,* which is the basis (although few modern urbanites would want their personal motivation identified with such a traditional, and therefore feudalistic, concept as *ninjō*).

In this personal type of gift-giving, in contrast to the *giri*-based type, the giver cares a great deal about what he gives because he is not simply meeting an unpleasant obligation. Much thought goes into the choice of the gift; he does not simply buy something of proper monetary value or resort to *taraimawashi,* as mentioned above. Moreover, the concept of balanced reciprocity, so important in *giri*-based gift-giving, here breaks down. In *giri*-based gift-giving, it is extremely important to consider the value of the gift in relation to what it is a return for, if it is a return gift, or in relation to the relative social status of giver and receiver and the specific occasion for which the gift is intended. In the personal gift, one may choose to give very little, or something of great value. Since mutual trust is already established between the giver and the receiver, it is not necessary to regard gift-giving as an indication of the giver's social character, whereas in *giri*-based gift-giving, it may be recalled, one's character was judged to a considerable degree by the extent to which one observed gift-giving etiquette. Thus the personal type of gift-giving is associated with a whole complex of different attitudes. These attitudes have come into being as a result of the process of individuation that modern city life encourages.[26]

Another innovation associated more with urban than rural Japan is what I might call "collective" gift-giving. It occurs most often in situations in which personal gift-giving described above is likely to occur (such as school or work), but it may also be seen in the neighborhood, since the basic unit of "collective" giving may be either the individual or the household. Whichever the unit may be, givers in this type are either already organized into a group—such as clubs at school or neighborhood associations—or organize themselves into a group on an *ad hoc* basis. Each member of the group contributes an equal amount of money, and the total collection is then given as a cash present to the recipient, or a gift is purchased with the collected money and given him. This type of gift-giving is suitable when the giver does not feel very close to the receiver and does not wish to spend much money or time in buying a gift, but he nonetheless feels the obligation to give. In short, "collective" giving occurs as a response to the dilemma in which urbanites are often caught between the lack of personal motivation to give and the persistent social obligation—*giri*—to give.

A third type of gift-giving practice more characteristic of the harsh competitive world of cities than of the corporate community of rural Japan is one based on ulterior motives.[27] Since a gift traditionally comes wrapped, since the giver, according to etiquette, belittles the content of the gift, and since a gift should not be opened in front of the giver, it is impossible to foresee the value of the gift, which may far exceed the amount deemed proper by the normal measure of balanced reciprocity. In addition, the obligation to accept, once a gift is presented, is as bindings as the obligation to give and to return. These norms governing the ritual of gift-giving provide the giver with a vast advantage—unfair though it is—in furthering his objectives. The social obligation thus created by an expensive gift requires in return a special favor for the giver which the receiver would not perform under normal circumstances. It is possible to cancel the debt incurred by the expensive gift by returning an equally expensive gift. But ordinarily the circumstances make it evident that the giver wants a special favor in return. For example, a teacher who receives a very expensive gift from his student's father is fully aware that the father wants to have his son's grade improved.

We regard this type of gift-giving as bribery in America. But because gift-giving is so pervasive in Japan, and the obligations to give, to receive, and to reciprocate are so strongly entrenched in the traditional social system, it is extremely difficult, if not impossible, to discern whether a gift is legitimate or illegitimate. As Dore notes, "only a hair-line separates the mere token of gratitude from the bribe."[28] Because the term "bribery" has a narrow legalistic tinge and because it is difficult to tell when gift-giving is bribery, we shall use the term "ulteriorly motivated" gift-giving. This type of gift-giving is an expression of urban conditions where anomie prevails; that is, emphasis on goals has taken precedence over the culturally approved means of achieving the goal.[29]

One final type of gift-giving should be mentioned briefly. I refer to altruistic donation. Donation as such is nothing new in Japan. It is collected in the village association, in the neighborhood association, in the PTA, etc., for constructing a community hall, a school gymnasium, or recreation facilities for children. Such a donation, however, is not usually based on true altruism. Instead, it is a way of expressing one's loyalty to the group, of demonstrating one's economic affluence, or of impressing other members of the group with the important contribution one is making for the group. In short, most Japanese make donations in order to fulfill their social obligations or social ambition. This type of giving is not an expression of altruism, since the motivation is based on considerations of the psychological reward one receives from others through their approval, esteem, or even envy.

True altruism, on the other hand, is based strictly on the satisfaction derived from the simple act of giving. No one has to know one has given, or how much one has given. True, such altruistic giving is not unknown in Japan. Even before the war, for example, commuters saw students standing in front of train stations asking for donations to help starving farmers of Tōhoku, where severe cold had destroyed crops. In the postwar years, we see other kinds of street-corner donation drives, such as the "red feather" or "green feather" donations, copied after the American Community Chest. Although no one knows how much such strictly altruistic donation amounts to in Japan every year, the amount probably is not very large. For such donation is based on a universalistic orientation, in which one does not seek through the donation the approval of "meaningful others," such as kinsmen, friends, and neighbors who "count" in one's social life. To the extent that Japanese are highly interdependent in their emotional patterning,[30] they find meaningful social life in particularistic relationships with others. Altruistic donation is not likely to be very successful in this sort of social context.

CONCLUSION

LET us now enumerate the significant cultural features of traditional Japan that are discernible in gift-giving practices:

1. The supernatural significance of magical contagion through communion and commensality as well as through gifts of food.
2. The household as a basic social institution.
3. *Giri* as a central motivational value in maintaining the custom.
4. Reciprocity as a principle of interaction.

While all these features except the first are still prevalent in modern Japan, there are new trends and changes that are discernible, particularly in urban areas. Let us list these:

1. Secularization, or a gradual loss of religious and magical meanings in gift-giving.
2. Individuation—the opportunity of individuals to interact as individuals and to express personal affect.
3. Instrumentalism, or ulterior-motivated behavior.
4. Weakly developed altruism.

These old and new elements of Japanese culture revealed in gift-giving practices indicate something of the general trend in the modernization of Japan. First, secularization—the decreasing reliance on religion and magic for solving worldly problems—is a natural evolutionary process.[31] Along with the secularization of the society in general, it is to be expected that gift-giving would have less and less religious and magical significace. Second, as Dore has observed, the complex city life of industrialized society encourages individuation; as social interaction is conducted on an individual basis rather than on the traditional household basis, it is natural for gift-giving to express this changing social pattern.

Third, I have alluded to the concept of *ninjō*—a concept as old as kabuki—in reference to the increasing tendency for expression of individual affect in modern Japan. But there is a basic difference between *ninjō* and the modern expression of personal affect—not so much in their contents as in their social contexts. In traditional Japan *ninjō* was placed in opposition to *giri*, as Benedict elucidated years ago.[32] The concept of *giri* defined proper conduct, whereas *ninjō* implied human failure to carry out *giri*. Society thus had no legitimate place for *ninjō*. Expression of personal affect, on the other hand, is now beginning to win a legitimate status in the modern social order side by side with *giri*.

Fourth, while the society is changing in a secular and individuated direction, it has also retained certain traditional features, such as the concepts of household and *giri*. What is important to note here is that these features are not simply anachronisms, the cuff buttons of modern Japan. Instead, they have played a crucial role in effectuating the process of modernization in Japan.

Lastly, the weak development of altruism also points to the strength of such traditional values as *giri*, which emphasize one's obligation in a particularistic setting. Since the roles of individuals are by and large defined in particularistic terms even in modern Japan, the most effective way to get things done is to take advantage of traditional motivational values. Basing social roles on universalistic criteria, on which altruism is ultimately dependent, is correspondingly rare in Japan. Altruistic gift-giving therefore will probably remain insignificant in Japan as long as the basic value orientation of the people does not change from particularism to universalism.

These observations lead us to consider Japan's modernization from the theoretical standpoint. There are two possible positions one might take. On the one hand, one may argue that in spite of an outstanding performance in the economic sphere, Japan lags behind in its social and cultural modernization, since it retains many traditional elements. On the other hand, one may argue (and many scholars have) that Japan's spectacular economic achievement has been accomplished by exploiting its traditional social and cultural patterns. The former position is based on the assumption that modernization as an end-state ultimately implies a uniform cultural manifestation, disregarding the heterogeneity cultures may display in the process of arriving at the end-state. The second position, which has been advocated by, among others, Ichirō Nakayama,[33] argues for a parallel development, namely, that although modernization may denote technological efficiency, for which all modernizing nations strive, there are different avenues by which to arrive at it, and moreover that in its social and cultural spheres a modernized nation can retain its traditional patterns.

Although the future is anyone's guess, the "uniform end-state" theory takes a position which has not been empirically demonstrated. The parallel development theory, on the other hand, is based on the widely substantiated position that each modernizing culture, while striving toward a common goal of more efficient integration and organization of its cultural legacy, attempts to achieve this goal through its unique set of cultural "equipment." In conclusion, then, those cultural patterns of Japan that are adaptable to and facilitate modernization will probably remain, and gift-giving as a medium for expressing these patterns will similarly be found in Japan for years to come.

NOTES

1. In most statistics, figures for expenditure of gifts are included in the category of "social expenses" (*kōsai hi*) along with expenditures for entertaining guests. Data published by the Japanese government (Japan, Office of the Prime Minister, Bureau of Statistics, *General Report on the Family Income and Expenditure Survey*, Tokyo, 1964, pp. 24–5, 58–9, 280–1) show that figures in this category range from about 1 per cent 3 per cent of the total household expenditure, the percentage increasing as the income level rises. R.P. Dore's *City Life in Japan* (University of California Press, Berkeley and Los Angeles, 1959, pp. 400–3) is probably the only publication to provide a separate category for gift items in the analysis of household expenditures in Japan. His table shows 17 households in Tokyo, spending 0.8 per cent to 19.4 per cent of the total household expenditure on gifts. (Dore's definition of "total household expenditure" is, however, slightly different from that of the government in the publication cited above.) Unfortunately Dore's sample does not reflect a larger population of which it is a part, since the sample was not randomly selected.

2. Japan National Commission for UNESCO, *Japan, its Land, People and Culture*, Printing Bureau, Ministry of Finance, Tokyo, 1958, p. 950; Sakurada Katsunori, "Noshi," *Nihon shakai minzoku jiten*, Seibundō-shinkōsha, Tokyo, 1957, III; Segawa Kiyoko, *Nihonjin no ishokujū*, Kawadeshobō, Tokyo, 1964, p. 245; Yanagita Kunio, *Shokumotsu to shinzō*, Sōgen-sha, Tokyo and Osaka, 1940, pp. 249–74.

3. E. Ishida, "Unfinished but Enduring: Yanagita Kunio's Folklore Studies," *Japan Quarterly*, 1963, X, pp. 35–42.

4. I wish to express my gratitude to the Center for Japanese Studies, University of Michigan, for providing financial aids in carrying out interviews on gift-giving with Japanese nationals resident in Ann Arbor in 1965–6. I wish to thank Mr. Makio Matsuzono for conducting the interviews and making initial analysis of the data. Thanks are also due Professor Takashi Nakano, who served as a teacher, consultant, and informant for the writer.

5. For an overall discussion of old beliefs surrounding food and food production and consumption, see K. Segawa, *op. cit.*, pp. 208–46.

6. Minzokugaku Kenkyūjo, ed., *Minzokugaku jiten*, Tōkyōdō, Tokyo, 1951, pp. 418–19.

7. Sugiura Ken'ichi, "Minkan-shinkō no hanashi," in K. Yanagita, ed., *Nihon minzokugaku kenkyū*, Iwanami-shoten, Tokyo, 1935, pp. 128–32; K. Yanagita, *op. cit.*, pp. 191–7. Wakamori Tarō *Nihon minzoku-ron*, Chiyoda-shobō, Tokyo, 1947, pp. 199–200.

8. G. DeVos and H. Wagatsuma, eds., *Japan's Invisible Race*, University of California Press, Berkeley and Los Angeles, 1966, pp. 370–2.

9. *Ibid.*, pp. 370–1.

10. Shiibashi Yoshio, *Amazake to kisetsu*, Minkan denshō, 1942, VIII, pp. 21–3.

11. Mogami Takanori, "Kōeki no hanashi," *Nihon minzokugaku kenkyū*; T. Wakamori, *Shakō to kyōyō*, Minkan denshō, 1944, X, pp. 447–8.

12. Kurata Ichirō, "Toshidama kō," *Minkan denshō*, 1943, VIII, pp. 497–502.

13. K. Sakurada, "Zōtō," *Nihon shakai minzoku jiten*, 1954, II.

14. E. Norbeck, "Yakudoshi, A Japanese Complex of Supernatural Beliefs," *Southwestern Journal of Anthropology*, 1955, XI, pp. 105–20.

15. J. Embree, *Suye mura, A Japanese Village*, University of Chicago Press, 1939, p. 104; T. Wakamori. *op. cit.*

16. K. Yanagita, *op. cit.*, pp. 101–29.
17. This token gift does not cancel the debt created by the gift brought. It simply symbolizes the good wishes of the receiver, who is in effect saying through the token return gift, "Please accept the supernatural power inherent in me which I hope will help you in some way." To reciprocate the gift and cancel the debt, the receiver must let some time elapse and then return a gift of appropriate value. A sick patient generally cancels his gift-debt by holding a feast when he recovers, to which he invites all those who paid him a visit during his illness.
18. K. Segawa, *op. cit.*, p. 228.
19. Oomachi Tokuzō, "Kankonsōsai no hanashi," *Nihon minzokugaku kenkyū*.
20. The social framework of gift-giving, especially in relation to the concept of reciprocity, has been discussed in my paper, "Gift-giving and Social Reciprocity in Japan, an Exploratory Statement," *France/Asie*, 1966/69, xxi, pp. 161–78.
21. M. Mauss, *The Gift, Forms and Functions of Exchange in Archaic Societies*, Free Press, Glencoe, 1954.
22. Furukawa Tetsushi, "Giri," *Nihon shakai minzoku jiten*, 1952, i, p. 291; Mori Yukiichi, "Mura no kōsai to giri," in K. Yanagita, ed., *Sansonseikatsu no kenkyū*, Minkan-denshō no kai, 1937, p. 162; T. Wakamori, 1947, *op. cit.*, p. 198; *Rekishi to minzoku*, Jitsugyō no nihonsha, Tokyo, 1951; *Nihonjin no kōsai*, Kōbun-dō, Tokyo, 1953. Minzokugaku kenkyū-jo, ed., *op. cit.*, p. 164.
23. R.P.Dore, *op. cit.*, pp. 260–2.
24. Incidentally, *kōden*, which is now given in cash (hence the translation "incense money") and is used to supplement the cost of the funeral, originated as an offering of the new crop of rice to the dead. Cf. I. Kurata, "Kōden no konjaku," *Minkandenshō*, 1944, x, pp. 457–63.
25. R.P.Dore, *op. cit.*, pp. 258–62.
26. R. P. Dore, *op. cit.*, pp. 387–9.
27. T. Wakamori, 1947, *op. cit.*, p. 198, Takagi Masataka, *Nihonjin no seikatsu-shinri*, Sōgen-sha, Tokyo and Osaka, 1954.
28. R. P. Dore, *op. cit.*, p. 262.
29. R. K. Merton, *Social Theory and Social Structure*, Free Press, Glencoe, 1949, pp. 125–50.
30. W. Caudill and T. Doi, "Interrelation of Psychiatry, Culture and Emotion in Japan," in I. Galston, ed., *Man's Image in Medicine and Anthropology*, International Universities Press, New York, 1963; W. Caudill and D. W. Plath, "Who Sleeps by Whom? Parent-Child Involvement in Urban Japanese Families," *Psychiatry*, 1966; W. Caudill and H. A. Scarr, "Japanese Value Orientations and Culture Change," *Ethnology*, 1962, i, pp. 53–91.
31. L. A. White, *The Evolution of Culture*, Mc-Graw Hill, New York, 1959, Ch. 15.
32. R. Benedict, *The Chrysanthemum and the Sword*, Houghton Mifflin, Boston, 1946; T. Furukawa, *op. cit.*
33. Nakayama Ichirō, *Nihon no kindaika*, Kōdan-sha, Tokyo, 1965, pp. 86–7.

PART III
Socialization and Psycho-Social Development

Maternal Care and Infant Behavior in Japan and America

WILLIAM CAUDILL AND HELEN WEINSTEIN

Human behavior can be distinguished, in one sense, from that of other animals in the degree to which it is influenced by culture—that is, influenced by shared patterns of action, belief, feeling, and thinking that are transmitted knowingly and unknowingly from one generation to the next through learning. The influence of culture is universal in that in some respects a man learns to become like all men; and it is particular in that a man who is reared in one society learns to become in some respects like all men of his society and not like those of others. A general question underlying the investigation reported here concerns the degree of importance of particular cultural differences, as a variable in the understanding of human behavior.

We began the present longitudinal study of children over the first six years of life in Japan and America because we wished to explore how early in the lives of infants, and in what ways, cultural differences become manifest in behavior. Our focus on culture as a variable is in no way meant to deny the great, and interrelated, importance of other major sources of variation, such as genetic endowment and physiological functioning of the infant, psychological characteristics of the parents, and position of the family in the social structure. Rather, by either controlling for or randomizing the effect of these other sources of variation, we wished to estimate more clearly the amount of the total variance in our sample of human behavior which may be attributed to cultural differences.

In the present study, we selected a matched sample of 30 Japanese and 30 American three-to-four-month-old infants—

Reprinted from *Psychiatry* 32 (1969): 12–43.

equally divided by sex, all firstborn, and all from intact middle-class families living in urban settings—and carried out an observational study in the homes of these infants during 1961–64. This article gives the results of that study. Subsequently, we made observations in the homes of the first 20 of these same children in each culture at the time they became two-and-a-half years of age, and again when they became six years of age, but these data have not as yet been analyzed.

Earlier studies by ourselves and others in Japan and America have indicated meaningful cultural differences in values, interpersonal relations, and personality characteristics. On the basis of this previous work we predicted that our Japanese mothers would spend more time with their infants, would emphasize physical contact over verbal interaction, and would have as a goal a passive and contented baby. We predicted that our American mothers would spend less time with their infants, would emphasize verbal interaction rather than physical contact, and would have as a goal an active and self-assertive baby. Underlying these predictions is the assumption that much cultural learning takes place out of the awareness of the participants, and although the Japanese mother does not consciously teach her infant specifically to become a Japanese baby, nor does the American mother specifically teach her infant to become an American baby, such a process does take place. We therefore also expected that by three-to-four months of age, infants in the two cultures would behave differently in certain important ways.

Our hypotheses were generally confirmed, although there were some surprises, and we conclude that, largely because of different patterns of interaction with their mothers in the two countries, infants have learned to behave in different and culturally appropriate ways by three-to-four months of age. Moreover, these differences in infant behavior are in line with preferred patterns of social interaction at later ages as the child grows to be an adult in Japan and America.

BACKGROUND AND HYPOTHESES

Before we began our study we thought a good deal, in a conceptual and theoretical sense, about the sources of the wide variation that we expected to find in any of the dependent variables in our observations of the behavior of Japanese and American infants and their caretakers.

We planned to do our observations in the natural setting of the home and because of this we knew, of course, that chance events would contribute to the variation in the data. The main systematic sources of variation, however, we believed would arise from biological, psychological, social, and cultural dimensions of human behavior. Although all of these dimensions are interrelated in actual behavior, each is sufficiently distinct to be thought of as a separate system (Caudill, 1958). In the biological dimension we decided to control on birth order, age, and sex of our infants. We expected that the influence on behavior of *individual* differences in genetic endowment and physiological functioning among the Japanese and American infants would be randomly distributed in the two samples. We do not, however, know of any *group* genetic or physiological differences between Japanese and American populations that would meaningfully exert an influence on the behavior of infants. In the psychological dimension, also, we expected the influence of individual differences in the personalities of the mothers and the infants to be randomly distributed in the two samples.

There is a tendency in scientific writing to blur the distinction between social and cultural dimensions of behavior by the use of such combined terms as "sociocultural"; or by subsuming one dimension under the other, as in the work of many anthropologists who think of social structure solely as a part of culture; or by simply ignoring one dimension while concentrating on the other, as in the work of many sociologists who emphasize the effect of position in the social structure to the exclusion of culture. We think of the cultural dimension as particularly referring to those historically derived patterns of thinking, feeling, and behaving that are shared in large part by all members of a society—for example, those qualities that make Englishmen differ from Frenchmen. We think of the social dimension as particularly referring to the occupational and industrial structure that has developed along similar lines in many societies in accompaniment with technological advancement. This process is usually called "modernization" and results in a society that is stratified into social classes (or levels of responsibility) which are closely tied to position in the occupational structure. In this sense, middle-class managerial personnel in England and France may have more in common than either group has with working-class machine operators in its own country.

In the world at present, we believe that each of these dimensions—the cultural and the social—exerts a relatively independent influence on human behavior, and that both dimensions need serious consideration in any cross-national study. There is considerable empirical evidence in the literature, from our own work and that of others, to support these ideas.[1]

For the foregoing reasons we decided in our study to control on social class in the selection of the sample of infants, and thus reduce the variation in our data that might be expected if the families came from differing positions in the social structure. As noted, all families in our sample are middle-class, but we did divide the sample in each country into two groups: (1) the father is the owner or employee of a small, established, independent business; (2) the father is a white-collar, salaried employee in a large business or in government. This distinction between an entrepreneurial and a bureaucratic occupation, and its ramifications in family life, is an important one in Japan, and we expected to find some differences in the behavior of mothers and infants in the two types of families.[2] Despite the work of Miller and Swanson, who did find differences in child rearing in terms of this occupational distinction in their study of families in Detroit, we felt that this distinction would not be very meaningful in our American data.[3]

In the light of the sources of variation we expected, and the controls we decided to use, in the biological, psychological, and social dimensions of infant and caretaker behavior, we emerged, by design, with the cultural dimension as the main independent variable.

On the basis of our previous work in Japan over the past fourteen years, coupled with a study of the literature, we have come to feel that the following differing emphases on what is valued in behavior are important when life in Japan is compared with life in America. These differing emphases seem to be particularly sharp in the areas of family life and general interpersonal relations with which we are most directly concerned here, and perhaps to be somewhat less evident in other areas of life such as business, the professions, or politics.[4] Japanese are more "group" oriented and interdependent in their relations with others, while Americans are more "individual" oriented and independent.[5] Going along with this, Japanese are more self-effacing and passive in contrast to Americans, who appear more self-assertive and aggressive. In matters requiring a decision, Japanese are more likely to rely on emotional feeling and intuition, whereas Americans will go to some pains to emphasize what they believe are the rational reasons for their action.[6] And finally, Japanese are more sensitive to, and make conscious use of, many forms of nonverbal communication in human relations through the medium of gestures and physical proximity in comparison with

Americans, who predominantly use verbal communication within a context of physical separateness.[7] One particularly pertinent example of the latter point is that a Japanese child can expect to co-sleep with his parents until he is ten years of age, and that in general a person in Japan can expect to co-sleep in a two-generation group, first as a child and later as a parent and grandparent, over half of his life span; to sleep alone is considered somewhat pitiful because a person would, therefore, be lonely.[8] In this regard, things are quite different in America, and the generations are usually separated in sleeping arrangements shortly after birth and remain so throughout the life cycle of the individual.[9]

In summary, in normal family life in Japan there is an emphasis on interdependence and reliance on others, while in America the emphasis is on independence and self-assertion. The conception of the infant would seem to be somewhat different in the two cultures. In Japan, the infant is seen more as a separate biological organism who from the beginning, in order to develop, needs to be drawn into increasingly interdependent relations with others. In America, the infant is seen more as a dependent biological organism who, in order to develop, needs to be made increasingly independent of others. Our more specific hypotheses in this study came from this general background of family life and interpersonal relations in the two cultures.

As indicated earlier, we expected that our Japanese mothers would spend more time with their infants, would emphasize physical contact over verbal interaction, and would treat them as objects to be acted upon rather than as objects to be interacted with. But, more than this, we expected the quality of the interaction to be differently patterned in the two cultures, and in Japan for it to be a mutually dependent, even symbiotic, relation in which there was a blurring of the boundaries between mother and child.[10] In contrast, we expected that our American mothers would spend less time with their infants, would encourage their physical activity and chat with them more, and would treat them more as separate

Table 1. Distribution of Cases in Terms of Independent Variables

Sex of Infant	Japanese (30 cases) Father's Occupation		American (30 cases) Father's Occupation	
	Salaried	Independent	Salaried	Independent
Male	9	9	10	5
Female	6	6	10	5

objects to be interacted with. And we expected the interaction in America to give evidence of the self-assertion of the child and his budding awareness of separateness from his mother.

By focusing on the contrasts in the behavior of mothers and infants in the cultural dimension, we do not mean to imply that we thought of child rearing as completely different in the two countries; we anticipated that we would find many similarities centering around the basic biological needs of the infant and the necessity for the mother to care for these needs. The differences we expected refer more to the "style" of caretaking and its effect upon the child. Equally, we do not mean to imply that one style of caretaking is "better" or "worse" than the other. An individual mother can do a good or a poor job of caretaking within either style. Our emphasis, rather, is upon the effect of differences in behavior as these are repeated day after day in the simple routine of life.

If we find that by three-to-four months of age Japanese and American infants have learned in some ways to behave differently in response to the culturally patterned behavior of their mothers, then this is a fact of great practical and theoretical importance. It means that, out of the direct awareness of mother or child, the precursors of certain ways of behaving, thinking, and feeling that are characteristic of a given culture have become part of an infant's approach to his environment well before the development of language and hence are not easily accessible to consciousness or to change.

DESIGN AND METHOD

The design of our study called for 30 Japanese and 30 American normal infants, who at the time of observation would be between three and four months of age and would be matched as previously described. Our plan was to gather data on the Japanese infants during 1961–62, and then to match the Japanese sample as closely as possible on all characteristics with an American sample that was to be studied during 1962–64. We were able to carry out this plan, although with some variation in the number of cases in each cell. The number and distribution of cases in the final sample used in the analysis of data are given in Table 1.

The Japanese families are of solely Japanese ancestry, and the American families are white and at least second-generation families of European ancestry. All of the Japanese families are nominally Buddhist, and the American families are divided among Protestant

(18 cases), Catholic (9 cases), and Jewish (3 cases) affiliation.

In both cultures we checked carefully with the infant's pediatrician and mother concerning any anomalies at birth or special developmental problems during the first three months of life. We decided to use firstborn infants not only to control on birth order, but also because the observational situation would be simpler if there was only one child in the home. Thus, strictly speaking, our results are applicable primarily to firstborn infants, and to mothers who are caring for their first child. We chose the age level of three-to-four months because we felt the relationship between mother and infant would have settled into a pattern by that time, and also because the observational method we planned to use had been worked out with infants of that age in mind. The age in days of the infants is quite close in both samples—a Japanese median age of 103 days, and an American median age of 109 days—and a comparison of the two samples in a rank-ordered distribution is not significant. There are more males (18 cases) than females (12 cases) in the Japanese sample because of the limited time we had for research in Japan coupled with the immediate availability of families who met our criteria in other respects.

Japanese mothers in the sample are somewhat older on the average (26.6 years) at the time of birth of their first child than the American mothers (23.7 years). Similarly, Japanese fathers are somewhat older on the average (29.7 years) than American fathers (26.7 years). These differences are in line with the reality in the middle class in the two countries concerning the age of marriage.[11]

All of our families are intact, and the largest number of households (15 Japanese and 25 American) in both samples consists of father, mother, and new baby—that is, the nuclear family. For the Japanese, those households with additional members (usually the father's parents) are mainly independent business families.

All of the families are residents of large cities. In the Japanese sample, we selected 20 cases from Tokyo and 10 from Kyoto because we wished also to take a look at the differences, if any, in child rearing in the two cities. The general way of life in Tokyo is thought of as more modern, and in Kyoto as more traditional. We did not find any significant differences between the two cities as measured by the dependent variables for infant and caretaker behavior, and have combined the cases from the two cities. In the American sample, all cases were selected from the metropolitan area of Washington, D.C.

All of the families are middle class as measured by the occupation and education of the father, and the education of the mother.[12] Although the Japanese sample is equally divided into 15 salaried and 15 independent business families, the American sample contains 20 salaried families and 10 independent business families because we had trouble in locating American cases in which the father was engaged in a small independent business.

The Japanese sample was obtained through pediatricians at St. Luke's International Hospital and at Tsukiji Maternity Hospital in Tokyo, and at Kyoto Prefectural Hospital in Kyoto. In Japan, middle-class mothers, in general, take their babies back to the hospital in which they were born for check-ups, so that the hospital is a normal channel for obtaining cases. Since the normal procedure for American middle-class mothers is to take their babies to the pediatrician's office for routine check-ups, the American cases were obtained from pediatricians in private practice.[13] In both cultures, the pediatricians selected cases from their practice which met our criteria, and they explained our work to the mothers by telling them that we were interested in studying the ordinary daily life of babies in different countries. If the mother agreed to participate in the study, the pediatrician introduced us to the mother and we carried on from there. In addition, in a few cases in both cultures, a mother with whom we had already worked would refer us to a mother who was a friend of hers and who met our criteria for inclusion in the study.[14] We did not pay our families for their time, but in each case we did give a present at the end of the observations.[15]

The data on the Japanese cases were gathered by Mrs. Seiko Notsuki, a psychologist; the data on the American cases were gathered by Mrs. Helen Weinstein, an anthropologist and the junior author of this article. Both are married and citizens of the country in which they worked. These circumstances were helpful in establishing easy and friendly relations with all of our families.

Before beginning the collection of data, the senior author trained his colleague in each country in the observational method used in the research. This was done by discussion of the variables, and by jointly conducting observations in a few pilot cases in each culture. After this training period, the senior author, in company respectively with his colleague in Japan and America, gathered actual data on several cases in order to involve himself directly in the collection of research material, and also to obtain duplicate records to be used in a check on the reliability of observations.

At the time of the initial contact with a mother we further

explained our study, and told her that we wished to observe the ordinary daily life of her baby. We requested that during our observations she go about her normal routine in the home, including leaving the house if this was her usual activity. We received excellent cooperation from the mothers in both cultures, and in this regard it is important to note that we stressed that our focus was on the life of the baby, and not directly on the behavior of the mother. As explained to the mothers, our method of observation calls for the observer to be near the infant at all times, and if a mother (or other caretaker) leaves the room, the observer stays with the infant.

Upon completion of our observations in the home, we also interviewed the mother for several hours to obtain information on the course of her pregnancy, the birth and subsequent development of the infant, and the general background of the family. A second purpose of the interview was to gather material on those aspects of the current life of the baby that we were not likely to observe because of the particular hours during which we were in the home.

We worked with each family for two days; usually these were consecutive days, and they were never separated by more than a few days. In general we spent about four hours on each day with a family, starting at nine in the morning on the first day, and at one in the afternoon on the second day. In planning our visits, we avoided days on which the mother or baby was ill, and in both cultures we spaced our work throughout all seasons of the year.

In making the observations we used a time-sampling procedure adapted from that originally developed by Rheingold. In this method, one observation of approximately one second in duration is made every fifteenth second in terms of a set of predetermined variables concerning the behavior of the infant and the caretaker. We designed an observation sheet that listed the variables down the side of the page, and provided columns for 40 observations across the page.[16] For each observation, a decision was made for all variables as to their occurrence or non-occurrence, although only occurrences received a check mark on the observation sheet. Four observations were made each minute, and thus a single observation sheet covered a period of ten minutes, or 40 observations. Upon completion of an observation sheet, the observer took a five-minute break during which she clarified, if necessary, the data recorded on the completed sheet, and also wrote descriptive notes concerning the context of the behavior that had just occurred. At the end of this five-minute break, another sheet of 40 observations was begun.

On the first day, observations were made from 9:30 A.M. until noon, and on the second day, from 1:30 P.M. until 4:00 P.M. Thus, 10 sheets, or 400 observations are available for each day, resulting in a total of 800 observations per case for the two days. This is a key number to be kept in mind because it forms the basis upon which the statistical analysis of the data is carried out.

In making the observations, the observer used a simple clipboard with a stopwatch mounted on the top. She sat in a convenient corner of the room and participated minimally in the ongoing situation. The observer would look for one second, and then would check what she had seen in terms of the predefined variables on the observation sheet during the next fourteen seconds. At various points in the observations the mother would carry the baby from one room to another, or into the yard, or onto the street. At these points, the observer followed along and continued to make her observations. Such transition points were naturally more "busy," but things usually settled downw ithin a few observations once the new situation was established.

After a few training sessions this method proved to be very simple to use and to produce reliable data. For example, the simplest situation is that in which the baby is alone, in bed, and asleep. In this case, the same observation concerning the sleeping baby merely moves across the sheet. A more complicated situation is exemplified by the following: At the beginning of a sheet the baby is alone and asleep; he awakens and cries; the mother comes into the room, looks at and talks to the baby; she begins to diaper the baby, with the baby shifting from crying to being happily vocal. Despite the general sequential nature of the observations, it must be remembered that the period of 14 seconds between observations is unrecorded. In this article, therefore, we will only present data on the behavior of the infant and the caretaker in terms of frequency of occurrence within a time-sample of 800 observations made over a five-hour span.

Definition of Dependent Variables

On the original observation sheet the 40 dependent variables were grouped under four headings: (1) Who is the caretaker (4 variables)? (2) Where is the baby (7 variables)? (3) What is the baby doing (14 variables)? (4) What is the caretaker doing (15 variables)? A detailed definition for each variable was established prior to the collection of data. In the process of analysis we have omitted, collapsed, or subdivided some of the variables. Results are presented here predominately in terms of 12 variables for infant behavior and 15 variables for caretaker behavior (see Tables 3 and 4). The definitions for the variables used in this analysis, and how we arrived at them, are as follows.

The basic problem under the heading of "Who is the caretaker?" is how to define a caretaker. Excluding the observer, a caretaker is any adult who is able, at a moment's notice, both to see and to hear the baby.[17] Usually this means that the caretaker is in the same room, but we also define a caretaker as present if the adult is in an adjoining room and can still both see and hear the baby. If the observation is made outside of the house, the same rule of being able both to see and hear the baby is applicable.[18] In all other situations, the baby is considered to be alone. Since the two variables, *caretaker present* and *infant alone*, are reciprocal, only the first is used in this analysis, and is placed under caretaker behavior (see Table 4).

When present, a caretaker can be actively caretaking (doing one or more of the caretaker behaviors listed in Table 4), or can be merely present. When several adults are present, the one who is actively caretaking is considered to be the caretaker. In those rare situations when two adults are equally active, the person who is closer in biological relationship to the infant is considered the caretaker (e.g., the mother rather than the grandmother, or, in the one possibly ambiguous case, the mother rather than the father). When several adults are merely passively present, again the person closer in biological relationship is considered the caretaker.

In recording, we always identified the caretaker by means of a simple code ("M" for mother, "F" for father, "GM" for grandmother, etc.). Empirically, the caretaker is the mother in over 90 percent of such observations in both cultures. In this paper, therefore, we will use the terms "caretaker" and "mother" as equivalent, and will not make any further distinction as to who is the caretaker.

The basic question for us under the heading of "Where is the baby?" finally became whether or not the infant was in close physical contact with the caretaker. An infant is defined as in close physical contact if he is being held in the caretaker's arms or lap, or is being carried by the caretaker; otherwise he is not in close physical contact. In this analysis the variable *in arms* is placed under caretaker behavior (see Table 4) and means close physical contact by being held in arms or lap, or being carried in any fashion. Since the variable is reciprocal with *not in arms*, it is only analyzed here in its positive sense.[19]

Under the heading of "What is the baby doing?" the basic distinction is whether the baby is *awake* or *asleep*. We define these two states largely in terms of whether the infant's eyes are open or closed, coupled with the degree of relaxation of the body. Since the two variables are reciprocal, we only present the results for *infant awake* (see Table 3). If the infant is awake, then he can also be engaged in one or more of the other behaviors.

Breast or bottle must be in the infant's mouth at the time of observation in order to be scored. On the observation sheet these were separate variables, but they are combined here into a single category meaning "attempting intake of liquid nourishment" because there was so little breast feeding in the American cases.[20] When we discuss our results we will give the findings for breast and bottle both separately and in combination. In addition to milk, mothers also gave water, fruit juice, and (in Japan) weak tea by bottle. The attempted intake of these liquids is also scored under the variable of *bottle*.

In America it is usual to start babies on semi-solid food at about the end of the first month of life, but in Japan this type of feeding is delayed much longer and is not typical until about the fourth month. On the observation sheet we had a separate variable labeled "food," under which we scored semi-solid food, or any harder food such as a cracker, when it was in the mouth of the infant at the time of observation. We will later give our findings for this variable separately. Since the data from the Japanese cases are rather scanty,[21] we made a composite variable called *all food* in which we combine the observations of breast, bottle, and food. This variable may be thought of as "attempting intake of any nourishment."[22]

All infants (and adults too) do a certain amount of sucking on "nonnutritive" objects. The variable of *finger or pacifier* denotes this behavior and includes all such actions as sucking on a finger or hand, or sucking on other objects, like a pacifier or the edge of a blanket.

In the area of infant vocalization, it is important to note that we mean any expressively voiced sound, and we did not include hiccups, coughs, and so on, in any of the definitions. *Unhappy vocal* means any negatively voiced sound, and was initially divided into "protest" (a weak negative vocal) and "cry" (a strong negative vocal). *Happy vocal* means any positively voiced sound, and was initially divided into "vocal to caretaker" if the caretaker was in close proximity, and "vocal" if the caretaker was at some distance from the infant or absent. Since the categories of infant vocalization are additive, we also use a composite variable of *total vocal*, which is defined as any vocalization by the infant.

Active means gross bodily movements, usually of the arms and legs, and does not include minor movements such as twitches or startles.

Toy, hand, and *other object* are all categories in which the baby is playing with an object. "Toy" means an actual toy; "hand" means playing with a part of the body, such as the hands, arms, legs, or toes; and "other object" means playing with another object, which must be specified—such as a blanket or the edge of the crib. These variables are mutually exclusive for a single observation, and hence may be added together to form a composite variable called *baby plays*, which may be thought of more conceptually as "baby explores his physical environment."

Under the heading of "What is the caretaker doing?" we have omitted "talks" and "bathes," which were on the original observation sheet. "Talks" was defined as talking to a person other than the infant, and is omitted here because it is not a direct caretaking action.[23] "Bathes" is omitted because the customary time for the Japanese infant to be given a bath is in the evening, whereas the American infant is usually given a bath in the daytime. Since our hours of observation were restricted to the morning and afternoon, we saw only a few Japanese babies being bathed.[24] In designing our study we had to make a choice between (1) standardizing our periods of observation and concentrating on studying simple events which would frequently occur in both cultures (e.g., the infant's vocalization and the caretaker's talking to the baby), or (2) letting our periods of observation vary while studying fewer and more dramatic events (e.g., how the baby was bathed or put to sleep at night) at whatever time they happened. We chose the former course.[25]

The caretaker variables of *feeds, diapers, dresses,* and *positions* are all reasonably self-explanatory. The caretaker is scored as feeding the infant whenever she is offering him the breast, bottle, or food at the time of observation. Diapering is restricted to the checking for wetness and the taking off and putting on of the diaper and its cover, plus assisting the baby to urinate or defecate, and the cleaning, powdering, and oiling of the baby's body. All other removal, putting on, or rearranging of clothing is scored as "dresses." "Positions" is the manipulation of the baby's body to make him more comfortable and can occur whether the infant is "in arms" (e.g., shifting the baby from one shoulder to the other) or not "in arms" (e.g., shifting the position of the baby in an infant seat).

Pats or touches is another combined variable. "Pats" can occur whether the infant is "in arms" or not, and consists of a rhythmic stroking or gentle striking of any part of the baby's body with the apparent intent of soothing or burping. "Touches" can occur only when the infant is not "in arms," and means that the caretaker's hand is resting on the baby's body, again with the apparent intent of soothing.

Other care is a general category under which are scored other caretaking acts which must be specified in writing on the observation sheet—such as "wipes baby's face" or "takes baby's temperature."

Plays with means that the caretaker is in direct interaction with the baby and is attempting to amuse or entertain him by such acts as playing peek-a-boo or pat-a-cake, bouncing him on her knee, or showing him how a toy works. The somewhat related variable of *affections* is sharply delimited and means that the caretaker kisses the baby, or snuggles her face against the baby's body.

Looks at is combined from two mutually exclusive variables, "looks" and "looks at," on the observation sheet. "Looks" means that the caretaker glances at, or directs her visual attention to, the infant from a distance of more than six feet. "Looks at" means that the caretaker is within six feet of the infant or is holding the infant "in arms" and looks directly at the baby's face.

Talks to means that the caretaker is talking, or otherwise vocalizing, directly to the infant. We have subdivided this variable, making use of the descriptive notes on the observation sheets, into *chats* and *lulls*. "Lulls" is a very delimited variable and means that the caretaker is softly singing or humming a lullaby, or making repetitive comforting noises, with the apparent intent of soothing and quieting the baby or getting him to go to sleep. "Chats" includes all other vocalization to the infant, such as talking to him, singing to him in a lively fashion, and playing word games ("boo," "goo," etc.) with him.

Rocks includes all conscious acts of the caretaker to cause the baby to sway rhythmically back and forth. Rocking usually occurs when the infant is "in arms," but can occur when he is not "in arms"—as when the mother rocks a cradle or a baby carriage. "Rocks" is not scored when the infant is "in arms" and is merely being moved up and down by the normal walking motion of the caretaker.

Reliability and Standardization of Data

Reliability was checked between two observers in 7 Japanese cases, using every other case among the first 14 cases completed, and in 3 American cases, using the first 3 cases completed. The senior author was the "constant" observer in the reliability check, being paired with Mrs. Notsuki in Japan and with Mrs. Weinstein in America.

In our approach to the question of reliability, we chose to use severe criteria, and to look at agreement between observers at the level of the individual observation. In assessing reliability we made both an "exact check" and what we call a "contiguous check." In an exact check, the two observers must agree about the presence of a category of behavior in exactly the same observation. In a contiguous check, the two observers must agree about the presence of a category of behavior within the limits of two observations.[26] The contiguous check seems to us to be a reasonable procedure because of the difficulty of keeping stopwatches synchronized, and because of the visual difficulty in picking the correct column in which to place an observation while moving across the sheet. In some places in the raw data, the observers have obviously recorded the same behavior for the infant and the caretaker over a ten-minute sheet, but are consistently off one column across the entire 40 observations. In Table 2, therefore, the percentage agreement between observers is given in terms of the contiguous check. In general, the reliability of the dependent variables is satisfactory in both cultures. There are only two instances in which reliability is poor, both in the Japanese data—a level of 49 percent agreement on "positions," and of 61 percent on "affections."

As we checked reliability, we also became aware that a variable could be satisfactorily reliable and still be "biased." By this we mean that compared to the scores of a constant observer (Caudill), the observers in the two cultures (Notsuki and Weinstein) might differ in the same direction (that is, both observers would have proportionately greater or fewer observations on a variable than the constant observer, but the proportions would be meaningfully different); or, what is worse, the observers in the two cultures might differ in opposite directions (that is, one observer would have proportionately greater and the other proportionately fewer observations than the constant observer). For example, on the variable of "active" in the Japanese cases Caudill had 91 percent as many presence scores as Notsuki, but he had only 75 percent as many

Table 2. Observer Reliability and Weights Used for Standardization of Frequencies of
Observations Across Cultures

Dependent Variables	Japanese (7 cases)			American (3 cases)		
	Average Frequency per Case	Average Percent Agreement per Case†	Weight Used for Standardization‡	Average Frequency per Case	Average Percent Agreement per Case†	Weight Used for Standardization‡
Infant Behavior						
Awake	497	98	—	430	100	—
Breast or Bottle	56	99	—	16	100	—
All Food	56	99	—	25	99	89
Finger or Pacifier	105	92	—	253	84	94
Total Vocal	111	91	1.04	126	80	.86
Unhappy	63	89	1.05	70	88	1.07
Happy	56	70	1.10	58	70	.64
Active	87	69	.91	104	74	.75
Baby Plays	145	85	.96	115	93	1.07
Toy	72	90	.94	83	95	1.05
Hand	29	79	1.04	11	87	1.12
Other Object	43	84	—	26	94	—

Caretaker Behavior

Presence of	574	99	—	275	100	—
Feeds	64	99	—	37	100	—
Diapers	17	95	.98	2	96	.93
Dresses	13	84	1.06	15	99	1.03
Positions	12	49	1.75	12	77	.71
Pats or Touches	44	78	.82	39	87	.84
Other Care	29	85	.97	19	85	.86
Plays with	26	67	1.34	34	86	1.16
Affections	9	61	1.44	6	74	1.11
Looks at	233	94	—	170	90	1.06
Talks to	120	90	—	85	83	.83
Chats	91	90	—	82	83	.83
Lulls	29	94	—	3	100	—
In Arms	158	100	—	91	99	—
Rocks	66	90	.95	3	88	—

†Agreement between two observers as to the presence (Yes) or absence (No) of a behavior is classified within four cells: (a) Yes/Yes, (b) Yes/No, (c) No/Yes, (d) No/No. Percent agreement is computed as the ratio of (2a) to (2a + b + c), thus avoiding the use of the somewhat spurious agreement on absence of behavior.

‡Weight used to standardize frequencies across cultures is computed as the ratio of (Sum of Caudill's Presence Scores) to (Sum of Other Observer's Presence Scores).

presence scores as Weinstein in the American cases; on the variable of "total vocal" Caudill had 104 percent as many presence scores as Notsuki, but only 86 percent as many presence scores as Weinstein.

Because of these differences in proportions, we computed a weight for each variable which would standardize the scores to those of the constant observer. Thus, for example, on the variable of "active," we reduced Notsuki's scores by applying a weight of 0.91, and reduced Weinstein's scores by a weight of 0.75. Similarly, in the variable of "total vocal," we increased Notsuki's scores by a weight of 1.04, and decreased Weinstein's scores by a weight of 0.86. The weights used to standardize all of the dependent variables are given in Table 2. The use of this method effectively eliminates the error introduced by the other observers' being "off" in differing proportions (and directions) from the constant observer, and permits a more accurate comparison of scores across cultures.

We believe that, as a general methodological point, the issue of standardizing scores has great importance; and, so far as we know, this is the first time it has been met directly in cross-cultural research. Without standardization, it is quite possible to have satisfactory reliability among observers within several cultures, but not to know whether the general perception or "set" of the observers is the same or different across cultures.

Techniques Used in Analysis of Data

The major results reported here (see Tables 3–10) were arrived at through use of multivariate analysis of variance.[27] The collection of the data over 800 equally spaced observations in each case makes the use of this technique of analysis very appropriate. In the analysis, the dependent variables were divided into two groups, 12 infant behaviors and 15 caretaker behaviors. Within each group, dependent variables were analyzed singly, and in combination (by means of canonical correlation as discussed later), in relation to three independent variables—culture, father's occupation, and sex of infant. The results for any one independent variable were always controlled in terms of the effect of the other two independent variables. In Tables 3–10, all means given for an independent variable are adjusted (that is, they are co-varied) for the effects of the other two independent variables.[28]

In addition to the analysis of the data over the total sample of 60 cases, we always also split the sample by culture into two groups of 30 cases each and ran duplicate intra-cultural analyses on all dependent variables in relation to the two independent variables (and their interaction) of father's occupation and sex of infant. We do not present the results of these intracultural analyses in tabular form in this article, but we will refer to these further analyses as they become important for the development of our argument.

In evaluating results we give two measures of the effect of an independent variable upon a dependent variable. The first measure is a correlation, and is an estimate of the magnitude of the effect (the proportion of the variance of the dependent variable attributable to the independent variable). The definition of the correlation coefficient used in this analysis is given in the footnotes to Table 3.[29] The second measure is an estimate of the significance of the effect (the likelihood that the null hypothesis can be rejected), and is derived from the F ratio obtained in an analysis of variance. All tests of significance reported in this paper are "two-tailed," meaning that for statistical purposes we take the conservative position that we have not predicted the direction of the finding.

The canonical correlation which is given at the bottom of Tables 3–10 is a very useful summarizing statistic. In descriptive language, the computer is programmed to develop what is, in effect, a composite dependent variable from the set of dependent variables through a process of discriminate function analysis.[30] Thus, in Tables 3–10, the composite dependent variables corresponding to the canonical correlations may be thought of as "infant behavior in general" and "caretaker behavior in general."

A few words need to be said about the use of percentages in the analyses that led to the development of Tables 6–10. After finishing work with the total frequencies (see Tables 3 and 4), we classified the 800 observations in each case in terms of their occurrence in six "states," which were defined by the infant's being either asleep or awake, and by the caretaker's doing caretaking, merely being present, or being absent (see Table 5). Because each case varies in the frequency with which its observations occur in the various states, we converted the frequency of occurrence of the dependent variables to percentages (that is, the frequency of occurrence of a dependent variable in a given state relative to total observations in that state).[31]

Finally, we ran a correlation matrix (Pearsonian r) over the frequency tabulations within each culture for the 12 infant and 15 caretaker variables for all of our analyses both in terms of total frequencies, and in terms of the frequencies in each of the states.

Table 3. Adjusted Mean Frequencies, in Total Observations, of Infant Behavior: By Culture, Father's Occupation, and Sex of Infant

| | | | | Adjusted Mean Frequencies | | | | | |
| Categories of Infant Behavior | Culture | | | Father's Occupation | | | Sex of Infant | | |
	Japanese	American	Correlation†	Salaried	Independent	Correlation†	Males	Female	Correlation†
Infant Awake	494	493	.01	474	521	.20	498	488	.04
Breast or Bottle	66	55	.11	59	62	.03	63	57	.06
All Food	68	74	.06	71	71	.00	74	68	.06
Finger or Pacifier	**69**	**172**	**.44****	116	127	.06	124	116	.04
Total Vocal	94	116	.25	100	112	.13	108	102	.07
Unhappy	**66**	**45**	**.33**	50	64	.21	55	57	.03
Happy	**30**	**59**	**.51****	45	44	.02	48	41	.14
Active	**51**	**95**	**.45****	73	74	.02	73	73	.00
Baby Plays	**83**	**170**	**.50****	129	124	.03	133	199	.09
Toy	**48**	**82**	**.28**	66	64	.01	76	52	.21
Hand	**14**	**27**	**.33**	21	20	.01	21	20	.01
Other Object	**22**	**57**	**.47****	41	38	.04	34	46	.18
Canonical Correlation‡			**.80****			.24			.38
Total Cases	30	30		35	25		33	27	

†This partial correlation is the square root of the ratio of (a) the sum of the squared deviations from the mean attributable to the independent variable in question, to (b) the total sum of the squared deviations minus the sum of the squared deviations attributable to the control variables and their interactions. When this partial correlation is squared, the result is a measure of the proportion of variance attributable to the independent variable in question. The means and partial correlations for all findings significant at $p < 0.05$ are printed in boldface. One asterisk (*) indicates $p < 0.01$, two asterisks (**) indicate $p < 0.001$.

‡The variables of "Total Vocal" and "Baby Plays" are not included in the canonical correlations because of linear dependency with their constituent variables "Unhappy" and "Happy," and "Toy," "Hand," and "Other Object." The means for the constituent variables do not, however, add exactly to the mean for the corresponding total variable because of rounding and the weights used to standardize frequencies of observations across cultures as indicated in Table 2. The variable of "Infant Awake" is also omitted from the canonical correlations in this table to make them comparable with the canonical correlations in Tables 6, 8, and 9.

We are not presenting these correlation matrices in tabular form in this article, but we will refer to pertinent patterns of correlations as they relate to our results.

RESULTS

Total Observations

The results of the analyses of the main effects of the independent variables over the total 800 observations in each case are given in Tables 3 and 4.[32] A general inspection of the tables will quickly indicate that culture is by far the most important variable in accounting for the differences in infant and caretaker behavior. Before turning to a detailed examination of the results by culture, however, let us dispose of the findings for the other two independent variables.

As can be seen in Tables 3 and 4, there are no findings by sex of infant for the behavior of either the infant or the caretaker. Equally, an examination of the intra-Japanese and intra-American analyses reveals no significant findings by sex of infant.

Father's occupation does not produce any findings for infant behavior, but it does produce an interesting pattern of findings for caretaker behavior. As can be seen in Table 4, mothers in small independent business families are present more, and lull, carry, and rock their infants more than mothers in salaried families. When, however, we look at the separate intra-cultural analyses, there are no significant findings by father's occupation in the American data. In the Japanese data, on the other hand, all of the findings in Table 4 are significant in the same manner, and in addition there are two further findings in the same direction on "infant awake" and caretaker "talks to" baby. Thus, the pattern of findings in the intra-Japanese analysis is that in the small independent business family the baby is awake more, and the caretaker is present more and doing more talking to, lulling, carrying, and rocking of the baby than is the case in the salaried family. It seems evident, therefore, that as a minor theme, occupational style of life does make a difference in Japanese culture, but not—at least in our data— in American culture.

Let us look now at the results of the analyses by culture in more detail. We will consider the areas of similarity in behavior before turning to the areas of difference.

As can be seen in Table 3, the types of infant behavior in which there are no differences between the two cultures are those clearly concerned with biological needs. Thus, there are no significant dif-

Table 4. Adjusted Mean Frequencies, in Total Observations, of Caretaker Behavior: By Culture, Father's Occupation, and Sex of Infant

Categories of Caretaker Behavior	Culture			Adjusted Mean Frequencies Father's Occupation			Sex of Infant		
	Japanese	American	Correlation†	Salaried	Independent	Correlation†	Male	Female	Correlation†
Caretaker Present	**541**	**421**	**.37***	**437**	**543**	.33	471	494	.08
Feeds	74	71	.03	71	74	.04	78	65	.13
Diapers	23	17	.24	19	21	.08	20	20	.02
Dresses	12	13	.03	12	14	.11	13	12	.05
Positions	**8**	**19**	**.49****	13	14	.02	15	12	.17
Pats or Touches	34	47	.23	38	43	.08	41	39	.04
Other Care	17	23	.15	21	19	.05	19	22	.10
Plays with	39	24	.25	29	35	.10	34	28	.10
Affections	7	9	.09	7	10	.17	9	7	.20
Looks at	**242**	**299**	**.27**	247	302	.26	278	260	.09
Talks to	101	123	.21	101	127	.24	116	107	.09
Chats	**79**	**120**	**.42****	94	108	.25	102	96	.06
Lulls	**22**	**3**	**.44****	**8**	20	.28	14	11	.09
In Arms	**197**	**139**	**.27**	**133**	**217**	**.36***	163	175	.06
Rocks	**46**	**20**	**.35***	**22**	**47**	**.34**	39	25	.19
Canonical Correlation‡			**.79****			.52			.51
Total Cases	30	30		35	25		33	27	

†See footnote in Table 3 for explanation of this partial correlation. The means and correlations for all findings significant at $p < 0.05$ are printed in boldface. One asterisk (*) indicates $p < 0.01$, two asterisks (**) indicate $p < 0.001$.

‡Canonical correlations do not include the variable of "Talks to" because of linear dependency with the constituent variables "Chats" and "Lulls"; the means of the constituent variables do not, however, add exactly to the mean for the total variable because of rounding and the weights used to standardize frequencies of observations across cultures as indicated in Table 2. In addition, the variable of "Caretaker Present" is omitted to make the canonical correlations in this table comparable with those in Tables 7 and 10.

ferences in the amount of time awake, sucking on breast or bottle, or intake of all food.[33] Technically, there also is no difference in the amount of total vocalization, but the correlation is .25, which is just short of being significant ($F = 3.7$, $df = 1/52$, $p < 0.058$).

For the caretakers in the two cultures, most of the areas of similarity indicated in Table 4 are concerned with basic functions involved in caring for the infant's biological needs for nutrition, elimination, and physical comfort. Thus, there are no significant differences in "feeds," "diapers," "dresses," "pats or touches," and "other care." Also, there is no difference in the overall amount of talking to the infant, but the manner in which this talking is done is clearly different. Affectionate behavior toward the infant may or may not be a requirement of basic caretaking, depending on one's point of view, but, in any event, there is no difference in such behavior between the two cultures. Finally, playing with the baby, which is not a requirement of basic caretaking, shows no difference in a technical sense, but the finding has a correlation of .25, on the borderline of significance ($F = 3.8$, $df = 1/52$, $p < 0.058$).

To generalize, the areas of similarity in both cultures point to the expression of biological needs by all of the infants, and the necessity for all of the mothers to care for these needs. Beyond this, however, the differences lie in the styles in which infants and mothers behave in the two cultures.

The American baby appears to be more physically active and happily vocal, and more involved in the exploration of his body and his environment than is the Japanese baby, who, in contrast, seems more subdued in all these respects. These differences can be seen in Table 3, which shows the American infant as more active,[34] more happily vocal (and quite possibly more totally vocal, as indicated earlier), more exploring of his body by greater sucking on his fingers (or by putting other parts of his body and objects into his mouth),[35] and more exploring of his environment in playing with toys, hands, and other objects. The Japanese infant, on the other hand, is only greater in unhappy vocalization.

These differences, moreover, do not just occur singly, variable by variable, but appear to be interconnected. For example, the physical activity of the American baby is negatively correlated with "finger or pacifier" ($-.42$), and positively correlated with "total vocal" (.71), "happy vocal" (.80), "baby plays" (.64), "toy" (.56), "hand" (.45), and "caretaker present" (.38). On the other hand, the physical activity of the Japanese baby shows much less patterning, and is only correlated with "total vocal" (.59), "unhappy vocal" (.39), and "happy vocal" (.43).[36]

The differences in styles of caretaking in the two cultures appear to be equally pronounced. The American mother seems to have a more lively and stimulating approach to her baby, as indicated in Table 4, which shows the American caretaker as positioning the infant's body more, and looking at and chatting to the infant more. The Japanese mother, in contrast, is present more with the baby, in general, and seems to have a more soothing and quieting approach, as indicated by greater lulling, and by more carrying in arms, and rocking.

It may also be that the Japanese mother plays with her baby more, but of even greater interest is the very different pattern of intercorrelations for this variable in the two cultures. The Japanese mother's playing with baby is negatively correlated with "hand" (−.39), and "other object" (−.36), and positively correlated with "caretaker present" (.48), "affections" (.63), "looks at" (.53), "talks to" (.77), "chats" (.65), "lulls" (.66), "in arms" (.76), and "rocks" (.61). At the least, this pattern means that those Japanese mothers who play more with their babies also do more soothing of their babies. In contrast, the American mother's playing with baby is correlated with "positions" (.36), "pats or touches" (.57), "talks to" (.47), and 'chats" (.47). There is no suggestion in the American pattern that a mother who plays more with her baby is also likely to do more soothing.

The key link between the infant and mother in the American culture seems to us to show up in the pattern of correlations with infant's "happy vocal." For the American infant, "happy vocal" is correlated negatively with "finger or pacifier" (−.41), and is positively correlated with "total vocal" (.92), "active" (.80), "baby plays" (.55), 'toy" (.48), "hand" (.39), "caretaker present" (.48), "affections" (.37), "looks at" (.39), "talks to" (.39), "chats" (.39), and "rocks" (.38). We feel that the link between baby's happy vocalizations and caretaker's chatting with baby is especially important, as it indicates a major type of communication between the American infant and his mother that is not found in the Japanese data. For the Japanese infant, "happy vocal" is correlated only with the following: negatively with "rocks" (−.36), and positively with "active" (.43) and "other care" (.48).

In summary, then, of the analyses by culture of the total observations, the expression of the infant's biological needs, and the mother's basic caretaking of these needs, are the same in both cultures; but beyond this, the styles of the infant's behavior and the mother's care are different. The Japanese baby seems passive, and he lies quietly with occasional unhappy vocalizations, while his mother, in her care, does more lulling, carrying, and rocking of her baby. She seems to try to soothe and quiet the child, and to communicate with him physically rather than verbally. On the other hand, the American infant is more active, happily vocal, and exploring of his environment, and his mother in her care does more looking at and chatting to her baby. She seems to stimulate the baby to activity and to vocal response. It is as if the American mother wanted to have a vocal, active baby, and the Japanese mother wanted to have a quiet, contented baby. In terms of the styles of caretaking of the mothers in the two cultures, they seem to get what they apparently want. That these two patterns do, indeed, discriminate between the cultures is indicated by the significant canonical correlations for infant behavior (.80) and for caretaker behavior (.79).

Division of the Data into States

Our next step was further to refine the data by grouping them into what we call states. The six states are made up of the combination of the infant's being either awake or asleep in relation to the caretaker's doing active caretaking, being present but not doing caretaking, or being absent. We divided the 800 observations in each case into these six states. The results of an analysis of variance for "time in state" in terms of culture can be seen in Table 5.[37]

The first thing to note in Table 5 is that the amount of time spent in doing caretaking when the baby is awake (State One) is not significantly different in the two cultures. Thus, the styles of caretaking and of infant behavior are different, but the mothers in both cultures do caretaking about the same amount of time during the daytime hours. This finding contradicts the popular notion that the Japanese mother is more attentive to her baby. What is true, however, is that the Japanese mother does seem to spend more time simply being with her baby when he is awake as indicated by the finding in State Two. And yet, in State Three, when the infant is awake and alone, again there is no significant difference between the two cultures. The canonical correlation over the three states in which the baby is awake is not significant, and perhaps the best general statement we can make is that there is not a significant difference between the cultures in the amount of time a mother is present or absent during the time that her baby is awake.

Table 5. Cultural Comparison of Adjusted Mean Frequencies for Time in Six States

Culture	Infant Awake			Infant Asleep		
	Caretaker Present and Caretaking (State One)	Caretaker Present but Not Caretaking (State Two)	Caretaker absent (State Three)	Caretaker Present and Caretaking (State Four)	Caretaker Present but Not Caretaking (State Five)	Caretaker Absent (State Six)
Japanese (30 cases)	286	**103**	106	52	**100**	153
American (30 cases)	321	53	119	16	32	**259**
Correlation†	.16	.34	.08	.37*	.45**	.42**
Canonical Correlation‡	.37			.58**		

†See footnote in Table 3 for explanation of this partial correlation. The means and correlations for all findings significant at $p < 0.05$ are printed in boldface. One asterisk (*) indicates $p < 0.01$, two asterisks (**) indicate $p < 0.001$.

‡It is not possible to obtain a canonical correlation over the six states because of linear dependency. Canonical correlations are given, however, for States One, Two, and Three in which the infant is awake, and for States Four, Five, and Six in which the infant is asleep.

Table 6. Adjusted Mean Percentages, in State One, of Infant Behavior: By Culture, Father's Occupation, and Sex of Infant

Categories of Infant Behavior	Adjusted Mean Percentages								
	Culture			Father's Occupation			Sex of Infant		
	Japanese	American	Correlation†	Salaried	Independent	Correlation†	Male	Female	Correlation†
Breast or Bottle	**24**	**14**	**.31**	20	18	.08	19	18	.04
All Food	24	20	.14	24	20	.13	23	22	.02
Finger or Pacifier	6	9	.17	7	9	.15	7	8	.13
Total Vocal	**14**	**22**	**.45****	18	18	.03	18	19	.07
Unhappy	10	8	.17	9	10	.09	9	10	.13
Happy	**5**	**11**	**.62****	8	7	.13	8	8	.03
Active	**5**	**15**	**.60****	11	10	.08	10	10	.03
Baby Plays	**11**	**25**	**.65****	17	19	.14	19	17	.13
Toy	7	9	.10	7	9	.12	**10**	**6**	**.35***
Hand	**1**	**4**	**.51****	2	3	.18	3	3	.01
Other Object	**3**	**11**	**.63****	7	7	.01	6	8	.20
Canonical Correlation‡			**.84****			.34			.49
Total Cases	30	30		35	25		33	27	

†See footnote in Table 3 for explanation of this partial correlation. The means and correlations for all findings significant at $p < 0.05$ are printed in boldface. One asterisk (*) indicates $p < 0.01$, two asterisks (**) indicate $p < 0.001$.
‡See footnote in Table 3.

Table 7. Adjusted Mean Percentages, in State One, of Caretaker Behavior: By Culture, Father's Occupation, and Sex of Infant

| | Adjusted Mean Percentages | | | | | | | | |
| Categories of Caretaker Behavior | Culture | | | Father's Occupation | | | Sex of Infant | | |
	Japanese	American	Correlation†	Salaried	Independent	Correlation†	Male	Female	Correlation†
Feeds	26	21	.16	26	21	.15	24	24	.01
Diapers	9	6	.25	8	6	.16	7	8	.01
Dresses	4	4	.05	4	4	.07	4	4	.01
Positions	**2**	**6**	.62**	4	4	.12	4	4	.09
Pats or Touches	11	14	.25	13	12	.10	12	13	.03
Other Care	5	7	.18	6	5	.20	5	6	.15
Plays with	**12**	**7**	.34*	10	9	.07	10	9	.06
Affections	2	3	.14	2	3	.09	3	2	.21
Looks at	77	89	.42**	84	81	.11	83	83	.03
Talks to	33	39	.22	36	36	.01	36	36	.02
Chats	**28**	**39**	.45**	34	31	.13	32	34	.09
Lulls	**6**	**1**	.46***	2	5	.24	4	3	.10
In Arms	**55**	**42**	.35*	46	53	.20	45	52	.20
Rocks	**12**	5	.38*	7	**11**	**.28**	10	7	.19
Canonical Correlation‡			.85**			.57			.49
Total Cases	30	30		35	25		33	27	

†See footnote in Table 3 for explanation of this partial correlation. The means and correlations for all findings significant at $p < 0.05$ are printed in boldface. One asterisk (*) indicates $p < 0.01$, two asterisks (**) indicate $p < 0.001$.
‡See footnote in Table 4.

The three states in which the baby is asleep, however, show a sharper contrast between the cultures. In State Four, the Japanese mother is clearly doing more caretaking for the sleeping baby, and we will return later to this question of what it is that Japanese mothers do to sleeping babies. In State Five (as in State Two) the Japanese mother is again simply present more. It follows, therefore, that in State Six, the American infant is alone more when asleep than is the Japanese infant. The overall pattern of cultural difference for the three states in which the baby is asleep is confirmed by the significant canonical correlation (.58).

A further insight into the patterns of behavior represented in Table 5 comes from a different type of analysis that we are in the process of applying to the basic data. Because the 800 observations follow along in regular sequence over the data sheets, it is possible to define various kinds of "episodes" that have a definite beginning and ending. From this type of analysis, we know that caretaking for the American mother is largely an "in" and "out" affair. When she is in the room with the infant she is usually doing active caretaking, and upon finishing this she goes out of the room. The Japanese mother, although not engaged in active caretaking any greater amount of the time, is passively present in the room with the infant to a greater extent. This behavior of the Japanese mothers in our sample is not due to a shortage of other rooms into which to go (see footnote 18), but is again more a matter of style of caretaking.

We turn now to a consideration of what is going on in the various states, as measured by the dependent variables for infant and caretaker behavior. By definition, nothing is happening in States Five and Six beyond their occurrence, and we will, therefore, confine the discussion to States One through Four.

Analyses by States

As can be seen in Table 6 and 7, which give the results for infant and caretaker behaviors in State One, when the baby is awake and the mother is doing caretaking, the general picture is mainly a more sharply focused version of that obtained from the analysis of the total observations. Once again, culture proves to be the most interesting independent variable, although there are a few findings by sex of infant, and occupation of father.[38] Let us discuss the latter findings before turning to the analysis by culture.

In Tables 6 and 7 there is only one finding by sex of infant, and this is that boy babies play with toys more than girl babies. Upon inspection of the intra-cultural analyses, however, this turns out to be solely an American finding. In the intra-American analysis, boy babies play significantly more with toys, and, in addition, American mothers show significantly more affection to boy babies. These findings hint at the possibility that the American mother does, in some ways, treat her boy baby differently from her girl baby. In the Japanese data this is clearly not the case, and there are no findings by sex of infant in the intra-Japanese analysis.

By father's occupation there is one finding in Tables 6 and 7: Caretakers in independent business families rock their infants more than caretakers in salaried families. This finding proves to be solely an intra-Japanese finding, and there are no findings for infant or caretaker behaviors by father's occupation in the intra-American analysis. The intra-Japanese analysis shows that mothers in independent business families rock their babies more, but that mothers in salaried families look at their babies more and perform other care for them more. This contrast by type of family between rocking and looking at suggests that the mother in the salaried family is beginning to give up some aspects of traditional Japanese child care, and is moving toward what she considers a "modern" kind of care.

Turning to the analysis by culture in State One, the similarities and differences in behavior for Japanese and American infants and mothers are much the same as those described earlier for the total observations. For infants in State One, it can be seen in Table 6 that there is no difference in the variable of all food—that is, in the total intake of nutritive substances. In contrast to the analysis by total observations, however, Japanese babies in State One suck more on breast or bottle than do American babies.[39] Also in contrast to the total observations, there are no significant differences in "finger or pacifier" and "unhappy vocal" in State One, probably because mothers in both cultures are, by definition in this state, present and doing caretaking.

As can be seen in Table 7, the findings on similarities in caretaker behavior in State One are almost a duplicate of those for total observations. There are no significant differences in the proportion of time that mothers in both cultures devote to the following activities: "feeds," "diapers," "dresses," "pats or touches," "other care," "affections," and "talks to." Thus, in the more sharply focused situation in State One, where the mother is doing caretaking for an awake infant, once again the similarities in the behavior of the infants in the two cultures are centered on biological needs, and the similarities for the mothers lie in basic caretaking for these needs.

The differences in the behavior of infants and caretakers in State One are also quite clear and in line with the results from the total observations. As can be seen in Table 6, the American infant is more happily vocal (as well as definitely more totally vocal) and is more active, and more engaged in play—specifically with his hand or other object. In State One the Japanese infant is greater only in sucking on breast or bottle. And, as can be seen in Table 7, the American mother is doing more positioning of, looking at, and chatting with her infant, while the Japanese mother is doing more playing with, lulling, carrying, and rocking of her infant.

A particularly interesting and suggestive finding concerning cultural differences in the style of communication between mother and baby emerges from the correlational analyses of the data in State One. In each culture, the caretaker's chatting to infant shows a strong patterning of correlations with other variables,[40] but the key difference is that the American mother's "chats" is significantly correlated with the infant's "happy vocal" (.66) and not with his "unhappy vocal" (.29), whereas the opposite is true for the Japanese mother's "chats," which is significantly correlated with the infant's "unhappy vocal" (.44) and not with his "happy vocal" (.30). Apparently, the mother's chatting to infant serves a different purpose in each culture, and probably also serves to reinforce the happy vocalization of the American infant, and the unhappy vocalization of the Japanese infant. The American mother would appear to be using chatting as a means of stimulating, and responding to, her infant's happy vocals. The Japanese mother, however, would appear to be using chatting to soothe and quiet her infant, and to decrease his unhappy vocals. In support of the latter point, it should be noted that the Japanese mother's chatting is significantly correlated with "lulls" (.40), but this is not so for the American mother (where the correlation is only .14).

The preceding line of thought receives further confirmation from the patterning of the correlations associated with "lulls" in each culture. The American mother's lulling is only significantly correlated with one other variable—"rocks" (.42). On the other hand, the Japanese mother's lulling shows a strong pattern, and is significantly correlated with "total vocal" (.61), "unhappy vocal" (.65), "active" (.38), "baby plays" (.64), "toy" (.63), "pats or touches" (.44), "plays with" (.67), "affections" (.57), "looks at"

(.49), "talks to" (.74), "chats" (.40), "in arms" (.68), and "rocks" (.57). At the least, this pattern suggests that those Japanese mothers who do more lulling, carrying, and rocking, have babies who are more vocal, active, and playing. In future work with the data, we plan to explore further the context of communication between caretakers and infants in the two cultures by making use of the sequential nature of our observations in an analysis of "vocal episodes."

In conclusion of the discussion of State One, it should be noted that the canonical correlations in Tables 6 and 7 for the effect of culture on infant and caretaker behavior are significant, whereas those for father's occupation and sex of infant are not.

States Two and Three, in which the infant is awake and the caretaker is either passively present (Table 8) or absent (Table 9), can be discussed more summarily because the major results are variations on an already familiar pattern of infant behavior. In both states, culture is the most meaningful independent variable, and sex of infant and father's occupation are of minor importance. Both of these states are of particular interest because the infant is behaving in them without direct stimulation from the caretaker. Because the patterns of behavior are so familiar, however, we believe the infants are behaving the way they do in each culture on the basis of what they have already learned from their caretakers.

In State Two (see Table 8),[41] in which the infant is awake and the caretaker is passively present, the effect of culture on infant behavior shows the familiar pattern: The American infant is more active and more engaged in play, whereas the Japanese infant is more unhappily vocal. The canonical correlation is significant for culture, but not for the other two independent variables.[42]

In State Three (see Table 9),[43] in which the infant is awake and alone, the effect of culture on infant behavior shows the same pattern: The American infant is more happily vocal and active, and plays more, whereas the Japanese infant is only more unhappily vocal. And again, the canonical correlation is significant only for culture.[44]

State Four, as indicated in Table 10, presents us with the interesting question of what mothers are doing to sleeping babies.[45] There are no general findings by sex of infant or father's occupation.[46] The effect of culture, however, is strong, and in Table 10 it can be seen that American mothers are proportionately greater in looking at sleeping babies, but Japanese mothers are greater in the feeding, dressing, giving other care, carrying, and rocking of sleeping babies. From our beginning analysis by "episodes" over the observation sheets, we know that the pace of the Japanese mother is more leisurely. She tends to continue her caretaking activities after her baby has fallen asleep more than does the American mother. The proportionately greater amount of time spent looking at the baby for the American mother occurs because she has left her sleeping baby alone, and then returns periodically to the door of the room to glance at him.

Specifically with reference to feeding, the Japanese mother is more content to continue sitting, holding the baby who has fallen asleep with the nipple of the breast or bottle in his mouth. By definition then, in this situation, the mother is still scored as feeding. The American mother, in contrast to the "slow motion" feeling in the Japanese situation, is more brisk, and usually gets up and leaves once her baby has fallen asleep.[47]

A comparison of the canonical correlations for States One through Four is an illuminating way of summarizing the results of the analyses in this section. As indicated earlier, the canonical correlation shows the magnitude of the effect of the independent variables on the entire set of dependent variables for infant behavior (Tables 6, 8, and 9) and caretaker behavior (Tables 7 and 10). In States One through Four none of the canonical correlations is significant for sex of infant or father's occupation, and all of the canonical correlations are significant for culture.

We have three chances to examine the effect of culture on the behavior of awake infants—in State One, when the infants are in interaction with their mothers, and in States Two and Three, when the mothers are either passively present or absent. Although all three of the canonical correlations are significant, the effect of culture is greater when the infants are in interaction with their mothers than when they are not. The highest correlation (.84) occurs in State One, when the mothers are doing caretaking, and accounts for 71 percent of the variance in the general behavior of the infants; when the mothers are only passively present, in State Two, the correlation (.67) is lower and accounts for 45 percent of the variance in the behavior of the infants; when the infants are alone in State Three, the correlation (.60) drops a bit more and accounts, for 36 percent of the variance in behavior. Thus, it would seem that culture definitely does make a difference in the behavior of infants, and it makes more of a difference, as would be expected, when the mothers are directly engaged with their babies.

Since the mothers are adult members of their cultures, while

Table. 8. Adjusted Mean Percentages, in State Two, of Infant Behavior: By Culture, Father's Occupation, and Sex of Infant

| | Adjusted Mean Percentages | | | | | | | | |
| | Culture | | | Father's Occupation | | | Sex of Infant | | |
Categories of Infant Behavior	Japa-nese	Ameri-can	Corre-lation†	Salaried	Inde-pendent	Corre-lation†	Male	Female	Corre-lation†
Breast or Bottle	0	0	.14	0	0	.14	0	0	.11
All Food	0	0	.09	0	0	.11	0	0	.12
Finger or Pacifier	17	20	.08	**14**	**24**	**.29**	15	22	.19
Total Vocal	22	20	.05	19	23	.15	21	20	.02
Unhappy	**14**	**7**	**.28**	**7**	**16**	**.32**	10	12	.12
Happy	8	11	.21	10	8	.18	11	7	.22
Active	**15**	**23**	**.31**	19	18	.06	18	19	.02
Baby Plays	**23**	**45**	**.40***	39	28	.20	37	31	.13
Toy	**12**	**26**	**.31**	22	15	.16	22	15	.16
Hand	6	8	.06	9	5	.12	7	7	.01
Other Object	6	11	.26	8	8	.00	8	9	.04
Canonical Correlation‡			**.67****			.46			.40
Total Cases	30	30		35	25		33	27	

†See footnote in Table 3 for explanation of this partial correlation. The means and correlations for all findings significant at $p < 0.05$ are printed in boldface. One asterisk (*) indicates $p < 0.01$, two asterisks (**) indicate $p < 0.001$. Mean percentages of less than one-half of a percent are indicated as zero.
‡See footnote in Table 3.

Table 9. Adjusted Mean Percentages, in State Three, of Infant Behavior: By Culture, Father's Occupation, and Sex of Infant

Categories of Infant Behavior	Adjusted Mean Percentages								
	Culture			Father's Occupation			Sex of Infant		
	Japanese	American	Correlation†	Salaried	Independent	Correlation†	Male	Female	Correlation†
Breast or Bottle	0	1	.10	1	0	.09	0	1	.14
All Food	0	1	.16	0	0	.03	0	1	.08
Finger or Pacifier	26	23	.09	26	22	.11	**20**	**30**	**.27**
Total Vocal	30	29	.02	27	33	.19	33	25	.26
Unhappy	**24**	**14**	**.31**	17	21	.15	20	17	.12
Happy	**7**	**13**	**.39***	10	11	.07	**12**	**8**	**.27**
Active	**18**	**30**	**.34**	22	28	.21	26	22	.10
Baby Plays	**21**	**50**	**.53****	37	33	.08	40	30	.22
Toy	**10**	**32**	**.46****	22	21	.03	26	15	.26
Hand	6	6	.01	7	4	.18	6	5	.07
Other Object	**5**	**11**	**.29**	8	8	.01	7	9	.07
Canonical Correlation‡			**.60**			.39			.47
Total Cases#	29	30		35	24		33	26	

†See footnote in Table 3 for explanation of this partial correlation. The means and correlations for all findings significant at $p < 0.05$ are printed in boldface. One asterisk (*) indicates $p < 0.01$, two asterisks (**) indicate $p < 0.001$. Mean percentages of less than one-half of a percent are indicated as zero.

‡See footnote in Table 3.

#One infant (Japanese, Independent, Female) was never in the condition of State Three.

Table 10. Adjusted Mean Percentages, in State Four, of Caretaker Behavior: By Culture, Father's Occupation, and Sex of Infant

Categories of Caretaker Behavior	Culture			Adjusted Mean Percentages Father's Occupation			Sex of Infant		
	Japanese	American	Correlation†	Salaried	Independent	Correlation†	Male	Female	Correlation†
Feeds	**13**	**0**	**.44***	6	6	.02	7	6	.04
Diapers	1	0	.19	0	0	.16	0	0	.03
Dresses	**1**	**0**	**.34**	1	1	.03	0	1	.11
Positions	5	2	.18	5	2	.20	4	4	.03
Pats or Touches	12	6	.21	10	7	.11	10	7	.09
Other Care	**14**	**6**	**.31**	10	9	.05	9	11	.11
Plays with	0	0	.01	0	0	.18	0	0	.18
Affections	0	0	.01	0	0	.06	0	0	.13
Looks at	68	**98**	**.53****	87	79	.18	84	83	.01
Talks to	4	5	.04	5	3	.11	7	1	.23
Chats	1	5	.17	4	1	.14	5	0	.18
Lulls	3	0	.25	1	2	.01	2	0	.16
In Arms	**46**	**9**	**.52****	26	29	.06	24	31	.11
Rocks	**11**	**3**	**.28**	7	6	.03	9	4	.20
Canonical Correlation‡			**.78****			.49			.47
Total Cases#	26	28		32	22		30	24	

†See footnote in Table 3 for explanation of this partial correlation. The means and correlations for all findings significant at $p < 0.05$ are printed in boldface. One asterisk (*) indicates $p < 0.01$, two asterisks (**) indicate $p < 0.001$. Mean percentages of less than one-half of a percent are indicated as zero.

‡See footnote in Table 4.

#Six caretakers were never in the condition of State Four. Using the obvious abbreviations, these 6 cases have the following classification: JSF, JSM, JIF, JIM, ASM, AIF.

the babies are only very junior members of theirs, it seems sensible that the canonical correlations for the effect of culture on caretaker behavior in States One (when the baby is awake) and Four (when he is asleep) should be more similar. The correlation (.85) in State One accounts for 72 percent of the variance in caretaker behavior, and the correlation (.78) in State Four accounts for 61 percent of the variance.

DISCUSSION

We feel that the most parsimonious explanation of our findings is that a great deal of cultural learning has taken place by three-to-four months of age, and that our babies have learned by this time to be Japanese and American babies in relation to the expectations of their mothers concerning their behavior. Nevertheless, we are aware that some of our findings might be thought of as due to group genetic differences, or to group differences in rates of physiological development. These questions cannot be answered with finality within the limits of our sample, but we did what checking we could on biological dimensions in our data that might be related to the infant's physical activity and total vocalization, as these are two central areas of difference between the cultures. A thorough check of the data (by Spearman's rank-order correlation) for the variables of "active" and "total vocal," both in terms of all 60 cases and of the 30 cases in each culture considered separately, did not reveal any significant differences in the relation of either variable to the independent variables of birth weight of infant, age in days of infant at time of observation, age of mother at time of birth of infant, or type of feeding of infant (in terms of breast, bottle, or mixed feeding).[48]

There is considerable experimental and observational evidence, on the other hand, that supports our conclusion that infants have learned by three-to-four months of age to respond in culturally appropriate ways. For example, Weisberg has shown experimentally that the vocalizing rate of three-month-old American infants can be increased (operantly conditioned) by the social consequences provided by the experimenter (briefly touching the infant's chin, smiling, and talking to him), but not by nonsocial consequences (the ringing of a door chime), nor by the mere presence of an inactive adult. This experimental result closely approximates the results obtained in the comparison of the observed behavior of American and Japanese caretakers in our study.

Our results on activity, playing, and vocalizing are also reflected in a study by Rubenstein of maternal attentiveness and exploratory behavior in American infants. In her study, maternal attentiveness (as defined by the number of times the mother was observed to look at, touch, hold, or talk to her baby) was timesampled in the homes of 44 five-month-old infants who were later examined at six months for exploratory behavior. Three groups of babies were distinguished at five months of age as receiving high, low, or medium attentiveness. At six months of age, the high-attentiveness group significantly exceeded the low-attentiveness group in looking at, manipulating, and vocalizing to a novel stimulus presented alone, and the high-attentiveness group exceeded both other groups in looking at and manipulating novel stimuli in preference to familiar ones. Rubenstein interprets her data as suggesting that maternal attentiveness facilitates exploratory behavior in the infant. We would agree on the basis of our results, if we conceive of attentiveness mainly in terms of stimulating the infant to activity, play, and vocalization, as appears to be the pattern for the American mothers in contrast to the Japanese mothers.

The observational study by Moss in the homes of 30 firstborn American infants equally divided by sex, at one and three months of age, is, in its latter phase, almost exactly the same as ours. Using a series of dependent variables for infant and caretaker behaviors, he made observations by a time-sampling procedure, using a unit of one minute in which behavior could occur or not occur, over eight hours, resulting in a total of 480 observations per case. Many of the variables used by Moss were defined in almost exactly the same way as our, and by converting his data and our American data to percentages of total observations, a direct comparison is possible. When this is done, either for the total samples, or separately by sex, the results of the comparisons (by means of a Mann-Whitney U test) show no significant differences for the infant behaviors of "awake," "finger or pacifier," "active," or "unhappy vocal." The data for the infants in the Moss study on his variable of "vocalizes" (which includes our variable of "happy vocal" plus "neutral" vocalizations such as grunts) significantly exceed those for our variable of "happy vocal." Equally, for caretaker behaviors, there are no differences in the two studies on the variables of "feeds," "looks at," "talks to," "in arms," and "rocks." It is therefore fairly obvious that much the same results would be achieved in a comparison of infant or caretaker behaviors in America and Japan, whether we used our American data or used the data from the Moss study.

Finally, we wish to draw attention to the detailed study by Arai, Ishikawa, and Toshima of the development of Japanese children from one month to 36 months of age, as measured by the Gesell norms established on American children.[49] The Japanese investigators used a sample of 776 children in the Tōhoku area (the northern part of the main island of Japan near the city of Sendai), equally divided across the age range of one to 36 months. In the areas of motor development and language development, which are closest to the variables in our study of physical activity and total vocalization, the findings of the Japanese study were that the Japanese infants matched the American norms in both respects in the age period from 4 to 16 weeks, but after that there was a steady decline from the norms in the Japanese scores for both motor and language development from 4 months to 36 months of age. In general across the entire age range, Arai, Ishikawa, and Toshima say: "For children having a developmental quotient between 90– 119,... motor behavior is 71.5 percent of the norms, social behavior is 70.4 percent, and language aptitude (the weakest behavior) is 66.0 percent."[50]

It seems likely from the results of this study in the Tōhoku area of Japan that there are no differences in motor or verbal behavior of Japanese and American infants during the first several months of life. If this is so, it strongly supports our contention that these are learned more than genetic or maturational differences.

CONCLUSION

In this report of work with Japanese and American middle-class mothers and their firstborn, three-to-four-month-old infants, our analysis quickly revealed that of the three independent variables considered, culture is by far the most important source of difference in the behavior of these infants and caretakers. This is followed by father's occupation, which is important in the Japanese situation but not in the American. Sex of infant, at least at three-to-four-months of age, is of little relevance.

Reviewing our findings in reverse order of importance, there is a hint, stemming from the intra-cultural analyses, that American mothers may give somewhat more attention, particularly of an affectionate sort, to their boy babies, but this is a tenuous finding in the American data, and there are no findings by sex of infant in the Japanese data.

The analysis by father's occupation produced more results, but all of these, upon further examination, proved to be important only for the Japanese data. In the Japanese independent business families the infant is awake more, and the caretaker is present more, and talks to, lulls, carries, and rocks the infant more than in the salaried families. In contrast, the caretaker in the salaried families is only greater in looking at the infant when compared with the caretaker in the independent business families.

In the single matter of looking at her infant more frequently, the mother in the salaried Japanese family seems more like the American mother, who, in the general cross-cultural analysis, looks at her infant more often. But the American mother also chats with her infant frequently, whereas the Japanese salaried mother is more silent than the Japanese independent business mother. If, as is reasonable, we consider the salaried mother in Japan to be more "modern," then, in her move toward modernity, she seems to have substracted from traditional ways of caretaking rather than to have added anything new. If anything, the independent business mother in Japan is closer to the American mother in the extent of her direct involvement with her infant. Thus, with regard to the relation of child care to social change, there would not seem to be any simple connection between a move toward modernity for the family in general and a shift toward Western patterns of child care.

The preceding findings, although of interest, become pale in the light of the strong findings of cultural differences. American infants are more happily vocal, more active, and more exploratory of their bodies and their physical environment than are Japanese infants. Directly related to these findings, the American mother is in greater vocal interaction with her infant and stimulates him to greater physical activity and exploration. The Japanese mother, in contrast, is in greater bodily contact with her infant and soothes him toward physical quiescence and passivity with regard to his environment. Moreover, these patterns of behavior, so early learned by the infant, are in line with the differing expectations for later behavior in the two cultures as the child grows to be an adult.

For now, we believe we have arrived at distinctive patterns of learned behavior for infants in Japan and America. Analysis of our data for the first 20 of the same cases in each culture at two-and-a-half and six years of age will establish whether these patterns persist and jell in the behavior of the children we are studying. Our prediction is that this will happen, because of the strong external pressures for conformity and the strong internal pressures toward being accepted favorably by one's fellows, in any culture.

If these distinctive patterns of behavior are well on the way to being learned by three-to-four months of age, and if they continue over the life span of the person, then there are very likely to be important areas of difference in emotional response in people in one culture when compared with those in another. Such differences are not easily subject to conscious control and, largely out of awareness, they accent and color human behavior. These differences add a zest to life and interpersonal encounters, but they can also add to bewilderment and antagonism when people try to communicate across the emotional barriers of cultures.

We hope that our analysis helps to illuminate the reasons for some of these difficulties in cross-cultural communication despite the seeming increase in similarity between countries in the modern world. One may wish, on moral and practical grounds, for greater real understanding by people of each other across cultures, but it is a moot point whether the world would be a better place in which to live if such cultural differences were to be obliterated.

NOTES

1. In work with our colleagues on the symptoms of Japanese and American psychiatric patients, we find both social-class similarities and cultural differences in the characteristics of patients in the two countries. See Schooler and Caudill; and Caudill and Schooler. An especially pertinent example also comes from the work of Pearlin and Kohn; in a comparative study in Italy and the U.S. of parents' values concerning their children's behavior, they demonstrate that middle-class parents in both countries are more likely to value the child's self-direction, while working-class parents in both countries place a greater emphasis on the childs conformity to external proscription; but equally, and from the same data, they show that regardless of social class, American parents are more likely than Italian parents to value happiness, popularity, and consideration, while Italian parents more than American parents tend to value manners, obedience, and seriousness.

2. We predicted that the Japanese mother in the small-business family would spend more time with her infant, would carry him more, and in general would be more attentive than the Japanese mother in the salaried family; and, because of the greater attention, we believed that the infant in the small-business family would be more responsive than the infant in the salaried family. Detailed information on the differences between these two occupational ways of life can be found in Dore; Vogel; and Plath.

3. The work of Miller and Swanson is very suggestive as to differences in child rearing in entrepreneurial and bureaucratic families, but their study is subject to some criticism on methodological grounds.

4. Even in the latter areas, however, the differences in emphasis are still evident. See Nakane.

5. See Caudill and Scarr; and Caudill and Doi.

6. See Reischauer, esp. Part III, "The Japanese Character"; and Nakamura, esp. Ch. 35 and Ch. 36.

7. See Caudill, 1962. Specifically with reference to Japanese reticence, Fisher and Yoshida comment upon their analysis of the nature of speech according to Japanese proverbs as follows: "Basically, the most ubiquitous lesson about speech in Japanese proverbs is, 'Shut up'" (p. 36). For example, they cite the following proverbs: *Kuchi o mamoru kame no gotoku su* ("One treats one's mouth like a guarded jar"); *Kuchi wa motte kuubeshi, motte iu bekarazu* ("Mouths are to eat with, not to speak with").

8. These patterns of sleeping are not a function of "overcrowding" in the Japanese home, but rather are a matter of choice, as is shown in Caudill and Plath. Much the same point can be made concerning bathing. Starting at approximately the beginning of the second month of life, the Japanese infant is held in the arms of the mother or another adult while they bathe together in the deep bathtub (*furo*) at home or at the neighborhood public bath (*sentō*), and this pattern of shared bathing will continue for a Japanese child until he is about ten years of age, and often much longer (see Vogel, pp. 229–232). In contrast, the American mother seldom bathes with an infant; rather, she gives him a bath from outside of the tub, and she communicates with him verbally and by positioning his body.

9. Although Japan is at one extreme in the length of time spent co-sleeping in a two-generation group, America is probably at the other extreme in this, and in many matters concerned with child rearing. Indeed, compared with the rest of the world, family life in the United States is in many ways rather peculiar. See Stephens, esp. Ch. 8.

10. This hypothesis concerning the greater mutual dependency of mother and child in Japan will become more pertinent as we analyze in the future our great wealth of data on children in the two countries at $2\frac{1}{2}$ and 6 years of age. But it is symbolized at birth by the widespread custom in Japan for the hospital to present the infant's navel cord (*heso no o*) to the mother upon discharge. The cord is sprinkled with preservative powder, and placed in a neat wooden box which is tied with ribbon. This is, of course, not too different from the custom of some American parents of saving locks of hair, baby shoes, and other objects as mementos of their child's infancy. The difference lies in the "directness" of the relation of the symbol to its meaning in Japan, and to the history of the symbolic object thereafter. In Japan the cord of the new infant is only one of many such cords of other family members that may be kept in the home, either in the household Buddhist altar or in a safe place in a bureau drawer. Custom varies from region to region, and household to household, as to the subsequent disposition of the cord. If the infant is a girl, she may be given the cord to take with her to her husband's household upon marriage; or the mother may retain the cords of all of her children, and these may be placed with her body in the coffin upon her death. In our interviews with the 20 Japanese mothers whose children we followed up at $2\frac{1}{2}$ years of age, we inquired about whether they had received their first child's navel cord and what meaning this had for them. We did not ask similar questions of our American mothers as it seemed inappropriate to do so. Of the 19 Japanese mothers from whom we have relevant information, 17 had received their cords from the hospital. Of the two mothers who had not, one was sad about this as she was keeping her own cord with that of her second child, which she had received since the second child was born in a different hospital. All of the 17 mothers who had received the cords kept them safely, and

8 mothers said the cord had real meaning for them; the other 9 mothers said that the cord only represented an old custom, but they usually added, "... but you can't just throw it away."

11. The age of marriage in Japan is increasing, and has been consistently later than that in the United States for at least the past 35 years. See Blood; Taeuber, p. 227; and Japan, Bureau of Statistics, Table 3, pp. 72–73.

12. In the Japanese sample, 12 of the fathers are college graduates in professional or managerial positions (8 are salaried, and 4 are independent), and 18 of the fathers are college or high school graduates in white-collar or highly skilled trade jobs (7 are salaried and 11 are independent). In the American sample, 14 of the fathers are college graduates in professional or managerial positions (10 are salaried, and 4 are independent), and 16 of the fathers are college or high school graduates in white-collar or highly skilled trade jobs (10 are salaried and 6 are independent). Of the Japanese mothers, 7 are college graduates, 19 are high school or technical school graduates, and 4 have less than a high school education. Of the American mothers, 9 are college graduates, 20 are high school or technical school graduates, and 1 has less than a high school education. In devising procedures for estimating social-class position, we made use of the work of Hollingshead on American populations and modified it to approximate the Japanese situation along lines suggested by the work of Odaka. See: Hollingshead and Redlich, particularly Appendix 2, "The Index of Social Position," pp. 387–397; Nihon Shakai Gakkai Chōsa Iinkai Hen; Odaka and Nishihira; Odaka; and Ramsey and Smith.

13. We wish to thank Dr. Hirotoshi Hashimoto, Dr. L. Takeo Doi, and Dr. Takajiro Yamamoto at St. Luke's International Hospital; Dr. Shigeki Takeuchi at Tsukiji Maternity Hospital; Dr. Fumio Nakamura, Dr. Tsuneo Nakamura, and Dr. Shigeo Imagi at the Kyoto Prefectural Hospital; and Dr. Emilie Black, Dr. Carol Pincock, Dr. Morris I. Michael, and Dr. Stanley I. Wolf in the Washington, D. C., area. We are indebted to Mrs. Seiko Notsuki of the St. Luke's International Hospital for carrying out the interviews and observations with the Japanese cases, and to Mrs. Mieko I. Caudill for her constant help in all stages of the research.

14. Because the pediatricians selected the bulk of our cases for us and had already received a positive response from the mothers before we met them, there were no refusals to participate in the study after we had made our contact with the mothers. It seems likely, however, that our mothers were a bit more adventuresome than most, but this would be true in both countries. In general, the mothers were pleased that their babies had been chosen for observation, and that they could be of help in a scientific way; on the whole, however, the mothers did not show any particular intellectual interest in our work. After the observations were completed, we invited the mothers to ask questions about the research, but if there were any questions, these usually simply concerned the mothers' wish to know how the behavior of her child compared with that of other children in our study.

15. In both cultures we gave the families copies of the best pictures we had taken of the infant and the mother during our work, and also often brought a toy for the infant. In addition in Japan, as is customary, we gave a modest amount of money in a white envelope suitably inscribed with the message that it be used in some way for the child's enjoyment.

16. An illustration of the original observation sheet may be found in a

preliminary report of this research, given at the Ninth International Seminar on Family Research in Tokyo in 1965. See Caudill and Weinstein.

17. We are not saying that only adults can be caretakers of infants, but we did not expect to find many older children acting as caretakers of young babies in our study because all of the infants are firstborn and do not have older siblings. In the actual observations on the 60 cases, there were only a few times when an infant was with older neighborhood children without an adult caretaker also being present. In these few situations we scored the infant as alone—that is, without adult supervision.

18. The rule that a caretaker is present even if in an adjoining room was made because of the nature of housing in the two countries. In Japan, the interior walls separating most rooms are usually made of sliding doors (*fusuma*) that are frequently kept in the open position (resulting in an opening which is half of the total wall space for the most usual four-door wall) during the day. In America, there frequently is no wall at all in the L-shaped living room and dining area. In either country, an ordinary door can, of course, be left open between rooms. In Japan it is easier for a caretaker to be outside and still "present", even though the baby is inside because the exterior walls of much of the standard Japanese house are made of sliding latticed panels covered with paper (*shōji*) which are frequently kept open during the day. At night these panels are closed, and in addition sliding solid wood doors on separate tracks (*amado*) are locked into place just beyond the *shōji*. In our judgment, based on the floor plans we drew of the housing of each family, the American families probably had on the average more total floor space, but the Japanese families had on the average more rooms. This is because in the two samples of fairly recently married couples, the Americans tend to live in apartments (21 of the 30 families), and the Japanese, in houses (22 of the 30 families).

19. On the original observation sheet this variable was represented by two additive variables: (1) being carried on the caretaker's back, and (2) being in the caretaker's arms or lap. The specific variable "on caretaker's back" was initially included because, in general, young Japanese children are often carried there. As we found out, somewhat belatedly, the Japanese infant at three-to-four months is not very frequently carried on the back because the mother feels the infant's neck muscles are not yet strong enough, although this becomes common a month or so later and varies by social class and occupational style of life. The infant was carried on the back during observations in only 3 of our Japanese cases, and we have therefore recorded these data as "in arms or lap." When the infant was not on the caretaker's back or in arms or lap, we originally recorded what sort of receptacle he was in (in bed, in bath, in infant seat, and in others place—such as playpen or on a *zabuton*, that is, a flat cushion on the floor). These variables did not prove to be very useful. As a subclassification of "in bed" and "in other place" we scored whether the baby was lying on his stomach or back. It is of interest that the Japanese babies were almost always on their backs, whereas the opposite tended to be true for the American babies. The reason for the difference, especially when the baby is asleep, is that the Japanese mother has been told that the baby might smother if placed on his stomach, and the American mother has been told that he might choke if left on his back.

20. At the time of our observations, 18 Japanese and only 5 American

mothers were continuing breast feeding. In many of these cases, particularly among Japanese mothers, there was a combination of breast and bottle feeding.

21. Only 6 of the Japanese mothers gave their infants semi-solid or harder food during the observations, whereas 21 of the American mothers did so.

22. Although it is a minor matter in terms of number of observations, the giving of liquid vitamins to the infant is scored under bottle if the vitamins are given by dropper, and under food if the vitamins are given by spoon. The action of the caretaker in giving the vitamins is always scored under "feeds."

23. All of the mothers in both cultures did some talking to other persons, including the observer, during the observations. The amount of this is almost the same in each culture. Using an analysis of variance, the mean number of observations of talking to other persons is 53 for Japanese caretakers and 55 for American caretakers ($F = 0.7$, $df = 1/52$, not significant). The targets of the talk, however, were in some respects different: Japanese mothers did more talking to tradesmen coming to the door, and American mothers did nore talking on the telephone to friends and to their husbands at the office.

24. During the observations, 4 of the Japanese and 16 of the American mothers bathed their infants, with an average of 22 observations in the Japanese cases, and 17 observations in the American cases. Using these data in an analysis of variance over the total sample of 60 cases, the mean number of observations is 3 for the Japanese and 9 for the American cases ($F = 5.6$, $df = 1/52$, $p < 0.05$). These numbers, however, have little meaning considering the difference in the customary time of day for bathing, and the qualitative difference in the context in which bathing takes place (see footnotes 8 and 25).

25. We believe this was a wise choice, particularly because the differences between Japanese and American family life in such more dramatic events as bathing and sleeping (see footnote 8) are so pronounced as scarcely to require detailed observational study. Specifically in our samples, as determined from the interviews with the mothers, all of the Japanese infants bathed together with their mother or another caretaker (usually the father or the father's mother if she was living in the household); and all of the Japanese infants co-slept with both parents, who had no intention of terminating this arrangement for several years. All of the American infants were bathed from the outside of the tub or bathinette by their mothers; 17 of the American infants slept alone in a separate room, while 13 infants slept in a crib in the parents' bedroom. In the latter cases, the young couple was living in an apartment with one bedroom, and without exception, each couple planned to move to a dwelling with two bedrooms so that the infant could have a separate room by the time he was one year old.

26. To illustrate, using the exact check the observers must agree, for example, that the caretaker looks at the infant in observation 24; using the contiguous check, there must be agreement by the observers either within observations 23 and 24 or within observations 24 and 25. The limits of the contiguous check are, obviously, foreshortened in observation 1 and in observation 40 of an observation sheet.

27. The computer program we used is called MANOVA, and is described in Dean J. Clyde, Elliot M. Cramer, and Richard J. Sherin, *Multivariate Statistical Programs,* Coral Gables, Fla., Biometric Laboratory, Univ. of Miami, 1966 (revisions issued Dec., 1967). On analysis of variance in

general, see Blalock. We earlier did a separate and complete analysis of the data by use of a nonparametric statistical technique, the Mann-Whitney U test. Such a technique does not, however, easily allow for the testing of one independent variable while controlling for the effect of others, and the testing of interactions is not feasible. The results of the earlier analysis were essentially similar to those presented here, but much less controlled and refined. See Caudill and Weinstein.

28. We also tested for all possible three- and two-way interactions of the independent variables. Two-way interactions were controlled in terms of the effect of the three independent variables considered separately and the effect of all other two-way interactions. Three-way interactions were controlled in terms of the effect of the three independent variables considered separately and the effect of all two-way interactions.

29. The correlation coefficient used here has the utility that it can be determined by computer through use of an option in the MANOVA program (see footnote 27). Elliot M. Cramer has suggested another correlation coefficient which is the square root of the ratio of (a) the sum of the squared deviations from the mean attributable to the independent variable in question, to (b) the total sum of the squared deviations. Two other correlation coefficients, *eta* and *epsilon,* might be used. Both are derived from the F ratio in conjunction with the degrees of freedom between and within cells. *Epsilon* is the more conservative of the two measures, and is to be used in evaluating the results obtained from small samples, such as are used in the present research. The formulas for these measures, and an excellent discussion of the need for an estimate of the magnitude as well as the significance of an effect, can be found in Cohen. In practical terms, if an effect is a strong one, there is little difference between the four measures in our data. For example, in Table 3 for the dependent variable of "baby plays," the effect of culture results in a correlation of .50; Cramer's measure also gives a correlation of .50; the formula for *eta* gives a correlation of .51; and the formula for *epsilon,* a correlation of .49. In all of these cases, when the correlation is squared, the amount of variance attributable to culture is about 25 percent of the total variance.

30. In technical language, the canonical correlation is a multiple correlation of one or a set of independent variables to a set of dependent variables. More precisely, it is the maximum correlation between linear functions of the two sets of variables. See Cooley and Lohnes.

31. In all of our analyses by states, we did an analysis of variance both of frequencies (ignoring time in state) and percentages. Obviously, however, the percentage analysis provides more pertinent information for this article because it answers the question of, relative to time in state, what the infant or caretaker is doing in terms of the dependent variables. One difficulty that may arise in doing analysis of variance with percentages is that the mean and variance for such binomial data are not independent. To meet this situation, especially in the case of percentages derived from small frequencies, it is appropriate to use an arc-sine transformation to gain independence of mean and variance. We did a thorough check of our data by comparing the results when using the arc-sine transformation with the results when using straight percentages. In no case did the use of the arc-sine transformation result in making a significant finding become not significant or vice versa. We have therefore presented our results (in Tables 6–10) in terms of straight percentage analyses because this procedure involves less manipulation of the basic data. See Snedecor, pp. 445–448.

32. An examination of the interactions of the independent variables in the analyses of total observations produced very little of interest. There are no significant three-way interactions for the 12 infant or 15 caretaker dependent variables. There is one significant two-way interaction out of 36 tests for the infant variables, and there are two significant two-way interactions out of 45 tests for the caretaker variables. Because of the large number of tests, these findings could easily be due to chance alone. We have no ready explanation for the two-way finding on "unhappy vocal," which shows an interaction between father's occupation (S or I) and sex of infant (M or F): SM 56, SF 40, IM 56, IF 77 ($F = 4.8$, $df = 1/52$, $p < 0.05$). The finding on "lulls," which shows an interaction between culture (J or A) and father's occupation (S or I) is obviously an artifact that is better explained by a one-way finding in the intra-Japanese analysis, as indicated later in the text. The interaction is: JS 15, JI 34, AS 2, AI 3 ($F = 4.1$, $df = 1/52$, $p < 0.05$). The finding on "plays with" infant, which shows an interaction of culture and father's occupation, strikes us as more pertinent to the argument of this paper because it suggests that an independent occupational style of family life has a different meaning for child care in the two cultures, and is particularly distinctive in Japan, as will become evident from other results. The interaction on plays with infant is: JS 29, JI 51, AS 27, AI 15 ($F = 5.0$, $df = 1/52$, $p < 0.05$).

33. As indicated earlier, there was very little breast feeding among the American mothers, and, hence, "breast" and "bottle" were combined. As is to be expected, the finding on the variable of "breast" considered separately shows the Japanese infant to be greater, with a mean of 30, compared to the American infant with a mean of 3 ($F = 10.1$, $df = 1/52$, $p < 0.01$). On the other hand, "bottle" considered separately is not significantly different, although the Japanese mean of 37 is lower than the American mean of 51 ($F = 1.0$, $df = 1/52$, $p < 0.32$). When semisolid food is considered as a separate variable (see footnote 21), the American infant is greater, with a mean of 19 compared to a Japanese mean of 2 ($F = 16.2$, $df = 1/52$, $p < 0.001$).

34. We are particularly interested in the category of "active," and we thought that the greater occurrence of gross bodily movements among the American infants might be related to the difference in temperature in the homes, especially in the winter, in the two cultures. In general, we avoided doing observations during particularly hot or cold days—when the outside temperature was above 85 or below 45 degrees Fahrenheit. The temperature inside of the homes in Tokyo, Kyoto, and Washington, D. C., is about the same during the warmer months of May–October, but during the cooler months of November–April the temperature in the Japanese homes probably averages about five to ten degrees less than that maintained in the American homes. During the cooler months, Japanese infants wear more clothing and are under more covers than American infants. Fortunately, roughly half of the cases in each culture were observed during the warmer months. For the American infants, there is no difference between the active behavior of the cases observed during the cooler (a mean of 125 observations) and warmer (a mean of 128 observations) months (using a Mann-Whitney U test of the rank-order of the frequencies, $z = 0.18$, n.s.). For the Japanese infants, however, the cases observed during the warmer months (a mean of 65) are more active than those in the cooler months (a mean of 34) ($z = 2.1$, $p < 0.05$). Nevertheless, in the cross-cultural comparison of the infants observed only during the warmer months

the American babies are still the more active ($z = 3.0$, $p < 0.01$). Naturally, then, the American infants are also the more active ($z = 3.8$, $p = 0.001$) in the comparison of cases observed during the cooler months. It appears, therefore, that temperature of the home and heavier clothing make some difference, but not enough to account for the greater activity of the American infant.

35. The occurrence of behavior in the category of "finger or pacifier" appears to be related to breast versus bottle feeding in both cultures, although the Japanese infants are in general much lower in any sort of comparison. The clearest data on this question come from the comparison of those mothers who never breast fed versus those mothers who were feeding entirely by breast (no use of the bottle at all) at the time of observation. The 9 American infants who were never breast fed have an average of 196 observations in the category of "finger or pacifier," while the 4 American infants being fed entirely by breast have an average of 97 observations in this category. Among the Japanese cases, the 4 infants who were never breast fed have an average of 88 observations in the category of "finger or pacifier," while the 6 infants being entirely breast fed have an average of 42 observations in this category. Thus, there is roughly twice as much finger sucking by babies who have never been breast fed in both cultures, but the average for the Japanese babies fed entirely by bottle is lower than the average for the American babies fed entirely by breast. It seems unlikely, therefore, that the greater average number of observations for the American infant in the variable of "finger or pacifier" is due to differences in methods of feeding. It may be due, however, to the greater use of a pacifier by the American mother, who often puts this device into her child's mouth as she leaves the room. The Japanese mother, in contrast, makes very little use of a pacifier.

36. As indicated earlier, these are Pearsonian r correlations, and a correlation matrix using the 12 infant and 15 caretaker variables was made separately for each culture. With an N of 30, using a two-tailed test, a correlation of .361 is significant at less than 0.05, and a correlation of .463 is significant at less than 0.01.

37. We did a complete analysis of main effects and interactions for the three independent variables of culture, father's occupation, and sex of infant. There are no significant three- or two-way interactions. There are no findings for the main effects of sex of infant, and also there are no findings for sex in either of the intra-cultural analyses. There are several findings of main effects by father's occupation, but all of these are explained by the intra-Japanese analysis, and there are no findings in the intra-American analysis. The intra-Japanese findings by fathers' occupation are that caretakers in independent business families spend a greater amount of time in State One (doing caretaking when baby is awake) than do caretakers in salaried families; and that with regard to State Six (baby asleep, caretaker absent), caretakers in salaried families are absent more than those in independent business families.

38. An examination of the interactions in the analyses of the data for State One provided little of interest. No three-way interactions are significant for either infant or caretaker behaviors. Of the 33 possible two-way interactions for infant behaviors, only one is significant. This is a finding on "toy" showing an interaction between culture and sex: JM 8%, JF 7%, AM 12%, AF 4% ($F = 5.2$, $df = 1/52$, $p < 0.05$). Obviously, this is not a meaningful interaction since the difference occurs only in the American data as discussed in the text. Of the 42 possible two-way interactions for caretaker behaviors, only one is significant. This is a

finding on "looks at" showing an interaction between culture and father's occupation: JS 82%, JI 72%, AS 87%, AI 92% ($F = 4.7$, $df = 1/52$, $p < 0.05$). In the intra-Japanese analysis of "looks at" by father's occupation, caretakers in salaried families look at their infants significantly more than do caretakers in independent families; the comparable test in the intra-American analysis is not significant.

39. The separate analyses of variance on the component parts of the variable of "all food" in State One are as follows: On "breast," which, of course, is greater among the Japanese, the Japanese mean is 9% and the American mean is 1% ($F = 8.6$, $df = 1/52$, $p < 0.01$). On "bottle" there is no difference, just as there is not in the total observations. The Japanese mean in State One on "bottle" is 14% and the American mean is 13% ($F = 0.4$, $df = 1/52$, $p < 0.55$). On the variable of "food," where, of course, American babies are given more semi-solid food, the Japanese mean is 1% and the American mean is 6% ($F = 12.4$, $df = 1/52$, $p < 0.01$).

40. The complete pattern of significant correlations (see footnote 36) for each culture is as follows: The American caretaker's "chats" is correlated with "finger or pacifier" (.57), "total vocal" (.64), "happy vocal" (.66), "active" (.58), "baby plays" (.57), "toy" (.40), "other object" (.41), "dresses" (.52), "positions" (.46), "pats or touches" (.55), "other care" (.43), "plays with" (.47), "affections" (.44), "looks at" (.73), "talks to" (.99), "in arms" (.43), and "rocks" (.37). The Japanese caretaker's "chats" is correlated with "total vocal" (.50), "unhappy vocal" (.44), "baby plays" (.57), "toy" (.58), "diapers" (.41), "positions" (.37), "plays with" (.65), "affections" (.63), "looks at" (.69), "talks to" (.91), "lulls" (.40), "in arms" (.76), and "rocks" (.66).

41. In State Two, no three-way interactions are significant. Of the 33 possible two-way interactions, two are significant, but both of these are explained by the intra-cultural analyses. "Total vocal" shows an interaction between culture and father's occupation: JS 16%, JI 28%, AS 21%, AI 17% ($F = 4.8$, $df = 1/52$, $p < 0.05$). The intra-Japanese analysis for "total vocal" by father's occupation is significant; the comparable test in the intra-American analysis is not significant. "Hand" shows an interaction between culture and sex of infant: JM 2%, JF 12%, AM 14%, AF 3% ($F = 7.8$, $df = 1/52$, $p < 0.01$). The intra-Japanese analysis for "hand" by sex of infant is not significant ($p < 0.14$); the comparable test in the intra-American analysis is significant ($p < 0.01$).

42. There are no findings in Table 8 by sex of infant for State Two. The intra-Japanese analysis has no findings by sex of infant. The intra-American analysis shows a single finding—male infants are greater on "hand" than are female infants (see footnote 41), but this could well be a chance finding. The two findings in Table 8 by father's occupation are better explained by the intra-Japanese analysis, and there are no findings by father's occupation in the intra-American analysis. In the intra-Japanese analysis, infants in independent business families suck more on finger or pacifier, and are more unhappily vocal; in addition, they also are greater in "total vocal." Quite possibly this is due to the passive presence of their mothers, because we know from the intra-Japanese analysis of the total observations that the mother in the independent family does more lulling, carrying, and rocking than the mother in the salaried family, and the infant in the independent family in State Two may be more aware of his mother's passive presence and

may be seeking attention by his greater unhappy vocals. Further evidence for this line of thought is that in the intra-Japanese analysis in State Two, the infant from the salaried family shows up as playing more by himself, which would indicate that he is more self-absorbed.

43. In State Three there are no significant three- or two-way interactions.

44. By sex of infant, the finding in Table 9 for "finger or pacifier" is better explained in terms of the intra-Japanese analysis, where female infants are doing more nonnutritive sucking than male infants; the comparison is not significant in the intra-American analysis. There are no other significant findings in the intra-Japanese analysis. The other finding by sex of infant in Table 9 shows male infants as more happily vocal when alone; in the intra-cultural analyses, this finding is of borderline significance ($p < 0.07$) in the Japanese data, where male infants may be more happily vocal, and is not significant ($p < 0.36$) in the intra-American data. The one significant finding in the intra-American analysis by sex of infant is that male infants are greater in "total vocal." There are no findings in Table 9 by father's occupation, and none in the intra-Japanese analysis. There is one finding in the intra-American analysis, which could be merely a chance finding—infants in salaried families play with their hands more than infants in independent business families.

45. In State Four, there are no significant three-way interactions. Of the 42 possible two-way interactions, one is significant but is explained by the intra-cultural analyses. "Looks at" shows an interaction between culture and father's occupation: JS 80%, JI 55%, AS 96%, AI 100% ($F = 61$. $df = 1/46$, $p < 0.05$). In the intra-Japanese analysis, "looks at" by father's occupation is significant; the comparable test in the intra-American analysis is not significant.

46. In the intra-cultural analyses for State Four, there are no findings in either culture by sex of infant. By father's occupation, there are no findings in the intra-American analysis, and only one finding in the intra-Japanese analysis. Japanese mothers in salaried families do proportionately more looking at sleeping babies than do Japanese mothers in independent business families (see footnote 45). This finding also occurs in the intra-Japanese analysis for State One (see footnote 38), and it does indicate, that in this regard, Japanese mothers in salaried families are closer to American mothers.

47. For further information on this general topic derived from our data, see Windle.

48. A further important source of evidence, although the research is only currently being developed, comes from the comparison of infants in Japan and America from birth through the first month of life. This work is being carried out by Dr. Peter Wolff of the Judge Baker Guidance Center in Boston, and by Dr. Yukio Okada of Kobe Medical College in Kobe. The data being gathered by these two workers are incomplete at present, and hence Dr. Wolff has strong reservations about any general statements, but his preliminary impression is, ". . . nothing in my data or the data that Dr. Okada and I put together would indicate essential differences between Japanese and American one-month-old infants" (personal communication). In addition, because obstetrical techniques vary somewhat between Japan and the United States, an additional indirect source of evidence indicates that "minimal brain damage" at birth is no more prevalent among normal elementary school children in Japan than in the United States. See Wolff and Hurwitz.

49. See also Toshima.
50. See Arai, Ishikawa, and Toshima, p. 269. (We are indebted to Miss Frederica M. Levin for her translation of this article from the French.) The authors of this study seem, in the discussion of their results, somewhat distressed that the Japanese mothers were so bound up in the lives of their infants that they interfered with the development of their infants in ways which made it difficult to meet the American norms. Our results agree in general with those of this Japanese study, but we do not agree with the concern over the lack of matching the American norms. We do not believe that the differences which we find are necessarily indications of a better or a worse approach to human life, but rather that such differences are a part of an individuals' adjustment to his culture.

REFERENCES

ARAI, S., ISHIKAWA, J., and TOSHIMA, K. "Développement psychomoteur des enfants japonais," *La Revue de Neuropsychiatrie Infantile et d'Hygiène Mentale de l'Enfance* (1958) 6:262–269.

BLALOCK, HUBERT M., JR. *Social Statistics;* McGraw-Hill, 1960.

BLOOD, ROBERT O., JR. *Love-Match and Arranged Marraige;* Free Press, 1967.

CAUDILL, WILLIAM. *Effects of Social and Cultural Systems in Reactions to Stress;* New York, Social Science Resarch Council, Pamphlet 14, 1958.

CAUDILL, WILLIAM. "Patterns of Emotion in Modern Japan," in Robert J. Smith and Richard K. Beardsley (Eds.), *Japanese Culture: Its Development and Characteristics;* Aldine, 1962.

CAUDILL, WILLIAM, and DOI, L. TAKEO. "Interrelations of Psychiatry, Culture and Emotion in Japan," in Iago Galdston (Ed.), *Man's Image in Medicine and Anthropology;* Internat. Univ. Press, 1963.

CAUDILL, WILLIAM, and PLATH, DAVID W. "Who Sleeps by Whom? Parent-Child Involvement in Urban Japanese Families," *Psychiatry* (1966) 29:344–366.

CAUDILL, WILLIAM, and SCARR, HARRY A. "Japanese Value Orientations and Culture Change," *Ethnology* (1962) 1:53–91.

CAUDILL, WILLIAM, and SCHOOLER, CARMI. "Symptom Patterns and Background Characteristics of Japanese Psychiatric Patients," in William Caudill and Tsung-yi Lin (Eds.), *Mental Health Research in Asia and the Pacific;* Honolulu, East-West Center Press, 1969.

CAUDILL, WILLIAM, and WEINSTEIN, HELEN. "Maternal Care and Infant Behavior in Japanese and American Urban Middle-Class Families," in Reuben Hill and René König (Eds.), *Families in East and West*; Paris, Mouton, 1970.

COHEN, JACOB. "Some Statistical Issues in Psychological Research," in B. Wolman (Ed.), *Handbook of Clinical Psychology;* McGraw-Hill, 1965.

COOLEY, WILLIAM W., and LOHNES, PAUL R. *Multivariate Procedures for the Behavioral Sciences;* Wiley, 1962.

DORE, RONALD. *City Life in Japan;* London, Routledge and Kegan Paul, 1958.

FISHER, J. L., and YOSHIDA, TEIGO. "The Nature of Speech According to Japanese Proverbs," *J. Amer. Folklore* (1968) 81:34–43.

HOLLINGSHEAD, AUGUST B., and REDLICH, FREDRICK C. *Social Class and Mental Illness:* Wiley, 1958.

JAPAN, BUREAU OF STATISTICS, *1960 Population Census of Japan, Vol. 2: One Percent Tabulation, Part 1: Age, Marital Status, Legal Nationality, Education and Fertility;* Tokyo, Office of the Prime Minister, 1962.

MILLER, DANIEL R., and SWANSON, GUY E. *The Changing American Parent;* Wiley, 1958.

MOSS, HOWARD A. "Sex, Age, and State as Determinants of Mother-Infant Interaction," *Merrill-Palmer Quart.* (1967) 13:19–36.

NAKAMURA, HAJIME. *Ways of Thinking of Eastern Peoples: India, China, Tibet, Japan;*

Honolulu, East-West Center Press, 1964.

NAKANE, CHIE. "Toward a Theory of Japanese Social Structure," *Economic Weekly* [Bombay], Annual No. 17, Feb., 1965, pp. 197–216.

NIHON SHAKAI GAKKAI CHOSA IINKAI HEN (Ed.). *Nihon Shakai no Kaisōteki Kōzō;* Tokyo, Yūhikaku, 1958.

ODAKA, KUNIO. "The Middle Classes in Japan," *Contemporary Japan* (1964) 28:10–32; and (1965) 28:268–296.

ODAKA, KUNIO, and NISHIHIRA, SHIGEKI. "Social Mobility in Japan: A Report on the 1955 Survey of Social Stratification and Social Mobility in Japan," *East Asian Cultural Studies* (1965) 4(Nos. 1–4):83–126.

PEARLIN, LEONARD I., and KOHN, MELVIN L. "Social Class, Occupation, and Parental Values: A Cross-National Study," *Amer. Sociol. Review* (1966) 31:466–479.

PLATH, DAVID W. *The After Hours: Modern Japan and the Search for Enjoyment;* Berkeley, Univ. of Calif. Press, 1964.

RAMSEY, CHARLES E., and SMITH, ROBERT J. "Japanese and American Perceptions of Occupations," *Amer. J. Sociology* (1960) 65:475–482.

REISCHAUER, EDWIN O. *The United States and Japan* (Rev. Ed.); Harvard Univ. Press, 1957.

RHEINGOLD, HARRIET L. "The Measurement of Maternal Care," *Child Development* (1960) 31:565–575.

RUBENSTEIN, JUDITH. "Maternal Attentiveness and Subsequent Exploratory Behavior in the Infant," *Child Development* (1967) 38:1089–1100.

SCHOOLER, CARMI, and CAUDILL, WILLIAM. "Symptomatology in Japanese and American Schizophrenics," *Ethnology* (1964) 3:172–178.

SNEDECOR, GEORGE W. *Statistical Methods* (4th Ed.); Ames, Iowa State College Press, 1946.

STEPHENS, WILLIAM N. *The Family in Cross-Cultural Perspective;* Holt, Rinehart and Winston, 1963.

TAEUBER, IRENE B. *The Population of Japan;* Princeton Univ. Press, 1958.

TOSHIMA, K. "Tōhoku Chihō ni Okeru Nyūyōji Seishinhattatsu ni Kansuru Kenkyū," *Nihon Shonika-Gakkai Zasshi* (1958) 62(11):1444–1450; 62(12):1550–1556; 62(12):1557–1563.

VOGEL, EZRA F. *Japan's New Middle Class: The Salary Man and His Family in a Tokyo Suburb;* Berkeley, Univ. of Calif. Press, 1963.

WEISBERG, PAUL. "Social and Non-Social Conditioning of Infant Vocalizations," in Yvonne Brackbill and George G. Thompson (Eds.), *Behavior in Infancy and Early Childhood;* Free Press, 1967.

WINDLE, JAN FOLK. "Feeding of Infants in Japanese and American Urban Middle Class Families," master's thesis, Dept. of Anthropology, Amer. Univ., Washington, D.C., 1968.

WOLFF, PETER H., and HURWITZ, IRVING. "The Choreiform Syndrome," *Developmental Medicine and Child Neurology* (1966) 8:160–165.

Who Sleeps by Whom?
Parent-Child Involvement
in Urban Japanese Families

WILLIAM CAUDILL AND DAVID W. PLATH

If a third of life is passed in bed, with whom this time is spent is not a trivial matter. As ethnologists, we expect co-sleeping customs to be consonant with major interpersonal and emotional patterns of family life in a culture, and at the same time to reflect cross-cultural differences.[1] Westerners viewing Japanese sleeping arrangements usually sense a high degree of "overcrowding," which they say results from lack of space in "densely populated" Japan. We argue that this apparent "overcrowding" in the bedroom is only in part a function of lack of space: It derives more directly from the strength of family bonds. We argue further that the frequency with which children co-sleep with parents expresses a strong cultural emphasis upon the nurturant aspects of family life and a correlative de-emphasis of its sexual aspects. We support our arguments by asking, of data from urban families, who sleeps by whom?

SELECTION AND CHARACTERISTICS OF THE SAMPLE

Co-sleeping in Japan usually occurs behind closed shutters and

Reprinted from *Psychiatry* 29 (1966):344–66.

The National Institute of Mental Health supported Caudill's fieldwork in Tokyo and Kyoto in 1961–62; the Ford Foundation foreign area training fellowship program supported Plath's fieldwork in Nagano in 1960. For field assistance, our thanks to Dr. Shigeo Imagi of Kyoto Metropolitan Medical School; to Mrs. Seiko Notsuki of St. Luke's International Hospital; and to Mr. Kan'ichi Mochizuki, then a student in Shinshū University, Matsumoto. For help during the preparation of the data we wish to thank Mrs. Mieko Caudill. For suggestions during the analysis of the data we are grateful to Dr. Carmi Schooler, Dr. Harry A. Scarr, and Mrs. Helen Weinstein of the Laboratory of Socio-environmental Studies, NIMH.

is not open to easy observation. Participant observation has its limits, and an ethnographer who asked to sleep all around town probably would not be welcomed. But both of us found that Japanese would willingly sketch their dwelling spaces and indicate where each person slept. We happened upon this independently and for different purposes, but have combined our data in a joint report.

The sketches were drawn in the course of individual interviews. The interviews in Caudill's research were conducted in 1962 at three hospitals, two of them in Tokyo and one in Kyoto. At each hospital, information was obtained from the first 100 mothers coming to the well-baby clinic who had, at the time of interview, a three- to four-month-old infant.[2] The interviews in Plath's research were conducted in 1960 in Matsumoto City, and information was obtained from fathers or mothers in 30 households in two neighborhoods.[3]

Discarding seven cases with inadequate data, we have a total sample of 323 households—198 in Tokyo, 99 in Kyoto, and 26 in Matsumoto. Each household consists of at least an unmarried child and both of his parents; and in many cases there are additional children, extended kin, and unrelated persons (maids, roomers, and employees in the family buisness). We examined household sleeping arrangements in terms of city of residence, size of household, number of generations living together, style of life, social class, and density. Statistically, density proved to be the most important single variable. Several of the other variables, however, were of minor importance in influencing co-sleeping patterns, and these results will be given at the appropriate points in the analysis. The meaning we assign to these variables is discussed in the following paragraphs, and the distribution of the sample in terms of them is given in Table 1.

In designing the research, our aim was to clarify parent-child co-sleeping patterns, and we chose our sample of households accordingly. We wished to obtain a sufficient number and spread of households on each variable to permit comparative analysis rather than trying to collect a sample that would be statistically representative of the general population. Thus, in contrast to the general population, our sample contains no one-person or two-person households, a greater proportion of three-generation households, more households whose main income is from a family business, and more upper middle-class and lower middle-class households.[4]

Table 1. Distribution of Households in the Sample by
Number of Generations, Style of Life, Social Class,
and Density

Category	Tokyo (N=198)	Kyoto (N=99)	Matsu-moto (N=26)	Total Households (N=323)
Number of generations in household				
Two	128	60	23	211
Three	70	39	3	112*
Style of life: main source of income				
Salary and wages	104	71	11	186
Family business	94	28	15	137
Social class				
Upper middle	65	60	6	131
Lower middle	71	29	8	108
Working	62	10	12	84
Density				
High	155	43	17	215
Low	43	56	9	108

*Includes 4 four-generation households.

City of Residence

Japanese tend to think of life in Tokyo as being more modern than that in other parts of Japan, and to think of life in Kyoto as being especially traditional. The image of life in Matsumoto falls between the two, and carries an aura of provincialism. From city to city there are minor variations in sleeping arrangements—notably in central Kyoto, with its older and larger houses, where families are somewhat more spread out in their sleeping arrangements than in Tokyo or Matsumoto. But if the data by city are controlled by any other variable, these differences vanish.

Household Size

The total sample has an average of 4.8 persons per household, and city-to-city differences are minor—5.0 for Tokyo, 4.6 for Kyoto, and 4.5 for Matsumoto. In this regard the sample is close to the 1960 census, which found (for households of like composition) an average of 4.8 persons per household for all urban areas, 4.9 for Tokyo, and 4.8 for Kyoto. Census figures for Matsumoto are not available to us.[5] As will be seen, size of household does prove to be a useful variable in certain respects.

Number of Generations

In line with the patrilineal emphasis in Japanese culture, 79 percent of the three-generation households in the sample include one or both of the husband's parents, while only 21 percent include one or both of the wife's parents. No household contains grandparents from both paternal and maternal sides.

Style of Life

The distinction concerning the main source of income for a household is related more to a "style of life" than to economic matters. Following World War II, the role of the "salaryman" has become more important and desirable, and is seen as a modern way of life free from some of the traditional constraints associated with working in a small family business. It should be noted that style of life is conceptually separate from social class.[6] And, as will be seen, style of life does play a minor role as a meaningful variable in sleeping arrangements.

Social Class

To determine social class, we first separated our households into five logical groups based on the occupation and education of the head of the household. Because there were so few cases in groups one and five, we combined the first two groups into an "upper middle class," we retained the third group and labeled it "lower middle class," and we combined the last two groups under the heading of "working class." We did not, however, find any important differences by social class in sleeping arrangements.[7]

Density

We define density as the ratio between the number of rooms available to a household for sleeping purposes, and the number of persons residing in the household. When there are fewer available sleeping rooms than persons, we call this *high density;* when there are as many or more sleeping rooms than persons, we call it *low density.*

It should be noted that we define density in terms of space available, not space actually used. In tabulating rooms available for sleeping, we excluded kitchens, baths, toilets, halls, porches, storage areas, and rooms used predominantly for business purposes (that is, the "shop"). We counted all other rooms as available for sleeping, including a room that a household might reserve for visitors during the daytime. Because of the ordinary construction of the Japanese dwelling, almost all of the rooms counted as available are mat-floored (*tatami*) rooms; people sleep in such rooms on quilts (*futon*), which are spread out each evening and taken up during the day. Ninety percent of the adults in the sample sleep in this manner, while 10 percent use Western-style beds. We shall return later to this question of bedding.[8]

As can be seen in Table 1, density varies by city, being highest in Tokyo. In this regard, the sample seems to reflect the fact that Tokyo's population has been increasing two to three times faster than that of Kyoto or Matsumoto; in addition, both of these latter cities have a larger proportion of old multiple-room houses because they were not bombed during World War II, whereas Tokyo was gutted by fire-bomb raids in 1945. Japan, in general, continues to suffer from a shortage of housing. Conditions probably have improved since 1955, the latest year for which we have reliable figures, but at that time in cities over 200,000 population the average dwelling space per person was still 10 percent below what it had been in 1941.[9] And the average Japanese urban household in 1955 had nearly twice as many persons per room as did its American counterpart —1.22 persons in Japan to 0.67 persons in the United States.[10] But if there is need for more living space in general in Japan, the need for more sleeping space in particular is less apparent.

AVAILABILITY AND USE OF SLEEPING SPACE

Our first question is: How much available sleeping space do the households in the sample have, and how much of it do they regularly use? Table 2 shows the distribution of the 323 households in the sample by number of persons in a household and number of rooms it has available for sleeping. The households to the left of the step-line have less than one sleeping room available per person, and these 215 households (67 percent) have a high density. The households to the right of the step-line have one or more rooms available per person, and these 108 households (33 percent) have a low density. These latter households could provide a separate room for each member if they chose to do so.

In contrast, Table 3 shows the distribution of all households by number of persons and number of rooms actually used for sleeping. There is a dramatic shift to the left of the step-line, and of the 108 households in Table 2 that could provide each member with a separate room, only one remains to the right of the line in Table 3.

A more detailed comparison of Tables 2 and 3 will show that three-person households in our sample prefer to sleep in one room,

Table 2. Number of Persons in Household by
Number of Rooms Available for Sleeping

Number of Persons in Household	Number of Rooms Available for Sleeping										Total Households
	1	2	3	4	5	6	7	8	9	10+	
3	31	45	17	8	10	3			1	2	117
4	6	20	15	17	3	2	2	1			66
5		8	4	13	9	4	3			1	42
6	1	1	3	7	7	8		2	1	2	32
7		1	1	7	6	2	3		1	2	23
8				7	4	2	4	4		1	22
9			1	3	3		1				8
10				1		1	1			1	4
11+				2		2	1		1	3	9
Total Households	38	75	41	65	42	24	15	7	4	12	323

Table 3. Number of Persons in Household by Number
of Rooms Used for Sleeping

Number of Persons in Household	Number of Rooms Used for Sleeping										Total Households
	1	2	3	4	5	6	7	8	9	10+	
3	102	14	1								117
4	23	41	2								66
5	5	25	11	1							42
6	1	8	17	6							32
7		2	11	10							23
8			8	11	3						22
9			3	3	2						8
10			1	3							4
11+				2	5	2					9
Total Households	131	90	54	36	10	2					323

whereas four-person households are more likely to divide into two
rooms. Given the household composition of our sample, this is
perhaps not so surprising, but if one continues to look in Table 3
for the modal frequency in terms of size of household relative to
number of rooms used for sleeping, the idea begins to dawn that
Japanese prefer to sleep in clusters of two or three persons, and prefer
not to sleep alone.

We do not, of course, expect every person in a household,
even if this were possible, to sleep in a separate room. It would be
highly unusual even among privacy-minded American households.
Each of the households in the sample contains at least one married

couple, and most of them also contain an infant. Presumably most of the married couples, and some of the mothers and infants, will co-sleep. This in itself makes it unlikely that many households will exhaust their available sleeping rooms.

But if some amount of co-sleeping seems likely a priori, the next question we ask is: To what extent does the amount of available space influence the degree of co-sleeping? If, for example, Japanese parents and children co-sleep simply because they lack space, then they should tend to disperse as more rooms become available. We can begin to test this as follows.

First, we exclude 38 households that have only one sleeping room available.[11] We assume that they have no opportunity to disperse, save that of bedding down members in kitchens or hallways. The remaining 285 households, however, have some freedom of choice in sleeping arrangements, since each of them has at least two sleeping rooms available.

Next, for each of these 285 households we compute two indexes. The first we call *use density*. To obtain this we divide the number of persons in a household by the number of rooms they now use for sleeping. For example, a four-person household sleeping in two rooms has a use density of two persons per room. The second index we call *available-space density*. To obtain this we divide the number of persons in a household by the number of available rooms, up to the point where the ratio equals one. For example, a four-person household with four available rooms has an available-space density of one person per room. A household with more available rooms than members would have a theoretical available-space density of less than one person per room, but we have set a lower limit of one for this index because it seems a bit unrealistic to expect a person regularly to use more than one sleeping room.

Finally, we examine the correlation (by the Pearson r method) between use density and available-space density for each group of households having the same number of members. There are nine such groups, ranging from three-person to eleven-or-more-person households (see Tables 2 and 3). The results of this analysis are: (1) the correlation is not significant ($r = -.05$) for three-person households; (2) the correlations are significant ($r = .25$, n.s.; $r = .29$ to $.89$, $p < .05$) for seven of the eight groups of households having four to eleven or more members; and (3) the correlation is significant ($r = .47$, $p < .01$) when all households having four or more members are considered together.

These results mean that three-person households do not tend to disperse for sleep even when rooms are available, but larger households do tend to disperse to some extent. For the larger households, the correlation tells us that the availability of space accounts for 22 percent (r^2) of the variance in the actual use of space. In other words, lack of space does make a difference in co-sleeping arrangements in our urban Japanese households having more than three members, but space alone tells only about one-fifth of the story. To fill out the story, we must ask, Who sleeps by whom?

SLEEP AND SOCIAL STRUCTURE

Our question now becomes: Which kinship roles are most likely to co-sleep, and which to disperse? Once again we exclude the 38 households having only one sleeping room available; and, for the households having at least two sleeping rooms, we consider separately the 86 three-person housholds and the 199 four-or-more-person households.

Each of the three-person households consists of a child with both parents—and in 79 of the cases the child is an infant of three to four months. Thus it is perhaps not too unusual that all members sleep together in one room in 71 (86 percent) of the households. Another 14 (16 percent) use two rooms; in 9 of these cases it is the child who is alone, but in 5 cases it is the father. In one household the three members each sleep alone.

Given the high number of infants in these three-person households, one might argue that the "instrumental need" to look after the infant at night would favor keeping him in the parental bedroom. But if convenience were the only consideration, the infant would probably be excluded from the room a few months to a year after birth. This tends to happen in American households but is much less true for Japanese housholds,[12] as will be seen in detail at a later point.

The next question we must ask is: What happens when a household becomes larger? We turn now to 199 four-or-more-person households in which density does make a difference. Remember that each of these households contains a father, mother, and child, plus some combination of additional children, extended kin, and unrelated persons. Table 4 presents data on sleeping arrangements by kinship category for all persons in these households. The table should be read horizontally: for example, of the 132 fathers in high-density households, 3 percent sleep alone; 97 percent sleep in nuclear family groupings, of two (15 percent), three (44 percent), and four-or-more (38 percent) persons; and one percent sleep with an extended kinsman. Complex-mixed sleeping groups are composed of three or more persons with at least one representative from each of the three categories—nuclear family, extended kin, and nonrelated persons.

The first point be made from Table 4 concerns the effect of household social structure on who sleeps by whom. As indicated by the percentages within the heavy lines, to a striking extent nuclear kin co-sleep with nuclear kin, extended kin with extended kin, and nonrelated persons with nonrelated persons. For the father, mother, and infant, the exceptions to this generalization are trivial; and for the child, extended kin, and nonrelated persons, the exceptions occur somewhat more often in high-density households. We did not fully anticipate this result, and it shows a highly regular sorting by social roles within the general tendency to cluster into co-sleeping groups.[13]

The second point to be made from Table 4 concerns the size of co-sleeping groups. Within the nuclear family, regardless of density, the three-person group is most common for the father, mother, and infant. This pattern is particularly apparent in low-density households, whereas high-density households have a substantial percentage of four-or-more-person groups. A child is found most often in a four-or-more-person group in high-density households, but in a two- or three-person-group in low-density households. If anyone sleeps alone in the nuclear family, it is most likely to be an infant in a low-density household.

Among extended kin, regardless of density, the most frequent pattern is to co-sleep in a two-person group, and the next most frequent is to sleep alone. Nonrelated persons are most frequently found alone, and this is especially true in low-density households.

The manner in which data are presented in Table 4 obscures two dimensions that require examination. First, the table does not fully indicate which persons are co-sleeping in terms of social roles. For example, it tells us that about one father in five co-sleeps with some one other person; it does not tell us who that other person may be. American common sense might suggest that it is his wife— but here American common sense is not the best predictor. Second, the table combines information from families that are at different stages in their life cycle. Let us re-sort the data with these points in mind.

Table 4. Percentage Distribution of Participation in Various Types of Co-Sleeping Groups by Kinship Category and Density of Household for All Persons in 199 Households Having Four or More Members

Kinship Category	Density	Sleeping Alone	Nuclear Family			Extended Kin			Nonrelated			Complex-Mixed		Total Percent*	Total Persons
			2	3	4+	2	3	4+	2	3	4+	3	4+		
Father	High	3	15	44	38	1								101	132
	Low	9	19	64	8									100	67
Mother	High		15	47	37							1	1	101	132
	Low		23	70	8									101	67
Infant	High	3	10	50	36							1	1	101	125
	Low	14	10	68	8									100	55
Child	High	2	19	13	53	6	4					3		100	120
	Low	8	40	30	17	6								101	34
Extended kin	High	22	3	*	*	44	18	3	2	*	*	5	1	98	231
	Low	35	2			52	6	4						99	92
Nonrelated persons	High	28				4		4	21	27	12	2	3	101	112
	Low	63				7			20	10				100	30

*Totals do not add to 100 percent because of rounding; an asterisk indicates less than .5 of a percent.

Co-sleeping and the Life Cycle of the Nuclear Family

From the point of view of the parents, the life cycle of a nuclear family begins at marriage; continues through the birth, rearing, and subsequent marriage of the children, until toward the end only the spouses remain; they are separated by the death of one; and finally the family ceases to exist upon the death of the other. We shall focus upon the intermediate stages of this cycle, since our data are inadequate for generalizations about the beginning and ending stages.[14]

Once again we exclude the 38 households with only one sleeping room. The remaining 285 households all contain a "primary" nuclear family that is in almost all cases a younger family in one of the early stages of the cycle. In addition, 110 households contain a "secondary" nuclear family, or the remnants thereof, which is in almost all cases in the later stages of the cycle. These older nuclear families make up the great bulk of the extended kin in Table 4.[15] Since we have already shown that there is little co-sleeping between extended kin and other groupings, let us also in a sense "stand the sample on its head" and look at sleeping arrangements from the point of view of these older nuclear families, being careful to note those situations in which older nuclears occur in the sleeping ranks of younger nuclears, and vice versa.

We have, then, 285 primary and 110 secondary nuclear families to consider across the stages of the nuclear family cycle. The sample can be divided readily into seven stages, of which the first three occur among younger nuclear families and the last four among older ones. These stages are: (1) both parents and an infant, (2) both parents and an infant plus one or more young children, (3) both parents and one or more older children, (4) both parents and one or more adult children, (5) both parents only, (6) one parent and one or more adult children, and (7) one parent only.

These stages are logically exclusive except for the line to be drawn between "older children" and "adult children" in stages 3 and 4. We decided this empirically by looking at sleeping arrangements in terms of the age of the child among the total 535 children in the 285 primary and 110 secondary nuclear families.

As can be seen in Table 5, the sharpest break in sleeping arrangements comes between the children who are 11 to 15 years old and those who are 16 to 20 years old. The former have a 50 percent chance of co-sleeping in a two-generation group (with a parent or extended kin member), whereas the latter have only a 17 percent chance of so doing. Moreover, although the numbers

Table 5. Percentage Distribution of Sleeping Arrangements by Age for 535 Children from Primary and Secondary Nuclear Families

Sleeping Arrangements	Age of Child						
	3–4 Months (N=259)	1–5 Years (N=103)	6–10 Years (N=28)	11–15 Years (N=28)	16–20 Years (N=46)	21–25 Years (N=38)	26+ Years (N=33)
Two-Generations	90	91	79	50	17	24	18
With parents(s)	90	79	68	46	15	24	15
With extended kin.............	—	12	11	4	2	—	3
One-Generation	2	7	11	36	46	40	33
With sibling(s)	2	7	11	36	46	37	21
With nonrelated person(s)	—	—	—	—	—	3	12
Alone	8	2	11	14	37	37	49
Total Percent*	100	100	101	100	100	101	100

*Totals do not add to 100 percent because of rounding.

involved are smaller, the break clearly seems to fall between children who are 13 to 15 years old and children who are 16 to 18 years old. The implication here is rather strong that puberty for the boy and the onset of menstruation for the girl set the stage for a withdrawal from co-sleeping with parents or extended kin. For these reasons we draw the line between stages 3 and 4 at 15 years of age. That is, we place a nuclear family in stage 3 if they have at least one child who is 15 years or younger. And we place a family in stage 4 if all of their children are 16 years or more.

Looking across the early years of life in a more general sense, it is apparent in Table 5 that from the point of view of a child he can expect to co-sleep with an adult until he is 10 years old. The period from 11 to 15 years is one of transition, with the greatest increase being in the co-sleeping with a sibling. After the age of 16, a child is more likely to co-sleep with a sibling or to be alone, but there always remains a fair chance (at about the 20 percent level) that he will co-sleep with a parent. As for sex differences, which are not shown in Table 5, there are none until after the 11 to 15 years old period. From 16 years on, there is a tendency for daughters more than sons to co-sleep with a parent. In these later periods both daughters and sons are about equally likely to co-sleep with a sibling, but sons are more likely to sleep alone than are daughters.[16]

Having established a reasonable cutting point between stages 3 and 4 in the nuclear family cycle, we show, in Table 6, the frequency distribution of the families across the seven stages. The table also gives the median ages of the parents and children at each stage. In these stages where data are drawn from several sources (that is, stages 1, 3, and 4), we first checked to see if the pattern of sleeping arrangements differed significantly according to the source. There were no differences, so we combined the cases to obtain the total families indicated in each stage.

The importance of the median ages given in the table will be explained more fully later. For now, we point out only that the median ages of the mother (26 years) and father (29 years) in stage 1 are in close agreement with findings in other studies. Since the infants in these families are three to four months old, it is likely that the parents were married one to two years earlier, on the average. At that time, the wife would have been about 24 or 25, and the husband about 27 or 28. In a study conducted in 1959, Blood found the median age of marriage to be 24 for wives and 28 for husbands among 444 young married couples living in three government apartment houses in Tokyo; and Taeuber cites data for 1935 on

Table 6. Source of Data on Nuclear Families Across the Stages of the Nuclear Family Cycle

Source of Data	Younger Nuclear Families			Older Nuclear Families				Total Families
	1 Both Parents, Infant Only	2 Both Parents, Infant Child(ren)	3 Both Parents, Older Child(ren)	4 Both Parents, Adult Child(ren)	5 Both Parents, Only Child(ren)	6 One Parent, Adult Child(ren)	7 One Parent Only	
Primary Nuclear Families								
From 86 three-person households	79	—	5	2	—	—	—	86
From 199 four-or-more-person households	92	88	16	3	—	—	—	199
Secondary Nuclear Families								
From 199 four-or-more-person households.	—	—	10	36	32	13	19	110
Total Families	171	88	31	41	32	13	19	395
Median Age:								
Mother	26	29	40	56	58	55	63	
Father	29	33	45	61	63	66	68	
Child	3–4 mos.	3–4 mos., 3 mos.	13	24	—	22	—	

Japan as a whole giving an average age of first marriage of 24 for women and 28 for men. It is also apparent from the 1960 census in Japan that the average age of marriage is increasing, particularly in densely populated urban areas.[17]

Parental Sleeping Arrangements in the Early Stages

Table 7 presents the data for sleeping arrangements from the point of view of the parents in stages 1 through 3. Four broad categories of sleeping arrangements are used, and these need a word of explanation. In the first category, *Two Generations: Together,* both parents and at least one child are co-sleeping. This category is subdivided into those families in which all nuclear members are literally together, in that both parents and all children share a sleeping room; and those families which are more symbolically together, in that at least one of the children co-sleeps with both parents. In the second category, *Two Generations: Consanguineous,* the parents separate in order to provide parental co-sleeping partners for the children. This category is also subdivided into those situations where each parent takes one or more children as a co-sleeping partner, and those situations where the father sleeps alone while the mother co-sleeps with one or more children. The third category, *One Generation: Conjugal,* is the usual "American" pattern where the parents are co-sleeping as a couple, and the children are elsewhere. Finally, in the fourth category, *One Generation: Separate,* the parents separate, each sleeping alone, and the children are elsewhere.

In stage 1 the overwhelming proportion (86 percent) of parents co-sleep with their infant. In 10 percent of the cases, the parents sleep conjugally, but we found no variable that distinguishes this group. And in a few cases, the father sleeps alone.

In stage 2 the most important change is the substantial increase (to 22 percent) in the *Two Generation: Consanguineous* pattern, even though the *Two-Generation: Together* pattern remains high (73 percent). Remember that in stage 2 each family has two or more children—an infant and at least one young child whose median age is three years. The amount of two-generation co-sleeping actually increases from stage 1 to stage 2 if the first two categories are added together (from 90 percent to 95 percent). It is as if the Japanese parents, wanting to provide a parental sleeping partner for all children at this stage and faced with the issue of sleeping four or more to a room, which they dislike (possibly because of the size of

Table 7. Percentage Distribution of Parental Sleeping Arrangements by Stage in Family Cycle for Younger Nuclear Families

	Stages in Family Cycle		
	1	2	3
Parental Sleeping Arrangements	Both Parents, Infant Only (3–4 mos.)* (N = 171 families)	Both Parents, Infant, Child(ren) (3–4 mos. and 3 yrs.)* (N = 88 families)	Both Parents, Older Child(ren)* (13 yrs.)* (N = 31 families)
Two Generations: Together............	86	73	52
Both parents and all children	86	53	29
Both parents and child(ren)—another child elsewhere	n.a.†	19	23
Two Generations: Consanguineous............	4	22	10
Separation of parents, each with child(ren)	n.a.	15	3
Exclusion of father, mother with child(ren)	4	7	7
One Generation: Conjugal	10	6	35
Parents together, all children elsewhere			
One Generation: Separate	—	—	3
Parents sleep separately, and children sleep separately from parents			
Total Percent‡	100	101	100

*Median ages for infants and children.
†n.a. = not applicable.
‡Totals do not add to 100 percent because of rounding.

the room, as indicated in footnote 8), have, in about one-fifth of the cases, decided to separate in order to meet the problem.

We have some evidence that spouses are not likely to separate if they have an alternative. And the preferred alternative is to send one or more children to co-sleep with a kinswoman. Of the 88 families in stage 2, 40 households include extended kin and 48 do not. Parents in the latter households are significantly more likely to separate than those in the former. This tendency can be seen even more sharply when we focus on the 30 families in stage 2 that are included in the sleeping patterns of both parents and one or more children (19 percent, or 17 families), and separation of parents(15 percent, or 13 families). Among the 17 families where both parents are together, 13 households contain extended kin, and four do not; on the other hand, among the 13 families where the parents are separated, only one household contains extended kin, and 12 do not (chi square $= 13.6$, 1 df, $p < .001$). Clearly, in households where there are extended kin, the parents have decided to remain together; when there are no extended kin available, the parents have decided to sleep separately.

We can explore this question further by asking where the "other" child sleeps among the 17 families in which both parents are together with one or more children. Four of these households do not include extended kin, and in all four the "other" child sleeps alone. But, in the 13 households that include extended kin, the "other" child co-sleeps with a kinswoman in 11 instances, and is alone only in two. Two points stand out here. First, it is always a child who goes to sleep with extended kin; the infant (and some-times other children) remains with the parents. Second, it is usually an older kinswoman who takes the child (the husband's mother in six cases, the wife's mother in two, the husband's unmarried sister in three). In short, if an older kinswoman is present during stage 2, she is likely to become a mother surrogate for co-sleeping.

Among the 13 families in which the parents are separated, the one household containing extended kin includes a husband's father who sleeps alone. Since in this pattern each parent is co-sleeping with one or more children, it is of interest to know how the children are distributed. The fathers in these families always co-sleep with a child and never with an infant, and the sex of the child apparently does not matter—in eight cases it is a son, and in five cases it is a daughter. The mothers always co-sleep with the infant, who is joined by a child in four cases (the additional child being a son in three cases and a daughter in one case).

In stage 2, the remaining sleeping patterns are not proportionately very important, but when the father sleeps separately (7 percent), he is most often alone, and the mother is with all of the children. Finally, in the few families in which the parents sleep conjugally (6 percent), the infant and a sibling usually share another room.

In stage 3, in which there are only older children and no infants, the total proportion of two-generation co-sleeping declines but remains high (62 percent). The decrease occurs primarily in the categories of parents co-sleeping with all children, and of parents sleeping separately—each with one or more children. The proportion of parents sleeping conjugally, however, rises nearly sixfold, although at 35 percent this still seems well below American norms.

In stage 3, if the nuclear family is not co-sleeping all together (29 percent), the parents usually keep the youngest child with them (23 percent). There are seven families in this latter pattern, and although there is no difference by density, it is informative to look at the three low-density families (which could provide, if they chose to do so, a separate room for each member). In the first case, the parents share a room with a 15-year-old son, while a 23-year-old daughter and a 19-year-old son share another room. In the second case, the parents co-sleep with a 10-year-old daughter, and two older daughters (15 and 13 years of age) share another room. And in the third case, the parents are with a 14-year-old daughter, and a 20-year-old daughter is alone.

In the consanguineous patterns (10 percent) there are only three cases. In two of these the father sleeps alone while the mother co-sleeps with all of the children, and in one case the father co-sleeps with a 10-year-old daughter and the mother with two other daughters (13 and 9 years of age).

Where the parents sleep conjugally (35 percent), the children also most often all share another room—about half of the time with a sibling of the opposite sex. Most of these cases are high-density families and are crowded for space as, for example, the family in which the parents share one room and the other room is occupied by four children (two sons, 23 and 16 years of age, and two daughters, 20 and 14 years of age). Still, the one low-density family arranges itself with the parents in one room and the two children (an 8-year-old daughter and a 14-year-old son) in another.

Finally, there is one individualistic family with three members, each of whom sleeps alone (father, mother, and 14-year-old daughter).

Parents' Sleeping Arrangements in the Later Stages

The data for parental sleeping arrangements in the later stages of the nuclear family cycle are given in Table 8. Remember that each of these 105 older families is living in the same household with a married child. This is a common—and preferred—situation in Japan. For example, a national survey on aged persons (65 years and over) conducted by the Ministry of Health and Welfare in 1960 found that in Japan's six largest cities, 51 percent of the households containing aged persons also contained a married child; in smaller cities the proportion rose to 64 percent.[18] It seems probable, therefore, that our findings should be valid for about half of the older nuclear families in urban areas.

In stage 4, in which the adult children have a median age of 24, for the first time the proportion of parents sleeping conjugally rises above the proportion of two-generation co-sleeping. There would seem to be three types of parents at this stage. The most numerous are those who have decided to sleep conjugally (68 percent), now that their children have become adults. A second group continues two-generation sleeping habits, either with an adult child or a grandchild (22 percent). And third, a small proportion separate and sleep alone (10 percent).

More in detail, among the 28 cases (68 percent) in which the parents sleep conjugally, the children sleep alone in 20 cases, with siblings of the same sex in four cases, and with cross-sex siblings in three cases; in one case a son co-sleeps with a male employee. Among the nine cases (22 percent) in which the parents sleep in some two-generation combination, seven cases involve children and two cases involve grandchildren. For example, the parents in a low-density family choose to co-sleep with a 24-year-old son; and the mother in a low-density family co-sleeps with her unmarried 35-year-old eldest son while the father sleeps alone (a younger son is married, and his family forms the younger nuclear family in this household). Finally, among the four cases (10 percent) in which the parents sleep separately, in one case three sons share a room together, and there are three rather peculiar cases in which not only the mother and father but also each of the children sleeps alone.

In stage 5 both older parents remain, but there are no unmarried adult children. In this stage, conjugal sleeping reaches its highest proportion (75 percent), followed by two-generation co-sleeping with a grandchild (19 percent), and with a small proportion sleeping separately and alone (6 percent). It would seem that

Table 8. Percentage Distribution of Parental Sleeping Arrangements by Stage in Family Cycle for Older Nuclear Families

Parental Sleeping Arrangements	Stages in Family Cycle			
	4 Both Parents, Adult Child(ren)* (24 years) (N=41 families)	5 Both Parents Only (N=32 families)	6 One Parent, Adult Child(ren)* (22 years) (N=13 families)	7 One Parent Only (N=19 families)
Two Generations: Together............	15	16	n.a.	n.a.
Both parents and child(ren).........	10	n.a.	n.a.	n.a.
Both parents and grandchild(ren)....	5	16	n.a.	n.a.
Two Generations: Consanguineous.....	7	3	62	32
Separation of parents, each with child(ren) or grandchild(ren)............	—	—	n.a.	n.a.
Exclusion of father, mother with child(ren) or grandchild(ren)............	7	3	n.a.	n.a.
Widowed parent with child(ren) or grandchild(ren)	n.a.†	n.a.	62	32
One Generation: Conjugal	68	75	n.a.	n.a.
Parents together, child(ren) or grandchild(ren) elsewhere				
One Generation: Separate	10	6	39	68
Parents, or widowed parent, sleep separately and alone				
Total Percent‡	100	100	101	100

*Median age for children.
†n.a. = not applicable.
‡Totals do not add to 100 percent because of rounding.

there are always about one-fifth of the grandparents in this kind of household who volunteer, or who are pressed into service, to care for the needs of a grandchild at night.

Stages 6 and 7 represent the fragmented remains of the nuclear family at the end of its cycle. The situations in these two stages appear to be reciprocal: In stage 6, where there is an unmarried child, the widowed parent tends to co-sleep with the child or with a grandchild (62 percent of the time); in stage 7, where there is no unmarried child, the widowed parent tends to sleep, at the end, alone (68 percent of the time) unless a grandchild is available.

In support of the above generalization, the 13 cases in stage 6 are made up of 10 widowed mothers and three widowed fathers who do have an unmarried child living in the household. Among the 10 mothers, six co-sleep with a child (four with daughters and two with sons), one co-sleeps in a cluster with three grandchildren, and three sleep alone. Among the three fathers, one co-sleeps with a daughter, and the other two sleep alone.

The 19 cases in stage 7 are made up of 16 widowed mothers and three widowed fathers who do not, of course, have an unmarried child living in the household, and must co-sleep with a grandchild if they are not to sleep alone. Among the 16 mothers, five co-sleep with a grandchild; and among the three fathers, one co-sleeps with a grandchild.

There is a further point of interest. If we combine the cases in stages 4 and 6, and the cases in stages 5 and 7, we have two types of older nuclear families—those that contain older parents and adult unmarried children (54 cases), and those that contain only older parents (51 cases). Here style of family life does make a difference. Households with a "small family business" style of life contain more older nuclear families having parents and adult unmarried children, whereas households with a "salaryman" style of life contain more older nuclear families having only parents.[19] It would seem that young married salarymen are willing to assume responsibility for their parents, but are less willing to have their adult unmarried siblings living with them. In contrast, adult unmarried siblings seem to be more welcome in small business households where they may more directly contribute to the work of the family.

Co-sleeping and the Life Cycle of the Individual

So far we have considered co-sleeping mostly in terms of the life cycle of the nuclear family. What about the co-sleeping career of an individual from birth to death? What are his co-sleeping "chances" at different ages? We have already seen (Table 5) that until the age of 15 a child has about a 50 percent chance of sleeping with one or both parents. From birth to age 15, a child's chances of co-sleeping with a sibling gradually increase; and before age 15 only a few children are likely to sleep alone.

In these early years of life, co-sleeping bears importantly upon questions of socialization and identity.[20] We have shown that, in general, when a family has more than one child, the parents may separate and each co-sleep with a child, or sometimes a child may be sent to co-sleep with an older kinswoman. On the whole we would expect that the older a child, the more likely he is to be removed from the parental bedroom. One way to test this is to contrast the treatment of infants and young children. Of the 88 families in stage 2, 73 have exactly two children—in each case an infant of three to four months, and a child with a median age of three years (see Table 7). We constructed a five-point scale of physical closeness to a parent in sleeping arrangements, and then asked of the data for each family: Who is closer, the infant or the child? The results are given in Table 9.

In each family, the infant and child are assigned a position on the five-point scale, and a tie occurs where both occupy the same position. The scale is as follows: (1) *Alone* means sleeping in a room by oneself. (2) *Other Person's Room* means co-sleeping in a room with a person other than a parent. This can occur when the infant and child are sharing a room (in which case it is a tie), or it can occur when the infant or the child is co-sleeping with an adult (usually a grandmother). (3) *Parent's Room in Own Bed* means that the infant or child is sleeping in his own Western-style bed or crib in the same room with both parents, or with either the mother or father separately. (4) *Parent's Room in Own Futon* means that the infant or child is sleeping in his own individual *futon* (quilts spread on the floor) with both parents, or with either the mother or father separately. (5) *In Parent's Bedding* means that the infant is sleeping in the same bedding (either in a Western-style bed or in Japanese *futon*) with both parents, or with either the mother or father separately.

We consider sleeping in one's own *futon* to be closer in access to a parent than sleeping in one's own bed or crib for this reason: the Japanese quilts of the several co-sleepers are usually laid out next to each other with the edges almost touching. This means that a parent need only reach over to care for an infant or child, without the necessity of getting up. In contrast, a bed or crib is a more distinctly separate "container," and a parent needs to get up in order

Table 9. Comparison of Closeness of Access to Parents in Sleeping Arrangements for Infant and Child in 73 Families Having One Infant and One Child

Scale of Access to Parents	Infant's Access to Parents					
	Alone	Other Person's Room	Parents' Room in Own Bed	Parent's Room in Own *Futon*	In Parent's Bedding	Total Cases
Child's Access to Parents						
Alone	1		2		1	4
Other Person's Room		4	5	4	2	15
Parent's Room in Own Bed	1		1			2
Parent's Room in Own *Futon*	1		18	12	2	33
In Parent's Bedding	1		8	8	2	19
Total Cases	4	4	34	24	7	73

to care for an infant or child. In fact, cribs are mainly used only during the first year of life; after this the crib is put away, and the young child is given his own *futon*. Even during the first year, the crib may be used only as a daytime container, and the infant will be brought down on the mats to sleep in *futon* during the night. Therefore, we scored beds and *futon* differently, but these points on the scale may be collapsed into a single category of *In a Parent's Room in Own Bedding*. We will give the results in both ways.[21]

In Table 9, cases falling on the diagonal represent ties between infant and child in closeness of access to a parent. Cases above the diagonal represent situations in which the infant is closer, and cases below the diagonal represent situations in which the child is closer.

Using the full five-point scale, it is clear that the child is closer to a parent than is the infant. There are 20 ties; the infant is closer in 16 cases; and the child is closer in 37 cases (chi square = 10.0, 2 *df*, *p* < .01). There is no significant difference in this pattern by density, social class, or style of life. There is a difference, however, by whether or not there are extended kin living in the household—a result which we have previously seen in the more general analysis of the data for stage 2.

In the data in Table 9 there are 33 families in which extended kin are present, and 40 families in which they are not. In the extended-kin families, the infant and child are equal in access to a parent (9 ties, 12 infant closer, and 12 child closer) because the child is frequently provided with a "substitute mother" and is sleeping in another person's room while the infant is with the mother (or with both parents). In the families with only nuclear members, the child is closer to a parent (11 ties, 4 infant closer, and 25 child closer). The comparison of closeness to a parent in these two types of families is significant (chi square = 8.2, 2 *df*, *p* < .02).

If the distinction between sleeping in own bed and in own *futon* is collapsed into a broader category of sleeping in own bedding, then the infant and child become equidistant in access to a parent (38 ties, 16 infant closer, and 19 child closer).

We conclude that, at the very least, there is little change in access to a parent in sleeping arrangements during the transition from infancy to childhood. In contrast, there is a sharp physical separation from the parents during this transition in the urban American family, if indeed such a separation had not already been made in infancy.[22] The relative conception of the path to be followed in the socialization of the young child would seem to be different in the two cultures. In Japan, the path seems to lead toward increasing interdependence with other persons, whereas in America the path seems to lead toward increasing independence from others. As we have shown, even in stage 3, at a time when the median age of the child is 13 years, the proportion of two-generation co-sleeping remains very high (see Table 7).

From the age of 16 to 26 or more (see Table 5), roughly 20 percent of the children continue to co-sleep in a two-generation group, mainly with a parent; and about 40 percent co-sleep in a one-generation group, mostly with a sibling. At this older age sleeping alone rises significantly, to 37 percent from age 16 to 25, and to 40 percent by age 26 or more. If our data included children living away from home,[23] then the total proportion of children sleeping alone between the ages of 16 and 26 and older would probably be over 50 percent.

As we have seen, however, daughters tend to marry in urban Japan around the age of 24 to 26, and sons a few years later around the age of 27 to 30. Presumably, after marriage the young couple sleeps conjugally for a year or two until the birth of their first child. But, from that point on, for at least the following 15 years the parents will usually co-sleep in a two-generation group containing one or more of their children. This repeats, of course, their own childhood experience, as can be seen in Table 10, which summarizes the data on sleeping arrangements across our seven stages in the nuclear family cycle.

Somewhere between stages 3 and 4, when the mother is in her middle to late forties and the father is in his late forties to early fifties, the balance shifts for the parents in favor of conjugal sleeping. This pattern persists through stage 5 and until one of the parents dies. Then, if there is an unmarried child available, the widowed parent tends to "revert" to the earlier pattern of co-sleeping with a child in stage 6. Finally, in stage 7, when there is only the widowed parent, the proportion of sleeping alone rises steeply.

In summary, then, an individual in urban Japan can expect to co-sleep in a two-generation group, first as a child and then as a parent, over approximately half of his life. This starts at birth and continues until puberty; it resumes after the birth of the first child and continues until about the time of menopause for the mother; and it reoccurs for a few years in old age. In the interim years the individual can expect to co-sleep in a one-generation group with a sibling after puberty, with a spouse for a few years after marriage, and again with a spouse in late middle age. Sleeping alone appears

Table 10. Summary Percentage Distribution of Parental Sleeping Arrangements across Stages in the Nuclear Family Cycle

	Stages in Family Cycle						
Parental Sleeping Arrangements	1 Both Parents, Infant Only (N=171 families)	2 Both Parents, Infant, Child(ren) (N=88 families)	3 Both Parents, Older Child(ren) (N=31 families)	4 Both Parents, Adult Child(ren) (N=41 families)	5 Both Parents Only (N=32 families)	6 One Parent, Adult Child(ren) (N=13 families)	7 One Parent only (N=19 families)
Two Generations: Together	86	73	52	15	16	n.a.*	n.a.
Two Generations: Consanguineous	4	22	10	7	3	62	32
One Generation: Conjugal	10	6	35	68	75	n.a.	n.a.
One Generation: Separate	—	—	3	10	6	39	68
Total Percent†	100	101	100	100	100	101	100
Median Age of Parents: Mother	26	29	40	56	58	55	63
Father	29	33	45	61	63	66	68

*n.a. = not applicable.
†Totals do not add to 100 percent because of rounding.

to be an alternative most commonly found in the years between puberty and marriage, and to be a reluctantly accepted necessity for the widowed parent toward the end.

We wish to make one broad generalization, and one speculation. The generalization is that sleeping arrangements in Japanese families tend to blur the distinctions between generations and between the sexes, to emphasize the interdependence more than the separateness of individuals, and to underplay (or largely ignore) the potentiality for the growth of conjugal intimacy between husband and wife in sexual and other matters in favor of a more general familial cohesion.[24]

The speculation concerns the coincidence of those age periods when sleeping alone is most likely to occur, with the age periods when suicide is most likely to occur in Japan. The rates for both types of behavior are highest in adolescence and young adulthood, and again in old age.[25] It might be that sleeping alone in these two periods contributes to a sense of isolation and alienation for an individual who, throughout the rest of his life cycle, seems to derive a significant part of his sense of being a meaningful person from his sleeping physically close by other family members. We are not suggesting that sleeping alone "causes" suicide, but rather that this type of separation is an added increment in the unusually difficult problems that Japanese young people seem to have in making the transition from youth to early adulthood as they shift from high school to college, enter the occupational world, and get married. Such transitions do involve the establishment of an identity more separate from one's natal family, and this is made harder by the long period of very close involvement in family life. Similarly, in old age, after a second long period of close familial involvement, to come finally to sleep alone probably carries with it a greater sense of separation than it does in the West.

CULTURE AND CO-SLEEPING

Others before us have hinted in a general way at the importance of co-sleeping in Japanese family life. But we believe that our work documents this with a degree of precision not achieved before, and at the same time demonstrates the wider relevance of what might otherwise appear to be only an offbeat sort of sociometry.

Dore, for example, writes of life in a Tokyo ward as follows: "Beyond the limits of actual cramped discomfort, crowded sleeping seems to be considered to be more pleasant than isolation in separate rooms. The individual gains a comforting security, and it is a sign that a spirit of happy intimacy pervades the family."[26] The co-sleeping-as-intimacy theme also occurs frequently in Japanese fiction and biography. For example, the twentieth-century social reformer, Toyohiko Kagawa, as a child prized—and later vividly remembered—opportunities to sleep by his elder brother. As a seminarian he was deeply impressed when a missionary offered to share his bed even though Kagawa was tubercular. When he recovered, Kagawa in turn shared his bed in the Kobe slums with criminals, alcoholics, the ill, and the destitute. And throughout his adult life he enjoyed praying in bed but was embarrassed because he feared the Almighty might take this as a sign of disrespectful familiarity.[27]

Evidence of a negative sort comes from "collective" societies that attempt to weaken parent-child bonds by requiring children to sleep away from the home. The Israeli kibbutzim are usually cited in this regard; two Japanese collectives tried this method but abandoned it after a period. For example, the Yamagishi community in Mie prefecture once had all children sleep in a dormitory from the age of three months, but now the children move to the dormitory in the third year of primary school (at about age 8). Also at the Yamagishi community, co-sleeping among adults is self-consciously used as a means of weakening interpersonal barriers. During training sessions for prospective members, they live together in one room and are expected to sleep in same-sex pairs. Trainees are told that co-sleeping will help reduce the strength of selfish desires.[28]

In another collective, Shinkyō village in Nara prefecture, a children's sleeping room was also tried, but at present children generally co-sleep with their parents. The following comment by one member is revealing:

> During the first stages of collective living, our plan to give the same love to every child led us at times to deliberately separate bawling children from their parents and make them sleep with other parents, and at times we had all the children sleep together. But lately we have not been particularly concerned about it either way; we are letting matters take their natural course. That is, a younger child sleeps with its parents, an older child sleeps with some other adult. Thus, there are couples who sleep by themselves even though they have children, and there are childless couples who sleep with other peoples' children. . . . Since we are all part of one family, these things can be arranged according to need. . . . Adults and children share their joys and sorrows alike, whatever their ages; so it is simply unthinkable that the emotional foundations of our collective life could shake over whether adults and children sleep together or not.[29]

Vogel's work is perhaps closest to our own, and we have earlier cited his data on sleeping arrangements for infants and young children.[30] He goes on to note: "When a second child is born, and the mother must sleep with the baby, the eldest child ordinarily stops sleeping with the mother and begins sleeping with the father or a grandparent. While elementary-school-age children often sleep in a separate room...it is not unusual for grown children to sleep next to their parents."[31] These observations are in general in line with the results of our analysis, although we believe we have defined the alternative patterns of sleeping arrangements more clearly, and shown that the separation of parents, each with a child, is an important variant pattern at the stage when there is an infant and one or more young children in the family.

Vogel stresses the "mutual dependency" of mother and child and relates it to what he feels is the basic alignment in the family: "mother and children versus father."[32] This alignment is not usually hostile, but refers to a real psychological and behavioral division within the family despite (or in some senses because of) the predominance of all-together sleeping arrangements. The relative lack of husband-wife intimacy in sexual and other matters is related to this division, as is the elaborate world of pleasure for males outside the home. This world of bars, restaurants, and clubs is, however, a great deal less sexual than Americans like to imagine. True, sex is available if a man has the money and time, and the motivation and energy, to invest in the relationship; but for the most part this world is a "play-acting" one which is entered for a few hours after work and then left for the long ride home to family and to bed.

Thus, our analysis of sleeping arrangements has ramifications beyond the confines of the family, and is related to the patterning of values and emotions in Japan in general. Japanese place great emphasis on collaterality (group interrelatedness) not only in the family but in many spheres of activity. They also find much of their enjoyment in the simple physical pleasures of bathing, eating, and sleeping in the company of others. Given these emphases in values and emotions, it is not surprising that individual assertiveness and the open indication of sexual feelings have negative connotations.[33]

A certain proportion of Japanese, however, as would be true among people in any society, have difficulty in behaving, thinking, and feeling according to the norm. Such variant persons may have good or poor adjustments to life. Among the latter, it is interesting that schizophrenic patients in Japan show more sleep disturbance and greater physical assaultiveness (especially toward their mothers) than do comparable American patients in the year prior to hospitalization.[34] There may, therefore, be something mildly ironic in the fact that it is usual to provide patients in small private psychiatric hospitals (which make up the bulk of psychiatric hospitals in Japan) with a personal female attendant who as a matter of routine care is with the patient throughout the day and sleeps in the room with him at night.[35]

In Western eyes, Japanese co-sleeping patterns may appear pathogenic, or at least to be taken as a denial of maturation and individuation. And yet, there is no evidence that on the whole people are not as happy and productive in Japan as in America, and there does not seem to be more grief in one country than in the other. It is true that the rhythm of life across the years is different in the two countries, and we have shown this particularly for sleeping arrangements. But two cautions are necessary here. First, we have little information about sleeping arrangements in America, but what we do have suggests more variation than might be supposed.[36] Because a child in middle-class America is given a separate room in which to sleep does not mean that he stays in it throughout the night; and how do the parents handle this situation? Secondly, the comparison of Japan with America results in sharp differences, but if the comparison were made between Japan and other Eastern or even European countries, the differences might be minor.

Finally, it seems that at least for the first few years of life, the tendency for mother and child to co-sleep is a "natural" one that human beings share in a general way with other mammals. Only recently has Western society tried to interfere. As Peiper notes:

> As late as in the eighteenth century the child slept with his mother. . . . The custom was so widespread—especially because it had such ancient origins—and the conditions so bad that legislators many times had to take measures against it. For example, as late as 1817 the general law for the Prussian States decreed, under threat of imprisonment or physical punishment: "Mothers and wet nurses are not allowed to take children under two years of age into their beds at night or to let them sleep with them or others."[37]

If the pattern of sleeping together was so common in the West as late as the eighteenth century, then we need more information about these matters over the years up to the present. Social change has been rapid in both Japan and America in recent decades, but it is likely that such changes have been greater in technological and occupational sectors than in patterns of family life.

In both cultures, in the flow of events across days and nights and years, as evening descends and the focus of the family turns from contact with the outside to the ordering of life within the house, who sleeps by whom is an issue with serious implications that warrant further study.

NOTES

1. See John W. M. Whiting, Richard Kluckhohn, and Albert Anthony, "The Function of Male Initiation Ceremonies at Puberty," in Eleanor E. Maccoby, Theodore M. Newcomb, and Eugene L. Hartley, editors, *Readings in Social Psychology;* New York, Holt, 1958. Roger V. Burton and John W. M. Whiting, "The Absent Father and Cross-Sex Identity," *Merrill-Palmer Quart.* (1961) 7:85–95.

2. The three hospitals used were St. Luke's International Hospital and Tsukiji Metropolitan Maternity Hospital in Tokyo, and Kyoto Metropolitan Medical School Hospital in Kyoto. In addition to having a three- to four-month-old infant, a mother selected for interview could, and frequently did, have other children as well. The several hospitals were picked so as to insure a good spread of cases by social class and style of life. The reason for focusing on mothers with infants was to provide background on various aspects of family life, not only sleeping arrangements, from a fairly large sample of such cases in order to supplement Caudill's intensive study in the homes of 30 Japanese and 30 American infants and their mothers. On this, see William Caudill and Helen Weinstein, "Maternal Care and Infant Behavior in Japanese and American Urban Middle Class Families," in Reuben Hill and René König (Eds.), *Families in East and West;* Paris, Mouton, 1970.

3. Matsumoto City, and life in it, is described in David W. Plath, *The After Hours: Modern Japan and the Search for Enjoyment;* Berkeley, University of California Press, 1964; see Chapter 2 in particular. Concerning sleeping arrangements in the Matsumoto area, Plath read a preliminary report, including 20 rural cases omitted here, at the 1964 annual meeting of the American Anthropological Association in Detroit.

4. The proportion of two-generation to three-generation households is roughly 2 to 1 in our sample, whereas it is roughly 4 to 1 in comparable households (census household types 4, 5, and 11, 12) for all urban areas (that is, "densely inhabited districts of all *shi*") in Japan. The proportion of salary and wage households to family business households is 1.4 to 1 in our sample, whereas it is 3.0 to 1 for all urban areas in Japan. There is no easy way to estimate accurately the distribution of households by social class from census data, but we are certain that our sample has more households in higher social classes than is true in the general population. See Bureau of Statistics, *1960 Population Census of Japan, Volume 2: One Percent Tabulation, Part 5: Household;* Tokyo, Office of the Prime Minister, 1962; Table 5, p. 137, and Table 13, p. 428.

5. The 1960 census data were recomputed, omitting households of two persons or less, so as to be in line with the household composition of our sample. See footnote 4, 1962; Table 1, pp. 20–21.

6. A person may be at the top of the social system working in a family business or an individual enterprise—for example, a well-known physician in private practice—or he may be at the bottom as the owner of a cigarette stand. Similarly, he may work for salary or wages as an executive, or as a janitor in a large company. In research in Japan, a use-

ful operational break can be made between these two ways of life by classifying businesses having less than 30 employees as "small independent businesses," and by considering owners or employees of such businesses as participating in a way of life that is meaningfully different, in occupational and familial terms, from that of owners or employees in "large businesses." Such a cut-off point is, of course, arbitrary to a degree, and the distinction is more readily apparent between businesses having less than 10 employees and those having more than 100 employees—and this latter classification would still cover the great bulk of cases. We have followed this sort of reasoning in our classification in this research, although our data on occupation of the head of the household are nòt sufficient for such precise placement. More generally, concerning the meaning of these two styles of life, see Plath, 1964 (footnote 3); Caudill and Weinstein, 1966 (footnote 2); and particularly Ezra F. Vogel, *Japan's New Middle Class;* Berkeley, Univ. of Calif. Press, 1963.

7. In devising these procedures for estimating social-class position, we made use of the work of Hollingshead on American populations, and modified it to approximate the Japanese situation along lines suggested by the work of Odaka. See August B. Hollingshead and Fredrick C. Redlich, *Social Class and Mental Illness;* New York, Wiley, 1958, particularly Appendix Two, "The Index of Social Position," pp. 387–397. Nihon Shakai Gakkai Chōsa Iinkai Hen (Research Committee of the Japan Sociological Society), editor, *Nihon Shakai no Kaisōteki Kōzō (The Class Structure of Japanese Society);* Tokyo, Yūhikaku, 1958. Kunio Odaka and Shigeki Nishihira, "Social Mobility in Japan: A Report on the 1955 Survey of Social Stratification and Social Mobility in Japan," *East Asian Cultural Studies* (1965) 4 (Nos. 1–4): 83–126. Kunio Odaka, "The Middle Classes in Japan," *Contemporary Japan* (1964) 28: 10–32; and (1965) 28: 268–296. See also Alex Inkeles and Peter H. Rossi, "National Comparisons of Occupational Prestige," *Amer. J. Sociology* (1956) 61: 329–339. Charles E. Ramsey and Robert J. Smith, "Japanese and American Perceptions of Occupations," *Amer. J. Sociology* (1960) 65: 475–482.

Our final three social-class groups may be described as follows. The upper middle class consists mainly of heads of households who are college graduates, and who are in professional or supervisory positions or are owners of substantial businesses. The lower middle class consists mainly of heads of households who are high-school graduates, and who are white-collar workers or owners of small businesses with paid employees. The working class is equally divided between heads of households who are high-school graduates and those who have less than a high-school education, and who are technicians, skilled or unskilled workers, paid employees of small businesses, or owners of small family shops with no paid employees.

8. Mat-floored rooms in Japanese dwellings lack the "specificity of purpose" usually assigned to rooms in Western dwellings. Thus, the ordinary Japanese house is not sharply divided into living rooms, bedrooms, dining rooms, recreation rooms, and so on. In part this reflects the relative sparsity of furniture in the Japanese house. Nevertheless, household members do tend to divide the space among themselves and to assign the use of a particular room to one or several persons. In addition, a household with multiple rooms is likely to set aside one of them as a "living room" or "guest room." The size of a room is usually given in terms of the number of mats it contains. One mat is roughly six by three feet in size and two inches in thickness, and it is made of packed rice straw covered with a finely woven rush. The edges of

better quality mats are bound in cloth. The most common sizes for rooms in Japan are six mats (roughly 9 by 12 feet) and four and one-half mats (roughly 9 by 9 feet). On these matters of use and construction of rooms see Ronald Dore, *City Life in Japan;* London, Routledge and Kegan Paul, 1958. Richard K. Beardsley, John W. Hall, and Robert E. Ward, *Village Japan;* Chicago, Univ. of Chicago Press, 1959. Bruno Taut, *Houses and People of Japan;* Tokyo, Sanseido, 1958.

9. See Alan H. Gleason, "Postwar Housing in Japan and the United States, A Case in International Comparison," in Univ. of Mich. Center for Japanese Studies, *Studies on Economic Life in Japan;* Occasional Papers, Number 8, 1964; pp. 1–36.

10. See footnote 9; Table 1 and note 3, p. 28.

11. Two of these households include extended kin; the other 36 are composed of nuclear kin only.

12. For example, in the observational study of 60 three-to-four-month-old-infants by Caudill and Weinstein (see footnote 2), 17 of the 30 American infants slept alone, and the parents of the remaining 13 infants planned to move to a larger apartment by the end of the first year so as to provide a separate bedroom for the baby. All of the 30 Japanese infants co-slept with their parents, to whom the idea of moving to provide more space for the baby never occurred. In other reports, Pease found that in one Tokyo suburb a child co-sleeps with his mother for an average of 92 months; and Vogel found that the interval varies from 35 months among Tokyo shopkeeping families to 130 months in a deep-sea fishing village in Miyagi prefecture. See Demaris Pease, "Some Child Rearing Practices in Japanese Families," *Marriage and Family Living* (1961) 23:179–181; and Vogel, footnote 6; pp. 229–230. In contrast, the only fairly large-scale study for the United States that we have found reports data on sleeping arrangements for children in Baltimore who were patients at a psychiatric outpatient clinic, and for a control group, in answer to the question: "Did your chlid ever sleep in the same room with you and his/her father?" This question assumes that co-sleeping may be an unusual and infrequent event (as at times of sickness), and thus the answers are not strictly comparable with our Japanese data, which are reported in terms of habitual sleeping arrangements. The Baltimore study found no differences between children who were patients and those who were controls. Of the total group of 370 children, 61 percent either had never co-slept with parents (39 percent) or had stopped by the end of the first year (22 percent). Of the remainder, 21 percent had stopped by the end of the fourth year, and 17 percent had continued beyond the end of the fourth year. These results are from unpublished data supplied by Martha S. Oleinick, Office of Biometry, National Institute of Mental Health. See also Martha S. Oleinick, Anita K. Bahn, Leon Eisenberg, and Abraham M. Lilienfeld, "A Retrospective Study of the Early Socialization Experiences and Intrafamilial Environment of Psychiatric Out-Patient Clinic Children and Control Group Children," unpublished manuscript.

13. Discussions of Japanese family life often stress the role played by the grandparents when they are present in the household—particularly the grandmother—in the rearing of children. Table 4 shows that 13 percent of the children in high-density families and 6 percent in low-density families co-sleep in some combination with an extended kin member who is, in fact, most often a grandmother. These percentages do not seem to represent a "considerable influence" in this regard on the lives of our group of children, but we defer discussion of this issue

until the next section of the paper. It is also not unusual to find reference to the importance of the role of a family servant in the rearing of children. And yet, in our data, no nonrelated person co-sleeps exclusively with a nuclear family member; and the likelihood of a nonrelated person co-sleeping at all with a nuclear family member is at most 5 percent in complex-mixed groups in high-density households.

14. We are indebted to Koyama for pointing out the necessity to consider the various stages in the family life cycle when analyzing social characteristics of the Japanese family. We have not made use of all of his stages here, and have made finer subdivisions in others. See Takashi Koyama, "Changing Family Structure in Japan," in Robert J. Smith and Richard K. Beardsley, editors, *Japanese Culture: Its Development and Characteristics;* Chicago, Aldine Publishing Co., 1962.

15. Within the 199 households represented in Table 4, there are 323 extended kin members (231 in high-density and 92 in low-density households). These members live in 123 households. Of these, 13 households contain only adult unmarried brothers or sisters of the husband or wife in the younger nuclear family. These unmarried brothers or sisters sleep alone, or co-sleep in same-sex groups of two. Our concern here is with the remaining 110 households that contain at least one parent of the husband or wife in the younger nuclear family, and may contain the other parent plus the parents' grown unmarried children.

16. In considering these data for children who are 16 years of age or more, remember that these show the sleeping arrangements of older children who are *living at home.* If they have left the home, and are living in company dormitories, rooming houses, apartments, and so on, their sleeping arrangements most likely would show higher proportions of co-sleeping with nonrelated persons, or alone. A survey conducted in October, 1965, by the Economic Planning Agency concerning the patterns of life of 2,500 young unmarried workers between 15 and 29 years of age in large companies in Tokyo and Osaka, found that 76 percent of the young women, and 44 percent of the young men, were living with their parents. See Japan Information Service, "Survey Taken on Finances of Young Japanese Workers," *Japan Report* (1966) 12 (No. 8, April 30): 5–7.

17. See Robert O. Blood, Jr., *Love-Match and Arranged Marriage;* book manuscript in preparation, Dept. of Sociology, Univ. of Mich., Ann Arbor, Mich. Irene B. Taeuber, *The Population of Japan;* Princeton Univ. Press, 1958; p. 227. Bureau of Statistics, *1960 Population Census of Japan, Vol. 2: One Percent Tabulation, Part 1: Age, Marital Status, Legal Nationality, Education and Fertility;* Tokyo, Office of the Prime Minister, 1962; Table 3, pp. 72–73.

18. Percentages for other types of households that include aged persons are: (1) In the six largest cities an additional 25 percent of the aged lived with adult unmarried children, and 18 percent lived with a spouse only or alone; (2) in the smaller cities an additional 17 percent lived with adult unmarried children, and 13 percent lived with a spouse or alone. The remaining percentages for the two kinds of cities include miscellaneous types of households in which the aged lived with grandchildren, with other aged persons, in institutions, and so on. All of these data are cited by Watanabe from The National Survey on the Aged published by the Ministry of Health and Welfare in 1961. See Sadamu Watanabe, *Old People in Transitional Japan;* Tokyo, pamphlet published by The Gerontological Association of Japan, 1963; especially pp. 6–7.

19. The data are as follows: Small business households contain 34 cases of parents and adult unmarried children, and 20 cases of only parents; salaryman households contain 20 cases of parents and adult unmarried children, and 31 cases of only parents. This fourfold comparison is significant (chi square = 5.9, 1 df, $p < .02$).

20. See footnote 1.

21. The main reason given by Japanese mothers for the use of cribs during the first year is that they are easier to clean than *futon* if the infant should soil his bedding. A secondary reason is the fear of rolling on the infant while asleep, although this applies mostly to the situation where the infant is sleeping in a parent's *futon* rather than in his own *futon*. The types of bedding used by individuals in our sample present some interesting contrasts. Restricting the analysis to the 259 households which include an infant and have two or more sleeping rooms, the following results are found. Among the 259 infants, 172 use cribs and 87 use *futon*; whereas among the 105 children in these households, only 10 use beds and 95 use *futon*. Thus, only 34 percent of the infants use *futon*, but 91 percent of the children do so. Among infants, the use of cribs is linked to higher social class ($p < .001$), to a salaryman style of life ($p < .01$), and to residence in Tokyo ($p < .05$). There are, of course, 518 parents of the infants in the 259 households, and the overwhelming proportion, 85 percent, of these parents sleep in *futon* (439 *futon* to 79 beds). Variations in parental use of beds or *futon* are influenced by several variables. First of all, beds are found in Tokyo more than Kyoto ($p < .05$), in low-density households ($p < .01$), among salarymen rather than small businessmen ($p < .001$), and are concentrated at upper social levels ($p < .001$). Secondly, double beds, in contrast to single beds, are used in high-density households ($p < .001$); and, equally, double *futon*, in contrast to single *futon*, are used in high-density households ($p < .02$). So it would seem that when things are crowded people adjust by using a container in which they can double up, whether they choose a bed or a *futon*.

22. See footnote 12.

23. See footnote 16.

24. To be sure, sexual relations between parents take place, but in what is reported as a brief and "businesslike" manner (for example, see Beardsley. Hall, and Ward, in footnote 8; p. 333). Vogel, citing his own data and that of Shinozaki in a larger study, indicates that, compared to American couples, Japanese couples have intercourse less frequently, and have less foreplay and afterplay (see Vogel, in footnote 6; pp. 220–222). As might be presumed from the sleeping arrangements shown in our data, sexual intercourse in Japan frequently takes place in the presence of sleeping children. The most usual answer given by the 30 Japanese mothers in an intensive case study of mother-child relations (see Caudill and Weinstein, in footnote 2) was that the parents wait until they think the child is sound asleep and then have intercourse. In addition, as Table 4 shows, the parents are usually the only *adults* in the bedroom, at least until they are in late middle age, and hence have a certain degree of privacy. In more traditional Japan, however, it was not too unusual for a young married couple to co-sleep with the husband's parents even though other rooms were available. In this regard, the famous Meiji reformer Fukuzawa urged that young married couples have a room apart from the husband's parents. Apparently Fukuzawa was not concerned about sex so much as he was with providing the young wife with at least a nocturnal sanctuary away from her

carping mother-in-law. However, Fukuzawa did not practice his own precepts. See Carmen Blacker, *The Japanese Enlightenment;* Univ. of Cambridge Oriental Publications, Number 10, 1964; pp. 88, 157–158.

25. In our data, as indicated, sleeping alone is most likely during the ages of 16–26 and after approximately age 65. Suicide in Japan, as De Vos and others have pointed out, is of special interest because of its sex and age distribution. The ratio of women to men is higher than in any other country, and the concentration of suicide in early life (15–24 years) and old age (60 years and over) is unique in having this U-shaped pattern. Moreover, these phenomena have occurred yearly as far back as reliable Japanese statistics have been kept. For example, in terms of the rates in Japan per 100,000 population for 1952–1954: For ages 15–19 the rate among males is 26.1, and among females is 18.7; for ages 20–24 the rate among males is 60.0, and among females is 35.5. In the United States, the comparable rates are: for ages 15–19, males 1.7 and females 1.6; and for ages 20–24, males 7.8 and females 2.8. In old age in Japan the rates for ages 60–69 are 58.1 for males and 34.6 for females; whereas in the United States the rates are 42.4 for males and 8.9 for females. See George A. DeVos, "Role Narcissism and the Etiology of Japanese Suicide," *Transcultural Psychiatric Research* (1966) 3:13–17; and "Deviancy and Social Change: A Psychocultural Evaluation of Trends in Japanese Delinquency and Suicide," in Robert J. Smith and Richard K. Beardsley, *Japanese Culture: Its Development and Characteristics;* Chicago, Aldine, 1962; pp. 153–171.

26. See Dore in footnote 8; p. 49.

27. On these aspects of the life of Kagawa see: William Axling, *Kagawa;* London, Student Christian Movement Press, 1932; pp. 22, 41–42. Emerson O. Bradshaw, *Unconquerable Kagawa;* St. Paul, Macalester Park, 1952; p. 84. Helen F. Topping, *Introducing Kagawa;* Chicago, Willett, Clark, 1935; p. 4.

28. See David W. Plath, "Utopian Rhetoric: Conversion and Conversation in a Japanese Cult," *Essays on the Verbal and Visual Arts: Proceedings of the 1966 Annual Spring Meeting of the American Ethnological Society.* J. Helm, ed. Seattle, University of Washington Press, 1967.

29. Yoshie Sugihara, *Shinkyō Buraku* (*The Shinkyō Community*); Tokyo, Shunjūsha, 1962; pp. 214–215.

30. See footnote 12.

31. See Vogel, in footnote 6; p. 231.

32. See Vogel, in footnote 6; p. 211.

33. On these broader issues see: William Caudill and Harry A. Scarr, "Japanese Value Orientations and Culture Change," *Ethnology* (1962) 1:53–91. William Caudill, "Patterns of Emotion in Modern Japan," in Robert J. Smith and Richard K. Beardsley, editors, *Japanese Culture: Its Development and Characteristics;* Chicago, Aldine, 1962; pp. 115–131. William Caudill and L. Takeo Doi, "Interrelations of Psychiatry, Culture and Emotion in Japan," in Iago Galdston, editor, *Man's Image in Medicine and Anthropology;* New York, Internat. Univ. Press, 1963; pp. 374–421.

34. See Carmi Schooler and William Caudill, "Symptomatology in Japanese and American Schizophrenics," *Ethnology* (1964) 3:172–178.

35. See William Caudill, "Around the Clock Patient Care in Japanese Psychiatric Hospitals: The Role of the *Tsukisoi*," *Amer. Sociol. Review* (1961) 26:204–214.

36. See footnote 12.

37. Albrecht Peiper, *Cerebral Function in Infancy and Childhood;* New York, Consultants Bureau, 1963; p. 611. For further information on this topic see also Philippe Ariès, *Centuries of Childhood;* New York, Knopf, 1962.

Parental Attitude Toward Twins in Japan

YOSHIKO IKEDA

Twins have been described as special human beings in myth, folklore, drama, and literature, including one of the oldest human documents, the Bible. Each culture shows it characteristic attitudes toward twins. Some cultures respect and worship twins as related to the supernatural, or welcome them as symbols of a good crop or sexual productivity. Other cultures reject or kill one or both of them as dangerous creatures with magical power, or receive them reluctantly as a penalty for the mother's sin, such as adultery or heterodoxy. Inoue and others reported in 1956 that the frequency of twin birth in Japan was assumed to be 0.47 percent, that is, one pair of twins in every 211 births, and the frequency of monozygosity (MZ) and dizygosity (DZ), 1.83 versus 1.0. Roughly speaking, twins seem to occur less frequently in Japan than in other countries, where the figure for MZ : DZ frequency is reversed.[1]

In the process of our long-term follow-up study of 20 pairs of twin children since 1952 (12 MZ pairs; 8 DZ pairs, including three different-sexed twins), we have finally come to realize that characteristic cultural and parental attitudes towards twins play very important roles in our culture. We have become especially interested in the incidence in Japan of (1) a general dislike of twins (2) discrimination between the elder and the younger and between a boy and girl, and (3) plural images of mothers (mother and grandmother).

GENERAL DISLIKE OF TWINS

According to a social survey conducted by the Ministry of Education in 1952, there were many superstitions about twins in all parts of Japan. The popular belief seemed to be that mothers were destined

To appear in *Youth, Socialization and Mental Health,* W.P. Lebra, ed. (Honolulu: The University Press of Hawaii) forthcoming.

to have twins as punishment for their sins, for disgraceful acts, or for violating taboos. To cite some examples, "When a woman has sexual intercourse over the seams of the Tatami mats," "When a woman eats a two-branched turnip," "When a woman cuts vegetables on the lid of a saucepan," "When a pregnant woman pulls a piece of cloth or paper with another woman, . . . then she is destined to have twins." It was also reported that a woman with criminal ancestors is fated to have twins. Another well-known belief was that different-sexed fraternal twins who were especially disliked were "reincarnations of men and women who committed double suicide."

In our 1952 study, we dealt with normal twin children. But they still told of suffering feelings of inferiority from being a twin. A monozygotic girl, aged 16 said, "I feel that people think twins are animal-like." "They must believe that twins are a kind of malformation" (a dizygotic girl, aged 16). "Children and adults gaze at us as if we are curiosities" (a monozygotic boy, aged 11).

When our contacts deepened, their mothers also began to complain of treatment they received. "My mother-in-law accused me of conceiving twins. She insisted that my husband's family never had any multiple births." "My husband and father-in-law persuaded me to give one of the pair to a distant relative, because they were ashamed of twins." "When it was found that I was pregnant with twins, I was forced by my parents-in-law not to go out and to give birth at home. It was clear that they wished the twins to die. The twins were unfortunately dizygotic. They said the mother's family was responsible for this. Feeling guilty, my own parents had to bring up one of the pair until the age of six."

Years have passed since our first survey in 1952, and many twin singers and actresses have become quite popular on television and radio. We wondered if under such influences any change had occurred in cultural and parental attitudes towards twins, and this led us to take up the following research.

In cooperation with the public health centers in N. city and I. city, we began a survey in 1967. We registered all the twins who were born in both cities from 1961 to 1966. First, public health nurses visited the mothers at home. Then we invited them to come to public health centers with the twins. Later our research team visited them at home and invited them to Japan's NIMH office regularly. We also formed a social group for mothers of twins.

The subjects of this study were 52 pairs of twins (25 pairs in I. city and 27 pairs in N. city) and their mothers. Their ages (Table 1) ranged from six months to six years. There were 68 premature infants and 36 normal infants. The age range of parents in shown in Table 2. The education of the parents (Table 2) and occupation (Table 3) of the fathers varied. When mothers learned that they were pregnant with twins, 69 percent of them felt unhappy and uncomfortable (Table 4). Only 7 percent felt happy. The rest were quite ambivalent. The main reason for unhappiness were (1) the anticipated difficulty of nursing two premature babies, (2) prejudices and superstitions against twins, (3) financial burden, (4) the anticipated difficulty of educating two children, and (5) the father's negative attitude. However, when the babies grew up, 23 out of 36 mothers began to feel happy about their twins. Nineteen of them had found that it was much easier to bring up twins than they had expected, and four of them believed that twins are welcomed by society. Twenty-four mothers still firmly believed that people in general disliked twins and were prejudiced against

Table 1: Age and Sex of Twins (1967)

Sex		Age							Total (pairs)
		Under 1	1	2	3	4	5	6	
M	M	2	1	5	0	2	4	3	17
F	F	0	8	4	3	4	2	1	22
M	F	1	2	3	2	3	1	1	13
Total		3	11	12	5	9	7	5	52

Table 2: Age and Education of Parents

Item	Father	Mother
Age:		
21–25	2	10
26–30	15	20
31–35	22	15
36+	13	7
Education:		
6 years	7	9
9 years	16	22
12 years	21	19
Through college	8	2

Table 3: Occupation of Fathers and Family Structure

Occupation	Family Structure		Total
	Nuclear Family	Extended Family	
Farmer	3	7	10
Merchant	5	6	11
Unskilled laborer	10	1	11
White-collar worker	15	5	20
Total	33	19	52

Table 4: Mothers' Initial Reaction to the Prospect of Twins

Reaction	Number (%)	Reasons	Number
Happy, satisfied	4(7)	I can get two babies by one delivery.	4
		It is easier to bring up two children together and simultaneously.	3
		Twins are evaluated highly by society.	4
Unhappy, dissatisfied	36(69)	It is difficult to nurse two premature babies.	32
		It is difficult to educate two children.	16
		Father's negative attitude.	4
		It is difficult to choose the heir.	1
		Financial burden.	23
		Social prejudices and superstitions.	24
Ambivalent	12(24)	——	

Table 5: Mothers' Descriptions of General Prejudice Against Twins

Superstitions	Twins are "animal-like."	2
	Twins are the result of sexual lasciviousness.	2
	Twins inherit bad traits	2
	Twins die early.	2
	Twins have defects.	1
	Different-sexed twins are reincarnations of men and women who committed double suicide.	1
	Others	5
Society's evaluation	Twins bring shame on parents-in-law.	9
	Twins give trouble to neighbors.	9
	Society makes a show of twins.	3
	Twins are injurious to family's reputation.	2
	Twins born of old parents are shameful.	1
	Others	1

them because they were animal-like; were the result of sexual lasciviousness; were destined to die early; had defects; or were shameful and gave trouble to their neighbors (Table 5). Parents in the lower social class received twins as punishment for sins such as an extramarital relationship, consanguineous marriage, or "runaway" marriage (without parental sanction). Because of physical fatigue and fear of having twins again, some mothers refused to have sexual relations with their husbands.[2] In 2 of the 52 families studies, the arrival of twins caused the final breakup of the family.

A few mothers felt happy being pregnant with twins. They expressed opinions that twins were very cute, lovable, and popular in society. These unusually exaggerated statements were never heard in cases of singletons and often reflected the mother's inner feelings of inferiority and, at times, strong exhibitionism.

Compared with the results of the previous study conducted in 1952, the results in 1967 showed slightly different attitudes toward twins. For instance, twin-like names were fewer in number in 1967. Only 50 percent of the mothers expected the twins to be discriminated as elder and younger (90 percent in 1952). However, this ratio later increased. Since the family structure changed, twin babies were mainly taken care of by their mothers. If the mother needed any help, the maternal grandmother or an aunt assisted her. (Previously, twins, especially the elder one, were brought up by the paternal grandmother.)

A few babies were given out for adoption. Compared with previous cases of adoption, motivations of mothers for giving away one of the twins seemed rather egocentric. It should be noted that in spite of the progress in obstetrics since 1952, 27 mothers out of 52 were not notified that they were carrying twins until the time of delivery or in the last month of pregnancy.

"ELDER BROTHER" AND "YOUNGER BROTHER" ROLE EXPECTATION

One of the most characteristic attitudes toward twins in Japanese culture is the different roles expected for the elder twin (the firstborn) and the younger twin (the second born). Even though the two reach the same level of physical and psychological development, and even if the elder is intellectually inferior to the younger, the elder one is still called "the elder" with honorifics and is expected to behave as the elder. On the other hand, the younger, who is called merely by his first name, is given the privilege of being the baby. What effects have the elder and younger role expectations on the mental health of the twins in childhood? I would like to present our observations of twin infants during a four-day camp held in the summer of 1968, and results from an 18-year case study of a pair of like-sexed fraternal twins.

The day camp was held at our National Institute of Mental Health by a research team consisting of psychiatrists, psychologists, pediatricians, and social workers. Eleven pairs of twins (7 monozygotic and 4 dizygotic, including different-sexed twins) were chosen from approximately 150 pairs of twin infants in the neighboring area. Their ages ranged from 2 years, 3 months to 5 years, 5 months. None had previously attended kindergarten or nursery school. Each pair was observed carefully from 9 a.m. to 4 p.m. while they were at free play, controlled play, swimming, and on picnic. They were also subject to psychological testing and experimentation.

We specifically examined the effect of the elder and younger role expectation on the twins' behavioral patterns by observing "separation from mother" situations each morning and carrying out three experiments causing anxiety, fear, and competitiveness. We found that twins designated the elder showed more difficulty parting from their mothers and participating in group activities. When the pair were left alone at free play, A (the elder) ordered B (the younger) around and took leadership. B was more modest and looked up to A as the boss. In the group and in experiments, however, A was more insecure, timid, and complicated than B. The younger twins behaved more freely and actively and were most tolerant to maternal separation. Mothers often described A as being careful and sensitive and readily becoming sulky and suspicious. From these findings, our team came to the conclusion that receiving the role of elder in early infancy made A feel more frustrated and dissatisfied regarding his dependency needs and attachment to his mother and made him more insecure in daily life than his younger twin.

A Case Study : Like-Sexed Dizygotic Twins

These twins were born as the eldest and second sons of a pharmacist who had come from a traditional, small town in the North and owned a store in downtown Tokyo. The mother was greatly shocked when twins arrived but was consoled when told by the father they were boys. (The couple's three older children were girls.) As a newborn baby, B, the younger, received more attention from the mother because he weighed less at birth and refused cow's milk. In infancy, A suffered from several diseases. As a result, he became closer to his mother. Parents treated A as the eldest son and called him "the elder" with honorifics, but called B only by his first name. B was frustrated at home because his father tried to correct his lefthandedness. A, on the other hand, liked to imitate and help his mother. B showed a better score in intelligence, social maturity, and vocabulary tests, but A was more self-confident and productive in other psychological tests including the Rorschach, CAT, PFT, and other experimental situations. As the superior. A commanded and protected B. In late infancy, B began to play with other boys outside the home and resisted A's orders. B insisted that he should be the elder because he was taller and stronger than A. They fought each other constantly.

In elementary school, the twins were placed in the same class for three years. B was ahead of A in school marks and better adjusted to the classroom. Eventually A revealed behavior problems including refusal to go to school, headaches, outbursts of violent behavior. Although the father tried to train A as the eldest son, A felt more and more insecure. Finally, sobbing, A said to his mother, "B is better than me. Please change our names. I can't be the elder. I will take B's name. I give mine to B." In psychological testing, interviews, and experiments, A showed hostility towards B. A also resented being a twin. A's responses were, "When I grow up, I shall put B in jail," "I am very happy when B fails in class," "I like to study when B is absent, for I feel inferior to B," "The elder brother is at a disadvantage because he has to be better than the younger," "If I have to be a twin, I would like to be ordinary twins who look very much alike." Accepting our advice, the parents put the boys in different classes from the fourth grade on and stopped discriminating in their role expectations for A and B.

In junior high school, B was still better in scholastic and athletic achievements. They were both attractive-looking teenagers, but B appeared more masculine. Accepting his wife's desperate request, the father permitted A to go to a private senior high school affiliated with a university. For the first time, A became active and could tolerate strict training for basketball. A gradually reached B's level in height and weight, and at one point A was even taller than B.

To fulfill his father's wish, A chose engineering at the university; B failed the entrance examination for a national university and the following year entered another university, majoring in physics. It is interesting to note that the twins again became close and began to attend our twin group meetings consisting of adolescents and youths. The pair was liked by younger twins, A as an effective speaker and B as a quiet but confident listener. Both took the role of the elder brothers toward the other twins. (See Table 6 for a summary of data for this pair.)

Table 6: Summary of Data for Case Study of
Fraternal Boy Twins

	Born November 1948 Father, pharmacist, age 39 Mother, housewife, age 37	
	A	**B**
Babyhood	Birth weight 2850 g Bottle-fed	2625 g Breast-fed
Infancy	Measles, Scarlet fever "Elder brother" role	Autointoxication? "Younger brother" role Lefthandedness corrected
	Dizygosity established	
	IQ 94 Social maturity, vocabulary good Psychological testing & experiments More confident, freer	IQ 97 Social maturity, vocabulary a little better Tense, Rejection More friends outside the home
	Fighting over "elder brother" role	
	1st grade–3rd grade same class	
Elementary School	School achievement low Refused to go to school Transient behavior problems IQ 97 Rorschach, SCT	School achievement high 9 cm taller in height 4 kg heavier in weight IQ 120 Rorschach, SCT
	4th grade+different classes, equal status at home	
Junior High School	Felt inferior to B Gradual improvement in school Rorschach, SCT	Better adjusted in school Pitcher on baseball team Rorschach, SCT
	Different Schools	
Senior High School	Private school affiliated with university basketball team	Public school Member of Students' Committee
	Physical growth about the same	
University	Course of Engineering	One-year *"ronin"* (college preparatory study at home) Course of physics the next year
	Friendship and Cooperation	

The Problems of Different-Sexed Fraternal Twins

Those who have the highest motivation for joining twin mothers' groups are mothers of different-sexed fraternal twins. These mothers are usually envied by mothers of girl twins. In actuality, however, they tend to be confused about disciplining the two-sexed twins. The mother wants to train the girl to become "girl-like" (*onnarashiku*) and the boy to become "boy-like" (*otokorashiku*). Needless to say, she has much higher expectations for the boy. She expects the boy to be bigger, stronger, and more independent. But girls develop and reach maturity much quicker than boys. The girl starts to talk earlier and is likely to show more social maturity and more interest in people. She is ahead of the boy in schoolwork through elementary school until the low-teens. At times, the strain of always trying to be "masculine" may impose a burden on him. He has the double burden of being the elder plus being a boy. In our twin clinic, we regularly saw more boys with behavior problems, including maternal separation anxiety and school phobia, than girls. Our experience with 13 pairs of boy-girl twins since 1967 and our survey of twin children in primary schools in K. city and S. ward in Tokyo seem to support our observation.

PLURAL IMAGES OF MOTHERS

I will touch on this problem very briefly. It was often observed along with elder/younger discrimination, especially in large families with grandparents and other relatives living together. In our 1952 group, the grandmother took responsibility for one twin in 17 of the 20 pairs. Usually the grandmother took care of the older one, especially if he was the eldest son. She tended to be overprotective and overindulgent. Thus, twins who were taken care of by grandmothers experienced very complicated and difficult interpersonal relationships.[3]

CONCLUSION

Through our follow-up studies on twin children and their mothers carried out in 1952 and again in 1967, we found that (1) superstitions and prejudices against twins and discrimination between the elder and the younger continue to exist in our culture today. (2) We found slight differences in attitudes toward twins between the 1952 survey and that of 1967, influenced by such factors as change in family structure, etc. (3) Even though in Japan twins may be considered a comparatively rare phenomenon and receive special treatment, there is much in common between Japanese public attitudes toward twins and those of other cultures in the historical past and even in developing countries of today. (4) We feel that much of what we have learned through our study of twins can be applied to the care of singletons as well, and that the rigid enforcement of parents' ideas as to the roles that children should play, regardless of level of psycho-physical development, may ruin or help the future prospect of that child.

NOTES

1. According to Komai, twin birth frequency is 2.7–4.5 percent in Nigeria, 1.4–1.6 percent in Sweden, 1.2 percent in England, and 1.1 percent among American Caucasians. The boy-boy: boy-girl: girl-girl ratio is 1:1:1 in America and 2:1:2 in Japan. Yamada investigated senile twins to examine the process of aging. He found that about 30 percent of them had been adopted immediately after birth. We presume that before 1948 there were many twins who were not registered as twins.

2. Leonard mentioned that American cultural attitudes toward twins are very positive. Therefore, thoughts of double trouble or of deeper emotional dissatisfactions are quickly put out of the mind of the mother. Burlingham described that the fantasy of having a twin was found among children after the Oedipal age in England. So far, however, we have never heard of such attitudes or fantasies in Japan.

   In the ancient days in Japan, twins or triplets were welcomed as harbingers of a good crop or as people possessing magical power. In myth, a hero-god who killed an eight-headed serpent was believed to be a twin. Also, early documents indicate that triplets born in Ise were given gifts from the Emperor and triplet girls served as ladies-in-waiting in the Imperial court.

   Western cultures have various interesting tales of twins in dramas, novels, and poems. But Japan has only three kabuki plays and one bunraku puppet show drama dealing with the subject. These are rarely performed, except "Sugawara Denjyu Tenaraikagami," in which triplet brothers meet a tragic fate. Regarding novels and folklore, we cannot recall anything popular.

   When and how Japanese cultural attitudes toward twins became negative is not known. Some believe that it had something to do with the feudal system of the Edo era, which emphasized male primogeniture.

3. A girl, age 12, DZ, told us, "I was very much relieved when my grandmother died. I felt sad, of course. I remember her devotion to me. But I always felt guilty toward my mother and my younger [twin] sister. Her death would probably improve my relationship with them." (On a home visit, we recall, her mother served her grandmother and her, like a servant.) Another boy, age 17, MZ, recalled, "When I entered elementary school, my grandparents bought me a leather school bag which was very expensive. They did not buy one like it for my younger [twin] brother. My mother bought him a cheap vinyl bag. When we went to school together, I felt uncomfortable carrying my shiny new bag."

"Graduation Phobia" in the Japanese University

YOMISHI KASAHARA

My reason for selecting this subject for a conference on youth is that one of the most pressing problems in Japanese universities has to do with those students who fail final examinations and yet who stay on year after year, either to graduate after a number of years or eventually to drop out. We use the term *ryūnen* to describe these students. To be accurate, *ryūnen* on campus should be designated potential dropouts. Every university in Japan contains a considerable number of such undergraduate *ryūnen*.[1] It seems to me worthwhile to consider this problem from a cross-cultural point of view, because I believe that the attitude in various countries toward college education comes out clearly in the way such students are handled. For these reasons I would like to comment briefly on how failing students are handled in Japanese universities.

In many Japanese universities, undergraduates who fail to earn enough credits for graduation within four years are allowed to stay for three additional years without special reason. Moreover, if the student has a valid excuse—physical or mental illness, financial difficulty, study abroad—he is allowed to take a leave of absence for up to four years, without losing his status as a student. Japanese custom permits such a vague reason as "personal affairs." Thus, the mentally disturbed, political activists, and apathetic students are able to utilize this excuse to prolong their stay on campus. Consequently, if these students wish to do so, they can stay for a maximum of eleven years before having to drop out of college.

According to a 1970 survey at Kyoto University, over one

To appear in *Youth, Socialization, and Mental Health,* W.P. Lebra, ed. (Honolulu: The University Press of Hawaii) forthcoming.

quarter of the senior class (888 students out of 3456) had postponed graduation for more than one year. Among these were many students, particularly in the Department of Technology, who decided to postpone graduation simply because they hoped to get better jobs the following year. Campus psychiatrists are particularly concerned about those *ryūnen* who have extended their stay for more than three years. We call these "long-term *ryūnen*" to differentiate them from those who stay for one or two additional years for understandable reasons. According to the survey, Kyoto University has 137 such long-term *ryūnen*. Their distribution by department follows in Table 1. It is interesting to note the high incidence of *ryūnen* in the Literature Department and the lowest incidence in the Economics Department. Table 2 shows the length of time of postponement and the reasons for it.

Table 1: Distribution of Senior-Class *Ryūnen* at
Kyoto University, by Department

Department	Enrollment	Total Ryūnen	Long-Term Ryūnen
Literature	388	186 (47.9)[a]	30 (7.7)
Education	98	26 (26.5)	3 (3.0)
Law	497	152 (30.6)	19 (3.4)
Economics	270	26 (9.6)	4 (1.4)
Science	452	115 (25.4)	17 (3.7)
Technology	1157	270 (23.3)	39 (3.3)
Agriculture	367	90 (24.5)	16 (4.3)
Medicine	135	14 (10.4)	7 (5.1)
Pharmacology	92	9 (9.8)	2 (2.2)
Total	3456	888 (25.7)	137 (3.9)
Distribution by Sex:			
Male	3297	857 (25.9)	134 (4.0)
Female	159	31 (18.5)	3 (1.8)

[a]Numbers in parentheses represent percentage of the enrollment of senior class.

It is obvious that among the reasons given by long-term *ryūnen* psychiatric disorders would be the most frequent. Twenty-eight students consulted psychiatrists one or more times. Some came voluntarily and others were referred by faculty or relatives. All 28 were given specific psychiatric diagnoses, e.g., schizophrenia, borderline syndrome, schizoid personality, other types of personality disorder, and severe forms of neurotic reactions. These we tentatively call "psychiatric *ryūnen*." Milder neuroses, behavior disorders of adolescence, and transient maladaptation syndromes are not contained in this category.

Table 2. Distribution of Long-term Senior-Class Ryūnen by Number of Years Repeated and Reason Given

Long-Term Ryūnen		Reason for Repeating						
Years Repeated	Number (% of senior class)	Psychiatric Disorders	Physical Illness	Financial Difficulty	Study Abroad	Personal Affairs	Not Clear	Excuse Not Yet Needed
3	79(57.7)	10	0	4	1	7	0	57
4	37(27.0)	6	0	2	3	16	0	16
5	11(8.0)	4	2	0	0	4	1	0
6	8(5.8)	6	0	0	0	2	0	0
7	2(1.5)	2	0	0	0	0	0	0
Total	137(100)	28	2	6	4	23	1	73

Perhaps the real number of psychiatric *ryūnen* is a little higher than reported because there may be some mentally disturbed among those students who offered the excuse "personal affairs." I have not interviewed all 137 long-term *ryūnen*, but it is my impression that most of the mentally disturbed among them should not be classified as psychotic but as suffering from behavior disorders specific to the late adolescence.[2]

For many years I have been very much interested in one of such behavior disorders, the apathetic state often found among long-term *ryūnen*. There is some evidence that a considerable number of the nonpsychotic long-term *ryūnen* are in this state. This condition, neither psychotic nor typically neurotic, seems to be rarely seen in the outpatient clinic of general hospitals or mental hospitals, possibly because apathetic people usually dislike seeking the help of others.

Without any realistic causes, such students show lack of interest in their major field of study and indifference to social activity. They complain of physical lethargy, intellectual impotence, and a feeling of emptiness. However, they are neither obvious slackers nor scholastic inadequates. But they do have many obsessive-compulsive features in their personalities and often have rather overambitious goals. They appear gentle and polite and have good insight. At least they do not show coldness and mistrust, as do those suffering from schizoid disorders, nor do they violate university rules as political activists often do. And we psychiatrists can differentiate between the apathetic and the typically depressive students, although the former may show transient depressive mood swings.

Several authors have already pointed out this apathetic state in late adolescence. In *The Student and Mental Health,* edited by D.H. Funkenstein (1959), there appears a chapter entitled "The Apathetic Student." It seems to me that the most detailed description of apathy in late adolescence was given by P.A. Walters, Jr. (1961). After naming this state "student apathy," he described it symptomatically: emotional withdrawal, lack of competitiveness, lack of commitment, inhibition of social activity, and a feeling of emptiness. He finally characterizes this state as "apathy prolonging late adolescence because of an unresolved conflict centering around the formation of a masculine identity" and psychodynamically detects in such a student "an unwillingness to commit himself to any action which would have a definite end in either success or failure." From my experience I believe that Dr. Walters' description is excellent.

I would like to present two cases of university students whom I have handled.

CASE I

A schoolmaster in an urban city made an appointment for his 23-year-old son, who, after postponing graduation for three years because of a shortage of only nine credits, had decided to take a leave of absence from law school. The patient was polite, gentle, and talked spontaneously. He said that since the middle of his senior year he had been unable to study. He would spend hours compulsively tidying up his desk, fiddling, and reading comics and magazines. He had given up attending classes and, instead, had developed an avid interest in Japanese classical literature, which in his middle school days had been his favorite subject. He had bought a tremendous number of books about the Japanese classics without considering whether he could afford them. Finally his interest had reached such a pitch that he attended several academic meetings on Japanese classic literature. However, except for this he had not shown any commitment to realistic activities.

It was interesting to me that in the interview he talked about his inner, irrational fear of taking final examinations. According to him, he could never take examinations, although he always made complete preparations for them. In spite of my suggestion to come to see me regularly for several weeks, he preferred to leave school and returned to his parents' home. During the next two years, at his father's suggestion, he worked every day as an assistant to a woodcutter. People were surprised at his hard work and wondered if he were normal. He never initiated anything, but read voluminously. Three years later, when he came back to the campus, I found that he had regained his interest in the study of law and was ashamed of his past attitudes toward life. I was not able to find any meaningful event prior to his improvement except for a new friendship with a professor in the Law Department whom he had admired for years. He graduated the following year after easily obtaining the nine credits, and he is now enjoying his work as a beginning lawyer.

After he passed his final examinations, he was able to interpret by himself that the fear (I think it better to call it "fear of the final exam") owed partly to apprehension about failure in examinations and partly to fear of leaving the university and going out into the world.

Case II

A 25-year-old senior was referred to the psychiatrist of the Student Health Center by his tutor. The reason for referral was that the patient had not attended any seminars or taken any examinations since the previous year. But he had come to the department office where the tutor and his assistants were working; there he worked hard to help members of the staff publish academic periodicals. He appeared lethargic, apathetic, and cold. He described himself as suffering from physical weariness, from insomnia, lack of affect, emptiness, and a complete inability to study. He confessed that he had been taking overdoses of sleeping pills. In answer to my questions, he talked about his history as follows. He came from the southernmost part of Japan, and his two brothers had always been successful persons and were famous as brilliant leaders in the labor movement. Immediately after admission to the college he began his political activities. In his high-school days he had decided to study Greek, so the major he selected was Greek literature. Two years later after working hard as a political activist, he gradually withdrew from social activity and at the same time lost interest in study. As I observed his way of talking, it was obvious that he was neither a schizophrenic nor an affective psychotic.

After the initial interview, he began to come to see me regularly, only because he could get sleeping pills more easily than before. There has been little change in him during the four years since the initial interview, but it is interesting that when a woman student from the same department taught him Greek grammar, he showed extraordinary ability to learn under her maternalistic sympathy. He has stayed on as a senior student, and although he does not try to graduate, it does not seem that he will drop out. It is obvious that he has completely retired from the world of competition, and he reacts and breaks his passivity only when someone like the girl student tries to help him.

The foregoing descriptions of the apathetic condition that is often found among long-term *ryūnen* on campus suggests that students are apt to show apathetic states in their senior year or just before graduation, when it is almost the time for them to leave school and enter the world of adults. Hence the reference to apathy among *ryūnen* as "graduation phobia."

Next, I would like to examine these things from the cross-cultural viewpoint. In the last fifteen years many cases of "school phobia" during preadolescence or early adolescence have been documented. I would like to comment briefly about these cases, because "graduation phobia" in late adolescence and "school phobia" in childhood seem to have some similar features.

Children with "school phobia" show marked resistance to going to school, although they have no realistic causes for this and their intellectual capacity is sufficient. If they are allowed to stay at home and withdraw from reality (i.e., school), hypochondriacal complaints begin and apathy and sometimes violence follow. The causes of "school phobia" are disputed but many authors agree that the families of those children have other difficulties, especially weakness or loss of authority on the part of father.

Comparing the graduation phobia of the college student with school phobia in children, the following similarities are apparent. Both show selective withdrawal from the competitive aspect of reality, i.e., school. In other words, persons suffering from both seem to be healthy except in competitiveness. Both states occur mainly among boys. It is clear that the core conflict of the apathetic student has to do with the male's need to assure himself of his masculinity. From my clinical experience it is also obvious that father figures are usually weak and vague for both types of patients. In this connection, I would like to mention that in Japan today attitudes toward authority are changing. Parents are afraid to try to exert authority, for they have been told that they must give their children freedom and that children resent controls which they think are out-of-date. These changes in society seem to play important roles in the development of such behavior disorders as apathy in late adolescence and refusal to go to school in early adolescence.

Of course, there are some differences between the two states. For example, the apathetic student suffering from graduation phobia is usually not able to attend classes but remains on campus and participates in club activities, etc. On the other hand, a boy suffering from a school phobia refuses to enter the school building or even to go near it. The difference, however, is not important and can be explained by the fact that the college student and the school boy are at different stages of emotional development. In short, it seems to me that the graduation phobia often found among long-term *ryūnen* on campus could come from the same emotional base as the behavior disorder called school phobia that is often found among preadolescent or early-adolescent boys.

I would like to mention another cultural factor that I believe helps explain the increase of such withdrawal reactions. In Japan today there is a greater emphasis on achievement than in the past.

This is seen in many areas, especially in industry. It seems to me that this tendency affects, directly or indirectly, the formation of the apathetic state in students. This is evident because these students are apt to show apathetic states often in their senior year or just before graduation, when it is almost time for them to enter the world of competition.

We also have to understand the attitude of the faculty toward such students to know why they linger so long on campus. As indicated above, students who are not able to get enough credits for graduation are allowed to stay on campus as *ryūnen* for too long a period, sometimes as long as eleven years. On the other hand, college students are not allowed to transfer freely from one college to another, and it is exceptionally rare for students who leave college to return later to the same college. Generally speaking, professors do not discriminate against, nor do they show any interest in, their apathetic students. If one does, he usually does not know how to help such students because they often show marked resistance to the educator's emphasis on academic achievement.

This fact may be also deeply connected with Japanese behavior. For instance, *amae,* passive expectation of another's love, the concept that Takeo Doi saw as a key for understanding the Japanese mentality, is found in both students and their families. In fact, there is a general feeling that graduation from college is a necessity for high status, so the student and his family do not want him to quit school but to be helped by the faculty, somehow or other. The over-permissive attitudes of the faculty toward failing students seem to be the counterpart of these attitudes toward them.

Further elucidation of the psychology of apathy is necessary to develop effective techniques for treating it. Though it is not within my province to discuss whether permissive attitudes toward failing students are right or not and whether permitting them to stay on campus for a maximum of eleven years is adequate from the educational point of view, I personally believe from my clinical experience of college students that such extra years provide the students, like the boy described in Case I, with a chance for a psychosocial moratorium, in the sense used by Erikson (Funkenstein, 1959). However, such students need psychotherapy or counseling. We have to work out subtle means of getting their cooperation so that we can treat them.

NOTES

1. Strictly speaking, there are two kinds of *ryūnen* in Japanese universities. One is the kind of student discussed here. Another is the student who fails to pass the exams at the end of the second year. Many Japanese universities test students at the end of the second year to see whether they have the ability to progress to professional courses, which begin in the third year. For several years, university faculties have been very much aware of these students who fail to pass the exams at the end of sophomore year, and there have been many discussions about them. However, the problem presented by *ryūnen* at the end of the sophomore year is different from the that of *ryūnen* who fail to pass the final exams and linger on at universities.
2. The ICD (International Classification of Disease)-APA (American Psychiatric Association)-WHO classification, divides neurosis into four groups as follows: transient maladaptation, behavior disorder of childhood and of adolescence, neurosis in the strict sense, and abnormal personality. The apathetic students discussed here belong, I think, to the second category, behavior disorder of late adolescence.

REFERENCES

Doi, T.L. 1962. *Amae:* a key concept for understanding Japanese personality structure. *In* Japanese culture. R.J. Smith and R.K. Beardsley, eds. Chicago, Aldine Publishing Company.

Funkenstein, D.H. 1959. The student and mental health. New York, World Federation for Mental Health and the International Association of Universities.

Marui, F. 1968. A counterplan for *ryūnen* students. *Kosei Hōdo* 22:18–26. [in Japanese]

Takagi, R. 1967. Family study of school phobia. Psychiatria Neurologica Japonica 69:1048–53. [in Japanese]

Walters, P.A. 1961. Student apathy. *In* Emotional problems of the student. G.B. Blaine and C.C. McArthur, eds. New York, Appleton Century, Crofts.

Sponsorship of Cultural Continuity in Japan: A Company Training Program

THOMAS P. ROHLEN

This paper will present data concerning the initiation and training of new employees in a Japanese industrial company. The significance of this material to (1) theories about the origin and function of initiation ceremonies, (2) selective processes in the reception of foreign cultural influence, (3) the course of industrialization in Japan, and (4) the persistence of Japanese patterns of interpersonal behavior will be discussed.

The company in question, which will be called Kogyo, was visited in 1965. The following account of its initiation and training program is based on information gained in a number of interviews with executives who were responsible for the program and from a twenty-minute movie taken by the company at its training camp. The material to be presented is not complete. Many questions remain to be answered, but enough is known to give an adequate description of the procedures involved and the material appears to be of sufficient interest to warrant presentation of this paper.

Kogyo is a rather new company. It was founded in 1949 by a group of former military officers who applied their engineering skills to problems of public sanitation. From a very simple beginning the company has grown rapidly and in 1965 employed over 3,000 men and women. It is one of Japan's largest installers of water-treatment equipment. Kogyo's main office is in Osaka, and it maintains branch offices in all other major cities. The company's success has been based in great measure on its excellent engineering staff and its readiness to adopt the most recent technological improvements

Reprinted from *Journal of Asian and African Studies* 5 (1970): 184–192.

in its field. Many of these improvements have originated in Europe or the United States, and Kogyo has been very active in contracting with foreign firms to borrow their technical know-how. Kogyo, in summary, is a successful and expanding company utilizing the most advanced technology. I have gone into some detail describing Kogyo, because of the usual assumption that as an industrial organization becomes more "modern" in technological matters and business organization "traditional" behavior patterns diminish or disappear, being replaced by individually oriented, contractual behavior. In Kogyo's case, however, technological advancement has been paralleled by the development of a training program designed to give increased vitality to traditional patterns.

Origin of the program

In 1950, Kogyo's officers instituted its first training camp for the explicit purpose of countering the "individualism" the Occupation's educational reforms were sponsoring. Kogyo's executives felt that the young men they were employing were poorly prepared to fulfill the requirements of participation in their strongly integrated and demanding company organization. The training camp was established to challenge the individual orientation of the new employees (all of whom were entering from high schools or universities) and to develop in them a spirit of cooperation and company loyalty. To attain this end they decided to create a training program modeled on the officer candidate training methods used in the former Imperial Navy. The navy training manual became their guide, and those executives acting as instructors at the camp who had not been in the navy were ordered to read the handbook and be guided by its philosophy, which can be briefly summarized as similar to the U.S. Marine Corps', but with greater emphasis on conformity and group loyalty.

Instruction in the technical and business aspects of the company was also given, but the purpose of the training program was primarily to mold the young men to the requirements of the company's tightly integrated and group oriented activities. It should be obvious that membership in a Japanese firm is strikingly different from employment in an American company. Many of the differences have been presented in Abegglen's *The Japanese Factory* (1959). The important point about the origin of the training program is that it was consciously developed to counter the influence of Western attitudes and values which appeared to threaten the cohesion of the company and the total complex of values, incentives, and rewards by which it operated.

The Present Program

At the time new employees are informed that they have been accepted by Kogyo they are instructed to appear at a dormitory in a rather remote rural district near Lake Biwa some forty miles from Osaka. The training program begins shortly after the students graduate from their high schools and universities in March. In recent years, Kogyo has been employing some 200 new members, all of whom go through training at the same time. Female employees attend a separate camp in the same vicinity. New employees range in age from 18 to 25 years old.

The program lasts for one month, during which time no trainee is allowed to leave the camp except in unusual circumstances.

Upon arrival at the dormitory each trainee is issued a set of uniforms which he is to wear throughout the training period. It consists of khaki pants and jackets which are worn for work and study and several sports uniforms for track, rugby and skiing. The new employees must deposit their money with camp officials and in exchange they are given some military-like scrip, which they may use at the dormitory canteen. Each is also issued a bed and cooking utensils. Finally, the trainees are placed in groups of 15 men supervised by an executive of the company. These groups form the basic units for all activities during the training period.

The daily routine will sound very familiar to those who have experienced military training. The men are awakened by loudspeakers at 5:30 A.M. and hustled out into the pre-dawn cold for a half-hour of exercises. They then return to their dormitory to straighten up their bedding and gear before going to help with the preparation of breakfast. Following the morning meal they clean their utensils and then the entire dormitory and its grounds. Inspections are made periodically by the instructors. From 8:00 A.M. until 3:00 P.M., with time out for lunch, the trainees receive lectures on all aspects of the company's business. Periodically, the smaller groups meet with their leaders. Questions may then be asked and the supervisor urges his men to greater effort and dedication to the group. From 3:00 P.M. until dinner everyone engages in contact team sports, particularly rugby and *bōtaoshi*, a navy game in which one team attempts to tear down a pole supported by its opponents. All sports events are organized strictly along team lines, each 15-man group forming a team. Occasionally long distance runs are held, and once during the period a nearby mountain is climbed. When conditions permit, skiing instruction is given. After dinner the trainees study until 9:00 P.M., when all lights are turned out.

Several aspects of the training deserve closer attention. The lectures delivered to the trainees are concerned not only with the operations of the company, but often deal with the attitudes and behavior expected of Kogyo employees. A persistent theme is the expectation that all will demonstrate a "fighting spirit," which was interpreted to me to involve determination, perseverance, and group loyalty. This theme was also a leading slogan of the Imperial Navy. Other lectures deal with subjects Americans would not consider remotely related to business. One, for example, on the subject of "love" instructs the new employees to make a success of their future marriages through a cooperative attitude and teamwork between husband and wife. Only when we realize that membership in Kogyo is regarded as a total lifetime proposition does such a subject have relevance in the training program. More revealing is the emphasis given to the 15-man groups. At no point is the individual selected out for general praise or condemnation; always, the focus is on his group. Competition is organized between groups, and rewards are exclusively alloted to these units. In the long distance run, for example, the individual's time is recorded only as part of his team's total time. Grades are also recorded on a group basis. At the end of the training period the standings are announced and the group with the highest achievements is rewarded by the company president.

The last day of training is the occasion for a series of ceremonies which mark the return of the participants to society and seal the bonds formed among the trainees and between them and the company. The girls come from their camp in the morning, and a general meeting is held in the main hall. Dressed in their business suits for the first time in a month, the men stand at attention while the president addresses them on the now familiar themes of cooperation, company loyalty, comradeship, and fighting spirit. Following the speech a formal toast is drunk with beer. Drinking together to seal a relationship is a common practice in Japan (Bennett and Ishino, 1963), and the symbolism is undoubtedly very clear to the trainees. The toast is followed by a singing of the company song, which all have been rehearsing, and the ceremony is closed with the traditional *banzai*. In the afternoon a rugby game is staged between the instructors and an all-star team of trainees. Finally, in the evening all gather around a campfire for singing and farewells since they will be separating the next day for their new assignments.

An immediate question is whether Kogyo's program is typical of most Japanese companies or simply an isolated exception. In several respects Kogyo is unique, but in terms of the purpose of its training, it is representative of a minority pattern. Perhaps only several dozen companies in the Osaka area now have training programs with a similar intent. Among the companies with such training there is considerable variation as to the specific methods used. Some send their new employees to Zen temples in Kyoto for a month of strict Zen discipline. Others have their employees go through the regular Self-Defense Forces boot camp. The essential point of similarity between all of these programs is their focus on adjusting new employees to the attitudinal requirements of company membership.

Though the number of companies that have instituted such programs is small, it is still significant. Before the war such training was not considered necessary, and it is the post-war changes in Japan which have stimulated executives to institute these programs. Kogyo claims to have been the first to see the value of such training and in the last decade many companies have come to Kogyo to ask advice about establishing their own programs. The movie I was shown, for example, was made by the company for the purpose of illustrating to others what they are doing. The number of companies using these methods is increasing, not decreasing, and several leading Osaka firms, including an important newspaper and a leading bank, are now training their employees in this manner. There are two obvious conclusions we may make at this point. First, that the university and high school graduates today are not as prepared psychologically to participate in institutions organized along the usual Japanese lines as were pre-war graduates, and, secondly, instead of welcoming this as a sign of modernization, consistent with the progress of their companies, many Japanese businessmen are anxious to remedy the situation by giving their employees the kind of education they feel is lacking in the public schools.

It is interesting to note Kogyo's opinion of the training programs utilizing Zen and the Self-Defense Force. An executive commented that these methods are fine as far as they serve to counter ideas detrimental to company loyalty, but they fail to establish any strong identity with the company since the training is done by outsiders. To be successful, Kogyo executives feel, a training program must not only counter the influence of the present educational system, but it must also replace such influence with a positive attachment to the company.

CONSIDERED AS AN INITIATION CEREMONY

In attempting to relate this material to the various theories concerning initiation rites some interesting points arose. Kogyo's program divides very readily into the three stages proposed by Van Gennep (1960), namely, separation, transition, and incorporation. Separation being emphasized by travel to a remote dormitory and isolation there, change to uniforms, loss of money, and introduction to unfamiliar routines, and the like. Transition occurs throughout the month as the individual is forced to adjust to the new and demanding situation by changing his perceptions, attitudes, and behavior to group-centered company norms. The concluding ceremonies, where business suits are again worn and tension is released through beer drinking, a rugby game against the instructors, and a campfire sing, serve to conclude the incorporation process and begin the process of return to everyday life.

The Kogyo example also fits well with Young's (1965) emphasis on initiations as dramatizations of solidarity, although the emphasis is not on universal male solidarity, but rather on company solidarity. Males and females are separately trained, and much of the male training, particularly the contact sports, emphasize Japanese male attributes of discipline and "fighting spirit." The basic distinctions underlined by the training program are, however, between the ideology of individualism emphasized in student life and the group orientation of company membership and, secondly, between membership in Kogyo and membership in all other organizations. The second distinction can be expected, given Japan's social complexity, where secondary groupings are much more significant than universal male solidarity except in situations such as armed conflict involving the entire nation. It should be pointed out that membership in a Japanese company, since it is a lifelong and nearly total affiliation, gives the boundary between one's company and all other organizations an importance it does not have in the West. The company takes responsibility for a greater part of its employees' lives and in turn the employees are expected to give their undivided loyalty and attention to the company.

Nathan Miller's proposal that there is a relationship between the elaboration of initiation ceremonies and the presence of external threat also seems consistent with the Kogyo case. He has asserted that "initiation rites are prosecuted with special vigor when the exclusive, personal interests of the group or class are threatened by exigencies, such as initial contact with alien peoples, migration, depopulation, threat of complete extinction or absorption into outside cultures, or the Heimweh provoked by a novel environment. The elders under these circumstances try to maintain group consciousness and custom largely through the extensive emotional and mental schooling of the manhood ceremonies, because only in this way can the social heritage be perpetuated as a living thing (1932: 49)."

We have seen that Kogyo's training was developed to counter the influence of Western-inspired educational reforms which appeared to the executives to threaten the cohesion of the company. Young (1965: 39) notes that there is little empirical evidence applicable to Miller's thesis since societies under such threat seldom survive. The opposite argument, that wherever we find initiation ceremonies we might assume that at some earlier time the society had been faced with a crisis which precipitated the practice, is similarly of conjectural value only. In the case of Kogyo, however, we have concrete evidence that the origin and subsequent elaboration of an initiation ceremony occurred in response to a perceived threat from outside and that the initiators of the initiation were quite conscious of its purpose.

When we turn to the theories of Whiting et al. (1958), we find that they do not apply to the Kogyo situation since it is not an initiation occurring at puberty and the emphasis is not on maleness. A case could be made, however, that Kogyo's training reinforces the values established by the Japanese family. Socialization in Japan emphasizes family or household solidarity, paternal authority and filial dependence (which becomes parent-child interdependence in adulthood). These are essentially the attitudes the company wishes to encourage. As the boy matures, some of the dependence originally focused on the mother is transferred to the father. Entrance into a company involves the transfer of much of this dependence from the family to the company. The initiation serves to dramatize this new orientation. Considerable attention has been devoted to the fictive-kin groups in Japanese economic and cultural life (for example, Bennett and Ishino, 1963) and there is general recognition that most other social groupings, from the PTA to the schools of flower arrangement, are formed along vertical axes similar to parent-child relations in Japan (e.g., Nakane, 1967). Kogyo's training is consistent with this emphasis as it serves to reassert traditional values associated with Japanese kinship.

We have seen that the training program was developed in response to social rather than individual needs. In the opinion of Kogyo's executives, it has produced the desired results. Morale in the company is high, no union has had any success in organizing the company, cooperation is excellent, and self-sacrifice for company goals has been marked. Employees are also apparently very happy with the company's system and atmosphere. The executives reported they felt most of their employees support the idea of the training program and said they were at no disadvantage in attracting new employees because of it.

This raises the question of how the training program affects the individuals who participate in it. Beside functioning as a mechanism of integration into the company, I feel it serves to re-establish the individual's connection with the mainstream of Japanese sociocultural life. To appreciate this we must first understand the position of Japanese youth in relation to their society. Robert Lifton, in a study of university students in Kyoto, has aptly described the alienation and disorganization experienced by most young Japanese. He notes "the absence in contemporary youth of vital and nourishing ties to their own heritage" (1962: 173) and the "exaggerated experimentation, of exposing one's self or being exposed to an extraordinary variety of cultural and ideological influences, each of which engages the young person sufficiently to affect his developing self-process, but never with enough profundity to afford him a consistent source of personal meaning or creative expression (1962: 175)." Lifton describes the great attraction of individual freedom as expressed in Western literature and movies, but writes that, "underneath this ideal of selfhood, however strongly maintained, one can frequently detect an even more profound craving for renewed group life, for solidarity, even for the chance to 'melt' completely into a small group (1962: 182)." With graduation and entrance into a company this dilemma normally fades as the individual adjusts to group membership. Kogyo's initiation serves to concentrate and speed up this transition. It unhesitatingly presents the standards and patterns of behavior expected and underlines the fact that membership in the company cannot be ambivalent. Rather than leaving the adjustment to the individual, Kogyo's training precipitates a minor crisis and crystalizes the young man's latent desire to reenter group life. Or stated another way, it facilitates the individual's return to an orientation and set of satisfactions similar to what he learned as a member of his family. The need for solidarity is not created by the initiation, but it is further developed and encouraged while the attractions of selfhood are suppressed. This explains, at least in part, the acquiescence of the trainees and their general satisfaction with the program. Obviously, those who are strongly disinclined to experience such a reintegration process will not join Kogyo, or for that matter any other business organization.

The fact that training programs are a recent phenomenon reflects not only increasing Western influence since the war, but also, I think, the growing confidence of some businessmen in the utility and correctness of opposing those aspects of Westernization which undermine Japanese group behavior patterns. What does this mean for the question of measuring and analyzing change in Japan? It points up the long appreciated, but little understood, process of selectivity by which Japan adjusts to foreign influences, filtering out or modifying whatever is disintegrative, while adopting the beneficial. Kogyo's training program is simply a relatively overt example of the filtering process involved in membership in most Japanese groups. It would seem that any new Japanese organization, of whatever form or function, whether conceived of as modern or not, is necessarily constituted of individuals who bring to the situation expectations and capabilities that are in great measure conservative since they are the products of former experiences with other Japanese groups (e.g., the family), and thus to ensure the success of the group, its organizers must recognize the importance of traditional patterns to its members. This example also illustrates the possibility of consciously developing mechanisms to maintain the continuity of social patterns in the face of strong foreign influence.

The inadequacy of simple assumptions that industrialization and urbanization lead automatically to Western-style individualism is underlined by the Kogyo example. Japan certainly has factories, unions, social welfare, political parties, etc., all of which have now assumed Western forms, but the informal principles on which these are organized remain essentially Japanese. The assumption, made for example by Abegglen (1958), that the inefficiencies of the traditional kinds of social organization will gradually lead to individual oriented contractual relations in industry may need closer scrutiny. No doubt there are many inefficient aspects to the existing organizational practices, but there are also a number of advantages, such as lower costs of training due to small labor turnover, reduced wage pressure, certain kinds of flexibility in personnel relations, and fewer strikes, which accrue from the Japanese system. In fact, American businessmen today are learning to appreciate some of these advantages enjoyed by their Japanese competitors. Japanese businessmen are not ignorant of the advantages of Western industrial organization, nor are they blind to the advantages of their own system. Today many appear to desire the best of both worlds, and a variety of experiments involving an increased degree of contractual organization and wage incentive are going on. But to a certain extent these are still experimental. The rejection of such ideas or their modification is always possible. Change in the direction of Western organizational emphases can certainly be expected, but replacement of group-oriented behavior by individualism as found in the United States is certainly no foregone conclusion for any point in the future.

In dealing with questions of change and persistence in Japan, or elsewhere, the time has passed when traditional behavior can be regarded as anachronistic or the product of a peculiar and vague "Japanese mind." We must analyze the social and psychological functions of specific group organizations and search for explanations of change or continuity in such terms. The dysfunctional aspects, social and psychological, of Westernization and the reactions they give rise to are as important as the more evident changes. Only when we treat questions of change and persistence in the same manner will adequate explanations for either be forthcoming.

BIBLIOGRAPHY

ABEGGLEN, J. G. 1958. The Japanese Factory: Aspects of Its Social Organization. Glencoe, Illinois: The Free Press.
BENNETT, John W., and Iwao Ishino. 1963. Paternalism in the Japanese Economy. Minneapolis: University of Minnesota Press.
LIFTON, Robert Jay. 1962. Youth and History: Individual Change in Postwar Japan. Daedalus 91:1:172–197.
MATSUMOTO, Y.S. 1960. Contemporary Japan: The Individual and the Group. Philadelphia: Trans. of the American Philosophical Society 50:1.
MILLER, Nathan. 1932. Initiation. Encyclopedia of the Social Sciences, New York: Macmillan 8:49–50.
NAKANE, CHIE. 1967. Tate shakai no ningen kankei (Human relations in a hierarchical society). Tokyo: Kodansha.
WHITING, J. W. M., Richard KLUCKHOHN, and Albert ANTHONY. 1958. The Function of Male Initiation Ceremonies at Puberty. In E. E. Maccoby, T.M. Newcomb, and E. L. Hartley (eds.). Readings in Social Psychology. New York: Henry Holt and Co. pp. 359–370.
VAN GENNEP, Arnold. 1960. The Rites of Passage. Tr. Monika B. Vizedom and Gabrielle L. Caffee. Chicago: University of Chicago Press.

The Psychological Interdependence of Family, School, and Bureaucracy in Japan

CHRISTIE W. KIEFER

Anthropologists have tended to look at socialization and formal education as equally important but somewhat independent processes when they occur in different settings. For one thing, the ethnographer's Freudian attention to "the life cycle" usually drops the discussion of socialization at about the beginning of latency, or at least by the end of puberty. In their classic work on cultural determinants in personality formation, Kardiner et al. (1945) found the school in a rural American community to be alien and even threatening to "primary" socialization practices. We are painfully aware of the contrast between primitive societies on the one hand, where continuity and consistency of experience draw no sharp distinctions between family-centered and community-centered socialization, and the complex modern state on the other hand, where schools and schooling are often the foci of conflicts that split communities. Then too, modern education is "rational" education, and even Durkheim, arguing with the Freudians over the value of collective morality (1925), thought of formal education as properly a process whereby the particularistic values of early childhood are rationally redirected to serve the larger society.

Recent developments in ego psychology (e.g., Hartmann 1958, Allport 1961, Erikson 1963) have lent popularity to a view of the personality as open to developmental changes from birth until death. Encouraged by this point of view, and by the growing anthropological literature that views crisis rites as symbolic reopen-

Reprinted by permission of the American Anthropological Association from *American Anthropologist* 72 (1970): 66–75.

ings of the primary socialization process (Roheim 1942; Whiting, Kluckhohn, Anthony 1958; Van Gennep 1908; Cohen 1964), the present paper tries to show how an education system sustains emotional habits learned in childhood, and channels them into the bureaucratic values of adult roles. I avoid the psychoanalytic vocabulary wherever possible because it evokes unwelcome associations to psychiatry, but the frame of reference is basically that of psychoanalytic ego psychology.

Throughout much of Japanese history, scholarship in letters, religion, and philosophy has been highly valued as a mark of moral integrity and leadership capacity, following the example of the Chinese "scholar gentry" pattern but more supportive of inherited social position in a feudal society (Dore 1965). Since the dismantling of the aristocratic system in the 1870s, however, education has become the main avenue of economic and social mobility. One would expect the content of public instruction to shift from that of moral philosophy and belles lettres to more purely technical matters best suited to a democratic industrial society, and this has been to some extent the case. One would also expect the development of criteria of learning ability for the recognition of academic talent, for the recruitment of students to high institutions (and keen competition for entry), and this has also been the case.

However, two features of the Japanese education system present rather striking differences to the U.S. case, and these have attracted the attention of other writers (Vogel 1962, 1963) since they seem to be in some ways "dysfunctional" in the modern Japanese economic and social milieu. The first of these is the relative emphasis still placed on moral discipline, at the expense of technical content. The second is the entrance examination system, usually referred to as *shiken jigoku*, "examination hell."

Success in achieving a secure place in Japan's expanding economic and political bureaucracies depends heavily on a successful academic career. The road to academic success varies according to locale and is sometimes artificially altered by methods such as bribery, but it usually depends on the passing of several successive entrance examinations, beginning most often with entrance into middle school (grades 7 through 9) and sometimes even with entrance into primary school. Competition for entrance into the best schools, even at the primary level, is keen, and students must observe a study schedule that is—by American standards—inhuman throughout their school careers, or at least from the third grade on, if they are to enter a prestigious university. Among middle class families, the task of preparing for the entrance examinations is not left to the children themselves, but is shared by their mothers, and success or failure in the examinations reflects seriously on the pride of the child's family and their "face" in the community (Vogel 1962, Kiefer 1968). The term "examination hell" thus accurately reflects the onerous labor that goes into preparation for the entrance exams and the anxiety of students as the test draws near. Says Vogel:

> Many Japanese parents and educators have remarked that entrance examinations are unfortunate because they force children to lead a very restricted life of study and worry about examinations. . . . Even children who do not become seriously emotionally disturbed cannot help being affected by the intense pressure placed on them at the time of entrance examination (1962:152).

Certain functions of the "examination hell" system are obvious even to the casual observer. Strict examinations in the higher schools do select the bright, hard-working students for promotion and discard the less able, thereby assuring that the former are recruited for positions of leadership and responsibility. Also, the fear of failing the examination raises student effort almost across-the-board, so that the quality of education remains at a high level. On the other hand, the same general results are accomplished by the American system of grading students on day-to-day performance, and the latter seems to place much less psychological strain on students and their families: the American system "cools out" academic failures; the Japanese system slams the door in their faces.

A second paradox of the system is that once a student has gained entry into a university, his bureaucratic future is practically assured regardless of how little he learns. The quality of education at the college level is consequently inadequate to supply competent personnel for business and government, so that considerable on-the-job training must take place after college graduation. It might be argued that this simply puts the burden of the expense for higher education on the employer rather than the general taxpayer or the student and his family, and that this might be a latent economic "function" of the system. The fact that the system requires vast manpower expense for college preparation, and causes vast manpower waste at the college level is harder to explain.

Ezra Vogel (1962, 1963) has addressed himself to this task and has made the following observations: First, competition within a face-to-face group is generally frowned upon and avoided in Japanese culture. Since (as Jules Henry [1963] has graphically shown) the American classroom fosters general competitiveness in its pupils and is itself the scene of intense rivalries, it is ill suited to a society that places high value on the sharing of responsibility and reward by members of primary groups. By means of the entrance examination system, competition is taken out of the classroom into an impersonal setting in which contact and communication between competitors is minimized. Second, according to Vogel, a generalized ethic of achievement has not yet taken hold in Japanese culture, so that achievement striving is focused in the somewhat traditional role of the scholar and soft-pedaled in other roles.

I am not convinced that a generalized achievement ethic is weak or absent in the nation that has had the world's highest economic growth rate for the past decade (Karsh and Cole 1968:47–48). McClelland (1964) found relatively low levels of achievement content in Japanese children's stories, and classified the country as *low* on achievement motivation. However, he also classified Japan as a country with low economic growth—a finding so contrary to casual observation that little faith can be placed on McClelland's methods, at least as applied to Japan. A recent report on cross-cultural differences in the semantic space occupied by certain affect-laden terms (Tanaka 1966), on the other hand, shows that Japanese evaluate the terms "work" more positively than do Americans or Dutch, and the word "wealth" more positively than do Dutch or Finns. The affective rating of both terms by Japanese agrees closely with that given by Frenchmen, a fact that lends some support to Bellah's (1957) thesis that a "protestant ethic" has long been a feature of Japanese values. Likewise, Japanese values as reported by Caudill and Scarr (1962) are predominantly future-oriented and tend to stress the "control" dimension of the man-nature relationship. DeVos and Caudill (1956) also found extremely high achievement drives in the personalities of Japanese immigrants in America.

Whether or not the examination system takes the place of a generalized achievement ethic, it apparently does help keep overt competition in the classroom low. Is this sufficient reason for the survival of the system in spite of its disadvantages? I doubt it, for the following reason: As Vogel clearly documented, responsibility for a student's success or failure in the examinations is intimately shared by his close kin—especially his mother. Mothers of children taking the examinations tend to avoid the topic and conceal information from their neighbors that might lead to discovery of a failure. They also tend to be critical of teachers and school administrators when they feel their children are not doing well, resulting in bad feeling between the supporters and the detractors of the neighborhood school. I have heard Japanese mothers accuse one another of being stingy in their relations with their neighbors in order to have money for private tutoring of their children. I have even heard of envy over a child's academic success resulting in a shouting fight between two mothers in the street of their community. The examination system encourages participation by families in the children's competitive struggle for education, because it shifts the emphasis from the classroom—where parents have little control over the children's behavior—to the home, where they have a great deal. I will argue later that given Japanese social structure this itself is probably a fundamental reason for the tenacity of the examination system, but here I only wish to point out the inconsistency in the "minimization of competition" model: The examination system does not eliminate or significantly relieve the strain imposed by competition on primary group relations in general; it merely displaces the strain from the classroom to the community. Might it be said that community solidarity is less valued in the abstract than classroom solidarity? I think not. "Community consciousness" (*kyōdō ishiki*) is frequently upheld as the opposite of selfishness and narrow familism even in modern middle-class suburbs where traditional forms of community cooperation have largely disappeared (Kiefer 1968).

The alternative model I will suggest here portrays the education system as a continuation of socialization trends begun in the family and as a bridge between the family and the socializing agencies of the educated adult, namely bureaucratic peer groups. To begin with the family system, we note the following gross differences between the American and the Japanese cases:

(1) In the Japanese middle class, the mother is the main agent of the child's socialization, and almost the entire responsibility for the child's education and conduct falls on her shoulders. In the United States, by contrast, the responsibility—if not the actual work —of socializing children is shared more nearly equally by both parents.

(2) In the Japanese family, there is a very close relationship between the child and his mother. In the middle-class family, where the father is absent from the home for long hours, he might be almost excluded from family intimacy, with the result that the child develops strong emotional bonds with the mother. This is especially

true of sons, in whose case the bond is much stronger than the American mother-son relationship because American mothers *expect* their sons to sever family ties when they reach maturity and leave home. In DeVos's terms, the ego boundaries of mother and child become "blurred" due to the intensity of their mutual identification (DeVos 1964).

(3) Since the Japanese family is an institution that binds the individual for life, he is encouraged to view his relationship with other family members as one of continuing mutual support and participation in common goals. The American parent, however, by physical punishment of the child for socially taboo behavior, says to the child, in effect, "Until you are grown, my commands are the law by which you must abide. Only when you are grown up are you free to decide for yourself." The family explicitly restricts what is felt to be his natural right as an adult, that is, his right to decide his own fate. It is easy to think of American socialization practices as "strict," and Japanese as "lenient," but I do not think this is necessarily the most useful view of the situation. Although the American child must be obedient to the specific demands of his parents, he is encouraged to develop as his inclinations direct him in all matters where the family has no strict jurisdiction. The Japanese child, on the other hand, learns at an early age to judge the consequences of *all* his acts in terms of their effects on his family. Japanese yougsters are in fact more obedient than their American peers, on the whole, due to their sense of the fatefulness of their antisocial impulses.

In the light of these differences between the Japanese and American families, we can examine the relationship between family and education system from a functional point of view. (Keep in mind that I am primarily concerned with education as it relates to the training of individuals for careers, and I will therefore address myself mainly to the education of boys.) First of all, the Japanese boy confronts a problem confronted by all boys everywhere—the problem of becoming a man—that is, like his father—in spite of the fact that his first and strongest identifications are with a woman —that is, his mother. This problem is relatively difficult for the Japanese boy, because of the emotional dependence on his mother I have mentioned above. Since the male child's first impression of his father is that of a competitor for his mother's affection, in his fantasy life the father is likely to be symbolized by the powerful and unloving villain. In both Japanese and American middle-class society, however, the mother seeks to teach the child that he must love the father if she is to love him. Once the child has learned his lesson, he is on the road to becoming a man; that is, "conquering" the father by "becoming" the father, and replacing him in his mother's affection. The better the child learns the social consequences of hatred, the less he is able to view his father as a villain, and the more his image of the father as "good" replaces his original "bad" father-fantasy. Whereas the child is emotionally weaned from the mother to some extent in America, in Japan he continues to hold the "bad" image of the father unconsciously as a result of his early experience of intense closeness with his mother to a later age, and simultaneously with his conscious image of the father as basically good.[1]

In the Japanese education system, the male teacher helps to resolve this difficulty by assuming some aspects of the mother's role, mainly the aspect of moral training. The teacher's similarity to the mother in this respect allows the male child to transfer some of his emotional dependence from his mother to a male figure. Anyone familiar with both the American and Japanese education systems will be aware of the relative emotional closeness of the student and the teacher in Japan, and of the greater role of male teachers in the education of male children. The identification of the teacher with the mother would not be possible unless the mother's emotional support mentioned above was transferred to the educational situation as well. Just as it does not make sense in the Japanese family for the mother to withdraw love and support from the child in order to teach him independence, so it does not make sense for the teacher to assume the role of the "bad" father by flunking his students. Here is the first important function of the "examination hell" system: as long as the students are allowed to expect the support of their teacher in spite of their progress, as long as they can *expect to continue as accepted members of their class* through the educational institution, the functional equivalence of mother and teacher survives. If on the other hand, the teacher were the one who decided which child should advance and which child should not, his role would cease to parallel that of the mother. He would be identified as a comparatively cold and distant authoritarian figure. To the extent that this latter role of the teacher works in the American system, its success is related to the greater similarity of maternal and paternal roles and the greater emphasis on autonomy training in the family.

But this is only the beginning. If the role of the teacher resembles that of the mother in Japan, then it can also be said that the classroom situation parallels the family. Just as the child's relationship with his family is strong and permanent, so his relationships with classmates tend to be strong and permanent also. The American education system places the responsibility for the student's success directly on the student (and less directly on his family), thereby fostering a sense of independence and a sense of competition between students. Since the American teacher holds the power of passing or failing his students, he maintains "social distance" from them. In the American classroom, students often cooperate for the purpose of asserting their own values in opposition to those of other students in the class, or those of the teacher himself. Institutionalized forms of competition are found in the classroom, such as the "spelling bee." In a word, then, the American classroom resembles a competitive arena, whereas the Japanese classroom resembles the training ground of a single team, learning how to play the game of life cooperatively.

EDUCATION AND BUREAUCRACY

I am not implying that all social behavior is more cooperative in Japan than it is in America and that this cooperativeness must be learned in the classroom, but rather that there are basic differences in *forms* of cooperative behavior and that different educational processes are suited to each. In Japan, the extended family has served as a model for cooperative social groups throughout history, with the result that modern Japanese institutions tend even today to be bound together by an intensity of commitment that is quite unfamiliar to their American counterparts. There is no need to go into this at great length. It has been dealt with extensively in the works of Benedict (1946), Bennett and Ishino (1963), Abegglen (1958), Matsumoto (1960), and others. In this essay, I am specifically interested in the "familistic" nature of bureaucracy—both governmental and industrial—and how the education system supports such a bureaucracy.

I referred earlier to the dependency of the Japanese child on his mother in the early years of his life and the continuity of his sense of obligation to his family into late life. This is a facet of Japanese culture that seems to have such wholesome economic and psychological functions that it has dictated the course of industrialization and stabilized Japanese society in periods of upheaval. Even today, however, the moral demands that the family makes on a Japanese adult—demands to support his kin when they need him, demands to sustain family traditions, to honor the spirits of family deceased, to avoid acts (such as divorce) that will bring shame on the family, and so forth—often place the individual in a moral dilemma when family demands conflict with the demands of his friends, his business associates, and his community. When a man's occupation directly involves his family, as is often the case with merchants and small manufacturers, there is little problem of conflicting loyalties, but *if he is a member of a bureaucratic organization,* his employer must have some guarantee of his personal commitment to his job; otherwise a bureaucracy cannot function.[2] The response to this problem in Japan has been to make use of concepts of loyalty learned in the family and to create a type of bureaucracy that mirrors the family; that is, one in which the individual normally commits himself to a job for life and in which the obligations of an employer to his employee are extensive and "paternalistic." The paradox of the Japanese bureaucratic system is that it makes *more* demands on members' loyalty than is the case in the United States, thus placing the bureaucratic employee in a double bind, because family loyalty must be extended to the bureaucratic setting without undermining the family itself. Undermining familism would mean undermining the fabric of bureaucracy.

In many societies, cultural patterns foster the development of beliefs and attitudes appropriate to one institution that must be radically changed when an individual achieves membership in other institutions, either in the normal course of maturation or as a matter of special privilege or obligation. In such cases, the individual is induced to question existing habits of thought, to reject them where they conflict with the requirements of the new role, and to assimilate new ones better adapted to his changed status. This process may be dramatic and violent, or it may be gradual. It may be largely unconscious, as in the traumatic "puberty rites" of nonliterate societies (Roheim 1942, Whiting et al. 1958, Cohen 1964). It may be calculated, as in initiation into elites or total institutions (Lynd 1958, Goffman 1960) or political conversion in totalitarian states (Lifton 1960).

In fact the conversion generally takes place on an unconscious level, and the converted are not aware of the change in their habits at first. This unconsciousness is necessary not only on the part of the converts themselves, but also on the part of those responsible for the conversion, when, as is often the case, both the "old" and the "new" values must coexist in the same society. An example will help to clarify the situation:

In some parts of China, such as the New Provinces, filial piety continues to be an important value in spite of growing economic strains on traditional morality. Women as well as men are exposed to this value incessantly from birth to maturity and naturally develop habits of thought by which their own kindred are regarded as the main source of spiritual and material good and the proper objects of their respect and devotion. At marriage, however, women must suddenly leave their kindred and join the households of their husbands. Because of the particularistic nature of the value of filial piety, the emotional ties of the new Chinese bride to her former home must be replaced by attachments to her new home; this is a very difficult task, for the bride herself and for both families. Potter[3] found that even today, in the New Provinces, brides undergo the kind of conversion procedure I have described as characteristic of this situation. Following the wedding ceremony, the bride is ridiculed and teased by members of her husband's family at every turn, until she is deeply depressed and frustrated. Since she is now separated from her own kindred and cannot turn to them for help, the stage is set for a loss of attachment to those emotional patterns that are now of no use to her. In psychoanalytic terms, her ego is weakened, and anxieties previously "bound" and allayed by her former attachment to her family are "set free," providing means by which she can be socialized into her new home. Since her hatred and fear of her new family cause her nothing but pain, she soon learns to turn the hatred in upon herself and thereby to accept *their* values and attitudes as the source of hope for her own salvation. Finding that she is rewarded to the extent that she performs the duties expected of her by her mother-in-law and other members of her new home, she gradually comes to see the good in herself in terms of her devotion to her new duties. She has been converted to a new system of belief.

Religious sects, criminal organizations, sports teams, and even learned societies practice this conversion-by-suffering, but here I am only interested in the function of "examination hell." I think the reason that the similarity between the "examination hell" phenomenon and that of the conversion ritual has not been recognized so far (to my knowledge) is that the psychological change that the taking of entrance examinations brings about is a very subtle one. There is no sudden switch of loyalties from the family to the bureaucratic group on the part of the student. Indeed, there is no such switch at all. Instead, the agony of studying late every night and the mounting fear as the examination draws near are imposed on the child by his own family. His successful passing of the examination is hailed with rejoicing by his own kin. His teachers and classmates support him in his belief that his mother and father are his closest allies. In order to understand the paradox of conversion-through-suffering that does not destroy the existing values of the child, three things must be kept in mind: First, as mentioned earlier, the Japanese bureaucratic structure could not exist without the moral basis of the family. What the "examination hell" ritual accomplishes in Japan is the extension of emotional habits learned in the family to the child's *group of age-mates*. Second, the ritual is not performed just once but several times, with increasing difficulty, as the child progresses up through the education system. Finally, the dramatic moment of the examination system, and the one from which it derives its psychological force, comes when the child is separated from his family and friends—that is, when he confronts the empty test forms in the examination room psychologically alone. Up to this point, his education has been a cooperative effort of mother and child, but now his mother is beyond his reach. He may cry, he may plead, but no one can help him pass the test. Studying the phenomenon of puberty rites in primitive societies. Cohen says:

> Very often, especially when boys are undergoing mutilation during the ritual, there occurs a dialogue of wailing between initiates in their secluded camp and their mothers and sisters in the distance. Unseen to each other, and yet of extraordinary significance in conveying to the initiates one all-important fact: cry and wail as they may—out of fright and true physical pain—or even stifle their cries of agony, their mothers and sisters answer and yet are powerless to help them. *This* is the true climax of the initiation ceremony. The profound but empty dialogue of wails and cries is the crisis of the deflection of energies away from the famliy. . . . It conveys to the groups their separateness; and with inexorable force it implants the notion in the youths that their families are out of their searching reach (1964:541–542).

Cohen discovered that puberty rites that inflict such suffering on the initiates are characteristic of societies in which socialization of the child is assumed by an organization of his age-mates at puberty and in which legal responsibility is also shared by members of the social group, both conditions that parallel the Japanese case in some respects.[4] The process by which the Japanese male learns attitudes appropriate to this role as member of a bureaucratic organization, then, is essentially this: First, he is encouraged to regard the classroom as a family by receiving the same kind of emotional support there that he receives at home. With the passing of his first major examination (for middle school), the classroom into which he passes as a result of the examination gains in import- ance for him, because it confirms his status as a student at a time when his faith in himself and his family has been seriously shaken by the trauma of the examination itself. With the passing of high school and college entrance examinations, he is socialized into an increasingly elite and close-knit group of age-mates, and the emo- tional significance of his classmates for him continues to grow as the examinations extend his energies toward the classroom— *without*, I repeat, undermining family roles. His final transition from school to office is made with relatively little effort and with the help of both school and family since the relationship between these three institutions in Japan is much closer than is typically the case in America and since the mutual emotional dependence of age- mates functions to bind the office group together in exactly the same way that it binds classmates together. Direct observation of many Japanese salarymen and students has convinced me that this is the case, and the fact is further implicitly recognized in the Japanese notion that certain companies have their own "personal- ity," and that they recruit students only from certain universities— universities wherein they are *given* the personality appropriate to the company.

As the young student's identifications are extended to include his peer group, both family and peer group receive psychological support from the externalization of the threat of failure, just as Japanese mothers often threaten their children with punishment from forces external to, and beyond the control of, the family (Lanham 1956, Kiefer 1968), with the usual result that the child values the more highly his intrafamilial relationships. In the American educational system, when the child learns new adaptive techniques for maximizing whatever psychological goods are to be had in the competitive classroom (irrespective of the *content* of his lessons), he gains thereby a measure of independent self respect. Since the content of the examinations cannot be known, the anxiety surrounding them cannot be put to rest by a similar development. The best defense against this kind of anxiety is the support of relatively powerful figures, especially teachers and parents who "know the ropes." The intense involvement of middle-class Japanese mothers in the education system—symbolized by the term *kyōiku mama* ("education mama")—may result from the realization that control over the children *in general* depends to some extent on their ability to fulfill the role of bulwark against examination anxiety.

The usefulness of this view of the Japanese education system as an instrument of personality development is apparent also in its application to another puzzling phenomenon: the political radicalism of Japanese college students. Westerners are often dumbfounded by the fact that Japanese college students who are militant leftists cease to be leftists at all when they graduate. We observed above that the Japanese teacher can be viewed as a "motherly father," helping his students accept their own masculinity in a culture that creates social distance between fathers and sons.

As a condition for accepting the teacher as a "good father," however, many young men are driven to seek objects for the hostile feelings they continue to have toward authority. In other words, the "bad father" image is projected onto politicians, business bosses, policemen, and soldiers—the impersonal male authorities usually selected as targets for student activism. Since, as I have argued, the education system forms a link between the family and the bureaucratic organization, these young men are able to extend their "good father" feelings to their employers after graduation from college (or at least to their school clique *within* the organization that employs them). The "bad father" feelings do not die off but are expressed in hostility for the *competitors* of their employer or clique. Leftism is simply the language by which these youths express their hostility toward authority, and it is a language both inappropriate and unnecessary to their roles as bureaucrats. Robert Lifton has portrayed the militant leftism (as well as militant conservatism) of Japanese youth as a kind of foreclosure of the crisis in indentity suffered by those facing adult responsibilities amid explosive social change "since [they] have been molded by a culture laying heavy stress upon the achievement of inner harmony through following closely prescribed emotional paths within a carefully regulated group structure (Lifton 1964:378)."

The point is well taken, but thanks to "examination hell," this particular identity issue opens late and briefly (and therefore violently?) for many Japanese men.

NOTES

1. In a recent paper, R. N. Bellah shows the similarity between the role of the emperor and the role of the mother in the Japanese psyche (Bellah 1967). I would take Bellah's analysis a step further, as I have done with the teacher, and suggest that the "good" and "bad" father images are resolved in the figure of the emperor.
2. Of course this is a problem in all industrial societies. The American

solution to the problem, described in such works as W. H. Whyte's (1950) and Riesman's (1958), shows the conflict between organization membership and individuality in this country.

3. Jack M. Potter (see Potter 1968) conducted research in a rural village near Hong Kong in 1961/62. This report is from unpublished field notes.

4. Moreover, in feudal times, members of Japan's ruling class actually underwent a puberty ceremony, or *seinenshiki*, during which the head of a boy was shaved and his status as a warrior conferred. Considering the similarity of the roles of the bureaucratic samurai of old and the modern salaryman—the "new samurai," (Vogel 1963)—it might not seem too ridiculous to say that the "priest's haircut" received by boys upon entry into middle school in modern Japan is *functionally* similar to the head-shaving of the feudal samurai. Both serve to remind the initiate that he has assumed new responsibilities.

REFERENCES

ABEGGLEN, JAMES G. 1958. The Japanese factory: aspects of its social organization. Glencoe: The Free Press.

ALLPORT, GORDON W. 1961. Pattern and growth in personality. New York: Rinehart & Winston.

BELLAH, R. N. 1957. Tokugawa religion. Glencoe: The Free Press.

———. 1967. The Japanese emperor as a mother figure. Mimeo. Center for Japanese and Korean Studies, University of California, Berkeley.

BENEDICT, R. 1946. The chrysanthemum and the sword. Boston: Houghton Mifflin.

BENNETT, JOHN W., AND IWAO ISHINO. 1963. Paternalism in the Japanese economy. Minneapolis: University of Minnesota Press.

CAUDILL, WILLIAM, AND HARRY A. SCARR. 1962. Japanese value orientations and culture change. Ethnology 1:53–91.

COHEN, Y. A. 1964. The establishment of identity in a social nexus: the special case of initiation ceremonies and their relation to value and legal systems. American Anthropologist 66: 529–552.

DE VOS, GEORGE. 1964. Role narcissism and the etiology of Japanese suicide. Mimeo. Paper presented to the Center for Japanese and Korean Studies, University of California, Berkeley.

DE VOS, GEORGE, AND WILLIAM CAUDILL. 1956. Achievement, culture and personality: the case of the Japanese Americans. American Anthropologist 58: 1102–1126.

DORE, R. P. 1965. Education in Tokugawa Japan. Berkeley: University of California Press.

DURKHEIM, EMILE. 1925. L'education morale. Paris: Librairie Felix Alcan.

ERIKSON, ERIK H. 1963. Childhood and society. New York: W. W. Norton. [Revised edition.]

GOFFMAN, ERVING. 1960. Characteristics of total institutions. In Identity and anxiety. M. Stein, A. K. Vidich, and D. M. White, eds. Glencoe: The Free Press. pp. 449–479.

HARTMANN, HEINZ. 1958. Ego psychology and the problem of adaptation. New York: International Universities Press.

HENRY, JULES. 1963. Culture against man. New York: Random House.

KARDINER, ABRAM, R. LINTON, C. DUBOIS, J. WEST. 1945. The psychological frontiers of society. New York: Columbia University Press.

KARSH, BERNARD, AND R. E. COLE. 1968. Industrialization and the convergence hypothesis: some aspects of contemporary Japan. Journal of Social Issues 24:45–64.

KIEFER, CHRISTIE W. 1968. Personality and social change in a Japanese danchi. Unpublished Ph.D. dissertation. University of California, Berkeley.

LANHAM, BETTY B. 1956. Aspects of child care in Japan: preliminary report. *In* Personal character and cultural milieu. D. G. Haring, ed. Syracuse: Syracuse University Press. pp. 565–583.

LIFTON, R. J. 1960. Methods of forceful indoctrination. *In* Identity and anxiety. M. Stein, A. K. Vidich, and D. M. White, eds. Glencoe: The Free Press. pp. 480–492.

———. 1964. Individual patterns in historical change: imagery of Japanese youth. Comparative Studies in Society and History 6:369–383.

LYND, HELEN M. 1958. On shame and the search for identity. New York: Harcourt, Brace.

MATSUMOTO, Y. S. 1960. Contemporary Japan, the individual and the group. Transactions of the American Philosophical Society 50(1).

McCLELLAND, DAVID C. 1961. The achieving society. Princeton: D. Van Nostrand.

POTTER, JACK M. 1968. Capitalism and the Chinese peasant. Berkeley and Los Angeles: University of California Press.

RIESMAN, DAVID. 1958. The lonely crowd. New Haven: Yale University Press.

ROHEIM, G. 1942. Transition rites. The Psychoanalytic Quarterly 11:336–374.

TANAKA, YASUMASA. 1966. Cross-cultural compatibility of the affective meaning systems (measured by means of multilingual semantic differentials). Journal of Social Issues 23:27–46.

VAN GENNEP, ARNOLD. 1908. The rites of passage. M. B. Vizedom and G. L. Caffee, trans. Chicago: University of Chicago Press. [1960]

VOGEL, EZRA F. 1962. Entrance examinations and emotional disturbances in Japan's middle class. *In* Japanese culture: its development and characteristics. R. J. Smith and R. K. Beardsley, eds. Chicago: Aldine. pp. 140–152.

———. 1963. Japan's new middle class. Berkeley: University of California Press.

WHITING, J. W. M., R. KLUCKHOHN, AND A. ANTHONY. 1958. The function of male initiation rites at puberty. *In* Readings in social psychology. E. E. Maccoby, T. M. Newcomb and E. L. Hartley, eds. New York: Holt, Rinehart, & Winston.

WHYTE, WILLIAM H. 1956. The organization man. Garden City: Doubleday.

PART IV

Cultural Stress, Extreme Responses, and Behavior Transformation

Self-Destruction in Japan:
A Cross-cultural Epidemiological
Analysis of Suicide

MASAAKI KATO

INTRODUCTION

Although it seems very clear to define suicide as "self-murder," that definition does not express its clinical and socio-psychological meaning. The meaning of suicide is at the crux of the study of suicide. Emile Durkheim has written that "the term suicide is applied to all cases of death resulting directly or indirectly from a positive or negative act of the victim himself, which he knows will produce this result."[1] However, his definition seems to me somewhat ambiguous, for an "act of the victim himself" depends upon the victim's subjective judgment of his own act, and his knowing that it "will produce this result" depends upon his ability to foresee the consequences of his behavior. This ability is necessary in order to distinguish suicide from other kinds of destructive behavior. In this connection, the Tokyo Municipal Medical Inspection Office reported that in 3.1% of the cases submitted for autopsy in 1961, it was difficult to judge whether the cause was suicide or accident. Dr. Edwin Schneidman noted that approximately 10% of the cases of attempted suicide in California are in question, i.e., of 100 cases, the cause of 11 was shifted from accident to suicide and that of 8 from suicide to accident. One of the difficulties lies in discriminating true suicide from "institutional murder" because of social pressure and "pseudosuicide" by persons who are unaccountable for themselves.

As examples of institutional suicide in Japan and India, most researchers cite *tsumebara* (enforced *harakiri*), *kamikaze*, *sati*, and

Reprinted from *Folia Psychiatrica et Neurologica Japonica* 23 (1969): 291–307.

jauhar. In Japan self-immolation (including *harakiri*) after the death of one's lord was sanctioned until 1863, when the Tokugawa Shogunate strictly forbade it. Injunctions aside, it was still practiced, in the most spectacular instance by General Maresuke Nogi, who with his wife committed *harakiri* after the death of Meiji Emperor Mutsuhito in 1912. Generally it is very difficult in these kinds of immolation to decide whether they are due to the victim's own will or some external institutional pressure. *Sati* and *jauhar* were forbidden even by King Akbar, who committed suicide in a previous life and was reborn as a king. As regards the Japanese suicide air force, *kamikaze*, and suicide submarines, *raiden*, in World War II, most foreign researchers look on them as examples of mass suicide. However, the persons involved did not think of these acts as suicide. After I interviewed three surviving *raiden* drivers fifteen years after the war, it became clear to me that they regarded their behavior as other-destructive, not self-destructive. Believing in immortality, they did not expect to die.

These situations are somewhat similar to the "pseudosuicide" of children or severely psychotic patients, i.e., unaccountable for themselves. If a schizophrenic patient obeys an invisible person's order to kill himself, or a manic patient who believes he can fly jumps from a 10-story building and dies, it depends upon his degree of responsibility for his acts whether it is suicide or not. The same difficulty occurs in the self-destructive behavior of children. Although Leo Kanner described the case of a three-year-old boy committing suicide, it is doubtful whether this child could foresee the result of his behavior. The line between "pseudosuicide" and true suicide is fine indeed. Consequently, I would define suicide as "an act of self-destruction carried out by a person with an integrated personality in the expectation that this act will result in his death."

ATTEMPTED AND COMPLETED SUICIDES

Erwin Stengel's hypothesis that distinguishing between attempted and completed suicides is very difficult is generally accepted. However, H. B. M. Murphy insists that attempted and completed suicides come from two different groups, even though part of these two groups might overlap: some of the attempted suicide group might die by chance, and some of the completed suicide group might survive. As J. W. McCulloch and A. E. Philip pointed out, "attempted suicide is neither a diagnosis nor a description of behavior and it is an interpretation of behavior which is difficult to make."[2] Owing to the difficulties of defining attempted suicide, unbiased comparison among nations of attempted suicide is more difficult than complete suicide. That is one of the reasons why the ratio of attempted suicide to completed suicide differs from country to country. For example, Schneidman detected 7.7 times more attempted than completed suicides in his 1957 survey in California; Paw Meng Yap reports 3.4 times more in Hong Kong, Japanese governmental statistics cite 0.15 times more attempted than completed suicides. However, it is notable that reliable statistics show in females and youth a higher incidence of attempted suicide than completed suicide.

In Japan we do not have reliable statistics of attempted suicide throughout the whole country. In 1957, this writer and others carried out a survey of attempted and completed suicide in a city of 150,000 population near Tokyo. Notwithstanding our effort to collect the data by visiting private practitioners and hospitals with the support of the prefectural health center and city police, we could find only 92 attempted vs. 231 completed suicides in this city from January 1, 1949 to December 31, 1956. This meant the ratio between attempted vs. completed suicides was 40:100, although these rates coincided with the general tendency of high rate in youth, low in the aged, and higher rate in female than in male which were contrary to those of completed suicide.

AGE AND SEXUAL FACTORS

Reliable statistical data in Western countries show that the rate for completed suicide is low in youth, rises in middle age, and is highest in the aged male and stationary or declines in the aged female (shown in the New York survey by L. Dublin, and the Leipzig survey by Feudel). Comparing the age distribution of completed suicides in Western countries, it is found that Hungary and Denmark show a rate which increases almost parallel with age, but the rate in the U.S., U.K., and Italy rises slowly with age and then declines in females over 80 years old. In contrast, the rates of Japan, Taiwan and Hong Kong show a characteristic curve rising in youth, declining in middle age, and rising again in the aged. These characteristics are most remarkable in the age distribution of completed suicides in Taiwan, although that in Hong Kong seems to be somewhat similar to the European curve. However, Yap mentioned that the main difference between the suicide rate in the U.S. and Hong Kong is in the fall of the female curve after menopause in the former.

Observing the rate of completed suicides in Japan during the past 10 years, it is notable that the rate among youth, particularly those from 15 to 24, has declined greatly. Immediately after World War II, the suicide rate in Japan rose rapidly, reaching a peak of 25.7 per 100,000 population in 1958, with a peak for males of 31.5 in 1955 and for females of 20.8 in 1958, then with a rapid falling off since 1961. It is significant that the completed suicide rate for males and females 15–19 years old decreased from 37.2 and 26.1 in 1955 to 8.8 and 6.1 in 1965, respectively, and for the 20–24 age-group decreased from 84.1 and 46.8 in 1955 to 23.3 and 18.3 in 1965, respectively, although the decline among the older groups was not as marked as is shown in Table 1 and Figures 1 and 2. Furthermore, the 1965 rate for the 15–19 age group was the lowest in 45 years and that for the age-group 20–24 was the lowest in 18 years.

Table 1. Fluctuation of Suicide Rates from 1900 to 1965 by
Sex in Japan per 100,000 Population

Year	Total	Male	Female	F/M
1900	13.4	16.9	9.9	58.7
1910	19.1	24.0	14.0	58.3
1920	19.0	23.3	14.7	63.5
1930	21.6	27.8	16.0	57.5
(1932)	22.2	27.8	16.6	59.7
1940	13.7	16.5	11.0	66.7
(1943)	12.1	14.7	9.6	65.3
1950	19.6	24.1	15.3	61.4
(1955)	25.2	31.5	19.0	60.3
(1958)	25.7	30.1	20.8	65.8
1960	21.6	25.1	18.2	72.5
1961	19.6	22.3	16.9	76.4
1962	17.6	20.4	14.8	72.5
1963	16.1	18.9	13.4	71.4
1964	15.1	17.5	12.9	73.7
1965	14.7	17.3	12.2	71.1
1966	15.0	17.1	13.0	76.0

Although different record-keeping practices and quality of vital statistics may bias the comparison of international statistics, I should like to cite the WHO *Statistic Annual* for 1964, Volume 1. According to this report, the completed suicide rate in Taiwan in 1964 is high among youth, declines in the middle aged, and rises again in the aged—a curve that is similar to Japan although much higher than that of the latter. That Taiwan's rate is higher may owe to differences in detection or definition of suicide; however, this

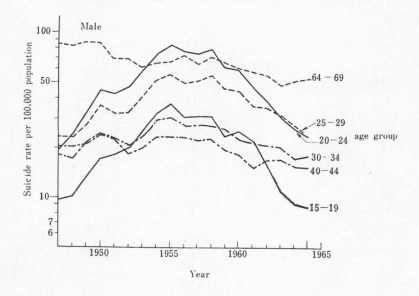

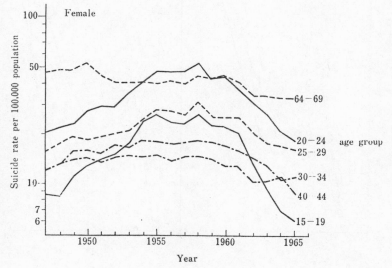

Fig. 1. Trends in the Suicide Rate in Japan by
Age Group and Sex, 1947–1965

does not invalidate the basically similar configuration of the curves of the two countries (Figure 3).

In this connection, Yap noted that in the completed suicide

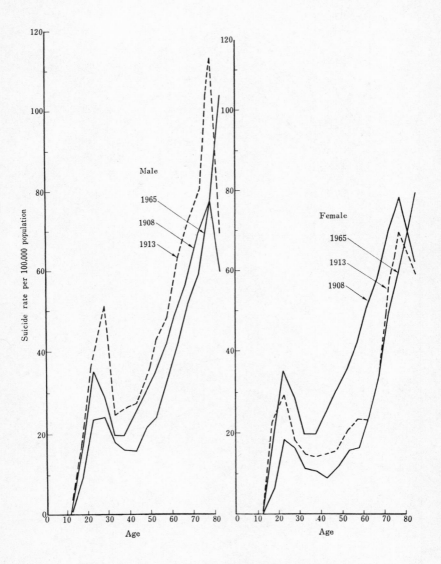

Fig. 2. Comparison of Suicide Rate in Japan by
Age Distribution per 100,000 population

rate in Hong Kong, "the male curve rises rapidly until the early thirties, when a plateau is reached, all the while keeping slightly

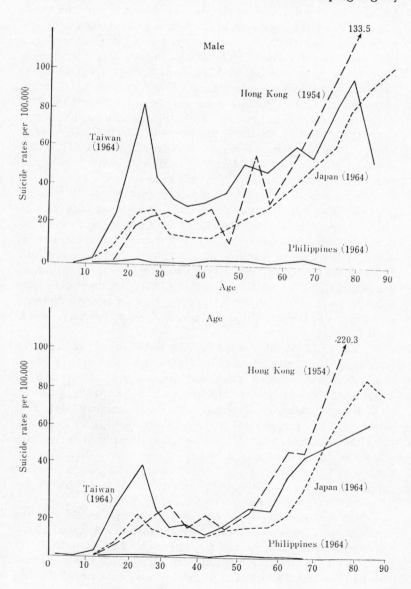

Fig. 3. Suicide Rate in Asian Countries

above the female. . . . These curves are similar to those found for most western countries, except that the plateau between 30 and 50 are unusual and that the female curve rises sharply after the menopause in Hong Kong, instead of reaching a peak at this period and then falling or remaining more or less stationary."[3] However, it must be noted that the WHO statistics dispute Yap's idea of the Western type, in showing that France, Portugal, and Hungary exhibit a rapidly rising female curve. However, the rapid decline of the suicide rate in Japan for the age-group 15–25 and the drop in the overall rate (total suicides) to 15.0 (approaching that of 16.1 in the U.S.A. and 13.8 in the U.K. and lower than that of Denmark, France, West Germany, Hungary, Sweden, Taiwan and Czechoslovakia) might mean that Japan's suicide rate curve is changing from the "Oriental" to the "Western" type.

As regards the ratio of female-male suicide, that in Western countries approximates one-third (33.3) compared with that in Oriental countries of two-thirds (66.7). However, in Japan the trend is toward a rise in the sex ratio, which seems against the general norm, as is shown in Table 2. The F-M ratio has increased from 58.7 in 1900 to 76.0 in 1966, and, if compared by age distribution, it is notable that the ratio for age-group 15–19 has decreased, from 152.9 in 1903 to 69.3 in 1965, although that for persons 20 years and older, particularly those 50 years and older, has increased in those 62 years.

As to the F-M ratio in the U.S.A., it is relatively high for the middle-aged and low in the elderly, although the total F-M ratio is as low as 34.8. Among other countries, the F-M ratio is high in Israel at 86.4 and low in Finland at 25.6. Generally speaking, those countries with a high suicide rate show a relatively low F-M ratio, such as Hungary (41.8), West Germany (51.5), Denmark (34.5) and Finland (25.6). In contrast, the following countries have a low suicide rate and high F-M ratio: Israel (86.5), New Zealand (63.9), Philippines (60.0) and the Netherlands (59.8). The exceptional country is Italy, which has a relatively low F-M ratio of 41.6 and a low suicide rate of 7.5 (Table 3).

Summarizing the foregoing results, it seems to me that the fluctuations of completed suicide rates are mainly influenced by the change in those rates for the age-groups 15–25 and over 65, in particular for males, although the high suicide rate in some countries like Finland, Sweden, and Australia is affected more by the rate among the middle-aged.

TRADITIONAL AND MODERN SUICIDE

Durkheim said that "having given a name of Egoism to the state of ego living its own life obeying itself alone, that of altruism adequately express the opposite state, where the ego is not its own property, where it is blended with something not itself, where the

Table 2. Fluctuation of Suicide Rates by Female vs.
Male Ratio in Japan from 1903 to 1965

Age	1903	1908	1913	1918	1935	1965
Total	60.0	64.4	59.8	65.6	62.9	71.1
15–19	152.9	135.9	113.1	121.0	83.6	69.3
20–24	68.9	66.4	72.1	68.7	62.6	78.9
25–29	57.3	57.1	58.2	64.9	57.8	65.3
30–34	60.7	61.0	59.8	67.0	78.6	61.7
35–39	52.7	62.6	53.4	55.3	60.5	67.7
40–44	48.1	54.4	53.7	59.9	64.0	56.5
45–49	45.7	50.8	47.0	57.3	51.6	54.6
50–54	36.6	47.5	47.0	53.4	51.8	63.0
55–59	38.8	43.4	46.1	41.4	41.2	48.9
60–64	43.1	45.6	35.6	48.5	44.9	55.6
65–69	55.5	51.6	46.6	52.8	47.0	64.2
70–72 ⎫		63.1	68.0	50.2 ⎫		83.1
75–79 ⎬	54.0	78.6	61.3	69.9 ⎭	57.1	78.2
80– ⎭		87.4	85.3	86.5	61.8	76.3

Table 3. Suicide Rates by Female vs. Male Ratio and by
Age Distribution in Several Countries

Hong-kong	(1954) F/M	Taiwan	(1964) F/M	U. K. (1964) F/M	Japan (1965) F/M	U.S.A. (1964) F/M
16–20	477.2	15–19	92.1	48.6	69.3	27.0
21–25	76.0	20–24	48.3	40.9	78.9	32.3
26–30	93.3	25–29	53.0	58.0	65.3	39.6
31–35	96.7	30–34	46.7	61.0	61.7	42.2
36–40	80.1	35–39	61.5	57.9	67.7	52.9
41–45	78.2	40–44	40.4	78.7	56.5	43.3
46–50	152.8	45–49	46.0	61.4	54.6	40.1
51–55	43.0	50–54	49.7	74.3	63.0	37.5
56–60	38.5	55–59	50.5	69.3	48.9	30.3
61–65	84.0	60–64	51.7	74.3	55.6	26.2
66–70	55.0	65–69	69.4	69.1	64.2	29.3
71–75	73.3	70–74	58.0	68.7	83.1	23.4
76–	165.0	75–79	51.8	48.2	78.2	14.9
		80–84	110.8	41.7	76.3	11.4
Total	67.6	Total	59.8	71.0	71.1	34.8

*Hungary 41.8, West Germany 51.5, Denmark 34.5

goal of conduct is exterior to itself, that is, in one of the groups in which it participates. So we call the suicide caused by intense altruism altruistic suicide. But since it is also characteristically performed as a duty, the terminology adopted should express this fact. So we will call such a type obligatory altruistic suicide."[4] That means not every altruistic suicide is necessarily obligatory, that there may be some option. In the traditional kind of obligatory suicide in Japan, inner and outer conflicts were closely connected with such traditional mores or morality as loyalty to one's lord and fidelity to one's parents (*on, giri, haji,* etc.). The sentiments most frequently expressed in ordinary suicide notes were *"Moshi wake ga nai"* ("There is no way to apologize"); *"Giri ga tatanai"* ("I cannot fulfill my obligations"); *"Shinde owabi suru"* ("I apologize by dying"); and *"Sakidatsu fukō o oyurushi kudasai"* ("Allow me to precede my parents in death").

Durkheim classified altruistic suicide into obligatory, optional, and acute types, regarding the military as a special environment where even today altruistic suicide is chronic. In this meaning, it might be presumed that in pre-World War II times, a kind of altruistic suicide still existed in Japan, but after the War the number of anomic suicides increased to a peak in 1955–58, and *both types of suicide have decreased since 1958.* As regards the egoistic type of suicide, Hiroshi Minami termed it "pure suicide," a type which is still rare even among modernized Japanese youth. Mamoru Iga declared, "if anomie is responsible for high Japanese suicide rates after the war, then lower suicide rates are expected when Japanese adjust to the social change since the war. . . . This lower 1963 figure may suggest not only the new adjustment but also the decline of suicide of more traditional Japanese type (e.g. altruistic or fatalistic types)."[5] He insisted, that egoistic goal, goal-means discrepancy, dependency and insecurity were the causal factors in anomie in Japan, in particular among the youth.[6]

Most foreign researchers of suicide in Japan consider "double or collective suicide" an example of traditional Japanese suicide. However, the writer thinks that most of the parent-child suicides are actually the mother's suicide with infanticide. Infanticide and suicide for love are not genuinely Japanese types of suicide. For example, Fumiki Okazaki noted that the proprotion of double suicide in Paris in 1927–1943 was 4.2%, while that in Japan in 1948–1960 was 3.6%, although the comparison of vital statistics in different countries might have many biases. Mikami and Takara insisted that double suicide for love in Japan was based on the religious belief in the future life, on the low value placed on individual life from the *bushidō* way of thinking, and on rigidly prizing women's chastity. T. Iguchi strongly opposes this view because it represents too broad an interpretation of the meaning of double suicide for love.

THE CHANGING PATTERN OF SUICIDE IN JAPAN

As mentioned above, the rate for completed suicide differs in time and area; thus, changing chronological, ethnological and sociological patterns should be investigated.

As regards chronological change, the suicide curve in Japan has been found to fluctuate with the business cycle and war; e.g., it rose in prewar times and during serious economic depression (1913, 1932, and 1934) and declined in wartime and with prosperity (1906, 1917, and 1960), as shown in Figure 4.

In the five years between the Japanese army's thrust into Manchuria in 1932 and the beginning of the Sino-Japanese War in 1937, the suicide rates leveled off and then declined rapidly after the outbreak of Sino-Japanese War. (There may, however, be many biases in the statistics of wartime, because suicides committed in foreign battlefields might be excluded, and even the completed suicides in Inland Forces might be officially attributed to accident or disease to protect the good name of the deceased. Nevertheless, the decline of the suicide rate during World War II and its rise in 1955–58 cannot be overlooked. The rise is probably closely connected with the financial, moral and political anomie of the times. What then, is the meaning of its decline in the past 10 years? Is it the result of financial, moral and political stability in Japan? Although I cannot deny the meaning of these factors, I should like to stress the importance of the changing pattern of expressing aggression, in particular that among youth.

As I mentioned above, the most striking fluctuation of the suicide rate is the change in the age-group 15–25, in particular for males. They reacted to outer social change more sensitively than did the aged. The aged, particularly the female, reacted very slowly. One of the hypotheses is that postwar "democratic" education was effective in changing them from passively dependent to more individually autonomic, and aggressive needs are becoming more ego-syntonic and dependent needs more ego-alien, just the opposite of youth before World War II. Stated another way, they have become more extrapunitive than intropunitive, easily express their aggressiveness toward others rather than suppress or repress it. In

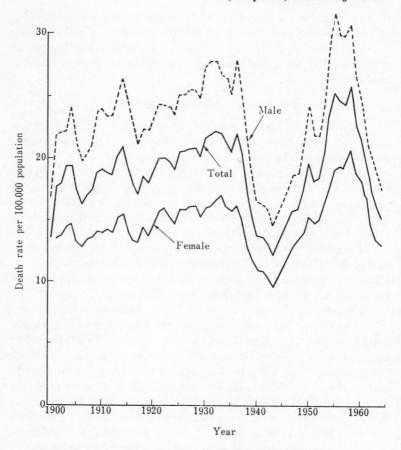

Fig. 4. Fluctuation of Suicide Rates in Japan from
1900 to 1965

this connection, the pattern of juvenile offenses should be compared
with that of suicide in the last 10 years.

According to the statistical report issued by the Young Adult
and Juvenile Section of the Japanese Ministry of Justice, the number of juvenile offenders in 1967 had increased 1.7 times over that
of 1957, although the number of adult offenders had increased
1.45 times in this period—juvenile offenders 7.1 per 1,000 population in 1957 to 11.1 in 1967, and adult offenders 8.2 in 1957 to
9.5 in 1967. The report showed 3.2 juvenile vs. 10.6 adult offenders
in 1936 and 3.4 vs. 7.7 in 1940. Since 1958 the proportion of juvenile
offenders overcame that of adult offenders. Michio Yasuda reported

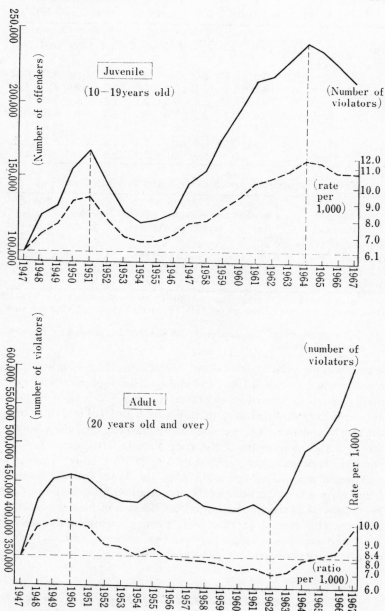

Fig. 5. Number of Penal Code Offenders Apprehended or Acted Upon by the Police and Their Ratio Per 1,000 Population in Japan, 1947–1967.

Table 4. Atrocious and Violent Crimes in Japan, 1956–1967

		Atrocious Crimes					Violent Crimes				
Age		1956	1964	1965	1966	1967	1956	1964	1965	1966	1967
	Under 14	0.04	0.07	0.07	0.05	0.05	0.09	0.30	0.24	0.18	0.17
	14–15	0.1	0.2	0.2	0.2	0.2	0.6	2.6	2.4	2.1	1.8
Juvenile	16–17	0.5	0.6	0.6	0.6	0.5	2.2	3.9	3.6	3.3	2.9
	18–19	0.7	0.8	0.7	0.7	0.6	3.7	4.5	3.9	3.6	3.4
	Total	0.3	0.4	0.4	0.3	0.3	1.3	2.3	2.2	2.1	1.9
Adult	20–24	0.6	0.5	0.5	0.4	0.4	5.1	4.3	4.2	4.2	4.0
	Total	0.2	0.2	0.2	0.2	0.2	2.1	2.0	1.9	1.9	1.8

Table 5. Homicide and Suicide Rates in Four Countries

Annual number per 100,000 population	Homicide offenders (a)	Homicide offenders who kill themselves	Suicide (b)	Suicide-murder ratio (c)
England & Wales	0.27	33% (0.09)	8.5	0.97
Denmark	0.53	42% (0.22)	21.0	0.98
U.S.A.	4.5 approx	4% (0.18)	10.0	0.69
Australia	1.7	22% (0.36)	11.0	0.87

(a) Figure taken from Interpol: International Crime Statistics for years 1959–60.
(b) Figures for years 1959 taken from WHO Epidemiological and Vital Statistics 1961.
(c) This ratio represents the number of homicide-suicides divided by the total number of suicides.

that atrocious crimes (intentional homicide, robbery, arson, and rape) reached a peak in 1960, and violent crimes (physical violence, bodily injury, intimidation, extortion) also reached a peak in 1964 and both have declined since then. Figure 5 and Table 4 show that the rate of violent crimes increased more markedly and the younger the age, the more marked the rise. Yasuda attributes the first postwar crime wave (September 1945 to 1951) mainly to poverty and moral and social confusion after the War, but the second crime wave after 1956 was closely connected with the consumption boom as well as the increase in leisure hours and pleasure-seeking impetus. However, I presume that these phenomena themselves are based on some changes in behavior patterns and the value system, particularly among Japanese youth.

SUICIDE AND HOMICIDE

As Schneidman pointed out, it is too simple to divide death from causes other than disease into natural death, suicide and homicide. Although it is said that homicide is an example of extroverted aggression in contrast to introverted aggression (suicide), this position is being reconsidered. For example, D. West noted that murder was followed by suicide in one-third of the cases in England, 42% of the cases in Denmark, 22% in Australia and 4% in U.S.A., although in some cases it was difficult to differentiate suicide from homicide (Table 5).

Although infanticide is said to be common in Japan, we have not enough data to confirm it. West mentioned that the natural psychological mechanism of identification, by which a mother feels her child a part of herself, has been carried to dangerous extremes by psychotic mothers in Western countries.

Eire shows a low rate in both categories; Finland has a high rate in both; Denmark is high in suicide and low in homicide; and Venezuela is low in suicide and high in homicide. Japan is similar to Finland in having a high rate in both categories (Table 6).

Table 6. Comparison of Suicide and Homicide Rates
in Various Countries in 1960

	Suicide and Self-inflicted Injury	Homicide and Operation of War
Eire	3.0	0.2
England and Wales	20.3	0·5
Switzerland	11.2	0.6
Belgium	14.6	0.7
West Germany	18.8	1.0
Canada	7.6	1.4
Australia	10.6	1.5
Italy	6.3	1.5
France	15.9	1.7
Japan	21.2	1.9
Finland	20.4	2.9
Ceylon	9.9	3.3
U.S.A.	10.8	4.5
Venezuela	6.6	8.7

Source: WHO Epid. and Statist. 1965, No. 15, p. 519.

A. L. Wood discussed the homicide and suicide rates in 36 countries, based on the average rate for the years 1951 to 1956, as given in the United Nations Demographic Yearbooks, eliminating the years in which a country was at war or in revolution. The median homicide rate was 1.7; the median suicide rate was 8.5; and a suggestive association emerged between high suicide rates and low homicide rates, and vice versa. This result would seem to lend support to the inverse relationship theory, notwithstanding the many exceptions and complicating factors (Table 7).

Table 7. Comparison of Homicide and Suicide Rates
in Thirty-Six Countries

Number of countries with	Low suicide rate (5.0 or less)	High suicide rate (12 or more)
High homicide rate (3.5 or more)	8	1
Low homicide rate (1.0 or less)	2	5
Totals of 36 countries	10	6

Although Durkheim presumed that altruistic suicide would occur with homicide and egoistic suicide would not, Henry and Short·noted that suicide was more frequent among people of high social status and those who live alone, contrary to homicide, which was more frequent among people of low social status and rare among the solitary elderly. They found that the rate of homicide and crimes of violence in the U.S. generally fluctuated conversely with the suicide rate and correlated positively with the business index. However, Fumiki Okazaki disagreed with the hypothesis of a reciprocal relationship between suicide and homicide, based on Japanese data from 1930 to 1959. Considering that in this 30-year period the areal correlation coefficient in 46 districts was only 0.08 and the chronological correlation coefficient was 0.647, he concluded that there was not a reciprocal proportion but rather a direct proportion between suicide and homicide. If Durkheim's hypothesis is correct, the direct proportion between suicide and homicide may indicate that Japanese suicides were mainly altruistic or anomic, with few egoistic suicides. More recent statistics confirm this, since suicide of an obligatory altruistic or fatalistic nature is decreasing, and anomic suicide rose until 1958 and has been declining since then.

Henry and Short consider child-rearing and personality development to be very important in determining the mode of expressing aggression. Persons of strong superego are likely throughout their lives to conform meticulously to society's rules, to feel guilty about even minor infractions, and to blame themselves and turn their aggression upon themselves rather than against others. The child-rearing practices of the middle classes are more likely to favor strong superego development than are those of the lower classes.

Since World War II, child-rearing in Japan has been changing. Traditionally in the Orient, parents have been very permissive and overprotective of their children in their infancy, which seems to most foreigners as a symbiotic relation between mother and child. As the child grows up, parental punishment becomes more severe. Through adolescence, he is most strictly trained until he becomes an independent member of society. This way of rearing is completely contrary to the Western way, where parents train babies with whip and candy, and are progressively more permissive as the child grows older. The contrast between the U.S.A., and Japan seems to be the most striking.

In prewar times Japanese children were enjoined to appreciate their parents for their *on* (indebtedness or obligation) toward them, and filial piety was one of the most important moral principles, together with loyalty to the Emperor. After World War II, these principles gradually lost their power, and the way of child-rearing is moving toward the Western way: i.e., severe rearing in infancy, becoming more permissive in adolescence. However, the writer is very reluctant to decide if the recent remarkable decline of the suicide rate and the rise in the rate of violent crime among Japanese youth might have some connection with changes in child-rearing, education and value systems caused by the rapid social change after World War II.

COMPARISON OF SUICIDE BETWEEN JAPANESE AMERICAN AND OTHER ETHNIC GROUPS IN HAWAII

Francis K. Hsu noted that the rate for completed suicide among the Japanese in Hawaii was not so high for youth and the aged as for Japanese nationals. However, Andrea Tyree has come to a different conclusion, based on statistics of the State of Hawaii from 1950 to 1960.[7]

1. The ethnic group having the greatest proportion of suicides was the Japanese, constitutiong 42% of the total. Caucasians (including Puerto Rican), with 29.5%, were a distant second.

2. Suicide rates by ethnicity ranged between 11.7 per 100,000 population for Japanese, 10.1 for Caucasian, 9.6 for Filipino, 8.5 for Chinese, 4.8 for Hawaiian, and 8.2 for others, based on 1955 population estimates, but Japanese do not show the highest rates until the 65 and over age bracket, and the Hawaiians, who have the lowest overall rate, have the highest suicide rate in the age category 25–34. (Table 8, Figure 6).

3. The only ethnic group whose suicide rate by age curve resembled the American national curve was the Caucasian group. It was hypothesized that the dissimilar curves of other ethnic groups resulted from social factors (status conflict or lack thereof) oper-

Table 8. Suicide by Age and Ethnicity, Hawaii, 1950–1960

Age	Caucasian		Chinese		Filipino		Hawaiian		Japanese		Other	
	No.	Rate	No.	Rate	No.	Rate	No.	Rate	No.	Rate	No.	Rate
65–	17	27.87	14	64.93	4	18.92	2	8.07	115	95.74	9	68.41
55–64	26	30.49	5	18.72	9	14.25	2	5.30	32	24.65	2	25.32
45–54	41	20.47	8	19.18	31	26.11	8	11.97	28	15.41	2	17.12
35–44	37	14.86	3	5.21	16	14.52	12	11.69	35	11.51	7	28.82
25–34	24	7.23	2	3.22	4	4.96	18	13.39	31	8.29	3	7.86
15–24	23	6.37	1	1.76	4	4.11	6	3.18	10	2.85	4	8.78
Total	168	10.09	33	8.50	69	9.64	48	4.79	251	11.70	27	8.18

Suicide rates are based in 1955 population estimates, averages of 1950 and 1960 United States census data. Source: *United States Census of Population: 1950, Hawaii.* Vol. 2, Part 52, p. 35: *United States Census of Population: 1960; Hawaii: Detailed Characteristics,* PC(1)–13D, p. 113; *United States Census of Population: 1960—Special Reports,* (PC(2)–1C), *Non-White Population by Race,* p. 254.

ating with varying intensity on the several ethnic groups at different points in their lives.

Tyree found that the correlation between occupational-ethnic status consciousness and the rate of suicide was − .509, and concluded that there was a relationship between suicide and status conflict except among the Japanese. They were greatly in excess of the total rank correlation across ethnic lines. Status sets of occupational and ethnic categories do not offer a source of status conflict for the Japanese in Hawaii. The relationship between status integration and suicide rates of these four ethnic groups is shown in the following Table 9.

However, Richard A. Kalish described different data on suicide rates in Hawaii from 1959 to 1965. His study was based on the data obtained through the Department of Health, State of Hawaii, and through a police inspector. It showed that the Hawaiians had the highest rate of suicide and the Caucasians were the second highest, although the Japanese male had a suicide rate

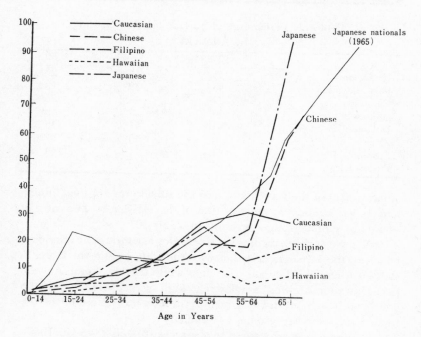

Fig. 6. Mean Annual Suicide Rate By Age and Ethnicity, Hawaii, 1950–1960 and Japan, 1965 (In Suicides Per 100,000 Population)

Table 9. Relationship Between Status Integration
and Suicide Rate in Hawaii

	Status Integration			Suicide	
Ethnicity	Measure	Rank		Rate	Rank
Caucasian	.2344	3		15.78	1
Chinese	.2449	2		14.48	2
Filipino	.2486	1		11.44	3
Japanese	.2256	4		14.48	2

Table 10. Suicide Rates by Ethnic Group in Hawaii,
1959–1965, per 10,000 Population

	Male	Female	Total
Hawaiian	2.48	1.02	1.78
Part-Hawaiian	0.97	0.40	0.68
Caucasian	1.52	0.83	1.23
Chinese	1.38	1.01	1.20
Japanese	1.53	0.39	0.94
Filipino	0.65	0.31	0.55

Table 11. Percentage of Suicide for Age Group
by Ethnicity

	10–29	30–49	50+
Hawaiian	55%	18%	27%
Part-Hawaiian	48%	39%	13%
Caucasian	24%	41%	35%
Chinese	14%	27%	59%
Japanese	15%	41%	43%
Korean	0	43%	57%
Filipino	33%	17%	44%
Puerto-Rican	33%	67%	0

equal to that of the Caucasian, and the suicide rate of the Chinese female was almost the same as that of the Hawaiian. The rates of suicide by ethnic group are shown in Table 10.

As regards the percentage of suicide for age groups by ethnicity, however, the Japanese, together with the Chinese and the Korean, showed a marked increase with age, while the Hawaiian and the part-Hawaiian showed a relatively high percentage among the youth, although he did not mention about the difference of the suicide rates for age groups by ethnicity.

It is not clear why these two surveys of Drs. Tyree in 1950–1960 and Kalish in 1959–1965 showed different rates of suicide by ethnicity, i.e., 11.7 vs. 9.4 in the Japanese, 4.79 vs. 17.8 in the Hawaiian, 10.09 vs. 12.3 in the Caucasian, 8.50 vs. 12.0 and 9.64

vs. 5.5 in the Filipino. The most remarkable difference between the results of these two surveys is that of suicide rates in the Hawaiian. However, one of the coincided results was that the age distribution of suicide in the Japanese, together with in the Chinese and the Korean, was low in youth and high in old age; in contrast, that of the Hawaiian was high in youth and low in old age.

It is suggested that almost all of these elderly Japanese are of the first generation (issei) to come to Hawaii as immigrants, and that they experienced many difficulties in becoming American citizens. Retaining the traditional Japanese way of thinking, they had many language problems and status conflicts. I presume that this high rate of suicide among the Japanese in Hawaii will decline in the future as the older generations die out, because the rate is low among young Japanese-Hawaiians. In the future, not only the suicide rates among Japanese in Hawaii but also those of Japanese nationals might become similar to the Western type, i.e., the age distribution of suicide rates will rise with age until age 65, when it will fall, particularly among the females.

SUMMARY

1. A simple comparison of vital statistics of suicide has many biases. For example, 3.1% of the cases submitted for autopsy by the Tokyo Municipal Medical Inspection Office were difficult to attribute to suicide or accident from the legal medical standpoint. Such cases as those of children or severely psychotic patients were sometimes almost impossible to determine. Many suicides were hidden by the victims themselves or by their families, largely because of the shame associated with the act of suicide. Notwithstanding these biases, the writer carried out an epidemiological analysis of the statistical materials of suicide to discern the characteristics of suicide in Japan. By the writer's epidemiological analysis, it is believed possible to discern the characteristics of suicide in Japan and compare them with those of other countries, notwithstanding the above-mentioned biases. This is because any errors could be expected to be randomized.

2. There are more difficulties in collecting reliable data on attempted suicide than completed suicide. The writer's survey in a city near Tokyo with 150,000 population in 1959 showed that only 92 cases of attempted suicide against 231 cases of completed suicide over a period of 8 years were obtained, notwithstanding the support of private practitioners, hospitals, health centers, and city police. However, the pattern in the attempted suicide rate of high rate in

youth, low rate in the aged and higher rate in female than male, as compared with completed suicide data, coincided with that for attempted suicide reported by many reliable statistics in Europe.

3. In this sense, it is notable that the rate of completed suicide in Japan during the last 10 years, particularly that for youth, has declined greatly. One of the characteristics of suicide in Japan, rising in youth, declining in the middle-aged and rising in the aged, which was the same as that in Taiwan, has begun to change to the Western pattern, increasing almost parallel with age.

4. The ratio of female-male suicide rates in Japan has risen during the past 10 years, in particular the ratio of the aged, as compared with that among youth, which has declined. Consequently, the writer presumed that the fluctuation of completed suicide rates in age and sex are mainly influenced by the change of those rates and ratio in the youth of 15–25 and the aged over 65.

5. It was suggested that in pre-World War II times, a kind of altruistic suicide still existed in Japan, but after the war the number of anomie suicides increased to a peak in 1955–58, and both types of suicide have decreased since 1958.

6. The suicide curve in Japan has been found to fluctuate with the business cycle and war; it rose in prewar time (1913, 1934) and serious depression (1932) and declined in wartime (1906, 1943) and prosperity (1917, 1960). The rise of suicide rates from 1944 to 1958 was probably connected with the financial, moral and political anomie of the postwar times. The decline of suicide rates since 1958 might be closely connected with not only financial, moral and political stability but also with the change of expressing aggression, in particular among the youth, i.e., transfer from intropunitive to extrapunitive responses. The statistics of the Young Adult and Juvenile Section of the Japanese Ministry of Justice showed that the rates of juvenile offenders decreased. It also showed that the proportion of juvenile offenders has overcome that of adult offenders since 1958 and the younger the age, the more marked the rise.

7. As regards the relationship between suicide and homicide, a direct relationship between suicide and homicide in the past 10 years in Japan might confirm the hypothesis that obligatory altruistic or fatalistic suicide is decreasing and anomic suicide is declining after a long rise.

8. Although two surveys on suicide rates in Hawaii by Drs. Tyree and Kalish showed different data by ethnicity, those rates for Japanese-Hawaiians were low in youth and high in old age.

The writer interpreted these data as follows: although the Japanese issei showed the same high suicide rate as Japanese nationals, the low rate of suicide in youth might suggest that not only the suicide rate among Japanese-Hawaiians but also that of Japanese nationals will become similar to the Western type in the future.

I wish to acknowledge the assistance of the Social Science Research Institute (NIMH Grant MH09243) and the East-West Center at the University of Hawaii in preparation of this paper.

NOTES

1. Emile Durkheim, *Suicide, A Study in Sociology*, trans. J. A. Spandling and G. Simpson, Glencoe: The Free Press (1951), p. 44.
2. J. W. McCulloch and A. E. Philip, *Social Factors Associated with Attempted Suicide, A Review of the Literature*, Brit. J. Pschiat. Soc. Wk., (1967), 9, p. 30.
3. Pow Meng Yap, *Suicide in Hong Kong*. Hong Kong University Press (1959), p. 14.
4. Durkheim, *op. cit.*, p. 221.
5. Mamoru Iga and K. Ohara. *Suicide Attempts of Japanese Youth and Durkheim's Concept of Anomie: An Interpretation*, Human Organization, Vol. 26, Nos. 1/2 (1967), p. 66.
6. *Ibid.*, pp. 62–64.
7. Andrea Tyree, *A Study of the Relationship between Status Conflict and Suicide*. University of Hawaii (1964), pp. 34–38.

REFERENCES

Dublin, L. I.: Suicide, a Sociological and Statistical Study. Ronald Press. N.Y. 1963.

Henry, Andrew and S. James: Suicide and Homicide. The Free Press. Glencoe, Illinois. 1954.

Hsu, K. Francis: Americans and Chinese, New York, 1953.

Iga, M. and K. Ohara: Suicide Attempts of Japanese Youth and Durkheim's Concept of Anomie: An Interpretation. Human Organization. Vol. 26, Nos. 1/2, 1967.

Iguchi, T.: Jisatsu no Syakaigakuteki Kenkyū (Sociological Study on Suicide) 1933.

Kalish, R. A.: Suicide, An Ethnic Comparison. In press, Bull. of Sociology.

Kang Sang: Suicide and Cultural Pattern in Japan. Collected Papers in Commemoration of Dr. C. W. Myung's 60th Birthday, 1965.

Kanner, L.: Child Psychiatry. 3 ed., Springfield, Ill., Thomas, 1957.

Kato, M.: Jisatsu (Suicide), Ijo Shinrigaku Koza, Vol. 5, Misuzu Shobo, 1967.

Kato, M.: Ichikawa shi ni okeru Jisatsu (Suicide in Ichikawa) Seishin Eisei Shiryo No. 5, Japan National Institute of Mental Health. 1931.

McCulloch, J. W. and A. C. Philip: Social Factors Associated with Attempted Suicide. British J. Psychiatr. Soc. Wk. 9. 1967.

Minami, H.: Ikiru Fuan no Bunseki (An Analysis of Anxiety to Live). Kobunsha. Tokyo. 1952.

Murphy, H.: Suicide in Singapore, Med. J. Malaya, 9.1. 1954.

Okazaki, F.: Satsujin no Kenkyu, Tokyo, Nihon Hyoronsha, 1963.

Schneidman, E.: Some Reflection on Death and Suicide, The 62th Annual Meeting of Japan Neuropsychiatric Association, 1965.

Stengel, E.: Suicide and Attempted Suicide, Baltimore, Penguin Books, 1964.

Thakur, U.: The History of Suicide in India, Munshi Ram, Manohar Lal, Delhi 6, 1963.

Tyree, A.: A Study of the Relationship Between Status Conflict and Suicide. Sinclair Library, University of Hawaii, 1964.

West, D. J.: Murder Followed by Suicide. Harvard University Press, 1965.

Wood, A. L.: Crime and Aggression in Ceylon. Trans. Am. Phil. Soc. 1961, 51, Pt. 8.

Yap, P. M.: Suicide in Hong Kong, University of Hong Kong Press, 1958.

Yasuda, M.: Juvenile Delinquency in Japan. Presented at the U.S.-Japan Joint Meeting of Legal Medicine, held on 2–3 April, 1968.

Delinquent Groups and Organised Crime

HIROAKI IWAI

One of the notable features of Japan's criminal statistics in recent years has been the increase in juvenile delinquency. Table I shows the quantitative variation in juvenile delinquency from 1956 to 1963. Offences by persons under 20, which had been increasing steadily after the end of the Second World War in 1945, reached a peak in 1951 and thereafter decreased until 1954. After 1955, however, the curve turned upwards again, exceeding in 1960 the 1951 peak, and has since continued to rise. Table II shows the offences by juveniles in 1963, analysed by type of offence.

1. Juvenile delinquency possesses several special characteristics, one of which is the tendency towards organised crime in this age group. As can be seen from Table III, showing the proportion of arrests under the Criminal Code involving complicity by two or more persons, the proportion of such offences by young people is far higher than for adults, being over a quarter (28.1%) of the juvenile offences in 1962, which is 2.6 times the figure (10.8%) for adult offenders. Moreover, the figures (23.1% in 1956; 24.6% in 1958; 26.5% in 1959) shows that the overall trend is for the proportion of offences involving more than one person to increase, despite a certain amount of fluctuation. Of course, since 'complicity' as defined in the criminal code involves the joint commission of certain specified offences, the figure is likely to be even higher if we include group actions of a less serious nature.

The figures given above refer to the country as a whole, but I

Reprinted from *Sociological Review Monograph* No. 10, 1966: 199–212, by permission of the Sociological Review Monographs, University of Keele, Staffordshire, ST5 5BG, England.

Table 1. Annual Increase or Decrease of Juvenile
Offenders (under 20) Under Penal Code (1956–1963)

Year	Number of Offenders	Increase or De- crease against the previous year	Estimated population by age groups (10 and over, under 20)
1956	127.421	+ 5.668	17.849
1957	144.506	+17.085	18.381
1958	155.373	+10.867	19.152
1959	176.899	+21.526	20.039
1960	196.682	+19.783	20.467
1961	216.456	+19.774	20.553
1962	220.749	+ 4.293	20.475
1963	229.717	+ 8.968	20.344

Table II. Number of Juvenile Offenders (under 20 years
old) by Classification of crimes (1963)

	Number	Percentage
Vicious crimes	6.960	3.3
Violent crimes	45.029	19.6
Theft	136.027	59.2
Immoral crimes	2.020	0.9
Other crimes	39.681	17.3
Total	229.717	100
Sexual crimes	5.458	2.4

Note: Sexual crimes are rape and obscenity. It is totalled repeatedly.

Table III. Situation of Complicity on Juvenile crimes
under Penal Code (1958–1962)

Year		1958	1959	1960	1961	1962
Total	Juveniles	24.6	26.5	25.5	26.3	28.1
	Adults	12.0	11.8	11.9	11.6	10.8
Vicious crimes		37.4	38.4	36.7	35.0	34.8
Violent crimes		30.7	31.4	30.6	29.9	31.4
Theft		26.5	29.2	28.5	29.3	31.0
Other crimes		5.8	5.5	4.6	5.0	5.5
Sexual crimes		35.4	33.9	31.9	29.5	27.3

should like to consider the situation in Tokyo and its environs in
order to get a deeper insight into the problem. The number of
juvenile delinquent groups taken under guidance by the Tokyo
Police Department in 1962 was 708, with a membership of 6,050.
Of these groups, 30.4% were groups of 5 members, 21.2% of 6
members, 11.9% of 7 members, 7.2% of 8 members, 6.2% of 9
members, while groups with 10 members or more accounted for

Table IV. Size of Groups (Kanagawa Prefecture, 1964)

	Number of members	Number of groups	Percentage
(A)	3–10	145	77.6
	11–20	29	15.5
	21–30	8	4.3
	31–40	4	2.1
	40–	1	0.5
Total		187	100
	Number of members	Number of groups	Percentage
(B)	3	24	16.5
	4	23	15.9
	5	34	23.5
	6	20	13.8
	7	14	9.7
	8	18	12.4
	9	6	4.1
	10	6	4.1
Total		145	100

23.1% of the total. However, this survey is not completely satisfactory, firstly because no mention is made of groups with less than 5 members, and then because no details are given concerning groups with 10 members or over. For this reason I have shown in Tables IV(a) and IV(b) the more detailed figures for Kanagawa Prefecture (an urban region adjoining Tokyo) in 1964. From this it can be seen that groups with a membership of 3 to 8 account for 71.1% of the total, the highest figure being for groups with 5 members.

These studies of juvenile delinquent groups have been carried out from many angles, analysing them by age composition, motive for formation of the group, places of activity and meeting, mobility, type of offence, seriousness of the offence, and degree of organisation, and there is a great volume of statistics and case studies on this topic. It is not my purpose, however, to summarize this research, but rather to point out a few of the most important features of this subject.

The first problem concerns the Japanese educational system. In the statistics for Tokyo quoted above, the largest number of delinquent groups (52.7%) were made up mainly of junior high-school students, then senior high-school student groups (17.4%), groups mainly of primary school students (3.9%), and others. The same situation exists in Kanagawa Prefecture, junior high-school students being the largest group. Japanese junior high-school students are aged from 12 to 14 years, in the final stages of their compulsory education, and at a point where they can see, just above them, the freedom enjoyed by students in senior high-school. The reasons for the large number of these students who join such groups should be looked for not only in physical and psychological factors due to the rapid physiological growth of children of this age, but also in the various social forces which they feel pressing in on them.

There is a link between the increase in juvenile delinquency and the extremely rapid pace of Japan's industrialization and the problems of concentration in urban areas which this has brought about. *Firstly*, although a high rate of economic growth has produced a so-called 'affluent society', it has also increased the will to consume by making consumer goods more readily available, and produced in the cities a flood of commercialistic amusements. Since even adults are susceptible to the stimulus of these new pleasures, it is inevitable that young people should be even more easily led astray. *Secondly*, there is the problem of the pressure of an exacting entrance examination system demanded by the need for higher education to keep up with a high rate of industrialization. A university education is regarded as normal for members of the middle class in Japan today. In favour of the examination system it can be said that, provided a child has ability, it guarantees him both status and a high income in the future, but on the other hand the high competition for high school and university places—as many as 30 applicants per place—turns what should be the happy period of adolescence into a grim struggle for survival. Students cannot enjoy the fruits of a prosperous industrial society, and have to renounce all pleasures in their efforts to succeed in examinations. Moreover, children without academic ability, particularly the children of poor parents, whose school records tend to be affected by their social circumstances, lose all hope for the future and react by abandoning themselves to enjoyment of the present. Junior high-school is the 'parting of the ways' where decisions about the future have to be taken, and this characteristic of the Japanese education system, which closes off the path to high social status as an adult at a very early age, is one of the factors contributing to the high rate of delinquency among fairly young children in Japan.

Researchers into the behaviour of delinquent groups hear a large number of statements which all consciously or unconsciously bear on this question. I should like to comment on a few examples of these statements.

One boy of 15 years old, who was a member of a violent group of juvenile delinquents told us: 'The others in my class spend all their time working; I've no hope of catching up with them. But I do have some pride. If I can, I want to be able to talk to them as equals in some way or other. So I decided that if I couldn't do it by being as clever, I'll do it by being as strong as they were.

Another 16-year-old delinquent said: 'School is useless. All they teach is how to study; they are not interested in anything else'.

Another boy: 'My family is poor, and won't let me go on school outings. This makes me ashamed in front of my classmates. My parents couldn't care less about school. I'm stupid, so whatever I do I get into trouble with the teachers. I don't like being the underdog, so I take it out on the people round me. I was being determined not to be looked down and that made me this way.'

An 18-year-old member of a group which had been threatening people in the street explained his feelings thus: 'I was caught, but I don't regret what I did in the least. The others in my school will graduate, move up to higher schools, and give themselves a foundation for going out into the world. Because I've come straight out into the world I don't count for anything. So I get together with my friends and push people around. Hard, sharp and quick, that's how I feel.'

Delinquent gangs are groups of fairly similar young people, their similarity lying in their failure to adapt to the society of home and school. Their groups are the natural attempt of youths alienated from society to satisfy their social nature and have their opinions heard. Association in coffee shops with members of the opposite sex; drives in stolen cars; loyalty to their leaders—all these have their roots in this same search for acceptance.

As delinquent groups move on to more serious offences, some sort of organisation begins to form, replacing the mob psychology which was their original reason for coming together. In general, we can divide delinquent groups into three main types—indulging in theft, in sexual offences, and in fighting with other groups. The fighting gangs in particular tend gradually to come in contact with groups of anti-social adults, as they prowl around the slums and entertainment quarters looking for likely adversaries. This problem is attracting more and more notice in recent years, and is linked with the anomalous fact that juvenile law in Japan still puts youths of 19 or 20, who are physically fully mature, into the category of juveniles. For this reason, I would like briefly to turn to the related question of organised crime among adults—in particular the phenomenon of the violent anti-social group.

2. The 1964 White Paper on criminal offences devotes a large number of pages to crimes of violence in general, and to organised violence in particular. Surveys for 1963 put the number of organised violent groups at 5,107, with a total of 184,091 members.

These violent groups, given the general label of *yakuza*, are made up of several distinct types—the *bakuto*, whose financial support is derived from organised gambling, the *tekiya*, who live on 'protection' money squeezed from open-air traders, and *gurentai*, gangs of violent hooligans. A characteristic common to these *yakuza* groups is their tight organisation with its strong traditional basis.

The basic unit of *yakuza* organisation is the *ikka*, a term whose original meaning is 'family'. 'Sumiyoshi-*ikka*' for example, means 'the House of Sumiyoshi'. This is not, however, a family group linked by blood ties, but a fictitious family composed of unrelated individuals. This group is often known as a *Kumi* (-*gumi* in combination with other words), as in Yamaguchi-*gumi*.

The head of the *ikka* or *Kumi* is known as *oyabun* ('having the status of the father'), and its members as *kobun* ('child-status'). A large organisation may have several *oyabun*, the chief of these being known as *sōchō* ('overall leader'). The *oyabun* under him, in charge of sections of the main group, bear the relationship of *kyōdaibun* ('brother-status') to one another.

The *oyabun-kobun* relationship is the central relationship unit in which the *yakuza* group is based. It is a superior-inferior relationship, with the *kobun* owing absolute obedience to the absolute authority of the *oyabun*. The ideal form of this relationship is exemplified in the *sakazuki-shiki* ('cup ceremony'). When this ceremony is to be held in all its formality, an auspicious day is chosen, and all members of the organisation will attend, with *torimochinin* or *azukarinin* ('guarantors') present as intermediaries. Rice, whole fish, and piles of salt are placed in the Shintō shrine alcove, in front of which the *oyabun* and *kobun* sit facing each other. The *torimochinin* arrange the fish ceremonially and fill the drinking-cups with *sake*, adding fish-scales and salt. (The details of the ceremony differ somewhat in different *kumi*.) They then turn solemnly to the *kobun* and warn him of his future duties: 'Having drunk from the *oyabun's* cup and he from yours, you now owe loyalty to the *ikka* and devotion to your *oyabun*. Even should your wife and children starve, even at the cost of your life, your duty is now to the *ikka* and *oyabun*,' or 'From now on you have no other occupation until the day you die. The *oyabun* is your only parent; follow him through fire and flood.' This ceremony is gradually disappearing today, and in practice the relationship between *oyabun* and *kobun* is one based on power. Nevertheless the cup ceremony is an expression of its original ideals.

The primary characteristic of this relationship is the unquestioning obedience of the *kobun* and the absolute authority of the *oyabun*. Nevertheless the *oyabun* also has responsibilities to provide for the upkeep of the *kobun* and his family. The *yakuza* will often say: 'The *oyabun* provides for his *kobun* whatever happens, and in return the *kobun* will give up his life for the *oyabun*. This is the best feature of our organisation.' In other words, the *oyabun* too has duties which he must perform, in his position as 'father' of a family, owing benevolence to its members. The relationship implies some 'give and take', the *kobun* ceasing to respect their *oyabun* if he does not care for them as he should.

Another relationship which helps to shape the *yakuza* group is that between the *kyōdaibun* ('brothers'). In the old groups of gamblers this relationship was divided up minutely, with fine gradations of status between the members. Their relative positions were defined as five-to-five (drinking equals), six-to-four, seven-to-three, eight-to-two, and so on, with different forms of address being used between the *kyōdaibun*, depending on their relative status. These five distinctions have now disappeared, however, and equals normally address each other as *kyōdai* ('brother'); superiors address inferiors as *shatei* ('younger brother'), inferiors using the word *aniki* ('elder brother') to their superiors. The *ikka* is the basic unit in *yakuza* society, members of the same *ikka* being referred to as *miuchi* ('members of the same body; relatives'). This reveals the character of the *ikka* as a closed, organic group, taking an exclusive attitude to the outside world. The name used by the *ikka* group represents its authority in underworld society.

The area controlled by a group is known as its *nawabari* ('roped-off area'), a word which is derived from the custom of roping-off the boundaries of one's own territory to distinguish it from the surrounding area. The term thus includes the concepts of a definite area of land, the right of absolute control within that area, and of a clear boundary separating that territory from the others surrounding it. From the fact that each group is continually attempting to extend the area of its own territory, the *nawabari* is also known as *shimori* ('defending to the death'), showing just how vital the defence of this territory is to the group. Before a *kobun* who had gone through the cup ceremony could achieve the status of *oyabun*, a long, severe period of apprenticeship was necessary. In the *bakuto* gambling groups, he would be given such jobs as polishing dice, cleaning the house of the *oyabun*, running errands, or baby-sitting. This type of menial service is disappearing today, but new *kobun* will be expected to act as *teppōdama* ('bullets') in fights with other gangs, standing in the front line, facing the guns and swords of the other side, risking his life for the sake of his *kumi*. In addition he owes complete obedience to his *anikibun* ('elder brothers') and in particular to his *oyabun*, with whom he will agree without question even if told that black is white. On occasion he will take the blame and go to prison for crimes committed by his *oyabun*. Only by this sort of unquestioning service will he rise in status little by little, eventually becoming an *oyabun*.

Atome, succession to the headship of the family by becoming an *oyabun*, is vital for the continuance of the group, and only those who have shown complete loyalty to the group and devotion to their *oyabun* will be considered eligible. In general it is not customary for the true child of an *oyabun* to succeed his father, the successor normally coming from among the *ichikobun* ('first rank *kobun*') within the group. Further, since the succession to the leadership and name of the group is a matter of vital concern not only to the group itself, but to the whole *yakuza* society, notices of a forthcoming succession ceremony are widely circulated, and a large number of people connected with the group will attend to celebrate the occasion. The *oyabun* too is expected to regard succession as a matter of extreme importance, and to be completely impartial in choosing his successor. There have been cases where dissatisfaction has arisen among the *kobun* over the question of a successor, the group splitting into two parties who have not hesitated to spill blood in order to advance their own claims. In such cases the *oyabun* will lose all authority within *yakuza* society. The cup ceremony mentioned in connection with the initiation of a new member of the group is also held—on an even larger scale—on the occasion of a succession to the leadership, and also to confirm the reconciliation after a dispute between two groups. On such occasions one or more peacemakers will bring the leaders of the two opposing parties together in the same room, in the centre of which will be placed two swords and offerings to the Shintō deities. As the ceremony proceeds, the peacemaker will come forward and tie the two swords together with a single cord. The representatives of the two sides will then drink simultaneously from cups of sacred wine, while all the participants clap their hands in a peculiar rhythm. This has given the ceremony of reconciliation its title—*teuchishiki* ('clapping ceremony').

Until quite recently the great number of formal ceremonies was a feature of *yakuza* society. An example of this is when two *yakuza* meet for the first time. Each of them will take up a pose: stepping forward, slightly bending his legs, clenching his fists and repeating at length his place of origin, present residence, the name of his *oyabun* and his own name in stilted archaic language. When one has finished, the same type of greeting is repeated by the other party. Even before the proceedings start, each of them will have yielded precedence several times to the other. This form of greeting, known as *jingi*, was also a characteristic of artisans in feudal Japan, when they travelled to other parts of the country and met members of the same craft, or master craftsmen from whom they wished to obtain employment. This custom disappeared long ago amongst craftsmen, but is still practised within the anti-social *yakuza* groups.

Another old custom originating in the lower orders of society is that of cutting off a finger to take responsibility or to show repentance for some offence. This custom existed over 200 years ago among prostitutes and other special sectors of society, but is practised now only in these professional criminal groups.

Many old customs handed down from medieval times still exist in *yakuza* society. The word *jingi* mentioned above originates from China, and originally referred to the Confucian virtues of love and duty. For this reason the *yakuza* see themselves as transmitters of the spirit of *bushidō*, and strongly resent being regarded as no more than American-style gangsters. Their actions, of course, are in no way different from those of the gangster and bear no relationship to the samurai tradition, but they like to regard their society as being based on principles of humanity and morality.

In discussing the group organisation and customs of the *yakuza*, the typical violent organised criminal class of Japan, I have tended to stress the traditional patterns of behaviour. Many of these have changed a great deal in recent years, and are still changing very rapidly today. It would therefore be a mistake to associate these groups with Shintō or *bushidō* simply because of these curious customs. In the final analysis their activities have their fundamental basis in criminal violence, in the acquisition of money without work, by illegal means.

These violent groups were able to wield their authority in the wilderness left after Japan had lost the Second World War. Their illegal activities were hostile to the peaceable members of society, while they used the traditions of ancient Japan to provide themselves with a false aura of respectability. They have therefore attracted the violent enmity of the ordinary citizen, and the police authorities have waged a continuous and widespread battle aimed at their complete eradication, with slow but encouraging results. The violent groups have, of course, tried to find countermeasures avoiding the net of the law by forming connections with prominent political figures or sections of the extreme right wing. These efforts have on the whole ended in failure under the sustained attack of society and the police. Their leaders are gradually being arrested, now making up quite a large proportion of the prison population.

3. As adult violent groups have been put on the defensive, and many of their members arrested, they have started to make use of groups of juvenile delinquents as a desperate countermeasure. In particular, the fearless energy of these young people is extremely useful in supplementing their depleted forces, and they are willing to extend extremely attractive bait in order to gain their allegiance. This is one aspect of the problem of juvenile delinquency which deserves very careful attention in the future.

Most groups of juvenile offenders of course, have no relations with adult groups. The great proportion of them have developed from groups of playfellows indulging in escapist activities. However, when these escapist activities reach a stage where the young offenders come into contact with adult groups, there is a tendency for the severity and viciousness of the offences to increase and for the group to take on a more organised form. This applied equally to groups of junior high-school children.

The usual organisation of groups of junior high-school students is the *banchō* group centred round the leader. This type of organisation is particularly common in the fighting gangs. (*Banchō* is their cant word for leader.) The result of a survey in 1962 of 136 *banchō* groups with 1,450 members is shown in Table V. In this table, A refers to groups having a clear connection with some adult violent organisation, B to groups led by older youths with a record of delinquency but with no such connection, and C to others. As the table shows, 66.9% of the groups act quite independently of any

Table V. 'Banchō' groups in Tokyo (1962)

			Number of Groups	Percentage
A	....	....	33	24.3
B	....	....	12	8.8
C	....	....	91	66.9
Total		....	136	100.0

other group, while 24.3% have some contact with adult violent organisations. It goes without saying that the higher the age of its members, the more likely is the group to have some such connection.

The form of contact between the two types of groups is not as a rule direct, but takes place through the medium of *chimpira*, youths of about 20 years of age. Figure I shows the age and composition of organised violent groups, and shows that 9.4% of their members are aged 20 or less. These are the *chimpira*, who form the base of the pyramid of *yakuza* organisation. As the chart shows, they are relatively few in number, but perform a vital role in the group. They may offer to protect juvenile groups with whom they come into contact from other groups, or allow them to use the name of the *ikka* or *kumi* as protection in the entertainment districts, and by such means contrive to draw them into their own organisation. There is no doubt that the name of a well-known *ikka* or *kumi* is enough to frighten other delinquent groups of the same age. Having won over a group of young people, the *yakuza* will then put them in the front line of their own battles. For this reason the existence of the *chimpira*, standing on the borderline where the juvenile and adult groups meet, is worthy of special note in any consideration of juvenile delinquency in Japan.

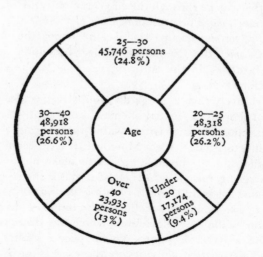

Figure I. The ages of members of violent groups (1963)

Apart from their usefulness to supplement the forces of the adult group, the patronage of juvenile groups has the additional advantage that the same offence when committed by a juvenile will be punished far less severely than when the offender is an adult. Further, rather than absorb the juvenile group into their own organisation the adult groups find it advantageous to allow them to have their own organisation. The characteristic of the *banchō* group is that it has no formal hierarchy other than the leader, so the adult group will often refrain from interference, exercising control through contact with leader alone.

As the *banchō* group member grows older and sinks deeper into delinquency, he finally matures into a fully-fledged *gurentai*. The implications of the term cannot be simply explained, but it is commonly used to refer to violent groups of young people based not on *oyabun-kobun* relationships, but on those between *kyōdaibun* only. (Another meaning is that of a recently formed *yakuza* group with no traditional 'family' name, but it is in the first sense that it will be used here.) The *gurentai* groups act as affiliates of the older professional criminal organisations. An example of this is a senior high-school gang which developed into a *gurentai* group called the Isseikai, and is now associated with the Machii-ikka, whose territory it helps to protect.

There are of course cases where the leaders of *gurentai* groups formed in this way go through the cup ceremony and formally enter the traditional *yakuza* organisation. One of these is the case of the Nandōkai, a *gurentai* group which came under the wing of the Yamaguchi-*gumi*, the Nandōkai leader becoming an *otōtobun* ('younger brother') in the adult organisation, while eight of the leaders became *kobun*.

It is relatively easy to break up groups of juveniles who are at the stage of shoplifting, sexual offences, and fighting 'for fun'. But once a connection is formed with an adult *yakuza* group they become far more difficult to deal with. Moreover, it has become more and more common for the juvenile groups to make positive efforts to form this sort of connection. One cause of this is the recent spate of films, popular songs and novels painting the *yakuza* as heroes. In particular one section of the declining film industry has produced a large number of films for television in which the *yakuza* is painted as a glamorous and heroic figure. Young people misinterpret their violent and destructive activities as the expression of a spirit of resistance, challenging the values of contemporary society. Their violent behaviour, bearing a superficial resemblance to the *bushidō* of the *samurai*, is taken to be the natural successor of the traditional Japanese spirit.

It would of course be a mistake to discuss juvenile delinquency and organised crimes of violence by adults as if the problems were one and the same, but it is also impossible to consider them as two completely unrelated problems. It would seem that in the United States there were few opportunities for members of juvenile gangs to enter the world of adult organised crime, and that the decrease in the number of juvenile offences when young people enter their early twenties is due to the fact that they themselves come to realise that they are unlikely to succeed in a group of adult criminals. The same cannot be said of Japan; juveniles coming into reform schools in recent years have often shown signs of being on the way to becoming *yakuza*. One survey shows that even in institutions with fewest of this type of inmate the figure was about 18%, and that in extreme cases some 60% of the inmates had either direct or indirect connections with a *yakuza* organisation. In a survey of the value-attitudes of youths in reformatories, we found that many of them mentioned value-concepts typical of the *yakuza*, such as the acceptance of violence, status-consciousness, and the concept of *giri-ninjo* ('duty and humanity', regarded by the *yakuza* as the moral basis of their society).

The *yakuza* as a violent criminal organisation is a cancer in the body of Japanese society, and must be speedily eradicated. But by the time a cancer is found, it is often too late for a surgical operation to be successful, and it would be far more satisfactory to diagnose and treat the condition effectively in the pre-cancerous stage. In other words, the task before us is to apply educational and social treatment at the stage where we are still dealing with groups of juvenile delinquents, and to find out how best to turn their abundant energy to constructive use in society.

Fear of Eye-to-Eye Confrontation Among Neurotic Patients in Japan

YOMISHI KASAHARA

I

Japanese psychiatrists have a terminology for phobia of interpersonal relations. This is not a peculiar kind of mental disorder specific in Japan (such as *amok* specific in Java, *koro* in Hong Kong, etc.) but is coincident with erythrophobia and allied conditions.[1] Since Casper in 1848, a dozen articles have been published concerning erythrophobia or ereuthophobia, and some of them described it as dysmorphophobia, a variation of ereuthophobia. This is the fear of deformity of some specific parts of one's body. Such phobic symptoms are well known to psychiatrists and psychologists in every culture. A Japanese psychiatrist, S. Morita, however, placed ereuthophobia, along with its allied conditions including dysmorphophobia, etc., under the comprehensive category of "phobia of interpersonal relations" (*taijin kyōfu*). Needless to say, a patient suffering from ereuthophobia actually fears that he may make a bad impression on others or make others become unpleasant by his blushing and, as a result, be humiliated by others. Consequently, patients may often withdraw from social relationships where there is a fear of this happening. In this sense, ereuthophobia and allied conditions are nothing but "fear of interpersonal relations."

It was in the early 1920s that Morita proposed this name and evolved for this group of neuroses a special method of treatment which was named after him. Since then, detailed studies of this

Reprinted from Working Papers, Culture and Mental Health Program, Social Science Research Institute, University of Hawaii, 1970. This paper was prepared while the author was in residence as a research fellow in a joint project of the East-West Center Senior Specialists Program and the SSRI's Culture & Mental Health Program (NIMH Grant MH-09243).

variety of neurosis have been made by many authors.[2] This is simply because ereuthophobia and allied conditions have been the variety of neurosis most frequently observed in Japan. This situation remains unchanged to this day. For instance, according to my statistics, of the 430 students who received psychiatric care at the Student Health Service of Kyoto University in 1968, one-half were neurotic. Out of these, 18.6 percent can be classified in the category with which we are concerned. This group ranks third after depressive reaction, accounting for 24 percent, and psychosomatic disorders, accounting for 20 percent.[3]

I wish to present here two subtypes of fear of interpersonal relations frequently found among Japanese youth with the hope that these data may be compared with neurotic patterns among youth in other cultures. The first is a fear of eye-to-eye confrontation, characterized by an anxiety of being looked at by others and an anxiety of unintentionally staring at other with strange looks. The second is a fear of emitting odor from one's body, classified as similar to fear of eye-to-eye confrontation. There are reasons to believe that in foreign countries these two types of neurosis do not occur as frequently as they do in Japan. Scattered references to the fear of emitting bodily odor are found in Western literature, but, to the best of my knowledge, the fear of eye-to-eye confrontation does not exist in the literature.[4]

II

A typical patient who has a fear of eye-to-eye confrontation complains as follows: "In the presence of others, I become tense and feel ill at ease. I am self-conscious of being looked at by others. At the same time, I am embarrassed as to where to direct my eyes. I cannot decide whether I should look away from other people's eyes or not. I cannot tell to what extent I should stare into the others' eyes. Meanwhile, my looks lose their naturalness and I end up by staring into others' eyes with piercing looks. Rather, it would be more accurate to say that my eyes become automatically glued to the other person's eyes. When this happens, rather than fear that I am being looked at, I feel that my eyes stare at others in an unnatural manner. This is because my unnatural piercing look hurts others by making them feel unpleasant. This is not merely imagination; it is indeed a fact for me. The reason I can insist on this is because I know intuitively by the way others behave towards me. Others look away from me, become restless, make grimaces, or leave their seat abruptly. It is psychologically so painful for me to embarrass people in this way that I end up avoiding people as much as possible."

The foregoing is a rough example of the complaints commonly made by severe cases of a fear of eye-to-eye confrontation. These symptoms usually develop between puberty and early adulthood. It is rather rare for these symptoms to persist with the same intensity after the age of 30, and after the age of 40 the onset of such a fear is extremely rare. In this sense, it can indeed be called a disorder peculiar to adolescence. There is no clear sex difference; however, it has been said that this pattern of neurosis is seen more among males. Blushing may be more acceptable socially for females than for males; therefore, the motivation to visit doctors may be weaker for females than for males. The more severe the symptoms of confrontation fear, the more restricted are the activities of daily life. Despite the persistence of their complaints and the intensity of their pathological convictions, patients appear to be normal. They tend to be more sociable than the average youth. A few cases border on overt schizophrenia.

Whereas in mild cases the fear of being looked at by others is predominant, in severe cases, as I indicated in the typical case cited, patients clearly suffer more from the fear of unintentionally staring at people with strange looks than from the fear of being looked at by others. It goes without saying that even in severe cases the fear of being looked at coexists. Thus, the combination of staring at and being stared at forms the pathological focus of this syndrome. Because the patient experiences the fear of eye-to-eye confrontation in the presence of others, I would like to further discuss complaints by patients in order to determine what kind of characteristics these other people have.

The patient does not experience any fear in the presence of doctors and counselors, or of his own relatives, with whom he has an intimate relationship. Conversely, he never experiences fear when he finds himself among total strangers in such places as a crowded street. The fear is induced in the presence of those who are neither particularly close nor totally strange, in other words, people of intermediate familiarity. This is especially so when he finds himself in a small group of several persons; he is most susceptible to fear in a small group where people are of about the same age and background as he. If they happen to be members of the opposite sex, the patient is particularly embarrassed. Male patients are usually too shy to make girl friends and tend to group among themselves, though they do not show overt signs of homosexuality.

Needless to say, the patient does not welcome making a speech on a stage in the presence of a large audience nor does he welcome being in the presence of his superiors. However, compared with small-group situations such as those mentioned above, these large-group situations are much easier to bear. This is because large-group situations do not involve the complex interpersonal relationships of being stared at and of being unable to help staring at others.

I will try to describe in more detail what happens when a patient grows phobic in a small group situation. The patient feels relatively at home when talking tête-à-tête with any person who happens to be around. But if a third person enters this situation his presence upsets the patient, no matter who he happens to be. The patient automatically directs his sight to this third person, and the patient feels that this action is repulsive and hurts the other's feelings.

The foregoing can be interpreted in the following manner. The patient is able to take part in a dialogue situation in which he can play the role of either the speaker or the listener. However, he cannot take part in a triangular interpersonal constellation. In such a triangular situation, the patient automatically shifts his eyes away from the person at the side, who, rather than the person in front of him, engages his central concern. If he is on a train or in a class-room situation, those who concern him are the ones seated by his side. Some severe patients insist that they look from the sides of their eye-sockets and their look pierces the person sitting right next to them. Also, they frequently complain that their sight field is too expansive or that they can see sideways more than they want to, suffering from their side-glancing obsession. I wish to call this characteristic feature "phobia of side-glancing," borrowing these patients' nomenclature. To avoid glancing sideways, they tend to develop various kinds of counter-reactions. Some patients try to prevent people from entering their sight by seating themselves at the very end of the first row in the classroom and some others by wearing sunglasses. Still others stare straight ahead as much as possible in order not to glance sideways and end up by actually developing a piercing eye-look.

In supplement, I wish to present the case of a patient suffering from the fear of bodily odor. The patient is a 19-year-old male college student majoring in a natural science. Convinced that his body odor makes others unpleasant, he tries to avoid approaching people as much as possible. In a classroom he seats himself in the back row and leaves the classroom the moment the lecure is over.

However, he cannot actually smell his body odor. At times he feels that the odor is peculiar, but most of the time he, himself, cannot understand the nature of his odor and consequently cannot describe it definitely when asked.

Therefore, the conviction that his body emits a peculiar odor is derived, not from his own perception but from observing the way others behave toward him. He intuitively feels that he is emitting a bad odor by observing people around him touching their noses with their hands, coughing, or laughing. Sometimes he can ascribe the sources of his odor to specific parts of his body such as the anus or genitals. Concluding from the foregoing, the form of this experience is not an olfactory hallucination but an idea of reference.

The preceding is an outline of the complaints commonly made by patients who fear their own body odor. This fear is similar to the fear of eye-to-eye confrontation on many important points. For instance, these patients do not give abnormal impressions, despite their delusional convictions. However, the fear of bodily odor is more serious than the fear of eye-to-eye confrontation because the former is more likely to show a short psychotic episode under stressful conditions than the latter.

It is obvious that patients with a phobia of interpersonal relations tend to suffer more from being repulsive than from being humiliated by others. Their complaints range from a fear of embarrassing others to a fear of giving an infectious look or radiating something from the body to paralyze others. What is of central concern in this context is the fear of hurting others. Therefore, we may be justified in labelling this kind of disorder as "altruistic phobia" as was suggested by Kaan (1892). This is to be set apart from "egoistic phobia" in which an external intrusion by phobogenic objects is feared.

However, as indicated previously, the patient suffering from altruistic phobia does fear humiliation by others. Actually, all phobias involve a fear of losing control of undesirable impulses and being humiliated as a result. For example, an elevator phobia is not the result of the possibility of physical danger involved in a falling elevator but is related to the necessity of being able to escape immediately from other people when one becomes anxious. The anticipation of panic, related to the need to move swiftly, causes anxiety to supervene and even a few seconds in going from one floor to the next floor become unendurable. If this interpretation is correct, the central problem of all phobias is the threat of public display of inadequacy and imperfection. Salzman (1968) states that "both phobia and obsession devices are attempts to control dangerous and undesirable impulses of a sexual or aggressive nature. It need not be necessarily a hostile or aggressive impulse. It may develop around the need to maintain pride and self-esteem. Loss of control and concern about humiliating consequences which might result are the factors that produce a phobia. The fear of losing control is in itself the threat of being humiliated." If this is true, there is no difference between altruistic and egoistic phobias, and consequently, concerning the threat of being humiliated, the phobia of interpersonal relations with which we are now concerned might be considered the most typical phobic reaction.

III

I would now like to consider these phenomena from a cross-cultural point of view. It should first be mentioned that it is extremely difficult to prove the hypothesis that a particular neurotic type is in the foreground in a given culture in a given period. Data being limited, I do not want to assert that phobias of interpersonal relations are in the absolute majority in Japan. In order to clearly establish this hypothesis, a precise comparative study of neuroses is necessary. However, if a particular variation of phobias of interpersonal relations is more liable to occur in a given culture than in others, this phenomenon should then be considered in relation to its background.

Phobias of interpersonal relations are nothing but variations of hypochondria in the sense that patients are overly concerned about their bodily self. What differentiates these phobias from other manifestations of hypochondria is the fact that patients feel that they are simultaneously repulsive to themselves and to others. In connection with this, it should be noted that the only parts of the body which patients are hypochondriacally concerned about are external, such as the face, body shape, body odor, etc. If we compare such neurotic patients in different cultures, we may discover what parts of the bodily self are psychologically most vulnerable in a stressful, interpersonal situation.

Ereuthophobia and allied conditions as a whole seem not to have been in the limelight in Western psychiatry. According to Dietrich (1962), there has been only one paper dealing with dysmorphophobia as its main theme in European literature during the previous two decades. Dietrich went on to say that ereuthophobia is very rare in Germany. When dysmorphophobia is mentioned in Western literature, one's nose, skin, hair, chin, teeth, shape of the skull, breast, and body weight are enumerated as common objects of concern. Body odor is rarely mentioned and the eye not at all. The fear of eye-to-eye confrontation no doubt exists in other cultures, but it may fail to attract doctors' attention.

In contrast to this, Japanese psychiatrists encounter the fear of eye-to-eye confrontation and body odor almost every day, while little mention is made of one's skull, breast, nose, skin, etc., by patients. I have encountered 39 cases of the fear of interpersonal relations among students of a Japanese university: fear of body odor, 11 cases; fear of blushing, 6; fear of eye-to-eye confrontation, 5; fear of voicing and stuttering, 2; fear of negligible scar on their face, 2; fear of hand trembling, 2; miscellaneous fears, 11. From this it can be stated with considerable probability that the fears of eye-to-eye confrontation and body odor are found frequently among young Japanese neurotics. This raises the question of why Japanese people exhibit a marked propensity to the themes of eye and body odor in their phobias of interpersonal relations. However, to consider these phenomena in sociocultural terms is a task for the cultural anthropologist, not a psychiatrist. I shall attempt to answer this question in terms of my impressions received through therapeutic experiences with the patients.

Let us consider, first, the reason Japanese are concerned about the eye. In everyday interpersonal relationships, the act of staring at the person to whom one is talking is quite extraordinary and considered to be rude. To be continuously stared at creates displeasure for the Japanese, except among very intimate relations. To look intently at the person to whom one is talking does not, for the Japanese, signify respect. Rather, a tendency to look downward is appreciated even today, especially among females, and is thought to be suggestive of a certain elegance. Thus, there exists a cultural characteristic which causes Japanese to be hypersensitive about "looking at" and "being looked at." Even today, Japanese parents often discipline their children by saying, "Neighbors are watching whatever you do." It is conceivable that Japanese children grow into personalities which incessantly watch those outside of their family circle, either consciously or unconsciously. There is in Japan a traditional children's game, "Niramekko," played between two persons who keep staring at each other until one of them breaks into laughter. The one who laughs first is the loser. I feel that this game should be called the game of eye-to-eye confrontation. As Dr. Sakuda (1967), a sociologist, points out, this kind of game has a close relationship with the so-called "shame culture" of Japan. This may have its origin in counter-reaction to the fear of eye-to-eye confrontation

In accordance with the avoidance of eye-to-eye confrontation in interpersonal relations, the mode of communication among Japanese is markedly nonverbal and indirect. Japanese culture esteems vague expressions and avoids frank talk. In this context, I feel that what those who fear eye-to-eye confrontation dread is another's rude, pointblank remarks in a given interpersonal situation. At the same time, they are also afraid that they may say something pointblank which is not in conformity with the established code of etiquette. The Japanese expect to understand and to be understood despite their use of vague expressions. Needless to say, these attitudes, in which we expect and depend upon another's benevolence, can be explained by the concept of *amae*, which has been illuminated by Doi (1962), one of the leading psychoanalysts in Japan, as the key concept for understanding Japanese personality structure.

It is also possible to detect some cultural influence in the "fear of side-glancing" observed among those who fear eye-to-eye confrontation. The sideward direction has a specific, intrinsic significance. The side, in contrast to above and below, represents a direction where equals are hand in hand, a space of friendship, or a space of conformity. It also implies something negative in that it could be a space where envy and competition lie. In making this point, recall the previous statement that a patient with a phobia of interpersonal relations finds it most difficult to deal with those who share similar backgrounds. Morita has also pointed out that, particularly in cases of shame, there lies a deep-rooted desire not to be defeated by equals and to surpass them. Psychoanalytic literature also points out that shame can be brought upon the individual in the process of comparing and competing with peers (siblings, schoolmates, gang, professional group, social class, etc.), and social conformity achieved through shame will be essentially one of identification. It seems meaningful that the direction about which many patients are concerned is neither above nor below but to the side.

Next, I shall consider why bodily odor concerns Japanese with phobias of interpersonal relations. To consider this in sociocultural terms is far more difficult than analyzing fear of eye-to-eye confrontation, for case reports concerning the fear of body odor are found in every culture, i.e., U.S., Germany, and France. With regard to Japanese culture, it can be said that Japanese tend to appreciate odorlessness more highly than fragrance. To the Japanese, cleanliness is a state where there is no odor rather than a state where there is a pleasant odor, perhaps owing to their religions, Shintoism, and to a lesser degree, Buddhism.

IV

Finally, I would like to comment on the method of treatment for phobias of interpersonal relations in Japan. In Japan, the phobias are usually treated by Morita psychotherapy. In this therapy a patient is usually required to be hospitalized for two months during which he is forbidden to talk (even with his doctor) about his symptoms. However, he is allowed to write down whatever he wishes in his diary. Morita and his successors have stated that in order to come to terms with neurotic suffering, one must not search for the cause nor try to eliminate it; rather, one has to accept it without fighting the symptoms. The characteristics of Morita therapy are clearly stated by him, "You should become the world's most well-known shy person showing your face can blush more than anyone else's. Don't fight against having a blushing face." This therapy does not deal with a patient's life history and unconscious. Because of this, Morita therapy stands in a position contrary to psychoanalysis.

The aim of Morita therapy—"not fighting against symptoms, but rather getting used to them and even having a friendly feeling toward one's symptoms"—has had wide appeal in Japan. Most psychiatrists who are not practicing Morita therapy and are not advocates of this therapy are often aware that in their approach to patients they make use of many aspects of Morita's method. Though not widely practiced in Japan at present, Morita therapy remains a special type of therapy.

During the past ten years, psychiatrists have often claimed that patients suffering from phobias of interpersonal relations have not reacted positively to Morita psychotherapy. My experience has been the same. The symptom has not been decreasing, but at present young patients are unable to accept the aim of Morita therapy—"not fighting but just accepting symptoms as they are." Some patients are persuaded to be hospitalized for Morita therapy but often leave the hospital in a week or so. Few consider that a treatment originated forty years ago can be applied to the present generation. I believe that Japanse psychiatrists are facing a critical problem in the treatment of phobias of interpersonal relations.

I am now tentatively trying two methods: psychoanalytically oriented group psychotherapy and behavioral therapy which Eysenck advocates.

V

In the preceding, I have described some cases of ereuthophobia and allied conditions observed frequently among the Japanese youth of today, and discussed them briefly in relation to the Japanese cultural background. I hope that well-designed cross-cultural studies can be conducted on these patterns of neurosis. I feel it would be most effective to compare neurotic types prevailing among college students in various cultures. College students form a social stratum which is comparatively alike in many important respect in many cultures today, and it seems to be more useful for the present purpose to compare data furnished by campus psychiatry rather than to compare statistics gathered from in- and outpatients in general hospitals.

I wish to conclude this presentation by stating that further elucidation on the psychopathology of these fears is necessary in order to develop more effective treatment techniques for them.

NOTES

1. In a strict sense, erythrophobia means "the fear of red." The fear of blushing taking place in the presence of others should be called ereuthophobia.
2. There are numerous English-language descriptions of Morita therapy. For a recent summary see Ikeda (1968).
3. The remainder comprised schizoid personality, obsessive neurosis, transient maladaptation, hypochondria, etc., each accounting for about 5 percent. The matrix group was ten thousand in number.
4. This is different from "stage fright" described by Fenichel, because patients having a fear of eye-to-eye confrontation clearly suffer more from the fear of unintentionally staring at people with strange looks than from the fear of being looked at by others.

REFERENCES

Dietrich, H. 1962. Uber dysmorphophobie (missgestaltfurcht). Archiv fur psychiatrie und nervenkrankheiten. 203, 501.
Doi, L. Takeo. 1962. Amae: a key concept for understanding Japanese personality structure. *In* R. J. Smith and R. K. Beardsley (eds.) Japanese Culture. Chicago, Aldine.
Eysenck, H.J., and S. Rochman. 1965. The causes and cures of neurosis. San Diego, Knapp.
Fenichel, O. 1945. The theory of neurosis. New York, Norton.
Ikeda, Kazuyoshi. 1968. Morita's theory of neurosis and its application to Japanese psychotherapy. *In* J.G. Howells (ed.) Modern Perspectives in World Psychiatry, II. London. 519–530.

Kaan, H. 1892. Der neurasthenische Angstaffekt bei Zwangsvorstellungen und der primordiale Grubelzwang. Wien and Leipzig, Deuticke (1892).
Sakuda, K. 1967. Haji no bunka saiko. Tokyo, Chikuma Shobo.
Salzman, L. 1968. The obsessive personality. New York, Science House.

A Psychotherapy of Neurosis: Morita Therapy

MOMOSHIGE MIURA AND SHIN-ICHI USA

A. The Origin and Development of Morita Therapy

The Morita Therapy is a unique psychotherapy which was originated and developed in Japan. Dr. Shoma Morita (1874–1938), Professor of Neuro-psychiatry at Tokyo Jikeikai School of Medicine, as a result of his 20 years of effort towards effective medical treatment of neurasthenia, arrived at this form of therapy. Around 1919 he founded this theory on his experience of a successful "conducting therapy in home setting" which was tried at his home on a few neurotic people.[1] Among references which, employed critically, became part of the background of this therapy, are the work therapy applied to psychotic patients, the fattening therapy of W. Mitchel of Philadelphia, the regulated living method of L. Binswanger, and the persuasive therapy of P. Dubois. During 10 years preceding the development of his therapy, Morita experimented with hypnosis. In the end he had become doubtful about this hypnotic method and, discarding it, began his new therapy. It must be emphasized here that the psychoanalytical therapy was well criticized in its early stage of development and incorporated into his novel therapy.

Shuzo Kure, a teacher of S. Morita's and pioneer of Japanese psychiatry, introduced and popularized the scholastic system of Kraepelin in Japan. He also recognized the therapeutic value of the scientific psychotherapy which was prevailing in Europe at that time. He presented the theme of psychotherapy to Morita, who was motivated to study this field. (Since his 16th year of age Morita

Reprinted from *Psychologia* 13 (1970): 18–35. The original appeared in Japanese in *Yonago Acta Medica* (organ of the School of Medicine, Tottori University, Yonago City, Tottori Prefecture) 14 (1970):1–17.

had suffered from neurasthenia, with palpitation, heavy feeling in his head and the like, but he was not cured by any kind of internal treatment. This may be also one reason why he took an interest in psychotherapy.) Morita had studied the German orthodox biological methods founded by Kraepelin, so it was natural that he should have opposed Freud's theory. But the so-called neurasthenia was classified, at that time, in the field of somatology which is concerned with etiology as well as treatment, so that not only the psychoanalysis introduced by Freud but also the psychogenic theory on nervous disease introduced by Morita, on which the psychotherapy was based, were out of the main current of psychiatry for a long time. Mitsuzo Shimoda, former Professor of Psychiatry at Kyushu University, however, was one of the few who supported this therapy.

The therapy was successfully applied and further developed by Morita's disciples, Gen-yu Usa, Takehisa Kora, Yoshiyuki Koga and Akichika Nomura, disciples of Shimoda, and Koji Sato, a psychologist, who was Professor at the Third National College at that time (now Kyoto University). As G. Usa originally was a Zen monk, he naturally inevitably developed the Morita Therapy along the line of Zen. So this therapy in the end also included the Zen mode of thought, though Morita did not receive it directly from Zen. Kora developed it with the background of European characterology, and Koga studied it in his field of psychosomatic medicine. Sato employed this method for student counseling and developed it in connection with Lewin's theory of causality. The actual value of Morita Therapy was gradually recognized by Japanese psychiatrists and psychologists, and after the Second World War it was introduced into the United States by the psychiatrists or clinical psychologists who had stayed in Japan as medical officers of the American army.

Karen Horney, who came to Japan in the summer of 1952, receiving a suggestion by Daisetz T. Suzuki, Zen philosopher, studied the Morita Therapy and Zen. She discussed the Morita Therapy with Kora in Tokyo, and G. Usa and Sato in Kyoto. But she could not utilize what she had found because of her sudden death at the end of the year. Akihisa Kondo, who was a disciple of Kora and Horney, wrote a treatise on Morita Therapy in Horney's journal in 1953. Sato read a paper on a case of treatment of stammering by Morita Therapy in the Inter-American Congress of Psychology in December 1955 and delivered lectures in U.S.A. and Europe to make it known world-wide. About this time Erich

Fromm showed interest in Morita Therapy and sought much explanation from D. T. Suzuki and Sato. In the same year Kora contributed an article to *L'Hygiene mentale,* and since 1957, Ingeborg Y. Wendt, German psychologist, has shown her interest in Morita Therapy and Zen. She visited Japan twice, and then wrote articles with a view in mind that the therapy should be adopted also in Europe. In summer 1958, Harold Kelman, successor of K. Horney in the American Institute for Psychoanalysis, visited Japan and emphasized the points of similarity between Morita Therapy and Zen. In the same year Kora and Sato introduced the therapy abroad from the point of view of "Zenish" psychotherapy. In 1962 Takeo Doi reported on "Morita Therapy and Psychoanalysis" and argued on psychopathology of *toraware* ("to be caught") at the conference of the National Institute of Mental Health. In 1963 Nomura explained the genealogy of Morita Therapy and discussed it in comparison with American and European psychotherapy at the Joint Psychiatric Meeting of Japan and U.S.A. held in Tokyo. In the International Journal of Psychiatry of October 1965, "Morita Therapy" written in 1964 by Kora, was reported in full, and a psychiatrist and two psychologists presented their opinions about it, to which Kora gave his answers.

B. MORITA'S THEORY OF "NERVOSITY"

The so-called neurasthenia or neurosis has been classified under many headings and there have been many opinions about its true form of cause. Morita summarized such diseases under the name of *shinkeishitsu* ("nervosity"), because neurasthenia, hypochondriasis, and obsession are based on the same predispositions. This denies the theory that they are caused by nervous exhaustion, and it is at the same time in opposition to psychoanalysis and the psychogenic theories. His explanation is based on his view that a hypochondriac temperament is the generation of nervosity and that the mechanism of psychic interaction is the condition inducing development of the disease.

Hypochondriac temperament is a kind of introvert inclination or predisposition, an extreme self-communion; that is, hypersensitivity to one's own physical and mental indisposition or any unusual, morbid sensation which threatens one's own existence. But it is the manifestation of the desire for existence which is inherent in human nature, a characteristic of every human. In cases of an extreme inclination, there develop a nervous tendency and then complicated symptoms of nervosity. This means that a man of nervous temperament has a sensitive, delicate feeling and also an extreme desire for completeness, an idealistic, intellectual attitude, and will to live. Kora gave it the name "inadaptability," which means the anxiety of a man who under his present conditions can not adapt himself to the given circumstances. This idea of his gives a broader meaning to the notion of hypochondriac temperament. He recognized its similarity with the basic anxiety alleged by Horney, but he thought the anxiety called "basic" to be not natural because the fear of death derives from the desire for existence.

Both hereditary and environmental elements influence the creation of hypochondria. Shimoda emphasized the element of environment and considered that one factor for its creation is over-discipline or overprotection in infancy. The intelligence of people of nervous temperament is on a level with that of normal men. Their extreme intellectual attitude is in striking contrast to the emotional inclination in cases of hysteria.

The second element of Morita's theory is the mechanism of psychic interaction. The mental process that Morita paid attention to in respect to nervosity is explained as follows: If attention is paid to some sensation, the sensation becomes very sharp; and by mutual interaction of sensation and attention the sensation will become more and more excessive. This process is named the mechanism of psychic interaction.

This is a kind of vicious circle which grows out of hypochondriac temperament, out of being prepossessed with one's own oversensitiveness, for example, headache, giddiness, absence of mind, heart acceleration, distraction, insomnia, inflating sensation of stomach, fear of epidemics, bashfulness when made an object of attention, sudden association of sexual excitation at the sight of the opposite sex, accidental fit of fear, fit of pain and so on. But if these symptoms are retraced back to their beginning, it will be made clear that these are normal sensations experienced by any normal man. The nervosity patient, however, out of his hypochondriac feeling, regards such reactions as unsound and unusual, is struck with fear of them, and at the same time anticipates them, so that by such mechanism of psychic interaction, these symptoms become worse and worse, he is captured therein, and the symptoms will be fixed for a long time in life.

Once having these symptoms, the patients believe in their reality and will continuously feel the distress of being confined in the subjectivity, as is shown in the dream. (G. Usa showed a case of mechanism of interaction in the afterimage of sensation of nervosity under the guidance of one of us (M.M.)). Autosuggestion is also one cause for the acceleration of adherence to those symptoms.

The patients can not compare themselves with others correctly because they are captives of their subjectivity; they can not feel sympathy for others and are not apt to take care of others in view of their own fear and distress. Therefore, the patients become egocentric and pity themselves and envy others; in their longing for sympathy they are always irritable and impatient. Such sadness and irritability are secondary emotions based on pessimistic thoughts caused by the misunderstanding of self-criticisms.

C. CLASSIFICATION AND STATISTICS OF NERVOSITY

Dr. Morita specified "nervosity" as the condition of mind in which, because of being self-introspective (introverted), one tends to become intellectual in the end. Therefore, he drew a clear line between nervosity and hysteria, because the former shows quite a different tendency from the latter in that hysteria means highly sensitive feeling in conjunction with extrovert mentality.

In classifying nervosity according to its elemental characteristics and not according to its external appearances, Morita regarded neurasthenia, anxiety neurosis, and obsession as diseases of the same type in their basic nature. The results of the therapy, and the fact that medical cures of these diseases require the same psychotherapy and almost the same period of treatment, demonstrate the sameness of the nature of these diseases.

Morita classified nervosity under the following three headings according to simplicity and complexity and general appearance. Of course, these three types of diseases may grade into or combine with one another.

1) Ordinary nervosity (so-called neurasthenia)

This means a peculiar nervosity in a narrow sense, including: heavy feeling in the head, headache, insomnia, stunned feeling, abnormality in senses, gastro-enteric neurosis, increase of fatigue, reduced productivity, reduced strength, bad memory, distraction of mind, vertigo (giddiness), ringing in the ears, tremor, writer's cramp, inferiority complex, shyness and worry for the future, sexual trouble, etc.

2) Paroxysmal neurosis (anxiety neurosis)

This is a kind of fit which a patient has subjectively the excitement of fear accompanied by the fear evoked in expectation of fit. The following come under this category: palpitation-fit, debility of arms and legs, vertigo, fainting-fit, nympholepsy, anxiety-fit, cold-fit, shivering-fit, pain-fit, dyspnoea-fit, etc.

3) Obsession (phobia)

This is a kind of mental complication caused by an antagonism in which a patient tries, by some means, neither to feel nor to think about certain unpleasant feelings or thoughts, regarding them with a hypochondriac feeling as morbid abnormality. The following come under this classification: homophobia (erythrophobia, look-in-the-face phobia, self-expression phobia, etc.), mysophobia, nosophobia, imperfection phobia, reading phobia, fainting phobia, agoraphobia, stammering phobia, crime phobia, aichmophobia, earthly thought phobia, acrophobia, inquiry phobia, etc.

As to the frequency of evocation of these diseases, the data issued by the Kora Kosei-in Hospital (1950–52) show that homophobia ranks first (38%), followed by heavy feeling in the head (11%), unstable nervous disease (8%), insomnia (5%) and nosophobia (4%) (44). However, a study of the materials of nervous diseases published by the Neuro-Psychiatry Department of Tokyo Jikeikai School of Medicine (1953–62) reveals that as the prime subject of complaint the physical condition comes first, showing almost the same percentage (35–40%) for every age (92). In regard to age and sex, the patients in their twenties lead the list, and of all patients examined 47% males and 41% females belong to this age. According to the statistics showing diagnostic distinction, of all the victims of nervous diseases, 55% are patients of nervosity (ordinary nervosity 35%, obsession 19%, anxiety neurosis 11%). As to the ratio of distribution by age of the three types of nervosity, ordinary nervosity is distributed almost equally (approximately 35%), while fear complex reaches a percentage of 36 at an age between 15 and 19, and shows a gradual decrease in percentage with increasing age. Anxiety neurosis occupies a little over 20 per cent between the thirties and fifties. No children under 14 years old are diagnosed as having nervosity. When classified according to sex, it is found that more persons of ordinary nervosity or obsession are found among the males, whereas more patients of anxiety neurosis (hysteria and psychogenic reaction, too) are among the females. In 1961, as against 1953, the victims of ordinary nervosity showed some decrease in number, while an increase in number was seen with the patients of obsession. Investigation with regard to the chief causes of the diseases reveals that in most cases domestic trouble and physical disorder result in sudden ailments. These are some of the causes of mental ailments: school problems of patients under the age of 19; domestic problems of people in their thirties or after; and various kinds of problems ranging from character disposition to love affairs of those who are between 20 to 29 years of age. The individual causes, however, do not greatly differ in percentage. Males are more troubled with problems concerning character, job and school affairs, while more domestic or housing problems worry females. More sexual problems are revealed by people below twenty. Insomnia gradually takes a more important position among the chief complaints with increase in age. The factors of heredity were found to be around 15% with all the patients of nervous disease examined. Among the factors, neurotic factors are the largest in number. The statistics published in 1960 by T. Suzuki reveal that among 1330 cases of nervosity 31.1% of patients had close relatives who were suffering from nervosity or had strong disposition to nervosity. He also reported that there is a high percentage of first-born children among nervosity patients, at a 1% level of reliability.

D. Principles of Morita Therapy

Since those who have a special psychical inclination towards nervous disease are apt to have an attack of nervosity due to some psychological mechanism, the method of treatment of this disease ought to be psychotherapy. The point aimed at by Morita's method is a training or drilling treatment of hypochondriac temperament underlying the disease, as well as the destruction of the psychic interaction in which the patient is caught. Some psychological bases in this therapy are as follows:

1. Contradiction of thought

Our thinking of what we wish to be or what we should be often brings about a contradictory result or a "fact," which was referred to as contradiction of thought by Morita. An idea or a thought is not always the same as the substance or the fact itself. Being unaware of this difference between idea and fact, not only the patients of nervosity but also sane people think of things that are not real just as if they were actually real. They do their best trying to change what is imagined into real facts by intellectual means, which results in contradiction of thought. The victims of nervosity may easily fall into contradiction of thought all the more because they so strongly long for perfection and they are such idealists. Generally speaking, our subjectivity and objectivity, our sentiment and intelligence, our understanding and realization—these things are frequently and very much contradictory, and hence do not accord with each other. The indistinctness in discrimination gives rise to the contradiction of thought. If a doctor tries to objectively persuade and control a patient of nervosity by telling him, "Try not to think of such a thing" or "Don't worry about that," he will not be able to succeed in attaining his object of curing this illness which is, after all, subjective. The unpleasant feeling we may have when we see cockroaches, for example, is feeling made into fact. In such a case, the patient of nervosity, if occasion demands, does not try to destroy the cockroaches, but by preserving this unpleasant feeling first suppresses his aversion against the insects, then becomes cool, and tries to do his best to approach them. This is also a feeling made into a fact by objective criticism, the fruit of intelligence, just like an attempt at the exclusion of fear of subjective death by saying, "Death is nothing to fear," which is nothing but a contradiction of thought. This attitude becomes one of the most important prerequisites in establishing an obsession.

2. Realization and understanding

Realization is self-consciousness obtained through the actual performance and experiences of our own, while understanding is abstract intelligence which fosters our judgment provoking us to say, "This ought to be so" or "That must be so" etc. by using our reasoning power. And, the deepest understanding is acquired through concrete experiences we actually go through, just as we can appreciate the taste of food only after we have actually eaten it. Our interests or hobbies, also, come to have meaning only after we have had actual experience. A patient of nervosity puts too much weight on his understanding by neglecting his own practical experience, so that he hastily concludes that the condition of his body and mind is so and so. Or if he thinks that interest is needed in the work he is to do, he does not try to set to work until his interest has been aroused. In such a situation, infused knowledge or thoughts prove to have little power of persuasion, unless the patient actually works and consequently creates a real situation. If the underlying tone of feeling of the patient is ignored, intellectual persuasion will bring him even further away from the realization.

3. Obedience to nature

It is a fact that the activity of our body and mind is a natural phenomenon. We can not control it by artificial means. However, our rational thinking suggests that we can control it as desired. The same is the case with mental phenomena. We have made the mistake of thinking that "only we know our own mind," or that "we can feel things just as we think we should," or that "we are free in thinking." To fear death, to hate discomfort, to grieve over a sad event, to complain about things that do not conform to our wishes—each of these is a natural manifestation of human sentiment. Even if we try to control ourselves as we want by such artificial means to our own advantage, after all matters will not go on as we wish. This frustration will begin to weigh heavy on our mind to no good and we will become incapable. Finally we will not be able to stand the pain. Then what we should do for our sake is to definitely abandon such artificial, poor behavior and to obey nature. Thereby, we will be able to attain the object of breaking down such contradiction of thought, by feeling cold as cold, by accepting pain or fear as it is, or by going through the agony itself. But we will never be able to succeed if we devise an artificial intellectual counter-plan. As the result of submitting to nature, we will lack a clear attitude of mind, and both physical and mental uncertainty will arise. Consequently the mind is always in a strain. But if the patient will adapt himself to the changes occurring in his environments, his attention will come into free play. As the symptoms of nervosity are caused by concentrated attention upon a point, the doctor should start by increasing the natural mental activity of the patient, enlarge the sphere of this activity and guide him to a free mental attitude.

E. PRACTICE OF MORITA THERAPY

Because nervosity is not directly related to nervous fatigue, rest and tranquilizers are not effective. Therefore, the Morita Therapy treats hypochondriac disposition by training the patients' characters and treats psychic interaction, which is the mechanism that aggravates the symptoms, by breaking the contradiction of thought, thereby breaking down the vicious circle of attention and sensation. We always endeavor to make patients grasp an attitude of life natural and obedient to their environment by their personal experiences and feelings.

Morita Therapy is a fundamental and natural method of treatment. It teaches the patients to obey their own nature and to have an attitude towards life appropriate to things as they are. Therefore, we do not stress suggestion or persuasion; nor is it necessary to pursue psychic conflicts to their sources. Instead, we direct the patients' lives, actions, and mental attitudes by the following method: We only criticize them through diaries and lectures. These directions and criticisms for their mental attitude are unique to Morita Therapy. The therapist does not direct the patients' attitude of mind to their symptoms but has them renounce all their intellectualized attitudes of mind, allow their symptoms to change as they will, and avoid being consciously concerned with their attitude of mind. As a general rule we have them enter the hospital, but also treat outpatients as an expedient means.

Four Stages of Treatment in Hospital

a) First stage: Period of absolute bed rest (4 to 7 days). In this period we isolate patients. Meeting with others, talking, reading and writing, smoking, eating between meals, and singing are forbidden. We have them be in bed except when they take meals, bathe, and excrete. We make them endure worldly thoughts and all of the pain which accompanies them, advise them not to avoid facing the agony. At the beginning patients are in great distress, but after about 4 days they are bored and tired of lying in bed. They want to get up and do something. And then, we direct them to get up. We give them printed instruction so that they will know and observe the rules. If they do not follow our directions, we sometimes tell them to leave the hospital. We interview patients every day for several minutes to see whether they are observing the instructions honestly or not. But the interview may be omitted, if during the period the patient complains of his symptoms.

b) Second stage: Period of light work after getting out of bed (3–7 days). This period is for an insulation method of treatment, too. Talking, associating with others, playing and reading are forbidden. Sleeping is limited to 7 or 8 hours. They must be out of doors in the daytime. To take a rest in the room is not allowed. On the first and the second day, we prohibit all actions requiring the use of muscles, such as looking at the sky, climbing an elevation, or using a bamboo broom, and also prohibit purposeless use of time in taking a walk without necessity, doing physical exercises, or playing with children or dogs, etc. We let the symptoms change as they occur, at the same time arousing a spontaneous desire to work, promote exact observation of animals or plants, and allow hand work like weeding or gathering dead leaves. Every day after supper they make entries in a diary, so that both their physical and mental conditions will become clear and the doctor will be able to criticize the contents of the diary and to make hints with regard to the mental attitude of the patients. For all the patients who are at the second stage or higher, lectures are held three times a week explaining the process of recovery in reference to the diary, and leading the patients to be able to discern between desires and facts. After having washed themselves in the morning and before going to bed at night, that is twice a day, they are required to read a convenient portion (or for five minutes) of a difficult classic book like the *Kojiki,* always from the beginning. But we induce them to read accurately only in pronunciation regardless of the meaning of the contents.

At this stage we let them perform necessary work at hand, not for fun or interest, but for them to be always in action, leave them in doubt about whether they will recover or not, keep them from devising treatment by themselves, and make them rely on the leadership of the doctor without reserve. We lead them not to tell the therapist about their symptoms in order to prevent them from observing their own progress and leave them to themselves according to the so-called "ignoring therapy" to ignore their complaints of pains. We lead them to stop taking an attitude of being ill, but rather to pretend that they are healthy, and to dissolve their fascination with contrasting phenomena of pleasure and displeasure, by stopping any discussion of a discriminating nature. There is no clear boundary in advancing to the next stage.

c) Third stage: Period of chores (7 to 20 days). In this period we have the patients work according to their state of health. They will become patient in working, before they know it, and happy in the discovery of their own courage and capacity for satisfaction in work. But we have to take care in this period not to let the patients be concerned with how they appear to others or with the dignity of their task. It is best for them not to have a choice as to what work to do; we have them do whatever they can. Their work extends to washing, cleaning the lavatory, kitchen work and so on. As they are working they come to realize that happiness lies, not far away, but in the immediate experience of daily life. Therefore, it is necessary for the therapist to devise directions so that they will gradually develop the ability to act voluntarily in any work. When the patients are so fully occupied with their work that they are unconscious of the passage of time, they are ready for the next stage.

d) Fourth stage: Period of complicated practical life (10 days). They learn patience through steady application of effort in work. While at the third stage their work depends on their interest, in this period they must work whether they are interested or not. Then they will come to adjust themselves to their varied situation. At the beginning of this period, patients are trained to lead a practical, ordinary life. They are permitted to read books and to go shopping. However, their reading is restricted to simple, practical, descriptive and scientific works; amusing, philosophical, and literary ones are to be avoided. We do not permit patients to sit and read in their rooms; they read at scattered odd moments during the day when they are free from work. We have them read any part of books and repeat several lines time and again without endeavoring to understand or memorize, whether they are difficult or not. During this period they are sometimes given permission to go to work or school outside the hospital. In this way, by continuing to have a realistic attitude towards life and work, the patients will be able, we hope, to fully experience their own lives and gradually realize what Morita called "pure mind." Morita Therapy achieves its aim when patients spontaneously concentrate on daily real life.

Kazuyoshi Ikeda, Professor of Kyushu University Psychiatric Institute, explained very well the meaning of these four stages in his paper (19). Let me quote some of his passages:

The first stage: The principle is to minimize the working span of 'contradiction of thought' or 'bad intellect', and to reduce the conflict to a simpler form of psychic interaction. The subsidiary meaning of taking rest is to recover from exhaustion and to induce spontaneous activities of the patient.

The second stage: A period of transition from rest to spontaneous activity. Here comes out the positive aspect of the Morita Therapy, that is, to break the contradiction of thought by making the patient concentrate on unrelated activities, and help him get insight into the dynamics of the paradox. At this stage the amount of work must be reserved so as to stimulate further spontaneous activity.

The third stage: An extension of the second stage. Varieties and heaviness of work increase, and they help the patient acquire self-confidence in his capacity. Individual differences come to appear at this stage in the type and the progress of cure.

The fourth stage: The preparation period for returning to actual life. Almost all the restrictions of life, including interpersonal relationships, are taken away. The responses of the patients show much more variety and complexity than in the previous stages. The theory of neurosis in the Morita school has not taken up the problem of character structure which underlies the symptom and has no hypothesis concerning it. The goal of treatment here is rather to bring about conditions under which the patient can develop his capacities to the utmost, keeping his native character as it has been.

Though the period of treatment is not fixed owing to the individual differences of the patients, an early recovery takes two weeks, and a slow recovery ten weeks, 40 days being the average. What makes it possible to build up such ability to adapt oneself to normal life in such a comparatively short period of time is the excellent originality of Morita Therapy. The problem of returning to their places in society after having left the hospital is not so difficult, because the patients, while in the hospital, have already been able to go to school or practice a profession at the fourth stage. Since the egocentric aspect of life has been broken down and a living attitude in which the patients are not too particular about the choice of the conditions of life has been cultivated, they are not forced to suddenly adapt themselves to changed conditions.

Though Morita Therapy originally was directed at a homelike therapy, there was also a kind of group therapy which only aimed at persons of nervosity, Morita himself living together with them. In orthodox Morita Therapy, it is obligatory that the therapist live not too far from the patients and pass much of his time with them; the doctor and his family, the nurses and the cooks take a consistent attitude towards the people of nervosity, and they treat them rather as lodgers than as patients, sometimes even as members of the family. Morita maintains that "A man of nervosity can not get well if treated as sick, but will soon get healthy when treated as if he were healthy." Therefore, the specific atmosphere in the therapeutic community is considered by William Caudill to be of great importance (4). Thus the therapeutic community is beyond the mere relationship between a doctor and a patient. This is one of the important characteristics of this therapy, since the lack of the usual one-to-one doctor-patient relationship is useful to raise the independence of the patients, and eliminate their dependence upon others.

Also the Sansei Hospital (Kyoto), which at present has 50 to 60 patients of nervosity, has adopted this therapy, and gradually perfected group psychotherapy. In this hospital, since 1956, leaders have been elected from among the patients of the third stage or higher. A group of 15 leaders takes charge of several tasks like cooking, gardening, postal service, and fire warden, and instructs the juniors, which system produces satisfactory results. The main points to be observed in guiding the patients by having them write a diary and hear lectures are as follows:

i. Lead them not to write about the symptoms of their

disease and about their own character in the diary, and not to speak with others about such things.

ii. Lead them to stop self-observing feelings and mental conditions, and urge them to draw their attention to the things happening around them.

iii. As to the symptoms, advise them to leave them as they are, *i.e.*, to let them change as they do without any treatment.

iv. The doctor does not attach importance to the symptoms, nor does he put any evaluating criticism on them, but tells the patients to bear distress even if it is painful.

v. Let them do necessary work without delay. In case the patients do not take pleasure in it, lead them to begin the work without noticing their aversion.

vi. Let them know through experience that a change in the kind of work means relaxation, and that it is possible to carry out two kinds of task or more at the same time (including mental work).

vii. Emphasize that the purpose of the work is not to expedite the recovery of the patient, but to complete the work itself.

viii. Lead them not to accumulate self-confidence from various experiences: aiming at attaining a specific mental state like the feeling of relief gives rise to an illusion of the reality of one's feeling, and results in establishing an imaginary self again.

ix. Let them assume full responsibility for their work, make them always bear the strains of life and, above all, meet the requirements of the public, And it is important that, when they are with other people, they always should try to be tactful.

x. It is not absolutely necessary that an explanation of the psychological mechanism of nervosity be given. On the contrary, intellectual interpretations and rationalistic comments may be a cause of strengthening the captivity in nervous temperament. C. Suzuki and A. Kumano pointed out that in the case of three physicians who tried to cure their own nervosity, their medical knowledge was absolutely of no value in the dissolution of this disease (84).

xi. Always give the patients a chance to behave like healthy members of society. Whether their feeling of being ill or imperfect still remains or not, they may even obtain an attitude aiming at lending their assistance to others.

F. Recovery by Morita Therapy

Patients who have been cured by this therapy have confessed to being in a mental state as if "having just awakened from a dream," or "the day has broken," or "the world has changed." But this does not mean that the anxiety and the feeling of discontentment have suddenly been taken away. As human life is a flexible thing, feeling is fixed in a stream of ups and downs and follows it obediently, but if once feeling has come in accord with nature, this means a first arrival at the absolute calmness of mind. The patients who have been cured by breaking down their hypochondriac temperament that had veiled their basic will to live, gain a more constitutive behavior and even a more active attitude towards society than they had in the days before they fell ill. When they do no longer need an intellectual support, intellect does not hamper their mind any more and can freely fulfill its original role of functioning as an outwardly-directed structure. Also from this point of view, the self-insight as devised in Morita Therapy is not limited, in its deepest meaning, to an intellectual understanding, but is that very condition which is brought to reality in the practice of daily life that may conveniently be called intuitive vision.

For measuring the results of Morita Therapy by means of psychological tests, Kataguchi used the Rorschach test and showed on the basis of the Basic Rorschach Score (BRS) that Morita Therapy, as compared with non-directive therapy, does not so easily bring about a change in human character (20). But Nakae, also by using the BRS, found that in other clinics, after the therapy had been finished, a remarkable change was observed (59), and he concluded that dissolution of the inclination to repressions, mental stability, feeling of sympathy, self-acceptance, and a nature-obeying attitude had been more improved than before. Using the RPRS (Rorschach Prognostic Rating Scale) according to Klopfer, one of us (S.U.) obtained the following results on personality changes in 114 patients who had been cured by Morita Therapy (101).

i. Between the prognostic rating score and the evaluation of results of treatment there exists a significant connection, and among the BPRS-factors M, Sh as well as FL indicate the efficiency in the healing prognosis.

ii. Concerning the personality changes before and after the treatment, a significant increase is obvious in the RPRS-factors, Sh and Col, of the treated group in comparison with the other groups, and also an improvement towards emotional integration.

iii. Among those who completed treatment at the hospital 3 to 35 years ago, the group that possessed a specific adaptability showed significant increase in m and Sh of RPRS as compared with the other groups, and for a long time they lived a community life tiding over difficulties they had never been faced with while they were in hospital. Hayao Kawai and S. Yamamoto found the score of the RPRS to be high on nervosity, and pointed out that the "unused egostrength" (Klopfer) of nervosity is strong (21).

Further there are studies on the relationship between the after-image time and treatment process conducted by G. Usa (94), on character tests (2) by T. Abe, on the P-F study by K. Takano (89), on the urine test by Y. Takahashi (87), and on the mecholyl test by B. Fujita (10) and Okuda (70), and these researches have obtained quantitative figures of the therapeutic effects of Morita Therapy.

The favorable results of the treatment are as indicated. About 60% of the patients were completely cured on an average after they had been in hospital for about 40 days. But even those who only improved in health will lead everyday life even if a few symptoms of the disease remain, and there are many who have completely regained their health after several months or years. There are also some who are suffering a renewed attack of disease and must once more enter a hospital, but according to Kobayashi's catamnestic observations over a long period of time, a comparatively great number of those who had to resort to hospital for a second time were hereditarily afflicted (26).

G. Criticism of Morita Therapy

Even in Japan Morita Therapy was not taken seriously at the beginning, since at that time the influence of the German psychiatric line of thought was considerable and no great importance was attached to psychotherapy in general. Today the actual value of Morita Therapy has been widely acknowledged, but nevertheless there is some criticism. From its early period this therapy has been in contradiction to Freudian psychoanalysis, as seen in the dispute between Morita, Sato, and S. Marui, who had introduced psychoanalysis into Japan (46, 74), and has encountered much criticism from this side. But properly speaking, there are only a few in Japan who have completed an exact training in the psychoanalytic way of thinking. Takamizu criticizes Morita Therapy from the psycho-analytic viewpoint, pointing out that it is not built up on a foundation of scientific theory, and that there is insufficient analysis of the complications occurring in the unconscious which may be the true cause for a neurosis (88). A. Jacobson and A. R. Berenberg, two American psychiatrists, stayed in Japan in 1950 through 1951 to participate in clinical practice and seminars at the Medical Department of Kyushu University. Their criticism of Morita Therapy was as follows (16): "They don't investigate the foundations and origins of neurotic behavior." "Techniques aimed at de-repression are looked upon as wasteful of time and antithetical to the goals they have set themselves." "Sources of conflict material are not sought after." "Dreams are given but scant attention." "Transference phenomena are not referred to." But their final conviction was that "Suppression is the dominant theme in therapy; conformity the goal!" From their point of view, the cure seemed to be chiefly "conforming behavior" rather than for the patient himself to have the feeling of being well without any conflicts. But with the above views in mind it was only natural that they were skeptical about the correctness of the very high recovery rate (cured, 76.2%; favorable progress, 7.6%) set forth by the Department of Psychiatry at Kyushu University. If emphasis is put on the cultivation of "personality," the lack of analytical research may be a weak point of Morita Therapy. But such arguments of these two American psychiatrists show the difficulty in understanding the intrinsic value of Morita Therapy.

A. Kondo, a disciple of Kora and Horney, argues on the future development of Morita Therapy as follows: In the first place, "It must utilize the rich achievements gained by the recent development of analysis in the western world, especially of the neurotic structure. Also the study of the patient's relationship with the doctor in the analysis surely will contribute a great deal to it." In the second place: "Reexamination of the whole system in the light of a reappreciation of Zen Buddhism can help this therapy develop more effectively and profoundly."(33)

In a discussion about Oriental Psychology and Psychotherapy held on the occasion of the Fourth International Psychotherapeutic Association Meeting in 1958, according to M. Kato's report, Kelman declared that in recent times in Japan there is an endeavor to unite Morita Therapy and psychoanalysis. It is true that in the previous two articles Kondo endeavored to make clear the fact that although there are strong differences between the Freudian orthodox school, Horney's school, and Morita Therapy concerning the theoretical structure, they have many factors in common with regard to the therapeutic mechanism. He demands the "acceptance" of those (35) and states: "There is some possibility of finding a method to adopt intellectual insight and emotional insight of psychoanalysis also into the Morita Therapy."(36) According to T. Doi's opinion, when explaining nervosity with the aid of the psychoanalytical method, it is found that the substantial common feature is "to be caught," which means something like "one cannot depend and presume upon another's benevolence even if one wants to (5,6)." And again, by elucidating the basic psychological structure of nervosity, he thinks that there exists no substantial difference between Japan and the Western countries, the difference between Morita's concept and Freud's concept being rather due to sociocultural variations (7).

According to K. Kakeda, in the Joint Japanese-American Conference of Psychiatry held in 1963 in Tokyo, the American participants critically commented on the report on Morita Therapy by A. Nomura (67), stating that, in a strict sense, it can not be classified under the notion of psychotherapy but under psychophysiological therapy. With regard to this, Nomura pointed out that the difference is mainly due to the different viewpoints on the part of the therapists, and that Morita Therapy takes as a starting point the biological, psychological and mental state, including the physical, and aims at normalizing the adaptability and leading the patients back to humanity in a wide sense. At this conference Z. Lebensohn said that the Sullivan school of psychotherapy, which puts emphasis on the peculiar human relations, has a deeper connection with Morita Therapy than has the Horney school, and that the method of leading even the outpatients to write a diary on events really occurring in everyday life will possibly also be adopted in America (8).

As Nomura also mentioned (65), many points of similarity between Morita Therapy and V. Frankl's *Logotherapie* are recognized by many Japanese psychotherapists. The practical techniques like the "Paradox intention" or the "Dereflexion" (9) are identical with Morita's nature-obedience and the conquest of the contradiction of thought, respectively. As devised by Morita, to give oneself completely up to the stream of natural feeling without putting any kind of significance on the things occurring, is one special feature of Oriental mentality.

As soon as Kora made public a detailed introduction to Morita Therapy in 1965, three American psychiatrists and psychologists responded with discussions on it (44). It seems that these criticisms have better grasp of Morita Therapy than former ones. Though the expressions of their opinions do not agree with each other, they have a common doubt about this therapy. The doubt raised is whether Morita Therapy can be applied not only in Japan but also in America and Europe. Y. Kumasaka, while appreciating Morita Therapy, maintains that thing-as-it-is-ness can not be accepted in America and Europe in the same way as in the East, for the American and European attitude towards nature consists not so much in merging into it as in challenging and conquering it. He adds that work therapy can not be adopted, because work is not much valued for its own sake in America and Europe as it is in Morita Therapy, in which work constitutes an important process in order to adapt to nature. Norman J. Levy considers that highly democratic countries would not adopt Morita Therapy because of its authoritative nature even if it is applicable to the Japanese, whose feelings easily submit to the will of authority. It is said that Kelman is of the same opinion. George A. DeVos affirms by the results of a test on Japanese, which he did with Caudill, that Japanese tend to lose their confidence when they fail to fulfill the expectations of authorities and families, but that Americans do not admit readily their lack of ability, and that they unconsciously think that they should serve others. He cites diligence as a fundamental character of the Japanese. He seems to consider that diligence not only takes part in nervosity but forms a ground for adopting Morita Therapy.

Kora answers to all these doubts, "It is often said that the Japanese easily accept nature, but actually it is not so. If the Japanese had been able to accept nature as easily as the Americans and Europeans think that they do, many cases of nervosity might have been avoided." "If one could accept mental facts as they are, as we recognize sensual facts as they are, as 'Flower is red, willow is green,' it would not be difficult to understand the standpoint of Morita Therapy irrespective of the East and West." He thus explains the possibilities of adopting Morita Therapy in America and Europe and refers to the fact that the Japanese do not behave so obediently as Americans suppose. He says that Americans and Europeans also, if they really want to cure their nervous diseases, have to follow doctors' directions. This probably isn't a question of being democratic or undemocratic. His proposal in his final passage corresponds to our own hope. "We hope that the Morita Therapy should be applied to many European and American patients so that Europeans and Americans may concretely examine where it is unacceptable and what its merits are." I.Y.Wendt has often expressed the same hope and proposes, "Japanese and Western doctors have to cooperate for purposes of research. In the beginning, therapy with Western patients should be done by Japanese doctors (with Japanese nurses) since the character of the method is nearer to their natural disposition."

Finally, it is a well-known fact that Morita owed very much to Oriental philosophy when he founded this treatment. Above all, so much importance is attached to the influence of Zen that Zen has sometimes been discussed in relation to "thing-as-it-is-ness" which forms the central tasks of this treatment. But, in fact, the Morita Therapy was never constructed on the ideas of Zen, nor was it explained in accordance with Zen. On the contrary, Morita absorbed knowledge about Zen from his patients, and his disciples praised his treatment as being one with Zen. In 1952, G. Usa answered to Horney that the founding of the Morita Therapy had nothing to do with Zen. Nevertheless Zen monk G. Usa had believed that the Morita Therapy had the same logic as Zen. He applied Zazen ("Zen sitting") to his actual treatment. This was because he had known the ultimate result of Zen and the Morita Therapy from the viewpoint of "Life without theory." It may be on the same background that K. Yokoyama uses for the Morita Therapy the Seiza ("sitting still") which was founded in Japan apart from Zazen.

NOTE

1. "Among some patients whom Dr. Morita was taking care of at his home there was a certain female, Miss Yatabe. She suffered from obsessive neurosis of mysophobia. She had been treated at the Sugamo Psychiatric Hospital for a long time, and had left the hospital without being cured. At his home Dr. Morita tried hypnosis, other usual methods of treatment, and his own method of persuasion, but had no success. He told me that sometimes he had lost his temper and struck her. To his surprise, however, the patient had been cured suddenly by herself when she abandoned herself in agony and despair. Dr. Morita studied this accidental case, and found the necessary conditions for this wonderful cure, which became the basis of his unique therapeutic method." (Shimoda, M., 1938)

REFERENCES

1. *Psychiatric Department Contribution in Memory of the late Dr. Morita, ed. by Tokyo Jikeikai School of Medicine, 1938. (Abbreviated in this Bibliography as *CM*)
2. *Abe, T. Supplementary study on nervosity, with special reference to personality tests. *Shinkeishitsu*, 1960, **1**, 137–156.
3. *Aoki, S. Studies on the report of Keigaikai (I) The life of M. Morita, orig-

inator of Morita psychotherapy. (II) Morita and Buddhistic thoughts. (III) Morita's critical comments on religion. *Shinkeishitsu,* 1962, **3**, 49–66.

4. Caudill, W. *The psychiatric hospital as a small society.* Cambridge: Harvard Univ., 1958.
5. **Doi, L. T. Psychopathology of "Shinkeishitsu," especially regarding the psychodynamics of its "Toraware." *Psychiat. Neurol. jap.,* 1958, **60**, 734–744.
6. Doi, L. T. Amae: A key concept for understanding Japanese personality structure. *Psychologia,* 1962, **5**, 1–7.
7. Doi, L. T. Morita therapy and psychoanalysis. *Psychologia,* 1962, **5**, 117–123.
8. Ewalt, J. R. East and west look at psychiatry. *MD, Med. Newsmagazine,* 1963, **7**, 77–81.
9. Frankl, V.E. *Theorie und Therapie der Neurosen* Wien: Urban Schwarzenburg, 1956.
10. **Fujita, B. Psychophysiological significance of the mecholyl test as applied in mental disorders, especially with reference to Morita's psychotherapy. *Psychiat. Neurol. jap.,* 1960, **62**, 831–853.
11. *Fujita, C. The view of human being in Morita therapy. *Shinkeishitsu,* 1960, **1**, 111–120.
12. *Fujita, C. On Morita therapy, with special reference to outpatients treatment. *Shinkeishitsu,* 1961, **2**, 34–38.
13. *Fujita, C. An application of psychodrama to the treatment of nervosity. *Clin. Psychiat.,* 1961, 3, 595–599.
14. *Fujita, C. A prospect of Morita therapy. *Clin. Psychiat.* 1965, **7**, 129–136.
15. *Furu, T. On the behavioristic moment of Dr. Morita's theory of nervous temperament. *Jap. J. appl. Psychol.,* 1934, **2**, 370–381.
16. Jacobson, A. and Berenberg, A. N. Japanese psychiatry and psychotherapy. *Amer. J. Psychiat.,* 1952, **109**, 321–329.
17. *Hotta, S. Nature and therapy of neurotic insomnia. *CM* 1938, 199–224.
18. *Iijima, Y. A study of TAT in nervosity. *Shinkeishitsu,* 1960, **1**, 177–187.
19. *Ikeda, K. Nervosity (Morita) and Morita therapy. *Clin. Psychiat.* **1**, 461–473, 1959.
20. *Kataguchi, Y. The application of Rorschach test to psychotherapy. *Shinrigakuhyoron,* 1958, **2**, 216–232.
21. **Kawai, Ha., Yamamoto, S. and Usa, S. A study on the validity of the Rorschach prognostic rating scale—applied to Morita-therapy. *Rorschachiana Japonica,* 1958, **1**, 95–106.
22. *Kawai, Hi. A supplementary psychopathological study on Morita therapy on neurosis. *Tokyo Jikeikai Ikadaigaku Zassi,* 1959, **74**, 1214–1230.
23. Kawai, Hi. and Kondo, K. Discussion on Morita therapy. *Psychologia,* 1960, **3**, 92–99.
24. *Kawai, Hi. Historical study on Morita therapy. *Shinkeishitsu,* 1962, **3**, 19–24.
25. *Kawai, Hi. A historical, sociological revaluation on Morita therapy. *Shinkeishitsu,* 1964, **5**, 33–41.
26. **Kobayashi, J. Catamnestic study on neurosis. *Psychiatr. Neurol. jap.,* 1960, **62**, 40–59.
27. Kobayashi, J. Studies on the formation of predisposition of neurosis. In *Clinical genetics in psychiatry.* Ed. by H. Mitsuda. Tokyo: Igaku-shoin, 1968.
28. *Koga, Y. Nature of gastroenteric neurosis and its treatment. *CM* 1938, 38–82.
29. *Koga, Y. *Neurasthenia can be cured without fail.* Tokyo: Shufunotomo-sha, 1956.
30. *Koga, Y. Cardiac neurosis, *Abnormal Psychology,* 1957, **3**, 55–108.
31. *Koga, Y. *Realities of neurosis and the way to make use of it.* Tokyo: Hakuyo-sha, 1957.
32. *Koga, Y. *How to cure anxiety and fear.* Tokyo: Shufunotomo-sha, 1958.
33. Kondo, A. Morita Therapy. A Japanese therapy for neurosis. *Amer. J. Psychoanal.,* 1953, **13**, 31–37.

428 *Stress, Responses, and Transformation*

34. *Kondo, A. Morita's theory of nervosity compared with the psychoanalytic theories of Freud and Horney on neurosis. *Tokyo Jikeikai Ikadaigaku Zassi,* **73,** 2077–2123, 1958.
35. *Kondo, A. Acceptance: its meaning in psychotherapy. *Shinkeishitsu,* 1962, **3,** 13–18.
36. *Kondo, A. Intellectual insight, emotional insight and intuitive insight in existential situation. *Shinkeishitsu,* 1962, **3,** 37–43.
37. *Kondo, K. A study of the socio-cultural backgrounds of anthropophobia. *Shinkeishitsu,* 1960, **1,** 157–175.
38. *Kora, T. Problem of "Shinkeishitsu (nervosity)." *CM* 1938, 1–37.
39. *Kora, T. *Character treatment of nervosity and neurasthenia.* Tokyo: Sanseido, 1933.
40. *Kora, T. *How to cure homophobia.* Tokyo: Hakuyo-sha, 1952.
41. *Kora, T. *Characterology.* New ed. Tokyo: Hakuyo-sha, 1955.
42. *Kora, T. Homophobia and Japanese historical social environment. *Kyushu Neurol. Psychiat.* 1955, **4,** No. 3 & 4.
43. Kora, T. and Sato, K. Morita therapy—A psychotherapy in the way of Zen. *Psychologia,* 1958, **1,** 219–225.
44. Kora, T. Morita therapy. *Int. J. Psychiat.,* 1965, **1,** 611–640.
45. Kumasaka, Y., Levy, N. J. and DeVos, G. A. Discussion on Morita therapy. *Int. J. Psychiat.,* 1965, **1,** 641–645.
46. *Marui, S. On neurosis. *Psychiat. Neurol. jap.,* 1938, **42,** 741–754; 797.
47. *Matsunaga, N. Clinical psychopathological study of the chronic obsessive-compulsive neurosis treated with Morita therapy. *Shinkeishitsu,* 1960, **1,** 189–214.
48. *Mikuriya, I. Statistical considerations of hypochondriac patients treated in the Psychiatric Department of Kyushu University during the recent eleven and half years. *CM* 1938, 225–234.
49. *Mizutani, K. and Shinpo, H. *Power to live truly.* Tokyo: Hakuyo-sha, 1963.
50. *Mizutani, K. *Self-realization.* Tokyo: Ikedashoten, 1965.
51. *Morita, S. *Therapy of nervosity and neurasthenia.* Tokyo: Nihon Seishin-igaku-kai, 1921.
52. *Morita, S. *Lectures on psychotherapy.* Tokyo: Nihon Seishin-igakukai, 1921.
53. *Morita, S. *Ways to the therapy of nervosity.* Vol. 1. Kyoto: Jinbun-shoin, 1935; Vols. 2 & 3. Tokyo: Shinkeishitsu-kenkyukai, 1937.
54. *Morita, S. *Fundamental therapy of neurasthenia and obsession.* New ed. Tokyo: Hakuyo-sha, 1953.
55. *Morita, S. *Nature and therapy of nervosity.* New ed. Tokyo: Hakuyo-sha, 1960.
56. *Morita, S. and Mizutani, K. *Desire to live,* Tokyo: Hakuyo-sha, 1956.
57. *Morita, S. and Mizutani, K. *Ways to the self-realization and awakening.* Tokyo: Hakuyo-sha, 1959.
58. *Morita, S. and Mizutani, K. *Questions and answers on nervosity.* Tokyo: Hakuyo-sha, 1959.
59. **Nakae, S. A study on the therapeutic effects reflected upon the personality changes of "Nervosität" by the Morita therapy. By means of the Rorschach test. *Rorschachiana jap.,* 1959, **2,** 86–101.
60. **Nakagawa, S. A study of prognosis of nervosity and its borderline cases. *Psychiat. Neurol. jap.* 1954, **56,** 135–186.
61. *Nishizono, M. A clinical study on neurosis. *Kyushu Neurol. Psychiat.,* 1954, **7,** No. 1.
62. *Noda, J. *Morita "nervosity" and its therapy.* Private publication, 1960.
63. *Nomura, A. Statistics on outpatients of nervosity. *CM* 1938, 234–244.
64. *Nomura, A. A historical study of neurasthenia and obsession in Japan. *Tokyo Ijishinshi,* 1953, **70,** 271–272; 325–327.
65. *Nomura, A. *Therapy of neurosis and the present-day life.* Tokyo: Nihonkyobun-sha, 1958.

66. *Nomura, A. A psychotherapy in Japan—Morita's psychotherapy. *Shinkeishitsu*, 1962, **3**, 25–29.
67. Nomura, A. Morita therapy found in Japan. *Folia psychiat. neurol. jap.*, 1964, **17**, Suppl., 133–138.
68. *Ohara, K. Changes of level of aspiration in the course of treatment with Morita therapy. *Clin. Psychiat.*, 1962, **4**, 395–399.
69. *Ohara, K., Aizawa, S., Kojima, H., Iwai, H. and Miyata, K. The current therapeutic trend of Morita therapy. *Clin. Psychiat.*, 1966, **8**, 249–258.
70. *Okuda, Y. Reaction on autonomic nervous center in mental illness. *Shinkeishitsu*, 1960, **1**, 43–64.
71. Okumura, N. Japanische Psychotherapie und Zen. *Berichte ü. die 3. Tagung d. Dtsch. allg. ärztl. Gesell. f. Psychother. in Wien am 6. u. 7. Sept.* 1940.
72. *Sano, A. Problem in the treatment of neurosis. *Shinkeishitsu*, 1961, **2**, 31–33.
73. *Sano, A. Limitation of Morita therapy. *Shinkeishitsu*, 1962, **3**, 7–11.
74. *Sato, K. A criticism on the psychoanalytic studies by Prof. Marui and others. *Psychiat. Neurol. jap.*, 1930, **31**, 687.
75. Sato, K. Psychotherapeutic implications of Zen *Psychologia*, 1958, **1**, 213–218.
76. *Sato, K. Zen and psychology. *Jap. J. Psychol.*, 1959, **30**, 286–295.
77. **Shinfuku, N. Psychopathology of neurotic preoccupations with reference to Morita theory. *Psychiat. Neurol. jap.*, 1954, **55**, 737–742.
78. *Shinfuku, N. On the relation of Morita theory to the psychoanalytical theory on neurosis. *Clin. Psychiat.*, 1959, **1**, 475–488.
79. *Shimoda, M. Preface. In memory of the late Dr. Morita. *CM* 1938, i–iv.
80. *Shimoda, M. *Lectures on mental hygiene.* Iwanami-shoten, Tokyo, 1942.
81. *Suzuki, T. *Solution of anxiety.* Tokyo: Ikedashoten, 1956.
82. *Suzuki, T. The Morita therapy for "Shinkeishitsu," especially regarding the relief from its "Hakarai." *Clin. Psychiat.*, 1959, **1**, 499–505.
83. *Suzuki, T. Psychotherapy—from a standpoint of Morita school. *Psychosom. Med.*, 1960, **1**, No. 1.
84. *Suzuki, T. *One way of life.* Tokyo: Hakuyo-sha, 1960.
85. *Suzuki, T. and Kumano, A. A few considerations given to anxiety observed in anxiety neurosis. *Clin. Psychiat.*, 1965, **7**, 789–795.
86. *Suzuki, T. *People free from anxiety.* Tokyo: Ikeda-shoin, 1961.
87. *Takahashi, Y. Psychophysiological study on neurotic patients treated with Morita therapy. *Shinkeishitsu*, 1960, **1**, 21–42.
88. *Takamizu, R. A medical view on insomnia. *Psychoanalysis*, 1952, **10**, No. 3. 12–15.
89. *Takano, K. Results of pictures frustration test with nervosity. *Shinkeishitsu*, 1961, **2**, 101–116.
90. *Takeyama, T. A study on impure types of nervosity. *CM* 1938, 142–168.
91. *Takeyama, T. Hypnosis and Morita therapy. *Shinkeishitsu*, 1961, **2**, 26–30.
92. *Takeyama, T., Ohara, K., Okuda, Y., Masuno, H., Aizawa, S., Shinozaki, T., Shimizu, M., Sato, H., Kojima, H., Iwai, H.and Miyata, K. Materials on neurosis. *Shinkeishitsu*, 1966, **6**, 18–29.
93. *Umasugi, T. Morita therapy viewed from Gestalt Psychology. *Clin. Psychiat.*, 1963, **5**, 711–713.
94. *Usa, G. Relations between after-image and mental set. *CM*, 1938, 83–108.
95. *Usa, G. *Persuasion therapy.* Kyoto: Jinbunshoin, 1936.
96. *Usa, G. *Self-realization therapy of nervosity and neurasthenia.* Tokyo: Hakuyo-sha, 1952.
97. Usa, G. *Treatment for nervous disease through Zen.* Mimeographed by Sansei Hospital, Kyoto, 1954.
98. *Usa, G. *Leaving self to the law of life.* (Posthumous manuscript) Kyoto: Sansei-kai, 1957.
99. Usa, G. and Usa, S. A case of nun, who suffered from visionary obsessions of snakes, treated by Morita therapy. *Psychologia*, 1958, **1**, 226–228.

100. *Usa, G. and Usa, S. *Living direct from the self.* Kyoto: Sanseikai, 1965.
101. **Usa, S. A study of the effects of the Morita therapy on neurosis as evaluated by Rorschach test. *Psychiat. Neurol. jap.*, 1961, **63**, 575–591.
102. *Usa, S. Morita therapy. In *Psychiatry.* Ed. by M. Murakami and H. Mitsuda. Igaku-shoin, Tokyo, 1963.
103. Wendt, Y. I. Japanische Psychotherapie. *Z. Psychother. med. Psychol.*, 1958, **8**, 203–223.
104. Wendt, Y. I. Eine japanische Klinik im Western. *Schweiz. Z. Psychol.* 1965, **24**, 366–370.
105. Wendt, Y. I. Japanese psychotherapy. *International Mental Health Research Newsletter.*, 1966, **3**, 2–9.
106. *Yamanoi, F. *A record of following the Morita Way of Life for thirty years.* Private publication, 1960.
107. *Yasuda, M. Supplementary study on nervosity. *Tokyo Jikeikai Ikadaigaku Zassi,* 1955, **71**, 12–28.
108. *Yokoyama, K. *Recommendation of Seiza* (sitting still)—*Seiza and Morita Therapy.* Private publication, 1965.
109. *Yora, K. A clinical study on the prognosis of nervosity. *Tokyo Jikeikai Ikadaigaku Zassi,* 1960, **75**, 302.

Shinkeishitsu is the magazine of Tokyo Jikeikai School of Medicine, Psychiatric Department, ed. originally by Prof. Morita.

*Written in Japanese.
**Written in Japanese with English summary.

Naikan Therapy

TAKAO MURASE

Naikan therapy (*nai*, meaning "inside" or "within," and *kan*, "looking"[1]) is a form of guided introspection directed toward attitude and personality change. It has been practiced in Japan for the past thirty years. Developed by a lay practitioner, Mr. Inobu Yoshimoto, Naikan therapy was originally employed in correctional institutions but is now widely used in medical and educational settings as well.

Although the method was derived from the Jōdo-shin sect of Buddhism, the most popular Buddhist sect in Japan, it is unrelated to any professional psycho-therapeutic form, Eastern or Western. Naikan therapy is based upon the philosophy that the human being is fundamentally selfish and guilty, yet at the same time favored with unmeasured benevolence from others. In order to acknowledge these existential conditions deeply, one must become open-minded toward oneself, empathic and sympathic toward others, and must courageously confront his own authentic guilt. Only then will he achieve new identity.

This Naikan philosophy is intimately related to Japanese culture and, at the same time, is firmly based upon the universal nature of the human mind. Both the culture-bound and the more universal aspects are found in the specific Naikan procedures and clients' behavior in Naikan setting. Let me start by describing the specific Naikan procedures.

THE METHOD

In short, Naikan therapy is a process of continuous meditation based upon highly structured instruction in self-observation and

To appear in volume IV of *Mental Health Research in Asia and the Pacific*, W.P. Lebra, ed. (Honolulu: The University Press of Hawaii), forthcoming.

self-reflection. Accordingly, the content of instructions and themes for meditation or reflection, as well as the way of giving instructions are of central significance.

The volunteer Naikan patient is asked to examine himself in relationship to others from the following three perspectives: (1) "Recollect and examine your memories of the care and benevolence that you have received from a particular person during a particular time in your life." (Beginning as a rule with an examination of his relationship to his mother, the client proceeds to examine, reexperience, and reflect relationships with other family members and with other persons whom he has been close to, from childhood to the present.) (2) "Recollect and examine your memories of what you have returned to that person." (3) "Recollect and examine the troubles and worries you have given that person." These three perspectives can be named, for the sake of convenience, "benevolence given," "benevolence returned," and "trouble given to others."

The examination is conducted in a boldly moralistic manner, placing the burden on the patient rather than on the "other." No excuses, rationalizations, or aggressions toward others are permitted except in the earliest meetings, when the counselor is more passive and tends merely to listen to what the patient describes to him. Following the introductory session, however, the counselor places more demands on the patient and is prepared to lead him if the patient faithfully follows the instructions. Mr. Yoshimoto used to give his clients such instructions as, "Examine yourself severely, like a prosecutor indicting the accused."

The patient begins his Naikan recollections and reflections at 5:30 in the morning and continues them until 9:00 in the evening. He sits in a quiet place surrounded on two sides by a Japanese screen and walls on the other two so that he is cut off from distractions and is free to concentrate exclusively on his inner world. Since he is not allowed to leave this very narrow space except to visit the bathroom or go to bed, the place inside the screen constitutes his whole environment. Such small confines facilitate concentrated self-reflection. For seven successive days he follows the same schedule so that at the end he has sat more than 100 hours almost continuously except while sleeping. This continuation of the same mental activity is essential for Naikan insight.

The counselor interviews the patient briefly (five minutes average) approximately every 90 minutes to ask what he has been examining. Total interview time amounts to 40–50 minutes a day.

The role of the Naikan counselor is very different from the ordinary role of the professional counselor or therapist. The primary function of the Naikan counselor is to directly supervise the patient in a highly specific routine of private meditation. He is mainly concerned with making sure that his patient is following instructions and reflecting successfully on the topics assigned for his self-examination. In this respect, the Naikan therapist is more concerned with procedure than with content or with the counselor-patient relationship. In other words, it is not necessary for the counselor to achieve a full, empathic understanding of the patient's intricate inner world. The counselor accepts and respects the patient as a person, as one who has the potential to realize himself; at the same time, the counselor is negative and critical about any non-Naikan or anti-Naikan attitude that the patient might have toward himself. In this sense, the basic counselor-patient relationship in Naikan is authoritarian. Although direct contact with the patient is sporadic, it is nevertheless intensive and highly directive. Accordingly, transference is kept as uncomplicated as possible.

Patients following the instructions often find them rather difficult. At first they may be unable to concentrate on specific themes in the way they are instructed. For some the psychological and physical isolation or confinement is too much to stand. The counselor uses several techniques to help them overcome the first barriers. Usually it takes two to three days for the patients to adjust to the new situation.

Occasionally and unexpectedly, forgotten memories come up and sporadic or diffuse guilt feelings and gratitude are experienced. At the same time, various kinds of resistance against the practice may come out, usually not the deeply rooted idiosyncratic resistance observed in psychoanalysis, but rather a more conscious reaction to such an unusual, harsh situation as Naikan. Patients are free to discontinue the method if it proves to be too difficult for them. Simple emotional catharsis is observed in some cases.

As the process goes on, the patient becomes more and more meaningfully involved with his past. For some the process is gradual, whereas for others abrupt insights into the guilty aspects of their present and past emerge. Insights into other people's love for them and their dependence upon them for this love also occur. Toward the end of therapy they accept the newly recognized guilt along with feelings of self-criticism and repentance. They also feel truly grateful for love from others and become empathic with the pain and suffering that they experienced.

THE OUTCOME

The most common result of successful Naikan therapy is an improvement in the patient's interpersonal relationships. The improvement is brought about by the increase in, or the fresh appearance of, real feelings of gratitude for others; an inclination toward self-examination rather than an extra-punitive or impulsive attitude; empathic and sympathetic ability; regard for others; and the realization of one's responsibility for his social role(s). From another angle, the establishment of identity; strengthening of ego-ideal; and achievement of security, confidence, and self-disclosure may be the most obvious factors in the improvement.

This method has proven effective with various types of patients, except psychotics, without any modifications of technique. Notable success has been achieved with delinquents, criminals, and drug addicts. Even though few scientifically rigorous follow-up studies have been done, in many correctional institutions the Naikan method has proven more effective than other methods of treatment.

CONTRAINDICATIONS AND ILL EFFECTS

As a rule Naikan is ineffective for patients who are diagnosed as having an endogenous psychosis. Severely self-punitive types of compulsive neurotics difficult to treat by any method may gain nothing from Naikan. It must be emphasized, however, that the depressive state that is accompanied by strong feelings of guilt is not necessarily a contraindication for Naikan, because the guilt and the self-criticism stemming from the systematic examination of objective experiences in Naikan differ essentially from feelings observed among depressed patients. This will be illustrated in the first case study, below.

CASE STUDIES

Case 1: a woman suffering from depressive reaction. Mrs. NGK was a middle-class housewife, 32 years old, when she began Naikan treatment. Previously she had worked as a primary schoolteacher. When she came in for treatment, she had been in a depressive state for 10 months, manifested by an increasing loss of interest in activities and a certain amount of obsession about her inability to accomplish things as she had before. She suffered from serious insomnia and had at times contemplated suicide. Her depressive reaction seemed to be precipitated by two incidents: maladjustment to her work following a change of teaching assignment two years previously, and an unexpected pregnancy several months before admission. The pregnancy increased her despair because losing her job as a result would have had harsh economic consequences for her family. Prior to these difficulties, she had reported no previous serious depressions. There were no reported familial or hereditary factors that might have effected her psychological disturbance. Medication given prior to Naikan treatment had been totally ineffective.

When she arrived for treatment, her motivation for Naikan was quite low. She cooperated with the treatment but in a very passive and almost reluctant manner. For three days she was not deeply involved in meditation but devoted most of her time to making accusations about her own incapacity and worthlessness. She seemed unable to adapt to the situation and was on the point of asking her father to take her back home. Her father, however, strongly encouraged her to continue trying. Mrs. Yoshimoto also strenuously encouraged the client to continue. Following this, after the third day, the patient suddenly began to be able to carry out the the practice of Naikan. She accepted the method with seriousness. She was then able to examine what her mother-in-law had done for her and through this was able to feel how deeply her mother-in-law cared for her. Following this emotional insight her whole attitude toward life underwent a drastic change. She found everything shiny and bright. Let me cite an interview from that time. Mr. Yoshimoto asked, "What have you been examining?" Mrs. N. replied, holding back the tears:

> Last year we bought a piano for our daughter. I realize now that this was only made possible by using the money that my mother-in-law had saved. I had forgotten this and thought that I had bought it with my own money, completely forgetting her contribution. I was so egocentric.
>
> When she was hospitalized, I only visited her once, bringing her a small gift, although my father-in-law visited her more frequently. (This was accompanied by a lot of self deprecatory crying.) When I was hospitalized after the delivery of my last child, she visited me almost daily, bringing expensive fruits and walking up to the fifth floor to see me in spite of her heart condition. At this time she very, very kindly took care of me and really acted like a loving mother. I think about that now and I am aware at last how egocentric and unaware I had been as a *yome* ("daughter-in-law"). I really don't know how I can express my gratitude to her now. I am full of the feeling that I wish to beg her pardon on my knees right now.

She spent the hours following this revelation reflecting on her relationship with her father-in-law, thinking about how he had expressed love and shown care for his daughter-in-law. She again realized how relatively ungrateful she had been, not only to her father-in-law but also to her real father.

Thinking about the troubles that she had given her father-in-law in the past, she realized that she had not been *sunao*,[2] "obedient." She described herself as feeling like a "poisonous snake." She also said that she had become increasingly aware of a tremendous amount of guilt toward people in her home and worried that she could not beg her father-in-law to forgive her for her faults and imperfections.

On the fifth day of Naikan exercise, Mr. Yoshimoto felt that she had become in some ways too dramatic and excited to continue the practice of Naikan properly. He therefore asked her father to come and discuss taking her back.

The father, on seeing his daughter's drastic change, was quite overwhelmed. They reunited, embracing each other in joyous tears. The day following her return home her excitement subsided but her improved state of mind continued.

When about two weeks had passed, she became unstable and a little depressed. But this time the amount of depression was significantly less than she had experienced prior to Naikan. She overcame the crisis by employing Naikan exercises at home by herself. Through this she regained courage and hope. Her former rigid attitudes toward life changed, and she became more flexible and accepting. She could relate herself to everything with gratitude, warmth, and naturalness.

Although at the time of my second follow-up study (one year and four months following her Naikan treatment) there was still a possibility of her becoming depressed in the future, her attitude toward life had fundamentally changed as a result of Naikan treatment. The likelihood of subsequent psychological disturbance seemed lessened following her treatment.

To summarize, this woman recovered from a severe depressive reaction by undergoing Naikan therapy for only a few days. Naikan brought her the insight that she had been very selfish and without any real regard for beneficence and love from others, especially her family members. This insight was accompanied by the deep feeling of authentic guilt and gratitude. Her strong defensiveness, which may have been mainly due to her distrust of others, was remarkably decreased, and her aggression toward herself seemed to disappear. She came to have a much better understanding of the feelings of others and gained vital hope for the future.

Case 2: a male student with ego-identity problems. Mr. M. was a male undergraduate student studying to be a primary schoolteacher. Although superficially his social and academic adjustments were normal, he seemed to be worried by emotional problems and wanted to "change himself." In the initial interview he told me that he had a feeling his personality was composed of a lot of small sins, which he was extremely afraid of facing. He had asked himself whether he could be a "real" adult since he realized he was dirty and "diffused."

After two days of the introductory stage he gradually became involved in examining himself. He kept thinking of his "dark" self and asking, "Who am I," and wondering how he could go on living. He recollected the warm treatment he received from his primary schoolteachers and realized that he had done nothing for them. He felt especially lonesome, miserable, and remorseful when he recollected an episode in which he accidentally broke a window in the school and his teacher did not reprimand him at all. With tears in his eyes, he kept on thinking about this incident. Then suddenly he felt alive, full of determination and insight. Sobbing, he told Mr. Yoshimoto, "Right now, at this very moment, I clearly realize what I should do right after graduation from the university; I must bring up children the way my primary schoolteachers did me. I believe this is my mission. That's all." Following this incident, when he was recollecting and examining his memory of the relationship with his mother, he had another experience of extremely strong emotion and feeling. When he was eight years old he still wet his bed, and whenever it happened his mother would change the wet sheet and let him come into her own bed. The recollection of the warmth of his mother's bed was combined with the recollection of another kind of warmth he experienced more directly in his babyhood, when he was carried by his mother in her arms or on her back. When he realized that he had completely forgotten this warmth up to the present, he felt so sad and sorry that he could not help but burst into tears. Sobbing, he went to Mr. Yoshimoto and asked for permission to go back to his parents immediately in order to do anything he could for them and also to tell them how his feelings and thoughts had changed. Mr. Yoshimoto advised him not to be so overwhelmed by sheer emotion but to try harder to examine himself. He simmered down and reached a tranquil state of mind.

Both of these experiences are primarily based on the acknowledgment of warmth from others. He said, "My mother and my first-grade teacher, these two persons are now closer to me, I feel."

In recollecting and reflecting upon his relationship with his father, he remembered one incident about which he felt deeply ashamed. Once when his father suddenly lost consciousness, his first worry was taking over his father's debts. Mainly for this reason he wished for his father's recovery. He also had to admit to himself that he had been jealous of his brother and had hated and distrusted him in spite of his brother's kindness to him. He found himself always being exploitative, not only of his brother but of others as well.

On the final day of his Naikan treatment he said, "Before Naikan, I wished I could completely forget such bad memories as having been slapped by my teacher or being a truant in junior high school days; but right now, I keenly feel that I exist here, now, only after I have done those things. That's why I really think I must not forget my sinful past." He felt strong enough to face the guilt squarely and found it most meaningful.

According to the follow-up interview and psychological testing carried out three months after he finished concentrated Naikan therapy, his interpersonal relationships in general showed marked improvement. His previous exploitative and antagonistic attitude toward others changed to a cooperative, accepting, and open-minded one. He began to listen to others and to see himself from another person's point of view. He also began to be more responsible, stable, and confident of himself, with greater hope for the future. The fundamental change in his attitude toward life made it possible for him to speak very easily in front of nearly 200 people in church. That he could do such a thing was beyond his imagination before Naikan therapy.

We must note, however, that in spite of the marked improvement in his attitude toward life, according to the TAT, his essentially negative relationship with his father seemingly remained almost unimproved.

Tentative Analysis of the Therapeutic Function of Naikan

The major task that the Naikan patient is asked to accomplish is to see himself in another's position and reflect on both the beneficence given to him and the harm he has done to others.

In vividly recollecting memories of "having been loved and cared for,"[3] especially by maternal figures, the Naikan patient reexperiences the deep security and satisfaction that he once had in his relationship with the person being recalled.[4] The Naikan setting reinforces the positive aspect of the client's image of others, especially his mother. His deep gratitude for his parents is transferred to others in general and he becomes more accepting of himself and others. He discloses himself, moves toward others, and becomes more empathic with them.

It may be also reasonable to assume that to recollect the experience of "having been loved and cared for" in earlier days gives the patient a feeling of inherent continuity and consistency between his present self and his basic trust of the world. This experience brings about a more solid and more integrated ego identity.

From the cultural standpoint, the character of the Japanese mother,[5] who is essentially very nurturant and interdependent with her child, may contribute in creating the above-mentioned therapeutic condition.

One additional significant therapeutic aspect of the acknowledgment of "having been loved and cared for" is that it prepares the ground for confronting and accepting one's guilt. One can never have authentic guilt feelings toward a person whom he feels he does not love or who he feels does not love him. This is probably the most decisive aspect of recollecting benevolence, because acknowledging guilt is, after all, the central experience of Naikan therapy.

Now let me discuss the therapeutic meaning of the acknowledgment of guilt. In contrast to the prevalent idea of guilt as being more or less negative and very often pathological, Naikan emphasizes the existentially positive meaning of guilt-consciousness[6] if one is able to confront it. Experiences related to guilt-consciousness tend to be forgotten and alienated from the ego unless one dares to face them. Once the person examines his past guilty conduct, relates himself directly with it, and accepts it as belonging to himself, he naturally changes his self-image and re-orients it toward responsibility, courage to be, and a humble attitude toward life. (He then achieves a broader and more integrated identity.) His selfish attitude and lack of empathy or sympathy lessens, often radically, when he realizes he is not qualified to demand and criticize others without respecting and understanding their feelings.

It is necessary to note that for a Japanese to do harm to those close to him, such as parents, is a severe violation of social morals. Thus, the acknowledgment of such misconduct produces especially strong guilt feelings in the Japanese. As R. Bellah (1957) and G. DeVos (1960) proposed, *on* obligation is very closely related with guilt among the Japanese. Naikan seems to facilitate guilt-consciousness skillfully by reinforcing the sense of *on* obligation, particularly the *on* obligation regarding one's mother. It is interesting to note that among Westerners, superego anxiety is said to have its origin in the father-son relationship, which is basically determined by fear of authority perceived in conjunction with sexual rivalry as well as by the more or less "universalistic" nature rather than by the "particularistic"[7] one. Japanese guilt, on the other hand, seems to be very closely related with the mother-son relationship, in which the fundamentally empathic and sympathetic attitude of the son toward his mother brings about guilt in him when he realizes he has done harm to his beloved mother, who may have raised her child in a rather "moral masochistic" (devotive), self-punitive way. He also tends to feel guilty when he realizes that he has had an unconscious intent to hurt his mother, due to the natural ambivalence that arises from living under very close parental control. The whole traditional social system of *on* obligation may reinforce this profound personal attitude toward guilt.

Thus, Naikan therapy utilizes very effectively such basic characteristics of the Japanese personality as strong potential guilt feelings, *on*-consciousness, the predominant significance of mother, and specific moral values in the context of highly "particularistic" interpersonal relationships. The more universal basis of Naikan may be found in its emphasis on insight into, and a positive relating with, one's guilt,[8] in contrast to the mere feeling of guilt.

ACKNOWLEDGMENTS

I wish to acknowledge the sincere cooperation of Mr. Inobu Yoshimoto, the founder of Naikan, and the patients who agreed to record their Naikan interviews, to have research interviews, and to take psychological tests. I also gratefully acknowledge the assistance of the Social Science Research Institute (NIMH Grant #MH09243) in the preparation of this paper. Lastly, I wish to thank Frank Johnson, M.D., who discussed the basic concept of Naikan with me and whose comments from the standpoint of a Westerner and a psychoanalytically oriented psychiatrist helped my thinking.

NOTES

1. *Kan* literally means "observation" but carries a specific meaning in the context of Japanese Buddhism. It implies observing or visually imagining an object during meditation with intensively integrated states of mind.
2. The Japanese word *sunao* is almost impossible to translate into English. It contains such implications as naturalness, naïveté, straightforwardness, simplicity, frankness, open-mindedness, mildness or gentleness, and compliance. Japanese culture attaches high moral value to this trait, and the word is often used in negative form by Naikan patients when they criticize themselves.

3. Discussing the dynamics underlying Naikan method may pose some difficulty for Westerners, since the recollection of affection for a parent (along with guilt about one's transgressions against the parent) is usually said to be discovered only after the analysis of unconscious anger toward the parent. Furthermore, for Westerners, hostility toward the parent often is deliberately intensified through the process of recollection and free association. This is much less prominent in Japanese patients than in Western patients. The cultural differences responsible for this may have to do with the different ways of gratifying dependency in Japanese culture when contrasted with a culture originating in Continental Europe (see Doi, 1961, 1962). The relative absence of aggression in Japanese family life cannot be accounted for simply on the basis of repression but is due to significantly different cultural practices in child-rearing and family life. I think that recognition of guilt and the realization of love in a way exacerbates and intensifies the conflict within the patient over his responsibilities for other people in his life.

4. In connection with the recollection of early experiences of being loved, it may be necessary to discuss the possibility of regression in Naikan therapy. We notice that many Naikan patients experience something similar to regression, though very mildly and temporarily. Since Naikan is an exclusively conscious and judgmental procedure, even though regression tends to occur, it is in conflict with the conscious, self-observational, and reality-directed way of thinking in Naikan and thus is readily and quickly suppressed. Although the therapeutic meaning of this oscillating process of repeatedly arising mild conflict and its resolution is not clear to the author yet, he assumes that the regression-like experience in Naikan must be therapeutic to a certain degree in making the patient relatively free from his perceived-reality-bound and rigidly patterned way of experiencing.

5. Those interested in the character of the Japanese mother can refer to Tomomatsu (1939), Yamamura (1971), and Caudill (1961). Yamamura, a Japanese sociologist, analyzed the image of mother among Japanese delinquents treated by Naikan therapy. In his findings almost all of the delinquent boys who underwent Naikan therapy realized either that they had returned evil for their mother's kindness or that they had been given love and care by their mothers in spite of the harsh treatment they gave their mothers.

6. Tillich (1952), Pattison (1969), and others call this recognition "existential (ego) guilt," which follows the violation of essential relationships between men. One might also call it "authentic guilt" after Buber (1958). This feeling should be contrasted with guilt based largely on repressed hostility since existential guilt involves realization and confrontation on a conscious level of actual violations of essential moral values in regard to a particular person. It is interesting to note that there is a striking similarity between what Buber (1958) proposed as the way of confronting and overcoming one's existential guilt and what Mr. Yoshimoto has actually practiced under the name of Naikan therapy.

7. "Particularism" is the term advocated by Parsons (1951) to refer to a specific value orientation based largely upon a particular person or a particular group; "universalism" refers to a value orientation that is based much more upon universal principles than upon a particular person or group.

8. Yasunaga (1967), a Japanese psychiatrist, contends that the significant therapeutic meaning of pure guilt-consciousness, which is defined as the feeling accompanied by the realization that one sees himself responsible

for his conduct, is that he also has done harm to a particular person. In this sense this "pure feeling of guilt" differs from the ordinary feeling of guilt. Yasunaga noticed that this kind of guilt feeling is brought about by a truly empathic understanding of another's pain and suffering. This experience of pure guilt has the positive effect of (1) melting away even the very strongest defense, (2) resolving one's *amae*, or dependent attachment on others, (3) successfully overcoming one's bitter consciousness of being hurt by others, and (4) increasing the possibility of confronting oneself honestly.

REFERENCES

Bellah, R.N. 1957. Tokugawa religion. Glencoe, Illinois, The Free Press.

Buber, M. 1958. Schuld und Schuldgefühle. *In* Martin Buber Werke, Erster Band. München, Kösel.

————. 1965. *In* The knowledge of man, selected essays of Martin Buber. M. Friedman, ed. New York, Harper & Row.

Caudill, W. 1961. Around the clock patient care in Japanese psychiatric hospitals: the role of the *tsukisoi*. American Sociological Review 26:204–14.

DeVos, G. 1960. The relation of guilt toward parents to achievement and arranged marriage among the Japanese. Psychiatry 23:287–301.

Doi, L.T. 1961. *Sumanai to ikenai*—psychodynamics of guilt in the light of Japanese concepts. Seishin Bunseki Kenkyu 8:4–7. [In Japanese]

————. 1962. *Amae*. a key concept for understanding Japanese personality structure. *In* Japanese culture: its development and characteristics. R. J. Smith and K. K. Beardsley, eds. Chicago, Aldine Publishing Co.

Parsons, T. 1951. The social system. New York, The Free Press of Glencoe.

Pattison, E. 1969. Morality, guilt and forgiveness in psychotherapy. *In* Clinical psychiatry and religion. E. Pattison, ed. Boston, Little Brown.

Tillich, P. 1952. Systematic theology. Chicago, University of Chicago Press.

Tomomatsu, E. 1939. Boshin (Mind of mother). Tokyo ,Kasei-sha. [In Japanese]

Yamamura, Y. 1971. Nihonjin to haha (Japanese and their mothers). Tokyo, Tōyokan Shuppansha. [In Japanese]

Yasunaga, H. 1967. Chiyu-kiten to zaiakukan (Healing and guilt feelings). Tokyo, Seishin Igaku 9:281–85. [In Japanese]

Taishu Danko: Agency for Change in a Japanese University

YASUYUKI OWADA
ALAN H. GLEASON
ROBERT W. AVERY

One of the unique features of the Japanese student movement in the latter half of the 1960's was the resort to a procedure for mass bargaining called *taishu danko*. The term itself derives from a similar term for the practice of collective bargaining in labor-management negotiations, but there the resemblance ends. *Taishu danko* has been described as a "public dialogue of uncompromising nature participated in by a mass of students and a great many faculty members and administrators."[1] This is a pale description in contrast to the striking variety of accounts which one hears from those who have seen a *danko*, or who have been caught up in one as a principal (as one of us was). From our own involvement in a series of these meetings at the International Christian University near Tokyo in 1969, we are suspicious of any dogmatic generalizations about them. We do not know of any agreed-upon definition.

We know that spectators and participants invoke many different metaphors when they describe what they saw. In conversation *taishu danko* has, at one time or another, been said to be a "public brainwashing," a "kangaroo court," a "spectator sport with audience participation," a "method for establishing real communications," "an explosion of destructive energy of young students," "thought control," and, depending upon the point of view of the speaker, either a "drama in which a University is radicalized"

Reprinted by permission of the American Anthropological Association from *Council on Anthropology and Education Newsletter* 2 (1971):9–12.

or a "drama disclosing the essential political nature of a University in a capitalistic nation." It is not precisely any one of these; on the other hand, it is all of them and more. Perhaps therefore we may be excused if we do not try to say what *taishu danko* really is.

At I.C.U. those who insisted upon *taishu danko* (many students and a few in the faculty and administration) regarded it as a genuine mode of communication through sincere confrontation. Those who opposed it believed that it was illegitimate because it was antithetical to the traditional means for resolving disagreements, i.e., through the *hanashiai* (mutual discussion and persuasion) which leads if possible to a decision by consensus.

In these uncertain circumstances the militant students (at the time, they were referred to as "the students," and we will follow that usage) provide a stable reference point, and moreover one which is useful to anyone who wishes to understand how *taishu danko* works. That is the central question for this paper. It is an exploratory description of the process of *taishu danko*, seen as a social vehicle for an ideological contest.

To get quickly to the point, it is necessary to omit almost all of the chronology of events (which began at least two years earlier) which led up to the students' demand for *taishu danko* at I.C.U., and to give equally short shrift to the moods of different groups on the campus, and to the intensification of these moods as the students defined an issue, announced three demands, summarized these in three slogans which captured the attention of the campus, organized a majority of students and student groups into a Zenkyoto ("all-campus joint struggle committee"), tried and failed to win accession to their demands through appeals to the president and other administrators, and then finally came to the faculty with one more demand, viz., that the issues be settled through *taishu danko*.

There had never been one before at I.C.U. When the students' demand was passed to the faculty in the midst of one of its meetings, there was a sudden silence, broken quickly by expressions of anxious concern. Probably every member of the faculty meeting had read about *taishu danko*, since reports of its use at other universities had been featured in news stories and on television. The apprehension probably did not exaggerate the subsequent reality.

First there was a preliminary negotiation between representatives from Zenkyoto and from the administration (or faculty). They mutually agreed upon a time and place, but most other matters were decided by the students. The students stipulated that they would appoint the co-chairmen for each session (they were always students), they would set agenda (usually some part of their announced demands), leaving for negotiation only such items as control over audience jeering, rest periods, certain parts of the physical arrangement, and the selection of non-principal university representatives who would sit at the negotiation table.

The five *danko*s took place in the University auditorium which had space and was usually filled (almost entirely by students). Each began shortly after noon and ran on until after the dinner hour, sometimes close to midnight. An oblong table which extended from front and center of the stage almost to the backdrop was the focal point. Six or seven representatives from each group faced each other across the table. The co-chairmen sat behind microphones at the far end of it. Behind the co-chairmen the Zenkyoto's red flag hung from the ceiling, flanked on either side by banners proclaiming the three demands. Many students, both on stage and in the audience, wore helmets. Beginning with the second session, many faculty members (including the writers of this paper) sat on the stage behind their representatives as an expression of identification with their colleagues who were facing the Zenkyoto representatives. This act was reciprocated by the presence on the other side of the stage of those students who represented different groups constituting the Zenkyoto.

The drama of *taishu danko* starts with its director, the Zenkyoto chairman, on stage, presenting a prologue. (The dramaturgical terms are ours, not the students'.) After a prologue, the "discussion" begins with one or more Zenkyoto representatives presenting specific demands which are on the agenda. This may take the form of a student asking university representatives to admit past acts, as interpreted by the students. The students then present their ideological justification with supporting factual evidence, and witnesses as the basis of their demands. Then university representatives respond in defense of their past actions and justify their views of the demands. Their views may be of such a nature as to accept in part the reasonableness of certain student demands, and to seek some compromise.

The faculty and administrators' defense of past actions and *their* ideological justification prepare the next stage of the "discussion." The students indict the faculty and administration for failing to accept their demands by the process of "correct" reasoning, that is, by following the reasons contained in the students' "logic." The student indictment is directed to the morality of their professors who demonstrate unwillingness to review the "reality" of actions as exposed by the students, thus continuing to evade confrontation with the "logic" of the students.

What frustrates the students most of all is the *attitude* or posture of recalcitrant faculty and administrators, rather than their unwillingness to give in to the demands. This recognition of the source of student frustration on the part of the faculty and administrators becomes a key to the next stage of the *taishu danko*.

Once this recognition is obtained, the discussion phase of the *danko* reaches its climax by public admission of collective "guilt" on the part of the university representatives. This is the point where debate ceases and the *danko* enters into the decisional processes. The admission of "guilt," that is, the public recognition of an error in their previous understanding and the acknowledgment of their unwitting responsibility for past actions as a consequence of this wrong attitude, is the necessary process of self-criticism before decision on the demands can take place. Through self-criticism, which is individual and simultaneously public and collective, the university representatives take upon themselves the task of reorienting their colleagues on the issues. They give their pledge to do so by signing their "confirmation" of actions contained in the student demands as decisions of the university.

At I.C.U. the five *dankos* proceeded pretty much in this fashion, over a period of two weeks. Several professors self-criticized themselves, and all confirmation statements were approved and signed.

The foregoing has described the setting and the outward sequence of the *taishu danko* which we saw. The outward features, however, get their meaning from the students' ideology. This ideology is so important to the successful (from the students' viewpoint) completion of *taishu danko* that we present it at some length, and as nearly as possible in the students' own words, as translated. (Words in quotes are fashionable idioms of the Zenkyoto students which carry a highly emotional charge as well as theoretical implications.)

> As a "pseudo-academic community" the present-day university owes its objective basis to its dependency upon the production relations of the capitalistic society. A university is an "individual educational capital" definable in terms of these relations. As such its function is to supply a labor force suitable in quantity and quality to the current mode of the capitalistic development. It appreciates the value of labor in the market through its reproductive processes called education. Students purchase their education in order to sell their labor more profitably as educated manpower in the highly industrialized society and its market. The faculty members are at the hub of this operation. They are engaged in selling their specialized knowledge

necessary for the production process of highly trained workers.

This is the historical reality of university education and its "alienation" from a true education. This is the basis of the students becoming alienated from themselves as "labor commodity reserve force" in response to the requirements for the development of Japanese capitalism. This is the basis of conflicts and contradictions we observe daily on the campus, and this is the reason why the so-called "academic community" becomes a facade for its managers to avoid or obstruct the penetration of the Zenkyoto "logic" which exposes its reality.

The complete "sublation" (or "supersession") of the alienated university as an "educational capital" cannot be accomplished without overthrowing the capitalistic production relations. Although the students cannot realistically engage in a direct and complete "sublation" of these relations, a campus struggle is meaningful in the following sense.

Through their campus "struggle" movement, the students demonstrate that it is a struggle toward "sublation" of the class relations that define the reality of university education. The students themselves must make an unrelenting effort to attain self-awareness as "contradictory beings" in this society and to overcome this state as "students" by rejecting the present and past mode of existence, their consciousness and activity. Their presence within the capitalistic system of education is in itself supportive of such a system. The students must clearly recognize this dilemma, and understand the nature of their existence by "perpetually" and "fundamentally" rejecting it. Thus, they engage in an unceasing struggle for "self-denial" and "self-revolution," through which they formulate and sharpen their "proletarian self-awareness." Whatever they do in promoting such a movement is subject to self-criticism.

Such a struggle also means that they place the equal demand of self-criticism on faculty and staff of the university in order that they may be awakened to the same "proletarian self-consciousness" as "educational workers." Then they will in turn join the struggle at their own stations toward the rejection of the university as an "educational capital." The development of such a struggle on an increasingly wider basis is a "medium" in relating the students to a perpetual movement aimed at the "sublation" of the capitalistic society as a whole. The Zenkyoto's three specific demands are the localized occasions of this perpetual movement.

We have described how one *taishu danko* worked, and we now turn to some implications. There was a reversal of roles on the stage of the I.C.U. auditorium, in two senses. The President and other administrators, the occupants of positions of University authority vis-à-vis all students, found themselves—during the hours of the *dankos*—in the position of subordinates who must decide whether to comply with demands being levied upon them. Of course they continued with their duties as "authorities" during the periods between *danko*s; this structure was not altered. Nevertheless the reversal in authority relations did follow the abrupt reversal in the customary direction and initiation of interactions between the University administrators and the students. This was made more visible because the ideologically based challenge to the way in which University administrators had exercised their authority in the past amounted to an attack by the students upon the *legitimacy* of the traditional structure of authority. It led to a later open discussion of the appropriateness of the bureaucratic form of general organization for International Christian University, with some faculty members taking the position that bureaucracy per se was inconsistent for an academic community which has addressed itself to a search for truth. On this point the students, throughout their protest movement, had been asserting in word and action the importance of the creation of a "true" academic community.

The second and simultaneous reversal placed professors in the (temporary) position of being students, while some of the student leaders behaved very much as professors might do who have grasped an important truth and seek to communicate it. The act which confirmed a "student's" achievement of this new understanding was that of self-criticism, delivered from center stage and usually in such moving language as to remove all doubt about its sincerity. Properly done, self-criticism not only acknowledged responsibility for past injustice done to "the students" and promised repentance; it also affirmed that the self-criticizer had acquired a new world view which cast very much of his past life into new perspective. Though not very many I.C.U. professors did all of this, those that did may well have undergone "ideological conversion" through the agency of *taishu danko* (we are less than dogmatic about this because we have no way of being sure whether the ideology which a self-criticizer expressed from the front of the stage had been his "real commitment" for some time or had come to him new and for the first time).

This was the education which the "students-cum-teachers-in-*taishu-danko*" sought to impress into all of their listeners, but especially upon their erstwhile professors. A few I.C.U. professors who sought the middle ground of confessing past sins while neglecting to mention ideological issues were not well received by their "new mentors." They were almost as likely to be targets for abuse as were those few professors who absented themselves from *danko*s and refused to have anything to do with them at all.

It is possible, as we have said, that there were no profound and long-lasting changes in ideological commitment within the I.C.U. faculty. We can still interpret *taishu danko* as an experience in desocialization and resocialization. Those who did publicly redefine their individual pasts in the ideological terms offered to them by "the students" did alter the definition of self which, in Erving Goffman's phrase, is "presented to others."[2] The complementary processes of desocialization and resocialization were taking place via the open denial of some features of one's "former self" and their replacement by avowed fealty to the new features.

This is, then, a summary description of the process of *taishu danko* as we saw and experienced it at one Japanese university, where it operated as an organized way to carry on an ideological contest between the faculty-administrators and the students. The first group attempted, on the whole, to sustain the ideology and the social structure of the status quo, while the second group sought fundamental changes in both the ideology and the structure. We have discussed how roles were reversed in the process of *taishu danko*.

NOTES

1. *Asahi Shimbun*, November 18, 1968.
2. This is meant to recall the title of Goffman's book, *The Presentation of Self in Everyday Life* (New York: Anchor Books, 1956).

Higaisha-ishiki: the Psychology of Revolting Youth in Japan

L. TAKEO DOI

Let me introduce at the beginning *higaisha-ishiki*, the Japanese word that appears in the title. Being Japanese, I am given to using Japanese concepts, and once in a while I come upon something quite excellent which I feel like introducing to English-speaking people. *Higaisha-ishiki* is one such concept. Not that the meaning of this word cannot be rendered into English. But it happens to be handy and apt for describing a certain psychological attitude that is characteristic of the revolting youth in our contemporary world. It also has the advantage of suggesting the underlying dynamics of such an attitude.

Higaisha-ishiki is composed of two parts: *higaisha* and *ishiki*. *Higaisha*, meaning "one who is wronged" or "the injured party," seems to have been coined in the Meiji period as a legal term along with *kagaisha*, meaning "one who inflicts a wrong on others" or "perpetrator." *Ishiki* stands for "consciousness" and can denote "the mentality of" when used in combination with a noun that indicates a person. Thus, *higaisha-ishiki* means "the mentality of a person who is wronged, "in other words," victim-consciousness." Now *higaisha-ishiki* is quite widely used, apart from its originally legal implication, to refer to anybody who believes he has been wronged. In fact, Masao Maruyama, a well-known professor of political science at the University of Tokyo, wrote in his book *Nihon no Shisō (Japanese Thought)* that all Japanese, whether conservatives firmly placed within the establishment or progressives popular in communication media, tend to have *higaisha-ishiki*, a

To appear in *Youth, Socialization, and Mental Health*, W. P. Lebra, ed. (Honolulu: The University Press of Hawaii) forthcoming.

remark that I quoted in my paper on *giri-ninjō* (Doi, 1967). I shall come back to this point later.

What enlightened me on the importance of *higaisha-ishiki* as a moving force in our contemporary world was the recent student movement in Japan. Let me give a rough sketch of it. For several years, medical students fought for repeal of the law requiring internship on the ground that internship is useless and a waste of time. Their grievances were not necessarily unfounded, for postgraduate education in all fields of clinical medicine is very poor in Japan. In 1967 the medical students at the University of Tokyo, for instance, boycotted classes altogether for two months, demanding that the University Hospital provide proper training for all graduates. The professors gave in to their demands, and in the meantime the Government prepared a new law for postgraduate clinical training. In 1968 the students staged even a bigger strike, demanding a radical change in the medical education system. Their tactics became increasingly violent, and school authorities made a counterattack, taking disciplinary measures against those who menaced the hospital staff. This set the whole University on a general strike, and many young faculty members of various schools were drawn into the protest movement. At about the same time, similar upheavals swept through almost all campuses in Japan. This not only paralyzed higher educational activities for more than a year, but also brought considerable damage to school buildings and facilities. Now, the campuses are much more quiet than before, but a few professional associations that sided with the universities are in trouble. For instance, the Japanese Psychiatric Association has not held its regular annual meeting since 1969. The Psychiatric Department of the University of Tokyo remains divided in two opposing camps, one centering around a certain professor, and the other, led by New Leftists, fighting to oust that professor, whom they label a sympathizer of the Japanese Communist Party.

When the foregoing incidents took place, I was amazed most of all by the speed with which the revolutionary fervor seized all the campuses. It was not only that the school authorities and the majority of students could not come up with any effective measures to put down the rioting, but a great many students and even a number of professors, though they never participated in violent activities themselves, either voiced sympathy for the rebels or publicly defended their cause. Many leading newspapers also gave the impression of being on their side by not attacking the student violence directly, though they of course duly deplored it. I found all this very appalling and strange. It was not that I felt very harsh myself toward the rebels, differently from others. On the contrary, my initial reaction was that they would not have had the chance to cause such trouble if the authorities had been more understanding and imaginative in coping with them. I guess I even identified myself with them to some extent. All the more I wondered what it is that made the adult world so helpless vis-à-vis the rebellious students.

Soon it dawned on me that the reason for our adult helplessness was the guilt that revolting students aroused in us. Apparently they knew quite well what they were doing: they would urge those whom they had attacked, "Don't play *higaisha* because that is only to complain, which after all is motivated by your petty egoism; convert *higaisha-ishiki* into *kagaisha-ishiki* by realizing that you yourselves have been grossly guilty of complacency in overlooking the numerous social ills." This tactic seemed to work remarkably well. It was because of this that the rebels succeeded in recruiting many students into their camp in the first place and in silencing their critics. I wondered, then, how on earth they themselves could get away with their own guilt in the face of their almost criminal conduct, not to speak of the fact that they themselves had not done a thing to correct the social ills. This could happen, I thought, only because they completely identified themselves with the victims of the social ills, believing that they could thus negate their own privileged identity. Does it not prove, then, that they hid themselves in a sort of vicarious *higaisha-ishiki*? I think it does, only they refused to admit this to themselves. If they did, they would have had to face their own guilt by their own logic.

This identification with the supposed victims on the part of the rebellious became quite clear when a number of young radical psychiatrists began to attack the Psychiatric Association. They accused the leaders of the association of monopolizing it only to enhance their privileged position and of neglecting to improve the conditions of mental hospitals where patients were locked in and fed large doses of tranquilizers to make them amenable to control. They also opposed a plan, which the association was then considering, to launch a system of specialty training, the rebels claiming that it was only meant to divert young physicians' attentions from social action and to keep them securely in the confines of the universities or big hospitals. Unfortunately, their accusations were not entirely unfounded. At any rate, the leaders yielded to them without much resistance and the association became totally demoralized. So we are now in a worse state than before. When all this happened

I thought, It is just the reverse of the witch hunts in the European Middle Ages. Then, people projected their bad impulses onto the mentally deranged and persecuted them as witches; now, young psychiatrists project their humiliations onto the mentally deranged and completely identify themselves with the unfortunate. Both are the same in being paranoid. I warned them, "If you become too involved with *higaisha*, that is, victims, you are bound to become *higaiteki*." *Higaiteki* is an adjective often used by Japanese psychiatrists to indicate that the patient tends to have persecutory delusions. But they have not listened to my warnings.

I think it is now clear why I felt that the psychology of *higaisha-ishiki* is applicable to the youth in revolt. Of course, the phenomenon of dissident youth is not confined to Japan alone; on the contrary, it is spread through out the contemporary world. Almost identical student riots occurred at Berkeley, Harvard, in Paris, and many other places. As a matter of fact, I have often been struck by the similarity of the ideology and tactics used by youth in various countries. It followed that the psychology of *higaisha-ishiki* might also be applicable to the revolting youth in other countries besides Japan. This thought intrigued me because the psychology of *higaisha-ishiki* as I formulated it above is clearly a derivative of the psychology of *amae,* that is, the particular dependency need that manifests itself in a longing to merge with others in a loving relationship. Those who are totally engrossed in *amae* would develop *higaisha-ishiki* when they feel rejected. It is easy to understand, therefore, that the Japanese people tend to have *higaisha-ishiki,* as Professor Maruyama pointed out. One might even hazard the thesis that what motivated Japan to wage her last war against the United States is also related to this psychology. Justly or unjustly, Japan felt persecuted by the United States and started on a war which she did not believe she could win. She may have hoped that the United States would feel guilty afterwards; if so she was quite right. Because Americans had to feel terribly guilty, particularly after dropping the atomic bombs, the initial victim of Japan's surprise attack was made to feel like the guilty one in the end. In the words made popular by the recent Japanese student riots, in this instance *higaisha-ishiki* was more or less successfully converted to *kagaisha-ishiki.*

So there is a distinct parallel between the *higaisha-ishiki* of contemporary Japanese youth against the establishment and that of their fathers against the United States or other powerful foreign countries. But why against the establishment at the present time?

Also, how does one explain the fact that now youth in Western countries are also caught by *higaisha-ishiki*? It is interesting to note in this regard that it is the threat of nuclear holocaust that now prevents the conflicts between powerful nations from escalating into hot war, thus creating the precarious cold peace and leading to the revolt of youth against the established authorities in advanced countries. For a long time, the West enjoyed the aggressor role on the world stage because of its advancement in science and technology. But now, that very advancement has created new problems for the West such as environmental pollution. The West's liberation of its former colonies in the present century also owes to social changes created by the advanced technology. Thus, conditions became ripe for the youth in Western countries to develop *higaisha-ishiki*, either by anticipating the possible dead end of contemporary civilization or by identification with the underprivileged. It is significant that Erik H. Erikson (1970) calls the present youth unrest "revolt of the dependent," not "revolt of the oppressed." He must mean the same thing I mean by *higaisha-ishiki*.

I would like to add a few more words about the connection between *higaisha-ishiki* and paranoid thinking that I hinted at above. I think the usual psychiatric conception of persecutory delusions is that they represent projections of the patient's own hostile feelings onto the external object. This is quite right, but I wonder if Western people do not sometimes forget that the hostility is originally engendered by frustration of one's deep dependency wishes, that is, *amae* in Japanese. Though some psychiatrists in the West recently pointed out a connection between an initial traumatic experience and later paranoid development, they did so only in extreme cases like the Nazi survivors. Robert J. Lifton (1967) came to a similar conclusion by observing the acute suspicion of "counterfeit nurture" among the atomic bomb survivors of Hiroshima. Apart from these striking examples, however, it is my impression that Western people tend to overlook the paranoid reaction that is provoked by the frustration of dependency wishes, particularly when it is mild. This applies, surprisingly, even to a psychological genius like Freud.

Let me cite, for instance, from "Analysis of a Phobia in a Five-Year-Old Boy," a passing conversation between Hans and his father, who actually took the role of therapist for Hans through the help of Freud (1950). His father asks him, "What do I really scold you for?" He answers, "I don't know." His father presses, "Why?" to which he says, "Because you're cross." His father denies it, saying, "But that's not true," but Hans emphatically repeats, "Yes, it is true. You're cross. I know you are. It must be true." His father then notes the following. "Evidently, therefore, my explanation that only little boys come into bed with their Mummies and that big ones sleep in their own beds had not impressed him very much." Now one could have said that Hans projected his hostile feelings onto his father. But was he not right after all in insisting that his father was cross? (In the original German, "You are cross" is *du tust eifern*.) The father's flat denial of this charge rather makes one suspect that it was perhaps the father who projected his anger toward Hans, which was caused by his wife allowing Hans to sleep with her. The fact that this marriage eventually ended in divorce strongly supports this interpretation. However, Freud takes notice neither of such a paranoid feeling on the part of Hans' father nor of the possibility that the father's mute anger or the couple's incompatibility might have been a main contributing factor for Hans' phobic neurosis.

Interestingly, it seems that Freud himself experienced such a paranoid feeling at times without recognizing it as such. I shall cite one example. In *The Interpretation of Dreams* (1961), he faithfully recorded his reaction to what he heard from his colleague Otto about the condition of his patient Irma, whom he had treated only with partial success. "I asked him how he had found her and he answered: 'She's better, but not quite well.' I was conscious that my friend Otto's words, or the tone in which he spoke them, annoyed me. I fancied I detected a reproof in them, such as to the effect that I had promised the patient too much; and, whether rightly or wrongly, I attributed the supposed fact of Otto's siding against me to the influence of my patient's relatives, who, as it seemed to me, had never looked with favour on the treatment." Is it not quite clear that Freud was slightly paranoid here? It may be true that Irma's family did not feel kindly toward Freud's novel treatment and that Otto was not particularly sympathetic to it, either. Even if so, Freud had no reason to blame them. On the other hand, it is most certain that the treatment of Irma had left him unsatisfied and that is why he was so unduly sensitive to Otto's report about her. It can be said, therefore, that the famous Irma dream was actually a continuation of this paranoid reaction, but curiously so far no analyst has come up with such an impious interpretation.

It is my contention that this kind of paranoid reaction is widespread in the contemporary world. The examples I gave above are mild ones, but such a reaction can be quite destructive when it takes a mass form, as in the case of revolting youth. Unfortunately, nobody has paid much attention to the psychological aspect of rebellious youth; such a phenomenon is usually analyzed only in sociological or political terms. Recently, however, Stuart Hughes, a distinguished Harvard professor of history, mentioned the present youth revolt in his special address to the 1969 annual meeting of the American Psychiatric Association:

> What has been unusual about the insurgent mood of the past half decade has been its juxtaposition of anarchism and the peremptory silencing of opponents, its peculiar blend of political puritanism and personal license, its cult of 'confrontation' as a quasi-religious act of witness. Together this complex of attitudes suggests something quite different from the conventional revolutionary aim of seizing the means of production or the implements of power and redirecting them for the benefit of the masses. It suggests, rather, a basically unpolitical aspiration to see through, to unmask, to strip—literally as well as figuratively—down to total nakedness. The goal is psychological, or, to use old-fashioned vocabulary, spiritual. And it marks the culmination of a quarter-century of amateur psychologizing among the young. (Hughes, 1969)

Evidently he was keenly aware of the psychological aspect of the present youth revolt, but I don't know of any American psychiatrist who sufficiently clarified the issue for him.

In this connection I would like to mention "Contestation," a brilliant study of the Paris student revolt of May, 1968, by two eminent French psychoanalysts, B. Brunberger and J.S. Smirgel (1969). It makes amply clear the paranoid nature of what motivated those youth who contested the authorities, and is in complete agreement with my own view of Japanese youth. But their emphasis is again on the projection of hostility. Though they noticed youth's identification with the supposed victims of society, they did so only in a tone of ridicule. They thus stopped short of recognizing the importance of frustrated dependency wishes in forming the paranoid reaction. In other words, the authors are not perceptive to the feelings of humiliation that must have existed deep down in the hearts of those youth who revolted. In my opinion, Western people generally, youth and professional adults alike, have not been attentive to such feelings of humiliation and do not dwell on them, either by repressing or suppressing them.

I am aware that I have put forward a very sweeping generalization. I did so not because I wanted to indulge in speculation, but because I felt it has a practical clinical merit. I only wanted to tell you that many young people who consult psychiatrists nowadays have the kind of paranoid reaction explained above, in other words, *higaisha-ishiki,* if not in a mass form, then as a solitary preoccupation. I conclude with a plea that psychiatrists, Japanese and non-Japanese alike, work to gain insight into this psychology and what lies behind it, that is, the particular dependency need called *amae.*

REFERENCES

Brunberger, B., and J.S. Smirgel. 1969. Contestation. Paris, Payot. [In French]

Doi, L.T. 1967. *Giri-ninjo:* an interpretation. *In* Aspects of social change in modern Japan. R.P. Dore, ed. Princeton, Princeton University Press.

Erikson, E.H. 1970. Reflections on the dissent of contemporary youth. International Journal of Psychoanalysis 51:11–22.

Freud, S. 1950. Analysis of a phobia in a five-year-old boy. Collected papers. Vol. 3. London, The Hogarth Press.

———. 1961. The interpretation of dreams. New York, Science Editions, Inc.

Hughes, E.S. 1969. Emotional disturbance and American social change, 1944–1969. American Journal of Psychiatry 126:21–29.

Lifton, R.J. 1967. Death in life. New York, Random House.

Contributors

Robert W. AVERY, Professor of Sociology, University of Pittsburgh.

Harumi BEFU, Associate Professor of Anthropology, Stanford University, Palo Alto, California.

William BROWN, Managing Director, Fuji National City Consulting, Ltd., Tokyo.

William CAUDILL, Chief, Section on Personality and Environment, Laboratory of Socio-Environmental Studies, National Institute of Mental Health, Bethesda, Maryland.*

George DEVOS, Professor of Anthropology, University of California, Berkeley.

L. Takeo DOI, Professor and Chairman, Department of Health Sciences, University of Tokyo.

Alan H. GLEASON, Professor of Economics, University of Toledo, Ohio.

Yoshiko IKEDA, Director, Division of Child Mental Health, National Institute of Mental Health, Ichikawa, Japan.

Eiichirō ISHIDA, Emeritus Professor of Cultural Anthropology, Tokyo University.*

Hiroaki IWAI, Professor of Sociology, Taisho University, Tokyo.

Yomishi KASAHARA, Professor of Psychiatry, Nagoya University.

Masaaki KATO, Chief, Division of Adult Mental Health, National Institute of Mental Health, Ichikawa, Japan.

Christie W. KIEFER, Human Development Program, Langley Porter Neuropsychiatric Institute, San Francisco.

Takie Sugiyama LEBRA, Associate Professor of Anthropology, University of Hawaii.

Momoshige MIURA, Emeritus Professor of Psychiatry, Tottori University, Tottori, Japan.*

Takao MURASE, Chief, Psychological Research Division, National Institute of Mental Health, Ichikawa, Japan.

Chie NAKANE, Professor of Social Anthropology, Institute of Oriental Culture, University of Tokyo.

Yasuyuki OWADA, Faculty Fellow in Anthropology, University of Redlands, California.

John C. PELZEL, Professor of Anthropology and Director, Har-'vard-Yenching Institute, Harvard University, Cambridge, Massachusetts.

David W. PLATH, Professor of Anthropology, University of Illinois, Urbana.

Thomas P. ROHLEN, Assistant Professor of Anthropology, University of California, Santa Cruz.

Harry A. SCARR, Research Scientist, Human Science Research, Inc., McLean, Virginia.

Shin-ichi USA, Director, Sansei Hospital, Kyoto.

Helen WEINSTEIN, Research Assistant, Section on Personality and Environment, Laboratory of Socio-Environmental Studies, National Institute of Mental Health, Bethesda, Maryland.*

---

* Deceased